THE AUTOMOBILE
The First Century

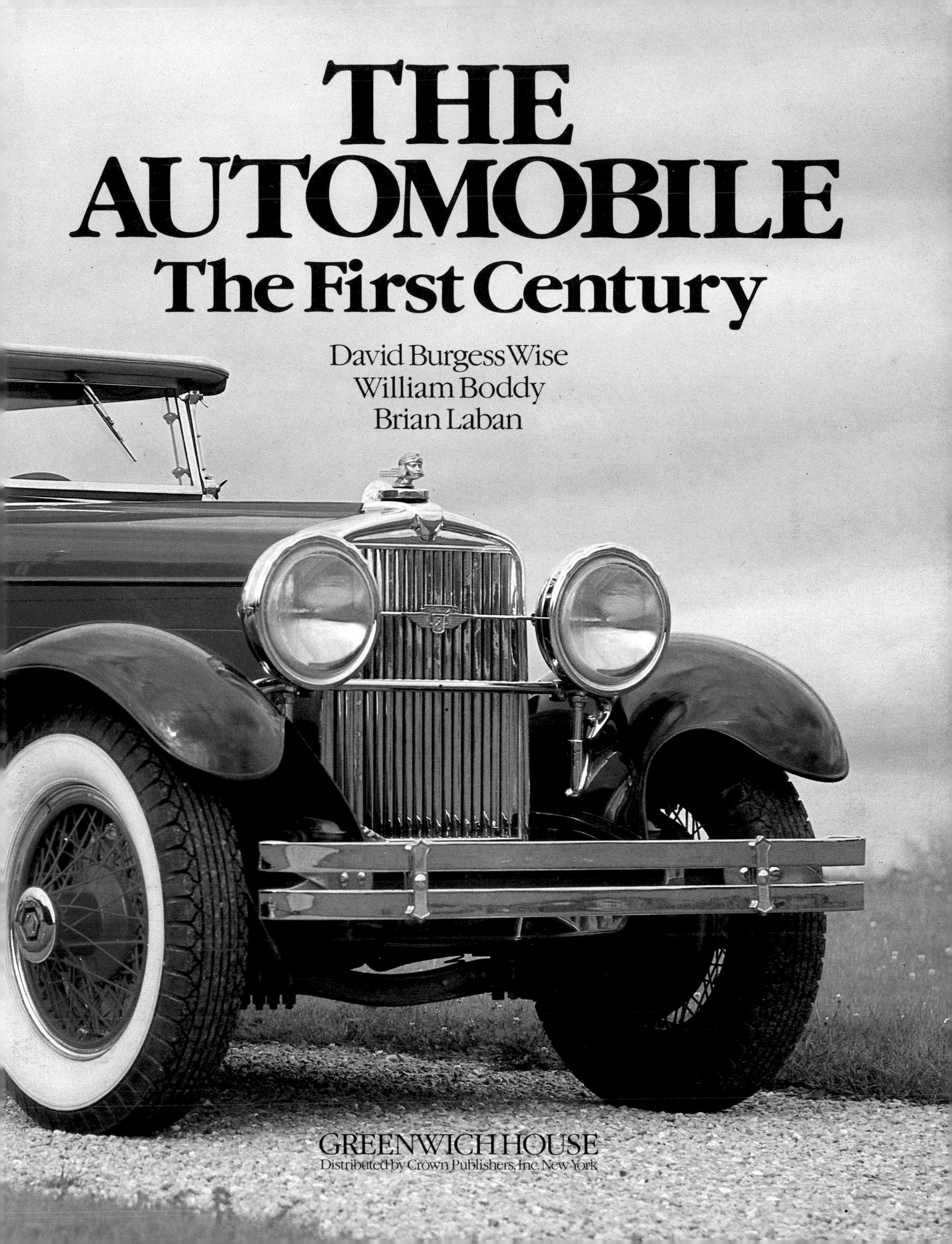

THE AUTOMOBILE
The First Century

David Burgess Wise
William Boddy
Brian Laban

GREENWICH HOUSE
Distributed by Crown Publishers, Inc. New York

Acknowledgements

Orbis Publishing is indebted to the following for allowing their cars to be photographed:
Château de Grandson, Switzerland; Cheddar Motor Museum, England; Coventry Motor
Museum, England; Donington Collection, England; Fiat Centro Storico, Italy; Peter
Hampton, England; Lancia Collection, Italy; Dr John Mills, England; National Motor
Museum, England; Peugeot Collection, France; Saab-Scania, Sweden; Franco Sbarro,
Switzerland; Hank Schumaker, England; Science Museum, England; Skokloster Museum,
Sweden; Stratford Motor Museum, England; Totnes Motor Museum, England; Rob Walker,
England; J. T. Williamson, England; Ben Wright, England.

Photographs were supplied by Alfa Romeo, Aston Martin, Audi, Autocar, Automobile Museum
Turin, BMW, Michael Bailie/News Feature International, Bayer Armeé Museum, Belli, Biscaretti
Museum, Jeff Bloxham, W. Boddy, British Leyland, N. Bruce, Bundesarchiv, C. Burgess-Wise,
Camera Press, Chrysler, Citroën, Daimler-Benz, M. Decet, Deutsches Bunde Library, Martin
Elford/*Automobile Sport*, Ford, G. Gauld, General Motors, G. Goddard, A. Heal, P. Helck,
Hull Museum, Robert Hunt Picture Library, Jeff Hutchinson/IPA, Archivio IGDA, Imperial War
Museum, Keystone, L. Klemantaski, Charles B. Knight/Motofoto, Brian Laban, LAT, Mansell
Collection, Mercedes Benz, A. Morland, *Motor Magazine*, Museé de la Guerre, Museé National des
Techniques, NSU, National Motor Museum, J. Neal East, John Overton/*Automobile Sport*,
D. Phipps, C. Posthumus, Publifoto, *Quattroruote*, Renault, Rolls-Royce, Sport & General, Keith
Sutton/*Automobile Sport*, Suzuki, Tatra Museum, J. Tipler, John Topham Picture Library,
M. Turner, Volkswagen, Volvo, N. Wright.
Other photographs were taken specially for Orbis by L. J. Caddell and J. Spencer Smith.

Juan Manuel Fangio

Jackie Stewart

Material in this book was originally published in the U.S.A. in *The Motor Car:
An Illustrated International History* by David Burgess Wise
and *The History of Motor Racing* by William Boddy.

Library of Congress Catalog Card Number 83–80847
ISBN: 0–517–414732

Printed and bound in Yugoslavia by Mladinska Knjiga
h g f e d c b a

Contents

Foreword

Henry Ford's dictum 'History is bunk' may be a colourful reminder of the man who probably did more than any other to bring motoring to the masses, but it is not wholly true when it comes to the story in which he played so great a part.

That the motor car is one of mankind's pivotal inventions is beyond dispute. Man has always sought mobility and ultimately sought mobility free of the restrictions of animal power and the whims of nature, yet in spite of numerous fanciful schemes and frustrating near misses the first practicable motor vehicles did not appear until the mid-1880s. They developed slowly at first and then, as the twentieth century dawned, by leaps and bounds. 1984 will be the motor car's one hundredth year and in that first century both the car and the world itself have changed immeasurably. This book traces the story from the pioneering days, often frustrated by irrational prejudice, to the present day and the coming of the 'world car' – the modern equivalent of Henry's Model T or the ubiquitous Volkswagen.

The development of the motor car has always relied heavily on practical experience as a means to confirm theory and nowhere has the pace of progress been more intense than in motor racing. What began as an inevitable attempt to express individual superiority soon became the manufacturers' proving ground and one of the most popular sports in the world; here, its contribution to the history of the motor car is charted side by side with the growth of the industry in which it plays such an important part.

Motoring history has not stopped, it is still being made. This is the story so far.

Below: this cartoon depicting a steam-engined tricycle of 1818 can now be found in France's Conservatoire des Arts et Métiers in Paris. It seems that even in those days motorists had fuel-price problems because, in the cartoon caption, the driver is haggling over the price of a sack of coal. By 1818, of course, the Golden Age of Steam was well under way but the vehicles produced were still 'carriages' rather than 'motor cars' as we have come to know them

Chapter 1

In the Beginning

ON THE ROAD

Below right: early trials of Cugnot's *fardier* revealed shortcomings in its controllability, graphically illustrated by this scene from its first trials, in which it demolished part of a wall

'There is in this city,' wrote the Parisian Gui Patin in January 1645, 'a certain Englishman, son of a Frenchman, who proposes to construct coaches which will go from Paris to Fontainbleau and return within the same day, without horses, by means of wonderful springs . . . If this plan succeeds, it will save both hay and oats . . .'

So it was, over three hundred years ago, that the first horseless carriages crept onto the scene, not with the hiss of steam or the bark of internal combustion, but with the whir of clockwork and the rumbling of crude wooden gearing like that of a mill. Travellers and tradesmen had long dreamed of being free of the constraints of animal power; the seventeenth, eighteenth and early nineteenth centuries were replete with fanciful schemes vying with springs and cogs to realise that freedom. Wind power, by sails, strings of kites or whirling mills, and steam power, with pistons, turbines or the simple power of an escaping jet all had their advocates. It was an age of inventors, most with ideas more romantic than practical . . .

Wind and steam were not to be the answer. The wind was fickle and when it obliged by blowing it was difficult to harness. Steam was only a little better; on the scale of the railways it was soon to open up whole continents, but with the technology of the day it simply did not translate into personal mobility on

the prevailing, rudimentary road system. True, it had its successes, but almost invariably in the fields of coaching or cartage, where big was not so bad. By the time the increasing popularity of the bicycle had brought a new lightness and finesse to engineering there were new ways of turning the wheels.

It was not until the 1850s that a viable alternative to steam power for road vehicles became available. It had long been known that certain gases – notably oxygen and hydrogen – could be combined in certain proportions and ignited within a closed container to give a powerful explosion. The difficulty lay in harnessing the power of that explosion.

The first practicable gas engine was patented in 1853 by two Italians, Barsanti and Matteucci, innocently ignorant of previous attempts to construct such a power unit. Eugenio Barsanti, a priest who taught in Florence was the theorist and Felice Matteucci the engineer. Barsanti's first design was a twin-cylinder engine in which free pistons rotated a flywheel shaft through a rack-rod system and it operated on a complicated three-stroke cycle, induction and explosion occurring during the same stroke. It was demonstrated in May 1856, driving a drill and shears. The following year, Barsanti, incapable of following one line of thought to a conclusion, devised an engine with two pistons working in tandem in each cylinder, followed in 1858 by an unsuccessful opposed piston design. The partners later quarrelled, Matteucci retired and Barsanti returned to his tandem piston design of 1857 until dying, shortly after, of Typhoid fever.

Already Barsanti's engines had been supplanted by a superior design devised by the Belgian Jean-Joseph Etienne Lenoir, a consulting engineer to Gauthier & Cie of Paris. In 1859 they formed the Societé des Moteurs Lenoirs to exploit Lenoir's invention, a two-cycle engine in which the gas was ignited electrically at atmospheric pressure; it was quiet and extremely inefficient, developing just two horsepower from 18 litres, but it was reliable and over 500 were built within five years.

The young Gottlieb Daimler visited the Lenoir factory in 1860, and dismissed the new engine as too expensive to run, and operating at too high a temperature; but already Lenoir was attempting to adapt his power unit to the propulsion of a road vehicle. On 16 June that year, *Le Monde Illustré* published an engraving of 'a carriage recently built by M Lenoir', commenting: 'The casing which encloses the motor doesn't in any way encroach upon the passenger space. The gas is contained in the tank A. The rear wheels are driven by an endless chain running on two sprockets. The car is steered by a steering wheel on a vertical shaft placed in front of the driver. This shaft carries at its lower end a pinion acting on a semi-circular rack fixed to the forward wheel, which it obliges to swivel to right or left, thus changing the direction of the vehicle.'

It seems as though this report was a trifle premature, for Lenoir's carriage did not manage to make any sort of journey until 1863; indeed, this may have been an entirely new vehicle. Recalled Lenoir: 'With this, we went from Paris to Joinville-le-Pont (a village some 9 km from Paris); an hour and a half to get there, as long to return. The carriage was heavy; the motor, of $1\frac{1}{2}$ horsepower, with a fairly heavy flywheel, made 100 revolutions a minute.' But those 100 revolutions a minute were hard-earned, for the journey was punctuated with breakdowns, and the consumption of fuel and water was 'considerable'.

Lenoir sold his patents to the Compagnie Parisienne du Gaz in 1863, although he seems to have retained the car; and in 1864 he received the world's first export order, from the francophile Tsar of all the Russias, Alexander II Nicolaevitch. The car was shipped to Russia . . . and vanished, its fate unrecorded.

It was the Lenoir gas engine which had inspired a German clerk, Nikolaus August Otto, to attempt to develop an internal-combustion engine which could be used in situations where steam power was impracticable. After numerous trials, he met a wealthy engineer named Eugen Langen, and together they developed a free-piston engine, which was patented in 1866, and which went into commerical production in 1872. Otto and Langen's company was reorganised as the Gasmotoren-Fabrik Deutz, and a 38-year-old engineer named Gottlieb Daimler was appointed factory managed, with his protégé, Wilhelm Maybach, as chief designer. They reorganised the factory, creating an efficient production system, and by 1875 had increased annual sales to 634 engines with a total of 735 horsepower; the workforce had increased to 230, and Maybach was now receiving a bonus of one thaler for every engine delivered satisfactorily.

Already, however, the free-piston engine was reaching the limits of its development potential: although, by the standards of the day it was reliable, it was also noisy and inefficient. Output was limited to about three horsepower,

Far left: pioneers of the petroleum-engined motor car, Karl Benz, *above,* and Gottlieb Daimler, *below*

Left: Daimler's singly-cylinder, half-horsepower engine, constructed in 1885; this was first fitted to a boneshaker bicycle, but was later tried in a 'horseless carriage'

Below left: completed in 1885 and first run in early 1886, this Daimler wagon was built by Wimpff and Son of Stuttgart. As Daimler wanted to keep this project secret until the wagon was fitted with his 1.1 hp engine, he told the builders that it was merely a present for his wife; they thought the carriage would be horse-drawn

Above: beating the Daimler into manufacture by a couple of months, this famous Benz three-wheeler was generally acknowledged to be the world's first successful petrol-engined motor car

Above: an early Benz catalogue

Left: Gottlieb Daimler is seen here sitting back and enjoying being driven by his son, Adolf; this is Daimler's first vehicle, on trial in 1886

and at that rating the engine needed an overhead clearance of around thirteen feet to allow for the movement of the piston rod. Inspired by the early success of the engine, the Deutz company began an overambitious programme of expansion, and when sales began to tail off, the board ordered Daimler to start development of a 'petroleum engine'.

Eventually, Otto returned to the four-stroke engine, a line of development which he had abandoned in 1861–2; in 1876 his new chief engineer, Franz Rings, drew up an engine of this type for the first time, and this was running in prototype form that autumn. Otto attempted to gain a monopoly of the gas-engine industry by patenting the four-stroke cycle, forcing other experimenters to concentrate on the two-stroke or risk prosecution. But in 1886, after two years of litigation, Otto's patent was overthrown on the grounds that an obscure French civil engineer, Alphonse Beau de Rochas, had, in a long-winded and rambling leaflet which he had distributed in 1862, described the four-stroke cycle and patented the concept.

Although this was, naturally enough, a matter of some chagrin for Otto, it was a vital step in the development of the motor car: inventors, who had been diverted into developing engines which avoided the Deutz patents, could now concentrate on the relatively simpler task of making engines which would run reliably.

Leading the field were Gottlieb Daimler and Karl Benz. Daimler had broken with Otto in 1881 and he was working with Wilhelm Maybach in the shed of his house in Cannstatt to develop a rapid-revolution motor, suitable for vehicle propulsion, using Maybach's patented hot-tube ignition system, which was cruder – but more reliable – than existing electric ignition systems. Benz, who had been operating a machine shop in Mannheim, Germany, since 1871, had hoped to overcome his financial problems by mass-producing tin-working machinery; when this plan had failed, he decided to develop an engine.

He was successful in building a two-stroke engine, which first ran on New Year's Eve, 1879, and received backing for this project from Emil Buhler, the court photographer, who encouraged Benz to form the Gasmotorenfabrik Mannheim in 1882. After only three months Benz resigned from this company, found new backers, and again began producing internal-combustion engines. Already he was considering the manufacture of a motor vehicle, so when, in 1884, it became evident that Otto would almost certainly have his four-stroke patent cancelled Benz started to build a four-stroke engine as part of the 'vehicle with gas-engine drive', which appeared in 1885–6.

The Benz car was one of the great highwater marks in the development of the motor car, for it was the first successful machine designed as an entity, and not just as a horse-drawn carriage with a motor added. The 0.8 hp four-stroke engine was mounted at the rear of the tubular chassis, which obviously owed much to bicycle technology in its construction. There was only a single front wheel, freeing Benz from the necessity of developing the geometrically accurate steering which would have been necessary with two wheels, and the engine drove the big, cycle-type rear wheels through a flat belt, a cross-shaft, fitted with a differential, and side chains. The power unit had its heavy flywheel mounted horizontally; this was because Benz feared that the gyroscopic action of a vertical flywheel might upset the steering.

Ignition was by coil and battery, with a spark plug made by Benz; the carburettor was a simple affair, a tank in which the volatile petroleum spirit gave off its rich fumes, which were then sucked, together with the requisite volume of air, into the cylinder. The engine speed was controlled by regulating the amount of air taken in, thus altering the fuel's ignition characteristics.

By the summer of 1886, the Benz car was sufficiently reliable to be able to make its trial runs in public. On 3 July, a local paper noted: 'A velocipede driven by Ligroin gas, built by the Rheinische Gasmotorenfabrik of Benz & Cie, already reported in these pages on 4 June, was tested this morning early on the Ringstrasse, during which it operated satisfactorily'.

Benz's partners found his preoccupation with the car an annoyance, for it prevented him devoting all his energies to the manufacture of gas engines, on which the company relied for its somewhat precarious existence. But he persisted, no doubt encouraged by press reports like the one which appeared in the Mannheim *Generalanzeiger* on 15 September 1886. 'The very first time that we saw it we were convinced that Benz's invention had solved the problem of

Below: Gottlieb Daimler's first mobile test bed, built in 1885; the wooden-framed 'boneshaker', with stabiliser wheels and steel rims, housed Daimler's 260 cc, single-cylinder engine, which produced a half-horsepower at about 600 rpm. The machine, which weighed 90 kg, was capable of around 12 kph. When this vehicle proved the engine's efficacy, Daimler ordered a 'solidly built' four-seater phaeton as the basis for his next development

building a road vehicle driven by a basic power source. However, as was to be expected, many deficiencies came to light which will have to be corrected by further experiments and improvements. The difficult task of inventing it may now be considered over and done with, and Benz intends to proceed with the manufacture of these vehicles for practical use. This motor vehicle is not meant to have the same purpose and characteristics as a velocipede, which one could take for a pleasurable spin over a smooth, well kept country road; rather, it is conceived as a cart or peasant's wagon, suitable not only for travelling fairly good roads, but also for carrying heavy loads up steep inclines. For example, it would enable a commercial traveller to take his samples from one place to another without any difficulty . . . We believe this wagon has a good future, because it can be put in use without much trouble and because when the speed is made sufficient, it will be the most inexpensive promotional tool for travelling salesmen, as well as a way for tourists to get around.'

Despite such eulogies, the car was not yet ready for sale, but by 1888 Benz judged that the time was ripe to put the new, sturdier version of his three-wheeler on public display. That September, he took it to the Munich Engine Exposition, and gave a number of demonstration runs in that city.

'Seldom, if ever,' ran one newspaper report, 'have passers-by in the streets of our city seen a more startling sight than on Saturday afternoon when a one-horse chaise came from the Sendlingerstrasse over Sendlingertorplatz and down Herzog Wilhelmstrasse at a good clip without a horse or shafts, a gentleman sitting under a surrey top, riding on three wheels – one in front and two behind – speeding on his way towards the centre of town. The amazement of everyone on the street who saw him was such that they seemed unable to grasp what they had before their eyes, and the astonishment was general and widespread.'

To temper such uncritical praise, the *German Yearbook of Natural Science* growled: 'Benz also has made a petrol car which caused some stir at the Munich Exposition. This employment of the petrol engine will probably be no more promising for the future than the use of the steam engine was for road travel.'

And certainly there were no buyers. Benz advertised his car as 'an agreeable vehicle, as well as a mountain-climbing apparatus', but the truth was that when his family borrowed one of the first cars for an impromptu motor tour, they found that its single-speed transmission was sadly deficient in hill-climbing powers. There were perhaps a couple of Benz cars in private hands; one was owned by the Parisian agent for the Benz gas engine, Emile Roger, another survives today in London's Science Museum, possible the first motor car to have been imported into Britain.

Benz had conceived his power unit as an integral part of a purpose-built motor vehicle; Daimler, on the other hand, saw his engine as a universal power unit, for industry as well as for vehicles, and made his preliminary tests in November 1885 with a 0.5 hp engine mounted in a boneshaker bicycle frame. only when this had proved itself capable of driving a vehicle did he consider fitting an engine in a carriage; and even then it was installed in a four-seater phaeton made by a firm of coachbuilders who were ignorant of the fact that it would not be drawn by horses.

Daimler, indeed, made no special stipulations when ordering the vehicle save that it should be 'handsome, but very solidly built', as it was to be a birthday present for his wife; he wanted, it seems, to keep the secret of his engine as long as possible.

When the carriage arrived, the power unit and transmission were installed by the Esslingen Engineering Works. The upper part of the engine protruded through the floor ahead of the rear seat, while final drive was simple, a two-ratio belt drive rotating a countershaft with pinions at each end engaging in toothed rings attached to the rear wheels.

Despite its crude design, the Daimler car seems to have performed successfully, but it was just an interlude in the production of engines for all kinds of uses, from firepumps and saw benches to primitive airships. Demand for these power units grew to such an extent that Daimler and Maybach had to move into larger premises, taking over an old nickel-plating works. It was here that the partners developed one of the crucial power units of the pioneering days of motoring, the V-twin; this 565 cc engine, with its cylinders set at 20 degrees, possessed an excellent power-to-weight ratio and turned at the rapid rate of 630 rpm, far faster than any contemporary gas engines. It was to remain the most advanced power unit available to car constructors for several years. Wilhelm Maybach designed a car round the V-twin engine; this 'steel-wheeler' followed, like the Benz of four years earlier, contemporary bicycle practice, and was a much neater design than the original Daimler car. It was shown at the 1889 Paris World Exhibition, where it attracted much attention. One of its kewnest passengers was Réné Panhard who, together with his partner, Emile Levassor, and Levassor's lady friend, Louise Sarazin, a widow whose late husband had represented Deutz in France since 1874 (and had told his wife on his deathbed to continue the business association with Daimler), planned to build Daimler engines for stationary use; after the Exposition, Mme Sarazin signed an agreement giving her the French and Belgian rights for Daimler petrol engines. In 1890, Levassor married Louise Sarazin, and Panhard and Levassor began manufacturing Daimler engines. They could see no future for the horseless carriage, however, and transferred their rights to use these power units in a carriage to Peugeot, who were already established as bicycle manufacturers, and who, although keen to build automobiles, had just decided against making Serpollet steam cars.

While these men were stumbling towards the beginnings of series production, others were still groping for the secret of making an engine that would drive a carriage. Most notably the Austrian Siegfried Marucs, who was said to have fitted a crude atmospheric engine to a wheelbarrow in 1870, the whole confection, with its tall guide rode for the piston, looking remarkably like a portable guillotine. Little more advanced than the 1805 De Rivaz, it ran only 200 yards before breaking down.

Siegfried's idyll had started in the mid 1860s, when this dilettante inventor had devised a 'carburettor' in his first-floor workshop in the Mariahilfstrasse in Vienna. Intended to vaporise petroleum spirit for lighting purposes, this device was scarcely suitable for adaptation to a road vehicle: for one thing it was so big it virtually filled the room . . .

Marcus was one of those typical Victorian inventors who, scarcely having proved that an idea might work, was immediately away in pursuit of another chimera. He seems to have built another motor carriage in the late 1870s,

Left: Enrico Bernardi, born in Verona on 20 May 1841

Below: one of Bernardi's tricycles of 1896; it was powered by a single-cylinder engine of 624 cc, which produced 2.5 hp at 800 rpm

Below right: the first Panhard & Levassor car, built in 1891; later cars had front engines (as opposed to the rear-mounted unit of this car) and featured the first gearboxes

which was reported, somewhat unreliably, to have made a 12 km journey to Klosterneuberg, and about 1888-9 had a third vehicle built which, with its strange 3–4 hp 'grasshopper' engine and rudimentary construction, looked a good deal older than it was. And so it was, when the Nazis celebrated the fiftieth anniversary of Benz's first patent, that the Austrians chauvinistically claimed that the Marcus car, which was still preserved in a Viennese Museum, preceded Benz by a decade – and added that its inventor had been Jewish . . . This so incensed the Germans that during the war they sought to destroy the Marcus car, thinking that this would eradicate any claim on Benz's priority . . . but the Viennese had foreseen such a move, and hidden the car away safety. The '1875' dating, however, stuck for many years afterwards.

Another experimenter whose work promised more than it delivered was Edouard Delamarre-Debouteville, of Fontaine-le-Bourg, younger son of the owner of a weaving works. In 1884, he drove through the town on a heavy tricycle powered by compressed gas. Passing over a crossroads, the rubber tube linking the gas containers burst with a terrifying explosion and Delamarre-Deboutteville decided to try some more amenable motive power.

Aided by his mechanic, Malandin, he fitted a twin-cylinder petrol engine into his father's old horse-break. It seems to have made one short test-run, which terminated in the chassis coming in two, after which the two experimenters converted their engine to a stationary power unit, and later marketed a developed version of this. Indeed, one of Delamarre-Deboutteville's descendants probably contributed more to the progress of motoring in his position as marketing manager of Ford-France in the 1930s . . .

To fond parents, the motor car was now a commercial proposition, but, for a prospective purchaser, to buy one would be an awfully big adventure. When in 1888, Emile Roger took his new Benz away from the works, he had been personally coached in its care and maintenance by 'Papa Benz' himself. After it had been duly transported back to Paris, however, the car refused to start, and Benz had to follow it, to instruct a mechanic in its handling. Curiously enough, Roger had garaged his car in the workshop of Panhard & Levassor, who also manufactured Benz two-stroke engines under licence, in addition to their Daimler activities. They showed as little interest in the vehicle as did the rest of the public, and no sale was forthcoming.

To Benz's partners, Rose and Esslinger, his preoccupation with the motor vehicle was becoming a threat to the business. 'Herr Benz', Rose would complain, 'we've now made a nice pile of money, but you had best keep your fingers out of that motor car or you'll lose everything'. Then he would sigh and add 'My God, my God, where is this all going to end?'.

It ended for Rose and Esslinger in 1890, when they resigned from the

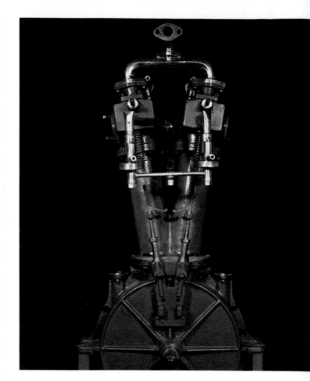

Above: a Daimler V-twin engine of 1892, with hot-tube ignition; although seemingly crude, this form of ignition was more reliable than the electrical units of that early period

Below: part of the extraordinary Millet tricycle of 1887; the power unit is a five-cylinder rotary engine

Below left: a Benz of 1888. The single-cylinder, four-stroke engine produced around 1½ hp between 250 and 300 rpm and drove the generously proportioned rear wheels through chains. This is the car about the intricacies of which 'Papa Benz' coached its owner, Emile Roger

Above: a two-cylinder petrol engine provided the power for this 1883 wagon built by Delamare–Deboutteville; unfortunately, on its first run, the chassis broke in two. This model is now in the Budapest transport museum

Above right: steel wire wheels gave this car, which Daimler sent to the 1889 Paris World Fair, the name 'Stahlradwagen'. A 1½hp, 'high-speed', vee-twin motor, of Daimler's own design, was fitted in the rear of a two-seater, tubular-steel, four-wheeled chassis. The car was instrumental in influencing Peugeot and Panhard & Levassor to begin production of Daimler-engined vehicles in France

company, to be replaced by two more accommodating businessmen, Von Fischer and Ganss, who had useful experience of selling in foreign markets. From then on, progress, if not swift, was at least positive.

On New Year's Day 1891, a postmaster named Kugler wrote to Benz, intrigued by the latter's suggestion that the motor car might prove useful to the postal authorities. 'I am positive that your ingenious and most practical invention will be crowned with a great success, I an not only thinking of its usefulness to the postal services, but I am utterly convinced that it would be most excellent for a country doctor. Not every doctor in a small village has box stalls, horses and a farm to maintain them, yet some kind of a cart is essential for a doctor who has to make calls in a number of places distant from each other. How often is a doctor called on during the night, and how else is he meant to get where he has to go? Before he has roused the sleep-drunk peasant from his bed and got him to put the bridle and harness on the horse, a lot of valuable time has been lost.

'There is another thing about your vehicle: it comes to a halt and turns off and that's it. It doesn't need any feed, or any groom, no blacksmith, no danger of having a horse shy; it just moved along as though a ghostly hand were pushing it – and one stroke of the brakes and it stops. That is what makes it so inexpensive to operate. Even the stupidest blockhead must be able to see such an immense advantage as this.

'The vehicle in motion does have something comical in its appearance from the aesthetic point of view, and someone who did not know what it was might think it was a runaway chaise he was looking at. That is because we have not yet grown used to it.

'But here also, in my opinion, a lot of minor changes and adjustments can artfully be made to improve its appearance without in any way losing sight of the characteristics that serve its purpose. If this were done, the lack of an animal in front to pull it would not be so striking to the beholder.'

Benz was, indeed, already planning changes, most important of which was the development of a four-wheeled car with geometrically accurate steering; meanwhile, the automobile workshop at Mannheim was concentrating mainly on the production of motor boats, which were proving quite popular in Germany. In 1893, the first Benz four-wheeler was ready to be put on the market; its inventor called it the 'Viktoria' because it represented victory over a tricky design problem (he was, apparently, ignorant of the invention of the king-pin steering system patented in 1816 by Georg Lankensperger – coachbuilder to the Royal Court of Bavaria – and later pirated by Rudolf Ackermann).

It was also the first time that a car had been endowed with a glamorous model name, and really marks the beginning of serious sales of motor vehicles to the public, for Benz put the Viktoria into series production.

It was a heavier-looking vehicle than the old three-wheeler, and had a 3 hp engine with a vertical flywheel, which was easier to pull over to start the engine, and which presumably did not upset the new improved steering.

Obviously alarmed by the spectre of motor car-choked roads, the Minister of the Interior of the Grand Duchy of Baden formulated regulations governing the behaviour of automobiles on highways, which he forwarded to the Benz company at the end of November 1893: '. . . Speed on the open road shall not exceed twelve kilometres per hour outside the towns, and within town limits and around sharp corners it shall not exceed six kilometres per hour . . . Upon meeting carts, dray animals or saddle horses, road speed shall be even further diminished . . . The probationary permission being granted to drive motor vehicles on public roads, extending from 1 January to 31 December 1894, inclusive, may be withdrawn immediately in the interest of public order and safety, or further restrictive conditions may be added'.

Benz managed to get the authorities to take the sting out of these regulations,

Above: Karl Benz on his Viktoria follows another Benz family member driving a Velo. This photo was taken on a family outing in 1895

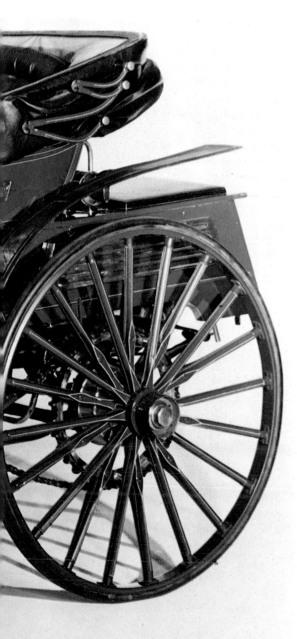

Below: an example of the 1893 Benz Viktoria, the first four-wheeled car built by the company. The car's single-cylinder engine produced 3 bhp at 700 rpm and could propel the vehicle at 25 kph

but his annual production was hardly enough to cause any road congestion problems, nor were the few owners of motor cars keen enough (or foolhardy enough) to undertake long journeys.

An exception to this was the rich German industrialist Theodor von Liebig, who in July 1894 drove his Viktoria from Reichenburg, Bohemia, *via* Mannheim and Gondorf, on the Moselle, to Reims and back. The trip was not exactly trouble free, and he only kept note of his progress as far as Gondorf, where he computed that he had used 140 kg of gasoline to travel 939 kilometres, and that the radiator had consumed 1500 litres of water. Von Liebig, though, concluded that the journey had revealed 'the delight of passing through beautiful landscape by an entirely new means of transportation', and had thus been well worth while.

By now, Benz was attempting to popularise the motor car, groping his way towards a primitive form of assembly-line production, and, on 1 April 1894, he delivered the first 'Velo', a smaller, lighter version of the Viktoria, with a $1\frac{1}{2}$ hp engine, which cost only 2000 Marks in its most basic form.

In 1895, out of a total output of 135 cars, 62 were Velos and 36 were Viktorias, the remainder being made up of various larger models like the Phaeton, the eight-seat Jagdwagen (shooting break), the eight passenger Landau and the stage-coach-like Omnibus. Developments of the Velo were to maintain the popularity of the Benz marque into the 20th Century, while the simplicity of the design ensured that it was widely copied by British and French manufacturers. Yet, even when it appeared, the Velo was a somewhat passé design. The truth of the matter was that, like so many innovators, Karl Benz was strictly a one-note man, and all the cars produced under his aegis were recognisably descended from the original 1885/6 model, with rear-mounted engine and belt-and-chain final drive. Having created what he was convinced was the ultimate design of motor car, Benz stuck doggedly to it, even when it proved commercially foolhardy. This form of shortsightedness was not unique to Benz, as can be seen from inventions as diverse as the Wright Flyer, the Edison Phonograph and the Ford Model T, all of which were produced long after progress had rendered them obsolescent.

However, compared with the cars being turned out by Gottlieb Daimler, the Benz Velo was the height of modernity. Daimler had signed contracts with a gunpowder manufacturer named Max Duttenhofer and another industrialist, W. Lorenz, to gain the necessary capital for expansion of his engine-building activities, a move which resulted in the formation of the Daimler-Motoren-Gesellschaft on 28 November 1890. Daimler and his new partners soon fell out, though, and at the end of 1892 he and Maybach broke away from the company to set up their own experimental workshop in the great summer hall of the defunct Hotel Hermann in Cannstatt. Here they developed the successor to the V-twin power unit, an equally outstanding engine which they called the Phönix. This had two cylinders in line, and was fitted with Maybach's new invention, the spray carburettor, which adjusted the gas/air mixture according to the engine speed and the load imposed on the power unit. This seems to have been an excessive amount of refinement for the inflexible tube-ignition system, which was happiest running at a constant speed.

Having developed an excellent power unit, Daimler and Maybach then totally nullified their achievement by fitting it in a belt-driven car of unbelievably retrograde design, which remained in production even after Daimler and his partners had resolved their quarrel, in 1895. It is hard to comprehend how Maybach could have produced this clumsy vehicle, with its centre-pivot steering, in 1893, when only seven years later he was to conceive the most advanced car in the world.

In fact, it could be argued that the principal effect of all this hard work by the Germans was to establish the French as the world's leading motor manufacturers for the ensuing decade, for the French were willing to experiment and alter, while the Germans seemed content to progress along the lines that they had established several years earlier. The French, too, seemed far more confident of the potential of the motor vehicle: in 1891, Peugeot dispatched one of their earliest cars on an ambitious foray, following the competitors in the

Right: René Panhard and Emile Levassor

Below: a fine example of Peugeot's early *vis-a-vis* design, albeit with more ornate bodywork than would be normal. These vehicles had engines of 1018 cc and could attain a speed of 30 kph. This particular example was built in 1892, along with 28 other cars
(Peugeot collection, France)

Far right: the Velo was what Karl Benz called the ultimate design of motor car and he continued to market developments of the one basic theme right into the 20th century; the success of the vehicle blinded Benz to the need to move forward with more advanced designs

2047 km Paris–Brest–Paris cycle race. It covered the distance in 139 hours, 'without a moment's trouble', a feat which helped Peugeot to sell five cars to private owners that year, and to boost output to 29 in 1892.

The cars which Peugeot were making echoed the company's long experience in cycle manufacture, with tubular chassis (through which the cooling water for the engine circulated) and spindly spoked wheels. The rear-mounted Daimler engines were purchased through Panhard and Levassor until Peugeot developed their own power unit in 1896.

Having seen the results obtained by his friend Peugeot, Levassor decided to build a horseless carriage for himself, prompted, it seems, by his go-ahead wife, the former Mme Sarazin.

The first Panhard & Levassor car appeared in the late summer of 1890. It was a dogcart with the engine mounted between the seats, similar in conception to the original Daimler carriage of 1886. It was not, apparently, an unqualified success, and Levassor would grumble-gently: 'If Daimler can make a carriage run at eighteen kilometres an hour, so can I . . .'

After building a couple of cars with the engine at the rear, Levassor settled on a front-engined layout, with the unit contained under a square bonnet, driving through the famous 'brusque et brutale' gearbox (which had four speeds forward, four speeds in reverse, and operated completely al fresco, devoid of any protective—or oil-retaining—casing) to the countershaft and side chains which gave the final drive.

'Build heavy', said Levassor, 'and you build strong!'. He also, it seems, built reliable, for with his second car (still rear-engined) he was the very first Parisian to make the summer drive that is now an annual ritual, from the capital to the coast, covering the 225 km from his works in the Avenue d'Ivry to his summer home at Etretat in a total running time of 23 hours 15 minutes on 31 July/ 1 August 1891. The greatest annoyance he found was the need to stop every so often and refill the surface carburettor, which also acted as a fuel tank, and only held 1.3 litres. 'It's true', he philosophised, 'that I made use of the halts to fill up the water tank and grease the car'.

This journey, however, was eclipsed less than two years later when his partner's 23-year-old son, Hippolyte Panhard, set out from the factory bound for Nice, driving the 2 hp car which his father had bought at a specially reduced price of 4318 francs on 28 August 1892, as a present for the young man. Leaving Paris via the Bois de Vincennes, Hippolyte drove the solid-tyred vehicle gingerly over the cobbled quais at Alfort, which had last been paved during the reign of Louis XIV. Once he reached the smoother roads beyond the city, though, he engaged the third speed, and allowed the carriage to reach a heady seventeen

kph. 'It's possible to attain twenty kph, but such great speeds require considerable attention on the part of the driver, and are not always advisable', warned the company's catalogue. Pausing for an excellent lunch at Fontaine-bleu, Hippolyte, who was accompanied by his uncle Georges Méric, covered 140 km in the day, noting in a letter to his father that 'some undulations of the terrain often compelled the use of second gear'.

Their progress was also impeded by the fringed canopy attached to the car, which caught the wind, so they abandoned it the next morning. Obtaining fuel was another problem, and they had to search for sources of supply: at Pouilly they were given 23 litres of gasoline by the owner of an 'oil-engined plough', while in another town, Hippolyte had to buy his fuel in a grocer's shop.

'Unfortunately, I had stopped behind the grocer's handcart. As I got down from the car, I pushed the clutch lever and the car jerked forward, overturning the handcart. Cost: 10 francs . . .'

As the car stuttered through villages, it attracted a vast amount of attention. 'Urchins, dogs, cats and chickens all rushed after us, each making their own distinctive noise. It was a dreadful racket . . .'

The important factor was that Hippolyte and Georges Méric were not making a test run: they were touring, and touring in a relatively relaxed manner. 'Yesterday at dinner there were five exquisite courses, much appreciated by Uncle Georges. Dinner, two rooms, stabling for the car and breakfast cost us a total of 10 francs. It's really not expensive . . .'

There were few mechanical annoyances on the road. Descending the steep Col de la République, they free-wheeled, and the car ran 'silently, like running on velvet', but the brakes overheated badly, and Georges Méric had to hold a bucket of water between his legs and cool the brakes with a wet rag. Nearing their destination, the travellers paused at Hyères, where Belhomme, a mechanic from Ivry, replaced Méric. It seems that a few components had dropped from the car during the eight day run (the French still call spares 'detached pieces'!) and a request for replacements was telegraphed to Levassor.

In Cannes, Nice and Monaco, the Panhard was the centre of attention, and Hippolyte showed it off at the best hotels, theatres, casinos and promenades, in front of prominent personalities.

Above: a famous name in motoring was born in 1886, when the old woodworking machinery firm of Périn and Pauwels passed to René Panhard and Emile Levassor on Périn's death. The earliest Panhard & Levassor cars had their engines either at the rear or in the middle, but by 1893 the partners had established what was to become the classic layout – front engine, central gearbox and rear-wheel drive. This 1892 example has a rear-mounted $2\frac{3}{4}$ hp engine. This was the first season in which Panhard & Levassor offered their clientèle the option of solid rubber tyres, though this car has iron tyres

Right: setting the classic pattern for motor vehicles is this 1894 Panhard & Levassor. It has a front-mounted engine, gearbox in the middle and rear-wheel drive

Above: the Honourable Evelyn Ellis proudly displays his Panhard & Levassor at the first ever exhibition of motor vehicles, held at Royal Tunbridge Wells in 1895

Below: by the mid 1890s, the motor car was becoming an accepted form of transport. This 1895 Panhard & Levassor publicity photograph is one of the first to link glamour and the motor car. It is unlikely that the two young *cocottes* would have ventured out alone on the primitive Panhard

However, the clutch (which was Levassor's eccentric 'brush' design) was beginning to play up: 'M. Levassor will say that I drove the car very badly, but I assure you that I took every possible care of it and did not try to climb hills more quickly by slipping the clutch'. And there were demonstration runs to be given to important prospective customers . . . 'a whole heap of Englishmen and the Grand Duke of Mecklembourg, cousin of the Grand Duchess Michael'.

The Grand Duchess Michael was keen to buy a car and drive it herself, and asked Hippolyte to drive her party to the Golf Club of which her husband was president.

'There will be three or four of them', wrote Hippolyte to his father, 'and it seems that they are all big and fat . . .' The reason for his anxiety was that misbehaving clutch. 'I'll try and put a wedge behind the clutch spring which, by the grace of God, will make it engage better. It would be awful to fail in front of all those grand people.'

The clutch did not fail, luckily, and the car continued to attract attention during Hippolyte's stay at Nice. On the way home, though, the young man tempted fate by driving into the mountains beyond Grasse and, sure enough, the clutch packed up, and the car had to be hauled to the next village behind horses. 'Anyway, it's been a picturesque journey', said Hippolyte philosophically.

It had been a journey, too, which could hardly have been made anywhere else but in France and emphasised that country's lead in the construction and use of motor vehicles.

In America, for instance, the number of successful gasoline carriages which had been built up to that date could be counted on the fingers of one hand, even though George Baldwin Selden had made his first patent application for a 'reliable road locomotive, simple, cheap, lightweight, easy to control and powerful enough to climb any ordinary hill' in 1879, and on the basis of this patent (which was not published until 1895!) attempted to gain a monopoly of the nascent American motor industry.

The first American motor vehicle appears to have been the unsuccessful Schank tricycle exhibited at the 1886 Ohio State Fair. This had an engine 'as big as a kitchen stove', and was chiefly important in having inspired young Charles Duryea, a cycle manufacturer from Peoria, to start experiments with an 'atmospheric engine'. Curiously enough, American pioneers seem to have almost wilfully ignored the fact that perfectly good power units were readily available to them on a cash and carry basis as early as 1891, when Gottlieb Daimler's friend William Steinway (of piano fame) began building Daimler

engines under licence in his Long Island factory, a venture which lasted until 1896.

It seems that the first successful American car was the three-wheeler built by John W. Lambert, of Ohio City, which was running—and photographed—in January or February 1891. The same year, Henry Nadig of Allentown, Pennsylvania, built a four-wheeler vehicle with a single-cylinder power unit, which does not seem to have been too successful, for it was replaced two years later by a twin-cylinder engine, in which form the car was operated until 1903 (it still exists, as does the 1892 Schloemer from Milwaukee).

In September 1893, Charles Duryea and his brother Frank made their first successful trials with a horseless carriage in the streets of Springfield, Massachussets. However, Frank recalled fifty years later 'because of its friction transmission, the car was barely operative, and I was never able to give a demonstration to a prospective client'.

More success and a measure of financial backing were forthcoming eventually, and in 1895 the Duryeas founded America's first motor-manufacturing firm, the Duryea Motor Wagon Company, in Springfield. The following year they set up an agency in London, under the aegis of one J. L. McKim, but this pioneering venture was short-lived.

In any case, Britain was far from being an ideal market for would-be motor magnates: successive Governments had compounded the asininities of the Locomotives on Highways Act to the point of absurdity by insisting that lightweight motor cars should be subject to the same regulations as adipose traction engines, especially with regard to having a crew of two aboard to attend to the mechanism, plus a third to walk ahead to warn of the vehicle's approach. Thus, those who wished to experiment with self-propelled vehicles had to behave like clandestine criminals, and some of the most able, like

Above: advertising for the 1896 Duryea, said to be America's first series-production motor car. In 1896 the Duryeas set up an agency in London but, largely thanks to short-sighted legislation, England was not ready

Above: the 1894 Bremer, a Benz-influenced machine built by Frederick W. Bremer, a young engineer from Walthamstow, disputes the title of Britain's first four-wheeled, internal-combustion-engined car with the contemporary Knight

Left: London did not have to wait for the motor car to bring traffic chaos. Save for the motive power, little has changed since this scene at the Mansion House of around 1900

Below: pioneer motorist Henry Hewetson had a cynical method of beating the 'Red Flag Act'. A boy on a bicycle went on ahead to watch for policemen; if he saw one, he reported to Hewetson, whose youthful passenger then dismounted and walked ahead of Hewetson's Benz carrying a 'flag' consisting of a red ribbon attached to a pencil!

Edward Butler, of Newbury, who built an ingenious petroleum tricycle in 1888, abandoned their vehicles in disgust. Frederick Bremer, of Walthamstow, a young cycling enthusiast, who had conceived the idea of fitting a gas engine to his cycle during the 1880s, began building a tiny, Benz-inspired car in 1892, which he completed a couple of years later. He ran it very little, and always after dark, to avoid infringing the law, and eventually abandoned it in his garden shed, from which he disinterred it some forty years later and presented it to the local museum. It was restored during the 1960s and successfully completed the London–Brighton Veteran Car Run.

John Henry Knight, of Farnham, Surrey, who had built a steam car in the mid 1860s, and who now owned the Reliance Motor Works, builders of stationary engines, had a three-wheeled car constructed there in 1895; in its later, four-wheeled form, it is now preserved in the National Motor Museum at Beaulieu. Knight was understandably bitter about the anti-motoring attitude of the British Government: 'It is this prejudice which has allowed England to be flooded with French and German motor cars, and the sum of money that has crossed the Channel for the purchase of these cars must have been very considerable', he wrote in 1902. 'Money lost to this country, because our legislators refused to allow motor cars to run on English roads! Had it not been for these restrictions, we might have taken the lead in self-propelled carriages, instead of leaving it to the Germans and French. A lost trade is seldom if ever recovered. French-made cars are now to be found in most foreign countries and our colonies, and we may be sure that these makers will do all they can to keep the trade they have obtained—partly through the want of foresight on the part of our House of Commons.'

Certainly, the manner in which the Daimler patents were handled in Britain in the early 1890s compared very unfavourably with the situation in France. Frederick Richard Simms, a young mechanical engineer from Warwick, had met Gottlieb Daimler at an exhibition in Germany at the end of the 1880s, and had acquired the Daimler rights for the United Kingdom and its colonies (except Canada). However, he found it difficult to popularise this power unit, due to the restrictive laws which dissuaded most people from attempting to go motoring. So, the first public demonstration of the Daimler engine in Britain

took place in 1891 with a motor launch brought to London from Cannstatt, with which trials took place on the Thames at Putney.

Nevertheless, Simms formed the Daimler Motor Syndicate Limited, to handle Daimler products, and an arch was rented at Putney Bridge Railway Station, where the Syndicate's main activity consisted of converting launches to petrol power (around this time three young brothers called Lanchester were also experimenting with a petrol launch powered by their own engine).

In 1895, Simms imported the first Cannstatt-Daimler car to be seen in Britain, and was approached by a syndicate which saw the possibility of vast profits in the new invention, and were willing to pay a considerable sum of money to acquire the Daimler rights. Prominent in this syndicate was Harry J. Lawson, an engineer turned company promoter. He had received his training in raising large amounts of cash for dubious projects during the bicycle boom of the early 1890s at the hand of the notorious Terah Hooley, whose name had become synonymous with the securing of capital for companies whose potential never quite managed to match the glowing terms of the share prospectus.

Lawson's training as a cycle engineer, and his experience of the cycle boom,

Above: the 1895 Knight, challenger to the Bremer's claim to be Britain's first petrol-driven road vehicle. John Henry Knight adapted one of his 'Trusty' stationary engines to drive what was originally a three-wheeler, the fourth wheel being added for the 1896 Crystal Palace Motor Show

convinced him that once the law with regard to motor vehicles was relaxed, a similar boom in self-propelled transportation could occur, and he intended to be the one to profit from such a situation. To which end, he set about systematically acquiring the British rights to all the leading Continental patents (although he also acquired a considerable amount of costly dross along the way), and then launched a manufacturing group to exploit them.

In January 1896, he floated the Daimler Motor Company, and set about publicising the 'new locomotion', especially through the columns of *The Autocar*, one of the very first motoring journals, which had been founded in November 1895 as the mouthpiece of the Lawson organisation (and which was to prove infinitely more durable than its sponsor).

By continued lobbyings, Lawson persuaded Parliament to change its attitude to the motor car (the Marquis of Salisbury, whose Conservative administration was then in power, subsequently became a keen motorist himself) and to bring in a new Act which freed motor carriages weighing less than three tons from the need to carry two people, and abolished the peripatetic harbinger altogether, raising the overall speed limit to 12 mph.

To commemorate the 'throwing open of the highways', Lawson organised a run from London to Brighton, on 14 November 1896—'Emancipation Day'.

The administration of the event was maybe a little dubious—at least one of the vehicles which reached Brighton did so by courtesy of the Southern Railway Company—but at least Britain was now on the way to being a country with its own indigenous motor-manufacturing industry, and could begin to make up the ground which had been lost to it by the Law.

Now the motor car had to find its market:

'What is it?
'It is an Autocar.
'Some people call it a motor car.
'It is worked by a petroleum motor.
'The motor is of four horsepower.
'It will run sixty miles with one charge of oil.
'No! It can't explode – there is no boiler.
'It can travel at 14 mph.
'Ten to eleven is its average pace.
'It can be started in two minutes.
'There are eight ways of stopping it so it can't run away.
'It is steered with one hand.
'Speed is mainly controlled by the foot.
'It can be stopped in ten feet when travelling at full speed.
'It carries four gallons of oil and sixteen gallons of water.
'The water is to keep the engine cool.
'It costs less than three-farthings a mile to run.
'The car can carry five people.
'It can get up any ordinary hill.
'It was built by the Daimler Motor Company of Coventry and cost £370.
'We have come from John O'Groats House.
'We are going to Land's End.
'We are not record-breaking but touring for pleasure.'

These words, printed on little cards which were handed out to members of the public along the road from John O'Groats to Land's End, were the bare facts behind the first epic drive on British soil. It was, after all, less than a year since 'Emancipation Day', and the infant British motor industry had done little except relieve credulous investors of a considerable amount of money. Indeed, when Henry Sturmey, founding editor of *The Autocar*, set out on this marathon drive in his newly delivered Daimler on 2 October 1897, the Daimler company had been building cars for only a few months. During 1896 and most of 1897, they had been importing Daimler and Panhard cars from the continent, and their first production models were, indeed, straight copies of the contemporary Panhard. They constructed the frames and engines. Their associates, the Motor Manufacturing Company, produced the carriagework, and it was a toss-up whether the finished vehicle was sold as a Daimler or an MMC.

Left: an example of the first Daimler to be built in Great Britain; a two-cylinder machine, it was constructed on contemporary Panhard lines and had a four-speed-plus-reverse transmission. Prices ranged from about £360 to £420

Sturmey's long drive, on which he covered a total of 1600 miles, and took seventeen days (including three days' rest) to cover the 939 miles from furthest north to furthest south, showed the basic reliability of the design. He had no trouble apart from clutch slip brought on by a howling gale which drenched the entire car, its occupants and its mechanism, and the total failure of the inadequate braking system on the descent of the Kirkstone Pass. The car ran away, attaining the suicidal velocity of 30 mph, Sturmey avoiding disaster by sitting tight and steering like a demon. He rammed a bank when the car attempted to repeat the episode a few miles further on!

However, not all the pioneers enjoyed such little trouble – after all, Sturmey

Below: an 1898 Decauville *Voiturelle* built by a French railway locomotive firm. This vehicle featured sliding pillar front suspension, although the designer, naval engineer Joseph Guédon, omitted to provide any springing at the rear. As with most vehicles of this type and age, the manufacturers went to De Dion for their power units, in this case a twin-cylinder unit of 489 cc

Above: based on the original Renault, this 1899 car has a slightly longer wheelbase than that machine to accommodate a third 'spider' seat. It is powered by an air-cooled 1¾ hp De Dion engine, driving the rear wheels via a three-speed gearbox, propeller shaft and differential (Skokloster Museum, Sweden)

Below: even as early as 1895, Daimler could advertise 'Over Ten Years Practical Experience' on the cover of the very first edition of *The Autocar.* Over eighty years later, the magazine still survives

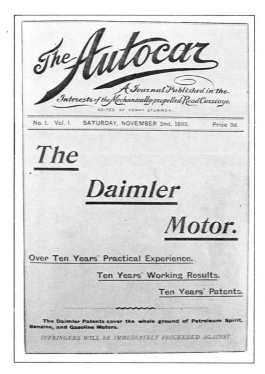

was a director of the Daimler Company, and his car had doubtless been assembled with more care than a less-exalted order would have received. Among those who suffered from the awkward temperament of the early tube-ignited motor cars was the author Rudyard Kipling, who in a letter written in 1904 looked back over his motoring experiences with wry amusement. 'I like motoring because I have suffered for its sake. I began seven years ago in the days of tube ignition, when 6 hp was reckoned fair allowance for a touring car, And fifteen miles an hour was something to talk about. My agonies, shames, delays, rages, chills, parboilings, road-walkings, water-drawings, burns and starvations – at which you laughed – all went to make your car today safe and comfortable. If there were no dogs there would be no vivisection, and people would still be treated on the lines of Galen and Avicenna. Any fool can invent anything, as any fool can wait to buy the invention when it is thoroughly perfected, but the men to reverence, to admire, to write odes and erect statues to, are those Prometheuses and Ixions (maniacs, you used to call us) who chase the inchoate idea to fixity up and down the King's Highway with their red right shoulders to the wheel . . .'

However, it was not just mechanically that the pioneers suffered. Harry Lawson's house-of-cards empire started running into trouble within two years of its inception. Most of the components of that empire were housed in the Motor Mills, a converted four-storey cotton-mill building on a thirteen-acre site near the Coventry Canal, which had been acquired in 1896 (and advertised as 'the largest autocar factory in the world . . . for the manufacture of autocars under the Pennington, Daimler and Bollée systems . . . 200 highly skilled workmen' before the Lawson companies had even moved in!). Here at various times were housed Daimler, the Motor Manufacturing Company, the Great Horseless Carriage Company, Humber & Company, the British Motor Syndicate, the Beeston Pneumatic Tyre Company, the Coventry Motor Company . . .

These companies lived, for the most part, a curiously incestuous existence, robbing Peter to pay Paul by complex financial double-shuffles like the 1898 acquisition of the Great Horseless Carriage Company by the British Motor Syndicate, where some £300,000 did a now-you-see-it-now-you-don't vanishing trick to, it seems, the complete satisfaction of 4000 out of 4070 shareholders who did not realise they had been comprehensively gulled . . .

Right: a Delahaye *vis-a-vis* of 1898, again, a fairly conventional design of small car, with a rear-mounted 'slow-running' engine (Château de Grandson, Switzerland)

Left: the Swiss Jules Weber and the Croatian Franz Brozincevic collaborated to build the Weber car in Zurich between 1899 and 1906. Powered by a rear-mounted 6/8 hp engine, this 1901 *vis-a-vis* features variable-ratio belt transmission, which was later to appear in the DAF cars of the 1950s (Château de Grandson, Switzerland)

Below: this 1899 Coventry Daimler, belonging to the Hon John Scott-Montagu, competed in the 1900 Thousand Miles Trial. Boasting four speeds forward (and four in reverse!) it was restored to original condition by John Scott-Montagu's son, Lord Montagu of Beaulieu who drove it in the 1970 re-enactment of the Thousand Miles Trial

The British Motor Syndicate, indeed, does not appear to have actually *built* anything. True, it issued some very handsome brochures, although half the vehicles in these were total improbabilities and the other half consisted of imported Panhards (which, Lawson generously conceded, with somewhat less than a regard for the truth, had been 'built under British Motor Syndicate Patents'). It did, however, rigorously pursue those hapless individuals who were presumed to have trespassed against those expensively bought patents.

Take the case of the would-be motor manufacturer from Birmingham against whom the Syndicate took action in 1896. 'An order was immediately made restraining the defendant from proceeding further with the infringement, and a wholesale order was made for the destruction of the parts produced'.

Added Lawson, casually: 'I am sorry to say that the man committed suicide . . . in the circumstances, and on representation being made to me, the directors accepted £150 instead of £600, due under one head of the infringement . . . The case proved that the patents are the absolute property of the Syndicate, and as much property as freehold land'.

This, when the Syndicate was little more than a squatter on the freehold of other men's ideas, was rankest hypocrisy. However, one gets the impression that Lawson was so puffed up with vanity that he could not see the dubiousness of the premises from which he was arguing. His father had been a Methodist minister, and it seems as though Lawson regarded himself as a prophet sent to lead the faithful into the promised land flowing, if not with milk and honey, at least with unlimited share capital.

For all his ridiculous posturings and grandiose schemes, Lawson did attract some able men into his organisation, among the charlatans like E. J. Pennington, the American inventor who matched Harry J. at his own game by selling him the rights to some pretty amazing vehicles, none of which was capable of running more than a short distance without mishap.

Among the gems in Lawson's dross were a young man named Percival Perry, who was later to head the Ford organisation in Europe, and a brilliant electrical engineer, Walter C. Bersey, who had built an electrical omnibus as early as 1888, while he was still in his teens.

Silent and elegant, Bersey's electric carriages caused a great sensation in London (where, indeed, he was issued with the last summons under the old Locomotives on Highways Act). In 1896, a correspondent from the *East Anglian Daily Times* was a passenger on one of Bersey's many demonstration runs. 'Observing a crowd assembled by the Northumberland Avenue entrance of the Grand Hotel, our correspondent found that it was occasioned by a very smart yellow-wheeled Landau, driven by a gentleman whom he afterwards found to be the inventor of the carriage, which it appeared was owned by the Great Horseless Carriage Company . . . our correspondent was at once recognised and invited to take a seat . . . The carriage, therefore, amidst a dense crowd which had already assembled, started with a living freight of no less

than seven persons, who anticipated that their driver would take them along the less frequented Thames Embankment. On the contrary, the intrepid Mr Bersey sharply turned round, and with *coeur leger* dashed into the thick of the Strand traffic and into the thick of the light badinage in which the London bus man and cabby are so gifted and fluent.

'Onward we sped, amid cries of "A penny all the way", "Whip behind" and "Where's your 'osses?" – and very instructive it was to observe the sudden

Right: the imposing 4 hp Orient Express of 1898. The firm of Bergmann's Industriewerke built Orient Express cars in Gaggenau between 1895 and 1903. This particular car has ten hand controls and one pedal, which works the warning bell; the main brake is controlled by the passenger! Immortalised in the 1902 motoring novel *The Lightning Conductor* as the 'Brute Beast', the Orient Express was reckoned one of the worst cars of all time by motoring pioneer St John Nixon, protégé of S. F. Edge

Left: a scene in Billancourt in 1898; Marcel Renault, on the left, is in the front of a contemporary quadricycle, his brother, Louis, is at the wheel of the prototype Renault car in the centre and Paul Hugé is in the first production Renault. The Renault's power unit is a De Dion 273 cc, air-cooled, 1¾ hp engine, driving through a three-speed-and-reverse gearbox. In the first six months, the Renaults sold over sixty cars

Below: Edward Joel Pennington sits proudly on his Torpedo in 1896. Pennington, 'imposter par excellence', claimed he owned the largest motor vehicle company in the world, but it was nothing more than a small firm with outlandish ideas that were hardly ever likely to transform the industry in the way he would have liked

surprise of the foot passengers as they realised that the handsome carriage which whisked past them was propelled silently and swiftly without the aid of the patient, nervous, skating quadrupeds to which they were accustomed. As we sped past them, we could easily have thrown one of the early Christmas oranges which were offered us into the gaping mouths of the startled foot passengers.

'Instructive was it to see the problems which the jealous Jehus set our driver by pulling their clumsy buses and cabs across his path, but calm and unmoved our skilful coachman brought his obedient motor carriage to rest within a few inches of the adversary, and when they gave him the slightest chance, flew, without apparent movement, swiftly and resistlessly past every vehicle, all the while having his machine under absolute control.

'Our correspondent, having no business instincts, had no thought beyond the absolute comfort of being propelled with the touch of the tiny lever at will, without effort, and without work or suffering to dumb, patient animals, wheresoever he wills. In his mind's eye, he beholds the streets of the 20th Century free from the crack of the cruel whip, the struggles of terrified animals, with traffic swiftly and silently passing through comely and cleanly streets, emancipated from the tyranny of the merciless "friends of the horse" . . . To show the docility of the electric carriage of towns, our driver assured us he had driven his chairman (the Earl of Winchelsea) and six other directors of the Great Horseless Carriage Company, from Westminster to Ludgate Circus and back (eight miles), through the thick of the Strand traffic, in thirty minutes. Welcome the motor car!'

Certainly, in the early days of motoring, it was the electric car which appealed most to the non-motoring classes. Bersey, who had invented a new type of dry battery which promised a longer service life than the lead-acid type, was obviously convinced that the electric vehicle was superior to its rivals, as he told the *Gentleman's Journal* in 1896: 'The petroleum motor carriage inevitably subjects its occupants to annoyances from which its electric rival is entirely free. The former is subject to excessive vibration, smell, noise and heat. From all these defects the electric car is free. Moreover, the petroleum motor requires an engineer to drive it, that is, if the danger of explosion is to be reduced to a minimum. The electric car is so simple that any coachman may learn to manipulate it in less than half-an-hour!'.

However, although Bersey attempted to popularise the electric by operating a fleet of cabs on the streets of London, the venture was short-lived. Right from the beginning, the major drawbacks which have always bedevilled the electric vehicle were apparent: the cabs could run no more than fifty miles on one charge, and then had to return to a generating station, either to take on fresh batteries (which weighed fourteen cwt!) or to be recharged (which took several hours), and, when the batteries reached the end of their service life, replacements were costly. With this constant need to return to base, no wonder that Americans nicknamed electric vehicles 'homing pigeons'!

The failure of the London Electrical Cab Company was one of the first cracks to appear in the elaborate corporate set-up of the Lawson organisation. Once one component had collapsed, however, the rest were not far behind; it was the affair of the Electric Tramways Construction and Maintenance Company which was to prove Lawson's ultimate downfall. In this instance, Lawson was acting as nominee for his old mentor, Terah Hooley, who, as an undischarged bankrupt, was debarred from trading. This company attracted official attention, however, with the result that Lawson and Hooley were committed for trial, charged with fraudulently creating a 'paper' company for the sole purpose of extracting large sums of money from the public, most of which had found its way into Lawson's pocket. Hooley, accustomed to nothing but the best, had hired the brilliant Rufus Isaacs as his advocate, and was eventually acquitted after a three-week hearing, but Lawson was found guilty of false statements and sentenced to twelve months hard labour. So the 'Father of the British Motor Industry' passed from the scene.

In any case, his hold on that industry had been too tenuous to be maintained for long. By persuading the Government to ease the restrictions on the use of motor vehicles on the roads of Britain, Lawson had prised open the floodgate to release a tide of imports and home-produced cars too strong to stem. Brilliant engineers like the Lanchesters were operating outside his organisation, using concepts which were years ahead of those costly 'master patents'.

Only Daimler ultimately survived out of Lawson's original companies, and prospered greatly under its new 'far-seeing and practical Board of Directors'.

Above: an early Georges Richard of the late 1890s; it was built on Benz lines and featured belt drive and three forward speeds

Below: not looking that much more advanced than the Viktoria and the Velo is this Benz Comfortable of 1898

Above: de Riancey of Levallois-Perret, Seine built cars between 1899 and 1901. This is their 1899 twin-cylinder model, one of only eleven built
(Château de Grandson, Switzerland)

Oddly enough, the most popular car of the era, the little belt-driven Benz, did not fall under Lawson's aegis, but was imported into Britain by a wealthy industrialist named Henry Hewetson, who had been one of the first owners of this marque in England, and had turned his hobby into a profitable business. The car was popular because it was relatively cheap, and simple enough to be worked on by someone who knew absolutely nothing about motor cars, and that was a very necessary thing, as the author Max Pemberton, who first rode on a Benz in 1896, recalled: 'Whenever we met a motor "hung up" by the road-side – and that was uncommon occurrence – be sure that it was a Benz in difficulties with its ignition. Carrying the engines aft, and access to them being by a door which let down in the manner of the flap upon a butcher's cart, the proprietor invariably wore the air of a man who was looking for a mutton chop he had mislaid, and would take some three weeks to find it'.

Despite this reputation for temperament, the Benz was still the world's most popular car. From 67 cars in 1894, output rose steadily until, in 1899, the year in which Benz delivered its 2000th car, production reached a record 572. The basic Benz design was now available in several variants, ranging from the little 3 hp Velo and Comfortable to the twelve-passenger Break, powered by the 15 hp opposed-twin Kontra-Motor announced in 1897. Demand reached its peak in 1900, when 603 cars were delivered, but collapsed the following year, when only 385 cars were ordered, as more modern designs began to undermine the popularity of the Benz.

Karl Benz would not – or could not – come up with a modern design to replace the old faithful, and so his directors first commissioned the company's chief design engineer, Georg Diehl, to produce an up-to-date car with shaft drive and a vertical-twin engine at the front, and then, when this had proved a disappointment, called in the French engineer Marius Barbarou, and commissioned him to design a whole new product range, from single-cylinder runabouts to a 60 hp, four-cylinder racing car. These were not an unqualified success, either, and Barbarou and his assistants resigned in 1904, but a pooling of the lessons learned from these German and French designs created a new range, called the Parsifal. Bitterly offended by the usurpation of his powers, 'Papa

Benz' had already left the company, although he returned briefly to help guide it through a sales crisis. He retired finally in 1906 and, with his sons, set up a little, limited-production car factory in nearby Ladenburg.

However, while it had been current, the belt-drive Benz had been an important factor in the creation of enthusiasm for motoring. Because it was simple, it was widely copied. Among the legions of Benz imitations were numbered the Star, the Georges-Richard, the Marshall, the Arnold, the Popp, the Hurtu, the Orient Express, the Hewinson-Bell . . .

Some ten years ago, an octogenarian survivor of the earliest days of motoring, who had carried a red flag for the North Oxfordshire Steam Ploughing Company in the late 1880s, and whose cycle repairer father had owned one of only six Hewinson-Bells ever made, recalled that the first time that a car stopped in the little Berkshire town where he lived, such a crowd gathered that he thought a circus was coming!

With so very few motor vehicles in existence, it was hardly surprising that the sight of one caused a sensation, and, right from the very beginning, motor shows were a popular form of public diversion. At the first indoor exhibition of

Left: S. F. Edge's 1900 Napier receives attention during the Thousand Miles Trial of that year. Unmade road surfaces wrought havoc with early pneumatic tyres and made scenes such as this commonplace. The boy behind the car is St John Nixon; the car's owner, novelist Mrs Mary Kennard, looks on

motor vehicles in Britain, at the Stanley Cycle Show in November 1895 (there were five cars on display), visitors were also regaled with another technological sensation, in the shape of a moving picture show on the Edison Kinetoscope. More shows followed, and soon became annual fixtures. One of the best of the early exhibitions, the Cordingley Show in Islington's Agricultural Hall, got away to a very curious start, for it was originally a sideshow at the Fourth Annual Exhibition of Laundry Machinery in 1896; two years later, the Laundry Exhibition still featured a 'moto-car section', although now this part of the display contained almost one hundred vehicles instead of the half-dozen or so at the first show. The august *Automotor and Horseless Vehicle Journal* rather sniffily looked down its nose at what it considered a vulgar display: 'If, however, the projectors of this Exhibition are going to continue to hold exhibitions of moto-vehicles, we would suggest the propriety of entirely dissociating them from any purely trade display such as the so-called Laundry Exhibition, because from the public point of view there is nothing in common between the automobilist and the laundry worker . . . we then utterly fail to see how it is possible that any good can result to the cause of automobilism by the association indicated. Moreover, we are by no means satisfied that the time is at all opportune for exhibition of moto-vehicles. It is not two years since the Locomotive on Highways Act was passed, and hence much progress is not to be expected'.

In passing, it should be observed that Stanley Spooner, who edited the *Automotor Journal*, did not learn to drive a car until 1926, when his colleague Edgar Duffield convinced him that the editor of a motor paper really should know how to drive, and persuaded him to buy an Austin Twelve. Further, Charles Cordingley, who organised the Agricultural Hall Show (which was soon to rid itself of its bagwash associations, and to survive another decade), also happened to be the publisher of the rival publication *Motor Car Journal*, and therefore Spooner's barbs might have been loaded with more venom than strictly necessary . . .

However, exhibitions and demonstrations still tended only to reach a localised audience, most of whom were already motoring enthusiasts. There were still millions of people in Britain who had never seen a motor car, and there was still much opposition to the new locomotion from those who made their living in one way or another from horses, and saw the motor vehicle as a threat to their livelihood. It was, thought Claude Johnson, the go-ahead secretary of the Automobile Club of Great Britain and Ireland (founded in 1897, and elevated to the title of Royal Automobile Club ten years later), time that some concerted demonstration was made to 'advance the automobile movement in the United Kingdom' and, accordingly, set out in November 1899 to survey the route for what would be the greatest trial of motor vehicles ever held in Britain, following a 1080-mile route linking most of the major towns and cities of England and Scotland. At Buxton, recalled G. F. Hodgkinson, Johnson's Daimler began playing up. 'My father gave the car some attention.

Below: as do most new fields of endeavour, the motor car soon attracted a press to report its progress and pitfalls to the rapidly growing body of aficionados

Below right: the Thousand Miles Trial was contested by 65 cars, representing most of the leading manufacturers of the day. Here the Hon C. S. Rolls and S. F. Edge contemplate Edge's 8 hp Napier. Edge was the company's first distributor and the 8 hp was their first complete car. It featured a front-mounted, 2.4-litre, twin-cylinder engine, four-speed gearbox and chain drive

By that time we had got a supply of petrol from Carless, Capel and Leonard, Limited, which used to arrive four two-gallon tins in a case, and come by rail. Claude Johnson stayed the night with us and then proceeded on his journey, and my father was appointed chief marshal and timekeeper for that section.

Young Hodgkinson, who seventy years later was still an active participant in Veteran Car Club events, had a part to play in the 1000-Miles Trial, too. 'These "engines of death" were not permitted to come through the main street of Buxton, because Buxton was a town which really catered for ailing people – rheumatism, arthritis, sciatica and all the other complaints – so it was my job to marshal the cars at the entrance to Buxton by a secondary road so that they did not come through the main part of the town. This I was doing with a $\frac{3}{4}$ horsepower Werner motor cycle with the engine mounted on the handlebars and driving the front wheel by a flat belt. It was very high and very liable to skid, and you could quite easily come off . . . When the Werner went out of commission, then it was my duty to pilot the cars on a pedal cycle.'

A total of 83 entries was received for the Trial, and 65 of these actually competed in the event, setting off on their trip round Britain from Hyde Park Corner on 23 April 1900.

Most of the leading designs were represented, with a preponderance of English Daimler and MMC cars; there were several Panhards, notably the

Right: the first Wolseley four-wheeler was built in 1899 and had a 3½ hp engine. This car successfully competed in the Thousand Miles Trial of 1900 and 70 years later covered the same route driven by another veteran of the 1900 event, St John Nixon

Below right: this Marshall-Benz *vis-a-vis* of 1901 was a licensed British copy of a French Hurtu, itself a copy of the Benz. It has a 2.9-litre, single-cylinder engine and belt drive

new 12hp model belonging to the Hon C. S. Rolls. This was the most powerful vehicle in the Trial, capable of some 40mph on the flat, although it was run pretty close by the 8hp Napier, the first complete car built by this London engineering firm, and driven by S. F. Edge, a former racing cyclist whose bombastic flair would soon put Napier in the forefront of the world's motor manufacturers. Other British car makers represented were Wolseley (makers of sheep-shearing machinery, whose chief engineer, Herbert Austin, was investigating the possibilities of motor-car manufacture) and Lanchester. There was, too, a representative cross-section of imported models: Panhards and De Dions from France, Benz and Orient Express cars from Germany, Locomobile and Brown-Whitney steamers from America.

The crowds who turned out to watch the event more than met the organising club's expectations. 'In the cities and towns, the footpaths and roads have been so densely crowded with spectators that only the narrowest passage remained through which the motor vehicles had to pass. At every cross road in the country there were knots of on-lookers from the neighbouring villages, the parson and his daughters on bicycles, the country squire on his horse, the old dowager safely ensconsed in her landau, coaching parties enjoying champagne lunches at the road side, and cyclists in legions. In villages, the children were given a "whole holiday", and were ranged on the school walls and cheered each motor as it passed. The confidence of the spectators in the control of their vehicles was, although flattering, decidedly embarrassing, for the crowds assembled at the bottoms of hills left a lane of barely seven-feet wide through which the vehicles had to pass at high speed. The police seemed to share with the public a keen enjoyment in seeing vehicles at thirty miles an hour, and sympathised with the rebukes which the crowd addressed to drivers who failed to go at top speed. Generally, the public looked on the passage of the motors as they do the passage of a fire-engine, namely, as a fine inspiring sight which makes the pulse beat faster and satisfies a craving for excitement.'

Seventy years later, one of the mechanics on the run recalled: 'Even if you broke down on a remote road, while you were doing a repair crowds of people would appear apparently from nowhere and gather round you so closely that you could not get on with the job'.

Breakdowns (at least of a major sort) were remarkably rare, although some of the more eccentric vehicles on the run proved somewhat accident prone. 'At Bath and Bristol, the Simms Motor Wheel skidded in the tramlines and upset, the man being thrown out. He got things right to a certain extent and arrived at the Bristol Drill Hall in good time. After a somewhat adventurous journey, during which the driver behaved with great courage and pertinacity, the vehicle disappeared after Carlisle.'

Some of these less successful vehicles, too, finished in much the same condition as the legendary Irishman's shovel: 'Motor Manufacturing Co's tricycle . . . new frame and wheels were substituted at Manchester, and a new motor was fitted to frame at Nottingham. This tricycle has since been withdrawn from Competition by the makers'.

Most of what a contemporary writer referred to as 'a legacy of annoyance and expense' was caused either by the imperfect design of the vehicles or by the sheer mechanical ignorance of their drivers, although some of the contestants in the Trial displayed a remarkable ingenuity, as one of the last survivors of the event, E. A. Rose, recalled at the end of the 1960s. 'Just before the speed trials in Welbeck Park, the car I was on as mechanic, the Marshall Dogcart driven by J. J. Mann, broke the drive to the water pump. It was driven by friction from the flywheel, and we carried out a wonderful repair. We got a cork and two pennies, drilled a hole through the cork and the pennies, shoved them on the spindle in some way and were able to get drive to the pump.

We were hours getting the pump going, and we did a rotten time in the speed trials . . . The Marshall was a belt-driven car, and you got this terrible slip on the belts. They stretched when they got wet, and you spent your time cutting and rivetting and putting resin on them to make them grip!'

Later in the Trial, Rose transferred to Alfred Harmsworth's Daimler Parisian Phaeton, driven by Sir Hercules Langrishe. Although 'Herky's' mount was a better-engineered machine than the little Marshall, it was obviously not entirely trouble-free. 'It had two cylinders, four seats and six horsepower. It was listed as weighing 16 cwt, but it felt more like two tons when you were pushing it! It was an unusual car; it had about ten lubricators on the dashboard, and the mechanic had to sit on the floor, with his feet just off the ground, ready to jump out if the car stopped on a hill. It was his job to see that the drip-feed lubricators did their work – so many drops per minute.

'Those Daimler cars were devils . . . for ignition, they had a platinum tube inserted into the cylinder head, and below the part protruding from the cylinder was a sort of metal cup which you filled with methylated spirits or petrol, put a lighted match to, and when the tube became red-hot, you then started your car. People often used to set the damned thing on fire!'

C. S. Roll's Panhard had both tube and electric ignition, but because the tube system was, although crude, more reliable than the primitive electric ignition, which at that stage relied on temperamental dry batteries (Bosch had only just invented the magneto), it was more frequently in use. Unfortunately for Rolls, 'Misfortunes seldom come singly, and it was therefore in the correct order of things that when Mr Rolls, between Keswick and Carlisle, had finished wrestling with a spiteful horseshoe which had punctured his front tyre, he should find the bonnet of his car in a blaze through a defective burner'. But this was nothing to Rolls's earlier escapade on the descent of the notorious Cat and Fiddle Hill when, taking a corner at high speed, he contrived to lose both his passenger and most of the luggage over the side of the car! Fortunately, Rolls managed to stay on board.

Climbing Dunmail Raise, the clutch of the 8 hp Napier failed, and the car ran away backwards, as the brakes did not work in reverse. Pushing his passengers out of the car, S. F. Edge steered the car to safety, no mean feat when you considered the undulating nature of the old road up Dunmail.

Quite the equal of this remarkable act was the ingenious way in which Monty Grahame-White overcame what could have been disastrous damage to his car. 'While attending to an adjustment, the tiller being temporarily in the hands of a passenger, Mr Grahame-White's car tried to jump a ditch and a hedge, resulting in the steering gear being broken. This occurred fourteen miles north of Alnwich, with 52 miles still to cover before reaching the Newcastle control. Towing or pushing would, with most people, have been an easy(?) solution to the difficulty, but Mr Grahame-White would have none of either, and determined to steer the vehicle with his foot, which he successfully accomplished by standing on the offside step, guiding the wheels with the hollow of his right foot on to the outside axle box, and thus wise did he travel right through to Newcastle, making his average speed for the day ten miles per hour. The only person who seemed to think nothing of the feat was Mr Grahame-White.'

Difficulties of quite a different kind were experienced by the journalist A. J. Wilson, who wrote for the cycling press under the pseudonym 'Faed' (he was stone deaf, and merely spelt his disability backwards as a penname). Much of the power of his Ariel tricycle was lost through an improperly closed compression tap. He could not hear the tell-tale hissing that indicated this fault, and just pedalled harder on hills to supplement what seemed to be a particularly unenthusiastic engine. He must have had legs like piston-rods, for the *Automotor Journal* reported: 'The time of Mr A. J. Wilson on his Ariel for Taddington Hill is remarkable, but it must be borne in mind that Mr Wilson's skill in pedalling is a factor in the case, which an ordinary flabby mortal under like conditions would have to allow for. When the longer hills had to be negotiated, Mr. Wilson's state of collapse was a thing to be seen, and not easily forgotten'.

For the record, Wilson pedalled up Taddington at an average speed of 18.91mph, compared with Rolls's Panhard, which achieved 17.77mph under full power . . .

Eventually, the competitors returned to London, and the Thousand Miles' Trial was brought to a successful conclusion. Then, as now, some manufacturers treated a minor class win as the occasion for vast, shrieking headlines in the motor press, a trend which offended the *Automotor Journal*: 'The public will be induced, by misleading assertions, to purchase vehicles which will disgust them once and for all with automobilism. The natural argument will be that if this is the sort of car that was able to be "first everywhere", a day spent in assisting an itinerant knife grinder now and again by way of relaxation would be equally exhilarating and less expensive'.

The Trial had done immense good in promoting goodwill for the motor car throughout England, although a few entrenched diehards still fulminated against it. At least one bastion of the Law was a staunch automobilist, though – Lord Kingsburgh, the Lord Justice Advocate of Scotland, who was a passenger in one of the competing cars. Summing up the achievements of the Trial, he concluded: 'One of these vehicles, going twelve to fourteen miles an hour, could be absolutely pulled up in less than its own length. That was an element of safety unattainable with horses . . . there have been several breakdowns, and some cars have been dropped, but in almost every case – indeed, in every case – the fault was not with the motor machinery, but because the coach-builder had not understood the proper strength of wheels or axles or springs

Right: frontal tubular radiators came into use on Panhard & Levassor cars in 1899, the year in which this 6 hp rear entrance tonneau was built. The bodywork on this example was built by Vincent of Reading. Around the turn of the century, Panhard & Levassor were perhaps the most progressive of manufacturers, their cars offering an enviable blend of performance and reliability which eluded many contemporaries

Right: the Type One Vinot et Déguignand built in Puteaux, Seine, in 1901. This car featured a 1½-litre, vertical-twin engine rated at 5½ hp. One unusual feature was the Vinot's vertical gearchange gate
(Château de Grandson, Switzerland)

to provide for such vehicles. Automobilism, in my opinion, is not only a sport, but provision for locomotion in this country which is needed and will be efficient'.

If in England motoring was just beginning to throw off the shadow of the Lawsonian era, American manufacturers were now faced with a far more pernicious patent monopoly, which was to create news, not only in the motoring world, for a long time to come.

George Baldwin Selden, having neatly bided his time until the first experimental cars were running on American roads, published his 1879 patent in 1895, and then claimed that all gasoline-driven vehicles developed since 1879 were infringements of that patent. He had not, let it be added, actually built a car to prove that his invention was practicable, although he had at one stage attempted to raise the capital to do so, only to frighten off the potential investor with the remark: 'Jim, you and I will live to see more carriages on Main Street run by motors than are now drawn by horses'.

However, the delay had proved fortuitous for Selden. By waiting until 1895, he had gained the maximum effective life for his patent, although at first he lacked the money to enforce it. In 1899, he began negotiations to raise the necessary capital, and was on the point of closing negotiations with five Wall Street bankers who were prepared to put up $250,000 when fate – and a gullible patent attorney named Herman Cuntz – stuck a far bigger fish on his hook, in the shape of the Pope Manufacturing Company, America's leading cycle manufacturer. They were considering going into car manufacture, and asked Cuntz to investigate any patents which might affect this multi-million-dollar venture. He had already come across the Selden patent, and attempted to proclaim its merits to his employers . . . whose engineering experts dismissed it at once. But ex-Navy Secretary William Whitney, head of the consortium which was providing the capital for the Pope venture, proved a more receptive audience for Cuntz and, on learning that Selden would rather his patent be administered by a car company than by investors, decided to make a deal, and took an option on Selden's patent until January 1900, in which the Pope-Whitney interests were given a 'definitive licence' – in effect an assignment of the patent – in exchange for $10,000 plus a percentage of any royalties collected.

The patent's validity having been attested by a British 'expert' named Dugald Clerk (who, although he knew a great deal about two-stroke gas engines, was far from being an authority on motor cars), the Pope-Whitney group – the Columbia and Electric Vehicle Company – was reformed as an

Above: there are few more famous names in the history of motoring than that of Henry Ford. Ford's vast manufacturing operation is based on a background of inspired innovation which was Henry's best known personal characteristic. The company began operations, shakily at first, in 1903 but by the end of that year they were firmly established. Ford himself died in 1947, aged 84, but the company carries on to the present with a strong family involvement

Left: this picture purports to show George Baldwin Selden on his vehicle of 1877 which incorporated his later patents. The picture, certainly taken at a later date, is so heavily and crudely retouched that Selden has gained an extra finger on his left hand as part of his rejuvenation!

Above: the Oldsmobile Curved Dash is regarded as the world's first mass-production car. It had a single-cylinder, 1.6-litre engine and chain-drive. In 1903, Whitman and Hammond drove a Curved Dash from San Francisco to New York and in 1904 production reached the 5000 mark
(Château de Grandson, Switzerland)

$18,000,000 corporation, the Electric Vehicle Company, and set about prosecuting manufacturers who were innocently transgressing.

With its vast finances, the Electric Vehicle Company had little difficulty in steam-rolling the token resistance put up by most American manufacturers into the ground, and by September 1902 the motor manufacturers were ready to negotiate. An Association of Licenced Automobile Manufacturers was set up, which paid 2/5 of 2.5 per cent of the retail price of each car to the EVC, retained 2/5 of that amount for its own coffers, and paid the remaining 1/5 to Selden (who seems to have paid half his share to the manager of the ALAM!). Not all the Association's concerns were monetary, however, for it made a genuine attempt to create uniform standards throughout the motor industry, establishing standard sizes for screw threads, copper and steel tubes, and many other common fittings. Moreover, association members could obtain access to all the latest technical information free of charge, enjoyed a standardised system of contracts, guarantees and agreements, and had their products featured in the ALAM's annual *Handbook of Gasolene Automobiles*, which claimed that 'each manufacturer or importer conducts his business entirely independent of the other and, of course, in open competition' (although the ALAM also seems to have existed as a price-fixing ring). Customers were assured, too, that buying a car manufactured under the Selden Patent was a 'guarantee . . . that secures to the purchaser freedom from the annoyance and expense of litigation because of infringement of this patent'.

Left: A Stanley Steamer of 1906, with the 'coffin' bonnet over the boiler, which characterised Stanleys from 1906 on; it was in 1906, that the famous Stanley called *Wogglebug* exceeded 127 mph with its specially developed streamlined body before taking off on a bump and crashing heavily
(Château de Grandson, Switzerland)

Below: this curious De Dion powered Quadricycle of 1898 is claimed to be a prototype built in Paris in 1898, though it has undoubtedly been heavily modified
(Château de Grandson, Switzerland)

However, as ALAM also chose who could be licensed, its activities represented a brake on free enterprise, and Henry Ford (who had founded the Ford Motor Company in the summer of 1903 after a couple of false starts) decided that it had nothing to offer him. His aim, after all, was to produce a $500 motor car which anyone could afford, and the average price of ALAM-built cars was $1382.

The first truly popular American car had been the little Locomobile steamer, designed by the Stanley brothers, which had enjoyed a great vogue – despite its many design shortcomings – in the period 1900–1903; it had been followed by the 'curved-dash' Oldsmobile, but even this fairly basic single-cylinder gas-buggy sold for $650 (and its makers were members of the ALAM).

At first, Ford found it impossible to rival these prices – his first car, the twin-cylinder Model A, sold for $850 – and production got off to a shaky start; soon, the company was courting bankruptcy. Then came the first order, from a Chicago doctor named Pfennig, which was followed in quick succession by a flood of sales. On 11 July 1903, the Ford Motor Company had been down to $223.65, and could not meet its obligations, by 20 August there was a balance of $23,060.67 in the bank.

Said Henry Ford: 'The business went along almost as by magic – the cars gained a reputation for standing up'. In its first year of operation, the company sold a million dollars' worth of cars, establishing itself high in the ranks of the Detroit motor-manufacturing companies, which included Cadillac, Olds and Packard. Already, the city was becoming the motor capital of America, with

fourteen companies assembling 11,180 cars in 1905, as well as component and coachwork manufacturers.

The growth of the American car industry had been phenomenal: in 1899, an estimated 57 companies employing a total of 2241 people had been involved in the manufacture of motor vehicles. By 1904, the total number of companies had risen to 178, employing over 12,000 workers, and producing over thirty million dollars' worth of automobiles.

At the end of 1904, Ford began to transfer production to a new, purpose-built factory on Picquette and Beaubien Avenues, and by the following spring, output had risen to a peak of 25 cars a day, although prices still remained at the $800–$1000 mark for the best-selling Fords, while the $2000 Model B, produced at the insistence of Ford's wealthy coal-merchant backer, Alexander Malcomson, was selling rather badly (Ford, wanting the freedom to make his own decisions, would eventually buy out all the other partners in his business, thereby achieving complete control).

S. L. Smith, who provided the backing for Oldsmobile, was also convinced that there was a future for the expensive car, even though sales of the little Olds runabout had risen from 4000 in 1904 to 6500 in 1905, and forced R. E. Olds and the team who had made the runabout successful to resign. He then promoted the high-priced models, which did not sell well, with the inevitable result that the company sank deep into debt.

Ransom Olds decided that the time was ripe for him to retire, leaving Smith and his son Fred – who was Secretary and Treasurer at Oldsmobile – to run the company: 'We had done so well by that time', he recalled, 'that I thought I had about all that I needed, and rather than hamper the ideas of the rest of the group I sold out my stock and decided to take a long vacation'. In fact Olds' own stock at the time amounted to a meagre five per cent, which made his bargaining position rather tenuous, to say the least.

Olds left in August 1904, and it was while he was taking his 'long vacation', in Northern Michigan, that he received a telegram asking him to return to Lansing. 'As I stepped off the train', he explained, 'I was met by an old friend who handed me an interesting looking paper. Reading it, I found that a group of my friends had organised a half-million dollar company, of which I was to be the head, and within three hours had raised the money to finance it. Of this I was to have a controlling interest, $260,000'. Thus, Reo was born, going into production in October 1904 with an Oldsmobile-like single-cylinder runabout, and quickly achieving spectacular sales success. In the first season's trading, sales reached $1,378,000. By the following year Reo had more business than it could handle.

There was a shadow over the Ford success, however, for in 1904 the ALAM had begun proceedings against the company for infringement of the Selden Patent. The young company confidently stated, however: 'To dealers, importers, agents and users of our gasoline automobiles . . . we will protect you against any prosecution for alleged infringements of patents'.

Furthermore, Ford was confident of victory: 'The Selden Patent is not a broad one, and if it was, it is anticipated. It does not cover any practicable machine, no practicable machine can be made from it, and never was, as far as we can ascertain. It relates to that form of carriage called a FORE Carriage. None of that type have ever been in use; all have been failures'.

Indeed, the Selden case did end in victory for Ford, but the hearing dragged on until January 1911, and involved legal costs of over a million dollars. Selden's patent, although judged valid, was ruled to apply only to vehicles powered by the obsolete Brayton engine: everything else was exempt. By that time, too, the patent had nearly run its course, and would have expired anyway within eighteen months. The case established Henry Ford as a popular folk hero: the David who had slain a monopolistic Goliath, and further enhanced his reputation as a builder of cars for the masses.

Both in Europe and America, manufacturers were paying increasing attention to the 'motor for the man of moderate means'; on the forefront of this movement was the De Dion-Bouton Company, of Puteaux, near Paris, whose proprietors, the Comte de Dion and Georges Bouton, had originally colla-

Right: this twin-cylinder De Dion Bouton *conduite interieure* of c1908 is an elegant town car of the Edwardian era, with painted-on 'canework' and silk upholstery; like all pre-World War I De Dions, it has a *decelerator* pedal
(Château de Grandson, Switzerland)

Below: one of the first of Renault's 1100cc, twin-cylinder machines, the AX; this particular example was constructed in 1910, although the type was introduced in 1905. The AX was a forerunner of Renault's famous *Taxis de la Marne*
(Château de Grandson, Switzerland)

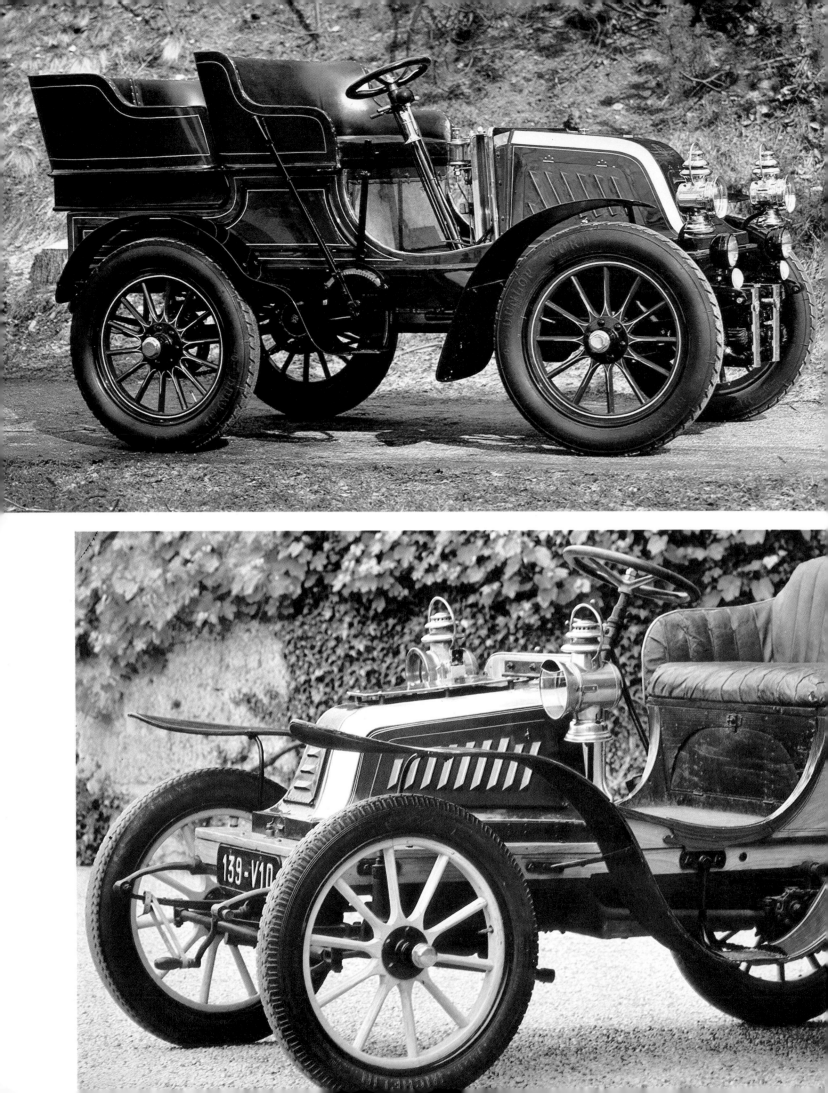

Left and above: Scania, now better known for their commercial vehicles, produced cars from their Malmö factory between 1902 and 1912 (cars were manufactured under the name Scania-Vabis between 1914 and 1929). This is a 1903 rear entrance tonneau, with a twin-cylinder Kamper engine
(Saab-Scania Collection, Sweden)

Below: built at Puteaux, Seine, the 1903 Prunel 'Apollo' phaeton was powered by a 6 hp De Dion engine. The firm built cars from 1900–1907
(Château de Grandson, Switzerland)

borated, in the 1880s, in the production of light steam vehicles. Since the mid 1890s, however, they had become increasingly interested in the high-speed petrol motor, initially used on lightweight tricycles and then, since 1899, in voiturettes, starting with the rear-engined Type D, with its curious *vis-à-vis* coachwork, and then in more orthodox models with the single-cylinder power unit at the front, under a coal-scuttle bonnet. Additionally, engines were produced in unprecedented numbers for other manufacturers all over Europe, the speed of operation being so rapid that any engine which failed to perform properly on the test bench was not rebuilt but simply dismantled to give spare parts for other units.

'In point of numbers', wrote Roger H. Fuller in 1902, 'the firm of De Dion-Bouton et Cie, of Puteaux, Seine, are the largest manufacturers of the modern light automobile, there being over five hundred of their voiturettes and light cars now in use in the British Isles, and the firm have sold 26,000 of their motors from $\frac{3}{4}$ hp to 10 hp. It is, therefore, not surprising that dozens of motor-car manufacturers have adopted the De Dion-Bouton motors for their cars, thereby being undoubtedly assisted over one of the most difficult problems of automobile manufacture. I counted no fewer than fifteen exhibitors at the recent Automobile Show who had adopted the De Dion-Bouton motor . . . A De Dion is generally admitted to be the easiest of all cars to learn, and is very suitable for ladies to manage. A beginner can hardly do much damage to the mechanism by ignorance and incompetence; in fact, I have often heard the remark made that the De Dion $4\frac{1}{2}$ hp car is almost "foolproof"'.

However, at a selling price of 300 guineas, the $4\frac{1}{2}$ hp De Dion was, although popular, still only within the reach of a fairly well lined purse; nor was it, as a 1902 diary proves, entirely 'foolproof'. 'Left Menai 9 am. Called at Bangor for a new tyre, could not get one; ran over a sheep; at Bethesda changed gears so rapidly that I broke the connecting rod of the steering gear; being at the top of a long hill there was nothing for it but to go down the hill backwards in the hope of getting to the bottom alive and finding a blacksmith; this was done; slate quarry workers on strike and much interested in car; after wait of $2\frac{1}{2}$ hours blacksmith finished his job; but the product of his labour was 1/16th of an inch too small; waited another $2\frac{1}{2}$ hours; this time successful result. Going round a sharp corner nearly ran into a big lake; down a steep hill in Bettws-y-Coed skidded on slippery surface and ran into front steps of hotel on my right; fielder suggested the back yard would be a cheaper and quicker way of entering. It was getting dark and I was getting so fed up and weary that I determined to sleep in the next available building, it was at Pentre Voelas, and it was a good thing for me that I did so. The next morning I had not gone more than a mile before I came to an absolutely rectangular corner going up a steep hill; there was a little wooden notice with the word "Danger" on it; had I continued in the dark of the night before I never could have seen it, and we should have been precipitated over the edge to the bottom of the ravine. Total distance accomplished – twenty-five miles.'

Part of the trouble, of course, was that the men who were adopting automobilism were, for the most part, mechanical illiterates, with absolutely no idea how their machine worked; it is on record that the owner of a De Dion living in North Wales telegraphed the company's London depot in some distress, saying that he was quite unable to start his car. Fortunately, a friend's mechanic diagnosed the trouble, otherwise De Dion would have had to have sent a man on a two-and-a-half day, 480-mile round trip just to discover that the motorist had forgotten to turn on the petrol tap of his car!

An additional hazard in Britain was the attitude of the police, who enforced the open road speed limit of 12 mph with severity, often prosecuting motorists on the flimsiest of trumped-up evidence . . . *The Autocar* published a road map each week, showing the location of all the latest speed traps, and a cycle patrol operated on the Brighton road by the London motor agents Jarrott and Letts in the summer of 1905 grew into the Automobile Association, whose scouts warned motorists of looming police traps by failing to salute and by wearing their lapel badges red side out instead of white. In many cases, prosecution of motorists was totally unjustified, but there was a hard core of 'scorchers' who antagonised the public by the speed with which they hurtled along the dusty highways. These adventurers not only took their own lives in their hands, but those of other roadusers, too, and they usually deserved the punishment they received.

They had been encouraged by the introduction of cars that were increasingly powerful and expensive. The manufacturers of such vehicles at first gained extra power by adding more cylinders, doubling up from two to four, then by increasing the capacity of those cylinders. In an age when there was no testing of drivers' abilities at the wheel, small wonder that the owners of such juggernauts often succeeded in reducing their vehicles to a heap of metallic flinders. But, wrote the famous artist, Sir Hubert von Herkomer (who instituted an international reliability trial which bore his name) in 1902: 'The real weak point in the present state of motoring is not to be found in the car, but in the present supply of drivers. You see mere boys driving – boys who can have had no training or experience . . . the present law insists on a licence, but does not insist on any qualification for which this serious licence is granted. Anyone, blind or lame, can get it'. To prove which, *The Autocar* obtained a licence for a blind beggar, whom they then photographed, sitting in a car, with a card labelled 'blind' hung round his neck.

The epitome of high-powered cars was the Mercédès, originally developed by Wilhelm Maybach out of the succession of rapid Cannstatt-Daimlers evolved for the rich Herr Jellinek and put into limited production (and mainly sold by Jellinek to his wealthy acquaintances, one of whom, Baron Henri de Rothschild, recalled: 'I drove to Stuttgart to take over the car, and found it by no means elegant, but the price was certainly proportional to the weight, its great size creating anything but a favourable impression amongst people who preferred the light carriages of 8–12 horsepower constructed by the French makers'). Out of this ponderous machine, Maybach evolved the lithe and elegant Mercédès; the contract to produce for Emil Jellinek the first batch of this 'car of the day after tomorrow' – thirty cars worth over half-a-million marks – was signed less than a month after the death of Gottlieb Daimler in March 1900, and the new model made its début at Nice the following year, causing an immediate sensation with its advanced technology – pressed-steel

Left: Decauville's 'Voiturelle' was a huge success at the turn of the century. The four-wheeled car was powered by a rear-mounted, air-cooled, $3\frac{1}{2}$ hp, vertical-twin engine. It is memorable as the first petrol-driven production car to use independent front suspension

Right: the American Cameron company was reorganised eight times in its nineteen-year history which ran from 1902 to 1921. This is a 1904 example built by the James Brown machine corporation of Pawtucket and, like the majority of Cameron cars, has an air-cooled engine
(Château de Grandson, Switzerland)

frame, mechanically operated inlet valves, low-tension magneto ignition and selective 'gate' for gear-changing.

Within a few years, there was a considerable market for such expensive machinery, as the motoring author A. B. Filson Young noted: 'One would think that there cannot be a great many people anxious to spend from £1500 to £3000 on a motor car. Nevertheless, the number of cars of this type bought in England and America is astonishing, and when one considers the complaints of "bad times" which seems to have become habitual with a certain class it is not a little surprising to realise that more and more money is being spent daily on luxuries – among them that most elaborate and costly form of luxury, the high-powered, sumptuously fitted motor car, which as a means of travel has in the few years of its life eclipsed the railway train in speed, comfort and convenience'.

Provided then, that you had the money, this was the dawn of the first golden age of motoring, especially, as Filson Young remarked, in France, with the 'vista of roads that lie visible before you for five or six miles, straight as a gun barrel, empty as the blue sky – these are conditions at which a speed of fifty or sixty miles an hour can be kept up through mile after mile, not only with pleasure and convenience, but with perfect safety'. In direct contrast were the rolling roads of England, where, as you went to Birmingham by way of Beachy Head, you would find 'every mile had its score of lurking dangers, its sudden corners, high hedges, crowded villages, busy farmhouses, sheep and cattle, hens and dogs, children shouting and playing in the roads, heavy wagons creaking along

on the wrong side, with the driver dozing on his load. Obviously, the English roads could be very dangerous and the British driver had to be far more aware than any in France.

'On the French road there was nothing to do but open wide the throttle, advance the spark and sit and sing like a bird while the engine sent you swooping and skimming as fast as a swallow over the world . . .'

It must have been exhilarating driving in the early part of the century with just you, the car and the open road . . .

Within a decade the motor car progressed from a stuttering novelty into a reliable means of transport, and the underpowered creepabout of the 1890s had been supplanted by vehicles that were high-powered, fast, well appointed . . . and expensive, both to buy and to operate.

'I heard', confided Max Pemberton in 1907, 'of the owner of a 100 hp Rochet-Schneider who offered a great firm of tyre makers £1000 a year to keep his car supplied in tyres, and met with but a chilly response . . . If men will drive engines of 60, 80, or 100 hp, they must foot the bill and foot it cheerfully. Even the possessor of a 40 hp car, should he make considerable use of it, will find himself £400 or £500 out of pocket at least at the end of his first year . . . Motoring in its speedier phase is one of the costliest pursuits we can follow – racing and yachting apart.

'I have taken the account books of three careful friends of my own – each owner of a 40 hp car – and I find that their expenditure upon tyres for the year just ending has been £580, £667 and £700.'

Or, in 1970s terms, an annual tyre bill of around £7000 . . . and that, as a 45 hp Hotchkiss proved on an observed Royal Automobile Club trial in mid 1907 could be over a mileage as low as 15,000, during which the Hotchkiss devoured the astonishing total of 46 tyres costing £12–£13 each.

Ironically enough, the Hotchkiss had a six-cylinder engine, a pattern claimed to be easier on tyres than big four-cylinder models – and a pattern, moreover, which had been established by the British motor industry, which was at last able to compete in terms of quality with the leading Continental manufacturers.

'In December of 1904,' recalled a correspondent to *Country Life* two years later, 'I wandered in the Grand Palais inspecting many motor-cars with an interest and delight to which there was but one drawback. Many cars were present from many countries, but to an Englishman, commercially as well as sentimentally patriotic, it seemed that not nearly enough of them were of English origin. Still wandering, I came across rather an insignificant little stand occupied by two gentlemen, a two-cylinder voiturette chassis of 10 hp, three sets of two cylinders of the same casting mounted on a base chamber, and a handsome body mounted on a frame, but lacking the organs or mechanism essential to life and motion. The gentlemen, it seems, were more interesting than the machines, for they were the Hon. C. S. Rolls, already well known as a

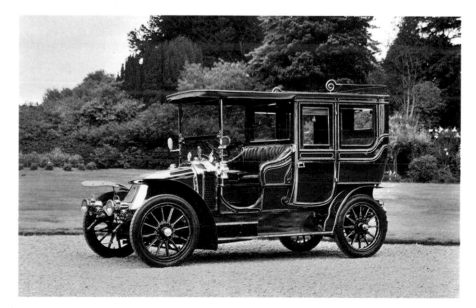

racing driver, and Mr Claude Johnson, who, as the first secretary of the Automobile Club of Great Britain and Ireland, had, by universal consent, proved himself to be an organiser of the most remarkable ability . . . I ventured to ask what the special and characteristic features of that car might be, whether it contained any new and striking departure, and so forth. The answer impressed itself deeply on my memory. It was to the effect that this was an effort to combine in one engine all the best features of many engines, which seemed an eminently sensible if not very original method of reaching a good practical result . . . It was with some pleasure, but not with any high anticipation, that I accepted an offer from Mr Rolls to try a similar two-cylinder car then and there on the Champs-Elysees. It was, in a single word, a revelation . . . Never before had I been in a car which made so little noise, vibrated so little, ran so smoothly, or could be turned about so easily and readily in a maze of traffic. Indeed, the conclusion that I almost reached there and then was that the car was too silent and ghostlike to be safe . . . When, wandering again through the Grand Palais in 1906, I came across a six-cylinder Rolls-Royce in one of the galleries, the extraordinary measure of progress which had been achieved in the interval, and the shortness of the interval, came upon me in a flash, and struck me "all of a heap", as the saying goes'.

In 1906, the 30 hp Rolls-Royce six-cylinder model defeated a four-cylinder Martini in a reliability trial which received the popular title 'the Battle of the Cylinders'.

Shortly afterwards, J. E. Vincent drove from London to Norfolk in the victorious Rolls-Royce: 'There was no reason in life against a good spin at top speed except that superstitious regard for the letter of the law which not one man in a thousand really has. The car simply flew forward; the speed indicator marked 25, 30, 35, 40, 45 and even 50 miles an hour; the road seemed to open wide to our advent, to stretch out its arms, so to speak, to embrace us; the motion, smooth, swifter and swifter still, even as the flight of the albatross, that stirreth not his wings, and absolutely free from vibration, was, in a single word divine'.

Right: a 1905 Rolls-Royce 30 hp six-cylinder, the model which was the immediate forerunner of the 'Silver Ghost'

Below, far right: this 1903 Spyker racer was the world's first six-cylinder car. The 8.7-litre engine drove all four wheels and each wheel was braked. Although the six-cylinder racing car was never put into series production, several 32/40 hp four-cylinder examples, with four-wheel-drive and four-wheel-brakes, were built

Below right and bottom right: three views of a 1907 Napier 60 hp, restored as a replica of the car with which S. F. Edge averaged 65.91 mph for 24 hours at Brooklands in that year. The engine is 'square' with 127 mm × 127 mm bore and stroke; this, in six cylinders, gives a displacement of 9653 cc

Below: Peugeot's type 818 torpedo of 1906; this four-cylinder, 12 hp machine was built in the same year as Robert Peugeot began building his Lion-Peugeot machines, having previously constructed motor cycles; the two companies were reunited in 1911, although the 'Lion' part of the name survived until 1913 (Peugeot collection, France)

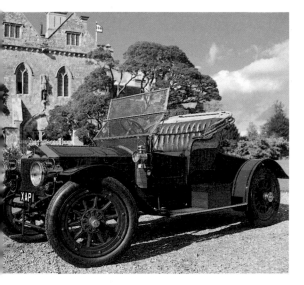

Yet the 30 hp Rolls-Royce was supposed not to have been a particularly successful model . . . In fact, after only half-a-dozen had been produced, the 30 hp was replaced by the illustrious 40/50 hp six, which was soon christened the 'Silver Ghost' after the most famous of the early examples produced, which in 1907 was subjected to a 15,000 mile trial by the RAC. It had already travelled from Bexhill, in Sussex, to Edinburgh and Glasgow, using only direct-drive third gear and overdrive top, at an average fuel consumption of 20.8mpg!

On the sixth day of the 15,000-mile test, a petrol tap vibrated shut, bringing the Silver Ghost to its only involuntary stop (apart from tyre trouble) of the entire run. At the end of the 15,000 miles, the RAC officials stripped down the car to see which parts, in their opinion, should be renewed in order to return the Rolls-Royce to 'as-new' condition: 'The engine was passed as perfect; the transmission throughout was passed as perfect; one or two parts of the steering details showed very slight wear, perhaps one-thousandth part of an inch, and the committee condemned these as not being "as good as new"; they also required the small universal joints in the magneto drive to be replaced, and the water-pump to be repacked; and this was all that was required for making the car equal to new after a mileage which many cars do not cover in three years' work'.

Some of the credit, however, should be given to the car's mechanics and chauffeur, for during the trial, it spent 40 hours 'in the motor houses . . . for repairs, replacements, and adjustments'. Concluded the RAC: 'The running of the car was excellent, except for a slight tendency to misfiring at low speeds during a part of the trial. The car (as a whole) and the engine (in particular) were exceptionally quiet (especially on the third speed, direct drive) and free from vibration. The springs, however, at the back of the car were scarcely stiff

Left: a 1911 Delaunay-Belleville H6B 30 hp six-cylinder of 4.4 litres, complete with compressed-air starter; unless otherwise specified, the chassis for the cars sold in Britain were sent to Aberdeen by sea to be clothed by the Shinnie Brothers, a subsidiary concern of the Burlington company who handled sales of this high quality French car in Britain
(National Motor Museum, England)

Below left: Martin Fischer built his first Turicum (Latin for Zurich) car in that Swiss city in 1904. Steered by twin pedals, it was just 180 cm long and was constructed in a disused skittle alley. The second Turicum was also foot-steered, but more conventional single-cylinder cars followed, as did a move to a larger factory. Four-cylinder models appeared in 1908 followed a year later by this twin-cylinder model. Not listed in any Swiss Turicum catalogue, it may have been licence-built in Czechoslovakia. All Turicums were friction-drive; over a thousand were built from 1904 to 1914

Below: one of motoring's best known masterpieces, the 1907 Rolls-Royce 40/50 hp, chassis number 60551 – 'The Silver Ghost'. 1907 saw the company adopt a single model policy with the 40/50, which survived until 1922. It was not until the advent of the 40/50 hp New Phantom in 1925 that the rest of the earlier 40/50s were dubbed 'Silver Ghost'. The car used a 7046 cc, six-cylinder engine and weighed almost two tons. With a power output of 48 bhp at 1200 rpm The Ghost proved capable on one economy test of returning 23.25 mpg

enough for the load carried. The front footboards became uncomfortably warm'.

The results of the Trial proved the built-in durability of the 40/50 hp Rolls-Royce (due mainly to Henry Royce's early training as a locomotive engineer), and established this well-constructed, if scarcely innovative, car as a claimant for the coveted title of 'The Best Car in the World'.

But the Rolls-Royce hadn't started the six-cylinder trend; that honour belonged to the British Napier company. Although Spyker in Holland and Automotrice in France had constructed six-cylinder cars before Napier, it was the British firm which had established the configuration as a production model, thanks to the remarkable selling powers of Selwyn Francis Edge. As a motoring writer with the pen name 'Auriga' noted in 1907: 'Mr S. F. Edge has shown, indeed, a rare and almost unique combination of the abilities, mental and physical, and of the spirit of enterprise tempered by prudence, which is exactly calculated to carry a man to the highest place with the automobile movement'.

'Auriga', apparently, had ridden on one of the very first Napier sixes in 1904 (the first, built in 1903, was sold to a Mr W. Bramson . . . his purchase was 'rather a brave thing to do', thought Edge) and noted: 'A good six-cylinder car is perceptibly and unmistakably more comfortable, more luxurious, less vibrant, less noisy than the best four-cylinder car that ever was built. Some say she ought not to be; but the fact remains that she is and she can be built to what power one pleases. She is easy on tyres, too, and as for her petrol consumption, I am afraid it does not worry me. It is the sort of thing which troubles an omnibus company desirous of making a profit, but it does not cause any anxiety to the rich men and women, of whom the supply is seemingly unlimited, who buy Napier six-cylinder cars. To such people also the argument that the extra luxury is not worth the extra money has no meaning. Like the difference between first and third classes in a railway train, it is worth buying for people who like comfort, and there are many to whom the cost is a matter of no moment'.

At first, though, there seem to have been other considerations than luxury, as Edge recalled over twenty years later: 'I read a paper at the RAC on the advantages of six cylinders over four, and I remember Rolls said that one of the advantages was, you had six strings to your bow instead of four, which rather goes to show the kind of straws we clung to in the early days of motoring. What was in Rolls's mind was that you were more likely to have one cylinder left firing if you had six of them than if you had only four!'.

Those early sixes had one major drawback, for the crankshaft damper had not yet been invented, and so they had critical engine speeds at which unpleasant vibrations occurred. Edge tried to explain the phenomenon away as the 'Power Rattle' . . . but whatever you called it, it could still snap a crankshaft.

Nevertheless, the overall performance of the Napier was so good that the six-cylinder layout was widely copied: by the end of 1906, claimed Edge, there were 141 different makes of six-cylinder car on the market.

Some, of course, were awful – it wasn't every engineer who could make one carburettor feed six-cylinders with the requisite smoothness, as gas-flow was, at best, an imperfectly understood science – but others were worthy to vie with Rolls-Royce and Napier for quality. Like the Delaunay-Belleville, introduced at the 1904 Paris Salon in four-cylinder form, and first available as a six-cylinder in 1906 in the shape of the monstrous 70 hp, which had a swept volume of 11,846 cc. The distinguishing feature of these cars was the circular radiator and bonnet, which recalled the company's origins as marine engineers, and, indeed, the excellent system of high-pressure lubrication incorporated in their power units had been developed as early as 1897 for the Delaunay-Belleville high-speed steam engines, which were built with power outputs of up to 7000 hp. The quality of the engineering fully justified the company's slogan 'The Car Magnificent', and the President of France and the Tsar of Russia were both enthusiastic users of the marque; the Tsar, in fact, was such a regular customer that one of the firm's more ostentatious sixes – a development of the 70 hp – was named the 'SMT' ('Sa Majesté le Tsar') in his honour. From 1910, Delaunay-Bellevilles could be fitted with a particularly refined form of self-starter, *Le Démarreur Barbey*, which operated by compressed air generated by a four-cylinder pump mounted between the dumb-irons; 'The driver, sitting in his seat, need exert no strength to operate the Starter. A tiny lever within the reach of his hand allows him, with two fingers, in one simple movement, to effect, almost instantaneously the engagement of the starter with the engine, its withdrawal and replenishment'.

Of similar quality to the Delaunay-Belleville – and, indeed, also endowed with a circular radiator and bonnet (which *Country Life* thought 'peculiarly ugly') – was the Hotchkiss, built by the famous armament factory founded in 1867 by a Connecticut Yankee called Benjamin Hotchkiss. Coincidentally, both the Hotchkiss and the Delaunay-Belleville were built at St-Denis-sur-Seine, 6 km north of Paris.

However, if such cars showed the luxury aspect of the big six, others merely represented it taken to absurd lengths, with cylinders like cannon bores and sumps the size of hip-baths – even a comparatively common model like the Napier 60 had a sump getting on for six feet in length! Imagine then, the sheer bulk of the power unit of the 50/60 hp Ariel-Simplex of 1907–8, which had a swept volume of 15,904 cc, making it the second-biggest car ever catalogued, and surprisingly good value for cubic centimetres at a chassis price of £950 – Napier's biggest, the 14,565 cc 90 hp of 1909–12 cost £1500. Surprisingly, the most cubically capacious car ever catalogued was the four-cylinder 200 hp Benz of 1913–14, with a 21,504 cc engine, or well over five litres per cylinder!

Only Fiat could do better, and their 300 hp was a one-off record-breaker which boasted a 28,353 cc four-cylinder engine which made infrequent appearances on the speed tracks from 1911 onwards, and managed to clock 132·37 mph at Ostend in 1913 (bigger engines have subsequently been used, but only in 'straight-line' land-speed-record contenders).

Reverting to road cars, wealthy megalomaniacs could also toy with such volumetric inefficiencies as the 60 hp Leader, one of the first production V 8s, which had a 15,505 cc engine and cost £1500 complete with bodywork in 1906 (its maker, Charles Binks of Nottingham, subsequently became better-known as a manufacturer of carburettors, including the celebrated 'rat-trap' pattern favoured by sporting motor cyclists). Contemporary with it was the 40 hp Adams V 8 built in Bedford; although its engine was only half the size (7274 cc) of that of the Leader, it had a more lasting claim to fame, for its power unit was a French Antoinette, designed by Léon Levavasseur, a power unit more often found in early flying machines, for which its compact construction and relatively light weight made it admirably suitable. Adams also built V 16 Antoinette engines under licence, but does not seem to have succumbed to the obvious temptation of installing one of these in a car . . .

Although the rich Edwardians loved a long bonnet, surprisingly few straight-eights made their appearance, and almost all were exclusively racing machinery. However, at the 1902 Paris Salon the firm of CGV (named after the triumvirate of racing drivers – Charron, Girardot and Voigt – who had founded it) showed a prototype touring eight-cylinder power unit. At the end of March 1903, the motoring correspondent of *Country Life* sampled the finished car: 'Her quietness and smoothness was almost astounding. The engine is a comparatively slow one, running at only 900 revolutions a minute when accelerated, while, of course, the mechanically operated valves make it very quiet at low speeds. The noisiest items of the engine are the gearwheels on the half-time shafts, but when cogs of fibre are substituted for the present metal ones, everything about the motor will be practically inaudible. Its elasticity is delightful to experience in actual use. M. Voigt, who drove the car, was able to thread his way through Piccadilly blocks at a mile an hour, yet the car is capable of travelling up to fifty times that speed. Only one speed is fitted, and inasmuch as it is possible to start on this, although geared to fifty, it is obvious that if a low speed were fitted for starting purposes and steep hills, the present gear could be considerably raised. A reverse is also needed, but we understand that both the items named will be embodied in the next eight-cylinder vehicle, the present one being regarded only as an experiment which must be pronounced as highly interesting and in a large measure successful'.

It failed to reach production status, though maybe the prospect of devoting

Above: Swazi chiefs visiting London prepare to board a luxury six-wheeled De Dietrich 40 hp *limousine de voyage* en route for an inspection of King Edward VII's horses in December 1907. The De Dietrich was based on the designs of a military engineer named Lindecker. The outer two pairs of wheels steered the vast vehicle

Below: Lion-Peugeot cars were originally built in the old Peugeot motorcycle factory at Beaulieu–Valentigny, between 1906 and 1910, when they merged with Automobiles Peugeot at Audincourt, the Lion-Peugeot marque lasting another three years. This 10 hp VC2 single-cylinder phaeton dates from 1909 (Peugeot collection, France)

over half the vehicle to the engine was too daunting, even for the most megalo-maniac motorists!

Nearly every manufacturer of note succumbed to the craze for engines of vast capacity; Gobron-Brillié, famed for their opposed-piston engines, built a vast six-cylinder 70/90 hp of 11,404 cc between 1908 and 1910. As its combustion chamber was formed by the crowns of the opposing pistons, and thus varied in size as they approached and recoiled, the giant Gobron was apparently particularly smooth-running.

Of course, the ostentation of the chassis had to be matched by similar excess in the coachwork department. The growth in the demand for luxurious coachwork can be traced in the rise of the Rothschild coachbuilding company of Levallois-Perret, which traced its origins back to horse-carriage days, but which had since the turn of the century devoted itself to building high-class motor-bodies, setting a long-lasting fashion by the creation, in 1902, of a particularly voluptuous body on the 40 hp Panhard belonging to the King of the Belgians. Coming at a time when the sinuous curves of *l'Art Nouveau* were all the rage, the *Roi-des-Belges* body was widely copied by coachbuilders everywhere, as Rothschilds had neglected to patent the design.

Even so, Rothschild bodywork had an extra flair that most other coach-builders could only envy; it was partly due to the fact that while the elders of the company's proprietors, Rheims, had been a carriage-builder for many years, the younger, Auscher, had been a sporting motorist since the 1890s, even riding in motor races so that he could better appreciate the stresses put on automobile coachwork.

The Rothschild factory had to be doubled in size in 1904, by which time the company held one-sixth of the coachwork market; the new factory employed 600 men, of whom 180 were employed in the blacksmiths' shop alone. The varnishing shop could hold thirty cars at a time, and was equipped with ovens to hasten the drying of the final colour and varnish coats. Output of new bodies was two per day in 1905, plus repair and conversion work on existing coachwork, and the manufacture of wooden wheels, in which the company held a monopoly in the French industry; they even deigned to build the odd horse-drawn carriage, although these were regarded as very much out-of-date!

Perhaps the most sensational bodies of all were the *limousines de voyage* built for the automotive grand tour, but they had nothing in common with modern GTs, with their smooth lines and low headrooms. These were machines complete with every possible luxury – one wealthy American even specified a built-in flush toilet in his 75/90 hp, 12,868 cc Charron – and one of the most sybaritic was built around 1907 for the rich Parisian Count Boni de Castellane, who had married Anna Gould, daughter of the American Millionaire Jay Gould. Boni de Castellane's 40 hp Panhard Pullman Limousine de Voyage was built on a chassis with a wheelbase stretched to 12 ft 6 in, and its coachwork was panelled throughout in satinwood, with polished mahogany mouldings inlaid with silver. In the panel which divided the front and rear seats were a folding table, a small electric heater concealed in a frame of polished copper and a silver washbasin. This was fed with hot or cold water from two tanks concealed in the roof, hot water being provided by the engine. And on either

Right: a 1905 CGV 40 hp, with Rothschild *Roi des Belges* coachwork. Founded by Ms Charron, Girardot and Voigt the company numbered many of the world's richest men – W. K. Vanderbilt, James Gordon Bennett, Waldorf Astor – among its glittering clientele, which also included kings, princes, counts, dukes and the author Octave Mirabeau, who immortalised his own CGV in a novel, '628–E8' which took its title from that car's registration plate

side of the central division were cabinets equipped with cocktail, toilet, manicure and vanity-case requisites.

In the rear compartment were two adjustable armchairs, upholstered in Rose Dubarry silk brocade, and capable of being transformed into a comfortable bed. The windows, of bevelled glass, were fitted with roller blinds and curtains to match the upholstery, and the interior was lighted by four electric corner brackets and a countersunk ceiling light, all silver-gilt.

The exterior of the body was finished in de Castellane's racing colours, and all exterior metalwork was of silver-plated copper, except for the doorhandles, which were of solid silver. On the dashboard, the usual controls were augmented by a barometer, altimeter, route indicator, speedometer, clock and thermometer. And the final touch to this extraordinary car was added by de Castellane's companion, a pedigree-bred bulldog with a silver-mounted collar two-inches wide, studded with diamonds and rubies, and hung with an 18-carat gold St Christopher medallion.

The appearance of this flamboyant vehicle incensed de Castellane's rival, the Baron von Eckhardstein, who swore to eclipse its magnificence at the forthcoming Concours d'Elegance Automobile at Nice, where all might see. His was an even more exotic vehicle. Like the Panhard Pullman, it was furnished throughout by the Paris branch of Maple & Company. The centre portion of the body resembled a stagecoach, and once again featured silk chairs which could be turned into a bed. Between the seats were sliding doors leading to the rear of the body, which housed a fully equipped kitchen, in which the Baron's corpulent chef, Emile, cooked meals for his master *en route.*

However, the most remarkable feature of Von Eckhardstein's car, which was reputed to have cost £4000 (or £3300 more than the standard 35 hp De Dietrich on which it was based), was its chassis, which had six wheels, with the front and rear axles steering, and the central axle drove. This curious layout, which also incorporated an unorthodox disposition of the springs, was the invention of a military engineer named Lindecker, who had persuaded De Dietrich to take it up around 1905. It was supposed to soak up all the unevenness of the road, enable the vehicle to run smoothly over potholes and hump-backed bridges, with 'comfort, sweet running, positive steering and safety'.

The Baron had wagered de Castellane that the De Dietrich would 'knock the feathers out of his blasted cocked hat at the Concours', but in fact both cars won high awards.

Perhaps the most consistent of all the concours set was the wealthy Englishman Montague Grahame-White (the same man who had steered his Daimler in the Thousand Miles' Trial by kicking the hub after the steering had broken, and whose brother, Claude, was the most famous British aviator of the day). Grahame-White loved big motor cars, and loved nothing better than to take an already huge vehicle and make it even more eye-catching by lengthening the wheelbase to absurd proportions.

Left: Le Zèbre of Puteaux, Seine, built cars between 1909 and 1932; their first cars, like this 1909 model, were powered by 5 hp, 600 cc engines, driving the rear wheels through a two-speed gearbox and a shaft (Château de Grandson, Switzerland)

Left: An experimental Peugeot quadricycle of 1905, in which the driver sat on a saddle behind the passengers and on top of the rear engine
(Peugeot Collection, France)

Below: the seemingly vast bonnet of the 1908 Sizaire-Naudin hides a single-cylinder engine of 1335 cc with an overhead inlet valve. Between 1905 and 1910 Sizaire power units grew from 918 cc to around 1500 cc, then to be supplanted by four-cylinder units. This car, designed by Maurice Sizaire and Louis Naudin, used sliding-pillar front suspension with a transverse leaf spring

In 1911 Grahame-White owned the biggest of all the pre-war Mercédès, the six-cylinder 75/105hp model, of 10,179cc. This was a chain-driven behemoth with canework panelling round the top of its tourer body. Fitted spanners were concealed in the hinged upholstery of the doors and plate glass panels in the top and sides of the bonnet displayed the gun-barrel finish of the cylinder blocks and the highly burnished pipework. A spectacular enough machine, you might think, but it was not enough for Grahame-White. In December 1911 the Mercédès was returned to the coachbuilders, who lengthened the wheelbase to 15ft 6in, fitted an aggressively pointed radiator of special design, along with giant Rushmore acetylene headlamps and new mudwings.

'Monty' was still creating such vehicles during the 1920s; but most of them had long since vanished. Let the epitaph of the Edwardian monsters be Grahame-White cruising down the long, straight avenues of poplars in Burgundy at a steady 90 kilometres an hour on his way to Monte Carlo, pausing only to sample the superb cuisine and the occasional bottle of Chateau Mouton Rothschild '99 – 'no more costly than a Beaujolais in many West End London hotels before the 1914 war'.

'There will always be snobs willing to pay Fr10,000 for the name on the bonnet of their car,' wrote Comte Pierre de la Ville-Baugé in 1905, 'but wouldn't it be interesting, in the cause of furthering the spread of motoring, to enable us to avoid this by listing conscientious firms who give value for money?

'What purchasers want is a reliable car comfortable and commodious enough for their needs, at a reasonable price; it's too much to ask for if you want one of these snob's cars, but not impossible to find, I reckon, outside this aristocracy of motordom . . . The interests of tourists are becoming more and more divorced from those of racers, for whom cost is nothing, and the leading marques are wrong to make so much of these attention-grabbing vehicles to promote their ordinary cars.

'If you haven't Fr20,000 or more to invest in a car before taking four passengers on a tour in hilly country, should you give up this mode of transport . . . or make your will before leaving? I don't know . . .'

It was a difficult problem to resolve, for there was still an immense gulf between the *voiture de grande luxe* and the light car: if you bought cheaply, you usually bought a vehicle in which everything had been pared to the bone. And perhaps the most successful example of minimal motoring was the Sizaire-Naudin, introduced at the Exposition des Petits Inventeurs in March 1905. Commented *La Vie Automobile*: 'New ideas are plentiful in this little car; almost everything about it is original, and, even better, properly carried out. The main aim of the designers is extreme simplicity. In this voiturette, everything possible has been omitted; the remaining parts have been so designed that the costs are reduced to a minimum without, however, neglecting the quality of construction.

'Apart from the chassis and wheels, the voiturette consists of: a 6hp single-cylinder motor mounted at the front of the chassis, a multi-ratio final drive and irreversible steering'. It also had independent front suspension, but not even the makers realised the advantages of this. They had done it for lightness, using a transverse spring.

The rear axle was an ingenious affair, for it gave three speeds forward and reverse through the medium of a crown wheel and four pinions of differing sizes, which were engaged by a curiously-contoured cam, which moved them both laterally and longitudinally.

'This system presents not only the advantage of a great simplicity, but also that of efficiency, for in every one of the forward gears there is only one intermediary between the engine and the wheels.' It also presented the disadvantage that a silent gearchange was virtually impossible . . .

Even the electric wiring was reduced to a minimum: the coil and batteries were housed in a box in front of the engine (helping to fill the aching void under the ample bonnet) so that only a few inches of wire were needed to link coil and contact breaker, while the 'plug lead' was a length of metal spring from the box to the sparking plug.

Right: priced at $750, the Model S Ford was a 1908 compromise between the basic Model N and the 'more pretentious' Model R. All three shared a common chassis and bi-block 15 hp engine; from them sprang the immortal Model T

Left: the car with which Ford brought motoring to the masses; the Model T came in many guises from sporty roadster to delivery truck and, at least between 1914 and 1925, in 'any colour so long as it's black'. This is a 1913 four-seat open tourer built in the British Ford factory at Trafford Park, Manchester. The 'T' used a 2.9-litre, four-cylinder, side-valve engine and pedal-controlled, two-speed transmission. In a nineteen-year production run, over sixteen million Model Ts were built (Hendy-Lennox, Bournemouth)

Although the Sizaire enjoyed several years of popularity and even achieved a number of sporting successes, its formula was obviously a sterile one, for, having reduced a vehicle to the absolute basics, its designers could only elaborate it as customers demanded extra refinement; and the Sizaire-Naudin would end up as a staid – and rather corpulent – light car of conventional design.

What then was the answer to the problem of designing a car for the masses? Already Henry Ford was practising the economies of scale, by raising production and reducing prices. In 1906, for example, he replaced the old Model F, with its twin-cylinder engine beneath the seat, with the four cylinder Model N, a far more sophisticated machine. Model F had cost $1000; Model N was only $600 ('It carries no equipment, it is "just automobile – all automobile"', announced the company) and was exported to Britain where it sold for around £125, a price which caused the deepest suspicion among the home industry. 'Nothing so cheap can be any good,' they said . . . and were duly surprised by the model's success, with annual British sales of 600. Ford, however, had even greater things in mind . . .

'The automobile of the past,' said Ford at that time, 'attained success in spite of its price because there were more than enough purchasers to take the limited output of the then new industry. Proportionately few could buy, but those few could keep all the manufacturers busy, and price, therefore, had no bearing on sales. The automobile of the present is making good because the price has been reduced just enough to add sufficient new purchasers to take care of the increased output. Supply and demand, not cost, has regulated the selling price of automobiles.

'The automobile of the future must be enough better than the present car to beget confidence in the man of limited means and enough lower in price to insure sales for the enormously increased output. The car of the future, "the car for the people", the car that any man can own, who can afford a horse and carriage, is coming sooner than most people expect.

'A limited number of factories can supply all the demand for high-priced cars, but the market for a low-priced car is unlimited. The car of the future will be light as well as low in price. This means the substitution of quality for quantity, even to the use of materials not yet discovered'.

Sometime early in 1907, Ford began development of his own personal vision of that 'car for the people'; already, despite the relatively high price of automobiles, America was becoming a nation of car-owners at a spectacular rate. In 1902 there had been one car to every 1,500,000 citizens of the USA; by 1905 the proportion was one to every 65,000, and in the spring of 1907, one American in 800 owned a car. Now Ford was after the remaining 799.

In the little experimental room, only 12 ft by 15 ft, at Ford's Picquette Avenue plant (which the company had occupied for only a couple of years, yet was already outgrowing) Henry Ford and his associates, C. H. Wills, C. J. Smith and Joseph Galamb were working on the successor to Model N. Models R and

S had been de luxe versions of the N, so the new car was to be called the 'Model T'.

Joseph Galamb, a young Hungarian engineer who had worked with the F. B. Stearns company before joining Ford, would draw up Ford's ideas on a blackboard, while Henry Ford, sitting in a big rocking chair that had belonged to his mother, would watch and comment. Then the ideas were translated into metal and tested. Much use was made of vanadium steel and special heat treatments of the metal, which gave the new design lightness combined with durability. Transverse springs fore and aft, combined with three-point suspension of the power unit, gave the car a unique ability to cross uneven ground without undue chassis distortion, while a pedal-operated epicyclic transmission developed from that of the Model N gave clash-free gear-changing (a notable boon in those pre-synchromesh days) though it only possessed two forward speeds. This wasn't such a disadvantage as it might have seemed, for the Model T had a 2892 cc engine, which, while its power output was restricted by narrow gas passages, had ample low-speed torque.

When news of the Model T was released to Ford dealers – especially its price of $850 – some of them informed the factory that they had hidden the advance catalogues of the car as its low cost and improved specification would render all the old model Fords still in stock quite unsaleable.

'High priced quality in a low priced car!' shrieked the advertisement which announced Model T to the public on 3 October, 1908, adding: 'We make no apology for the price – any car now selling up to several hundred dollars more could, if built from Ford design, in the Ford factory, by Ford methods, and in Ford quantities, be sold for the Ford price if the makers were satisfied with the Ford profit per car'.

In fact, by the standards of the Model N, the Model T got away to a slow start, only 309 were built in the first three months of production, while Model N output had been running at an average of 70 to 80 cars *a day* during the summer of 1908, reaching a peak of 101 a day as the final orders were met.

By the summer of 1909 output was nudging 2000 cars a month, and the Ford company was claiming 'the largest shipment of motor cars in one consignment in the history of the trade . . . a train of 41 cars, loaded with three motor cars, 123 motor cars in all . . .'. Already, however, it was becoming uneconomic to ship built-up motor cars over long distances, and Ford began to set up branch assembly plants, to which components were shipped in knocked-down form; by 1912 they owned sites in Kansas City, St Louis, Long Island City, Los Angeles, San Francisco, Portland and Seattle, while the first overseas assembly plant had just been established in a former railway carriage works on Britain's first industrial estate, at Trafford Park, Manchester. The plant produced 1485 cars in 1911 and 3081 in 1912, which put it in the front rank of British car manufacturers in terms of volume.

It was just a drop in the ocean against Ford's total output that year in its Detroit factory of 82,400 Model Ts . . .

An important factor in the growth of the Ford Motor Company had been their removal, in the New Year of 1910, to a magnificent new factory at Highland Park, to the northwest of Detroit. Four stories high, 865 feet long and 75 feet wide, this 'Crystal Palace' boasted 50,000 sq ft of glass, and was the largest building under one roof in the state of Michigan. The 60-acre site on which it stood was soon filled with subsidiary buildings. The old Picquette Avenue plant, of which Ford remarked proudly 'As good as, perhaps a little better than, any automobile factory in the country', was sold to Studebaker.

Ford was only following a long American tradition in insisting upon complete and absolute standardisation of components; Samuel Colt, for instance, had used interchangeable parts in his gun factory half-a-century earlier. But at Highland Park, Ford was moving towards a new concept of mass production. It didn't come all at once; there were brilliant individual aspects like the machine which dipped wheels six at a time into vats of paint, spun them round to throw off the surplus and put them out to dry, turning out 2000 wheels a day; or the radiator assembling machine which assembled 50 tubes and plates into a complete matrix in one operation. Then there was the drilling machine

Below: the 20 hp, 2471 cc Lanchester was current from 1904–11. Like all early Lanchesters, it was unorthodox yet advanced, with oversquare, ohv engine, transmission disc brake, power unit between the front seats, side tiller steering (only abandoned in 1909), epicyclic gearbox and worm final drive. The cantilever springs were designed to give the same motion as a walking man, but Lanchester's advanced theories themselves were out of step with the fashionable mainstream of design and his cars never enjoyed the success they deserved. This 1908 Single Landaulette cost £600 new (National Motor Museum, England)

which bored 45 holes at four different angles in the cylinder block in one operation; most significant was the sub-division of magneto flywheel manufacture into 29 operations performed by 29 men seated along a moving belt, a step which cut the time taken to assemble a magneto progressively from 20 to 13 minutes, then to 7 minutes and finally to 5 minutes.

A similar process was soon adopted for the assembly of the engine, and in the summer of 1913 experiments began in hauling a line of chassis on a rope, six men following each chassis as it was dragged past piles of parts brought to the line in little trucks. An overhead chain hoist dropped the engine into each chassis at the appropriate point. This improvised experiment cut the time taken to assemble each chassis from $12\frac{1}{2}$ hours to 5 hours 50 minutes. Moving production lines were soon installed on a permanent basis, and work further subdivided, so that by the beginning of 1914 it only took 1 hour 33 minutes to assemble each Ford chassis.

Such moves gave spectacular impetus to Ford output; in 1913, 199,100 chassis were produced at Highland Park, while in 1914 the figure rose to 240,700. In 1915, which saw the production of the millionth Model T, 372,250

Fords were manufactured, an achievement which was eclipsed in 1916, which saw 586,202 Ts leave Highland Park, while the following year witnessed the building of 834,662 Ford cars.

It was a total which more than fulfilled the apparently rash statement made a few years previously by Ford's rival, Billy Durant, that one day the American public would buy 500,000 cars every year. Durant, who had tried – and failed – to buy out Ford, had united the Buick, Cadillac and Oldsmobile marques in an organisation which he called General Motors, and for which he had raised capital of $12,500,000. It was, apparently, a winning line-up, especially as Cadillac was headed by Henry M. Leland, the 'Master of Precision', who worked to limits of 100/000th of an inch, and who had won the British Dewar Trophy in 1908 when three cars had been dismantled, their parts jumbled, and reassembled in the most convincing demonstration of standardisation that had yet been given. However, to its four profitable lines – Buick, Cadillac, Oakland and Oldsmobile – General Motors now added unremunerative dross like the Ewing, Elmore, Cartercar and Rainier, which dragged the group down until, in 1910, the bankers were forced to take over and oust Durant. Under its new president, Charles W. Nash, appointed in 1912, and its works manager, Walter P. Chrysler, General Motors made a spectacular recovery – without the dross.

Durant made a reappearance on the scene as the backer of the new Chevrolet company, which he changed in character from a producer of quality cars to a builder of medium-priced vehicles, made $6,000,000 in six years and regained control of General Motors.

Above: one of the last Lion-Peugeots, built after the merger of the two Peugeot car companies under one roof at Audincourt. The C3, of which this is a fine example, was equipped with a V4 engine, pressure lubrication and four-speed transmission. Lion-Peugeot were renowned for their racing voiturettes, which culminated in the 1910 vee-twin VX5, with an 80 mm bore, and stroke of no less than 250 mm; the driver had to look around, not over, the immensely tall engine (Peugeot collection, France)

Right: a 1911 Cadillac Model 30, from the stable of Henry M. Leland – 'Master of Precision'. The Model 30 had a four-cylinder engine of 4.7 litres, and a year later Cadillac made history by standardising electric lighting and starting (Hillcrest Motor Co, Beverley Hills, California)

Against such spectacular growth, the achievements of such mass-producers as Hupmobile, with their annual sales of around 12,000, looked a little wilted, although they were still able to compete in the low-priced car market; in 1913 a survey showed between 23 and 30 car makers active in the 'under $1000' sector.

However, they could not hope to compete on equal terms with the big boys as far as bulk buying of components was concerned; even then, the annual raw material consumption of a major producer like Ford was pretty awe-inspiring. In 1913, the company ordered: 1,000,000 lamps; 800,000 wheels; 800,000 tyres; 90,000 tons of steel; 400,000 leather hides; 2,000,000 sq ft of glass; 12,000,000 hickory billets for wheel-spokes . . .

That America (for so long the backward cousin of the European motor industry) had now taken over as the world's leading car manufacturing nation, was a proven fact. The biggest European companies were no more than dwarfs by New World standards; the total output of the entire British motor industry in 1912 was only 23,200 vehicles, and even the major producers like Wolseley only turned out some 3000 vehicles yearly. Of course, in Britain the car was still regarded as a luxury, not a necessity, a fact proven by Lloyd George's introduction in 1910 of a taxation system for cars based on the horsepower of their engines, measured under the somewhat dubious RAC rating formula, which took only the bore of the engine into account, and thus bred generations of cars with long strokes and narrow bores. Under the 1910 taxation formula, cars of up to $6\frac{1}{2}$ hp paid £2 2s in tax, and larger vehicles were taxed in a progressively steepening ratio up to a rating of 60 hp and over, which attracted an annual impost of £42, a frightening figure when translated into modern terms, but doubtless just about bearable by rich owners accustomed to paying over £500 per annum for replacement tyres.

The inevitable result was the encouragement of smaller and smaller vehicles and, before long, a new word was enriching the motoring vocabulary: 'Cyclecar'. The name was an amalgam of the two terms 'motor cycle' and 'car', and usually seemed to be applied to a vehicle which combined the worst features of each in the interests of simplicity and cheapness. Perhaps the most revoltingly crude vehicle of this type was the Dewcar of 1913/14, which had a 'chassis/body' unit consisting of two planks butted at their extremities, and with a viciously pointed petrol tank mounted immediately above the single-cylinder motor-cycle engine, in just the right position to cause a merry blaze at the least spillage of fuel. The opportunities for self-destruction with a vehicle of this type were endless; and yet they were bought and driven with enthusiasm, their owners professing

Left: the extremely imposing Valveless was the first car to be built by David Brown Ltd. The 1914 19.9 hp model shown here was the last of the marque. It started life in 1910 as a 25 hp model, but the engine was later reduced in size to bring it within the 20 hp rating (National Motor Museum, England)

Above, centre: the 1912 Hispano-Suiza Alfonso was named after the King of Spain, who was an enthusiastic driver

Above right and below: the 1913 Daimler Cranmore Laudaulette, with 4.9-litre, six-cylinder, 30 hp Knight double sleeve valve engine

disdain for the humble Ford (which at £125 cost little more than the average cyclecar, and offered accommodation for five against the maximum of two small people which could be forced into the cyclecar's cramped cockpit).

Only two British makes of cyclecar exhibited any lasting merits, and these were the four-wheeled GN and the three-wheeled Morgan, which was the better-engineered of the two.

The prototype Morgan was built in the workshops of Malvern College by young H. F. S. Morgan while he was convalescing from a crash on his Peugeot motor cycle, and represented car design reduced to a workman-like minimum. The chassis was based on a tubular-steel backbone down which ran the propellor shaft, at the forward end of which was hung the big V-twin engine from the Peugeot and at the rear of which was a two-speed bevel box (this not only drove the single rear wheel *via* twin chains, but also served as a mounting point for the quarter-elliptic rear suspension). A tubular framework at the front of the chassis carried sliding-pillar independent front suspension with coil springing. The prototype had tiller steering, but when popular demand spurred Morgan to put the little vehicle into production, high-geared wheel steering was adopted. The bottom tubes of the chassis also served as exhaust pipes, thus keeping the number of parts to a minimum.

Its excellent power-to-weight ratio gave the Morgan a particularly sporting performance, a fact which was not lost on H. F. S. Morgan, who began to enter competitions; he found an enthusiastic, if somewhat unorthodox, 'public relations officer' in his clerical father, Prebendary H. G. Morgan of Stoke Lacy, Worcestershire, who wrote enthusiastically to the press about his son's achievements. He even turned up, clad in top hat with side strings, frock coat and dog-collar, to watch H.F.S. cover sixty miles in the hour at Brooklands in 1912 at the wheel of a special single-seater Morgan. Although various makes of V-twin power unit – MAG, Green-Precision, Blumfield – were used, it was the JAP power unit which became identified with the Morgan.

In the 1913 French Cyclecar Grand Prix, a Morgan came first, and was immediately reclassified as a motor cycle and sidecar by the French authorities for having had the temerity to beat Gallic cyclecars like the Bédélia and the Violet-Bogey; it retained the moral victory.

The Bédélia, produced by two extroverts named Bourbeau and Devaux, was a tandem-seated device which also had its origins in components retrieved after a motor-cycle accident. However, its crude centre-pivot steering, controlled by steel wires wrapped round the tubular column, and belt drive (with ratio changing controlled by the front-seat passenger on racing versions) were symptoms of a somewhat more casual attitude to design than that of the Morgan's progenitor . . .

Its protagonists called the cyclecar movement 'The New Motoring', although much of it was really a restatement of mistakes that had long been forgotten. Nevertheless, at its peak in 1913/14, it attracted a large number of would-be motor tycoons to chance their arm at entering the market with totally unproven designs, some of which seemed remarkably tenacious of life, like the Carden, a narrow-tracked projectile with centre-pivot steering, which carried its power unit at the rear of the bodywork. It started off meekly enough, with a single-cylinder 4 hp engine, but then developed a lethal sting in its tail, like an earthbound *kamikaze* bee, with a V-twin JAP engine of around 1000 cc, whose weight and power must have reduced the already minimal directional stability of the machine to almost negative proportions. Yet, this offence against all engineering decencies was revived after World War I and continued to be manufactured, under the new alias of 'AV Monocar', until 1926.

To show the depths which cyclecar manufacturers were prepared to plumb, it should be noted that the constructors of the Globe cyclecar of 1913/16 were the well-known firm of sanitary engineers, Tuke & Bell of Tottenham, better known for custom-built sewage-disposal plants . . .

Just before the outbreak of war, there were dozens of different makes of cyclecar on the British market, and there was the inevitable tendency for them to grow into proper little cars. Many lapses of good judgment occurred during this growing-up period, like the unfortunate case of the 1095 cc V-twin

Far right: from 1910 to 1950, Morgan three-wheelers were very little changed, having a tubular chassis with sliding-pillar front suspension and quarter-elliptic springs at the rear; engines, however, were another matter, various makes of vee-twin being fitted. The prototype used a Peugeot 7 hp power unit, but the cars which went into production had all kinds of engine, such as JAP, MAG and Blumfield

Below and right: before World War I, the Star Engineering Co of Wolverhampton, a descendant of the Star Cycle Co, was one of the six largest car manufacturers in Britain. This is a 3-litre, 15.9 hp Star Torpedo tourer, which cost 400 guineas new in 1914, fitted with a 'streamline body of most pleasing lines', cape cart hood and dynamo lighting set

Buckingham exhibited at the 1913 Motor Cycle and Cyclecar Show. On this belt-driven and somewhat sketchy chassis, the car's designer, J. F. Buckingham, caused a dainty saloonette body, replete with lace curtains and cut-glass flower holders to be erected. He called it, of course, the 'Buckingham Palace'. Mr Buckingham was to achieve greater fame during the ensuing world conflict as the inventor of a particularly anti-social device known as the Buckingham Incendiary Bullet, much favoured by the British and allied forces for shooting Zeppelins down in flames.

Herbert Austin, who had resigned from his job as chief engineer at Wolseley in 1906 to form his own car-manufacturing company, building mainly large, powerful four and six-cylinder cars, went to the opposite extreme in 1910/11. His new car used an 1100cc single-cylinder engine (built by Swift) and cost £150; it was not a success, and was soon dropped. Thereafter, the smallest model in Austin's pre-war lineup was an 1145cc 10hp, uprated in 1913 to 1452cc. In that year, incidentally, Austin increased his factory area to nine acres, an addition of 25 per cent, and modernised the production machinery to meet the demand for his products (although the area was marginally reduced again early in 1914 when suffragettes burned down the employees' library).

Others were more faithful to the small-car concept, partly because it brought a new type of customer onto the market: the woman driver. It is often claimed that it was the introduction of the self-starter by Cadillac which really attracted

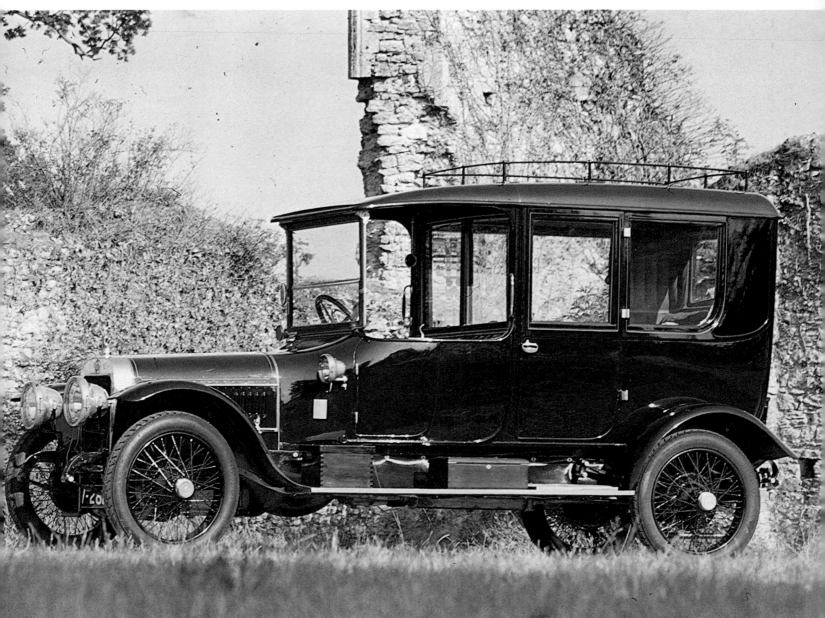

Above: an early example of a 7 hp Austin, not to be confused with the famous car of the 1920s; this 1910 machine was really a Swift, made in Coventry and sold under two names. It was equipped with a single-cylinder power unit of 1100 cc
(National Motor Museum, England)

Left and above: by 1913, Argyll of Glasgow was the fifth-largest manufacturer in the British Isles, turning out quite a large range o cars. This is a 1913 15/30 hp
(National Motor Museum, England)

the lady motorist, but in fact the electric starter was a necessary evil which had to be developed once the old trembler-coil ignition system had been ousted by high-tension-magneto or battery-and-coil installations for, while a car in good tune would start on the tremblers once its cylinders had been primed, the more up-to-date ignitions lacked this useful facility.

The advent of lady drivers was not altogether welcomed by a generation of males somewhat apprehensive of the outcome of the emancipation movement. 'Several prominent gentlemen have been assuring us lately that our comrades of the other sex are something of a terror on the roads. If memory serves rightly, most of these gentlemen are somewhat advanced in years. Possibly, when a man has turned the corner of, say, fifty, he objects to piling his new £500 car up the bank in order that a lady piloting her 8 hp two-seater may wobble past', commented W. H. Berry in April 1914. 'But, come, sirs! What do we do when any other road obstruction causes delay to our imperial progress? Why, slow down and, if necessary, stop until the danger is past . . . We cannot claim that all women are unsuited to be drivers, forsooth, because some few are inclined to be wobbly on the road. For weal or woe we must make up our minds that the lady driver will be seen on the roads in increasing number . . . Manufacturers are catering specially for the lady driver. They are building cars for her particular benefit, and she is seizing advantage of the opportunity in order to do her shopping and to take out her friends and to run down to town and to the links. What difficulty does the little Swift, or the Humberette, or the Singer, offer a lady driver? Is there any reason why a woman should not handle a Rover, or a Darracq? Assuredly not. Very well then!'

Berry's choice of typical light cars is interesting for, while the Swift and the Humberette were unashamedly cyclecars, albeit of the better-designed sort, the Singer was one of the nicest of all the 'big cars in miniature' to appear in the years immediately preceding World War I. With a four-cylinder engine of 1097 cc, the Singer Ten sold for £185 and lasted in basically the same form until 1923. It was a brisk performer, despite having its three-speed gearbox in unit with its rear axle, and it was with a highly tuned version of this model that Lionel Martin, progenitor of the Aston Martin, was to gain experience of rapid light cars.

However, the Singer was only one of several attractive small four-cylinder cars of around 1–1·5 litres capacity to make their début at this period; Calcott and Calthorpe were honoured names, whose origins went back to bicycling days, while Swift added a Ten to their range in 1913 (although it was not nearly as popular as their cyclecar). In Oxford, a successful cycle and motor agent called William Morris was just beginning to market a diminutive model, mostly assembled from proprietory parts. It had a handsome 'bullnosed' brass radiator, a feature shared with the little AC from Thames Ditton, Surrey, which was built as a handsome sporting model as well as in standard two-seater form.

One of the smallest four-cylinder cars to be produced was the little Bébé Peugeot, designed by Ettoré Bugatti, who had not long set up in business as a maker of very expensive, but inordinately rapid, small cars of 1327 cc; his Bébé, a design which he had sold to Peugeot, had a monobloc four-cylinder engine of only 855 cc and a curious transmission in which the ratios were provided by concentric propeller-shafts terminating in pinions of differing diameters. Normally, the Bébé was endowed with two-seater bodywork rather reminiscent of the bath in which Marat was assassinated, but the little engine was powerful enough to permit at least one example of this model being fitted with a diminutive two-seater coupé body of undoubted charm, if minimal practicality.

Perhaps the oddest marketing technique employed by any Edwardian light-car maker was that employed by Motor Schools Limited, who built a friction-drive 10 hp car with a 1244 cc Chapuis-Dornier four-cylinder engine. As their name implied, Motor Schools ran a training institute where drivers and mechanics received instruction at fees ranging up to £25 for 'three-months practical work in garage and works, 72 driving lessons and daily attendance at class lectures'. They had what was claimed to be the largest fleet of dual-control vehicles – fourteen of them, and probably of their own make – and also published a little *aide memoire* booklet entitled *200 Practical Points on Motoring*. With every copy of this was given a coupon entitling the purchaser of the book to enter a competition in which the prize every month was a £150 Car and Course of Instruction FREE'. The car, of course, was their own little friction-drive Pilot 10hp, and the competition was one in which competitors had to fill in the missing words in a story which throws an uncomfortable light on the problems of small-car owners of the day (and the answers to which were to be found – surprise, surprise – on a diligent reading of *200 Points* . . .).

'While travelling between Uxbridge and Ruislip in our car, we heard a sharp metallic click, as if something had been picked up by the wheel and hurled against the front mud-guard', ran the puzzle story. 'On examination, we found that (1) . . . had worked loose, with the result that (2) . . . had come off, and evidently been thrown up by the wheel. Fortunately, we had another with us, and were soon off again. Much to our dismay, after stopping for petrol, we found on turning the starting handle, that we could get no (3) . . . but we soon found the simple cause of the trouble. The next day we found it necessary to use the spare (4) . . . This is one of the spare parts that *200 Practical Points on Motoring* advise all motorists to carry. Everything went all right on the way back until after lunch. Somehow we had lost the (5) . . . but what would have been a problem to us amateurs was solved by the answer to question No. (6) . . . in *200 Practical Points on Motoring*.'

Indeed, if contemporary instruction books are to be believed, the average journey by light car was fraught with such nameless perils. Spectacular collisions must have been commonplace, for manuals gave graphic, if improbable, instructions on how to get home if a crash carried away the front wheels ('For one wheel smashed, replace it with a skid made from a purloined fence post, for two wheels smashed, borrow a coster cart, fasten it to the front axle, and use reins to steer . . .'), while Sankey, makers of pressed-steel artillery wheels advertised how their products withstood violent impacts, like Lionel Martin's crash with his Singer in the 1914 London–Gloucester Trial: 'For no apparent reason, for there was no evidence whatever of a skid, the car left the road at high speed, dashed into the grass at the roadside, jumped a three-foot gulley, was hurled sideways and overturned. The front axle was twisted, the springs torn off, and the nearside chassis member snapped in half – yet in spite of this wreckage, the Sankey Wheels which took the brunt of the impact were absolutely unharmed'.

It is hardly surprising that in the same issue which described this crash, *The Motor* ran a leading article entitled 'Subtleties of Insurance Policies', just to help out readers.

In fact, although petty annoyances could still mar an outing by car (the author's great-uncle, who was one of the first Ford agents in Britain, and often drove with S. F. Edge, recalled having to spend nights sleeping by a broken-down car on a heap of roadside gravel at this time), the internal-combustion engine was becoming increasingly more reliable, its development immeasurably aided by the opening of Brooklands in 1907 as a venue where endurance, as well as sheer speed, could be tested.

Quite the most remarkable proof of the growing maturity of the motor car was given on 15 February 1913, when Percy 'Pearley' Lambert covered 103 miles 1470 yards in an hour at Brooklands driving a 25 hp Talbot, basically a production touring model, endowed with wind-cheating single-seater body. The fact that, without excessive modification, a car which could be bought for only £515 could put 100 miles into an hour caused a sensation among the motoring public, especially since the speed limit on British roads was only 20mph (and would remain so until 1930!).

Sunbeam snatched Lambert's record from him with a purpose-built racing car, and 'Pearley', attempting to regain his honours before the opening of the 1913 Motor Show at Olympia, crashed, was killed, and was buried in Brompton Cemetery in a coffin streamlined to match the contours of his car, quite a fitting epitaph to the man.

Above: the 1913 Bébé Peugeot had an 850cc engine and a strange two-speed rear axle with twin concentric propellor shafts and two rows of crown-wheel teeth. Designed by Ettore Bugatti, the 6 hp Bébé represented the best light car design of the time, with an engine capable of a heady 2000 rpm. Bugatti had signed the design contract on 16 November 1911 (Château de Grandson, Switzerland)

Right: this elaborately equipped 1914 Turner was originally purchased by a military officer, who was killed shortly afterwards. The car was then stored for sixty years before being found, in original condition (Cheddar Motor Museum, England)

It was the achievements of men like Lambert which built up the motor business in Britain, despite hostile legislation and official apathy, to the status of a major international industry. In 1905, exports had been only £501,802; in the year ending 31 March 1914, Britain's motor industry exported cars worth £4,324,000. A far sterner test of the industry's abilities was imminent . . . on 4 August 1914, World War I began, and with it came the first demands for mechanical transport for military purposes. Although the horse was still favoured by the army at this time, the motor vehicle, in various forms was becoming rapidly more efficient and the needs of war would force this progress to an even greater degree.

Military vehicles had first appeared, except for steam-traction engines, during the Boer War, when a couple of MMC tricycles and a Locomobile steam car had been tentatively used by officers in the British Army, but they had proved of limited utility. The War Office obviously had some idea of the potential of self-propelled vehicles, for they held trials for lorries as early as 1901, and there had been a number of experiments with motorised troop transport on manoeuvres, notably a London–Hastings run organised by the Automobile Association in conjunction with the Guards.

However, the military hierarchy was still enamoured of the horse and, when war broke out in 1914, the Army was woefully short of fighting vehicles. A subsidy scheme had been in operation for some years, under which lorry owners whose vehicles conformed with certain specifications received payments from the War Office on condition that their vehicles were made instantly available for military use on the outbreak of war. The Army obviously had need of them, for its own motorised strength in August 1914 only amounted

to some eighty vehicles. Subsidy lorries brought the strength of the British Expeditionary Force's motorised units up to 1200 vehicles. To supplement this inadequate force, the authorities commandeered some 1300 London buses which were shipped over to France for troop transport. Eventually, when time permitted, they were repainted in olive drab, but at first they ploughed their stolid way across the Flanders fields flaunting the bright red livery and boldly lettered advertisements that they had worn on the streets of London.

London taxis, too, were commandeered for service in France, but it was the French who made the first decisive use of internal combustion for military purposes when the military commander of Paris, General Gallieni, commandeered the city's taxis to rush French reinforcements to help stem Von Kluck's advance on the city. It was a decisive move in the Allied victory in the Battle of the Marne, and one of the Renault taxis was preserved for posterity in Les Invalides. Incidentally, the cab-drivers not only received the full cab fare shown on their meters, but also a 27 per cent tip!

Some of the first British vehicles to reach France were quickly involved in the fighting. One three-ton Leyland truck, still bearing the name of 'John Jackson & Son of Bolton & Manchester' on its headboard, was captured by the Germans and later recaptured in damaged condition by Lancashire troops.

Some of the first buses taken over for military use were stripped of their bodywork by the Royal Naval Flying Corps and fitted with boiler-plate armouring. Noted the *War Illustrated*: 'There are a number of British armoured cars at the front, and their services are invaluable for obliterating small parties of German cavalry. The horsemen stand no chance against these swiftly moving and well protected engines of war, unless they vault hedges and ditches

Below: this 1913 Vauxhall Prince Henry is a 4-litre development of the 3-litre car designed by Laurence Pomeroy Snr for the 1910 Prince Henry Trials. With a four-cylinder, 75 bhp engine it originally sold for £615. It has a top speed of 75–80 mph. Worthy of note is the distinctive fluted vee-radiator; the flutes, so long a traditional feature of Vauxhall styling, were inspired by the contours of a wardrobe in the bedroom of a Vauxhall director (National Motor Museum, England)

and take to the woods, where, naturally, the motor car cannot follow. In the matter of putting an end to the sneaking services of German spies, they are also useful'.

War Illustrated also commented on the activities of one of these motor heroes: 'Commander Samson, the best known of our naval airmen, has added to his renown by a dashing exploit. On 16 September, near Doullens, seventeen miles north of Amiens, he went out with a small armoured-car force and encountered a patrol of five Uhlans. He killed four of them and the fifth was wounded and captured. The British party suffered no injury. Commander Samson was the airman who, three years before, flew over the German Emperor's yacht when it arrived in the Medway. On that occasion, the Kaiser admired his daring, and Commander Samson is evidently determined to continue to merit his admiration'.

This was the stuff of high adventure and, before long, armoured cars were being featured in the stirring tales of authors like Percy F. Westerman, in which the heroes were inevitably plucky, resourceful, lantern-jawed British lads of around fourteen years of age . . .

Private-car chassis were used as the basis for armoured cars, too: the Belgian Minerva company, whose factory at Antwerp was right in the path of the German advance in 1914, hastily turned its workforce to converting its 7·4-litre 38hp chassis into armoured cars, some of which could even boast a rotatable domed gun turret at the rear. These were used for forays from Antwerp and against the German cavalry, although one naval airman in command of a Minerva threatened a patrol of German cycles with his machine-gun, whereupon 'those that were not killed left their machines and hid in the woods'.

However, of all the chassis used for armoured cars, the most outstanding were the Rolls-Royce and the Lanchester, both capable of attaining speeds of up to 50mph against the 16mph or so of the normal army truck.

Apart from minor modifications to the suspension and running gear, both were based on standard touring-car chassis, yet withstood the extra weight of the armour-plating with complete reliability. Some of the Rolls-Royces used in Arabia which survived World War I, were active in the local skirmishes of the 1920s and 1930s, and fought in World War II, by which time their original wheels had been changed for a later pattern carrying large-section tyres, as the original beaded-edge high-pressure type had proved incredibly vulnerable in service. In fact, except when in action against the enemy, the Rolls-Royce armoured cars were limited to 20mph, as they were quite capable of gobbling up a dozen tyres in a day.

The Lanchesters, on the other hand, with their all-round cantilever suspension, were markedly kinder to their footwear, and did sterling service on the Russian Front. Also, their mid-mounted engines were less likely to be damaged by enemy fire. The Lanchesters fought in squadrons of six, supported by

Left: a Büssing armoured car, based on an 80 hp Daimler truck chassis and made for the German army during World War I; this machine was equipped with four-wheel drive and steering, together with a driving position at each end so that the machine was truly reversible; it had a top speed of about 30 mph

Right: De Dion Auto-Canons were used successfully to defend Paris against Zeppelin attacks during World War I and, indeed, were brought to England to help protect London against the same threat; this is a 1914 example, based on the De Dion V8 chassis

Left and right: two views of an early 10 hp AC armoured car, built as an experiment in 1914. As can be seen, the most vulnerable parts were the wheels and particularly the tyres, which were very prone to punctures. In the photograph *left* the radiator armour in closed, making the vehicle less exposed but more prone to overheating

three high-speed service vehicles on the same chassis (a general-purpose lorry, a mobile workshop, and a field kitchen). This chassis was also used, incidentally, for searchlight tenders and powered winches for observation balloons.

Nearer home, the raiding of London by Zeppelins, which began in 1915, prompted the authorities to institute a mobile air-raid defence system based on the V8 De Dion Auto-Canons which were being successfully used by the resourceful General Gallieni in the defence of Paris. In charge of the project was Commander Rawlinson of the Naval Armoured Car service, who duly collected his auto-canon and its attendant *caisson*, or ammunition truck, from Paris in September 1915: 'Although driving an exceptionally fast car and sending it along at its best speed, it was no easy task to catch up the gun, as that most remarkable machine, the Auto-Canon, with well over 100 horse-power, did an easy 50 miles an hour on the level, although its weight of over five tons delayed it somewhat on the hills'.

At first, the De Dion was based in the RNVR Armoured Car Headquarters in the Talbot Works in Ladbroke Grove, and its firing position was on the

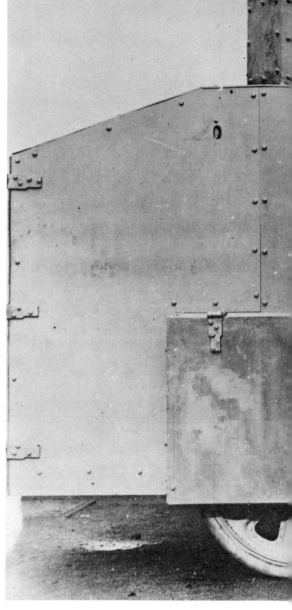

Above: an armoured car prototype of 100–120 hp, designed by Charles Jarrott and submitted to the French Government for appraisal

Artillery Ground in Moorgate, for it was reckoned that this would be the ideal place to defend the Bank of England against airship raids. However, from the way that Rawlinson's detachment went into action, it seems as though the Zeppelins were the lesser menace!

'At that time, there was no system of "air-raid warnings", "raid shelters", or "maroons", such as was organised later on, and the streets on this occasion were crammed with vehicular traffic and pedestrians . . . the *most pressing* and *most vital* thing they had to do was TO GET OUT OF OUR WAY . . . omnibuses in every direction were seeking safety on the pavement . . . people were flattening themselves against shop windows . . . sinking the hill in Holborn . . . my speedometer registered 56 miles an hour.'

At this point, Rawlinson was going so fast that he could not stop when he came upon a section of the road blocked off for repairs, and had to charge through the barriers. The whole journey across London was so rapid that, twenty minutes after leaving the Talbot factory, the Auto-Canon was set up and firing at a Zeppelin that was dropping bombs on Moorgate. The airship was frightened off, but apparently undamaged.

More 'Automobile Anti-Aircraft Guns' were now constructed on Daimler and Lancia chassis, and a 'Mobile Anti-Aircraft Brigade' was formed under Rawlinson's command, and billeted in the stables of the Grand Duke Michael of Russia's palatial house, Kenwood, in Hampstead; total strength was now seven automobile guns, as well as fourteen other vehicles.

Although the Auto-Canons do not seem to have scored any positive successes against the Zeppelins, they did at least scare several marauding airships into releasing their bombs before they could do any damage on their prime targets.

Left: in the early days of World War I, Ford light trucks, many of them built in Britain, had to face the most appalling hardships. These Model Ts shared – with only the aristocratic Silver Ghost – the distinction of being capable of coping with conditions such as encountered here in the deserts of Mesopotamia

More effective as a weapon was the Tank, developed in great secrecy by the British motor industry, and based on such pre-war experiments as the Ruston & Hornsby caterpillar-tracked vehicles and the Diplock Pedrail attachment for traction-engine wheels.

The prototype tank was nicknamed 'Willie', and was completed in December 1915 at the Lincoln works of William Foster & Company; its top speed was $3\frac{1}{2}$ mph.

By the summer of 1916, the Tank was a fighting proposition, and fifty were sent to France. For security, the units which later became the Tank Corps were then known as the Heavy Branch, Machine Gun Corps. Psychologically, these first 'Land Ships' were a terrifying addition to the machinery of war (although that ingenious author, H. G. Wells, had forecast such a weapon several years earlier in a short story called 'The Land Ironclads'), and they terrified the Germans, whose rival experiments were fruitless.

The British Tanks went into action on the Somme on 15 September 1916, and were soon to play a significant part in the winning of the war, turning the static fighting of the trench lines into a more mobile battle. At Cambrai, for instance, in November 1917, 378 tanks penetrated 10,000 yards behind the Hindenburg Line.

This took just twelve hours, compared with the three months it had taken British troops to advance this far at Ypres, at the cost of 400,000 casualties and millions of pounds in ammunition – the preliminary bombardment alone had

Above: motor cars also played their part in carrying the War to the air. In this 1911 photograph, a 26 hp, eight-cylinder De Dion is being used as an aircraft tender

represented £22,000,000-worth of shells. At Cambrai there was no preliminary bombardment and only 5000 casualties. Petrol power was proving its worth in warfare.

Even more spectacular was the Allied victory at Amiens, in August 1918, in which the Tanks played a decisive role; the German commander Von Ludendorff called this the 'black day of the German Army', but less than 1000 Allied troops were killed or wounded.

It's instructive to look through photographs of the War to realise how quickly the motor vehicle ousted the horse from the roles which it had played in battle for hundreds of years. In 1914 photographs of the fighting forces, horses predominate, with only the occasional motor vehicle visible; by 1918 the situation is entirely reversed. Some idea of the rapid increase in numbers of military motors is given by the fact that when the British Government took stocks in 1919, it found that it had 165,128 self-propelled vehicles of all kinds on the strength, of which some 100,000 were overseas – and that didn't include all those vehicles which had been damaged beyond repair.

Indeed, so rapidly did the tempo increase that in 1915 the commercial vehicle manufacturer AEC became the first British company to follow the Ford example and install a moving production line to increase output (although in AEC's case production seems to have run at about thirty vehicles a week, so the line must have moved somewhat glacially.

Right: a Cadillac model 55 of 1917; this had a 5.1-litre, V8 engine, producing over 70 bhp and it was in this year that the company introduced detachable cylinder heads for the engine, first produced in 1915. The V8 Cadillac was widely used by the US Army during World War I (Skokloster Museum, Sweden)

The initial stages of the war in Europe had seen no American-built Fords on active service: Henry Ford was a pacifist, and at first refused to build for the warring nations. His overseas factories, in Manchester, Bordeaux and Canada, took a different view of things, and supplied Model Ts by the thousand to the Allies. British-built Ford light trucks were especially useful in Mesopotamia, where they proved to be one of the only two types of vehicle – the other was the Rolls-Royce Silver Ghost – capable of withstanding the tough desert conditions.

Once America had come into the war, however, the American Government set the ball rolling by ordering 2000 ambulances from Ford's Detroit factory; among the diverse orders which followed were those for 820,000 steel helmets, naval patrol boats and V8 and V12 Liberty aero-engines and cylinders. Henry Ford also formed a new company to produce the Fordson tractor, thousands of which were shipped to Britain at the order of the Ministry of Munitions to enable farmers to improve the yield of home-grown produce.

In fact, the War taught many motor-manufacturing companies how to diversify their products; Austin built complete aircraft; the Clyno motor-

cycle company and the Guy truck company both built ABC Dragonfly aero-engines; others produced shells, fuses, paravanes for minesweepers and a host of other military requirements which had little in common save that they were made of metal.

Prominent among British aero-engine makers was Rolls-Royce, whose excellent Eagle power unit had six cylinders and an overhead camshaft, and could develop 225 bhp on its first trials in October 1915, a figure which had increased to 360 bhp by the Armistice.

Strangely enough, after the war, Continental manufacturers generally put the lessons they had learned in aero-engine design into the power units of their motor cars; in Britain, almost without exception, makers stuck stolidly to side valves (admittedly Wolseley, who had built Hispano-Suiza V8 aero-engines, *did* produce a range of overhead-camshaft engines, but these failed to realise their potential to such a degree that their makers might just as well not have bothered . . .).

Standardisation was a wartime lesson that many quickly forgot, too: once

Above: another De Dion V8 chassis of 1914, in this case specially modified and put to use as an ambulance; despite the obviously cold weather, this particular example seems to have overheated, a not uncommon problem in the days before thermostats and reliable antifreeze, when cold air could freeze the water in the radiator even with the engine running

Right: a Scania-Vabis ambulance of 1914, based on the combine's 20 hp model; the four-cylinder engine was made with a one-piece cylinder block, as opposed to the two-piece version of the 60 hp model of the same period
(Saab-Scania collection)

the armed forces had built up their requirements by commandeering a wide variety of machinery, they then chose a limited number of makes which would be the standard military issue for staff cars. Roughly, in descending order of rank, the list ran: Rolls-Royce (for the *very* top brass), Vauxhall, Daimler, Sunbeam, Wolseley, Austin and Singer. So strictly was this adhered to that when Sunbeam's output of aero-engines became so great that the company couldn't continue building cars, Rover were contracted to build Sunbeams under licence, even though the Rover car was fully the equal of the Sunbeam for quality.

The Royal Flying Corps (which became the Royal Air Force on 1 April 1918) was an individualistic sort of a service, so it exercised its own choice of motor vehicles, most of its heavy trucks being Leylands, most of its staff cars and tenders Crossleys. So closely did the air service and its transport become linked that the terms 'RAF Leyland' and 'RFC Crossley' were often used as model names.

Individualistic, too, seems to be the only word to describe the attitude of a large part of the French Army to motor transport. Although there was, of course, much standardisation, there were also eccentricities which could not have happened elsewhere. Ambulances were a fruitful medium for self-expression: one conversion consisted of a tandem-seated Bédélia cyclecar (which was driven from the back seat) with a stretcher mounted over the front seat, engine and petrol tank, the last of which was apt to leak on to the hot cylinders and set off a merry blaze. One can imagine the hapless *poilu* pleading to be left to die in peace where he was rather than be rushed off to the field hospital on such a crazy device. An even more casual casualty wagon had appeared in the early stages of the war, however; fitted on the back of a 12/15 hp Mors chassis was a sort of three-storey dishrack, in which the injured were stacked in tiers, completely exposed to the open air. 'Science is required in carrying wounded, a lack of which would often have fatal results', added a cryptic caption. 'Our allies' simple but ingenious method of quickly conveying wounded soldiers from one place to another has proved invaluable in practice.'

Above: the Germans' answer to the armoured vehicles of the allied forces; ludicrously, great pains were taken to protect the mechanical parts and the occupants, but the pneumatic tyres were left totally exposed

Left: an Ehrhardt armoured car, built for the German forces by a Düsseldorf-based company that had been the first in Germany to introduce four-wheel brakes (in 1913)

A more sensible French conception was the conversion of motor buses into mobile operating theatres.

Where the English used motor cycles for carrying despatches, the French used Bébé Peugeot cars; but where there was a need for rapid communications, Gallic ingenuity received free rein. When war broke out, the Mercédès company, which had just gained a one-two-three victory in the French Grand Prix, was celebrating its win by displaying one of the team cars (under false colours, as they had repainted it with the winning number!) in their showroom on the Champs-Elysées. Noted *The Autocar*: 'One of the high officials of the French motor transport service, requiring a car with which he could reel off three or four hundred miles between breakfast and dinner, secured possession of it, to find that connecting rods were broken and the bearings had gone. Put into good mechanical condition, fitted with a windscreen and mudguards, the enemy car rendered valuable service, frequently covering the three hundred miles separating Lyon from Paris after morning business had been attended to, and making another run of about a hundred miles to Châlons, or another point behind the lines. This experience showed that a racing car can be used very successfully for long distance travel, for the officer who had charge of the Mercédès states that his petrol consumption was eighteen miles to the gallon, that tyre trouble was practically nil, and that the car was so easy to handle that after three hundred miles he was not too fatigued to work'.

Another ex-racing car used for high-speed dashes was the Renault which had won the 1906 French Grand Prix; this car was appropriated by the celebrated Escadrille Cigogne ('Stork Squadron') of the French Air Services, who thought that it would be 'a suitable machine for wild dashes from the front to the base, from camp to Paris or from point to point of the line'. Despite its 10 mpg petrol consumption, and tyres which refused to last for more than 500 miles, the Renault was used with success by the leading French air aces – Guynemer, Fonck, Nungesser and Navarre.

Perhaps the most hilarious conversion was that carried out by the Italians on the 115 hp Itala which Henri Fournier had driven in the 1908 Grand Prix at Dieppe; this was converted into an ambulance to make a nightly climb up a mountainside in search of wounded on the border between Austria and Italy. But the machine was so unsuitable for the task, and ran so badly that the secret police became suspicious of its activities, and arrested the driver and passenger, keeping them under observation for twelve hours until their innocence could be proved . . .

Keeping all these diverse Allied vehicles supplied with petrol was an immense task in itself, and sterling work was carried out by the petrol companies, both in shipping crude oil from the oilfields, despite the constant threat of U-Boat attack, and in refining it and getting it to the Front. Shell, indeed, built a refinery, shipped it across the Channel one weekend, and had it working within 36 hours. Even the humble two-gallon petrol tin played its part: a special factory was set up for the manufacture of this indispensible item, which, when drained of spirit, was used for countless purposes in the trenches – even as building blocks for shelters and, after being beaten flat, as flooring.

The Germans, who had entered the war somewhat better equipped with military motors than the Allies – as early as 1900 the Kaiser had offered a prize equivalent to £4000 for the 'best automobile war carriage which will combine all the requisites for service in the field' – suffered badly from the British naval blockade. As their supplies of rubber dwindled, the Germans were forced to resort to all kinds of substitute spring metal tyres, which proved a great hindrance to their mobility. Their choice of staff cars fully reflected their highly class-structured society, ranging down from Field Marshal Von Hindenburg's 21-litre Benz tourer (which still exists in England . . .) to the sub-utility 10 hp Phanomobil, which had its single-cylinder engine mounted above the front wheel.

The unparalleled use of mechanical traction during World War I was to prove of major significance in the future growth of the motor industry. Thousands of men, whose peacetime experience of motor vehicles was no more than a rare ride on an omnibus – if that – had been trained as drivers and mechanics, and tasted the rare mobility that only the rich motor owner had known pre-war. Having tested, and fought for, that sense of freedom they were unlikely now to look back.

Below: a strange German vehicle, the Phanomobile 6/12PS; this particular example, with a transverse, air-cooled, four-cylinder engine mounted over and chain-driving the tiller-steered front wheel, was manufactured in 1922, but earlier examples of the model had been used by the German army as ambulances during World War I. Primary drive was by friction to a two-speed epicyclic gearbox, while, as the photograph shows, cooling was aided by twin fans
(National Motor Museum, England)

Chapter 2

Pioneers of the Track

THE CARS: 1894-1914

Motor racing is nearly as old as the motor car itself. The early motor races were contested over the ruler-straight *Routes Nationale* of France, and for a good reason. Firstly, the French received the emergence of the horseless-carriage as a practical means of transport with more understanding and far fewer restrictions than those it was plagued with elsewhere, particularly in England. Secondly, the pioneers were faced with the task of making carriages drawn by mechanical means (instead of behind horses or other suitable animals) prove that they could, in fact, represent an effective replacement. For this reason their primary concerns were making the new-fangled vehicles run with a modicum of reliability and safety and then to show that these autocars, automobiles, motor cars, as they were variously called, were able to cover a reasonable amount of ground and at far higher speeds than animal-propelled carts and carriages were capable of doing.

Thus, the best means of both proving these matters to a sceptical public and of improving the design and construction of the motor car itself, was accomplished by organising races, which were thus generally well supported by those who saw a big commercial future for the motor car and by those who, liking these new exhilaratingly fast vehicles from the sporting viewpoint, realised how essential it was for them to prove themselves, so that authority would not frown on them. In the next chapter we shall see how the then deserted, unfettered main highways of the European continent were ideal for such

Below: one of the 30 hp, 6.3-litre lightweight Renaults which competed in the ill-fated Paris-Madrid race of 1903; it was in one of these cars that Marcel Renault crashed and was killed, causing the race to be stopped. The maximum weight limit for the event was 1000 kg, so the chassis of the cars were drilled as much as possible in order to reduce the overall weight and allow for big engines; this process undoubtedly took away a substantial amount of strength. The optical phenomenon of the forward lean of the car, typical in photographs of this period, results from the use of a focal plane shutter camera. As the shutter moves across the image, the tops of the wheels, being recorded on the film slightly later than the bottoms, have advanced slightly – hence the 'crouch'

Above: the Peugeot Vis-à-Vis which passed the finishing line first in the Paris-Rouen Reliability Trial and shared the prize money with the second-placed Panhard; the car was driven by a Monsieur Doriot who is seen here seated next to Pierre Giffard, the organiser of the Trial

pioneer motor races, which were at first great town-to-town contests, regarded with awe by the horse-minded fraternity, but all the time teaching lessons to those who designed and built the competing cars. Because these grew rapidly ever larger, more powerful, and therefore faster, they made it plain that the horse had met its match and that even express trains might soon be unable to match the performance of these new petrol-burning motor vehicles.

The first proper motor race, contested in 1895, was the Paris-Bordeaux-Paris race, but the Paris-Madrid race of 1903 which was stopped at Bordeaux by order of an irate Government due to the many accidents which happened, caused future contests to be held over properly policed closed roads. But these were still public roads fenced off and guarded for the purpose, usually triangular circuits of considerable length. This continued to be the norm up to and even after World War I. The result was that cars were raced, and thus demonstrated, under normal road-going conditions, having to contend with hills, conventional corners, cambered road surfaces, dust and other natural hazards of the kind encountered by travellers. As time moved on, it became logical to institute classes for the various-sized vehicles that were avidly entered for such exciting contests of speed and endurance, and eventually to impose certain restrictions on the engineering factors of the motor cars

Above: a 1901 Napier 50hp model competing against a diminutive De Dion tricycle in a British speed-trial

that were soon being specially constructed for racing purposes and growing ever faster.

From primitive things that were decidedly experimental and, in fact, mere horseless-carriages, they quickly became fast, then very fast, decently reliable and controllable by the standards of their time. For this reason, those long-ago, courageously fought motor races of the pre-1915 period were exciting to watch, and important to analyse after they had been run off. The cars that contested them, from the earliest Panhard & Levassor to those $4\frac{1}{2}$-litre overhead-camshaft Mercédès which put up an all-conquering 1-2-3 victory in the 1914 French Grand Prix (to the consternation of the French on the eve of war), are now if immense historical interest, and the handful that have survived and have been restored to original condition and running order are fine machines to own and drive.

Before the first full-scale motor race was run in 1895 there had been the important Paris-Rouen Trials of 1894. The best performance in these was made by a De Dion steamer which was able to carry six persons. This was really a steam tractor and, although it headed the finishers, which comprised thirteen petrol cars and seven more steam vehicles, it was not given a prize. The important cars at the time were the Peugeots, which had Panhard & Levassor engines which were hung at the back of a low chassis frame made of hollow steel tubing, through which the cooling water circulated. Final drive was by side chains but the whole conception of the carriage was crude, to later eyes, with wheels of different sizes front and back, although some did have wire-type spokes, and steering by a lever atop a vertical column, as was then customary practice.

The 1894 Panhard & Levassor cars had already set the fashion others were ultimately to follow, in mounting their engines at the front of the frame. The engine itself in these cars was a V-type Daimler motor, the larger of the two sizes used being of 75 mm bore × 140 mm stroke. This power unit, which had its two cylinders angled at fifteen degrees from the vertical, developed about $3\frac{1}{2}$ hp at 750 rpm. Ignition was by the prevailing hot-tube, obviating electrics, and a surface carburettor was used, although the Panhard engineers already had a float-feed carburettor on the stocks, which was fitted to one of their Paris-Rouen entries. The drive from the V-twin engine went through a double-cone clutch to a gear chest which gave three, or in some models four, forward speeds, it being notable that these gears were not always enclosed in any form of casing. Reverse was obtained by keying one of two gears to an intermediate shaft, from which the final stages of the transmission consisted of single or double chains. This short-wheelbase, high-perched Panhard was controlled by a left-hand steering lever that was said to transmit jolts from every stone or rut encountered by the front wheels. The driver had quite a handful to contend with, as the throttle and governor controls were before

Right: the only surviving example of the 1899 Cannstatt-Daimler 'Phoenix' racer; these cars exhibited several advanced design features, including a honeycomb radiator (probably the first such example) and a gate gearchange

him and with his right hand he worked the levers for changing gear, reversing and applying the side brakes. There were also the usual pedals, and foot and hand brakes were interconnected with the clutch. Radius rods tensioned the driving chains.

Thus, the first-ever competition cars! They had low-power governed engines with unpredictable carburation, and ignition at the whim of the wind, which could snuff out the burners on which the platinum hot-tubes relied. They were terrible to steer, and gear-shifting was a difficult accomplishment. But at least they pointed the way to better, and certainly far faster cars to come, and were just about practical, which cannot be said of those Paris-Rouen entries which proclaimed motive power achieved by gravity, hydraulics, compressed-air, multiple levers, pendulums or just the weight of the passengers! Indeed, most successful of these 1894 primitives, the Peugeot, covered the $78\frac{3}{4}$-mile course at an average speed of $11\frac{1}{2}$ mph.

By the year 1895, when the first real motor race took place between Paris and Bordeaux, Panhard & Levassor had progressed further. They had their own engine, which they called the 'Phönix', a vertical twin-cylinder power unit. Still a very crude, short-wheelbase machine, nevertheless, the advent of the ever-more powerful engine must be recognised. This successful 1895 Panhard & Levassor had solid rubber tyres and retained hot-tube ignition, although as it had its engine at the front the burner was less affected by the wind than those of the Peugeots, with their low-hung rear-placed engines close to the draught and the dust. The Panhard's steering gear was still direct-acting and reversible, thus calling for great strength and continual concentration. The winning Panhard & Levassor weighed 604 kgm, and its engine developed some 4 hp at 800 rpm, from cylinders of 80×120 mm, which was sufficient to give it a maximum speed of $18\frac{1}{2}$ mph. The gears were now enclosed to protect them against dust and road grit. It is interesting that at this stage of automobile development, although the pneumatic tyre for racing had made its appearance, it was quite unreliable and it was the solid rubber tyre, as used on the 1895 winning Panhard & Levassor, which ruled supreme, superior to the iron tyres which were employed on some of the competing vehicles.

Ever-more-lusty power units were the hallmark of these early motor races. The four-cylinder 8 hp Panhard & Levassor engine had appeared in that 1895 Paris-Bordeaux event and when this type of race was repeated the following year it was just such a car that proved victorious, averaging $14\frac{1}{2}$ mph over $1062\frac{1}{2}$ miles of decidedly indifferent roads, for the race was not only out of Paris to Marseilles but the competitors had to return to Paris. So, we find the monster racing car already in evidence as early as 1896, because in those days of insipid little cars of $3\frac{1}{2}$ to 4 hp, an eight-horsepower Panhard was indeed a monster. Yet, exciting as such giant racers seemed to the ordinary automobilist of eighty years ago, it must be remembered that they relied on crude brakes, a spoon on the back tyres supplemented by a contracting band on a drum on the transmission; that after dark they had to rely on candle-lamps for illumination of the tree-lined unlit roads they raced over, and that suction-opened

Left: the 4-litre De Dietrich of 1903, similar to the Charles Jarrott car which started first in the ill-fated Paris-Madrid race of that year

Below: it was a Mors like this which Henri Fournier drove to first place in the celebrated Paris-Berlin race of 1901. The drive chain broke as he was about to start the victory parade!

Below right: driving a borrowed 60 hp Mercédès touring car like this, Belgian Camille Jenatzy won the 1903 Gordon Bennett cup at Carlow, Ireland

automatic inlet valves were as commonplace as the solid tyres, tiller-steering and tube-ignition. Yet, it was these great town-to-town contests that were forcing the pace of design and evolution, both of racing cars and ordinary automobiles and were also making the name of Panhard & Levassor famous and France the premier country among the car-building nations.

From that time onwards, it was a case of increasing the size of engines to force more speed from these wooden-framed, cart-sprung racing *bolides*. Engines ran at virtually a fixed speed, so increasing the rate of crankshaft revolution, as was done later to obtain a gain in power, was out of the question. Instead, cylinders were made ever larger, the old adage that there is no substitute for cubic inches being very much to the fore, and big gilled-tube radiators were used to cool these enormous engines.

So much was this the case that by 1898, classes for the different-sized cars that were entered for races had been instituted. Starting with motor cycles of less than 100 kgm and then those two-wheelers of over 100 but weighing not over 200 kgm, the cars were divided into those of 200 to 400 kgm and those which turned the scales or tipped the weighbridge at over 400 kgm. That year

the 8 hp Panhard & Levassor had wheel-steering, its 80 mm × 120 mm four-cylinder engine making it a very fast car by the leisurely standards of the day. Electric coil ignition was taken up by Panhard, following the Peugeot fashion, and the power race continued. Mors stole the advantage from Panhard and by 1901 progress had dictated that equal-sized wheels be used at both ends of these racing cars. It was the 24 hp Cannstatt-Daimler racer of 1901 that set the ultimate fashion, that of using a radiator of honeycomb tubes. Mercédès pushed home their technical superiority, with a pressed-steel, channel-section chassis frame, the new type of radiator and a gate gear-change. This soon became the accepted format and it was then a case of engines becoming bigger and ever bigger in respect of the swept volume of their cylinders. The high-tension magneto replaced the low-tension magneto machine which had necessitated mechanically interrupted breaker-points within the actual engine cylinders, where they soon sooted-up (although Itala retained low-tension ignition for Grand Prix racing cars as late as 1908) and the automatic inlet valve gave place to mechanically operated poppet valves, with Fiat pioneering the placing of all such valves in the cylinder heads.

The speed of these racing cars must not be under estimated. By the time of the 1908 French Grand Prix, when giant power plants were being installed in flimsy chassis, over 100 mph was attained on straight stretches of the road circuit, in spite of the fact that wind-cheating bodywork was not normally resorted to. There had been attempts at so-called streamlining, notably with the inverted-boat type of body fitted to the Mors car which made the best, meteoric, showing in the ill-fated 1903 Paris–Madrid race until this was stopped at Bordeaux. But on the whole, it was power, the brute force of really enormous engines, that made these road-racing cars go so quickly. The 1902 racing season had seen the advent of the famous, or notorious, 70 hp Panhard & Levassor, which contrived to have a 13.7-litre engine in a wooden chassis weighing, to comply with the contemporary racing rules, under one ton. The engine may have been absolutely massive, with its great 160×170 mm cylinders, but it was not very highly developed, being of the constant-speed concept, in which 1500 rpm represented maximum crankshaft speed. There was no valve overlap in those days of suction-operated inlet valves (of which the Panhard had three per cylinder) and splash lubrication sufficed for the big-end bearings. The cooling water was contained in copper jackets surrounding the cylinders, with the usual big gilled-tube radiator on the nose of the car and, to reduce the weight of the cast-iron pistons, their skirts were drilled, and, like-wise, the connecting rods to which they were attached.

Above : the 1913 Peugeot racing car, seen here in the hands of Georges Boillot at Boulogne. Boillot started his career in the Targa Florio, retiring from the 1908 and 1909 events, but winning the following year's race. By 1913 he was one of Europe's top drivers. He won the French Grand Prix in 1912 and 1913 and failed to take his third successive victory only due to engine problems one lap from the end of the 1914 race. He finished fourteenth at Indianapolis in the same year and set fastest lap in that race. A pilot in the French Air Service, he was killed in action in April 1916

This huge engine was rigidly mounted in the chassis, instead of being given a separate sub-frame as previously, and metal plates reinforced the frame. Front springing was by a transverse spring of three leaves, whereas Panhard had previously had a fancy for semi-elliptic springs to tie the front axle to the car. It is said that this transverse spring on the Seventy was located by rods – the advent of the 'Panhard rod' so well known today. Final drive was by the accepted side chains, to a dead axle beam. This enormous racer was able to make some 90 mph with its engine running at 1200 rpm, and the iron pistons sweeping up and down the bores at a speed of 1400 feet per minute. It was able to run away from all competition, but smaller-engined cars were not too far behind.

The battle of the cylinders existed in the Napier's use of a six-in-line engine, which was to achieve great things on the Brooklands track from 1907 onwards. But for road-racing, the four-cylinder engine ruled supreme. When the first of the French Grand Prix races as we know them today was held at Le Mans in 1906, the winning car, a Renault, was able to show that the simple L-head side-by-side-valve power plant was still viable, but its capacity was 12,970 cc, obtained from four cylinders of 160 × 150 mm, the over-square configuration, ahead of the cooling radiator. Renault even made use of a three-speed (instead of a four-speed) gearbox and at this date detachable wheels were disallowed, so that punctured or burst tyres, of which there were many, had to be changed on the fixed wheels; Renault had had the foresight to fit his cars with the newly arrived Michelin detachable rims. The biggest

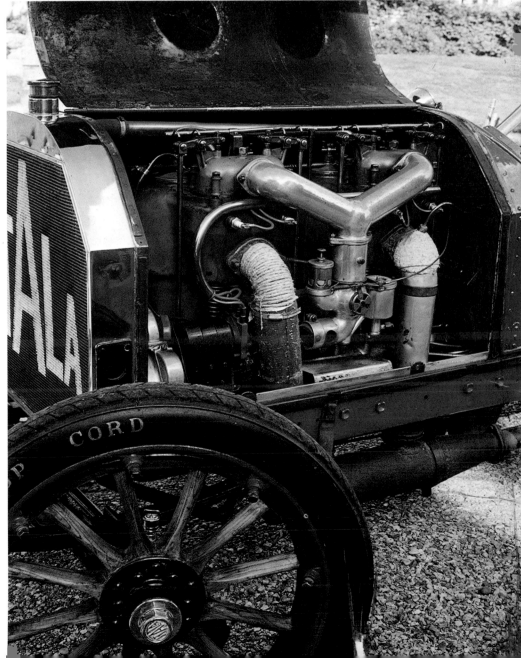

Right: what many early cars lacked in sophistication, they attempted to make up by sheer brute force. A classic example of the latter-day adage that there is 'no substitute for cubic inches' was the 1907 120 hp Itala. The four-cylinder engine displaced 14,432 cc, giving a top speed of just 100 mph at a leisurely 1100 rpm. This particular car won the 1907 Coppa della Velocita at Brescia in the hands of Cagno (National Motor Museum, England)

engines in that race were those of the Panhard & Levassors, at 185×170 mm, giving a swept volume of 18,279 cc. There were also the 18.1-litre De Dietrich engines; the Itala, Fiat and Hotchkiss entries for the Grand Prix were all of over 16 litres, making the $7\frac{1}{2}$-litre Grègoire look like a light car.

That was the trend for many years, and it was one that the race regulations, which at different times imposed a fuel consumption limit or a restriction on engine-cylinder-bore diameter, rather than the designer's whim, finally broke down. Even when the latter artificial limit was imposed for the 1908 Grand Prix at Dieppe, being set at 155 mm, with 127 mm set as the maximum bore in a six-cylinder engine, huge power units still prevailed. Biggest were the Clément-Bayards and the Opels, at just under 14 litres, but engines of well over 12 and 13 litres were commonplace and the victorious Mercédès was a giant of 12,831 cc. All this, of course, implied very excessive piston speeds and already the idea existed that power could be better weaned by having a short-throw crankshaft with thus more lightly stressed pistons and crankshafts. Then higher rates of revolution could be used, and power output boosted not through capacity but from efficiently running and breathing power units.

The adoption of overhead valves and an understanding of overlap in camshaft timing made this possible, and it was quite soon to be exploited, not only in the *formule libre* races but also in light-car or *voiturette* contests, in which the short-stroke four-cylinder engine was to oust the abnormally long-stroke twin-cylinder entries.

Racing for the Grand Prix was abandoned for political reasons between the years 1909 and 1911 when long-distance events were boycotted out of jealousy by the major French and German manufacturers. When it was revived in 1912 at Dieppe, Ernest Henry had brought about a revolution in racing-engine layout with his Peugeot Grand Prix cars. These had the epoch-making feature of overhead valves inclined in the cylinder heads and operated by two overhead camshafts, and the formula followed ever after for the majority of top-racing power units. By having a camshaft above each line of valves, the lightest possible operating gear could be applied to them, killing valve float; the use of inclined valves meant that the hemispherical combustion chamber of maximum efficiency could be used. The then existent problems of the noise of driving two camshafts situated so far from the engine crankshaft and the manufacturing expense of the whole set-up were not problems that governed the design of a racing engine. The Peugeot not only won the 1912 French Grand Prix with this new remarkably efficient engine of 7602cc (from a Fiat possessed with a vast engine of 14.1 litres) but in voiturette racing a 3-litre Peugeot to the refreshing new Henry formula was remarkably successful.

Top left: a man and his car: Fritz von Opel in the four-cylinder, 12-litre Opel, one of the largest cars in the race, at the start of the 1908 French Grand Prix at Dieppe. Opel finished 21st and a similar car driven by Jörns came in sixth

Above and right: the 1908 Austin 100 hp Grand Prix car was, like many of its contemporaries, loosely based on a road-going production car. Shown here is the impressive 9677cc, straight-six engine, which unfortunately lacked sufficient power for what was quite a heavy car (National Motor Museum, England)

The twin-cam Peugeot racing engines were the product of this brilliant Swiss engineer Henry and the Peugeot racing drivers Goux and Georges Boillot. They used a still-excessive piston stroke for their 7.2-litre GP cars of 200 mm, in conjunction with a 100 mm cylinder bore, so that with these new high-speed engines running at a maximum of 2200 rpm and producing some 130 bhp, the piston speed was as high as 2900 feet per minute. But it all held together to give a race average speed of nearly $68\frac{1}{2}$ mph for this gruelling two-day 956-mile race of 1912.

This Peugeot advance set the fashion for the future but was not immediately taken up universally. While shaft instead of chain final drive was now the vogue and detachable wheels with centre-lock hubs had facilitated tyre-changing, there were those who went cautiously towards twin overhead camshafts. Certainly, for the 1913 French Grand Prix at the Dieppe circuit, run again on a fuel-consumption basis, the 5.6-litre Peugeots ruled supreme. But in the dramatic race of 1914, over the Lyons course, five single-overhead-camshaft $4\frac{1}{2}$-litre Mercédès racing cars dominated the scene. This was as much due to the Teutonic care taken to prepare for the race and the use of team tactics, or at least of having sufficient cars in the race to break up any opposition, as to the design of the winning engine, which was of modest capacity partly because efficiency could now be gained from a comparatively small, fast-revving engine; also, because the race rules limited engine size to 4500 cc. And just as the result of this oft-quoted 1914 French Grand Prix on the eve of the war was no proof that the single-overhead-camshaft engine was superior to the twin-cam power unit, nor was it conclusive over the matter

Left: the aviation-type engine of the successful 1914 Grand Prix Mercédès had 115 bhp (20 fewer than the 1908 cars). However, the engine was powerful enough to help the cars to a 1-2-3 victory in that year's Grand Prix

Below: three of the famous Mercédès Grand Prix machines of 1914, complete with their distinguished drivers Lautenschlager, Salzer and Wagner (from left to right) celebrating their 1-2-3 victory in the French Grand Prix, on their return to Germany

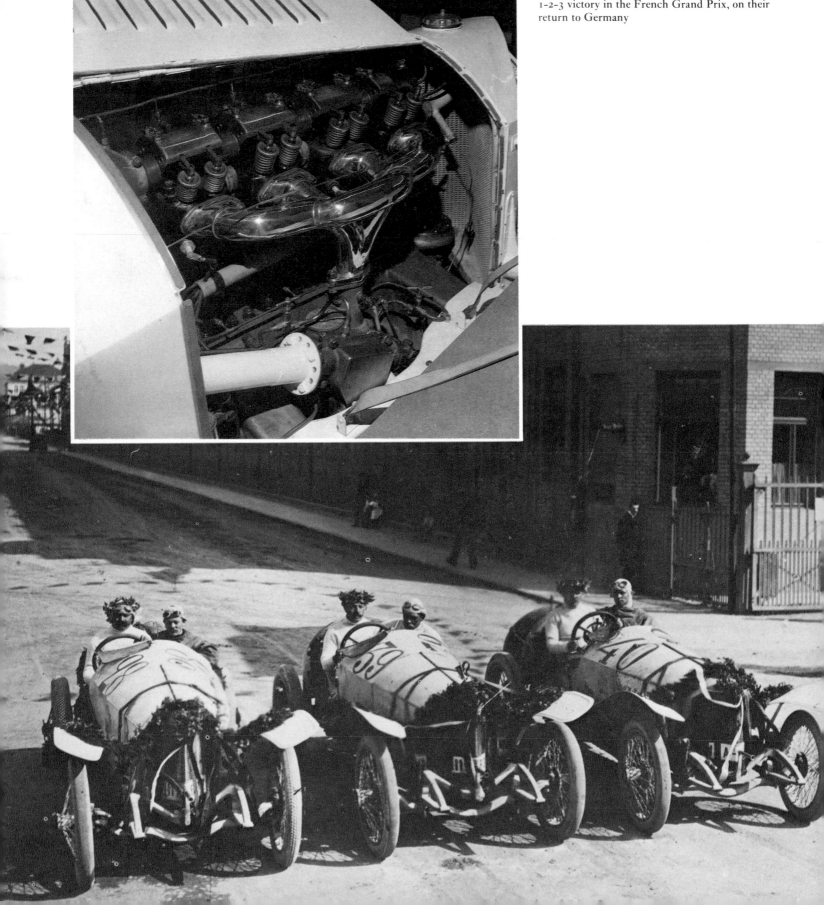

of racing-car brakes. The Mercédès team had rear-wheel brakes, of expanding shoes within rear-axle drums cooled by air fins, supplemented by a brake on the transmission, as was commonplace from around 1904; they won against cars with the latest front-wheel brakes, as used by Peugeot and Delage. That the Peugeot was able to outbrake the Mercédès in this event is indisputable, but this ability was no match for team tactics as employed very professionally by the Mercédès organisation.

After the Armistice, as we shall see, both twin-cam racing engines and four-wheel brakes ruled supreme; at first, servo assistance was used for the brakes, but it soon became unnecessary.

In the light of modern knowledge it is seen that Ernest Henry did not, in 1912 and the remaining pre-war years, exploit to the full his splendid new engines. The hemi-head that his properly actuated inclined overhead valves made possible was less suited to the comparatively low crankshaft speeds he envisaged than for quicker-running engines, and another pre-eminent aspect of his design, namely the use of four valves to each cylinder, was at the time more a concession to its ability to combat valve breakage than a serious endeavour to obtain optimum breathing through the additional, if smaller, inlet valve ports. But these comments notwithstanding, the advance was of great significance. Indeed, overhead valves were soon to become universal for specially constructed racing power units and it is worth remembering that when Fiat first used their push-rod overhead valves on their 1905 racing engines, they also had the valves inclined at 45 degrees and were able to extract a useful 120 bhp from these 16-litre 180 × 160mm power units, even though the crankshaft speed was restricted to around 1100 rpm when flat out.

Ernest Henry added the refinement of a camshaft above each line of valves by 1912 and the previous remark that he used four valves to a cylinder to combat exhaust-valve failure requires the endorsement that he was apparently also anxious to overcome the then-prevalent unreliability of valve springs, designing special tappets that relieved his valve springs of the necessity of closing the tappet mechanism. His first 3-litre engine was not an extreme power producer, giving perhaps 90 bhp at 3000 rpm in its 1912 Coupe de L'Auto form, which was its first high-speed application and it was comparable to the side-valve Sunbeam cars which created a furore by finishing 3rd, 4th and 5th in the Grand Prix itself. Even though output was only around ten horsepower above that of the L-head Sunbeam's engine, and the Peugeots were hampered by not adopting the streamlining then in vogue thanks to the influence of track racing at Brooklands, Henry still went on to develop his design much more effectively for the 1913 Coupe de L'Auto competition. He inclined his four valves at 60 degrees instead of at 45 degrees for that race and drove his 'upstairs' camshafts by a train of gears instead of by a vertical shaft. No more power was claimed but the engine was now the epitome of efficiency, producing its 90 bhp at 3000 rpm on a compression ratio of only 5.6 to 1. For the still-born 1914 light-car race of the aforesaid title, Henry had a four-cylinder engine of 75 × 140 mm built to comply with the race limit of 2½ litres. This car did well after waiting for the war to finish, winning the 1919 Targa Florio race. The 1913 3-litre Peugeots were within 5 mph of the top speed of the far bigger 1912 full Grand Prix cars, and the 1914 version, giving 80 bhp at the customary 3000 rpm, was capable of some 92 mph. Thus, the most advanced racing engine design of this pre World War I period appeared, with great success, in 7.2-litre, 5.6-litre, 3-litre and 2½-litre forms. It was to be widely copied by Sunbeam and Humber before the war, and set

a fashion for the immediate post-Armistice era, until Henry advanced again, with his straight-eight-cylinder Ballot engines.

At this formative period of racing-car development, ball and roller crankshaft bearings were accepted as a way round lubrication problems that had been far from solved at this date, and castor-base lubricants instead of mineral oils were the norm. Valve gear was semi-exposed in many cases even though engine speeds were increasing. From driving on the ignition and governor controls, the racing driver for some years prior to the war had had to make full and proper use of his gearbox with, of course, no aids of the synchro-mesh kind. Indeed, he had to be able to change gear without the clutch if need be and the practice of heeling and toeing was rife, whereby the accelerator was pressed to speed up the engine revs to accommodate the gearbox, at the same time as the foot brake was being applied to slow the car for a corner, round which it would be driven in the lower gears. This need to change difficult gears constantly while braking with indifferent brakes, using outside handbrake as well as prodding the brake pedal while changing gear, together with wrestling with insensitive steering and a cord-bound steering wheel that would kick and cut the hands, made driving these pre-1914 racing cars in the long engagements that were normal to them, a very tiring and tough proposition, suitable only for the very fit. But their worst feature in this respect was the hard springing, from leaf springs that scarcely 'gave'.

Below: a 1912 Coupe de L'Auto Sunbeam, built for a light-car race at Dieppe in which it was part of a British 1-2-3. After competition, this car saw road service until it was stored in 1930. 1958 was the year when it was retrieved from mothballs and renovated; it is still able to travel at 85mph, by courtesy of its 2996cc side-valve engine
(National Motor Museum, England)

Yet, all things considered, it can be said that in the two seasons preceeding World War I, the road-racing cars, whether restricted by race rules or not, were very fast, not too unreliable, and generally pleasant vehicles, pointing the way directly to a forthcoming generation of what were to be known as 'sports cars'. The W. O. Bentley-designed 3-litre Bentley of 1919/21 is proof of this. . . .

In the field of the *voiturette* or lightweight racing cars, the general trends followed those of the bigger cars. The freakish twin-cylinder Peugeots with very long stroke engines gave place to the beautiful little four-cylinder Hispano Suiza of 1910, which had a 65 × 200 mm engine that gave something in the order of 52 bhp and was the forerunner of another pioneer sporting car, the 80 × 180 mm Alfonso Hispano Suiza. From there, as we have seen, Ernest Henry of Peugeot went ahead, with immaculate twin-cam racing 3-litre motor cars.

Down all these experimental and exciting years there were naturally attempts to break away from the conventional progression of racing-car evolution. The two-stroke power pack was tried, and discarded, Gobron-Brillié got further

Right : Léon Molon is seen at the 1913 Gaillon hill-climb with his Hispano-Suiza. This Hispano used an ohc engine, of 85 × 130 mm dimensions, based on the supercharged unit which was to have been raced in 1912. The cars were more reliable in normally aspirated form. Due to their odd shape, they were known as 'Sardines'

Below : one of the unsuccessful cars built by Humber for the 1914 TT. This, like many other cars of the period, used a Peugeot 'crib' engine, being of the classic twin-overhead-camshaft, sixteen-valve, four-cylinder type

with engines in which the pistons moved in opposition and required two crankshafts, connected together. Marc Birkigt, who was responsible for the Alfonso Hispano Suiza and those magnificent post-war production models of this illustrious make, tried to perfect the supercharged engine but forced induction of the mixture was left to Mercédès after the war, and for Fiat to render practical on the race circuits. Up to the war, multiple carburettors were far from being fully exploited and Henry was content with a single instrument. This is explained by the fact that valve overlap was little understood at this time and was at first applied only to late closing of the exhaust valves, because the idea of opening an inlet valve early to apply some ram filling was quite foreign to contemporary thinking. But over-large choke tubes in the carburettors were frequently found on racing engines, which were not expected to pull properly at much below 2500 rpm. These aids to an unobstructed gas flow contrasted oddly with the tortuous inlet manifolds through which the up-draught carburettors invariably fed the cylinders.

Plain big-end bearings were possible, especially if dry-sump lubrication assisted the less refined oils of those times to remain decently cool. Petrol would be fed by air pressure, usually from a drum or bolster-type fuel tank set across the back of the chassis; in those days, a riding mechanic was invariably carried and he had to operate a hand air-pump as well as watching the oil gauge casting glances astern for overtaking cars.

When Brooklands opened in the summer of 1907 in Surrey, it forced the pace of race-engine improvement, because on a banked course the throttle is open fully, or nearly so, for very long periods. Thus 'run' bearings, through over-hot oil, burnt-out exhaust valves and seized pistons, were more often the cause of defeat than in road racing and the track tuners were soon to learn the disasters that resulted from running the fuel mixture too weak, of not allowing sufficient cooling air to penetrate to the sump or oil tank, and of trying to obtain flat-out speed with piston and bearing clearances too tight. But sheer maximum speed was of the essence down at 'The Track', which is why it was not long before very advanced thinking was applied to reducing the wind drag inherent in chassis and bodywork. Radiators were cowled in, leaving only a slit or hole through which cooling air could reach their tubes, thus, incidentally, sometimes improving their capacity in that important direction. Bodies with long tails of tapering or 'airship' shape were quick to appear, and to carry out this so-called 'streamlining' to its ultimate, a long undershield would enclose the bottom of the chassis, as was done on road-going cars to exclude road dirt and dust. The extremists even fared-in front axles and small protruding parts such as spring hangers and dumb-irons with carved wood and fabric, one droll sight being a certain 1912 Lorraine-Dietrich with a vast area of exposed flat-fronted radiator, beneath which was a carefully streamlined axle! All this attention to reducing the drag of the wind undoubtedly paid off, enabling more speed to be realised for less power.

From the first Brooklands racers which were virtually stripped chassis that had worn touring and even closed coachwork until their competition débuts, the trend swung away to these splendidly sleek specially bodied track cars. It was but a step from fully faired two-seaters to the genuine racing single-seater, because a riding mechanic was not so necessary on the wide expanses of the Weybridge concrete as on a narrow, dust-obscured road circuit. These monoposto or single-place racing and record-breaking cars were only wide enough at the cockpit to accommodate the driver, and further drag-reduction was achieved by putting discs over their wheels. An even more extreme idea, pioneered by the Sunbeam engineer who was so keen on racing his products to endorse their worth, namely the great Louis Coatalen, was to isolate the radiator from the engine compartment, so that drag should not develop beneath the engine bonnet. It was Coatalen who had first thought of using a large aeroplane engine in a motor-car chassis and his 1913 V12 aero-engined Sunbeam of 9 litres capacity, endowed with the typical slim single-seater long-tailed racing body of the period, was a successful experiment in this empirical age. Another experiment sometimes attributed to a much later period of automobile evolution was four-wheel-drive, tried out on the big Spyker racing car as early as 1903, and front-wheel-drive, as used a little later on the transverse-engined American Christie racing car.

The real lesson of racing as it was up to the outbreak of World War I was that power from the petrol-burning internal-combustion engine could be efficiently raised by using the twin-overhead-camshaft engine, which was superior in making high crankshaft speeds possible, which the side-by-side valve formation could not encompass. This is reflected in the fact that the 1912 Coupe de L'Auto Sunbeams were the last successful side-valve racing cars, apart from minor races, and the T-head valve layout, as used for the Alfonso Hispano-Suiza *voiturettes* (that is to say having the inlet valves on one side of the cylinder block and the exhaust valves along the opposite side, necessitating two separate camshafts in the crankcase), did not survive the war. The racing-car engine had paved the way for the powerful overhead-valve aeroplane engines of the war years and those Mercédès which dominated the last Grand Prix to be held before hostilities broke out had engines significantly similar to those in the first German fighters to appear over the Western Front. So, racing was improving motor-car design, which in those earlier years was its purpose.

Braking, roadholding, speed and streamlining being the main headings under which the fierce incentive of competition had forced the pace. By 1914, the then-current four-cylinder long-stroke twin-cam engines were good for 130 bhp in Grand Prix form, although this output of 30 horsepower per litre left room for great strides after the war; indeed, supercharging made such progress easily attainable.

In the emerging days, Panhard & Levassor had gradually been overtaken by Mors, which put up such a great performance in the Paris-Bordeaux portion of the 1903 Paris-Madrid race, although the Renault light cars of the time were almost a match for the Mors. After this, Napier made some inroads with big six-cylinder cars. But Fiat raced away with their overhead-valve (pushrod) racers, until Peugeot got ahead with the twin-cam sixteen-valve engine. During this pioneer period, Britain was out-classed, apart from Sunbeams making the simple design of side-valve power unit perform well, and developing the Brooklands type of pure track-racing car, a sphere where Sunbeam, Vauxhall and Talbot were to the fore, the last-named make being the first to cover over one hundred miles in one hour.

Racing continued for a while in America at Indianapolis where these pre-1914 racers were able to hold their own. But it is to the post-war era that we have to look for the next stages of racing-car development. Better fuels and improved tyres aided the effective use of the higher speeds made possible by much higher rates of crankshaft rotation and by the use of forced induction.

THE RACES: 1894-1914

The motor-racing contests of that empirical period prior to World War I were regarded with probably more awe, excitement and possible alarm than we devote these days to space travel and scraping Mars for dust samples. The motor car was scarcely established as a decent form of transport before the turn of the century, and was the subject of a good deal of open hostility and official threats. Yet, in the midst of all this, here were the new-fangled motor-carriages actually racing one another in smothering clouds of dust, along the ruler-straight roads of Europe. By 1902, these petrol-carriages, which were certainly not to be encouraged, were attaining quite respectable speeds on the straight stretches of virtually unpoliced public *Routes National*: about half as fast again as you could travel in the comfort and security of the best express trains.

Yet all this frenzied obsession with speed in the new age of motors was to improve these vehicles quickly and surely, so that within a few years of these first motor races, the motor car was a quiet, docile and swift form of everyday transport. We owe the greatest respect, therefore, to those brave men, the conductors of the early, very primitive racing cars: men who drove furiously into the unknown, striving to leave one town and arrive as quickly as possible at the next. Unprotected by crash helmets, protective clothing or Armco barriers, over routes sparsely marshalled and unpractised, they raced, as Charles Jarrott put it, over the never-ending road that led to the unobtainable horizon. Speed, ever more speed, was then the order of the day, at the expense of safe controllability, and driver comfort. Yet, there was never any shortage of keen amateurs who were prepared to pit their strength and improving skills against the hazards of racing, if they could only lay their hands on the steering wheel of the latest racing monster from the Panhard & Levassor or Mors factories.

Above: Charles Jarrott and his mechanic Cecil Bianchi on board a 1904 Wolseley

Below: one of the works twin-overhead-camshaft 3298 cc Sunbeams raced at the Isle of Man, where Kenelm Lee Guiness won for the team; he averaged 56.4 mph over 600 miles of racing. The cars featured four valves per cylinder, hemispherical heads and roller-bearing crankshafts

It all commenced calmly enough. In 1894, *Le Petit Journal* had the initiative to organise a competition for *Voitures sans chevaux*, to be run from Paris to Rouen, a distance of 78¾ miles, which was to be judged by the paper's staff and a number of consulting engineers. This significant and historic event, which took place on 22 July, attracted the remarkably large field of 102 vehicles. The entrants included Pousselet, Pellorce, De Dion Bouton, Lemaitre, Roussat, Gautier, Hidien, Victor Popp, Scotte, Klaus, Tenting, Panhard & Levassor, Quantin, Rodier, Archdeacon, Le Blant, Periere, Letar, Gaillardet, Varennes, Vacheron, Coquatrix, Leval, Peugeot, Darras, Geoffrey, Gillot, Loubiere, Duchemin, Ponset, Lemoigne, Bargigli, Le Brun, Spanoghe, De Prandieres, Corniquet, Martin-Cudrez, . . . the list is seemingly endless and all these pioneers really deserve to be listed, for they were the true forerunners of every competition exponent who followed them. Suffice to say that, adventurous as they obviously were, with very few exceptions such as Peugeot, Panhard, Jeantaud, Landry et Beyroux, Bellanger, and De Dion Bouton, their names did not continue into the future of motor racing.

Indeed, this first run was not a race at all. It was a trial, and the ingenious means of locomotion announced by many of the entrants were too optimistic to persist and were soon to reduce to steam, electricity and petrol. But that Paris–Rouen Trial was what sparked-off the great motor races that were to follow. As has been said, these divide into clearly defined types. Up to 1903, when the Paris–Madrid race was stopped at Bordeaux by order of the French Government because of accidents that had happened along the inadequately marshalled public road, the important races were from one town to others, which were designated low-speed Control areas, the route either ending at one of them or turning back at the final town. Thus they were road races pure and simple. They might be divided into classes, with the competing vehicles defined by weight or other limits, but speed was the vital ingredient. After Paris–Madrid, such races were, with a few exceptions that persisted into post-World War II times, run over closed circuits, which were shorter and could thus be properly controlled. These road circuits were invariably formed of temporarily closed public roads, often provided with temporary safety fencing to keep spectators off the course, pedestrian-bridges or tunnels.

The second sub-division of motor races in this experimental period from 1895 to 1914 involves the purpose behind all the racing. The very earliest contests were mainly a proving ground for the motor vehicle itself, although the better makes gained notice by coming through victorious in this latest sport. The French makes led the way for a long time and then came the Gordon Bennett races, for which teams of three cars had to be entered by each competing country. The cars themselves, all the components used in their construction including the tyres, and the drivers were required to be of the nationality of the entrant. Thus motor racing became not a mere proving ground but a battle of the nations. Emphasis was placed on this by the ruling which said that the next year's Gordon Bennett race would take place in the country of the winner, which caused Britain to search for a course in Ireland for the 1903 contest. This series lasted from 1900 to 1905 inclusive, and the victors were France four times, Britain once and Germany once.

Other nations having tired of French supremacy, and the Gordon Bennett regulations being difficult to enforce, the nationalised series of races gave way to the French Grand Prix, first held in 1906 and won by Renault. Fiat were victorious in 1907 and Mercédès in 1908. This was the most important race of them all, until other nations followed suit and held their own Grands Prix. The idea was to vary the race rules from year to year to promote advance in racing-car design and construction and to stage great international contests in which *make* raced against *make*, instead of, as in the Gordon Bennett races, nation competing against nation. This was a great success until 1909, when the major manufacturers refused to compete in long-distance events through a suspicion that they might lose to a smaller concern like Delage or Bugatti. Thus, the French Grand Prix was abandoned until 1912 and small-car or *voiturette* races were held instead.

Following the 1894 Paris–Rouen Trial, which sparked off all this auto-

Left: Percy Lambert aboard his 1913 Talbot, 25/50hp seen at Brooklands; it was with this car, in February of that year, that he put 100 miles into the hour. Lambert was killed in the following November while trying to regain his record from Peugeot: he crashed on the Members' Banking at the Weybridge track

Below: the first Indianapolis winner was Ray Harroun, who took the flag in this Marmon 'Wasp' in 1911 (averaging 74.61 mph); according to legend, his was the first car ever to feature a rear-view mirror

motive activity, the first proper motor race was held, in 1895, in the form of the Paris–Bordeaux–Paris contest, organised by the newly formed Automobile Club de France. It was a struggle occupying three days, from 11 June to 13 June 1895, with a field of 22 out of 46 somewhat optimistic entries; eleven reached Bordeaux and nine ran the entire distance of 732 miles. Whilst this sounds unremarkable by today's standards, the distance alone on those primitive carriages over such difficult going defies imagination! Most epic was the drive of Emile Levassor, who insisted on conducting his famous No 5 Panhard & Levassor without relief for fear of losing his lead, pausing every 100 kilometres or so to take on fresh supplies, but his total stopping time was a mere 22 minutes, on a journey lasting 48 hours 48 minutes! At Tours on the return run back to Paris he had a lead of 4½ hours over his nearest rival, a Peugeot. Immense enthusiasm greeted him as he drove to the finish by the Porte Maillot, where, in true Gallic fashion, a monument was later erected to mark the finish of the very first motor race. In fact, as Levassor carried but one passenger he was not awarded the first prize (31,500 francs), which went to Koechlin's Peugeot, a carriage which had been on the road for 59 hours 48

minutes. Whereas Levassor had averaged 15.0 mph, this Peugeot had run at an average speed of 12.2 mph and another Peugeot, not eligible for the first prize, at 13.4 mph. Of those which retired, a Serpollet steamer broke its crankshaft and the Jeantaud, the only electric car to start, had axle trouble.

From this first race came others, faster and better supported, over longer distances. In 1896, they raced from Paris to Marseilles and back, a little matter of 1063 miles, and the winning Panhard, driven by Mayade, averaged 15.7 mph, proof that the motor car was both fast and a stayer. Panhard cars, in fact, walked away with that one. In 1897, they tried shorter races, the 149-mile Paris–Nice–La Turbie going to the Count de Chasseloup-Laubat, whose De Dion steam-brake averaged 19.2 mph. The Paris–Dieppe race of just over 102 racing miles was divided into classes for motor tricycles, *voiturettes*, six seater, four seater and two-seater cars, and Jamin's little Bollée contrived to do 25.2 mph, whereas the fastest car, in the four-seater section, was Count de Dion's De Dion, with a speed of 24.6 mph. Finally, there was the 107.7-mile Paris–Trouville contest, won by a Panhard at 25.2 mph.

In 1898, the race was from Marseilles to Nice, the celebrated driver Charron getting there first on his 6 hp Panhard at 20.4 mph, followed in by two more Panhards. Charron then won the Paris–Amsterdam race, averaging 26.9 mph for the $889\frac{1}{4}$ miles, with Giradot's Panhard second.

Not only were speeds higher but the number of recognised events increased. The season opened in March with the 75-mile Nice–Castellane–Nice race, this new pursuit of motor racing having by now extended from the capital city to the fashionable Mediterranean watering place. An entry of 24 cars and fifteen tricycles had been obtained and Peugeot-Frères gave Lemaitre the new big Peugeot, the 140×190 mm two-cylinder engine of which was sufficient to give this driver victory at 26.0 mph over Giradot on the four-cylinder 80×120 mm Panhard, a smaller Peugeot finishing in third place. The racing motor tricycles were nearly as quick: Teste on a De Dion averaged 25.1 mph, but their riders were apt to be badly hampered, even involved in accidents, due to the dust flung up by the cars.

The Panhard drivers, Charron, de Knyff and Giradot, filled the first five places in the Paris–Bordeaux contest, the winner's speed for the 351 miles being almost 30 mph; a Mors finished 6th. Flag signals were used throughout the Tour de France, which covered 1350 racing miles and was again dominated by the Panhard Company's entries, the big 16 hp racer of de Knyff winning at

Left: the Paris–Rouen Trial of 1894. The most important cars were the Peugeots like this example of Kraeutler which averaged 10.1 mph over the 78¾ miles. These cars were fitted with Panhard & Levassor engines and chain drive; steering was by a single lever mounted on a vertical column

Below: in the last Gordon Bennett Cup event of 1905, Léon Théry repeated his victory of the previous year, accompanied in his Brasier by Muller, his mechanic; as an extra reward for this performance, Théry was made an honorary member of the Academie Française

30.2 mph. Note how speeds were for ever creeping up as engines increased in size. These *average* speeds are most impressive if you can imagine the conditions under which cars raced in 1899. On the downhill straights on their top speed (or gear) such racers were truly awe-inspiring. Gerald Rose, the first writer to chronicle the great motor races of that period, recalled 'the tremendous rush and roar of one of the big racers coming down the straight towards Dieppe at 100 miles per hour, the driver crouching under the wheel and the mechanic's head just visible above the high scuttle', a thrill modern racing cars and conditions can never repeat. He wrote that of the 1908 Clement–Bayards in the Grand Prix, but the spectacle must have been just as thrilling before the turn of the century as the higher, more unwieldy racing giants and their intrepid pilots battled over the long French highways at speeds of over 60 mph.

Back in 1899, there was the little jaunt from Paris to St Malo, accomplished by Anthony's Mors at 30.7 mph, while in the Paris–Ostend 201-mile race the forthcoming struggle between Panhard and Mors was beginning, Giradot and Levegh respectively on these rival makes both averaging 32.5 mph, with a Peugeot third for good measure. Then, in the Paris–Boulogne race, Giradot's Panhard & Levassor was the victor at 33.5 mph but Levegh on a Mors tailed

him home, and was only 0.3 mph slower. To give a sense of proportion, in 1899 came a novel contest, run between Paris and Trouville, in which pedestrians, horses, cyclists, motor cycles and racing cars took part, over a distance of 104½ miles under a handicap to end all handicaps. Thus, the runners got an allowance of twenty hours, the horses were given fourteen hours, the cyclists five hours, the motor bikes 3¼ hours and the racing cars had to do the course with a start of three hours. It was rather a snub to progress, as they finished much in that order, except that two horses arrived first and second, and a motor cycle was two seconds ahead of the first car. The average speeds are interesting: runners, 4.9 mph; best horse, 8.5 mph; fastest bicyclist, 19.4 mph; best motor cyclist, 32.5 mph, fastest racing car, a Mors, 35.2 mph. Motor traction had justified itself, but perhaps the racing men were glad to return to normal contests.

Racing recommenced in February 1900 with the *Course du Catalogue* which was sub-divided on a chassis/price basis and which Girador dominated on a big Panhard. The season was one fought out between Panhard and Mors, until things changed with the advent of the first race for the Gordon Bennett cup. This trophy had been donated by Mr James Gordon Bennett, Paris-based proprietor of the *New York Herald*, maybe with the idea of getting America into motor racing and breaking the hold which France had established. The races were team affairs between the National Automobile Clubs, who had to choose their own teams of drivers and cars. They held eliminating contests for this purpose but much bickering resulted. The route of each race had to be of not under 550 km and the event was to be given its baptism in France on 14 June 1900. A course was found from Paris to Lyons, via Orleans, Nevers and Roanne. No very severe mechanical restrictions were imposed, perhaps because Mr Bennett was not an automobilist, but two side-by-side seats, occupied throughout the race, were insisted on and the minimum empty weight of each competing car had to be over 400 kg. As this was a nation-against-nation contest, national colours for the cars emerged, blue for France, white for Germany, red for America (which in later years became the Italian colour) and yellow for Belgium. At first, this novel race did not attract much enthusiasm but it is an important motor racing landmark in the period 1900–05.

The first race could boast only five runners: three four-cylinder 5.3-litre chain-drive Panhard & Levassor's representing France, a Snoeck-Bolide from Belgium, that had a 10.6-litre engine with its four cylinders horizontally opposed and final drive by belt and chain, and from America an antiquated single-cylinder Wilton with a piston stroke of 177.8 mm, driven by chain. The 24 hp Panhards had little difficulty in preserving their status for, although Baron de Knyff retired, having lost top gear as well as hitting several stray dogs, many of which were run over along the route, Charron came in the winner at 38.6 mph, and second place went to Giradot's Panhard at 33.4 mph. The American and Belgian entries both retired, so there were only two finishers.

Above: the enormously successful René de Knyff was always recognisable by his flowing beard and habitually worn yachting cap. Pictured here in 1907, the Panhard director listed among his victories the 1898 Paris–Bordeaux–Paris, the 1899 Tour de France and the Marseilles–Nice–Marseilles race of 1900. He went on to become President of the CSI from 1922 to 1946 and died in 1954, aged 90

Left: a contemporary illustration by Reginald Cleaver shows the finish of the Marseilles–Nice race in March 1898. The report read: 'The motor-car race from Marseilles to Nice was attended with very bad weather, the roads from the pelting rain were dreadfully wet, and both cars and occupants were covered with mud soon after starting . . . Many of the carriages broke down on the road from various causes, their occupants finishing the journey by train'

Above: Fernand Charron, one of the first successful racing drivers, who won the 1898 Marseilles–Nice and Paris–Amsterdam races for Panhard. He was also victorious in the first Gordon Bennett trophy race from Paris to Lyons of 1900, despite a dramatic off-road excursion

However, the race was not entirely lacking in drama. Charron hit a big St Bernard dog, which jammed the car's steering, causing the Panhard to career across the road, over a ditch, through a gap between two trees and across a field, whence it regained the road by taking another gap in the trees, ending up facing the wrong way. But it was the heroic age of the game and the luckless riding-mechanic, Fournier, later to become a great Mors driver, got down and cranked-up the engine; the car restarted with Fournier holding the now disorientated water-pump against the flywheel, from which its friction-drive was obtained. The Panhard had bent its back axle when striking a bump near the start, but everything held well enough together for Charron to take the coveted Gordon Bennett cup. Giradot was likewise not without trouble, as in swerving to avoid a horse near Orleans his steering had also been damaged. That was motor racing over the open roads of 1900.

Because of the small entry and comparative public disinterest in the 1900 Gordon Bennett race, the AC de France decided to take steps to improve the situation before the 1901 contest was due to be run. As victors the previous year, the French had, under the rules, to host the race. The great Paris–Toulouse–

Above: the Automobile Club de France's Paris to Bordeaux race in 1901 was won by Henri Fournier's Mors, seen here. He completed the 327-mile course in just over six hours, averaging 53 mph

Paris event of the previous year, in which Levegh's 24 hp Mors had won at 40.2 mph for the 837 miles, had made the Gordon Bennett look rather anaemic. To give it more of the big-time appearance in 1901, it was to be combined with the race from Paris to Bordeaux. Alas, it did not work out that way. The complete race of 327 miles had the usual good entry and was won by Fournier on a powerful 60 hp Mors. This completed the course in 6 hours 10 minutes 44 seconds, an average speed of 53 mph, staving off the might of the 40 hp Panhards, which came home in the next five positions, Maurice Farman's averaging exactly 49 mph; the day of the brute force racing monster had dawned! However, in the Gordon Bennett division the winner was a mere tenth in the race overall, this being Giradot, on another 40 hp Panhard & Levassor, at a speed of 37 mph, his race time being nearly three hours longer than Fournier's. But France had at least retained the right to hold the Gordon Bennett race in 1902, although neither of her other team entries, a Mors and a Panhard, finished the course. Britain should have been represented in the 1901 Gordon Bennett race by S. F. Edge on his enormous 50 hp Napier, but the car was so heavy that its British tyres would not stand the strain and with French tyres it was not eligible for the Gordon Bennett race. The green car started, however, but retired with clutch failure. Nevertheless, it thereby set this colour – Napier green, as the British motor-racing hue, not always copied very exactly for the future.

Before we look at the 1902 Gordon Bennett race, it is necessary to describe another great race of the preceding year; this is the one which took place from Paris to Berlin. There were 53 Controls to be arranged along the 687-mile route, where the competitors had to be accurately timed in and out and led through the towns, usually behind official cyclist-marshalls. Local persons of import-ance had to be appeased in this era of ever bigger and faster racers capable of raising ever taller columns of dust and making ever louder noises – their exhaust notes were likened to the sound made by Gatling guns! Soldiers had to be found to police the long course, augmented by experienced flagmen, and buglers were needed to proclaim the passage of a car racing at express-train pace. *Pavé* still existed in places; elsewhere, dust was the menace – apart from straying dogs and cattle – and to combat that proper exhaust-boxes were specified. M. Serpollet drove over the entire route to see that everything was ready for this three-day racing epic. There were the usual three classes – Heavy cars, Light cars and *Voiturettes*. A highly satisfactory entry had been received,

Left: many were the adventures experienced by the competitors on the 1902 Paris to Vienna event. Here is the eventual winner, Marcel Renault, with his 3.7-litre car; he surprised everyone by his early arrival, and he won everlasting fame for his company

Below left: Marcel Renault and his 30 hp car about to embark on what was to become their last race, the 1903 Paris to Madrid. He died when his car overturned at Coune-Verac (*below*). His brother, Louis, finished first on the road and second overall in the event, and later decided to withdraw the Renault cars from competition for a year

33, 27 and 11, in these respective categories, of such renowned makes as Mors, Panhard, De Dietrich, Serpollet steamer, the new very technically advanced Mercédès from Germany, and the lighter but very game Panhards, Gladiators, Darracqs, and finally the little Renaults. The smallest cars were now able to keep up speeds faster than the biggest motors of a few years earlier, so the interest in this race must have been intense and its usefulness to the new motor movement was inestimable. The winner was due to pull up in front of the Kaiser's tribune and the competitors who made the arduous journey successfully were to go in a great procession along the Brandenburger Tor and down the Unter den Linden. There was even a class for tourist cars, which took nine days to do the route, and one for racing motor cycles, filled with 7 hp 170 kg De Dions.

It was no wonder such races caused a sensation; spectators would wend their way out to the start in their thousands, the cyclists carried Chinese lanterns to probe the early-morning mists, and horse-drawn carriages mingled with the few touring motor cars. As the racers went on their headlong way, the police had great difficulty in forcing the onlookers back to give them passage. It was a foretaste of the 1903 disaster – and the route was marked in the

more populous places by flowers, flags, even triumphal arches, erected by citizens who knew of the official lunches, dinners, receptions and fêtes that followed in the wake of the big and important motor races. The Mors might now be superior to all other cars and the great Fournier at the height of his skill and fame, but as the racers became heavier and faster, their crude tyres became the great levellers. Punctures resulted in delay if nothing worse, driver and mechanic wrenching off the ruined cover and tube with their bare hands, in order to fit a fresh cover from those piled up behind their seats. This could give the less-powerful autos a chance, so the result at the finish-line over 680 miles distant from the Paris start, was very much open to conjecture. They were racing for the Kaiser's cup, the Grand Duke of Luxembourg's trophy and other fine prizes, not forgetting £500 presented by the City of Hamburg, so they were unlikely to waste any time! In fact, it was the bearded Maurice Fournier who came through triumphant, ahead of the Panhards of Giradot and de Knyff, with another Mors fourth. Fournier's huge Mors had averaged 44.1 mph and it is worth reflecting on how a modern family car would have fared, before the days of universal *autoroutes*, over this formidable route!

Right: S. F. Edge, who devoted thirteen years, from 1900, to the promotion, racing and sales of Napier cars, the most important of which were the six-cylinder vehicles, the first to be built in large numbers. As a driver, his first major success was in the 1902 Gordon Bennett Trophy, after which he became British team captain

Far right: Mme du Gast on her 5.8-litre De Dietrich during the infamous Paris–Madrid race; she finished at Bordeaux in a lowly 77th position, but she would have been much better placed had she not halted to extricate Stead from under his inverted De Dietrich

Below: De Bron's 9.8-litre 45 hp De Dietrich prior to the start of the Paris–Madrid contest; the sound of the cars' exhausts was likened to that of Gatling machine guns

Panhards took the first three places in the Light-Car class, Giraud leading them in at $35\frac{1}{2}$ mph. The lightweight Renault of Louis Renault was beginning its great run of success in the *Voiturette* class, averaging a noteworthy 36.9 mph, while the best of the motor cycles was Osmont's De Dion, at an even more impressive average of 36.4 mph. That, then, was the form that open-road motor racing took, just after the turn of the century; enormously exciting it must have been, too!

The importance of the Paris–Berlin race of 1901 was that it showed the progress of racing-car development. In fact, glorious victors though Henri Fournier and his Mors were, a chain broke as the post-race parade was commencing: he had grasped his success by a very slender margin. 1902 marked further advances, both in racing *bolides*, built to the new 1000 kg weight limit but still very powerful, and in the persuading of the French Government (which disliked motor racing) to sanction the Circuit du Nord event, where the competitors would be running on alcohol fuel. This was for the most part a success for it was very well organised, with bombs let off to announce the imminent arrival of the racers, but very few spectators turned up to watch them. The

winner of the Heavy Car Class was Maurice Farman's 40 hp Panhard, at 44.8 mph; in the Light Car category, Marcellin's 24 hp Darracq, averaged 41.2 mph, and the fastest *voiturette* was Gruz's 9 hp Renault, which managed an average speed of 33.6 mph.

All this was a preliminary to the important Paris–Vienna race of 1902. This race very nearly did not take place, however, as the French authorities were reluctant to grant permission for it, even with the 1000 kg weight limit imposed to reduce the size of the engines that could be crammed into racing chassis. The Bavarians and the Swiss actually refused to have any racing on their territory and the route of this four-day, 615-mile race had to be continually changed. Nevertheless, the Viennese were keen to host the event and even put up special prizes. The climb of the Arlburg Pass, over which the route went, was the supreme test and resulted in two comic incidents. This section of the course was more like a trial than a motor race, with the snow just gone in time from the narrow unguarded precipices, where the ascents and descents were of startling steepness and torrents from the rivers had to be crossed on improvised bridges. It was here that Max, driving a small Darracq, struck a boundary stone, the car going some way over the edge and his and his mechanic's seats breaking away from the chassis. This left the former occupants safe a little way down the hillside, while the car itself plunged 100 feet further down. Max took a look at his wrecked racer, then climbed back to the road just as Barras arrived on the scene. The story circulated that Max had escaped death from under his car and he made excellent use of this dramatic story when he reached the finish. Then there was Derny, whose motor cycle ran away down one of the hills. All he could do was cry out in alarm, not knowing that De la Touloubre (whose real name was Captain Gentry) was up ahead in his Clément

car, and who, with the true racing driver's calm skill and reaction, would pluck him safely from the saddle of his run-away machine as it shot past the car. Or so legend has it!

Many cars had to be pushed up fearsome gradients but Teste's Panhard climbed at better than 23 mph. His was one of the new 70 hp Panhard & Levassors, which were enormously powerful for their light overall weight. Count Eliot Zborowski, father of the Zborowski who later thrilled English race-goers of the 1920s with his Chitty-Chitty-Bang-Bangs, did what he could to combat these fire-eating monsters from France, on his advanced 40 hp Mercédès. Even so he had to be content with second place in the unlimited class, behind Henri Farman's 70 hp Panhard. The other 70 hp Panhards of Maurice Farman and Teste, and the 40s of Pinson, de Crawhez and Chauchard filled the 3rd, 4th, 5th, 6th and 7th places in this class, with Edge's 40 hp British Napier beating the Mors Sixty of de Caters into 8th position. However, the hero of the Paris–Vienna event was Marcel Renault, whose little 16 hp Renault ran so well and so fast that he drove into the finishing enclosure, a trotting-track at Prater just outside the city of Vienna, long before the officials and spectators expected him. Indeed, Marcel made his circuit of the trotting track in the wrong direction and was made to go out and come in again the intended way, but he was still comfortably ahead of Zborowski's Mercédès and had vanquished no fewer than five of the 24 hp Darracqs. This excellent showing by a small car was a pointer for the future. Renault had averaged 38.9 mph, compared to Farman's 38.4 mph and Zborowski's 37.9 mph. The best of the 24 hp Darracqs had done 38.1 mph and the fastest *voiturette* was Guillaume's 12 hp Darracq which, averaging 30.6 mph, just turned the tables on the 8 hp Renaults. The winner was declared as Marcel Renault, and fame immediately engulfed the expanding company from Billancourt, on the Seine.

The 1902 Gordon Bennett Trophy race had been incorporated with the Paris–Vienna and appeared to have been taken by Zborowski on his all-German Mercédès but it was found that he had incurred penalties, so Edge and the big Napier were announced as the winners, after a drive of 11 hrs 2 mins 52.6 secs over 351.46 miles of the route, an average speed of 31.8 mph.

It was just as well that Britain had won the Gordon Bennett, because there was growing resentment over road racing in France and, had a French car won, it might have been difficult for that country to stage a decent race for the Trophy in 1903. As it was, the British now had this problem to face. In Belgium, the idea of racing over a closed circuit was instituted, with the Circuit des Ardennes race, on a pattern soon to be the accepted form. This 'circuit' consisted of a 53-mile route out from Bastogne and back, to be covered six times in the morning, before the motor cyclists had a two-lap race over it in the afternoon. The point, however, was that this race was devoid of 'controls' as it did not pass through congested towns. It was also primarily for amateur drivers and attracted great interest, the town of Bastogne being full long before the start. Britain's Charles Jarrott, an experienced racing driver of the day, equipped himself with one of the 70 hp Panhards and won at 54.0 mph, after taking the lead on the third lap. The celebrated driver Gabriel was second on a Mors Sixty, another of those fine cars driven by Vanderbilt finishing in third place ahead of Eliot Zborowski's 40 hp Mercédès. The fastest lap was turned in by Baron P. de Crewhez' 70 hp Panhard which came in 13th, followed by Baron J. de Crewhez on yet another 70 hp Panhard.

So, we come to the fateful year of 1903, which changed the very face of these early motor races. Even more ambitious than previously, the Automobile Club de France decided to have a massive contest from Paris to Madrid. They were, however, working in an atmosphere of restriction. The French Government had refused to authorise the Pau Week of Speed in February 1903 and permission was not granted for a race from Nice to Salon and back. King Alfonso was quite happy to allow racing on Spanish soil, however, so the section to Madrid was assured. Little was known about the route here but it was felt that the crossing of the Guadarrama mountains would present very little difficulty to those who had conquered the Arlburg Pass in the Paris–Vienna race. Eventually, even the French authorities gave in, and the great race was on. It

Camille Jenatzy working very hard to keep his 60 hp Mercédès ahead of René de Knyff's 80 hp Panhard on his way to winning the 1903 Gordon Bennett race between Carlow and Athy, Ireland

is significant that it attracted no less than 230 entries – which makes the support for classic races over seventy years later look rather poor by comparison. This excellent entry was made up of 98 Heavy Class cars, 59 *voitures legeres* and 35 *voiturettes*, as well as 38 motor cycles. That was the *early* entry-list, with over three months to go! Finally, with a few cancellations and many additions, Paris–Madrid had 314 runners, and these included sixteen Panhards, fourteen Mors, twelve Mercédès – but sadly lacking Zborowski's entry as he had been killed in a hill-climb at Nice – ten De Dietrich, seven Serpollet steamers, six CGVs, and even four Wolseleys from Birmingham. The new 90 hp Mercédès cars were the favourites, and the use of light chassis frames and light alloy in the engines had resulted in ever-more-powerful machines, now capable of some 100 mph on the open road, while carrying two persons and fuel for a long run.

The start of what should have been a stupendous race was as spectacular as ever. It was deemed too dark at 3.30 am in the morning to risk letting the racers go, but by 3.45 am, with thousands of onlookers pressing round the cars, which had to force a way through them, Charles Jarrott's huge De Dietrich set off towards Bordeaux, the spectators just opening up a path sufficient for him to get through. De Knyff followed Jarrott, then off went car-manufacturer Louis Renault. With hindsight, the tragedy can be seen staring us in the face. It was almost dark, while vision was later obstructed by

great dust clouds that made it necessary for the drivers to steer by looking at the line of the road-side tree tops. It was impossible properly to police this very long public-road course, along which cars sped at upwards of 90, even 100mph; the cars were top-heavy with poor brakes, and dogs, cattle and children were free to wander on the roads. News of fatal accidents began to come in and although, over the years, these have been exaggerated they were none the less appalling. Marcel Renault died when his 30hp Renault overturned at Thery. Barrow's riding mechanic – they used to sit low on the side step – was killed when his De Dietrich ran so forcibly into a tree that it disintegrated and one of its front dumb-irons was driven far into the tree trunk. Leslie Porter ran into a wall when cornering too fast and his mechanic Nixon was killed. In trying to avoid a child, Tourand shot into the crowd at Angoulême, causing the deaths of his mechanic and a soldier. There were many other accidents, but with less serious consequences it is important to remember, because history will tell you of *hundreds* killed. This *was* enough, however. The horrified French Government demanded that the race be stopped at Bordeaux, 342 racing miles from Paris. It would not even permit the racing cars to be driven to the station for their ignominious return to the Capital: they were dragged to the train behind horses. It was as disastrous as the Le Mans accident of 1955 and it was immediately to change the type of racing allowed in France. Through all this calamity, though, let us not forget Gabriel and the epic per-

The Panhard team poses before the 1903 Gordon Bennett event at Athy; Henri Farman and René de Knyff occupy the centre and right-hand cars

formance he put up in his 70 hp streamlined Mors. Starting No 168, he passed all but two cars, along this very demanding course. He won the Heavy Car class at 65.3 mph, after racing for more than $5\frac{1}{4}$ hours. But it was Louis Renault who had arrived ahead of everyone who had not either crashed or retired, his lightweight Renault averaging a magnificent 62.3 mph, which gave him second

place, a triumph short-lived when they broke to him the news of his brother's death. Salleron's 70 hp Mors was third, at 59.1 mph. Even Masson's Clément *voiturette*, an 18 hp machine which could be comfortably out-performed by a modern family car managed 47.2 mph, to win its class. Remember, that these are *overall* speeds and top speeds reached were probably half as fast again.

That was how it ended in 1903, most subsequent racing being on closed circuits. The Circuit des Ardennes was held again in Belgium and was a Darracq victory, and by charm and persuasion, especially among influential ecclesiastics, the British contrived an elaborate two-circuit course in Ireland for the fourth Gordon Bennett race, contested over 327½ miles. This time there were a dozen runners, including a team of three Napiers from Acton, London, with America, France and Germany against them. Alas, the Napiers failed and, rather surprisingly, so did the 80 hp Panhards. It was the red-bearded Jenatzy, 'The Red Devil', who brought his Mercédès Sixty (a stripped touring car used after a factory fire had destroyed all the intended· 90 hp Mercédès racers) home the victor, at 49.2 mph. The Panhard aces, De Knyff and Henri Farman, had to accept second and third placings.

Although high quality racing was spreading to other countries, with the Florio Cup being held in Italy and the Vanderbilt Cup in America, the Gordon Bennett, with its unique rules making it a test of motor-manufacturing nation against motor-manufacturing nation, remained in the public eye. The 1904 race had to be held in Germany, the 87-mile course had to be covered for a distance of 317.86 miles and the June day of the race was declared a public holiday. Jenatzy tried hard to keep the Cup in his car's native land but it was the steady driving of Théry on an 80 hp Richard-Brasier which triumphed, his winning average being 54.5 mph to Jenatzy's 52.8 mph.

That took the Gordon Bennett back to France in 1905, the last time the race

Below: the tyres on Salleron's Mors being cooled with wet rags and buckets of water at a control point in the 1904 Gordon Bennett

was held. Entries had been increasing but, with the automobile now well established, its makers were anxious to race against one another and not be hampered by the Nationalistic GB rules. For this reason, the Gordon Bennett motor race (there were GB balloon and aeroplane races as well) lasted but one more year. In 1905 it was held over the great Auvergne circuit, in France, which incorporated such severe bends that it was said that at one corner the inmates of the houses could watch the racers pass from the parlour and then run across to their kitches to see them accelerate away! Once again, Théry won for the organising nation, on a Brasier, but a new challenge was rising in International racing, and two Italian Fiats followed Leon home.

Italy had held the mountainous Florio Cup race in September 1904, fore-runner of the very testing post-war series, and Lancia's Fiat had beaten the French and German entries. The 1904 Circuit des Ardennes had reached a satisfactory peak that year, a big entry and close racing ending with a win for Heath's Panhard, with Teste's Panhard (both of which were of 90 hp) only 1 min 55 secs slower, after battling for nearly 367½ miles. In 1904, too, the American Vanderbilt Cup race began, for a Trophy presented by W. K. Vanderbilt Jnr to the AAA. A triangular circuit was found not far from New York, on Long Island, using two time controls, through which the competitors had to tour for three and six minutes, respectively. Heath went over and drove to victory on a 90 hp Panhard, at 52.2 mph, and a Clément-Bayard was second. Third place went to Lyttle's 24 hp Pope-Toledo and other American cars racing included such makes as Packard, with the 'Grey Wolf' track racer, an S & M Simplex, with a big engine installed in a touring chassis especially for the race, and a Royal, which was just a tourer stripped for racing. It was the commencement of America's participation in road-racing events as distinct from track racing, however.

The Florio Cup was to flourish, too, and the 1905 race, held at Brescia, was won by Raggio in a gigantic 112 hp Itala, from a De Dietrich, with Vincenzo Lancia's Fiat third. America was taking enthusiastically to motor road-racing, the Vanderbilt Cup being over 283 miles in 1905, with no Controls to observe. Moreover, although it was won by a Darracq, with a Panhard second, an American 90 hp Locomobile, driven by Tracy, secured third place.

So, 1906 was set for the first of the great French Grand Prix races. There are historians who will prefer to regard the 1906 event as the ninth of the series, because, retrospectively, the Automobile Club de France called the eight pre-ceeding contests by this title. Thus, the first of these races, by this reckoning, was the Paris–Bordeaux–Paris race of 1895, followed by the 1896 Paris–Marseilles–Paris race, the Paris–Amsterdam race of 1898, the 1899 Tour de France, Paris–Toulouse–Paris in 1900, Paris–Berlin in 1901, the Paris–Vienna in 1902 and the Paris–Madrid (Bordeaux) race of 1903. Although the flirtation with speed, achieved by increasing engine size, continued unabated most of us prefer to think of the new type of race that followed the Gordon Bennett series in 1906 as the first of the Grands Prix. This was organised by the ACF, the leading French Club, and not to be confused with the Grand Prix de France, which was a less important event. The Grand Prix as staged in 1906 was clearly intended to ensure a French victory by simple preponderence of numbers. France was the biggest producer of automobiles at that time, measured in numbers competent to race, and therefore if she was not restricted to teams of three National entries, as she had been in the Gordon Bennett races, she stood an excellent chance of winning the greatest prize in the motoring world year after year.

So, the ACF went happily ahead with its plans: the Grand Prix was to be run under the same technical regulations as the Gordon Bennet, ie, there was to be a maximum weight limit of 1000 kg, or of 2204 lb, with a supplementary 7 kg if a magneto or engine-driven dynamo was needed for ignition. For the first time, it was stipulated that any repairs or adjustments required to a car during the race must be carried out only by the driver and riding mechanic. Such work was intended to be carried out at the 'pits' which, although taking their name from sunken replenishment depots, were, in this instance, at road level. They were on the outside of the course so as to be accesible to cars running on the right-hand side of the road, but the grandstands that overlooked them were on the inside of the circuit. Originally, it was intended to lap the course clockwise but, in the end, the rule which had applied since the days of the Roman chariot races prevailed and an anti-clockwise direction was used; a fine triangular course of 65 miles per lap had been selected just outside Le Mans. That races really were true tests of endurance and gave spectators and competitors perhaps more than their money's worth, in those times, is emphasised by the six laps that were required to be completed on two consecutive days, giving a race distance of a fraction under 770 miles. Another innovation was the absence of any form of 'control', whereby drivers previously had to run through danger areas at normal speeds or even behind bicycles. The closed circuit made this possible except where the course passed through St Calais, and this place was by-passed by a wooden road specially made for the purpose.

As had been intended and anticipated, the entry list was mostly comprised of French-built cars, of which there were 26, compared with six Italian and three German examples. Big engines also predominated, all being over 12 litres, with Panhard-Levassor using 18-litre power units. To reduce the time two men took to slash punctured tyres off fixed wheels, detachable rims were adopted by Brasier, Fiat, Itala and Renault.

The Grand Prix commenced at 6 am on 26 June when Gabriel on a De Dietrich was flagged away; in fact, he stalled his engine and it was Vincenzo Lancia whose Fiat crossed the start line first. Thereafter, the cars left at 90-second intervals. Barras on a Richard Brasier led the first lap, at the best speed achieved, 73.3 mph, but the Hungarian driver Szisz, on the big works Renault, took the lead after three circuits and, at the close of this strenuous day's racing, he was still in that position, having averaged 66.8 mph. He was challenged by Clement's Clement-Bayard in second place and the third man home, Felice Nazzaro who drove an Italian Fiat. The cars were to be started on the second day of the race in the order of finishing the first day's racing, but it is significant that Renault refused to hurry, Szisz taking twelve minutes in his pit having

new tyres fitted and the essential fluids topped-up. Clement, too, took five minutes over similar precautions, whereas Nazzaro went immediately into action. Nevertheless, as he completed his opening lap, Szisz found that eleven cars had still not been flagged-off and he was so far ahead of his rivals that he could drive comparatively easily. The coal-scuttle-bonneted shaft-drive Renault from Billancourt gave no anxiety and thus won the 1906 French Grand Prix race in the formidable overall time of 12 hrs 14 mins 0.07 secs, which represents a speed of 63 mph. Nazzaro took his Fiat into second place but was well over half-an-hour slower than the French car, while Clement was third: a convincing French victory.

There were but eleven finishers out of the 32 who had set off. It is interesting to note that, although Szisz did not have to press-on at fastest-lap speeds, the winning Renault was, nevertheless, the fastest car through a timed kilometre, at 92.2 mph, compared to Nazzaro's Fiat, which was clocked there at only 87.2 mph. After this very worthwhile success, Renault did not trouble to contest the 1906 Circuit des Ardennes event, but France retained her supremacy there, since Duray's De Dietrich won, and a Darracq made the fastest lap.

Right: François Szisz – his Hungarian christian name was Ferenc – entered competitions as Louis Renault's riding mechanic in 1900, progressing to chief tester and racing driver. After numerous successes, the unflustered Szisz retired in 1908, reappearing briefly in 1914 to contest the French Grand Prix in an Alda – an outclassed car – and a French road race at Rochefort, which he won in a 12-litre Lorraine-Dietrich. He died in Hungary in 1970, aged 97

Below: François Szisz and riding mechanic Marteau in the 13-litre, 90 bhp Renault, which won the 1906 Grand Prix at Dieppe, averaging 63 mph over 12 hours 14 minutes (two days racing). These cars could approach 100 mph and were fitted with quick-release wheel rims in case of punctures

All this activity on the part of the French encouraged Germany to stage an important contest in the Taunus Mountains, over a 73-mile circuit. However, to encourage more ordinary cars she restricted engine size to 8 litres, which seemed a good move as an entry of 92 was received. To Germanic regret, however, the winner of the eliminating rounds and of the final was Nazzaro's Fiat, although a Pipe and two Opels were next home.

It was the Grand Prix in the automobile-pioneering country of France that at this period held the greatest appeal and attracted the most attention, however. For 1907, the ACF moved the locale to Dieppe, and imposed different rules, the consumption of fuel being limited to 30 litres per 100 km. This works out at 9.4 mpg and, while this was a move to try to improve engine efficiency, it was not of great inconvenience to competitors, and big engines remained the norm. Renault had sold their successful 1906 cars (the winning one for an astronomical sum it was rumoured), but they built a set of replicas for this 'second' French Grand Prix. The race was to be over a flat, triangular 47¾-mile circuit, lapped ten times in a day, a single day's racing now being recognised as more convenient for everyone. National racing colours were also

insisted on for all the runners in this 1907 Grand Prix, whereas the previous year, as if to mark the end of Gordon Bennett Nationalism, they were not, the winning Renault being painted red, the hue of Italy.

Eleven teams of French cars were entered for the 1907 GP against one each representing Belgium, Italy, Germany, America and Great Britain. This worked out to 38 top-rank racing cars starting, and they were all the mighty four-cylinder racing monsters we can now scarcely visualise, although the Dufaux, Porthos and the Weigel entries were far in advance of their time in having eight-cylinder in-line motors. The first car was again dispatched at the early hour of 6 am, the rest going away at 60-second intervals. The previous Renault/Fiat duel again emerged, with De Dietrich well up. Louis Wagner led for three laps for Fiat, at a sizzling average of 72.1 mph. After he had retired

Above: Louis Wagner's 8-litre Fiat leading the 1908 Coppa Florio at Bologna, in which he averaged 90 mph

Inset, far right: Arthur Duray, born in New York but later taking French nationality, began racing Gobron Brilliés in 1902. After breaking the land speed record in 1903, at 83.46 mph, he moved to Darracq and in 1905 joined De Dietrich. It was in 1906 that he achieved his first success – the Circuit des Ardennes. Duray continued to race and attempt speed records until he retired in 1928

it was Duray who led, but eventually his De Dietrich seized its gearbox. This moved Nazzaro into the lead, with Szisz chasing him, but the red Fiat had an unshakable lead and won at 70.5 mph from the French car, with Barras' Richard Brasier third. It was a Fiat domination, although Duray had made fastest lap, at 75.4 mph. It was felt, however, that, whereas Fiat paid little heed to running out of fuel, which the petrol consumption limit made probable, Szisz may have been a trifle over-cautious in this respect. Fuel limits for racing were unpopular for this reason but this was still the golden age of motor racing for, if the great town-to-town contests were the ultimate, these enormous cars on the closed circuits, their big cylinders firing about 'once every telegraph-pole', must have been a most intriguing spectacle, as they battled for the *blue riband* of the motor-racing world.

The Grand Prix continued in much the same form in 1908 and the venue had not been changed, although certain improvements were introduced. By way of regulations, engine size was now limited to a maximum piston-area of 117 sq in, so that, at last, rather smaller engines were to be seen and, instead of a maximum weight-limit, it was decided to eliminate dangerously light cars by having a *minimum* weight-limit of 1150 kg, or of 2534 lb. On the Dieppe course, the inconvenience for the public, of having to get to grandstands on the inside of the circuit was changed by placing them outside it and, in consequence, the replenishment pits really were pits, sunk below the level of the road in order that the view of the spectators was not impaired. Moreover, the road to these pits was set back from the course proper, as was done as a safety measure in much more recent times. The surface of the road had deteriorated, so that much tyre-changing was the order of the day, the winning car stopping nine times for this reason and a Clement Bayard nineteen times. That speeds were rising is evidenced by the fact that of the 48 starters more than twenty were timed at over 100 mph through a flying kilometre. There were fewer French entries than before and French hopes were low when it was seen that it was a

Near right: Felice Nazzaro was a Fiat apprentice, whose skill as a driver, mechanic and diplomat earned him drives in Vincenzo Florio's Panhard; in 1905, he graduated to the position of works Fiat driver alongside Lancia. In 1907, he won the Targa Florio, the French Grand Prix and the Kaiserpreis. Like Lancia, he went on to build his own cars, but mechanical failures precluded notable success. Nazzaro continued to race until 1929, having been appointed head of the Fiat competitions department in 1925

German Mercédès that led on the first lap, and at a record 73.7 mph. However, this car failed to keep going and Fiats took its place; these in their turn retired and, after that, the race was a German procession, Lautenschlager's Mercédès winning at 69 mph from Hémery's Benz, with third position occupied by another Benz, this time of Hanriot.

This overwhelming German victory, coming as it did after the Fiat success of 1907, was a grave blow to the French motor industry. Design was by now advancing for, whereas the 1908 Mercédès cars retained the popular side-chain final drive, they used the honeycomb radiators which this manufacturer had pioneered, as did many other makers, and high-tension magneto ignition was normal, while inclined overhead valves and even the single overhead camshaft had arrived. The French manufacturers, however, found racing as a means of improving the breed and publicising their individual wares very costly and, after the Mercédès and Benz domination, they looked with very luke-warm interest on another Grand Prix in 1909.

The Automobile Club de France tried to persuade them to build cars for a race at Anjou limited to four-cylinder machines with a cylinder-bore not exceeding 130 mm and of a maximum weight of 900 kg. But the Club required an entry of forty cars at least to make such a race viable and, at the end of the year, had only nine entries. So, the idea was abandoned and the mighty French Grand Prix faded away for three years, to be replaced by a series of *voiturette* contests. There was a much less important Grand Prix held in 1910, at Le

Below: Lautenschlager's 12.8-litre Mercédès hurtles out of the pits past Jenatzy's 12.8 Mors during the 1908 Grand Prix at Dieppe. Lautenschlager inherited the lead after another Mercédès and the Fiats retired, and he went on to win, while the 100 hp Mors was unsuccessful

Right: Christian Lautenschlager joined Daimler in 1900, becoming foreman-inspector, and won his first major race, the 1908 Grand Prix. His driving style was steady and unspectacular, aiding the works Mercédès assault on the 1914 French Grand Prix, in which Lautenschlager took the laurels. He continued racing after World War I and remained in the employ of the Daimler concern

Mans, under the title of the Grand Prix de France, and even that was won by a 10-litre touring-type car built by Fiat. It was, admittedly, driven by Victor Hémery, but it did seem that, for the moment at least, the French could no longer win.

Meanwhile, these small-car races, organised by the influential French motor journal *L'Auto*, accelerated the efficiency of the current light motor cars, so that in the comparatively short period from 1909 to 1911 the ridiculously long-stroke, freakish, single-cylinder cars of Sizaire-Naudin (which used independent front suspension as a sop to progress) and Delage had given way to beautiful little four-cylinder racers, culminating in the 65 × 200 mm Hispano-Suizas, designed by the Swiss engineer Marc Birkigt and driven with verve and skill by, among others, the celebrated Zuccarelli. All this was too much for the French manufacturers of the bigger and more illustrious cars. If the Grands Prix were to be revived in 1910 or subsequent years they realised that such a great race might well be won by one of these newcomers to the motor-racing game, and, anyway, they were giving away publicity to them by not racing. It was an unhappy thought so, by the end of 1911, all arguments against the non-revival of the ACF's Grand Prix, were put aside and the race was held again, at the Dieppe circuit, in June. They even reverted to the ambitious scheme of having a two-day contest, to ensure maximum pressure, and thus, as the true Grand Prix cars again lined up, they were to race for a furious 954.8 miles.

Left: one of the four works 3-litre Sunbeams, which competed in the Coupe de L'Auto category of the 1912 Grand Prix. The car, driven by Rigal, took third place in the Grand Prix and won the 'L'Auto' cup

So, racing in the grand manner was on again and, to emphasise this, the ACF had imposed no restrictions on the entrants in the 1912 Grand Prix, apart from insisting that the competing cars carried bodies that were no wider than a maximum of 5 ft 9 in; and to this day no-one seems to know quite what they had in mind in so doing. A legacy of the light-car races that had flourished between 1909 and 1911, while the GP proper was in abeyance, was a separate section of the two-day race devoted to cars under 3 litres capacity, with their cylinders not less than four in number and with the stroke not less nor greater than twice the cylinder bore. To avoid freak entries, and no doubt with the new 'stick-and-string' cyclecars in mind, a minimum weight limit in this class of 800 kg (1763 lb) was insisted on and *L'Auto* gave the winner's cup. Surprisingly, this class was the more popular, for it attracted 42 entrants, out of a total of 56. Moreover, there were seven *Coupe de L'Auto* cars from Britain; four Sunbeams and three Vauxhalls. Naturally, all eyes were on the GP cars, from the stables of Lorraine-Dietrich, Peugeot, Rolland-Pilain, Excelsior and Fiat. The Fiat and Lorraine-Dietrich cars, with previous Grand Prix racing experience behind them, used enormous overhead-valve 15-litre engines and chain final drive.

However, the significance of the 1912 race was the appearance of the revolutionary new Peugeot four-cylinder, sixteen-valve, twin-cam, shaft-drive 7.6-litre racers. Whereas Fiat were claiming a developed horsepower of 200, these smaller Peugeots probably produced a genuine 130 bhp at 2800 rpm (they claimed 175 bhp) and the 'little' Sunbeams, still with L-head side-valve engines, around 80 bhp. Although the cars proved slower than those in the earlier races, the writing was on the wall – plain and easy for the knowledgable to read – that the day of the monster road-racing car was over. The Grand Prix resolved itself into a battle between the old-school Fiats, which were delayed by broken fuel pipes, and Georges Boillot's Peugeot of not much over half their engine size. The celebrated Boillot won, at 68.45 mph, from Wagner's big Fiat, which averaged 67.32 mph. The future was again underlined when one of the 3-litre Sunbeams, driven by Rigal, netted third place in the Grand Prix proper, at 65.29 mph, as well as winning the *Coupe de L'Auto*. Indeed, these Sunbeams, closely akin to ordinary fast touring cars, although having the benefit of Brooklands work behind them, came home 1-2-3 in the 3-litre race and third, fourth and fifth in the Grand Prix itself. As to top speeds, Boillot was timed at 99.86 mph during the race, Bruce-Brown on one of the gigantic Fiats at 101.67 mph, and Dario Resta in the fastest of the Sunbeam team-cars at 65.29 mph. The small car had arrived!

In competition with the great French Grand Prix, the AC de la Sarthe again held its GP de France at Le Mans, which was an opportunity for Boillot and Peugeot to show that their victory at Dieppe was no fluke. Boillot made fastest-lap, at around 80 mph, and Goux's sister Peugeot won the race, at 74.56 mph, both impressive figures over this course.

The Grand Prix proper was thus fully re-established. For 1913, the ACF set it on a new circuit, at Amiens, and, as before, reverted to a one-day contest, over a 19½-mile course to be lapped 29 times. A fuel-consumption limit was also re-imposed, twenty litres of petrol per 100 kilometres, or at the rate of a consumption of 14.2 mpg, the cars being required to carry regulation bolster petrol tanks, behind which streamlined tails were forbidden, either because they were thought dangerous or because they would have off-set the 'road' aspect of the racers. Each competing car had to weigh a minimum of 800 kg (1760 lb) before it was fuelled. They now ran *clockwise*, as contemplated by the organisers in 1906, enabling the grandstands to be placed outside the circuit, for easy access, and the replenishment-pits to be on the inside. Building a connecting tunnel and a concrete loop-road to avoid closing one main road that was near the course was nothing, now that the race was of such importance.

The shorter lap was nice for the onlookers but the new rules were not liked by the builders of racing motor cars and only twenty entries came in. Yet, design was very fluid; Peugeot had eared hub caps to enable the road wheels to be removed quickly with a hammer, and none ran out of fuel, with the 40½ gallons metered out to them before they were taken out to the start behind horses. New companies were now building special cars for racing, and Peugeot remained in the ascendant. Boillot won in a 5.6-litre car at 72.2 mph and was timed through the flying kilometre at 97.26 mph. His team-mate, Goux, was second, and one of the 3-litre *Coupe de L'Auto* Sunbeams came in third.

The GP de France, at Sarthe, had been reduced in distance and was of no great importance, except to Mercédès, who were using it before staging an impressive racing come-back, and to Bablot who won it in a fast Delage, at 76.8 mph for the 337½ miles, after recording the fastest lap at 82.5 mph.

So, we come to 1914, with Europe, about to be plunged into a holocaust of war, and Germany, in the form of the Mercédès Company, taking the greatest possible pains to dominate this last pre-war Grand Prix. It was run at Lyons, in the heart of industrial France, over an interesting course of over 23 miles to a lap, with a charming corner known as the *le piege de la mort*, to give a race distance of 466.6 punishing miles. The date was 17 July, 1914. Note the imminence of war! And it was the team of five white Mercédès, with slab petrol tanks and sharp-pointed radiators, white cars superbly prepared, which had the heels of all the others. For the first time, the race rules limited engine capacity to 4½ litres: quite small cars by previous standards! Mercédès elected to eschew the new idea of prodding overhead valves with two camshafts and used single-overhead-camshaft four-cylinder engines with sixteen inclined overhead valves. They were shaft-driven chassis, but with only rear-wheel brakes, and their drivers were good solid testers rather than racing drivers, certainly not aces with the flair of Georges Boillot. They had to race against the might of Peugeot, with their front-wheel brakes and proven twin-cam engines, and cars from the Alda, Nagant, Delage, Fiat, Piccard-Pictet, Vauxhall, Schneider, Opel, Itala and Sunbeam factories, in the tense atmosphere of that far-away summer of 1914.

Boillot did his utmost. But the sorely stressed Peugeot retired with maladies mechanical, probably a broken valve but the exact nature of which historians still argue over. The white German cars from across the border had their troubles, too. But there were five of them, so they could afford a pacesetter to break up the Peugeot attack. It was Lautenschlager, victor back in 1908, who swept to victory before a dazed French crowd, he and his aggressive Mercédès having made a speed of 65.3 mph over the distance. As intended, Wagner and Salzer followed him in, at 65.1 mph and 64.6 mph, respectively. Spectators were only stirred from their troubled meditation of the proximity of a German war by Goux bringing his blue Peugeot into fourth place, at 63.9 mph, ahead of Resta's British Sunbeam. Eleven had retired out of 37 starters and only the coming war could reverse the result and its impact on French minds.

Above: Georges Boillot was to epitomise the 'Spirit of France' in the early days of motor racing. He was always linked with Peugeot, starting with the smaller rival concern Lion-Peugeot until the companies amalgamated, and he raced with some success in all categories, including record attempts and hill-climbs. His last race was his greatest: the 1914 Grand Prix at Lyons, where he fought the works Mercédès virtually single handed in his 112 bhp Peugeot

Chapter 3

The Industry Returns to Work

ON THE ROAD: 1919-39

For a time after the Armistice it was only too easy to make money out of motor vehicles. There was a wider market than ever before, ranging from the war profiteer with a fortune to spend to the demobilised soldier with a hundred pounds or so for a motor vehicle of some kind. Between these two extremes, cars of all types were available, although in insufficient numbers, as it turned out, to satisfy demand. For many manufacturers who had spent the last four years engaged solely on war work, the buoyant car market proved propitious. Now that all the military contracts had faded away in the euphoria of peace, the aircraft manufacturers and munitions engineers needed to find something that would tide them over until the next bout of international unpleasantness brought the orders in again. So the Grahame-White Aircraft Company built bodies for luxury cars, wardrobes and even a crude cyclecar, while in France the two most famous native aircraft manufacturers, Voisin and Farman, metamorphosed into makers of quality cars. Of course, it was in many ways an artificial situation, for an aircraft industry can hardly have been said to have existed at all before the outbreak of war.

In one respect, the car buyers of 1919 were disappointed, for very few car manufacturers had incorporated the engineering lessons learned in the war – especially the war in the air – in their post-Armistice offerings. Most 1919 models, indeed, were almost indistinguishable from their 1914 counterparts except for a few details like the replacement of acetylene and oil lighting with electric light . . . and in respect of the price tag, for inflation had sent prices soaring. A car which had cost £400 before the war was now nearly twice as much; and it was impossible for a manufacturer to hold prices steady between the announcement of a new model and its appearance on public sale.

It was in this climate that the American manufacturers, many of whom who had stuck a cautious toe in the European water in 1914–15, before a total ban was placed on the import of cars for private use, flourished. Less affected by the hostilities than European companies, they had continued with the development of new manufacturing processes, so that, despite the $33\frac{1}{3}$ per cent import duty placed on their products by the British Chancellor of the Exchequer, Reginald McKenna, they could still undercut the home products – except in one important respect: economy of use.

American cars were designed for the wide-open spaces of their homeland, where a nationwide road-building programme was at last making possible long cross-country journeys. In America, fuel was cheap, and drivers disliked gear-changing, so engines were big – and thirsty, so thirsty in fact that one pundit suggested that the nation's oil reserves would all be exhausted by 1932. And in Britain, where petrol had been strictly rationed until January 1919, such prodigality was received with suspicion; indeed, running costs were a great source of worry to the motoring public, who in 1920 sent a nationwide petition to Lloyd George demanding a reduction in the price of fuel, which was then 3s 8½d a gallon (and was even more on the Continent, where in 1921 Frenchmen

were paying Fr10·50 for a gallon of petrol, equivalent to 5s 4d at the prevailing rate of exchange, while Italians, who bought their petrol by weight in *lattes* of 3·9 gallons, paid 62 lire for this quantity, which at 80 lire to the pound meant a price of 4s a gallon).

Despite the duties, which in total added over fifty per cent to the price, American cars could compete in price with the home product to such an extent that in 1920 over 33,000 of them were imported into Britain. Ford, with its factory in Manchester and its Irish plant, opened at Cork in 1917 to build tractors and provide castings and other components for the assembly lines at Trafford Park, did even better, for the Model T was becoming increasingly British in content (if not in design, for a Ford edict of 1919 specified that all Ford cars worldwide should be built left-hand drive, a state of affairs which prevailed until 1921); in 1919 two-fifths of all the cars on British roads were Model T Fords.

Then, at the end of 1920, the axe fell. The British Government completely changed the basis of car taxation, which had hitherto been based on a fairly nominal carriage tax according to the rated horsepower of the engine, allied to

a high petrol tax. In August 1920 petrol had reached its highest price level since the war – 4s 3½d a gallon – and the Taxation Committee set up by the first Minister of Transport, Sir Eric Geddes, decided that a horsepower tax should be substituted for the petrol duty. (Of course, by the end of the decade the hapless motorist was paying *both* taxes. . . .).

To cushion owners of high-powered pre-war models against the effects of £1 per horsepower, a reduction was given where a car was over ten years old, although this concession, too, was soon forgotten by the rapacious Ministry.

The effect of the new taxation was immediate: by 1922 imports of American cars had tumbled to only 14,000 annually, and, in order to minimise the effects on their own products of an outmoded rating system which only took the cylinder bore into account, British manufacturers began developing the classic long-stroke engines which were to characterise their products for the next twenty or thirty years.

If the introduction of the horsepower tax in 1921 was, unintentionally, a watershed in engine design, the proof of the value of the car as a means of private transport had come less than two years earlier, in the autumn of 1919, when Britain's railway workers went on strike. The weapon used to break the strike was the motor car. The Government took powers to commandeer motor vehicles, and Hyde Park became a vast clearing house for London's food supplies. Petrol rationing came into force for the duration of the strike, which collapsed on 15 October, largely due to the role played by the motor vehicle, which had now proved itself an alternative, not an auxiliary, to the railways.

But such labour troubles also proved the undoing of many of the optimistic firms which had so bravely plunged into the market in 1919, assembling cars in

Above: one of the original Thulin models of 1920, built in Sweden and based on the German Aga; fitted with a four-cylinder engine, it was characterised by its pointed radiator grille and concave body sides. Only three hundred examples of this model were made before the company went bankrupt in 1924 and when the concern, which had previously made aircraft, was reconstituted a new model was produced. Only thirteen of this Type B model were built before competition from the newly formed Volvo company forced Thulin out of business once more
(Skokloster Museum, Sweden)

penny numbers from bought-in components. Now, in 1920, foundry workers went on strike for four months, and the supply of iron castings ran short; other strikes, hold-ups and shortages combined to cause a major slump in the motor industry in 1920–21: similar conditions hit the American industry, even more vulnerable because of its great size and reliance on volume production for adequate profits, even harder.

In April, 1920, there was a collapse of automotive shares on the New York Stock Exchange, precipitated by higher interest rates and other restrictions which had limited hire-purchase sales of cars. However, although sales were falling, raw material costs remained high; in order to move ahead again, manufacturers would have to take drastic action, but they were quite unprepared for what the ever-surprising Henry Ford did . . .

Slashing prices by figures ranging from $165 on a $525 chassis to $105 on a $745 coupe and $180 on a $975 sedan, Ford announced: 'The war is over, and it is time war prices were over . . . Inflated prices always retard progress. We had to stand it during the war, although it wasn't right, so the Ford Motor Company will make the prices of its products the same as they were before the

Below: one of the most popular cars on British roads during the early 1920s was the Morris Cowley, with its bull-nose radiator. This four-seat, 11.9 hp Cowley was one of 6937 Morris cars built in 1922; the following year, Morris sold 20,024, thanks to aggressive pricing and production methods
(Coventry Motor Museum, England)

war. We must, of course, take a temporary loss because of the stock of material on hand, bought at inflated prices . . . but we take it willingly in order to bring about a going state of business throughout the country'.

What he didn't say was that with each car sold at a loss of $20 went $40-worth of spare parts on which there had been no price reduction, thus cancelling most of the loss. Other manufacturers were incensed by Ford's boldness, but the majority of them soon followed suit, and there was a brief Indian summer of reviving sales; then the sales graphs began to slide at a dizzying rate.

William Durant tried to save his General Motors combine by buying huge blocks of shares, but it was a futile operation, and the DuPonts and J. P. Morgan & Company bought him out for $27,000,000.

Ford owned most of the shares in his own company, and was soon to acquire the few that remained in outside hands, thus freeing himself from what he regarded as the menace of the bankers (save that he had a $25,000,000 loan to be repaid in the spring of 1921, a figure which, taken with outstanding tax bills and employee bonuses, added up to over $50,000,000 – or $30,000,000 more than the company's cash reserves). A crash programme of waste elimination was carried out, and the company stopped buying raw materials, and stock-piled cars using the materials on hand, thus saving costs.

Throughout November and December 1921, the leading motor manufac-turing companies began to close down their factories 'for stocktaking', and thousands of men were laid off. On Christmas Eve, Ford closed down 'for inventory' too. Within three months, the number of men employed in the motor industry in Detroit had fallen from 176,000 to 24,000.

Managers laid a machine-shop floor in the Ford factory, and when that was done, acted as watchmen, patrolling the empty buildings on bicycles and roller skates. Office staff were dismissed in their hundreds, and all the spare office and catering equipment was sold, raising an estimated $7,000,000. But these dark days were the nadir of the depression; in January there were signs that car sales were picking up again in New York, and some manufacturers began production again. The Ford plant remained shut, however, with demand met by dealers' stocks, built-up cars which Ford had stockpiled and vehicles assembled from spare parts at the Ford branch factories. At the end of January, Highland Park opened up again, and Ford began shipping cars out to dealers, to be paid for on delivery. Thus, instead of having to borrow the money needed to pay off his $50,000,000 debts, Ford compelled his dealers to borrow to pay for the cars. Most of them found little difficulty in disposing of the extra vehicles as sales continued to recover through the spring of 1921. Once again, Henry Ford had proved his ability to survive in adverse conditions.

The slump was slower in reaching Britain: the postwar boom began to collapse at the end of 1920, and it was not until the spring of 1921 that the full effects were felt. William Morris, now entering the mass-production market with his Morris-Cowley, saw sales plunge from 288 in October 1920 to 68 in January 1921. He reacted by following the Ford lead and slashing prices, knocking £100 off a £525 Cowley four-seater, and reducing other models by figures ranging from £25 to £90. Other makers, notably Bean, had earlier cut prices, but Morris had chosen the right psychological moment, and succeeded where the others had failed. Not only did his sales increase – his profits rose, too.

The collapse of the post-Armistice boom was also to provide Morris with his keenest competitor, although in a somewhat circuitous fashion. The Clyno Manufacturing Company of Wolverhampton were one of the country's most respected makers of motor cycles, whose machines had been widely used during the war (one of their motor-cycle machine-gun outfits can still be seen in London's Imperial War Museum), in which they had developed an ohv four-cylinder power unit originally intended as the motive power for a sidecar com-bination. However, Frank Smith, the company's Managing Director, was an enthusiast for sporting light cars, and decided to enter the car market after the war with a 10 hp ohv four-cylinder model using the motor-cycle engine, which could almost have been the British equivalent of the Brescia Bugatti; three prototypes were built before the company's backers, De La Rue, withdrew their finances and Clyno went into Receivership. Reformed in 1922, Clyno abandoned both motor cycles and sporting light cars and instead moved into the mass-production market, building a 10·8 hp model, largely from bought-in components, powered by a side-valve Coventry-Climax engine. Right from the start, Frank Smith followed the Morris star, continually trimming the prices of Clyno models so that they were identical to those of the equivalent Morrises. It was a policy which worked spectacularly well – at first – raising Clyno eventually to third place in the British production league behind Morris and Austin, at which stage they were producing 300 cars a week in a tiny factory in the heart of Wolverhampton, its inadequate floor space augmented by an asbestos roof over the dirt yard outside.

One of the reasons for the popularity of the Clyno was its excellent handling, which was apparent right from the earliest. In April 1923, *The Autocar* took one of the first few hundred Clynos on the road, and was highly impressed . . . 'It is curious how obvious in the running of a new car is the handiwork of the

Below: a 1927 10.8 hp Clyno Royal Tourer, with coachwork by Mulliner of Northampton. By following Morris's price-cutting marketing strategy, Clyno became Britain's third biggest seller, behind Morris themselves and Austin. Alas, Clyno's standards were forced into decline by this policy and the firm survived only until 1929. This particular car, originally owned by Blackpool's leading fruit and vegetable merchant, is believed to have covered some 300,000 miles from new, when it cost £199.10s
(David Burgess-Wise, England)

designer who is also an artistic driver. For example, the family model Clyno handles in such a way which suggests that those who are responsible for it understand very fully the finer points of roadworthiness and have attended to each with exceeding care. As a result, there is, indeed, very little to criticise and much to commend'.

One reason for the good handling of the car was the fact that one of the firm's backers apparently owned a Grand Prix Peugeot, and specified that the Clyno should have steering that was equally light and positive. In this, the Clyno's designer, George Stanley, who had previously worked for the Triumph motor-cycle company, was entirely successful: 'It must be admitted that the Clyno steering gear is one of the best . . . the necessity of effort is so small that the car is steered as unconsciously as a bicycle'.

Although the Clyno company built some components (like the gearbox) themselves, the Clyno was still largely an assembled car, albeit a very successful one. One reason for its steadily rising sales graph was probably that it bore an established and respected name with a good war record, which would have overcome the sales resistance felt by an entirely new marque. In this respect,

it is interesting to observe the fate of the Cooper, a handsome light car also introduced in 1922, which used almost exactly the same mechanical mix as the Clyno. This marque lasted one year, and produced perhaps forty cars; Clyno lasted nine years and sold nearly 40,000.

Another factor which sorted, in the public's eye at least, the sheep from the goats as far as light cars were concerned was the burgeoning number of trials.

These trials were not just Sunday afternoon map-reading exercises, either; take the 1921 Scottish Six Days' Trial, which covered 900 miles 'deliberately designed to smash up every frangible part of the machines'. It included such fearsome ascents as Tornapress and Applecross, where the road rose steadily for five miles on end, 'stony cart tracks in regions chiefly inhabited by sheep, eagles and deer . . . they have a knack of topping off a frightful bottom gear grind with two or three C corners on a grade of one in five, with a road width so restricted that a car must be reversed to get round. Or take Inverfarigaig Corkscrew, a 6 ft track, paved with dust or mud (according to the weather, and doubling back in itself six times within 800 yards; at each hairpin, the inside wheel must clamber up one in five or six, while the outer wheel races up a comparatively mild pitch of one in eight . . . The trial is run on a basis of 20 mph, plus or minus five minutes per hour. Twenty miles in sixty-five minutes on the Portsmouth Road is, of course, child's play, even for a tiny car, but Scotland has no equivalent for the Portsmouth Road. In the loch districts, a so-called main road swirls along in a precarious serpentine switchback, full of humps, dips, blind angles, and the most poisonous little skew bridges, too narrow for a pair of vehicles and generally quite invisible till the last second. Such a road spells violent acceleration and violent brake work . . . it makes for chassis testing'.

Above: the most famous precursor of the modern baby car was the Austin Seven. The Seven offered seats for four, 45 mph and brakes on all wheels. This is a 1923 'Chummy' with a fold-down hood. Like the Model T, the Seven came in many guises, from racing cars to delivery vans, and it was built under licence throughout the world. It fulfilled admirably the intention of its designer, Sir Herbert Austin, to bring motoring to a vast new market

Such conditions would prove a stiff test for modern small cars, yet of the fifteen light cars taking part in the trial, fourteen finished, ten won gold medals, one a silver and three were awarded bronzes. The car which retired was an 8 hp air-cooled, two-cylinder Rover, which ran off the road into a ditch and broke a spring. 'The other four Rover Eights all won gold medals, losing no time and climbing all the hills', reported *The Autocar*. 'This is simply a stupendous performance . . . They did not smoke, they did not smell hot and oily, and they very rarely gave an audible pink even when they had to pick up on a fierce grade after a terrible hairpin at the top of a long climb. They have scored a great triumph for air cooling, and their success possibly sounds the tocsin for the big sidecar.'

In fact, the car which was to prove the doom of the sidecar outfit as a common means of family transport was probably no more than a doodle on the back of an envelope when those words were written, for it was in 1922 that Sir Herbert Austin announced his new 7 hp baby car, which he had designed on the billiard table at his home to avoid the criticism of colleagues opposed to the project. The Austin Seven was designed to occupy the same ground area as a motor cycle and sidecar, and it *did* look ridiculously small and pramlike to British eyes (although the Continentals were well used to tiny cars); but, like the Model T Ford, it was designed for that section of the market that hitherto could not afford a car. The initial scorn and derision which greeted its announcement turned to admiration when the aviation pioneer E. C. Gordon England decided to prove the new car's mettle. Nearly fifty years later, the author interviewed him about the competition début of the Austin Seven, in 1922.

'I'd crashed in the *Daily Mail* gliding contest at Itford, in Sussex, and I was laid up in hospital at Eastbourne for some weeks with my leg in plaster right up to the knee. It was this that started me off, because I was lying in bed recovering and I read all about this new Austin Seven. One thing that became rooted in my mind was: "He'll never sell this thing, because it's being described in the motor press as a toy – and the public won't buy toys, they want cars".

'I went into it very thoroughly, and came to the conclusion that the Austin Seven would make a very good show as a racing car. So I wrote to Sir Herbert Austin, as he was in those days, and said: "I am intrigued by this car, but I don't see how you are going to get it over to the public unless you can hit them

Below: a 1923 Hotchkiss AM Tourer, with all-weather coachwork by Melhuish. The AM, built at St Denis, Seine, had a four-cylinder, side-valve engine of 2.4 litres, a four-speed gearbox and four-wheel brakes

squarely between the eyes from the word go – and the only way to do that is to race it. I've taken the trouble to go into the whole position very carefully, and I find that Brooklands has a whole series of 750 cc class records. Not one of them has ever been touched.

'"Therefore, if you do what I suggest, you can go out and get all these records – I'm certain you can set them at over 70 mph – you can go before the public announcing the availability of 'the Austin Seven, which has already taken all these records at Brooklands.'

'"At present, I am in hospital recovering from a damaged leg, but as soon as I'm mobile, may I come up and have a chat with you about the whole idea"?

'I got a very nice letter back, saying that he'd be glad to see me and perhaps I'd let him know when I was fit to travel. In due course, I was released from hospital, and the first thing I did was to go up to Longbridge. "Before I go and see Sir Herbert", I thought, "I'd better find out just what the climate is like here". Well, the climate was what I'd expected – I might almost say hoped! – the whole staff thought the old man was going soft in the head. I had a long chat with the sales manager, a very brusque fellow, who said "The whole thing's nonsense . . . they'll never sell!".

'"Isn't that marvellous", I thought. "This is the chap who's going to put this car on the market!".

'Having got this view, and one or two others quite similar, I marched in to see Sir Herbert Austin. Now he had a secretary called Howitt, who had a most peculiar squeaky voice. "He's in there", he said, nodding towards Austin's door, "but I don't think you'll do anything with him".

'However, I walked in, and Austin was perfectly polite, really . . . for him! He said, very gruffly: "Well, what do you want?".

'Then we had a two-hour battle straight off. He opposed every mortal thing I said – and I told him he didn't know what he was talking about. We really got down to a slogging match, which was inevitable with him – it was his nature – and I said: "Look here, I've been round your organisation, and you haven't got a friend in the place. They don't believe the Austin Seven's got any future at all. The only way you can get round it is by doing what I suggest".

'Towards the end of the two hours, I think I'd beaten him down on every point. He didn't like that very much, so his final gambit was, I think, a lovely one. Pointing at my leg in plaster, he said: "You'd make a bloody fine racing driver!".

'"You damned fool", I replied – we'd got to that stage then – "You couldn't build a racing car by the time that leg's all perfectly sound!".

'"Can't I?", he said. "All right, that's a bet!".

'And that's how we ended the conversation – he muttered something about "he'd bloody well show me". So I went home and carried on with my business, getting fit among other things. One day I received a telegram: "RACING CAR ON TRAIN NO . . . ARRIVING PADDINGTON . . . O'CLOCK. PLEASE MEET AND COLLECT. HERBERT AUSTIN".

'He'd won . . . I still had my leg in plaster. He must have gone at it like a bull at a gate to get the thing done. I went up to collect it, and there it was – shockingly badly interpreted from what I'd asked for, I thought, but the essentials were there. That was all I cared about. I knew I could do the rest. So I took the car straightaway to my little works at Walton-on-Thames, full of joy because I hadn't expected to get it so soon, and we set about making it run.

'In those days, I saw a lot of Sammy Davis. "I'm going for records at Brooklands", I said. "Can I count on you to come and help me?"

'"Of course you can", he said. Then I knew I had *The Autocar* behind me.

'Dear old Lindsay Lloyd, the Clerk of the Course at Brooklands, was himself all over . . . "You can't do anything in *that* car!", he said.

'"Never mind", I replied. "Will you be there, because we want all the tapes down for the mile and half-mile and so on".

'Well, as luck would have it, the little car behaved awfully well, and Lindsay Lloyd reported back that we'd done the half-mile at 75·8 mph, I think it was, and the mile at 72 mph. We'd lost some speed because we'd gone round on to the banking. Anyway, it was very good.

Below: the Austin Seven was built with many identities in many countries. This is a Dixi 3/15 hp, two-seater roadster, built in Germany. In 1928, the Dixi works were absorbed by BMW and the model continued as the BMW-Dixi

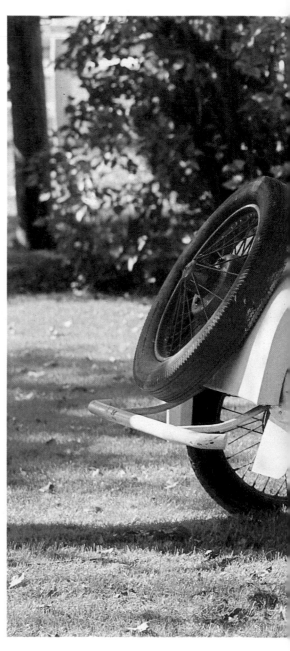

'I was able to telegraph back to Sir Herbert Austin that we had set up the records. And that was the beginning of the Austin Seven!'.

That, too, was the end of the cyclecar, which had reared its unlovely head again in the post-Armistice boom, due partly to the tremendous amount of Government surplus material which was dumped on the market at knockdown prices. Timber and ply featured large in the make-up of many of the nastier cyclecars – I once saw the remnants of a Gibbons, manufactured in suburban Essex by two incurable optimists named Gibbons and Moore: it resembled nothing more than a tea-chest mounted, somewhat haphazardly, on four old pram wheels, with a motor bike engine bolted on the offside. In 1921 this unlovely machine sold for £115 – which must have represented a profit of around 900 per cent on the material costs – and a 'set of fittings' (presumably luxuries like hood, windscreen and lights) was another £18.

The advent of the Austin Seven, a proper four-cylinder, four-seater car for £165 fully equipped, consigned such aberrations to the everlasting bonfire they so richly deserved; it also proved the salvation of the Austin company, whose other post-war products could be summed up as 'worthy'; well engineered, they were ponderous machines which had lost all the excitement of the pre-1914 Austins, which rejoiced in model names like 'Vitesse' and 'Defiance'. Herbert Austin's post-war policy had initially been to produce a 20 hp model which adapted American design philosophies to British taste, and, insofar as the

Austin Twenty was really rather a dull machine, he succeeded admirably; its younger sister, the Austin Heavy Twelve, which followed soon after as a sop to the horsepower tax, was another well engineered car which was totally lacking in 'sparkle', and was said to be much favoured by maiden aunts (as a digression, uncles seemed to go for Morris Oxfords, but one's father tended to favour the Clyno; thus early did popular cars acquire a 'market image').

More attractive light cars appeared in 1922: there was the pretty little 8/18 Talbot, designed by Louis Coatalen and sold in France with a different radiator as the Darracq by another component of the Sunbeam-Talbot-Darracq combine in one of the earliest successful examples of corporate badge engineering; there was the 8/18 Humber, with its close-coupled 'chummy' bodywork; there was the attractive Gwynne Eight, unique among British cars in being taken originally from a Spanish design, the Madrid-built Victoria, whose progenitor, Arturo Elizalde, was normally associated with the production of large, luxurious, sporting cars; and there was the Trojan . . .

The Trojan was designed by Leslie Hounsfield, who had made his name as

Below and right: what must have been one of the most successful 'unusual' cars ever built, the Leyland Motors-manufactured Trojan. This 1924 car featured a four-cylinder, two-stroke engine mounted under the floor. Although the power output from its 1½ litres was a miniscule 10 bhp, its pulling up steep hills at low speed was quite remarkable. Solid tyres were available on these cars right up until 1929 (National Motor Museum, England)

Above and far right: this fine example of the rare 1923 Humber Chummy was restored by Humber apprentices. It is powered by a four-cylinder 8 hp engine (Coventry Motor Museum, England)

a designer of steam-propelled military transport at the time of the Boer War, which may explain some of the more curious features of the car's eccentric make-up. Hounsfield had built a prototype of his 'people's car' as early as 1910, but it wasn't until he had attracted Leyland Motors, who had prospered greatly during the war, building trucks for the Government, to back the venture that production began. Surprisingly, Leyland chose the Trojan to supplant the super-luxury Leyland Eight car, killed by the slump after some fourteen examples had been built. You couldn't have found two more disparate designs – Leslie Hounsfield summed up his brainchild in the succinct phrase: 'It's weird . . . but it goes!'.

In many ways, the Trojan was the British equivalent of the Model T Ford: it was designed to be a go-anywhere car – simple to drive and cheap to maintain. Its two-speed epicyclic gearbox gave crashless gear changing and, by pulling up a hefty lever, the engine could be started from the seat, a notable advantage when few light cars had the luxury of a self-starter. Mechanically, it was like nothing else on the road: its 'chassis' was a sort of metal punt in which lay the odd, four-cylinder, two-stroke engine. This engine was said to have only seven moving parts, its cylinders being arranged in a square, each pair sharing a common combustion chamber. This arrangement was possible because the engine was a two-stroke and it gave maximum control over the timing of the induction and exhaust strokes. Each pair of cylinders also shared one long, V-shaped con-rod, which, instead of articulating as the pistons moved up and down the bores, simply flexed itself. Maximum power output of this strange 1529 cc engine was a puny 11 bhp, although, to compensate for this, bottom end torque was remarkable, enabling the Trojan to grind slowly up the steepest gradients with the inexorability of the mills of God (which is probably an appropriate place to remark that the Trojan was the only marque of the day to advertise in the *Church Times*, as its low price and commodious – and ugly – bodywork made it the ideal transport for impecunious clergymen with large families). Other idiosyncracies were chain final drive and long, supple canti-lever springs fore and aft, which were intended to take the jolts out of the narrow solid tyres which were the model's standard wear ('Wondersprings',

Left: André Citroën brought to the slightly *vieux style* French motor industry a breath of the mass production methods that car manufacturers in other countries had long regarded as *de rigueur*. While his countrymen clung to archaic methods of production, Citroën, in 1919, put his version of mass production into practice. This is one of his second generation of cars, the 1925 5cv tourer. The famous double chevron Citroën badge commemorates André Citroën's former trade as a gear manufacturer

the Trojan's promoters called them with pride). Because of the underfloor location of the engine, the bonnet held only the petrol tank, hooter, steering box, carburettor and lots of emptiness . . .

Leyland built the Trojan in its Kingston-upon-Thames factory, which during the War had been used to produce Sopwith Camels; at one time production reached 85 a week, for progressive price reductions made the Trojan as cheap as the British-built Model T Ford, at £125 for a fully-equipped four-seater in 1925. Then Leyland tired of it, and Trojan Limited took over manufacture in 1928.

One wonders how such a strange vehicle would have succeeded on the export markets, had anyone been particularly interested in selling abroad, for, having put up a high tariff wall, British manufacturers sat tight behind it and rarely bothered to sell their products overseas. One of the few manufacturers to establish an export department and to build a special 'Colonial Model' was Clyno, who, after the 1924 Empire Exhibition, received the following letter: 'I have corresponded with over sixty English manufacturers on the subject of trying to get into the Colonial trade during the last six months, and as far as I can see, you are the only people in Britain who have any ambition to do so. I must honestly say that, with the exception of yourself and one other firm, the correspondence I have had has made me feel ashamed to be an Englishman, and if your manufacturers persist in their attitude, England is doomed from a manufacturing point of view'.

Certainly no British manufacturer showed the enterprise of General Motors or Willys-Overland, who established factories in England, supplied with components, in General Motors' case, from their Canadian subsidiaries to minimise the rate of duty paid. Also, Britain was almost unique in the number of little 'localised' firms whose products rarely sold outside their own area; there was the Clyde from Leicester, the Jewel from Bradford and the Airedale from Esholt, Yorkshire. Only France could rival Britain in the production of such esoterica, and many French light cars were of a flimsiness of construction that beggared belief.

French mass-producers, however, built solid cars of almost indestructible reliability; and of those mass-producers the most spectacular was André Citroën, who had worked for Mors before the war, and had emerged in 1919 as the first European manufacturer truly to assimilate the Ford system of mass-production of a single model. In his new factory on the Quai de Javel, Citroën proposed to build one hundred cars a day, which would be sold, fully

Below: yet another Peugeot saloon to feature the Weymann-type fabric body was this 1928 190S saloon
(Peugeot collection, France)

equipped, at a moderate price . . . and received 30,000 orders before production began. Citroën's first car was the 10cv Type A four-cylinder tourer.

He was even inspired to announce grandiose plans for a factory in America, but this scheme was soon abandoned. However, Citroën did establish an assembly plant in England as well as subsidiaries in other European countries. The English works, at Brook Green, Hammersmith, was opened in 1923, by which time Citroën had announced the Type B, an improved version of the Type A, and the little 5cv which, since it was normally seen in bright yellow paintwork, was punningly known as the 'Citroën pressée', which phonetically could be rendered either as 'Citroën in a hurry' or 'lemon squash!'.

For the English market, Citroën imported the Type B in chassis form, coachwork, in the British idiom, being fitted by Short Brothers of Rochester, Kent, another firm of aircraft builders who had turned to car-body manufacture in the post-war slump. The little 5cv was imported complete from Paris. Then, in 1925, Citroën pioneered the all-steel body built under the American Budd patents, and proved the strength of this form of construction by standing an elephant on the roof. There were only three main pressings to this type of saloon body – the two sides and the roof. To the consternation of the panel-beaters of the day, these pressings couldn't easily be repaired if the car was involved in an accident; they had to be replaced complete. To a generation unaccustomed to the philosophy of repair by replacement, such a concept came as a shock.

Citroën always thought big: when the British Government announced that import duties were about to be reimposed, he ordered cars to be shipped to England in large numbers. Nearly 100 5cvs were parked on the flat roof of the Hammersmith works, the yard was crammed with Citroën taxi chassis, and storage space was hired for the 10cv models. And André Citroën – his rival, Louis Renault, called him sneeringly 'Le Petit Juif' ('The Little Jew') – was also an astute publicist, who from 1925 to 1934 hired the Eiffel Tower and turned it into France's biggest billboard, with his name written 100 feet high in a quarter of a million electric light bulbs.

Mass-production was spreading all over Europe: though Fiat was Italy's biggest car maker, it had hitherto built nothing in large volumes; or perhaps even that statement isn't strictly true, for Fiat's most popular pre-war model had been the 1847cc 'Zero', of which only some 2000 had been produced in a little over three years. 1919 saw the Torinese company with a brand new model designed for mass-production in a brand-new factory (five storeys and a test-track on the roof), even if Communist-inspired strikes prevented either from getting under way for a while, and forced Fiat, in order to remain active, to stick touring bodies on war-surplus 9-litre armoured car chassis (these were a Russian order frustrated by the Bolshevik revolution, so perhaps there was an ironic justice in this method of raising revenue).

The new model was the 1460cc Tipo 501, a slightly rotund vehicle of conventional design and refined construction, of which some 46,000 were sold between 1919 and 1926. The standard Italian coachwork wasn't too much liked in England, so once again Short brothers had to be called in, while bodies were also bought from the moribund Harper Bean concern, in receivership after an ambitious trade consortium called the British Motor Trading Corporation, had collapsed about their ears.

As motoring became more popular, so the number of accessories available burgeoned. Suddenly, there was sufficient traffic on the roads to warrant the sale of direction indicator devices and 'traffic warners' which gave illuminated advice of the drivers' attentions. Driving mirrors, which had first appeared on cars around 1905, became commonplace, while the increased price of petrol promoted an interest in fuel economy devices. There were, of course, plenty of fitments of dubious virtue available for those who made a fetish of adding to the equipment of their vehicle, fitments such as the 'More-Room' steering wheel, which was designed so that it could be slid forward to make it easier for portly drivers to get in to their seat, or the 'Kwiksail' car mascot, a small biplane fitted to the radiator cap in such a way that at speeds of over 15mph it began to rise up its mounting pole to a height of around 8 inches, with its

propeller revolving merrily. In France in 1921 there was understandable anxiety about the growing number of car thefts, so anxious owners could equip their vehicles with devices such as the Flic steering lock or, if they owned a Ford, the Rapid steering wheel. This could be unscrewed and removed from the car to prevent its being driven away, although what one was supposed to do with the detached steering wheel as one went about one's daily round on foot was not recorded. Nor was it mentioned how one guarded against astute car thieves who had troubled to equip themselves with their own Rapid wheel . . .

Tyres were still a perennial source of worry, as roads which had been neglected during wartime were, if anything, in even worse condition than the pre-1914 highways that had taken such expensive toll of pneumatics. To guard against unnecessary tyre damage, the Michelin Tyre Company introduced an 'ingenious device' at the 1921 Paris Salon. It was 'an invention for warning the driver that this tyre is becoming deflated', and, the reader was informed, 'consists of a tiny gun complete with lock and cartridges. The trigger is rubber-covered, and rests on the base of the rim. It cannot be released so long as there is adequate air pressure in the tube. To cock the gun it is only necessary to press a plunger, and, if a cartridge has been inserted, the device is ready for use. If the tyre becomes deflated, the lack of pressure on the beading releases the trigger, and a loud report gives the warning'.

Slightly less wearing on the nerves was the Jeff Patent Tube, an inner tube of curious construction – its inner surface was made up of overlapping flaps which were claimed to seal punctures as soon as the wounding instrument was withdrawn. *The Autocar* noted: 'At Christmas 1921 we fitted a set of Jeff Tubes to one of the staff cars and started by driving four large nails through the tread of one of the tyres so equipped. We have run the car for about five thousand miles, and have had no trouble at all in the way of air leakage'.

Like all parts of the motor car, however, tyres were becoming more reliable: now owners were claiming mileages of up to 20,000 miles a cover, and manufacturers could guarantee tyres against premature failure for up to 5000 miles.

In 1921, the Royal Automobile Club issued a report on the causes of breakdowns dealt with under their 'get you home' scheme, and found that the most common source of trouble was half-shaft failure, which accounted for no less than 13.9 per cent of all breakdowns. Running it a close second was ignition failure; both these factors, it was stated, were the result of poor maintenance and bad driving rather than any inherent defects, 'and pointed to the necessity for improved accessibility in view of the general disinclination of many owner-drivers to undertake any work on the car which is not rendered absolutely simple'.

'The owner-driver' – that is a phrase that sums up the essential difference between pre-war and post-war motoring in Britain, for the war had reduced both the number of people able to keep a 'motor-servant' and the number of those willing to undertake such an employment . . . and, of course, increased the total of those who regarded the possession of a car as a necessity, but one

Below: André Citroën, the man who revolutionised the French motor industry and publicity seeker par excellence

Left: Citroën hired the Eiffel Tower between 1925 and 1934 just to advertise his company. There are a quarter of a million lightbulbs in the display

Right: the first of the mass-produced Fiats was the 501, which appeared in 1919 with a 1½-litre, side-valve engine. This is the 1924 Torpedo, one of the second series of 501s on which were introduced front brakes and low pressure pneumatic tyres
(Centro Storico, Italy)

that they could only just afford. For such people, home maintenance was the only solution – and a dirty and depressing business it could be, especially when the majority of cars on the road had varnished coachwork and plenty of bright metal requiring frequent polishing to prevent tarnishing. For this reason, motoring still tended to be a seasonal business.

'In these days', grumbled a 1921 motorist, 'when to have a car washed by somebody else is a costly and slow process, even the most enthusiastic motorist, who is also his own cleaner, becomes a little tired of using his car during the exceptionally wet days of an English winter, for the simple reason that even an hour or two's run may entail a similar period splashing about in a cold and draughty yard endeavouring to remove the mud from the chassis and coachwork. Accordingly, the mileage of the car during the winter is liable to be limited; some people – the chicken-hearted, they say – even going to the extent of carefully greasing and covering their machines so that they may be laid up for a month or two at a time'.

Added to which, of course, was the important factor that the British railway network was still run by private enterprise, and therefore offered a reliable, and often more comfortable, alternative means of transport, especially over long distances, with branch-line communication to the most obscure corners of the country at reasonable cost. Just how attractive railway travel then was can be seen from Great Western Railway Statistics for the year 1921 (and remember that the Great Western had been astute enough to use motor transport as a feeder to the railheads as early as 1903). During the period April to October, some 64 million people travelled by Great Western, and the company was taking a million pounds a month from passenger traffic alone (and at least as much again from goods train receipts). In the month of November 1922 a total of 115,563 was run, the average number of minutes late amounting to just 2.3; no wonder people in those far-off days used to set their watches by the passing trains!

Against this, the motor car did offer the freedom to wander, to change one's plans on impulse, and the romance of the open – if ill-maintained – road inspired hundreds of touring articles in the motoring press of the period. It is interesting to note that motoring novels, which had enjoyed a vogue in the early 1900s and then faded away, were now back in fashion, usually featuring the sort of high-powered luxury car that the average motorist yearned for but knew he could never afford. Because of the romance and glamour attached to such exotic machinery, it is easy to fall into the trap of thinking that they were a commonplace sight on the roads of the early 1920s, just as one could be gulled, from reading certain motoring magazines of the 1980s, that there are nearly as many Lamborghinis on the road as Ford Escorts.

Of all the exotic cars of the 1920s, unquestionably the most glamorous was the Hispano-Suiza, known before the war as a well built, if conventional, car emanating from Barcelona, and designed by the Swiss Marc Birkigt. It had attracted attention chiefly because that most enthusiastic of motoring monarchs, the King of Spain, a patron of the marque, had been given one of their 15.9 hp sporting models as a present by his English Queen. They had even opened a French factory at Levallois-Perret to assemble their cars, of which this Alfonso XIII model was undoubtedly the favourite with the French. Among its high-society owners, one notes that the 15.9 hp Hispano was the chosen vehicle of that notorious society adventuress 'La Baronne De La Roche' (actually one Elise Delaroche); it was in this car that her lover Charles Voisin, the aviation pioneer, and brother of the more famous Gabriel Voisin, was killed in 1912.

A beautiful example of the Hispano-Suiza H6B, 37.2 hp model; this particular machine was specially commissioned by the Maharajah of Alwar in 1929 as a wedding present for his son and it has cabriolet-roadster bodywork by the French coachbuilder Kellner. The Hispano was intended primarily for panther hunting and the spotlights mounted either side of the windscreen were intended specifically for this purpose, having extendable arms which allowed them to be focussed on the prey. The bell, which can be seen in front of the radiator grille, could be rung from the cockpit and was used for clearing natives out of the car's path
(Stratford Motor Museum, England)

However, the firm's post-war glamour model had nothing in common with the Alfonso; instead, it drew heavily on Hispano-Suiza's contribution to the war, during which over fifty per cent of all allied aircraft were powered by Hispano-Suiza aero engines, either 'genuine' or built under licence. Until his mysterious disappearance in 1917, the French air ace Georges Guynemer was associated with Hispano-Suiza-powered aircraft, scoring his most famous victories on a SPAD biplane. Guynemer, with 53 victories to his credit, and France's other top ace, Rene Fonck, both flew with the famous Escadrille N3, the Hispano-powered French 'ace of aces' squadron, whose good luck emblem was a stork. Guynemer was a personal friend of Birkigt, and indeed designed his own deadly modification for the Hispano power unit, with results recalled by Captain W. E. Johns: 'In July, he took the air in a 200 hp Hispano-Suiza SPAD fitted with a gun of his own design. This was a light one-pounder which fired a shell through a hollow crankshaft; the shell came out of the propeller boss. He met an Albatros and fired his new gun at it from a distance of two hundred yards, and the black-crossed machine blew up in flames'.

Guynemer became part of French wartime mythology, and when the time came to choose a suitable radiator mascot for the new car, Birkigt commissioned a sculpture of the stork that had adorned the fuselage of his friend's SPAD. Launched at the 1919 Paris Salon, and intended for production at the Paris Bois-Colombes factory, opened in 1914, the new 32 cv Hispano H6 had a six-cylinder power unit which incorporated many of the features developed on the war-time V8 aero engine, like an alloy block with screwed-in steel liners and a single overhead camshaft. Designed for the elite few who could still afford the ultimate, the H6 was unequivocally the most advanced car of its day, with powerful servo-assisted brakes on all four wheels; when, five years later, Rolls Royce grudgingly decided to fit four-wheel-braking to their cars, they took out a licence to copy Birkigt's design.

It was no bad thing that the Hispano had such fine brakes, for the engine's 135 bhp at 3000 rpm endowed the car with a top speed of around 85 mph, while a light but very stiff chassis enabled the performance to be used to the full. The seven-bearing engine was also notable for an impressive helping of low-speed torque which, in spite of the use of a fairly high final drive ratio, could haul the big car from six to fifty miles per hour in top gear in just 21 seconds. It was one of the best all-rounders of the period, combining performance, reliability, comfort and style.

Only one thing marred the Hispano-Suiza, and that was its gearbox, a three-speed affair in unit with the engine; some years ago, the author drove a T49 Hispano, a 3750cc version of the H6 designed for the less well heeled Spanish market, in all respects save the smaller engine identical to its 6597cc French cousin, and noted that second gear had a scream like a sawmill – and that was on a low-mileage car! For the record, the author also recorded that the distance from the driver to the radiator mascot was exactly eight feet!

Although the H6 was a glamour car, it seems to have been pretty sparing in its public appearances in the early part of its life; reporting on the 1921 Glasgow Show, *The Autocar* remarked petulantly: 'At the opening of the Show, by the way, the Hispano-Suiza was conspicuously absent'.

What gave the Hispano-Suiza its especial cachet was the fact that, although it was a super-luxury car, it offered sports-car performance; André Dubonnet, the *aperitif* king, even entered his tulip-wood bodied Hispano for the Targa Florio – this was the 46cv, eight-litre 'Boulogne' model. A sister car, owned by Captain Woolf Barnato, covered 300 miles at Brooklands at an average speed of over 92 mph.

Such feats by the *richesse dorée* gave the Hispano-Suiza a romantic aura that was enhanced by its 'starring role' in that archetypal novel of the 1920s, Michael Arlen's *The Green Hat* . . . 'Like a huge yellow insect that had dropped to earth from a butterfly civilisation, this car, gallant and suave, rested in the lowly silence of the Shepherd's Market night'.

The French had their Hispano novel, too, in the pages of Pierre Frondaie's *l'Homme a l'Hispano*, written in 1924, but the car does not really feature as more than a passing shadow in this rather turgid romance about the tragic M. Dewalter's unrequited love . . . it is just there as a hint of his super-richness . . .

Unquestionably, such adulation gave the Hispano the edge in *chic* over its main rival in the Continental carriage trade, the straight-eight Isotta-Fraschini from Milan, but in any case the author has been informed by those who have driven both cars that the Hispano was without a doubt the better-handling vehicle. 'In comparison', they said, 'the Isotta drove like a truck'. Perhaps it is because the Hispano was designed for the man who drove himself, while the Isotta was meant to be driven by a chauffeur, who would not complain.

There was no direct equivalent for such vehicles in England, although the ingenious ohc Straker-Squire, 3.9-litre, six-cylinder car was a beautifully engineered high-speed tourer that promised great things, but failed to get into serious production. Interestingly enough, the engine design of the Straker-Squire was based on that of the war-time Rolls-Royce Eagle aero engine; Rolls-Royce seemed to have benefited not at all by their aviation experience and resumed post-war production virtually where they had left off, with the basically 1906-designed Silver Ghost, a very fine car, but not, as the company's advertising arrogantly claimed, 'The Best Car in the World'. In sympathetic hands, though, and fitted with appropriate lightweight coachwork, the Rolls could acquit itself creditably against its more technically sophisticated rivals, as G. R. N. Minchin noted in a letter written in 1922: 'The Alpine Eagle Rolls Royce . . . is a most wonderful car . . . One can run at 50 to 60 mph for mile after mile with absolutely not a sound but the wind and the noise of the tyres, with the springs gently absorbing the bumps in the road. It is such a fascinating motion, it tends almost to lull one to sleep, and one cannot believe one is

travelling so fast. No other car approaches the Rolls-Royce in this particular respect, and it is a sensation difficult to describe. One can drive all day at an average of over 40 mph and not feel tired or have a headache at the end. Coupled with this speed is such silence that with the car at rest passengers cannot tell whether the engine is running or not . . . The Rolls can be driven all out all the time, and it will never wear, nor flag, nor cause any trouble. It is one of the cheapest cars in the world to run and, should one want to sell it for any reason, its secondhand value is remarkable'.

The car which caused the greatest sensation among the British motoring public was the 3-litre Bentley, originally announced in 1919, and tested that year by S. C. H. Davis of *The Autocar*, but which did not get into production until 1921, mainly for reasons of finance. Its designer, W. O. Bentley, had been

Below: a beautiful example of 'The Best Car in the World', in this case a 1921 Silver Ghost; interestingly, the bodywork of this car was not fitted until 1925, having been built by Gustaf Nordberg's Vagnfabrik. It was restored by the same company thirty-five years later (Skokloster Museum, Sweden)

responsible for one of the better war-time aero engines, the Bentley Rotary, which was the most-sought-after power unit for the Sopwith Camel fighter; he had also pioneered the use of light-alloy pistons before the war, and the Bentley car used design features based on racing and aircraft-engine practice – although not on Bentley's aircraft engine, for its power unit was an in-line four-cylinder with an overhead camshaft. Perhaps the prettiest Bentleys were the few built without front-wheel brakes in the very earliest days of production, for these had, unmodified, the elegant radiator shell designed by that greatest of all motoring artists, F. Gordon Crosby (who also created the marque's winged badge). And the first of these was sold, in September 1921, to a wealthy young socialite named Noel Van Raalte, who had financed KLG sparking plugs and who owned Brownsea Island in Poole Harbour; while an undergraduate, he had raced round Cambridge, in reverse, in a Grand Prix Mercédès!

After a year of ownership of Bentley Number One, Van Raalte analysed his feelings about the car which, coincidentally, had a similar ring to Minchin's experiences with his Rolls: 'This chassis has a four-seated saloon body, and I employ no chauffeur. I can truthfully affirm that this is quite the most pleasing and satisfactory car of the many I have had. I find I can drive any distance up to 400 miles straight off in a day without feeling tired, which is an accomplishment I cannot achieve on anything else. The car is extremely fast, flexible and sweet-running. In traffic, it can be driven all day on top speed, except for an actual dead stop. It is not by any means cruelty to the car to do so, as it does it with great ease. Its petrol consumption in Scotland, where I live, and where the hills and roads are not, perhaps, of the most desirable, is over 20 mpg. The brakes and steering are better than any others I know of, and are all that could be desired. The suspension is excellent, and the way the car holds the road at high speeds is most remarkable. *The Autocar* recently stated that this car was a paradox in combining the qualities of the ultra-fast sporting car with those of the sweet running touring car. It can be used as either with great ease'.

The Bentley was also the most expensive car in its capacity class, costing £1395 in September 1922, equipped with a four-seater touring body; a comparable French car of similar conception, the six-cylinder Lorraine-Dietrich, cost £750 in London at the same date.

However, the Bentley's greatest rival among high-class fast touring cars was

Below: 'the Car Superexcellent', the magnificent, Grosvenor-bodied, 30/98 Vauxhall E-type of 1921, designed by Laurence Pomeroy and representing the peak of the company's achievements. The prototype appeared in 1913, with 4½-litre engine and a price of just £125, but only thirteen were built before war intervened. Post war, the car eventually sold for £1600 and, with a top speed of over 80 mph, it was one of the few rivals to the contemporary Bentley as a high-speed, high-class tourer

the 30/98 Vauxhall – 'The Car Superexcellent' – an inspired design by L. H. Pomeroy, which represented the high peak of the Luton company's achievements since their début in car manufacture in 1903. A few examples of this model had appeared just before the war, but it did not get into full production until after the Armistice. Compared with the Bentley, it was old-fashioned in concept, but sound engineering gave it a surpassing performance. It was the sheer joy of owning such a car that led one John Grange to write, in the spring of 1922, a tribute to his car which also encapsulates the heady pleasure of motoring in the golden days of the 1920s: 'I have covered about 3000 miles in my 1922 30/98 Vauxhall without the slightest trouble.

'The tyres are certainly not half worn, and 20 mpg can easily be attained with care. But what do a few drops of petrol, more or less, matter to the proud owner of a car like this? I am old in motordom. For eighteen years I have never been without a car. Yet each model I have possessed had its shortcomings, which became more and more flagrant as experience developed an exacting criterion. Hence my praise of any of my former possessions has always been meagre, restrained and qualified, because none captured the sanctions of my soul like my present machine has done. My pen seeks to portray the truth; and it is a verity that I have never seen a car so accurately described by its makers as the 30/98 Vauxhall. It is endowed with every virtue they claim for it. There is embodied in its vitals ample potency of incredible performance. It is a veritable miracle of mechanism. If one desires speed, it moves with might and majesty along the King's highway at the slightest touch of the accelerator pedal. It gulps giant gradients with greed and gusto. Yet withal the engine shows no symptom of punishment. So far no adjustment has been necessary. Oil consumption is alarmingly small, being more than 1000 mpg. The chassis is very strong indeed, for so light a body as the Velox. Its brakes are silent, sweet, efficient'.

If proof was needed that the motor car was an essential part of everyday life, then it came in May 1926, when the Trades Union Council called upon Union members throughout Britain to support the miners, whose industry had been badly hit by lower-priced German and Polish coal, as well as by newer sources of energy – oil and electricity. At midnight on Monday 3 May, in defiance of emergency regulations which made it an offence to 'prevent the proper use or working of any . . . railway, canal, bridge, road, tramway, vehicle . . .', railwaymen and transport workers joined the ranks of the strikers.

For a few hours, the nation ground to a halt, and then volunteers came in to keep the roads and railways moving; the 'unprecedented interference with routine' lasted until 15 May (although the miners stayed out until August). During that period, those who could drive took over trucks and buses – buses were festooned with barbed wire and carried a policeman to keep the strikers at bay, although the only serious incident occurred when strikers overturned a Tilling-Stevens petrol-electric of Thomas Tilling's fleet at the Elephant and Castle. There were, indeed, some curious sights; well-known racing drivers at the controls of lorries and buses, a $10\frac{1}{2}$-litre Fiat racing car delivering copies of the Government newspaper, *The British Gazette* . . .

The private car came into its own, carrying people to and from work, and London had a foretaste of things to come, with traffic jams and parking problems; Hyde Park was closed off, and became a distribution centre for milk and fish, while Regent's Park was used as a bus depot at night. Vans and trucks were converted into impromptu buses, too, carrying commuters in from the suburbs in extreme discomfort for 3d to 6d. There was, it seems, no problem in getting hold of petrol, and the brand-new miracle of wireless kept the nation informed of the progress of the strike.

It would be foolish to assume that things went on as normal, but thanks to motor vehicles, abnormality was kept to a minimum. And when it was all over, *The Autocar* commented: 'During the troublous times through which we have all passed one outstanding point emerges, and this is the paramount importance of road transport to the whole community. In the days before the motor vehicle had become a part of our national life the discontinuance of work on so gigantic a scale as that which took place when the general strike was declared would almost certainly have resulted in a paralysis of activity utterly disastrous to

every branch and section of the people. In our opinion, the escape of the country with wounds which, deep though they may be, will heal in time, is attributable to the fact that road transport of essential commodities was available to save the nation from irreparable disaster'.

Certainly, the Strike started the habit of commuting by car, and only a few days after one enthusiastic motorist was writing to the Minister of Transport suggesting that 'motorists who drive into London daily to business should be given special facilities in the parking places nearest their offices, and by being allowed a four hours stay instead of the two hours at present available'.

So, although parking restrictions were becoming necessary in London, outside the big conurbations, motorists still parked pretty much where they pleased. In villages and small towns, it was still the custom, a legacy of a more leisurely era, for the local *grande dame* to instruct the chauffeur to halt the limousine in the middle of the road outside a shop and sound the imperious hooter to summon the shopkeeper. He would then stand humbly by the footboard of the big car, noting down my lady's shopping list for subsequent delivery (probably by pony and trap).

Below and right: this imposing vehicle is a Standard 13.9 hp all-weather tourer of 1926, built by the Standard Motor Company of Coventry, which was founded by R. W. Maudslay in 1903. The 13.9 hp, introduced in 1924, used an overhead-valve engine and worm final drive; it was the company's most successful offering of the period. The radiator mascot, which was adopted in 1923, is the standard of the ninth Roman Legion

Anticipating the coming increase in motor traffic, various road-improvement schemes of more or less a practicable nature had been suggested. Proposals for special motorways restricted to cars alone dated back to the end of the 19th Century, while a circular road round London had first been suggested in Edwardian times. In the 1920s, the first scheme for a London to Birmingham motorway was published, but it got no further than some of the more fantastical proposals, such as a suggestion that main roads should be put into tunnels to preserve the rural beauty of England, or that in London, where the length of the average traffic jam had doubled since 1914, wide, straight roads should be constructed above the existing buildings to carry through traffic.

Slightly less impracticable was the 1924 proposal that elevated roads should be built above existing carriageways to carry cars along the main east-west through routes in the City of London. The motor age was certainly prompting the construction of new roads, but, far too often, these were hardly purpose-built motor roads, just wider versions of the old roads and, although they may have passed through open country for a good deal of their length, indiscriminate speculative building soon made them little better than the thoroughfares they were intended to replace.

It was around this time that the motoring author Filson Young took advantage of the new vision accorded by the aeroplane, over London's new roads . . .

'To realise the muddling and blundering that is going on . . . you must get up into the air and see what combined greed and lack of design may do to make the world ugly', he wrote. 'A glance at the Barnet by-pass on its way from Finchley to Hatfield told a tale that is to be seen repeated on the outskirts of nearly all the big towns in England. As soon as this road leaves the dense suburban belt that extends to Mill Hill, this dreary trimming of its edges by little houses begins and continues for miles; one comes to realise the extent of this new method of planning homes in mile-long ribbons along the arterial roads . . . Behind the noisy roads lie patches and spaces apparently unused by man; for the people who inhabit these ribboned roads have no contact with the land, and agriculture means nothing to them.

'Turning south-east from Hatfield, we crossed the end of Epping Forest and the North Circular Road and what I think is called the Eastern Avenue. We looked down upon a world that crowded along even these great arteries; they had been established so that men could escape from crowded populations, but the arteries were themselves becoming choked . . .'

So, for most people the romance was going out of motoring, that fact was reflected in the rise of the saloon car, which was rapidly overtaking the open tourer as the most popular type of coachwork. Not only that, but motorists obviously were not what they were, if an indignant correspondent to *The Motor* in 1926 is to be believed: 'Whilst travelling in my car on Sunday afternoon, 29 August, at 2.30 pm on the Great North Road, just beyond Bromham cross-roads, I was passed by a large touring car, travelling fast and driven by a lady. Seated at her side was a gentleman. A little farther ahead the large touring car ran into the rear of a stationary car, which was on the extreme left-hand side of the road in question. The "colliders" got out casually to view the damage, and obviously observing the stationary car was conveniently unattended, jumped, with guilty haste, into their own car. The gentleman, who now took the wheel, reversed the car, made the gears hum, and burst off at a great speed in the direction of Bromham. For the full benefit of those closely interested, I may say the damaged car happened to be a new Standard blue four-seater, bearing a trade number, the rear number plate and mudguard of which appeared quite "unhealthy" after the unwanted incident on what was to all events her "maiden voyage".

'I can honestly assure you that during my many years of motoring, I have never witnessed such a mean action performed upon a fellow motorist by another supposed loyal member of our colossal motoring fraternity. It completely filled me with utter disgust, and it is evidently some small sample of treatment that one may possibly expect to receive from some of the so-called "Ladies" encountered on the road'.

As a postscript, one may add that at this period – and, indeed, right up to 1930, there was no compulsion on motorists to take out insurance against accidents. Nor was there any form of driving test, two factors which add extra point to this account of a mid 1920s escapade which reads like the scenario of a Mack Sennett comedy: 'On coming to the crossing from the direction of Rugeley, it was apparently deserted, but, my attention being on the signpost ahead to find the road for London, I unfortunately failed to notice the turning coming out at an angle on my left, from which a number of cars and motor cycles were coming and evidently wishing to go to Warwick.

'Failing to locate the London road from the signpost, I decided to drive up to the policeman on the point to inquire. Shouts on my left caused me to realise that I had brought my car almost broadside on to the traffic emerging on that side.

'Seeing they had all managed to slow sufficiently to clear me, I again started to make for the policeman, when a car seemed to appear from nowhere, coming head on. Seeing a turning on my left I accelerated and swung into it, as my only hope of preventing a nasty collision, my action again throwing those unfortunate people on my left into confusion.

'At this moment, the policeman, who had evidently been taking a little relaxation from his undoubted strenuous job of regulating the traffic, woke up and in a loud voice inquired what game I thought I was playing. I did not stop to tell him, as I had done no damage, and shuddered to think of the names I might be called if I returned among my victims'.

Mind you, the motoring laws in Britain were so antiquated that it would have been difficult, even for the most law-abiding citizen, to have remained within them. George Bernard Shaw, always ready for a good controversy, claimed that between 1909 and 1929 he had covered well over 100,000 miles, and had never completed a car journey without breaking the law . . . at the time, he was addressing the Chief Constables' Conference! Shaw was quite proud of the fact that he had been summoned for speeding: 'I was informed that I had passed through a police control at a speed of twenty-seven miles an hour. There was no question. There was no room for argument. The constable and I were perfectly civil to one another. He was pleased when he got my name, because he knew he would be in the paper next day. And I was pleased, because what came into my head was that it was a mercy he did not catch me half an hour before, when I was driving at fifty!'.

So, motoring was becoming more commonplace. But what were the makes which made it so? Whose cars were the most popular? We can gain some idea, at least, from the various impromptu censuses which enthusiasts compiled for publication in the correspondence columns of the motoring press. On a Sunday afternoon in the summer of 1925, a motorist counted the number of cars using the Bognor-Littlehampton road during the space of an hour: 'Morris 29, Austin 15, Rover 15, Singer 13, Ford 11, Standard 8, Bean and Citroën 5, Wolseley 6, Dodge Brothers 4, Talbot 4, Daimler and Clyno 2, AC 4, Overland 4, Essex 4, Sunbeam 4, Buick 3, Napier 3, Hillman 3, Renault 3, Armstrong-Siddeley 4, Fiat 5, Morgan and Chevrolet 2, Crossley and Humber 3, Unic 2 and one each of the following: Studebaker, Swift, Delage, Charron-Laycock, Lancia, Riley, ABC, Cubitt, GWK, Star, Darracq and Jowett'.

On the Continent, obviously, things were a little different. Four years later, an inhabitant of that cosmopolitan and somewhat anti-motorist country, Switzerland, made a similar survey of the cars passing his house in Geneva between 5.50 pm and 6.20 pm one Sunday – and a curiously mixed bag they were: Citroën 43; Fiat 43; Peugeot 22; Renault 21; Chrysler 20; Buick 10; Ford 9; Whippet 7; Talbot, Donnet, De Dion, Nash, 6 each; Delage, Studebaker, 5 each; Ansaldo, Auburn, Erskine, Essex, 4 each; Amilcar, Cadillac, Chenard-Walcker, Pic-Pic, Voisin, 3 each; Martini, Benz, Imperia, Panhard, Packard, Willys-Knight, Wolseley, Victory, Austin, Bugatti, Minerva, Frazer-Nash, Aries, 2 each; Lancia, Sizaire, DeSoto, Opel, Falcon-Knight, Ballot, Berliet, LaSalle, Chevrolet, Maximag, Rally, Mathis, Hudson, 1 each. British cars, our observer added, were almost unknown on the roads of his country, only the odd Morris, Austin or Rolls-Royce serving to remind the Swiss that Britain did indeed have a motor industry.

Above: in May 1926 in Great Britain the Trades Union Council called a General Strike of workers throughout the country in support of a miner's dispute. This scene shows the 'changing of the guard', at the London Omnibus Depot, on 6 May 1926

Above right: crowds of striking workers line East India Dock Road in London as armoured cars escort a food convoy from the docks. Behind the leading armoured car is a Daimler lorry and the picture also gives an idea of the problems encountered when narrow road wheels met slippery tram lines

Right: the strike lasted from 3 to 15 May, during which time essential services were run by volunteers and the Forces, and the motor car was pressed into vital new roles. This scene from the eighth day shows a lorry leaving London's heavily barricaded Smithfield market

160

Below and far left: an Austro-Daimler ADS 19/100 hp of 1926, powered by a straight-six overhead-camshaft engine of 3 litres, whose 100 bhp can push the car along at a speed of 100 mph. This example is believed to be the 1926 Ulster TT machine

Left: the 11.9 hp AC of 1921, with a four-cylinder, side-valve Anzani engine with a three-speed gearbox, mounted on the rear axle; the car has a disc transmission brake plus foot brakes on the rear wheels (National Motor Museum, England)

Right: Peugeot's Type 163 of 1923, which is powered by a 1437 cc, 10 hp, four-cylinder engine. This is the Torpedo version, but the model was also available with de luxe Torpedo or boat-tailed, sporting four-seater bodywork (Peugeot Collection, France)

The sad thing about Britain's apparent indifference to export sales was that the average British-built car was demonstrably equal to the most extreme overseas conditions – a standard 10.8 hp Clyno, with no pump or fan to aid its cooling, was reported to be in everyday use in Aden without any overheating troubles. In 1926, Frank Grey, the former MP for Oxford, challenged the British motor industry to build him a car suitable for making the West-East crossing of Africa; the only response came from Jowett of Bradford. On 16 May 1926, Grey and his companion, Jack Sawyer, left Lagos in two two-seater Jowett 7 hp flat-twin cars. Sixty days and 3800 miles later, they arrived at Massawa, on the Red Sea, after an adventurous trip, during which they had freed a young native girl from slave traders. Jowett, who specialised in coining advertising slogans – typical samples included 'The little engine with the big pull' and 'The seven that passes a seventeen like a seventy' – now added 'The car that put the camel on the dole' to the list.

British cars, too, had made the first motor journey from Cape to Cairo a few months earlier; Major and Mrs Chaplin Court Treatt had started the epic 13,000-mile journey on 24 September 1924, driving a pair of 25 hp Crossleys, which reached their destination on 24 January 1926, having survived the muddiest rainy season on record. In 1927 Mrs Diana Strickland crossed Africa in a Wolverhampton-built 14/40 hp Star named 'The Star of the Desert'.

On other continents, too, British cars blazed the trails: in 1924 Major Forbes-Leith's Wolseley 14 had been the first car to make the journey by road from England to India.

The British did not, however, have a monopoly of long-distance motoring,

Above and below: this imposing vehicle is a 1925 Austro Daimler ADM/BK, powered by an overhead-camshaft, six-cylinder engine of 2650 cc designed by the brilliant Ferdinand Porsche
(National Motor Museum, England)

Below and bottom: while Citroën are justly famous for their front-wheel-drive cars, they have also produced some notable rear-drive vehicles, the most extreme of which was this half-track conversion by M Kegresse. Many French colonies were in inaccessible West Africa, protected by thousands of miles of desert. It was an expedition of comprehensively equipped Citroën Kegresses which made the first successful crossing of the Sahara, in 1922–3. Similar vehicles went on to make many other pioneering journeys

for Citroëns fitted with the half-track conversion devised by M. Kégresse, formerly in charge of the garages of His Imperial Majesty the Tsar of all the Russias, were renowned for opening roads across Africa, where the French had long been trying to establish closer links with their colonies; French West Africa was separated from Algeria by several thousand miles of desert. The equipment carried by the Citroëns, which made the first successful Sahara crossing in 1922–23 is worthy of note. Wrote André Citroën: 'The body was designed to give the maximum of comfort to the travellers. It had three seats, one of them reserved for a possible guide, boxes of provisions, camp requisites, maps and munitions – for, in the desert, one must think of defence, and the mission carried a rifle per man and three aeroplane machine-guns. Each car carried, rolled up on its side, a tent which could be built up in a few minutes. Two of them, called provision cars, carried from 60 to 120 gallons of

Right : Humber's 14/40 Doctor's Coupé of 1927;
it featured a four-cylinder engine of 2050 cc and
had a top speed of just on 60 mph
(Coventry Motor Museum, England)

Below and below right : the AC Six of 1925
featured a six-cylinder, overhead-camshaft engine
designed by John Weller. In 1991 cc form, the
engine produced a highly respectable 40 bhp, and
it was still in production, albeit in a modified
state, in 1963. By this time, it was producing over
100 bhp
(Peter Hampton)

petrol. The others had two tanks of 15 gallons each, making 50 gallons with the front tank. They also had two water tanks, holding four gallons'.

In 1924–25, came the famous *Croisière Noire* (Black Journey) in which eight cars were despatched from Algeria, to cross Africa, splitting into four groups which would reach the coast at Mombasa, Dar-es-Salaam, Mozambique and Cape Town, finally to rendezvous again on the island of Madagascar, having carried out 'a feat of transport unsurpassed in the history of the motor car'.

Then, in 1931, Georges Haardt, organiser of these two journeys, achieved the crossing of Asia from Turkestan to Peking at the head of an expedition of Citroën *auto-chenilles* christened *La Croisiere Jaune* (Yellow Journey), only to die from pneumonia in Hong Kong while planning the return trip.

Turning from the well planned to the near-farcical; in 1926 three Chinese men made the overland trip from Shanghai in a beaten-up Trojan, arriving in London to tumultuous apathy (although, along with Parry Thomas, who had just taken the Land Speed Record at 171.09 mph in his 27-litre *Babs*, they were honoured at a supper and concert party organised by Leyland Motors whose engine was used in Thomas's car).

Facing page : the last Mercedes-Benz car to be built at Mannheim and the last one designed by Dr Porsche – the Nürburg 460 of 1928. Power was from a straight-eight, overhead-camshaft engine of 4.6 litres and the car featured the classic Mercedes U-section frame, rigid axles and semi-elliptic springs

Below : by the time this Model T sedan was built, in 1926, sales of Ford's classic had begun a rapid decline from a peak of over two million in the 1923 fiscal year. While Henry Ford clung steadfastly to his devotion to the T, rivals reaped the benefits. Ford eventually admitted defeat in 1927 and the T was replaced

Then there was Michael Terry who, with £8 2s 3d in his pocket, set out in February 1923 at the wheel of a rickety Ford, accompanied by one Richard Yockney, to make the first-ever crossing of the desolate 'Never Never Land' of Northern Australia, covering 800 miles of trackless desert where, on occasion, the car could only cover ten yards at a time before becoming bogged down, and where four miles could represent a day's journey. And when they reached their destination in October (after running out of both petrol and water in the desert and almost dying before a search party found them), the explorers felt so uncomfortable in the soft beds of the hotel that they rolled themselves in blankets and slept on the bare boards of the verandah!

However, although the Model T Ford was still capable of conquering the desert, during the mid 1920s, its star, which had seemed permanently in the ascendant, began to wane with alarming rapidity as old age caught up with the 'Universal Car'. Sales, which had reached a peak of 2,055,309 during the company's fiscal year (August to July) of 1923, fell off, slowly at first, then with increasing rapidity as Ford's rivals introduced more attractive models that were not just a 1908 design gently warmed over like the Model T. Henry

Ford, who had envisaged the car going on for ever, was nonplussed as customers turned to the more stylish Overland, Essex, Chevrolet and Dodge models. As speculation grew that the T was approaching the end of production, with some 14 million of the type already built, Ford remained adamant, denying all rumours. 'We have no intention of introducing a "six"', he stated in December 1926. 'The Ford car is a tried and proved car that requires no tinkering. It has met all the conditions of transportation the world over . . . Changes in style from time to time are merely evolution . . . We do not intend to make a "six", an "eight" or anything else outside of our regular products. It is true that we have experiments with such cars, as we have experiments with many things. They keep our engineers busy – prevent them from tinkering too much with the Ford car.'

Ford had, indeed, planned a successor to the Model T, the unorthodox eight-cylinder X-Car, so-called because its cylinders were laid out in the form of two St Andrew's Crosses in tandem, but the engine proved too heavy, and the sparking plugs on the lower cylinders so susceptible to water and mud that the design was shelved in 1926, after six years of experimentation.

Rumours that the Model T was to be discontinued after nineteen years' production began to spread. On 26 May 1927, the fifteen-millionth Model T came off the production line, the event marked by a simple ceremony . . . and then Henry Ford passed the death sentence on the 'Tin Lizzy'. When the production lines finally stopped moving, some 15,500,000 Model Ts had been built, of which around three-quarters of this total, amassed since 1908, were still in regular use.

Reaction to the demise of the old model varied from one Ford executive's cynical 'The Model T lasted two years longer than it should have' to that of the old lady who bought and stored away seven new Model Ts so that she should never have to change her allegiance for the rest of her life.

Only when Model T had passed into history did Henry Ford command his company, which had neither advanced design engineering department nor proving ground, to develop its successor.

The first blueprints for the new car had been drawn up in January 1927; such was the speed at which new models were put on the market in those days that a prototype chassis was running inside three months. But it needed plenty more of the 'seat-of-the-pants' testing that was typical of Ford methods in those days. There was not even a full-time test driver; the man appointed to the task normally managed the Ford farms. Once again, Ford returned to his favourite development method of watching engineers draw his concepts in chalk on a blackboard, and only when he was satisfied with the drawing was it

Right: Morgan were responsible for bringing sporting motoring to those who could not afford large cars, their machines being light enough to be motor-cycle engined. This is a 1927 Morgan Aero, which features a JAP vee-twin power unit
(National Motor Museum, England)

Below: the passing of the Model T heralded the arrival of the Model A, which maintained Henry Ford's tradition of straightforward design. The A had a 3.3-litre, side-valve engine and a three-speed gearbox. The bodywork, styled under the supervision of Edsel Ford, was a smaller facsimile of the luxury Lincoln. In spite of the Depression, the Model A enjoyed outstanding sales success. This is a 1930 Sedan, equipped with period accessories
(G. W. Walker, Indianapolis)

translated into metal. Even when the first prototype was complete, Ford insisted on testing it, to 'represent the public' and, having hurtled it across a rough, obstacle-strewn field, insisted that hydraulic dampers were fitted to improve the ride.

By 10 August, development was complete, and the new car was ready for production. Meanwhile, of course, Ford sales were just coasting on the residue of Model T output and the manufacture of spare parts, so the company's rivals, especially Chevrolet, were able to make damaging inroads on Ford's section of the market. Public interest in the 'New Ford' was intense – probably no car before or since had attracted so much attention and speculation. The purchasers waited with increasing impatience as the weeks dragged into months, while the Ford factories throughout the world were totally reorganised for the manufacture of the new model; the measure of the confidence that the car-buying public had in Henry Ford was shown by the 400,000 orders that were received before anyone had even seen the car.

Production of the New Ford – which was given the designation 'Model A', as it represented a new beginning – began in limited numbers in November 1927, and the press were at last permitted a look at it at the end of that month. On its first public showing, 100,000 people crowded into the showrooms of Detroit just to catch a glimpse of the new car, which turned out to be as conventional as the Model T had been quirky, although its design was full of Ford ingenuity, like the petrol tank which formed an integral part of the scuttle, or the short copper strips which connected the distributor to the spark plugs. But what really set the Model A apart from its predecessor was its elegant styling, carried out under the supervision of Edsel Ford, who had created the car as a smaller facsimile of the luxury Lincoln, which had been produced as part of the Ford empire since 1922. For such up-to-date looks, the price was astonishingly moderate: the Model A Tudor sedan, at $495, was no more expensive than the equivalent Model T (and $100 less than the Chevrolet), the Fordor was $570 and the Coupe was $495. Development and new machinery costs totalled $250,000,000 – and Ford met this colossal bill with equanimity and cash from the company's reserves, for when Model T had ceased production, Ford could count $350,000,000 in the bank. . . .

By comparison, Europe could show nothing on so grand a scale: William Morris, who had built up production of his well liked Bullnose models to over 54,000 in 1925, and gained British market dominance, did not even have a moving production line until the early 1930s. Chassis were just pushed down the factory in rows, getting nearer the exit as they approached completion. The same, on a lesser scale, applied at Clyno, who were still matching Morris prices to the penny with a car that was in many ways superior. Then they made two fatal mistakes – building a huge new factory at Bushbury, a Wolverhampton suburb, and introducing a 9hp model to forestall the rumoured introduction of the Morris Eight. They tried to build a '£100' version of the Nine, but the

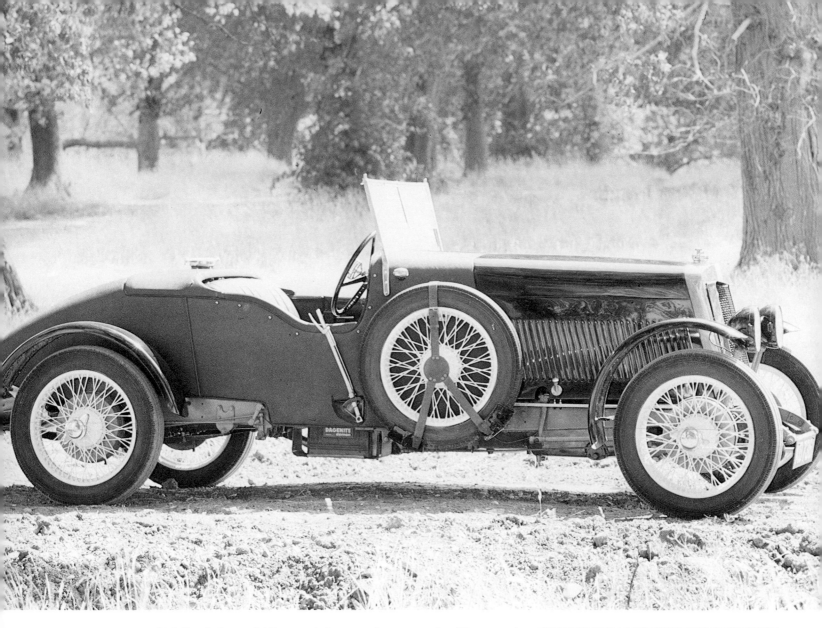

new model, officially christened 'Century', became known as the 'Cemetery', as its introduction was instrumental in sending Clyno to an early grave, one of the first victims of the depression that was about to force many motor manufacturers out of business. The Rootes Brothers, Kent-born motor traders who were building up a car-building empire by snapping up companies which had run short of cash, like Humber and Hillman, could have bought Clyno for around £86,000, but preferred to see this admirable make go out of business. Henry Meadows, a former works manager of Clyno, had plans to revive the marque during the late 1930s but re-armament put an end to them.

The depression proved that, henceforth, the race would definitely be to the strong, and lack of finance and the inability to compete on equal terms with the mass-producers, who could practise the economies of scale (and who, indeed, had often snapped up their former suppliers, to further minimise costs of components) drove some of the most respected names in the industry – Bean, Swift, Star, Calthorpe – out of business. One make, however, which had collapsed before the onset of the depression, had done so because of incompetent marketing. The shock was that much greater because the firm in question was Wolseley, one of the oldest names in the British motor industry, who had introduced a new model known as the 'Silent Six' for 1925; its radiator mascot was six little Klu-Klux-Klansmen standing in a circle. Customers, expecting the model to live absolutely up to its name, were apt to return their car to the factory for replacement if they heard the slightest sound emanating from the engine. The company ran into so much trouble from this cause that, by 1927, they were bankrupt, owing £2,000,000; William Morris stepped in and bought up Wolseley for £730,000.

Above and right: the Bean Company of Dudley, Staffordshire, produced cars between 1919 and 1929. However, this was just another firm which failed to survive the Morris price war. This is a 1928 Light 14, which used the 14/40 hp engine in the smaller 12 chassis to cut costs (National Motor Museum, England)

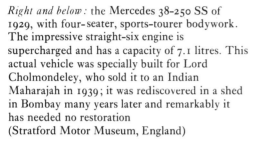

Left: a 1929 Lea-Francis Hyper, with a Cozette-supercharged Meadows engine of 1½ litres capacity. This is a replica of the car with which Kaye Don won the 1928 Isle of Man TT (Stratford Motor Museum, England)

Right and below: the Mercedes 38-250 SS of 1929, with four-seater, sports-tourer bodywork. The impressive straight-six engine is supercharged and has a capacity of 7.1 litres. This actual vehicle was specially built for Lord Cholmondeley, who sold it to an Indian Maharajah in 1939; it was rediscovered in a shed in Bombay many years later and remarkably it has needed no restoration (Stratford Motor Museum, England)

Right and below: one of the last steam cars to be made and sold in commercial quantities was this American Stanley 735-A of 1920; this particular example was used as the British importer's demonstration model. The 735 had its boiler under the bonnet and its double-acting twin-cylinder engine on the rear axle (National Motor Museum, England)

By the end of the 1920s, it was evident that the smaller independent motor manufacturer was a dying breed; in 1919, over eighty different companies produced a total of 25,000 cars (or an average of 300 per firm), while a decade later there were forty motor manufacturers in Britain, who built 239,000 cars between them, an average of 6000 each. The motor vehicle had obviously come to stay, for there were 2,260,500 motor vehicles on the roads of Britain, paying a total of £27,040,384 in licence duties; 1,042,300 of these were private cars, paying an average horsepower tax of £13 18s 6d each, while 339,500 were petrol or steam goods vehicles, average duty £26 5s 6d.

Perhaps even more significant were the statistics from the United States, where production during 1929 reached a record level of 5,337,087, a figure a million greater than the previous year's output, and one that would not be beaten for another twenty years. And of those cars, nine out of ten were closed, an exact reversal of the 1919 figures, when nine open tourers were sold for every sedan.

Cars were more powerful now and people needed a vehicle that could be used reliably in all kinds of weather and cars now developed rapidly, both technically and aesthetically.

The 1920s was a decade of sweeping changes, a decade in which the external form of the motor car altered radically, if not beyond all recognition, and in which its mechanics made unprecedented progress, most particularly in the opposed respects of starting and stopping. Electric starting and four-wheel braking became accepted as commonplace where, before the war, they had only been fitted by the most adventurous of manufacturers. Hydraulic brakes had been invented as early as 1918 by the aircraft manufacturer Malcolm Loughead (better known by the phoneticised version of his name – 'Lockheed') and first fitted in production to the Duesenberg of 1920, although as they were then truly hydraulic, using a water-based fluid in compression, such brakes were generally mistrusted. And when they appeared on the cheaper American cars, with their 'sudden-death' wraparound band brakes, vicious in the dry and totally useless in the wet, there was further reason to treat them with suspicion. Henry Ford, indeed, would have nothing to do with hydraulic brakes, and regularly published homilies on the superiority of mechanical brakes (although by that time hydraulics had become eminently trustworthy).

Other notable trends of the latter part of the decade were the adoption of coil ignition in place of the more reliable – but more complex and costly – magneto (and the relegation of the starting handle from its fixed abode on the nose of the crankshaft to the tool kit), the general acceptance of flexible engine mountings to minimise vibration, the abolition of scuttle-mounted petrol tanks feeding the carburettor by gravity in favour of the rear-mounted tank with some kind of pump or vacuum device for fuel supply. Cars became easier to look after, with the introduction around 1928 of cellulose paint in place of coach varnish and the availability of chromium plating, which reduced the care of brightwork from the daily rubdown with polish necessary in the days of brass, nickel plate or german silver to an occasional wipeover with a damp rag.

Transmissions, too, altered dramatically, with the announcement of syncromesh in 1928 and the relatively short-lived vogue for free-wheels in the final drive. In 1927, Packard introduced the hypoid-geared back axle, which permitted a dramatic lowering of the overall height of the car without the need for a dropped chassis; better roads were another factor permitting the building of low-slung vehicles.

One remarkable invention of the 1920s which failed to catch on was the original 'run-flat' tyre, invented by 16-year-old Fred Rapson, whose father was a noted tyre manufacturer. This tyre had an inner high-pressure tube within a low-pressure outer cover, so that in the event of a puncture, the motorist could drive to the nearest garage, with the weight of the car taken by the high-pressure tube. And the tread of the low-pressure tyre was detachable, so that it could be replaced when the tyre wore out. . . .

Body design showed many minor improvements, like the adoption of safety glass (although this didn't become compulsory in Britain until 1937) and the advent of the sunshine roof, which had been pioneered by a pre-war Labour-

From every angle the 1927 Packard Model 343 Murphy Convertible Sedan is a truly magnificent motor car. It somehow fits the scale of the country for which it was intended. This car was later owned by America's first World Champion racing driver, Phil Hill. With its superb straight-eight power unit, the Packard ranked as one of the finest cars in the world

dette limousine body on a Rolls-Royce Silver Ghost. Luggage boots began to be built into the rear of the body, and passenger comfort and roadholding were enhanced by the general adoption of shock absorbers on the suspension. By the end of the decade, cars were appearing on the road with independent suspension; front-wheel drive had made a tentative appearance, and the Armstrong-Siddeley and Cotal 'self-changing' epicyclic transmissions brought semi-automatic gear selection into practical use.

As the car was maturing, so the companies that built cars were changing. The older, smaller companies were either turning to the production of relatively high-priced specialist cars, or vanishing from the scene, unable to compete with the mass-producers. The great manufacturing corporations were gaining muscle; during the 1920s General Motors took a European stake with the acquisition of Vauxhall in Britain and Opel in Germany, while Morris and Rootes, both former cycle and motor agents, were expanding their manufacturing empires, Morris even attempting to compete in the French market by taking over the Léon Bollée factory at Le Mans to build a 12cv Morris-Léon Bollée which failed to achieve lasting success, although it was apparently better-built than the company's English products.

In the winter of 1927–28, somewhat implausible reports of an 'understanding' between Ford and General Motors began to appear in the Press; Henry Ford was stated to have agreed to purchase a 'substantial holding' in General Motors, while GM were supposed to have promised 'not to fight Mr Ford's new motor car if Mr Ford did not invade the high-priced motor-car field'. As Chevrolet was edging ahead of Ford in terms of sales, the whole business was obviously journalistic invention.

Yet the thing which really marked the 1920s was the rise of the small car, notable milestones being the Peugeot Quadrilette and the Austin Seven. In 1928, Morris had announced their Eight, which had an overhead camshaft, and which was thus a descendant – if on the wrong side of the blanket – of the Hispano-Suiza aero-engine, which Morris's new acquisition, Wolseley, had manufactured during the war years, applying the knowledge gained therefrom to the design of their post-war models. So the new Morris was really a Wolseley.

Soon, however, it had a companion which *did* admit its parentage, the Wolseley Hornet, the smallest six-cylinder car on the market, announced in the spring of 1930. But this Snark also turned out to be a Boojum, for the new car was almost indistinguishable from the Morris Eight, except for the two extra cylinders and a few inches of chassis added to accommodate them. The most noticeable difference was the price, which at £195 was £60 more than the comparable Morris, and the braking, which was Lockheed hydraulic rather than the mechanical system of the four-cylinder car. After the initial ecstasies – 'speed . . . effortless, exhilarating, from the staid forties through the smooth fifties to the swift sixties' – had died away, the customers decided that the Hornet wasn't exactly stunning value for money, and the model's sales began to

Right: the boat-backed Opel 8/25ps of 1920; this machine had a 2.2-litre, side-valve engine, with a four-speed gearbox, a transmission brake and shaft-drive
(National Motor Museum, England)

Below: a 1923 11.9hp Calcott, built by one of Britain's smaller manufacturers who were to succumb to William Morris's price war of 1921 and never recover. This car is powered by a four-cylinder, side-valve engine of 1645cc, and is of the type in production from 1920 to 1924. Calcott was taken over by the Singer concern in 1926
(National Motor Museum, England)

Left and above: two versions of Peugeot's 'sensation' of 1919, the Quadrilette; this model started life with a 628 cc, four-cylinder engine, but this had grown, by the time the car was withdrawn in 1929, to 694 cc; the three-speed gearbox was mounted in unit with the worm-driven rear axle. The 1921 car, *above*, has tandem two-seat bodywork, while the other version, made a year later, has offset, side-by-side seats (Peter Hampton and Peugeot, France)

fall away. So, after only eighteen months on the market, the Hornet, having failed in its manufacturer's aim of 'providing first-class express travel in a small car for the first time' was replaced by a design whose meretriciousness was far more studied.

The New Hornet cost only £3 10s more than its predecessor, and on the surface appeared to be an entirely new design, carrying a portly sixlight saloon body 7 ft long on a wheelbase of just 7 ft 6 in, and within an overall length of 11 ft 7½ in. This, of course, didn't leave much room for an item of such minor consideration as the engine, which had a few inches lopped off by replacing the vertical shaft which drove the dynamo and camshaft by a two-stage chain and belt drive. This was engineering by the standards of Procrustes, and, to carry the simile further, the docked power unit was shoehorned into the forward extremities of a chassis with the torsional rigidity of a bedstead. Pushing the engine forward over the front axle meant that the radiator had to lean over backwards to make room for it, while the forepart of the sump had to be amputated to accommodate axle movement. Ostensibly to increase passenger comfort, but probably also to reduce stresses on the flimsy, overloaded chassis, softer springs were fitted, and, to judge by contemporary opinion, all this jiggling

Right: representing the opposite ends of the 1922 motoring spectrum, an 11·9 hp Morris Cowley (*left*), William Morris's bullnosed 'motor for the masses' and a 10 hp Sporting Calthorpe, with alloy Mulliner bodywork and tuned engine good enough for a 60 mph top speed

about with weight distribution and suspension endowed the New Hornet with excellent road-holding – provided that it was going straight ahead on a perfect road surface. Corners proved the full horrors of letting the stylist and the salesman override the engineer's better judgment.

The cynicism which had overtaken the motor industry as manufacturers strove to maintain sales in the face of the depression was amply exemplified by the introduction seven months later of a sporting version of the Hornet, the Hornet Special, supplied in chassis form to coachbuilding companies, who cloaked its deficiencies in bodywork of exaggeratedly sporting aspect, so that the end result usually looked like something designed for the adolescent readers of the *Wizard* or *Hotspur*, with an aggressively louvred bonnet held down by leather straps, stoneguards on the headlamps and all the other accoutrements deemed necessary by the Walter Mittys of the Kingston Bypass.

Describing the new model, *The Autocar* hedged enough bets to build a maze: 'It is implied that the chassis is not sold as a racing job, but as a basis which is structurally correct and upon which keen coachbuilders can develop whatever they desire, for the capability of high performance is present in the design, and all the much desired refinements for speed work are already incorporated. The extent of the performance will largely be a matter of selected body style'.

Blame the shortcomings of the chassis on the coachbuilder, then . . . and perhaps the best summing-up of the Hornet Special came, again, from *The Autocar*: 'It is a most seductive motorcar'.

Seduction seems to have been the main aim of quite a few motor manufacturers in the difficult days of the slump as they busied themselves with the newly discovered art of selling sizzle, not steak, making plenty of employment for men such as C. F. Beauvais, an ex-staffman on *The Motor*, who suddenly blossomed forth as a much vaunted automotive stylist.

It was the activities of such window-dressers which prompted Ernest Appleby to remark, waspishly, in 1931: 'There are cars on the market today, the sales of which would not be increased by the bare chassis . . . there are one or two which as complete cars are most imposing, but when one opens the bonnet it is difficult to find in it the engine, so small is it in comparison with what one expects to find'.

It wasn't, of course, an entirely unexpected situation, for sales of small-engined cars had been on the increase for some time, and the most popular models were now those of 10 hp and under; the trouble was that motorists would insist on demanding all the equipment on a baby car that they had hitherto demanded on larger vehicles; and a crop of ludicrously proportioned saloons and coupés was the inevitable result. Final-drive ratios had to be lowered to cope with the extra weight, with the consequence that economy suffered and high-revving engines needed reboring at laughably short intervals – sometimes after 10,000 miles or less. . . .

Reading the correspondence columns of the contemporary press, one comes to the inescapable conclusion that motorists were then obsessed with running costs, but when an enterprising American firm attempted to abolish running expenses entirely, there were surprisingly few takers.

The company in question was the American Austin Company, of Butler, Pennsylvania, founded in 1930 with the bold idea of introducing the Austin Seven to the American market, which had been gravely affected by the depression to the extent that during the years 1930–32, personal income deteriorated by 42 per cent, car production fell by 75 per cent and expenditure on automobiles was down by 75.4 per cent. It was against such a backdrop that the American Austin firm launched 'the most sensational sales plan ever introduced in the motor world'. Quite simply, the scheme was to give every purchaser of a $435 Austin – or, at least, every purchaser living in Pittsburgh or Butler – free motoring for the first year (or 7500 miles) that the car was in his ownership. Provided that the owner always bought his petrol and oil from a Gulf Refining Company garage, and had his car serviced at the specified intervals, all the costs would be met by the American Austin company. It should have been a runaway success.

Russell K. Jones, sales vice-president of American Austin, explained the reasoning behind the scheme: '"Free Motoring" is the natural result of an analysis of our first year's sales and service experiences. There was a definite indication that Austin prospects and purchasers were always interested in the bantam's economy. Those who owned the cars knew about this economy. The public at large remained unconvinced and somewhat sceptical. We accepted the burden of proof and the result is "Free Motoring".

'The Austin under "Free Motoring" (or otherwise) offers the lowest cost power transportation in the world, including the streetcar and motor cycle. "Free Motoring" will rid us of the old sales bugaboo that "you could pay another hundred and get a larger four". You can; but under the new plan the Austin first cost of $435 does not have to be supplemented by any maintenance costs for 7500 miles, so that at the end of that mileage the cost to the purchaser is still $435. On the other hand, by adding the lowest average maintenance cost for other fours for 7500 miles to their lowest initial price, you get over $720. In other words, we offer a transportation saving of $285 or more for the first 7500 miles, or year, over that of our nearest price competitor. That means over $23 a month saving.

'Our plan, which will be tried elsewhere than in the places named when opportunity presents itself, is offered to persons with pruned budgets. We know it will work because in the last few days, when only a few persons outside

Above: even in very small packages, American cars of the 1920s and '30s radiated a certain style; this 1930 American Austin version of the Austin Seven exudes personality, but it was not to the taste of the American market, which, as before and since, fought off the incursion of the sub-compact. The company battled on through two receiverships to become the American Bantam Car Co in 1937, only to fold in 1941 (Ralph Davis, Glendale, California)

Right: a Pennsylvania gas station in 1935; the pumps advertised not only the price of the fuel, but also the taxes to be paid on it. In the state from which much of the period's oil originated, the car was a well established part of everyday life and this Chevrolet was one of the best sellers

our plant knew anything of it, we have been besieged with telephone calls, wires and letters asking for more details'.

Keen efforts were made to promote the scheme: a fleet of Austins fitted with radio loudspeakers cruised through the business districts of Pittsburgh and Butler broadcasting the details, but it seems that even in times of depression, the average American wasn't prepared to countenance motoring in something as tiny as the Austin, even though it had been restyled to suit indigenous tastes by Count Alexis de Sahknoffsky, better known for his work on Peerless luxury cars. The car was regarded as a joke, and appeared as such in a Laurel and Hardy film of the day, where its inability to accommodate Oliver Hardy's huge bulk was emphasised hilariously.

So the original manufacturers of 'the bantam car' went into liquidation in 1934; their successors fared a little better and, when the War came, designed the original Jeep. However, their factory wasn't capable of building the Blitz buggy in sufficient quantities, Willys and Ford came along with similar designs, and the company ceased production.

It's odd, because cars based more or less on the Austin Seven were successfully built in France (Rosengart), Germany (Dixi and BMW) and even Japan, where the Nissan Jidosha Kaisha built it as the Datsun (though they improved the styling and chassis design), which had the advantage that it was so small that its drivers didn't need to take a driving test.

If British-designed baby cars couldn't make the grade in America, an American-designed baby car could – and did – change the face of light car motoring in Europe. The story started in 1929, when Ford of Britain began work on an immense new factory on reclaimed marshland at Dagenham in Essex. While the factory was under construction, the depression hit Europe, and sales of the Model A Ford, even in its smallbore 14.9 hp 'beat-the-taxman' guise, began to sink. It was apparent that although the Model A was a light car in its homeland, it was regarded as over-expensive to run by European motorists. And when the vastly expensive Dagenham factory opened in 1931, having

cost £5 million – one would probably have to add two noughts to the figure to realise its present-day value – the company was desperate.

Not that it showed it to the outside world, however. To the motoring press, Ford of Britain seemed supremely optimistic and serene: 'In a period of difficulty and world-wide depression, the gigantic Ford undertaking at Dagenham was conceived and brought to fruition. It is an example of heroic pluck, the rearing of this hive of industry which stands like a lighthouse of hope in a storm-tossed sea of industry. It lifts the beckoning hand of faith in a time when many men are losing courage. It was not built in a period of boom when goods almost sold themselves; it was erected in a time of depression, its purpose and mission being to create international trade'.

Now, as Model A sales crumbled away, the company faced a make-or-break decision. Sir Percival Perry, the Chairman of Ford of Britain, wasn't at heart a small car man, and had been unmoved when, in 1928, Henry Ford had shown him drawings of a proposed new baby Ford to compete with the Austin Seven. Henry Ford retained his interest in the project, and in 1930 commanded a selection of 15 representative European light cars to be shipped to Dearborn for his inspection. Perry remained lukewarm until the sales position became so bad that he was forced to act. In the first five months of 1931, sales of cars over 10 hp fell by more than 10,000, while sales of cars under 10 hp rose by 2000.

'Every one in this country is agreed that the only path out of the present intense industrial depression is one of economy,' wrote Perry to Edsel Ford, 'and as this reacts upon the motor industry, it means that the tendency everywhere is to buy smaller and cheaper motor cars'.

Nevertheless, he sat tight for another three months before begging Henry Ford to let him have a light car that could be produced to save Dagenham from financial collapse. Ford agreed, and work on the design started in October. Engineering staff worked unceasingly on the task, even the 67-year-old Henry Ford wielding a spanner in the construction of the prototypes. Development time of this new 8 hp model must have been an all time record, for the designers first put pencil to paper in October 1931, and by February 1932 sixteen prototypes were running on the road.

Henry Ford wanted to produce this new model under a new marque name – 'Mercury' – and the prototypes were built with this name on their radiator badge, but Perry insisted that the car, soon christened Model Y, should be marketed as a Ford. It was unveiled to the public at the Ford Exhibition at the White City in February 1932 when the oldest Ford dealer, A. E. Rumsey of Bristol, dapper in gold-rimmed glasses and goatee beard, stepped forward to pull a dustsheet from one of the prototypes.

When they heard that the proposed price of this stylish little saloon was £120, which undercut both Austin and Morris, Ford dealers could scarcely contain their joy.

'Nothing like it has ever occurred in the motor industry in this country,' Perry wrote to Edsel Ford. 'Have never seen Ford dealers so enthusiastic . . . Public opinion and press everywhere proclaim 8 hp car just what is wanted here . . . Anticipate that many months will elapse before we can overtake the demand'.

Within a year of Perry's original request, the Model Y was in production and selling well. Out of 55,339 cars built at Dagenham in 1933, no fewer than 32,958 were Model Ys, and Ford of Britain was at last established as one of the Big Three in terms of sales.

The Model Y had dragged the company back from the edge of disaster, from a dreadful situation where Dagenham was living from hand to mouth; there was no exaggeration in the statement by a Ford director that: 'The Model Y was our only salvation'. By 1934 the Y held 54 per cent of the British market for cars under 9 hp.

Now Morris fought back, installing moving production lines at his Cowley factory and introducing a new 8 hp model whose styling was a blatant crib of that of the Model Y, but offering a number of refinements like hydraulic braking and a chassis strong enough to bear open tourer bodywork in unmodified form – the Dagenham directorate was always rather concerned about the

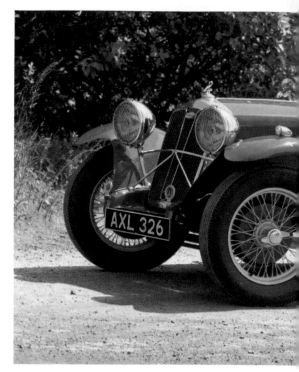

Above: small, relatively cheap, six-cylinder engines were the speciality of the Wolseley company in the early '30s. The Hornet Special sports car, of which this is a 1935 example, had a 1.6-litre, overhead-camshaft engine producing around 50 bhp and endowing a top speed of almost 80 mph

Above right: the Standard Big 9 saloon of 1932, with a 1287 cc, side-valve, four-cylinder engine, which gave the car a top speed of about 55 mph. In the background is an older Standard Nine, the Teignmouth of *c* 1930

Right: one of the early six-cylinder Volvos, the PV651-652 seven-seater, the first of which had appeared two years earlier, in 1929; this particular example has a 65 bhp engine and all-round hydraulic brakes. Earlier products of this Swedish concern, which began making cars in 1927, had been fitted with four-cylinder power units
(Skokloster Museum, Sweden)

rigidity of the Y's chassis when endowed with open bodywork, and only catalogued saloons, leaving outside specialists to cater to the fresh-air fiends.

The Morris Eight sold well – 100,000 by July 1936, less than two years after its introduction – but Perry had a dramatic ace up his sleeve. By cutting out unnecessary frills, the price of the Model Y was reduced from £120 to £115, then to £110. Finally, at the Ford Exhibition in the Albert Hall in 1935 came the dramatic announcement: 'A saloon car at £100, not only roomy and comfortable, but exceptionally economical'. Production costs and, more

Right: in 1932, Ford's British subsidiary moved from Manchester to Dagenham, where, initially, American cars were assembled. However, 1933 saw the introduction of the first all-British Ford, the 8 hp model Y, which was made available in two and four-door form, and was powered by a 940 cc, side-valve four. This example was made in 1936 and is typical of the £100 Ford Popular current from 1935 to 1937, the only fully equipped, four-wheeled saloon car ever sold at so low a price (National Motor Museum, England)

importantly, profit margins, had been cut to the very minimum to achieve this figure . . . but it achieved the desired result.

It was the first time a fully-equipped four-seater saloon car had been offered at £100; previous attempts to market a car at this figure had produced only austere open cars, like the Morris Minor £100 side-valve model announced as the chimes of midnight heralded the new year of 1931, and available only as a two-seater painted 'naval grey'. This didn't sell at all well, and Rover's contribution to the economy car stakes, the rear-engined £85 Scarab, didn't sell at all, for it was withdrawn from the market as soon as it was announced in 1931.

Now the Ford Popular struck exactly the right note, and once again saved the day for Dagenham: Ford's share of the '8hp and under' market, which had dropped to 22 per cent in 1935, soared to 41 per cent, giving the company over 22 per cent of the total market. Dagenham was firmly established as the biggest Ford operation outside the USA; although the Model Y was also built in Ford factories in France, Germany, Spain, Australia, New Zealand and Japan, it never achieved significant sales in those countries.

Its successor, the 7Y Ford Eight of 1937, was designed in Dagenham, and

Above: the Czechoslovakian Aero type 500 of 1933, fitted with a single-cylinder, two-stroke engine of 499cc, developing 10bhp at 2500rpm (Château de Grandson, Switzerland)

Above left: there were no breathalyser laws in the 1930s, when this 1932 Austin 16 was photographed outside the Church House Inn in Devon. The fabric-bodied saloon had a 2.2-litre, six-cylinder engine

Below: a 1936 Morris 8hp tourer, a splendid money-spinner for the company. Some 350,000 'Eights' of various types were sold, aided no doubt by the fact that it was a particularly easy car to drive and was both spritely and economical. Introduced in 1935, the Series I had a 918cc side-valve engine and sold for £132 10s in saloon form

was to set the style for British Ford economy models for more than two decades to come.

While mass-producers were coming to rely more and more on the smaller sorts of car as the Depression reshaped buying habits, luxury car makers went in entirely the opposite direction, building bigger and more flamboyant cars than ever. The 1920s had seen Ettore Bugatti's magnificent aberration, the Royale, with a straight-eight single ohc engine of 12.8 litres (the prototype's power unit displaced 14.7 litres!) based on one of Bugatti's aero-engine designs. But this car, originally intended for kings and heads of state, never reached its intended clientèle and, at half-a-million francs for the chassis alone, only found six purchasers among super-rich commoners between 1927 and 1933, so Ettore Bugatti, never one to let a good engine go to waste, adapted this power unit to drive high-speed railcars, one of which set a 122 mph record in 1936. All the Royales produced are now jealously guarded collectors' items, and at least one Bugattiste is so anxious to own an example of this model that he is reversing the original design progression by building a replica of the 'Golden Bug' round a railcar engine. . . .

Below and bottom: the Bugatti type 41 – the Royale – was intended by Ettore Bugatti as a car for kings; while no king ever owned a Royale, it became the king of cars, this magnificent 1929 example being one of only six Royales built, between 1927 and 1933. It is every extravagant inch a Bugatti and the magnificence of the engineering is beautifully demonstrated by the 250 bhp, 12.8-litre, straight-eight engine – destined, incredibly, to drive high-speed railcars. In recent years, at least one 'Royale' has been created round a railcar power unit

A year or so after the Royale appeared, the American Duesenberg brothers, Fred and August, put *their* concept of the super-luxury car on the market, encouraged by their backer, the flamboyant Erret Lobban Cord. Advertising superlatives (which for once in an American while were justified) greeted the appearance of the Duesenberg Model J in December 1928: 'It is a monumental answer to wealthy America's insistent demand for the best that modern engineering and artistic ability can provide . . . Equally it is a tribute to the widely-recognised engineering genius of FRED S. DUESENBERG, its designer, and to E. L. CORD, its sponsor, for these men in one imaginative stroke have snatched from the far future an automobile which is years ahead, and therefore incomparably superior to, any other car which may be bought today'.

The new Duesenberg had a straight-eight twin-ohc engine with four valves per cylinder displacing 6.9 litres, with a claimed output of 265bhp at 4250rpm: the chassis, which was exceptionally rigid in construction, came in two wheel-base lengths, short (11ft 10½in) and long (12ft 9½in), although one specially commissioned limousine had a wheelbase of 14ft 10in. The standard of engineering was exceptionally high, and much use was made of aluminium in the

Right: a Duesenberg Model J boat-tail speedster, with aluminium coachwork by Murphy and the 'basic' 265bhp, overhead-camshaft, straight-eight engine
(Donald L. Carr, Yellow Springs, Ohio)

Below: a 1935 Auburn 851, equipped with a supercharged, 4585cc engine, giving a power output of 150bhp and a top speed, via the two-speed rear axle, of 100mph. Each car was hand-built and carried a plaque to guarantee that it had been tested to over 100mph
(National Motor Museum, England)

car's construction; according to *The Motor*, the Model J was the world's most expensive car, with a chassis price of £2380, while typical American convertible bodywork brought the cost up to £3450. The Duesenberg looked better when it was fitted with open, sporty bodywork; somehow more formal carriagework didn't seem to suit the chassis so well. Not so long ago the author saw a Model J *sedanca de ville* which, although undoubtedly a very fine car, looked a little too high and narrow for its length. But the Duesenberg was a successful model considering the times that it was born in, with sales averaging one a week during its production life of 1928 to 1937, and is still one of the most sought-after of all antique cars. Current price, if you can find one, of a well preserved Model J Duesenberg is approaching £60,000 . . .

Doubtless you would have to pay even more for the highly exotic Model SJ Duesenberg, fitted, as its title suggests, with a supercharger, a centrifugal blower in the American idiom, running at five times crankshaft speed and boosting power output to a claimed 320 bhp, giving the car a top speed of 129 mph (the unsupercharged J was capable of 116 mph) and the ability to reach 100 mph from rest in 17 seconds. It was not a typical American car of its

Above: a 1932–3 version of the famous SS One fixed-head coupé, with a six-cylinder, 50bhp, side-valve engine
(Coventry Motor Museum, England)

Right: the Lagonda company produced its first V12-engined cars in 1937, in the shape of the V12 and Rapide; these were followed in 1938 by a more sporting version of the Rapide called the Le Mans, an example of which is pictured here. The 4480cc engine, common to both models, produced 225bhp in the Le Mans, 50bhp more than in the Rapide
(Stratford Motor Museum, England)

Below: a superb 1930 Duesenberg Model J convertible sedan. The Duesenberg was one of the few American cars with a true sporting pedigree. Although Fred and August Duesenberg were brilliant engineers, it took the skills of Erret Lobban Cord to sell the Duesenberg

day . . . or, for that matter, any other day but it remains one of the great American classics.

Nor, indeed, was the V12 Twin-Six Packard, whose 7298 cc power unit was silken-smooth, yet gave sizzling road performance. Introduced in 1930, this was Packard's second venture into dodecuplicity of cylinders, for they had built the original Twin-Six in 1916, and sold over 35,000 of them before production ceased in 1922. Designer of both Packard V12s was Colonel Jesse G. Vincent, who had gained his original inspiration from a V12 Sunbeam aero-engine imported into the United States just after the outbreak of World War I. This second V12 Packard lasted in production until 1939, and was bodied by the great American coachbuilders of the day; with a price tag of $4000–$6000, the Packard V12 represented excellent value for money, and a total of 5744 was built. A front-wheel-drive variant, built in 1932, didn't reach production.

Not that this was the only American V12, for Franklin, Lincoln and Pierce-Arrow announced luxury models with this engine configuration, while Cadillac, having persevered with the manufacture of V8s since 1915, brought out both V12 and V16 models during the 1930s. The other great American V16 of the 1930s was the Marmon, which had an 8-litre engine and made its appearance in 1931; to rival Cadillac and Marmon, another famous American quality car maker, Peerless, made plans for a V16, and built a prototype with an elegant Murphy body before falling sales caused them to abandon car production in 1931. Soon afterwards, however, prohibition was repealed, and Peerless resurfaced . . . as the Peerless Corporation, brewers of Carlings Ale, having decided that quenching America's thirst was a less risky business than pandering to its taste for luxury.

Nor were big V engines restricted to American manufacturers, for the Daimler company had been building their Double-Six since 1926, and continued to build it in capacities varying from 3743 cc to 7137 cc for the next decade, encouraged by Royal patronage; King George V had several Double-Sixes in his stables. Like its French contemporary, the Voisin V12, the Daimler Double-Six compounded complexity by not only having twelve cylinders but having twelve *sleeve-valve* cylinders . . .

Voisin, never noted for the conventionality of his engineering, also built a straight-twelve, again with the sleeve-valve engine that was his hallmark, while the Bucciali brothers, who used V12 Voisin engines in front-wheel-drive chassis, made a sixteen-cylinder 'Double-Huit'.

In 1931, Hispano-Suiza introduced their most spectacular model, the 9425 cc Type 68. As a publicity stunt, that great French motoring journalist Charles

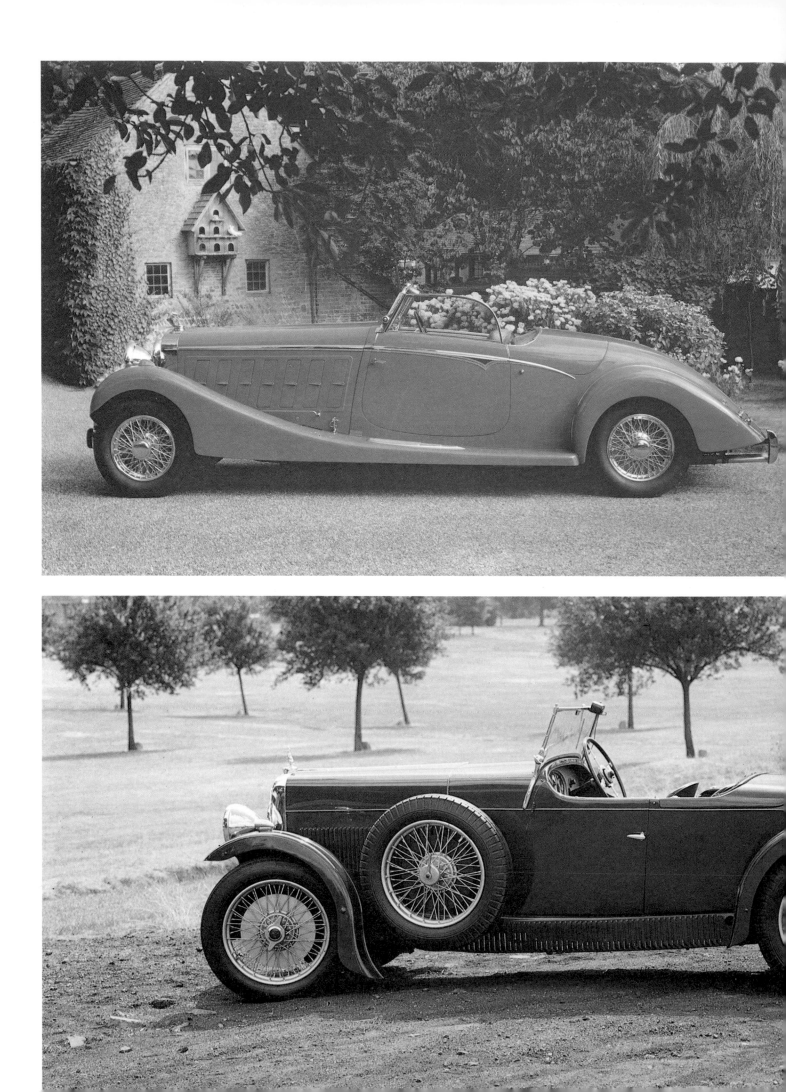

Left: a beautiful Hispano-Suiza 68bis, with Saoutchick coachwork and an 11.3-litre, 250 bhp, pushrod V12, built in 1934
(Peter Hampton)

Right: a 1931 replica of one of the 4½-litre, supercharged, short-chassis Bentleys raced by the Birkin-Paget team; this car was based on a production 4½-litre 'blower' – originally a drop-head coupé. The big Bentley, in supercharged and unsupercharged form, is one of the greatest and most famous British sports cars; the Birkin-Paget versions reached 125 mph
(National Motor Museum, England)

Below and bottom: the 1932 Alvis 12/60, with two-seat-and-single-dicky bodywork by Cross and Ellis, and its 1645cc, straight-four, pushrod engine, with SU carburettors, producing 52 bhp
(Coventry Motor Museum, England)

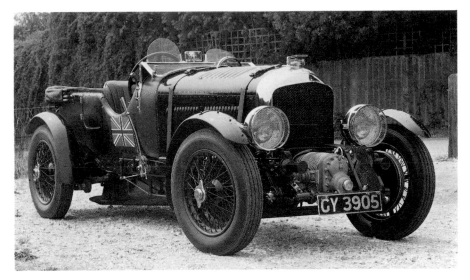

Faroux drove one of the first Type 68s at high speed from Paris to Nice and back, the car going straight from the run into Hispano's showrooms for the duration of the Paris Salon de l'Automobile. During that time, not one drop of oil is reported to have fallen from the hard-worked car. A couple of years later, the decision was taken to market the Type 68*bis*, which had a 20mm increase in stroke, bringing the swept volume to a respectable 11,310 cc, making this almost certainly the biggest production car of the 1930s.

By contrast the V12 Rolls-Royce Phantom III, announced in 1936, was almost a baby car, with an engine of 'only' 7.3 litres, but a performance that was decidedly un-Rolls-like. A couple of years ago, the author rode in a magnificently preserved Rolls P III belonging to the lady rally driver, the Hon Mrs Victor Bruce, who, despite her petite build and 79 years, was still capable of handling this massive car with perfect safety at speeds considerably over 80 mph . . .

Perhaps the most curious engine configuration of the 1930s was that announced right at the beginning of the decade by the National Factory of Automobiles of Barcelona. Although it never made production, the 3993 cc Nacional was a most interesting design, which had an engine constructed largely of elektron alloy with steel cylinder liners, and whose duralumin connecting rods ran directly on the crankshaft without bearings. Only two forward gears were provided, with maximum speeds in these ratios of around 40 and 80 mph respectively. So, what was noteworthy about the cylinder layout of the Nacional? It had ten cylinders in line.

A multiplicity of cylinders was not to remain the prerogative of the plutocrats for long: that arch-leveller, Henry Ford, worried by the fact that Chevrolet sales had overtaken Ford, due not only to the hiatus in production when the Model T gave way to the Model A, but also to the fact that the Chevrolet had six cylinders against the A's four, decided to bring the V8 engine, hitherto only used in expensive luxury cars, into the mass-production market.

The luxury V8 Lincoln was already being manufactured under the Ford banner but, like all the other V8s currently in production, it was costly to build, with its cylinders and crankcase cast separately. Ford was convinced that the way to mass-produce a V8 was to cast crankcase and cylinders in a single unit, a task then regarded as impossible by everyone except himself.

In May, 1930, the first experimental unit was completed; then followed months of trials as the design engineers attempted to build a prototype that could be translated into production terms. Some thirty different cars were made, and they even gave the octogenarian inventor Thomas Alva Edison a spin in one of them; but nothing seemed to satisfy Ford: 'He seemed to be getting madder and madder . . . he felt we weren't yet on the right track', recalled one of the engineers.

Then, in December 1931, the 68-year-old Ford personally took charge of the work, labouring like a human dynamo. The energy of the man must have

Left and below left: the 1½-litre Aston Martin 'Le Mans' of 1933, one of the first Astons to be produced after the company had been reorganised by A.C. Bertelli and W.S. Renwick. This car was fitted with the new single-overhead-camshaft engine, which featured dry-sump lubrication and gave the heavy car a top speed of 85mph. This was one of the most expensive 1½-litre sports cars made at that time, being offered at the same price as three MG Midgets or two Rileys
(National Motor Museum, England)

Below: the sports version, 508S Balilla, of Italy's most famous family saloon of the 1930s; this particular model was built in 1935 and was renowned for its excellent brakes and high gearing, the latter of which gave it a cruising speed of 70mph from its 1100cc engine
(National Motor Museum, England)

been amazing . . . and this must have been the most fascinating era in the Ford Company, for two immortal designs were being simultaneously developed under Ford's personal supervision, the V8 and the 8hp Model Y; both were ready for production in a staggeringly short space of time.

The V8 was announced to the public on 31 March, 1932; known in Ford terminology as the Model 18, it shared the streamlined radiator shell and more modern styling of the recently introduced Model B (Edsel Ford had insisted that the latter should be referred to as the 'Improved Model A', but his edict was generally ignored). Performance of the new model was electrifying, for it had a power-to-weight ratio unknown among its contemporaries: unfortunately, its cable brakes and overall chassis design were not really up to 80mph motoring, and it was not long before the Model 18 gave way to the vastly better Model 40. When that happened, the Model B was phased out, and soon all American Fords were V8s. But in Europe, where taxation authorities disliked powerful cars, the V8 attracted a high rate of duty, and several Continental countries were offered the B40, which retained the less heavily taxed Model

Left: a 1934 Talbot 105, designed by Georges Roesch, with a six-cylinder engine of 2970 cc, which gave the car a top speed of more than 90 mph; this model was fitted with a preselective gearbox, in conjunction with a centrifugal clutch
(National Motor Museum, England)

Right: the 1934 Graham-Paige Straight 8, which was fitted with a centrifugal supercharger rotating at $5\frac{1}{4}$ times engine speed, could reach 95 mph

Below: up to 1930, Nash concentrated on a range of six-cylinder-engined cars, but that year saw the introduction of a 4.9-litre straight-eight with overhead valves. This engine was steadily developed until 1942 and found homes under a great many different bonnets; the example shown here is a drophead coupé of 1932
(Château de Grandson, Switzerland)

B power unit which, incidentally, soldiered on throughout the decade in a variety of guises, surviving into the 1940s as the motive power for Spanish-built Ford trucks.

For those who could afford it, however, V8 motoring was a revelation, as *The Autocar* witnessed in 1936: 'To drive a V8 for the first time is to sample virtually a unique motoring experience. Everything that this machine does is achieved remarkably easily. It suits the laziest driving mood with its almost exclusively top-gear running abilities, as well as providing in the fullest measure a swift car for point-to-point travel when such is wanted. This car may be got moving by using first and second gears for just a few yards, and then the engine will pick up at once and pull away smoothly on the quite high top gear ratio. It runs thereafter even in slow-moving traffic and conditions that involve taking right-angle corners without the slightest need for a change-down to be made. Hills are the easiest prey to the car, all normal main-road gradients being treated as acceleration bursts if the driver wishes . . .'.

Forty years on, it's a view that can be endorsed wholeheartedly, for the author's first experience of 'the greatest thrill in motoring', as Ford advertising called the V8, was in Northern France with a 1936 Model 68 V8 which, despite the vast change in road and traffic conditions since it was built, could hold its own with most 1970s popular cars, cruised at 50–55 mph and had perfectly acceptable ride and roadholding. Yet in 1936 one could buy a fully-equipped Ford V8 saloon for just £250, a similar price to cars of only 10 or 12 hp from other British manufacturers (for by this time the V8 was built at Dagenham instead of being shipped over from Canada).

Indeed, the equipment and performance of these American cars put them in a class by themselves, even though their styling might not have wholly coincided with European taste. Some years ago, the author was talking to a motorist who had interspersed a succession of Rolls-Royces with a 5-litre Hupmobile Eight around the year 1936, and he remarked, 'the American car didn't suffer too badly in the comparison!'.

Features which we nowadays take for granted, such as radios, synchromesh gearboxes and independent front suspension, first appeared in mass-production terms on American cars.

Cheaper motoring really entered the realms previously reserved for the exotica when the straight-eight Graham appeared in 1934 with a supercharger as a standard offering. A six-cylinder version was announced in 1936, capable of 90 mph, and boasting overdrive on the upper two of its three gears; a button on the dashboard controlled the operation of this overdrive, which, when the button was pulled out, engaged automatically at speeds over 40 mph, and disengaged below 30 mph, when a freewheel came into operation.

Overdrive had first appeared in 1934 (although some earlier cars had a geared-up top speed, which wasn't quite the same thing) on that remarkable (and ugly) car, the Chrysler Airflow.

Above: Henry Ford rushed the 1932 V8 into production, so that early models had many minor teething troubles. But within a very short space of time the V8 had established itself as one of the all-time great cars. This 1935 Model 48 Roadster, fitted with non-standard steel wheels, shows the elegance of line achieved by the mid-1930s V8s

The greatest thrill in motoring.

Left: Ford advertised that driving a Ford was the greatest thrill in motoring a claim underlined by the sketchy brakes of the first, 1932 models which were not up to the V8's sports car performance

Brainchild of Cal Breer, the Airflow's 'back-to-front' design was the result of wind-tunnel testing, and proved to be too extreme for the average purchaser, who liked a car to have a recognisable bonnet (so later Airflows had a curious 'widow's peak' grafted on to their front contours). Although it wasn't a great success, the Airflow did condition the public for the streamlines that were to come from other makers, and, in this context, it's worth noting that the wind-tunnel had become part of the car stylist's stock-in-trade relatively early on, although its use was by no means universal. Ford had developed an experimental streamlined car in their wind tunnel as early as 1930, and in 1932 used wind-tunnel techniques to improve the airflow around their new Lincoln models. In view of this, recent claims that the wind-tunnel wasn't used in the development of the Lincoln-Zephyr, the first Ford product to have a monocoque body/chassis unit, seem surprising for its shape was every bit as slippery as that of the Airflow. Developed by Dutch-born John Tjaarda under the patronage of Edsel Ford, the Lincoln-Zephyr kept the Lincoln name afloat at a time when falling sales of its more conventional models seemed likely to cause the marque to vanish from the scene altogether. Its sleek, unconventional lines even drew qualified praise from the English press: 'A certain amount of adjustment is needed as regards the unusual appearance, but from all points of view a remarkable car has been produced'.

It wasn't long before streamlining was all the rage in Europe, too; Panhard gave birth to the curious 'Dynamique', with spatted front wings and 'China-closet' curved windows at the sides of its narrow windscreen (which boasted

Above: Henry Ford's once-avowed intention of never building 'an engine with more spark plugs than a cow has teats' had evaporated by the mid 1930, as Ford V8s maintained the marque's prodigious record of sales successes. Ford introduced the 3.6-litre V8 in 1932 at $460 and in 1935 one million were sold. This is a 1937 sedan, built in England but broadly similar to the American product

Below: Carl Breer designed a range of aerodynamic cars in the 1930s, which were sold as Chryslers and De Sotos. They were known as Airflows and pioneered 'overdrive' gearing. The engine was mounted well forward. This is the cheapest Chrysler version, sold in England as the Heston and powered by a 4.9-litre, eight-cylinder engine; it was made in 1937, the year in which the model was dropped (National Motor Museum, England)

Above: the strange rear-engined Crossley RE of 1932, based very closely on the earlier Burney Streamline, designed by Sir Dennistoun Burney. Various engines were tried by Burney, but Crossley used their own 2-litre straight-six, with a power output of 61 bhp (left). The model was notable only because of its unusual design and was not a success, soon being dropped from the range. Not how the designers of the 1930s were convinced that it was more important to streamline the tail rather than the front, of the car
(National Motor Museum, England)

Below: a 1935 Hillman Aero Minx, with bodywork by Thrupp & Maberley; this 10 hp, side-valve car was to form the basis of the Talbot and Sunbeam Talbot Tens
(Coventry Motor Museum, England)

Below: the 1935 Tatra type 77A built in Koprivnice, Czechoslovakia, was designed by Hans Ledwinka, regarded by many as one of the automobile industry's few geniuses. Ledwinka drew on the Hungarian Paul Jaray's very advance understanding of aerodynamics to determine the shape of the car, which was powered by a 3.4-litre, 70 bhp, air-cooled, V8 engine, mounted behind the rear axle. The car was capable of 95 mph even though its body had been developed theoretically, not tested in a wind tunnel

three wiper blades) and grilles over the headlamps which were miniature replicas of the sloping radiator grille. The Art Deco interiors of these Panhards were every bit as eccentric as their outward appearance.

Paul Jaray's work for Maybach attracted attention, too . . . but mostly was regarded as a Showtime eccentricity: 'Reminiscent of submarine practice, the Maybach', commented *The Motor*'s man at the 1935 Paris Salon, 'with barrelled body and wings . . . the headlamps are recessed into the wings'.

With his Aerosport, which appeared at the same Salon, Gabriel Voisin returned to a theme he had successfully used on racing cars a decade before: the body as full-width aerofoil, with wheels set in the pontoon wings which formed an integral part of the design. To the eyes of 1935, the Voisin looked thoroughly odd, but then the design was a quarter-century ahead of its time; it is, indeed, vaguely reminiscent of the Mark II Jaguar range of the 1960s . . . It was far more futuristic than the 'car of tomorrow' shown at the 1936 Salon by Peugeot, which would have passed almost without remark had it not been for the aircraft-type stabilising fin fitted at the rear of the bodywork. Because of this useless appendage, the Peugeot attracted more attention than another truly prophetic vehicle at the same show, the Czechoslovakian Tatra 77a, designed by Hans Ledwinka, which, like the Voisin, had full-width aerofoil bodywork, although it went further by mounting its air-cooled V8 engine and transmission at the rear of the backbone chassis. 'Everything', claimed the car's catalogue, 'which science has allowed to be conceived or established has been put to practical use in the design of the Tatra car, without regard for traditional attitudes. Everything is new about this car, whose bold concept attains perfection . . . The economy resulting from the latest developments applied to the Tatra is unbelievable. The car is so perfect that its engine works without effort with unequalled results. Its longevity is increased because it is mechanically more perfect . . . For twelve years, Tatra has been using independent suspension, and has been followed in this respect by manufacturers the world over, proving the correctness of the views of the pioneer'.

Above and left: streamlining found its way onto several cars of the 1930s, and some of those models were very sleek indeed. The Peugeot 402, which was introduced in 1935 with a 2.1-litre engine, was certainly streamlined, but its body was so wide that the chassis had to be fitted with special outriggers in order to support the weight. Even the headlights were concealed behind the radiator grille so as not to spoil the streamline effect as can be seen on the 1937 model pictured here (Peugeot collection, France)

Above: the amazing Panhard Dynamique of 1937. It featured, apart from unique styling, a backbone chassis, torsion-bar suspension, worm drive and a central driving position

Below: the Humber Vogue of 1936; this model was introduced by Humber in 1932 and was aimed at women drivers. Although not as slow as some of its predecessors, the Vogue was underpowered, having a heavy body and a 12 hp engine of 1700 cc
(Coventry Motor Museum, England)

Unfortunately, the Tatra achieved little success outside its homeland, unlike the contemporary light car, also streamlined and also fitted with an air-cooled rear engine, which was also shown for the first time in 1936 by its designer, Ferdinand Porsche. But then Porsche had a more powerful backer than Ledwinka, for his 'KdF-Wagen' ('Strength through Joy Car') had been developed under the patronage of that most enthusiastic of motorists, Adolf Hitler, who proposed that the car should be available to Germans at a price of around £55. The more who bought, the lower the price would be, Hitler claimed; but the true *raison d'être* of this 'People's car', or 'Volkswagen' was that it would keep the car-buying public's money inside Germany, thus strengthening the Fatherland's currency . . . moreover, when War inevitably came, it would be very easy to adapt the Volkswagen for military use.

At the 1938 Berlin Motor Show, Dr Goebbels, the Nazi Propaganda Minister, said 'The Twentieth Century is the period of the motor car. Since the National Socialist revolution, politics no longer lag behind the development of applied science. Politics show the direction applied science is to take . . . The export of motor vehicles in 1937 exceeded the 1932 production total'.

To emphasise the direction in which politics would now push applied science, the Führer opened the Show with a speech giving the official Party line on the Volkswagen. 'The people's car will soon be produced.', Hitler claimed. 'It will make life pleasanter and satisfy the longing of thousands for the motor car. In time, it will become the general means of transport for the German people.'

Excusing the delays in getting the Volkswagen project under way, Hitler

continued: 'If we have not progressed so rapidly in the production of this car as was done in other spheres, it is because there were two main difficulties to be overcome. First of all the requisite purchasing power had to be created and, secondly, lengthy research had to be made to produce this low-priced machine with a maximum performance for the minimum horse power. The proposed car will not only be the best, but the cheapest car in the world, and will give 100 per cent service'.

Few Volkswagens were, in fact, built before the war, and even Adolf Hitler, one suspects, might have been surprised that the car to which he had been sponsor would survive until the 1970s and become the best-selling car of all time in the process. It had been, apparently, originally inspired by one of Ledwinka's earlier designs . . .

At the same period that he was backing the Volkswagen, Hitler was also pouring money into the Mercedes and Auto-Union Grand Prix cars, to ensure Nazi dominance on the racing circuits of the world, and had ordered the construction of a system of high-speed motorways – *Autobahnen* – of which some 800 miles had been completed by 1937, at a cost of £56,000 a mile.

The construction of specially-designed motor roads had been mooted as far back as the 1890s, when schemes for a motorway from London to Brighton were published: but it took a dictatorship to introduce the concept to Europe.

Even outside the totalitarian states, the face of motoring was altering radically, with production concentrated more and more in the hands of the big batallions, who were thus able to educate the public into buying cars which were, in many ways, inferior to those they supplanted, though the new models were bedizened with all kinds of tempting gadgets. Many motorists of the 1930s were, anyway, first-time buyers, who didn't have a standard of comparison; and there was now a vast number of motorists – they were no longer an eccentric minority, for a survey taken in 1935 proved that there were some 35 million motor vehicles in use throughout the world.

Inevitably, this growth of motoring led to an increase in restrictions on the motorist. In 1936, for the first time, British motorists had to undergo a driving

Above: this straight-eight limousine was made at the height of Packard's 'classic' period in 1936. 1935 saw the first slanting radiator grille, while wire wheels, solid front axles, mechanical brakes and automatic chassis lubrication were major items which disappeared in the following year

Below: the most successful motor car ever, in terms of numbers sold, was the Volkswagen Beetle. Over 20 million have been built and the car is still in production in a number of developing countries

Above: one of the earliest British motor car companies was the Wolseley concern, whose first cars were designed by Herbert Austin, better known for selling cars under his own name. In 1927, however, the Wolseley organisation was forced into liquidation and was taken over by Lord Nuffield's Morris company; rationalisation of the range was slowly put into effect, thereafter, Morris engines replacing the Wolseley units, in all cases, by 1938. The model pictured here was made before this time, however, being a 1936 21 hp saloon, with a straight-six 3-litre engine. Somewhat inconveniently, the body was not fitted with a boot lid, access to the luggage compartment gained by folding the rear seat

test, and a 30 mph speed limit was imposed in towns. American motorists, it seems, fared even worse: 'Detroit motorists who get into trouble with the police are liable to be sent to the city's new psychopathic clinic, where experts decide whether or not the erring ones should be allowed to drive. Seventeen standard traffic offences are staged with the aid of model cars. "Patients" must spot them all, and also describe what action should be taken when various emergencies arise'.

By 1937, the American economy was on the upturn: sales of cars were second only to those in the record year of 1929, though because of this there were no startling innovations in the new car models. 'It is not the habit of the industry to make daring innovations in the midst of a good buying cycle,' wrote an American journalist. 'Such innovations are considered to be better saved for the day when car owners must be prodded to buy new vehicles.'

Right: Oldsmobile built a number of six-cylinder and eight-cylinder-engined models during the 1930s and this is the company's 'Six' of 1937, with a 4.2-litre engine producing 95 bhp at 3400 rpm
(Skokloster Museum, Sweden)

Nevertheless, there were improvements: wheelbases were generally longer and bodies larger to give more interior space, while headroom was increased by lowering the floor level, which also helped to give passengers more leg room. Seats were wider, by as much as six inches, and luggage boots were more capacious. Engine sizes were on the increase, always a good economic pointer, though some of the extra power was obviously needed to cope with the increased weight of those bigger bodies – and with all those accessories now deemed necessary by American motorists. Most of them now had heaters fitted to their cars, often in conjunction with windscreen defroster, while some 30 to 35 per cent of new car buyers were reported to be ordering radios to be fitted to their cars, though the general trend towards all-steel bodies had caused car radio manufacturers some reception problems. The all steel 'turret top' roof had appeared in 1935, and since then, bodies had become almost entirely made of steel, with wood retained only as a medium to nail the upholstery to; this development was due because steel mills were now capable of rolling wider steel sheets, and because the art of pressing and welding steel had made notable advances. But whether these new techniques really meant that Chevrolet were justified in describing the all-steel body on their 1937 models as 'crashproof' is a debatable point.

America was now unquestionably the world's most car-conscious country; the world-wide average number of people to each car was 66, in America the average was only 5.6. Second most car-conscious country, surprisingly, was New Zealand, with 10.5 per car, followed by Canada, with 10.9 per car and then Australia, with 13.8 per car. There were 24.5 Frenchmen to each French-

Right and below : the Packard 115 coupé, of 1937. This model had a great deal in common with the 120, which had been introduced two years earlier; one major difference, however, was that the 115 was fitted with a 3.6-litre, six-cylinder engine as opposed to the straight-eight of the sister car, which by 1937 had grown from 3.7 to 4.6 litres

Left: one of the great luxury cars, this straight-eight Packard of 1939 spent its working life with a Swedish tobacco company (Skokloster Museum, Sweden)

Bottom: this 1939 Cadillac 135 bhp V8 was part of the Swedish Royal Family's collection; this actual car was used frequently by King Gustav V (Skokloster Museum, Sweden)

registered car, while in the United Kingdom the average number of people to every car was 30.6.

At the far end of the scale came China, with no less than 13,123 Chinamen to each car . . .

Since many of the world's countries had no indigenous motor industry, there were obvious export outlets; America sold between 9 and 13 per cent of its total output to overseas customers during the 1930s, while Britain, admittedly with a smaller annual production, had increased its export sales to more than 17 per cent by 1937. The total export figure of 1936 was almost double the overseas sales made in 1933. The turning point in British car exports was apparently 1931, when Britain went off the gold standard, making English cars financially more attractive to overseas buyers. A typical example was that of Vauxhall, who in 1929 exported only 150 cars; in 1931 the figure had risen to 800, by 1932 it was up to 1750, more than doubled the following year to 3650 and in 1934 reached 6800. Of course, Vauxhall was helped by being part of the General Motors organisation, which meant that the company could take advantage of its adoptive parent's assembly plants across the world for sales and service facilities, as well as for the conversion as necessary to left-hand-drive.

Ford, of course, had assembly plants all round the world, and Rootes were also establishing footholds overseas, encouraged, no doubt, by reports like the one which stated: 'In particular, the Hillman Minx has proved a "best seller",

Left and far left: a 1934 Rolls-Royce Phantom II, with Thrupp & Maberley coachwork, commissioned by the Maharajah of Rajkot; the Maharajah's motto is displayed on the car and it can be roughly translated as 'an impartial ruler of men of all kinds of faith'
(Stratford Motor Museum, England)

Below and below left: commissioned by H.E. Nawab Wali-ud Dowla Bahadur, the President of Hyderabad State, India, this 1926 New Phantom 40/50hp Rolls-Royce saw service right up until 1948. The immaculate aluminium body was built by the Barker company
(Stratford Motor Museum, England)

not least because of its roominess in its own horsepower class – a point appreciated in most overseas countries, where men are men'.

They usually are, of course, and one can hardly imagine the overbodied Minx having much appeal as a virility symbol, though one Mr Bhattarchargee of Calcutta was recorded as owning a fleet of three of them. . . .

The Minx was introduced in 1932 with the object of moving Hillman into the mass market. It utilised the firm's 1185cc, side-valve engine and sold initially, on the domestic market, for £159. The model was very successful and was kept in the sales vanguard by virtue of progressive updating right up to the outbreak of war. Mr Bhattarchargee might well have added a little variety – even spice – to his collection with the sporting Aero-Minx, a variant which was introduced in 1933.

There were, too, the prestige sales of British cars to foreign royalty: Rolls-

Royce cars, of course, led this field, followed by Daimler and their alter ego Lanchester, for these two oldest of British firms had combined during the Depression. Humbler makes appealed to the humbler monarchs: Prince Mahomet Ali of Egypt had a Humber Pullman limousine, while an Armstrong-Siddeley was the chosen mount of the Attah of Igbitta Lokojo, from Nigeria.

On the other hand, during 1937 Britain imported £1,515,836-worth of motor vehicles and accessories; oddly enough, considering that there were already rumours of war in the air, the only country to have increased car sales to Britain was Germany, which in 1937 sold British motorists £86,202-worth of

Left : the archetypal British sports car of the 1930s was the MG – wind-in-the-hair motoring without bankruptcy and with a great sporting tradition. This is a 1937 TA, with long-stroke, 1290cc, pushrod-overhead-valve engine

Right and above right : this Alfa-Romeo 8C-2300 came second in the 1935 Le Mans 24-hour race and was later used on the road by Mike Hawthorn. The car was designed by Vittorio Jano and was fitted with bodywork by Touring of Milan; its twin-overhead-camshaft, eight-cylinder engine (*above right*) gave the car a top speed of 115mph from its supercharged 2336cc (National Motor Museum, England)

motor cars, against £5875-worth in 1936. All other countries showed a more or less marked drop in sales to Britain.

Just imagine . . . in the Spring of 1938 the British motorist with £700 in his pocket could choose from over 400 different cars of around 70 different makes, ranging from the 7.8hp Austin Seven at £112 to the 23.8hp Talbot at £695, and there were still the expensive models like the Alfa-Romeo, Bugatti, Bentley, Autovia, Rolls, Hispano *et al*, at prices in excess of £700. . . .

This was, however, the high point of the recovery from depression: by the summer exports and imports were both in decline. In the first seven months of

1938, American cars worth £415,322 were imported into Britain, compared with £841,585 for the same period in 1937. German imports, £54,720 in July 1937, plummeted to £8708 in July 1938.

Right: a 1938 BMW 328 and a Bucker Jungmeister trainer aircraft of the Luftwaffe

Then came Munich. Already the car manufacturing companies were involved in the setting up of 'shadow factories' for the production of war material: now the threat of war with Germany once again proved how vital the motor vehicle was to the nation. Cars were used to evacuate children, invalids and hospital patients from areas vulnerable to aerial attack; they were used to mobilise the ARP and the emergency services; they were used to transport the Prime Minister, Neville Chamberlain, to and from the aerodromes in Britain and Germany in his high-speed dash to the Four-Power Conference at Munich with Hitler, which averted the war for a year.

'And what of the private individual?' asked *The Autocar*. 'Supposing it had been necessary for London to be evacuated, then London alone had 140,000 private cars, capable of carrying, at need, some 500,000 persons, which might well have proved a vital factor in relieving other forms of transport.'

In their inimitable fashion, the British authorities rose to the occasion by discouraging people from owning cars by announcing an increase in the annual road tax from 15s to £1 5s per horsepower, and increasing the tax on petrol from 8d to 9d a gallon. This brought the amount contributed to the national purse by the motorist to £104 million, more than one-tenth of the total. Justifying the increase, which was to come into effect from the beginning of 1940, the Chancellor, Sir John Simon, showed once again that the motorist was regarded as having a bottomless pocket: 'Side by side with the reduction of income tax in 1934, my predecessor reduced the private car tax to 15s per horse-power. The users of private cars, who very largely correspond with the income tax paying classes, have, for five years, enjoyed the benefit of this reduced scale

Below: a rare convertible example, assembled in Britain, of Citroën's famous 7 cv model, with independent suspension, front-wheel drive and unitary construction. Produced from 1934 to 1957, the *Traction Avant* Citroën was, in its saloon version, the typical French police car of the period. President de Gaulle's personal car was a special, Chapron-bodied 15/6 *Traction* (National Motor Museum, England)

Below right: during the war, Ford built many four-wheel-drive vehicles; this is one seen leaving the Dagenham, Essex, factory.

of taxation. Therefore, I feel bound to ask them, in these stern times, to submit to a substantially increased scale.'

With bland ignorance of the possible consequences of his proposals, Sir John commented: 'We ought, I am sure, to avoid any measures which would have a generally depressing effect upon industry . . .'.

Shortsighted MPs welcomed the tax on 'luxury motoring' as a means of curtailing the manufacturer of motor cars and lessening the traffic on the roads, together with the burden of their upkeep. It was as though the 19th century mechanophobe, Colonel deLaet Waldo Sibthorpe, who regarded engineers as lower than vermin, was once again stalking the corridors of Westminster to heed the development and progress of the car.

Before the tax came into effect, however, a more effective curtailment of private motoring was declared, as Britain went to war against Germany. Once again the motor vehicle, reviled in peacetime as a rich man's plaything, would prove the vital hinge on which battles were won or lost. More than ever before, this was to be a petrol war. . . .

The French called it the 'Drôle de Guerre', the British the 'Phoney War'; under any name it meant that for a while after war had been declared,

little seemed to happen. There were a few air raid warnings, some women and children were evacuated from London. Industry, far from increasing output, actually had less work in hand than before. Although the Earls Court Motor Show was cancelled, some manufacturers actually introduced 1940 models. The original Ford Anglia, for instance, was a 'war baby', announced after the outbreak of hostilities.

Ford was in a particularly difficult situation, for the Government was reluctant to place orders with the company, maintaining that the situation of its factory at Dagenham, on the River Thames near London, was too vulnerable. So Ford camouflaged the factory site under the guidance of experts from the Royal Air Force: 'an elaborate picture was painted on the roof to make the buildings appear from the air as though they were a piece of marshland with tracks running through it'. Even so, most Government departments still hung fire, although the Ford company was still fulfilling a pre-war Air Ministry order for six-wheeler trucks and winches for Balloon Command, while there were small orders for five-ton trucks from other Ministries, and there was a special agreement with the Ministry of Agriculture and Fisheries, dating from the early part of 1939, that Ford should produce tractors against the eventuality of war being declared, to be stored in depots all over England until they should be needed. The Ministry had agreed to order 3000, with the proviso that if war didn't break out, the company would take them back at cost price. In fact, the tractors proved vital, for when war broke out, 3,000,000 additional acres of land were put under cultivation for food crops.

Apart from this, life went on pretty much as usual. Dagenham was still working a forty-hour week, there was plenty of food (although already rationed) in the canteens, cigarettes were still plentiful. However, heads of departments were given secret instructions for immobilising the factory in the event of enemy invasion.

Some V8 engines were supplied for use in a dangerous device called a 'degausser' used to explode magnetic mines from a distance: some of these units were installed in Wellington bombers so that they could detonate these mines by flying over them at a low level.

Then, early in April, Hitler struck. Denmark and Norway were invaded and suddenly the 'phoney war' had ceased to be a joke.

When the war broke out, the War Department owned just over 50,000 vehicles of all types, from motor cycles to three-ton trucks, and had commandeered another 26,000 from civilian users: but when the Low Countries and France fell, most of these vehicles were lost or abandoned at Dunkirk, and only 5000 returned to Britain.

Above right: the fire engine stationed at the Ford works had plenty of fires to put out during the blitz, even though the Ford complex was disguised by being painted to appear from the air to be marsh land

So motor manufacturers had to work flat out on providing replacements; they also had to adapt their manufacturing skills to the production of a wide variety of military equipment of all kinds under the 'shadow factory' scheme. Leyland Motors, for instance, had opened a vast new engine and transmission plant, which was now turned over to making tanks, bombs and other munitions. Daimler built two 'shadow factories' near its works in Coventry; these were initially wholly engaged in the production of Bristol Mercury, Pegasus and Hercules radial aero-engines.

As the centre of so much of the motor industry, Coventry was particularly important to the British war effort. The Germans, whose anticipations even ran to having aerial photographs of important car factories available in 1939, were obviously aware of this, and their attempts to bring the motor industry to a standstill added a new word to the English language – 'Coventrated', meaning complete and utter destruction by bombing. On the night of 14 November 1940, German bombers destroyed the centre of Coventry, and the raids continued until the following April. The city had preserved much of its medieval heritage, despite its industrialisation, and many historic buildings were destroyed (although the crazy buildings in Much Park Street occupied by Lea-Francis Cars, surely the oldest ever used as part of a motor factory, survived).

Around 170 high explosive bombs and mines were dropped on Daimler's Radford factory, which was seventy per cent destroyed – yet production was increased, as the company had expanded into 44 dispersal factories reaching from Newcastle to North Wales.

Among the other casualties of the blitz on Coventry was the famous Motor Mills, birthplace in 1896 of the British motor industry. Daimler had moved out in the 1930s, however, and at the time of its demise the building was being used as an Air Ministry store.

Daimler's contribution to the war effort was extremely varied – gun turrets, parts for Bren and Browning guns, rocket projectors, four-wheel-drive scout cars and armoured cars, buses, and, during the final year of the war, a large Government order was received for a fleet of cars for the use of high-ranking officers once Germany had been occupied.

Other companies, apart from using their normal production expertise, also contributed to the war effort with their byproducts: Dagenham byproducts were used in the manufacture of Toluole and Xylole for explosives and varnish for aircraft fabrics, while the slag from its blast furnace was converted into Tarmac, which was used to build runways for the Battle of Britain airfields. Before the war was over, the runways and dispersal points of fifty-six airfields scattered over ten counties had been constructed of Tarmac reclaimed from the slag from the Ford furnace.

Of course, the factories were always on the alert for enemy attack, although it was rare that an air raid was as leisurely as the occasion in 1940 when Ford workers were playing a local team at football on the Ford Sports Ground: the match had to be halted seven times due to enemy action, but was eventually played to a finish, the referee taking note of time lost in the air raid shelters so that full time was played. 'Fords won by four to two,' ran a contemporary report, 'and by the time the last whistle sounded, the field and the factory were ringed with smoke and fire, the largest conflagration being the oil tanks at Purfleet, which were belching flame and smoke many feet into the air.'

Often the raids had more tragic consequences, like the attack on Vauxhall's Luton factory in August of the same year, in which 39 people were killed and 40 injured: despite the heavy damage, the plant was back in production six days later. Vauxhall were another company with a widely varied war production, turning out 5,000,000 jerricans, 250,000 Bedford trucks, armour-piercing

Top: Field-Marshal Montgomery's staff car 'Old Faithful' was a 1941 Humber Super Snipe powered by a 4.1-litre engine. The car's body-work is by Thrupp & Maberley; it saw service with 'Monty' between 1942 and 1943 in the Western Desert campaign from the Nile to the Sangro
(National Motor Museum, England)

Above: vehicles in the element for which they were intended; the photograph shows heavily equipped infantry advancing in Jeeps and tracked vehicles along a road in Coutances, Normandy, in July 1944

Above: in the desert, four-wheel drive was a necessity and, as often happens, four-wheel drive development took great leaps to meet military needs

shells, 4,000,000 venturi tubes for rocket launchers, 95 per cent of the components for the first twelve British jet aircraft engines and Churchill tanks, which were developed from drawing board to production within a year. Over 5000 of these 38-ton tanks were produced, and a successor was under development when the war ended.

During the early part of the war, there were few restrictions on the movement of labour, and some workers even moved from Dagenham to Coventry in search of higher pay. Others joined up, but before long there was more need for skilled men in the factories than at the front. Yet by 1941 there was a shortage of suitable employees, and women were being trained for jobs which were formerly thought of as suitable only for men: when the war ended there were 3500 women employed by Ford alone.

Despite the difficult conditions that the motor factories were working under, the vehicles they produced were beyond reproach: they were even sought after by the enemy, as battle orders signed by Rommel, captured early in 1942, proved: 'For desert reconnaisance only captured English trucks are to be employed, since German trucks stick in the sand too often . . . all captured motor transport is to be distributed to the fighting companies for the transport of personnel . . . all German trucks are to be echelon transport (second line transport)'.

Praise came from the Allied commanders, too: Montgomery's famous caravan, and the truck which pulled it, were built by Ford. Three weeks after the invasion of Normandy, 'Monty' found time to write to Dagenham: 'The caravan which your works produced for me has come ashore safely in France, and since I came over here I have been using it to the full as my operations room. There is no doubt you have produced a most excellent vehicle'.

A Ford V8 utility car, equipped with desert tyres, was acquired by the Royal Air Force in Cairo in 1942: first it carried Air Chief Marshal Sir Arthur Tedder (who became Lord Tedder, Marshal of the Royal Air Force); then from El Alamein to Tripoli it was the transport of Air Marshal Sir Arthur Coningham. From Tripoli it was shipped to Malta and then to Sicily and Italy, carrying

Left: the Jeep in action; airmen of the 351st Fighter Squadron, 353rd Fighter Group, loading equipment for transfer to their aircraft, prior to the D-Day invasion of 6 June 1944

many notable Air Force Commanders, including Air Vice-Marshals Broadhurst, Dixon and Foster, ending its war in Linz, in Austria. In August 1945, Air Vice-Marshal Foster commented that the Ford, although somewhat battered externally . . . is still mechanically absolutely sound and in regular use.'

Officialdom was surprised by the scale on which the motor industry had become accustomed to operate. Although the Carden-Loyd Bren Gun Carrier had been designed round the engine and rear axle of the Ford V8, it wasn't until September 1941 that the Ministry of Supply asked Dagenham to build the complete vehicles. Their initial order called for 25 a week.

'That is too few,' the Ford management told them. 'With our capacity, at least a hundred a week can be built, and we do not believe in running our factory except at the highest possible pitch.'

Amazingly, it took several weeks to convince the Ministry that such a rate of output was possible, but in January 1944, two years after the Bren Gun Carrier had gone into production at Dagenham, the factory was turning out two hundred of these complex tracked vehicles a week. Nearly 14,000 were built before the end of the war in Europe.

Perhaps the most amazing achievement of the Ford production methods was the building of Rolls-Royce Merlin aero engines in unprecedented numbers in a shadow factory at Urmston, Manchester, not far from the old Ford factory at Trafford Park. The aero engine works, in production within a year from the start of work on the foundations, covered nearly 45 acres, and eventually employed 17,316 workers, of whom 7200 were women. Less than one hundred of this total had had anything to do with aero engines before joining Ford, and only three hundred or so knew anything about car engines. Nevertheless, before its closure in 1946, the Urmston factory had produced over 34,000 Merlin engines, not one of which failed the exacting requirements of the Royal Air Force. One intriguing aspect of this project is that the jig boring machines which were vital to its success were supplied by a firm from Switzerland in 1943, which meant that they were shipped to Britain via German-occupied France and Spain. The Germans had to agree to this unusual move because the Swiss insisted on their right, as neutrals, to trade with all belligerents. The Germans, who needed Swiss light machine tools, were forced to speed their own downfall. . . .

Sadly enough, when Ford of America were asked in their turn to produce Merlins (this was in 1940, before the USA entered the war), Edsel Ford and Charles Sorensen approved the venture, but were over-ruled by the 77-year-old Henry Ford, whose curious ideals of neutrality and pacifism dictated that no engines should be built for Britain . . . so Packard eventually took on the task. Later that year, however, Ford and General Motors cooperated in the production of Pratt & Whitney radial aero engines.

Although America didn't come into the war until 1942, its motor industry had been supplying the Allies since 1939: in 1939–40 the French government had ordered large quantities of trucks, which were being shipped when France fell to the Germans, so were hurriedly diverted to England. Here, improvised assembly plants were set up in all kinds of unlikely places, from the airship shed at Cardington, built for the ill-fated R101, to a tram shed in Wigan. Here, in June 1942, the first Jeep ever assembled in Britain was completed. The Jeep – officially known to the US Army as 'Truck, ¼-ton, 4×4, Command Reconnaisance' – was the result of a US Army specification of 1940, for which prototypes were built by the American Bantam Company (who had tried unsuccessfully to introduce the Austin Seven to the American market), Willys-Overland and, later, by Ford. The final design of Jeep was an amalgam of all three designs and, as such, was produced by all three companies, although Bantam switched to other war work before Pearl Harbor. Willys, on the other hand, persisted with the Jeep after the war, and a developed version is still in production, although it is now far more refined than the original 'Blitz Buggy', of which hundreds of thousands were built: at the peak of production, a Jeep was leaving the Willys assembly lines every 1 minute 20 seconds.

In March 1941, the American Government had passed the Lend-Lease Act, under which materials and know-how were made available to the Allies on the

Below: Ford lorries line up, waiting to be shipped into action. Their durability and ruggedness was remarkable, and some were still working, well into the 1970s, as tow trucks in France and Italy

premise that by pooling knowledge and resources, they could win the war more quickly. Under this scheme, the US supplied some $42,000,000,000-worth of material and services to 44 countries, especially Britain and the USSR.

Until Pearl Harbor, however, private car production continued almost unabated, with sales of well over four million cars in both 1940 and 1941, but once America entered the war, the skills of the industry were wholly employed in the manufacture of military equipment. There was little problem in the mass-production of trucks and Jeeps, and tanks and other fighting vehicles posed few difficulties, but at the request of President Roosevelt, Ford built a vast new factory at Willow Run, near Ypsilanti, Michigan, where four-engined Liberator bombers were to be built on production line methods. Needless to say, there were vast problems involved, and at one stage the venture gained the nickname 'Will It Run?'; but by late 1943 all the problems were solved, and in 1944 the plant was turning out three to four hundred Liberators a month.

The production figures achieved by the American automobile industry during the war were staggeringly huge: 4,131,000 engines, 5,947,000 guns,

Left : vital war work on four wheels did not just mean active service at the front; here, a Ford van, one of a fleet donated by Henry and Edsel Ford, is busy delivering food at home

2,812,000 tanks and trucks, 27,000 aircraft, and millions of smaller items from saucepans to atomic bomb equipment. . . .

Although the military vehicle in the front line had been afforded great – and well deserved – attention (after all it was the trucks of the 'Red Ball Express' which had kept the Allied armies in France supplied after D-Day), the poor motorist who needed a private car for his war work on the home front was hedged about with bureaucratic restrictions of the most annoying sort. New tyres were in short supply, yet motorists could be fined for using bald tyres while waiting for the new ones to arrive.

Petrol was rationed, yet the rationing seemed sometimes to be carried out on an arbitrary basis, as one British munitions worker complained in 1943: 'Drastic cuts long ago eliminated those who had any hope of getting to work by alternative means of transport. The remainder are so carefully controlled that the exact number of working days for the quarter is declared in advance and petrol is doled out to the nearest half-gallon. Even a single day lost through illness is reported to the Divisional Petroleum Office, and coupons for petrol to cover it have to be surrendered at the end of the period. Now, apparently on instructions from London, the DPO has slashed allowances so that people are

only able to go to work for 50 days out of the 75. They are invited to "stay with friends" or sleep at the office for the remaining nights. My only friend with a spare bed near my work happens to be of the opposite sex, and I don't think she would at all appreciate that suggestion. . . .

'It comes particularly hard when one sees American troops running round to the local dance hall with British girls in their Service vehicles at night and to read of MPs and Government officials using chauffeur-driven limousines to go to the theatre'.

There were, of course, ways round the regulations for the ingenious: cars could be persuaded to drag themselves along powered by cumbersome producer-gas outfits generating a fairly combustible gas from charcoal or manure, while those who could not obtain new pneumatic tyres were offered a curious device called a 'Getuhome', which consisted of wood segments linked together by a turnbuckle mechanism which tightened it on to the bare rim. 'Looks like an ordinary tyre, strong and durable and *will* get you home', claimed the optimistic manufacturer.

Despite all the restrictions, however, the private motorist could look forward

Above and top: the German equivalent to the Jeep was the Volkswagen Kübelwagen, based on the Volkswagen car chassis. The amphibious version, the Schwimmwagen, had a shorter chassis and four-wheel drive. It used an 1131 cc engine and could reach 50 mph on land and 7 mph in the water
(National Motor Museum, England)

with a degree of hope to peacetime, and vehicles making full use of all the technological lessons learned during the war. 'Wherever extreme conditions of service have to be met, or intricate machinery devised or constructed,' commented *The Motor*, 'technical knowledge of enduring value has been gained. Supplementing the laboratory and test track, many theatres of war have provided ready-made proving grounds where natural forces and conditions have caused nearly as much destruction as the direct attack of the enemy'.

For many motorists the anticipation was to be prolonged well after VE-Day, for the bureaucrats had also learned a great deal from war conditions. It was to be a long time before those war-developed cars were readily available to those who were placing orders for early delivery. . . .

Chapter 4

Improving the Breed

THE CARS: 1914-39

Even though the war was ushered in with an over-whelming victory at Lyons by a team of 4½-litre Mercédès racing cars of outdated design (their single-overhead-camshaft power units being contrary to the thinking of the Peugeot engineers with their twin-cam method of valve operation, dispensing with rockers), the period of hostilities was a time for aeronautical rather than motor car advancement. Nevertheless, when racing became possible again, after World War I, it was seen that even the racing car power plant had evolved to a significant degree. The frenzied production and continually enforced improvement of aero engines during the war resulted in useful advances applicable to racing engines and indeed to the power units of ordinary cars. Improvements in the fields of detail design, metallurgy and production methods were obvious, but it was the use of smaller, multiple cylinders, however, in which another great advance lay.

That the two significant new racing cars of the post-Armistice period were straight-eights has been attributed to the use of such an engine by Ettore Bugatti for a powerful aeroplane motor during the height of hostilities. He also made an aero-engine with two blocks of eight cylinders set up side by side, with separate crankshafts geared together, to produce a really beefy sixteen-cylinder engine. But it was the straight-eight principal that endeared itself to the planners of racing engines for the revival of the sport after the war was over; the chief protagonist was again Ernest Henry. He added this multi-cylinder concept to his pre-war Peugeot twin overhead-camshaft valve actuation, when commissioned by Ballot to build him racing cars for the first big post-war American motor race, the 1919 Indianapolis 500 Mile contest. Henry enclosed the previously exposed overhead valve gear but retained his system of having four valves for each cylinder, two inlet and two exhaust, these being set at a sixty degree angle in the fixed cylinder head. Henry also relied on the long piston stroke of his earlier engines, the straight-eight post-war Ballot being a 74 × 140 mm power unit, having a swept volume of 4894 cc. This was adequate to comply with American regulations, which called for a maximum engine size of 300 cu in, or 4917 cc. The long crankshaft required for such an engine, on this Henry-inspired Ballot, ran in five main bearings of the roller type, and it was a complex piece of work, in four separate sections joined together by a taper-and-key arrangement. In contrast, the big-end bearings were plain, with split bronze bushes between the con-rod and journal, these had white metal inner faces with bronze-to-steel rubbing in the con-rod. Dry-sump lubrication was resorted to, in order to reduce oil temperature, but the engine was susceptible to big-end oil starvation and was limited to a maximum crankshaft speed of 3500 rpm. While the big-ends were fed with oil through drilled crankpins, the main bearings were lubricated on the jet principle. Henry mounted this big engine on a sub-frame in a conventional chassis, with channel-section side members and semi-elliptic leaf springing. A cone clutch took the drive, through a four-speed gearbox, to the back axle via

Below: P. C. T. Clark at the Luton Speed Trials of 1948 in one of the victorious 1914 GP Mercédès cars

an open propeller shaft. Like Bugatti with his in-line eight-cylinder aero-engine, Henry used a 4-4 layout of the crankpins of his long crankshaft. Ignition was by a Bosch magneto, and two Claudel-Hobson carburettors supplied the mixture. Ballot must have been well pleased with these cars, the two costing him, it is said, £30,000, even though they had pre-war chassis characteristics and bolster petrol tanks ill-suited to the flat-out racing which Indianapolis involved.

The American firm of Duesenberg had also prepared straight-eight racing cars for the 1919 500 Mile Race. This engine was more closely related to the Bugatti aero-motor, as it had a single overhead camshaft operating three inclined valves (two exhaust and one inlet) per cylinder via rocker gear, the camshaft being driven from the front of the crankshaft by a vertical shaft and bevels. The cylinder head was detachable and, to simplify the valve gear, a

Right: Maurice Ballot stands between the two 4.9-litre, straight-eight Ballots of Albert Guyot (*left*) and René Thomas in Paris, 1919. Ballot built motor engines prior to World War I, and engaged the brilliant designer Ernest Henry to build Indianapolis cars for the 1919 race. Thomas made fastest lap at 104.2 mph and Guyot took fourth place

Y-shaped cam follower prodded the paired exhaust valves. Again, a 'four-four' crankshaft arrangement was employed and there were but three main bearings, two plain at the front and a ball-race at the back. The gearbox provided only three forward speeds, but a nicely streamlined body was used. Neither of these two revolutionary new post-war racers did anything much at Indy, where the winner was one of the 1914 GP Peugeots (Henry could still afford to smile), but they set a fashion which lasted into the mid 1950s, that of in-line eight-cylinder engines for racing. The disadvantages of a long and therefore likely-to-be-whippy crankshaft were offset by such merits as the ability to dispense with a heavy flywheel, good balance (which brought reliability with it), an increase in piston area from small light pistons (thereby increasing combustion chamber efficiency and rate of crankshaft revs) and excellent low-speed torque, although Henry threw away the latter quality in his 1919 Ballot engine because of big-choke carburettors. The problems of feeding fuel to a long eight-cylinder in-line motor were solved by having more than one instrument and overcome completely in later years when supercharging was the norm.

When the 3-litre maximum swept-volume rule came in, in 1920, both these Ballot and Duesenberg designs were reduced in size and, subsequently, fared better. Peugeot, on the other hand, having lost Henry to Ballot and later to Sunbeam, were handicapped by an over-ambitious engineer who concocted for them a racing engine of 80 × 149 mm and four cylinders which boasted five overhead valves each, three of which let the gas in, the other two being exhaust valves. There were three camshafts to operate this multiplicity of poppet valves, and eight sparking plugs; developing a claimed 108 bhp at about 3000 rpm, it was something to ignore, although it reflected the diversity of thought in racing-car drawing offices at this time. What this Peugeot and the 1920 3-litre Duesenberg did have in common was unit-construction of engine and gearbox, which pointed to a coming universal trend.

Another technical innovation which was, much later, to become universal

Right: the 3-litre straight-eight engined Duesenbergs took second, third, fourth, sixth and eighth places at Indianapolis in 1921. This is the car in which Jimmy Murphy won the 1921 French Grand Prix, and was the first American car to be equipped with hydraulic brakes all round

Below: the 1914 4.5-litre Delage Grand Prix car was fitted with four-wheel brakes, a twin-overhead-camshaft, four-cylinder engine, with desmodromic valve-gear, twin carburettors, and a five-speed gearbox. While the Delage was not particularly successful in the 1914 Grand Prix, W. F. Bradley took two 6.2-litre cars to Indianapolis and René Thomas won at 82.47 mph

for racing and road cars alike, was the use of hydraulic operation for the brakes. Duesenberg had this for their impeccably prepared 1921 3-litre car which won the French Grand Prix, providing a nasty shock for European constructors. In fact, the fluid used for this then-exciting new form of brake actuation was a mixture of water and glycerine, retained within the single master cylinder by the ground-to-fit piston! This fluid actually passed along the tubular front

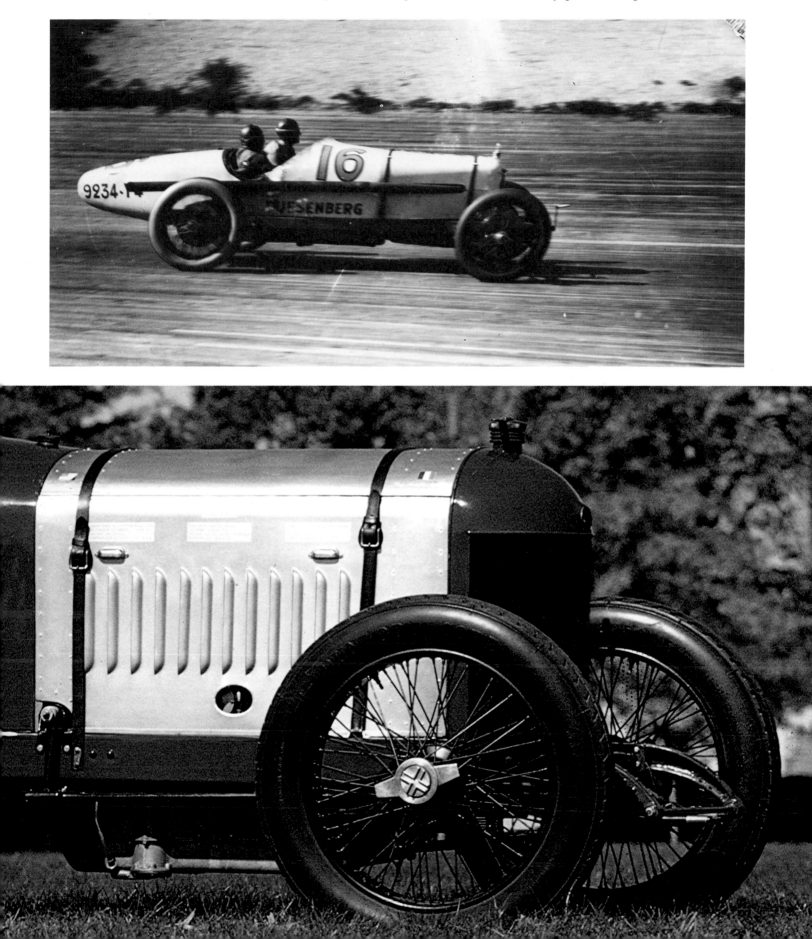

Right: originally entered in a Fiat, Louis Wagner drove a 3-litre Ballot at Indianapolis in 1921

Left: Fiat's 115 bhp, 3-litre straight-eight Tipo 802, built for the 1921 Grand Prix, had roller-bearing big ends fitted, but was uncompetitive

Below left: the 1.5-litre, four-cylinder Talbot-Darracq of Chassagne at the Brooklands 200-mile race of 1921, in which the team finished in the first three places

Below: Jimmy Murphy on his way to winning the 1921 French Grand Prix at Le Mans; where he averaged 78.22 mph to become the first American to win a major European motor race

axle and up through the drilled steering-pivot pins, to expand individual pistons that opened out the flexible spring-steel brake shoes. Other significant, if then individual, aspects of this GP-winning Duesenberg were torque-tube transmission, Delco high-tension coil ignition, and detachable wire wheels employing Rudge-Whitworth centre-lock hubs. The car was able to develop between 115 and 120 bhp at 4250 rpm and, with the help of its new-style braking system, this American Duesenberg took the European racing world by storm in 1921; the straight-eight racing engine was the fashion from then on. As others were to adopt the Ernest Henry twin-cam multi-valve cylinder head, so his pioneering of the eight-in-line cylinder layout was not disregarded, either. Ballot and STD used both for their engines of the new 3-litre racing formula, but for the latter cars (conveniently labelled Sunbeam, Talbot or Darracq, as and when it suited Louis Coatalen, who had built them, seven in number at a cost of some £50,000) a better bottom-end lubrication system was devised, using plain bearings for both mains and big-ends, again in conjunction with a dry-sump system. All these post-war racing eights, Ballot, Sunbeam and Fiat, were twin-cam engines of 65 × 112 mm in the prevailing long-stroke idiom. However, the Type 802 Fiat broke away from the Henry multi-valve school of thought, to set another lead in future design, as the engineer concerned, Fornaca, opted for two large valves per cylinder, set at 96 degrees: the classical hemi-head combustion chamber. He also used the cylinder and water-jacket construction, complicated but effective, which Mercédès had found practical in their pre-war racing car and war-time aeroplane engines, namely blocks of steel forgings, welded and machined with the water covers made up of sheet-steel welded in place. This notable Fiat engine had a single-

piece crankshaft instead of a built-up shaft, this being made possible by the use of split bronze bearing cages for the roller main bearings. The big-ends were of the same type and this all-roller-bearing power unit developed a useful 115 bhp at 4600 rpm. That was the norm for the 1921 Grand Prix season.

There was now a full appreciation of the value of four-wheel braking in the field of road racing. It not only reduced skidding but was almost as useful as good acceleration over a twisty course, in killing speed into the corners. To reduce the wear and tear on the drivers, servo operation of these mostly cable-operated brakes was usual, with the servo driven from the gearbox, which helped to apply the brakes when the pedal was depressed. This system was built into the great 37.2 hp Hispano Suiza touring-car chassis by the eminent Swiss engineer, Marc Birkigt. Racing bodywork, too, was evolving, into pointed-tail two-seaters, with decent protection for driver and riding mechanic in the prevailing long-road contests.

The influence of the big-time racers was handed down to the voiturette or 1½-litre class of racing car. Whereas the successful type immediately after the Armistice was the light-weight, four-cylinder, single-overhead-camshaft,

Below: Douglas Hawkes' 3-litre Bentley on its way to fifth place in the 1922 Isle of Man TT. Bentley won the team prize in the factory's second venture into competitions

sixteen-valve Brecia Bugatti, by 1921 and 1922 the twin-cam form of racing engine was supreme in this category. At first, it aped the bigger racing cars in having four valves per cylinder. In this form, the 1486 cc Talbot-Darracqs, another facet of Sunbeam Chief Designer Louis Coatalen's enthusiasm for racing, were producing no less that 50 bhp at 4000 rpm, which rendered them quite invincible.

We move now to the interesting 1922 racing season. This was run under the maximum capacity of 2 litres ruling. It was important because it brought some mixed design-thinking into the picture but it is remarkable that those companies which supported racing in the grand manner were willing to go to the expense of building entirely new racing cars every year; in recent times, of course, the 3-litre Formula One rule has remained unchanged to obviate this vast seasonal expenditure. Anyway, that was the position in 1922, with a minimum weight limit of 650 kg (1436 lb) to match this 2000 cc capacity ruling and the various manufacturers fielded many diverse configurations.

Ernest Henry changed from his straight-eight to a four-cylinder engine which he built for Sunbeam. It retained four valves per cylinder, now with the

Below right: Cushman's Brescia Bugatti prior to the 1922 200-mile race at Brooklands; basically a 1914 Type 13 model of 1.4 litres, the car was so named because of its surprising success in the 1921 Brescia event, the pre-war cars having been stored throughout the duration of hostilities

inlets at twenty degrees to the vertical, set higher in the heads than the forty degree exhaust valves, with two sparking plugs to each cylinder and twin carburettors. A plunger oil pump, a former Henry love, was used, feeding plain, white-metal, big-ends and the crankshaft ran in three ball-races, being the usual built-up affair. A cone clutch took the power to a four-speed gearbox and there were the expected mechanical gearbox-servo, cable-operated, four-wheel brakes. This was a retrograde design. The small piston area and restricted engine speed made these Henry-Sunbeams non-competitive, aggravated by a tendency to break their inlet valves. Yet, on ordinary petrol, these 2-litre compact 'four-potters' gave around 85 bhp at 4250 rpm.

Fiat countered the smaller engine-size by changing from the eight-cylinder to a six-cylinder engine and got 92 bhp at 4500 rpm – note that racing car engines did not rotate all that quickly – later increased to 110 bhp, which made Fiat the in-car of the 1922 season. If we accept this single-carburettor Fiat as the leading racing car of the period, we see it as a small 13½ cwt, staggered two-seater with a wheelbase of 8 ft 2½ in, its radiator neatly cowled, a full length undershield running beneath the wedge-tail body, and the exhaust pipe running for part of its length in a metal tunnel. The eight in-line engine still persisted, however, being used by both Bugatti and Rolland-Pilain, but Ballot had retrogressed to four cylinders. The lessons were plain to see. The future lay in light weight, multi-cylinders and roller bearings throughout the engine for high revs, with some attention being paid to low-drag bodies. There was Bugatti's plan of taking the exhaust-pipe out through the centre of a barrel tail,

and Grillot had gone to the terrible complexity of desmodromic mechanically closed valves on the Rolland-Pilain engines, a theme it was better to leave Mercédès to play with over three decades later!

The 1923 season was of less importance from the point of view of technical evolution, because supercharging was just around the corner, and would soon up-lift power output for a given cylinder capacity quite dramatically. In the meantime, what do we find? Coatalen achieved his burning ambition, that of winning the French Grand Prix, by the simple strategy of hiring Vincent Berterione away from Fiat to design for him a race winner. This Sunbeam six-cylinder looked outwardly and within much like the six-cylinder Fiats that swept all before them the previous year, for the Grand Prix formula remained at a top engine-size limit of 2 litres, as it was to do for a further two seasons.

Above: the 1922 Sunbeam Grand Prix team The drivers are Kenelm Lee Guinness, in number 16, and (Sir) Henry Segrave, in 21

Left: a 1922 Duesenberg; fitted with a Miller engine and rechristened the Murphy Special, Jimmy Murphy's Duesenberg won the 1922 Indy 500, while the car shown here finished second, driven by Harry Hartz

Above: the eminent Swiss engineer Marc Birkigt was responsible for preparing all competition Hispano-Suizas at the Levallois-Perret factory from 1911 until 1914

Above right: a 1922 straight-eight TT-type Sunbeam

Below: Sir Algernon Lee Guinness after winning the 1500 Trophy on the Isle of Man in 1922, with a four-cylinder, twin-overhead-camshaft Talbot Darracq

Below right: Sir Algernon on the famous Mountain course during his winning drive

Before we look briefly at other 1923 road-race designs, there were some racing cars built to compete in the rather odd 1922 Tourist Trophy Race to consider. This, belying its title, was for pure racing cars and was held over the well known Isle of Man course. The rules provided for cars of up to 3 litres capacity, with an additional 1½-litre race; the bigger cars had to weigh not less than 1600 lb. One of the straight-eight twin-cam Henry-style STD Sunbeams, based on the 1921 GP machines, but now with magneto ignition, twin Clauden Hobson carburettors, and a power output of 108 bhp at 4000 rpm, won a rather uninspiring race, and a 1½-litre 16-valve 'invincible' Talbot-Darracq was victorious in the *voiturette* section. A very complicated TT Vauxhall was evolved for the TT event. Its engine was a twin-cam four-cylinder of 85×132 mm, with sixteen ninety degree valves in a detachable bronze cylinder head that sat on an aluminium cylinder block, in which there were removable liners surrounded by the cooling water. The camshafts were gear driven, and the built-up crankshaft had a central flywheel and ran in six ball-races; the big-ends used double roller-races. This was a good engine, of rigid structure, the ignition was by Delco coil with dual distributors, and one twin-choke Zenith looked after the carburation. Although the compression ratio was a modest 5.8 to 1, this fine if complicated power unit rewarded Ricardo with an output of nearly 130 bhp at 4500 rpm. Alas, the chassis, designed by King, was also very complex, as well as too heavy, and it was further hampered by novel compressed-air servo brakes with steering-column control, allied to separate mechanical linkage. The body was just as odd, being a slab-tank two-seater

233

with rather sexy scuttle cowls. At the time, this ingenious Vauxhall was a failure but its day was to come, in sprints, when it was subsequently developed into the multi-blower Vauxhall Villiers Supercharged Special and successfully used by Ramond Mays.

The TT also saw a British Aston-Martin endowed with a twin-cam engine which was pure Ernest Henry Ballot so far as its sixteen-valve upper half was concerned. Continuing with the 1923 Grand Prix entries: although, as has been said, Sunbeam won, the significant cars were the supercharged straight-eight Fiats. Similar in design concept to the 1922 successful Fiats, but with gear-driven overhead camshafts, they used a Wittig vane-pattern blower driven off the nose of the crankshaft and for feeding air into the carburettor under pressure,

which the mechanic is supposed to have been able to control. These were the fastest cars racing, which were said to produce an effective 130 bhp. Alas, for Italy, the new-fangled superchargers were not impervious to road grit, and they retired. But the writing was on the wall in big, clear letters – very much so, for Fiat with the new supercharged engine won the Italian Grand Prix before the year 1923 was out. Of the others, Voisin ran weirdly streamlined Knight sleeve-valve-engined racers; Bugatti was also mad on good air-flow over the car, with short-wheelbase straight-eight cars endowed with all-enveloping tank-like coachwork, and there was a lone vee-twelve-cylinder Delage which was also of future significance, among one six-cylinder and two straight-eight Rolland-Pilains; the latter were not successful in the Grands Prix. Their six-cylinder racer had a Henry-Schmid cuff-valve engine.

The 1923 season of Grand Prix racing had seen the greatest divergence of engine, chassis and aerodynamic design since the sport was resumed after the end of World War I. The next season was just as significant, but in a more stabilised fashion, as the supercharger had by now been virtually perfected. Although the engine capacity limit of 2 litres still prevailed, the use of a blower brought with it a very considerable power increase, which made the swept-volume ruling an arbitrary one and gave greatly increased top speed and acceleration.

The racing car which won most races in 1924 was the P2 Alfa Romeo. Like the Sunbeams before it, this fine racer owed much to the Fiat influence, in that it was designed by the talented Vittorio Jano who had served with Fiat from 1911. The Alfa Romeo used a straight-eight engine with its cylinder blocks in four pairs, their bore and stroke being 61×85 mm, giving an engine size of 1987 cc. In the style of the day both big-end and main bearings were of the

Below: the start of the 1922 French Grand Prix, held over a distance of 498.85 miles at Strasbourg, with a Fiat in the lead

roller-type; welded-up water jackets surrounded the cylinder blocks, a permanently-engaged Roots paddle-type supercharger blew air through a Memini carburettor via a long cast-conduit in the light-alloy base chamber and, naturally, the two overhead valves in each cylinder head were inclined and

operated by twin overhead camshafts. This advanced, although conventional in the racing sense, power unit was installed in a compact chassis with a wheelbase of 8 ft 6 ins, using four-wheel-brakes with servo assistance. The cart-springing which was normal at that time was practically overcome by the use of big-section balloon tyres. Capable of well over 120 mph, the P2 Alfa Romeo became a legend in its lifetime. The claimed power output was 135 bhp at 5500 rpm, which was similar to the power developed by the 1924 Grand Prix Sunbeams, which were simply improved versions of the Fiat-based 1923 cars, although now supercharged, with a Roots blower compressing the mixture drawn from a Solex carburettor within the supercharger casing. The Sunbeam six-cylinder engine had dimensions of 67 × 94 mm and the very slight power advantage

made them faster than the P2 Alfa Romeos at the premier Lyons Grand Prix although they did eventually lose the race, due to faulty magnetos.

M. Lory had much improved his V12 Delage for the 1924 season, but it was not yet supercharged, as he had not yet perfected the layout of this car. This was not altogether a disadvantage, however, because it ensured reliability from the complex Delage power unit and netted the great French manufacturer second place in the Lyons Grand Prix.

The 1924 Grand Prix season is best remembered for the advent, although unsuccessful at first, of the new and extremely beautiful racing Type 35 Bugatti. It was as conventional in concept as the 1923 'tank'-bodied Bugattis had been unorthodox. With the shapely two-seater pointed-tail body and much-louvred bonnet behind the little Bugatti horse-shoe-pattern radiator, it blended well with the unusual wide-spoked aluminium wheels, whereby Ettore Bugatti sought to conduct heat away from the tyres and save unsprung weight at his axle extremities. These Type 35s were powered by a typical Bugatti straight-eight single overhead-camshaft engine of 60×88 mm (1990 cc) having three vertical valves in each cylinder, the cylinder block and head being in one piece. Bugatti was not only unconvinced at this period of time about forced induction,

Above: (Sir) Henry Segrave at the wheel of the 1923 six-cylinder, 2-litre Sunbeam Grand Prix car

Below: work in progress on the Alvis team cars prior to the Brooklands 200-Mile Race of 1923. The car in the foreground was driven by C. M. Harvey and went on to win the race when the Fiats expired. The Alvis Racing cars were based on the production 12/50 model

Right: the supercharged, 2-litre straight-six engine of the 1925 racing Sunbeam. This particular engine is fitted with the later SU carburettor in place of the original Solex unit

Right: the legendary Alfa Romeo P2, designed by Vittorio Jano and introduced in 1924. It earned a place in racing history in winning the first Grand Prix in which it was entered, the 1924 French race, with Campari at the wheel

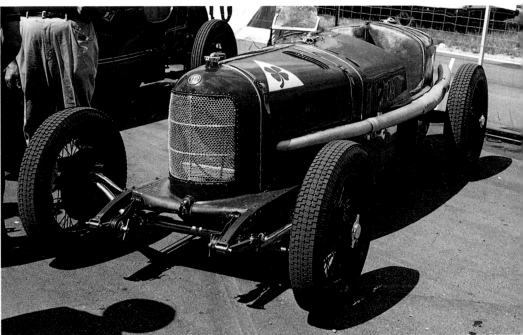

Right: E. Friedrich in the 2-litre, tank-bodied, Bugatti, on his way to third place in the 1923 French Grand Prix at Tours

he was avidly opposed to it, so twin carburettors sufficed to feed his angular power-pack. This artistic engine had a built-up crankshaft turning in three comparatively small ball-races and two larger roller-races while the light con-rods had roller big-ends. The drive went through a Bugatti multi-plate clutch to a four-speed and reverse gearbox, the torque of the open propeller shaft being absorbed by side radius rods. The chassis was also well-constructed; the side members were carefully stressed and the back axle suspended on reversed quarter-elliptic springs of leaf pattern. The splendid appearance of the 1924 GP Bugatti was notably enhanced by the tubular front axle which possessed forged slots through which the front half-elliptic springs passed. All this contributed to the Bugatti's legendary road holding. The engine was scarcely competitive in terms of horse-power, giving about 100 bhp at 5200 rpm on its first appearance. Reliability and cornering prowess, however, made the Bugatti the most prolific race winner of the 1924–39 era. At its début at the important French Grand Prix it appeared that the ingenious wheels may have transmitted too much heat because the tyres gave continuous trouble. Incidentally, the brake drums were detachable with the alloy wheels.

Right: Kaye Don in the 146 bhp supercharged two-litre Sunbeam of 1924, pictured here at Brooklands in 1928

Below: the powerful 1925 Delage was designed by Albert Lory and won the French and Spanish Grands Prix

Below right: the V12 engine of the 1925 Delage used twin Roots superchargers and developed 195 bhp at 7000 rpm

By 1924 it was all happening – the supercharger had been discovered in Europe and America. The applications in America were of very high-speed aircraft-type centrifugal compressors, running at up to four times crankshaft speed, which gave the Duesenbergs the edge over their rivals at Indianapolis. At the same time Miller produced their front-wheel-drive racer, for the same course, where the 500-Mile Race was held every May. A de Dion-type axle was fitted at the front of the chassis and the typical Miller straight-eight engine was turned back-to-front to provide a drive for the steered and driven front wheels. Later, of course, Alvis of Coventry were to experiment with this form of drive in both four and straight-eight cylinder racing and sports cars.

Mercédès returned to racing in 1924 with a Porsche-designed car, which followed the expected straight-eight cylinder configuration and had steel cylinders with Mercédès welded-on water jacketing, and dry-sump lubrication. The crankshaft ran in nine roller bearings, and other interesting aspects of the specification were four valves per cylinder, and a Roots supercharger blowing through the carburettor, in contrast to the sucking of air from the carburettor that Mercédès preferred for their sports chassis. Front springs passed through the axle although this was not actually a Bugatti preserve, as Fiat also did it. The Mercédès used sodium cooling for the hollow exhaust-valve stems and its engine was an impressive piece of work for 1924, developing perhaps as much as 160 bhp at the very high crankshaft rotative speed of 7000 rpm. Alas for German hopes, the poor road-holding made it highly dangerous, and it was in one of these Mercédès that the legendary Count Louis Zborowski of Chitty-Chitty-Bang-Bang fame was killed at Monza during the Italian Grand Prix.

The 2-litre ruling remained in force for the 1925 racing season but, as a change was suspected, new designs were not encouraged and the starting-grids were mainly composed of improved versions of the 1924 cars. Lory had done good work on his V12 Delage engine, which now boasted a notable power increase, through having twin Roots superchargers. These, and the large piston area, which the use of a dozen tiny pistons ensured, gave the potential of 190 bhp at 7000 rpm, nearly the dreamed-of 100 bhp per litre. However powerful the 1925 V12 Delage was, Alfa Romeo, with improved versions of the great

P2, was more powerful, and would undoubtedly have won the French Grand Prix at Montlhéry (over the artificial road-circuit) had they not withdrawn their cars as a mark of respect for their ace driver Antonio Ascari, who was killed when his P2 inexplicably overturned in a ditch when he was leading the race. Alfas ran on dope at this stage in their engine development, although ordinary petrol was still the norm for lesser racing engines.

Another important trend of 1925 was the elimination of the riding mechanic from the leading races. His chief tasks had been to warn his driver of overtaking cars, to maintain fuel pressure, to read the instruments and to keep an eye on the mechanics, while also assisting with tyre changes or similar operations away from the depot. The number of accidents in which the occupants of racing cars were involved now led the authorities to ban the riding mechanic, although for the time-being body widths remained of two-seater dimensions. Ettore Bugatti-the-Thoughtful faired over the passenger's seats of his Type 35s when he heard of this but, under protest, was obliged to have the metal cut away. In America, however, the centre-cockpit single-seater was already the accepted design for racing cars, and this was eventually adopted in Europe.

The 1926 International Grand Prix ruling for the maximum permitted engine capacity was 1½-litres (1500 cc), which remained unchanged until 1928. There was also a minimum weight clause of 600 kg (1322 lb) – a reduction of 108 lb over the 1925 rule for 2-litre racers and, despite the elimination of the mechanic, the bodies still had to seat two, and not be less than 80 cm wide. Only one mechanic was allowed to get into the road to assist the driver at the pits.

In voiturette racing, the Talbot-Darracqs of the STD combine, under Louis Coatalen, were still supreme. New four-cylinder 67 × 105.6 mm (1481 cc) cars had been designed by Bertarione for this class of racing, based on the successful 2-litre six-cylinder Sunbeams. The Grand Prix cars themselves were now built to the 1½-litre formula. The STD concern had more ambitious plans: they produced new, very low-slung, straight-eight supercharged racing cars of an interesting design. In compliance with the then-prevailing belief that fast cornering was enhanced by making a car's centre-of-gravity as low as possible, the Talbot's transmission was off-set in the frame, a gambit made possible because a mechanic no longer had to be accommodated. A double-reduction, back-axle final-drive lowered the actual height of these components and the driver sat on a cushion on the car's undertray. The chassis side-members were made of pressings, with vertical slots through which the back and front axles passed, suspended on semi-elliptic springs. The front axle of the 1926 Talbot was also a remarkable construction. It consisted of two tapering tubes, bored out almost to the steering pivots, bolted together at the centre, which was enabled, by the use of angled flanges, to be considerably lower than the front-wheel hub centres, and thus pass below the engine. This unusually rigid and very low chassis frame was enclosed by aluminium panels and nicely streamlined with a cowled sloping radiator. The engine had its steel 'pots' in two blocks with welded-on water jackets, as Bertarioni was responsible for the design. It was in accordance with mid-1920s practice, having twin overhead camshafts operating two inclined valves per cylinder and a nose-mounted Roots supercharger, twin Bosch magnetos, roller-bearing crankshaft, and a Solex carburettor for the blower to draw from. It developed some 145 bhp at 6500 rpm, and ran to 7000 rpm. A finned oil-cooler was fitted to the outside of the body. Transmission was now by torque-tube, and the front springs again passed through slots in the ingenious front axle. Top speed was in the region of 130 mph.

There was, at the time this 1926 Talbot was being tested, the popular idea that Grand Prix cars, intended to race over a road or artificial-road circuit, should be built as low as possible. This seemed to give them the ability to corner faster with a minimum of roll which, in those days of very hard non-independent suspension, could promote instability and skidding. It also brought with it the unfortunate factor that the driver was not always aware that forces were mounting to a point where his car would spin uncontrollably.

This notwithstanding, the Delage racers, which M. Lory prepared for the

Above: the accident which resulted in the banning of riding mechanics in racing cars. Kenelm Lee Guinness' badly damaged Sunbeam after he crashed during the 1924 Spanish Grand Prix at San Sebastian; his mechanic was killed

Above right: Robert Benoist on his way to winning the 1927 British Grand Prix at Brooklands. Delage took the first three places, their chief opposition coming from the Bugatti 35s, such as George Eyston's, being passed here by Benoist

Below: Rudolf Caracciola – *der Regenmeister* – on his lap of honour after his first major victory, in a Mercédès GP car, at the German Grand Prix, Avus, in 1926. Caracciola became known as one of the greatest ever Grand Prix drivers

new 1½-litre Formula, were also very low-hung, albeit with a more conventional chassis frame than those of the Talbots, swept down to pass below the back axle. It was the engine of the 1500cc Delage which was a truly remarkable piece of engineering. Ignoring expense, Lory used the expected straight-eight cylinder configuration, with a bore and stroke of 55.8 × 76mm, which gave him a swept volume of 1484cc. Two overhead camshafts operated the valves, two per 'pot', angled at a hundred degrees. This, too, was conventional stuff, but the complexity of almost watch-making precision came with the details. The camshafts were driven by a train of gears, amounting to twenty in all, counting the drives for the auxiliaries. There were roller and ball races in abundance, each camshaft running in nine such bearings, so that the total used was in excess of sixty. The crankshaft was a forged one-piece counter-balanced affair, and was again fully-rollered. This marvellous little racing power unit was given the required power output by means of twin superchargers mounted on the near side and driven by a shaft from the timing-gear train; they sucked from one carburettor apiece. There were two oil pumps for the dry-sump

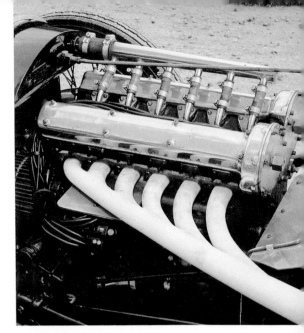

system, a water pump and a Bosch magneto. All this complexity gave Lory more than 160 bhp at the now acceptable engine speed of 7500 rpm. But what he had not allowed for was the difficulty of getting excess heat away from his wonderful power unit. This passed, via the exhaust pipe, too close to the driver's footboard and cockpit side, so that feet and torso were roasted in long races, like a loaf in a fierce oven.

This was unfortunate as these 1½-litre GP Delages were as fast as they were aggressive looking. On the low-height theme, the rather whippy chassis was so low that the tops of the front tyres were on a level with the top of the vertical radiator. The driver could touch the ground easily if he put a hand out of the car, and the height to the top of his scuttle was a mere 35½ in. The wheelbase measured 8ft 2½ in, while suspension was by short, very stiff half-elliptic leaf springs and there was a powerful servo braking system, with large ribbed drums behind the wire wheels. The front axle was a three-piece tubular one

Above: the Amilcar C6 of 1926, some 35 of which were produced. Designed by Edmond Moyet, the works cars won 74 events in the voiturette class during that year, outclassing the rival Salmsons

Top: the 1100 cc, dohc, six-cylinder engine of the Amilcar C6, which ultimately produced 108 bhp at 6000 rpm, powering the car to a top speed of 125 mph

Above: the magnificent V12 Sunbeam Tiger was the last World Land Speed Record car to be raced on a circuit. Only two of these cars were built, based on the 1925 2-litre Grand Prix model. Using a supercharged, 4-litre, V12 engine, this car took (Sir) Henry Segrave to a new record of 152.308 mph, at Southport in 1926, and subsequently went on to race at Brooklands, Boulogne and San Sebastian. Its Brooklands' record included victory in the Mountain Championship for Sir Malcolm Campbell in 1932

Top: the 3976 cc, V12 engine of the Tiger was based on two of the 1925, 2-litre, Grand Prix engines, mounted in a 75-degree vee on a common crankcase. The supercharged engine developed 296 bhp and was versatile enough to be used for both racing and record breaking

and Delage, in the face of a general change over to torque-tube final drive, retained an open propeller shaft.

By the time the start of the 1926 racing season had arrived, it was apparent that to build a competitive 1½-litre road-racing motor car had become an exceedingly costly process, and this sadly reduced the number of different makes who could afford to participate. The celebrated Welsh engineer and racing driver, J. G. Parry Thomas, had decided to come in when straight-eight racers were using his now-famous conception of a single-overhead-camshaft engine, with inclined valves opened by a common inlet/exhaust cam per cylinder and closed by leaf valve springs. He was even more extreme in hanging his chassis low on its springs (the frame passing below the axles and being only 5 in. from the ground) which were of the quarter-elliptic type at the rear and semi-elliptic at the front. The bodywork of these Thomas Specials was so low and flat that it is said the mechanics, when in playful mood, would turn the cars upside down and roll them along on their wheels just as easily as when

Left: Sir Malcolm Campbell and his fourteen-year-old riding mechanic, after a win at Brooklands in one of the 1927 World Champion 1½-litre Delages

Below: the supercharged 1½-litre Delages were instrumental in forcing Ettore Bugatti to adopt supercharging for the Type 39 racing car. Despite Bugatti's efforts, 1927 saw Delage as World Champions, winning every Grand Prix in which they started. This very compact machine was powered by a straight-eight engine, delivering a respectable 170 bhp to a five-speed gearbox, and remained remarkably competitive up to ten years later

they were upright. As a result, the Thomas creations became known as 'Flat-irons'. However, they had early gearbox troubles and were only competitive for outer-circuit racing and class-record breaking.

Ettore Bugatti was at last forced, by the 1½-litre Formula and the ambitious designs of his rivals at Delage and the Sunbeam/Talbot/Darracq combine, to resort to supercharging. Thus was created the 1½-litre Type 39 Bugatti. This was the straight-eight Type 35 that had made its début in 1924, endowed with a Roots blower on the side of the engine and with its stroke reduced from 88 to 66mm, thus getting it down from 2 litres to the required 1½. The supercharger was driven by a train of gears and a short shaft and it 'puffed' at around 10 psi. Because of the oven-like propensities of the Delage cars and the hasty preparation of the new Talbots, they only just scraped a victory in the JCC 200-Mile Race at Brooklands at the end of 1926, so Bugatti began to reap the benefit of a simple, proven design.

The 1½-litre ruling continued for 1927 and the Delages then became the World Champion racing cars. Lory had cured the drivers' objection to staying in them for the length of a race unless they could douse their scorched feet in cold water, by the simple, if technically expensive, expedient of turning the cylinder blocks round, so that the exhaust ports and off-takes were on the opposite side of the car. This was not such a simple alteration as it sounds. It necessitated removing the twin blowers; a single Cozette supercharger was substituted. The engine and its five-speed gearbox was then off-set 4 in to the left of the chassis centre line, to give more space in the cramped cockpit; the radiator was slightly inclined and the steering improved. By using dope fuel, a blend of straight petrol, benzole, alcohol (for cooling the engine internals) and ether (to aid starting up), this fine power-unit was now producing some 113 bhp per litre, and a maximum of 170 bhp without revving above 8000 rpm, which was not to be sneezed at. It enabled the 1927 Delage to win every Grand Prix race in which it started. Even so, with a supercharger pressure of only about 7½ psi, this engine had much in hand, as Ramponi was to prove to Dick Seaman ten years later, when he challenged successfully the new ERAs with one of these by then-ancient Delages. In contrast, money was running out for Talbot and this STD design was never fully developed.

Although Delage dominated the 1926/7 1½-litre Formula, there were a number of notable experiments at this time, which deserve mention, though they were unsuccessful. Itala made a V12 racer with two banks of cylinders at sixty degrees and horizontal valves, two per head, prodded from a central camshaft between the V of the cylinder blocks. There was a supercharger that blew air into ports uncovered when the pistons got to the base of the cylinders. This novel Itala not only had front-wheel drive, but independent suspension using transverse springs and rubber blocks. Built in 1100cc and 1500cc forms, this ingenious confection was never raced. Then Fiat returned, with a six-cylinder two-stroke racer possessing twelve pistons, as there were geared-together crankshafts one above the other, and common combustion chambers. This car was never raced . . . but the great Fiat Company did win at Monza with another remarkably ingenious design. It was a twin-six of 50 × 63 mm with its cylinder blocks side by side and the crankshafts geared together as on the two-stroke. Three twelve-cam camshafts were needed to operate the overhead valves and Fiat managed with plain bearings. This exciting swan-song of Fiat should have produced more victories, as the engine was giving 187 bhp at 8500 rpm on the bench. Known as the Type 406, this Zerbi-planned power unit was put into the light Tipo 806 chassis and, had it been developed, it might have offered a powerful challenge to the Delages. A team was said to be coming over for the 1927 British Grand Prix, but the Fiats were withdrawn and never seen again on a race course. In Britain, however, Alvis entered the field, with front-wheel-drive straight-eight cars, at first with horizontal overhead valves actuated by vertical rockers. The bore and stroke of the Smith-Clarke-designed, Coventry-built engine was 55 × 78¾ mm (1497 cc); later, conventional twin overhead camshafts were substituted.

All this 1½-litre 'F1' activity, led so ably by Delage, who showed that if sufficient time and money is spent, success should be comparatively easy to

achieve, reduced the former Talbot-Darracq dominated *voiturette* class to 1100cc, and sired the beautiful little Roots-blown twin-cam Amilcar Six and the less successful straight-eight Salmson, which was likewise supercharged.

So far as pure Grands Prix were concerned, the rule makers recognised that the very expensive small racing cars made artificially powerful (by dint of supercharging), would cease to be built, largely due to Delage's domination and the impending financial slump. Consequently, a period of free formulae was introduced, in which the older GP cars, stripped big-engined sports cars, like the Mercédès and the Bentley, and a few new large racing cars, too like Sunbeam's 4-litre V12 and the immortal Type 35B supercharged 2.3-litre Bugatti, all had occasional success. Then, for 1931, proper racing cars were back in vogue. At first, the rules were peculiar, insisting on two-seater bodies but no riding mechanics, under the agreement that had been in force for some years, and races were to run for at least ten hours. The period of racing was notable for the arrival on the circuits of the Tipo 8C, or Monza, Alfa Romeo, a straight-eight, twin-cam, Roots-blown sports car stripped for racing, and of the 2.3-litre, double-overhead-camshaft, Type 51 Bugatti. After looking closely at some twin-cam American Miller racers, Ettore had at last gone over to that form of valve gear in this car. From the Monza Alfa Romeo stemmed the invincible Tipo B, P3 or *monoposto* Alfa Romeo, call it what you will. This was a genuine, though rather wide, single-seater, using Vittorio Jano's Monza engine which

Above left: a classic design unclothed: the 1927 Bugatti Type 35B is a masterpiece of engineering and, even without its bodywork, is one of the world's most instantly recognisable racing cars. The car is powered by a 2.3-litre, supercharged, straight-eight engine and features the distinctive Bugatti, alloy-spoked, wheels

Above: the 1931 Bugatti Type 51 was a logical progression from the 35B and in this car Ettore Bugatti finally adopted twin overhead camshafts. In 1931 it raced to victory in Monaco, Montlhéry, Spa, Tunis, Morocco and Czechoslovakia and maintained its domination for two more years, until Alfa Romeo and Maserati finally brought their efforts to fruition
(Donington Collection)

had, along the years, been increased in size from 2.3 to 2.6 litres. The chassis, at first sprung on half-elliptic leaf springs, was only 26 in wide and was swept up compactly over the back axle. The clever thing about the *monoposto* Alfa Romeo was its transmission. Jano used twin propeller shafts, splayed out thirty degrees from a chassis-mounted differential, that was itself behind the gearbox. By doing this, he was able to sit the driver lower than in other racing cars where the seat was above the single propeller shaft. There were other advantages, too. The twin prop shafts with a drive on the chassis meant that, if the gear-ratios had to be altered quickly to suit a given race, they could be conveniently changed without stripping the back axle. Even better, by putting the differential unit up on the sprung chassis, unsprung weight on the back axle was reduced, with a beneficial effect on rear-wheel adhesion over bumps. Unfortunately the twin-bevel drives in this clever design made the axle somewhat heavier than if a single final drive had been used.

As the P3 Alfa Romeo was improved further over the years, it became one of the most famous racing cars of all time. The gear drive to the twin overhead-camshafts was taken up between the two separate cylinder blocks, which enabled the twin superchargers set beside the engine to be easily driven from them. Improvements in lubricants and bearing materials had given Jano faith in plain bearings for mains, big-ends and camshafts. The 2.6-litre engine of the P3 gave 180 bhp at the modest engine speed of 5400 rpm, a further reason why those plain bearings were adequate. In a car which tipped the weighbridge at just over 15 cwt, dry, here was a winner indeed. Moreover, the *monoposto* Tipo B Alfa Romeo was able to stand much development. Over the years its engine was increased to 2.9 and finally to 3.2 litres. It was made to handle better by using Dubonnet independent front suspension and, finally, in the period when the makers had retired from the racing game and *Scuderia Ferrari* was racing these splendid Alfa Romeos, the engine capacity went to as much as 3.8 litres. For a time, reversed quarter-elliptic rear springs were also tried. Nuvolari was able to defeat the German cars (of which more anon) on their home ground with one of these Alfas, at the 1935 Nürburgring German GP, in spite of a refuelling delay. In 1934, 68 × 100 mm, 2905 cc guise, this, the first of the European single-seater road racers, was capable of 145 mph.

The gambit of increasing the size of an engine was then universal. The Maserati which had evolved from the Diatto sports car into a straight-eight 2½-litre GP car by the 1930s, was later enlarged to 2.9 litres and was helped by hydraulic brakes, which Maserati had been quick to adopt around 1933.

Below : Vittorio Jano's masterpiece was the Alfa Romeo P3, a direct descendant of his Monza design. The P3 was technically very sophisticated, using twin propeller shafts, to allow a lower seating position, and a chassis-mounted differential to reduce the unsprung weight. The car was virtually invincible (Donington Collection)

Below right : the adjustable friction dampers of the P3 and one of the huge, finned brake drums (Donington Collection)

Bugatti had gone to 4.9 litres for Formule Libre races, apart from making a fabulous four-wheel-drive sprint car, just as Alfa Romeo made two twin-engined *Bimotore* cars. Maserati also built, in later years, a 4-litre V12 and an earlier twin-six racer. Likewise, Alfa Romeo had, in 1929, put two 2-litre eight-cylinder power units side by side to form a sixteen-cylinder, 4-litre Formule Libre racing car.

All was changed in 1934, by the new 750 kg Formula. This was aimed at preventing the overdose of absolute power which the authorities who governed motor racing felt the free Formula had dangerously encouraged. They reckoned without the strength of Hitlerian Germany. Hitler wanted propaganda through motor racing and was able to divert enough money towards Mercedes-Benz and Auto Union to enable these Companies to produce quite extraordinary racing and record-breaking cars. The employment of expensive light alloys defeated the new maximum-weight ruling, while by mixing fuel-brews of the most advanced nature, enormous power was developed by their big engines, which were at the same time sufficiently light to enable the complete car to pass the weighing-in ceremony. It was a new era of racing, which produced

Right: a picture that tells the story of the German domination of motor racing in the late 1930s. The Mercedes pit crew at the Swiss Grand Prix, at Berne, in 1937 shows their own team cars of Caracciola, Lang and von Brauchitsch in the leading three places, with Stuck – in the rival Auto Union – lying fourth

Below: in the hands of Tazio Nuvolari the 2991 cc, supercharged, eight-cylinder Maserati 8CM became a race winner. The wide lower half of the bodywork complied with the minimum body width requirement of the 1934, 750 kg formula, leaving the upper half in narrow, wind-cheating form. Although the car was very successful, it had a reputation for being extremely difficult to drive and cost several drivers their lives
(Donington Collection)

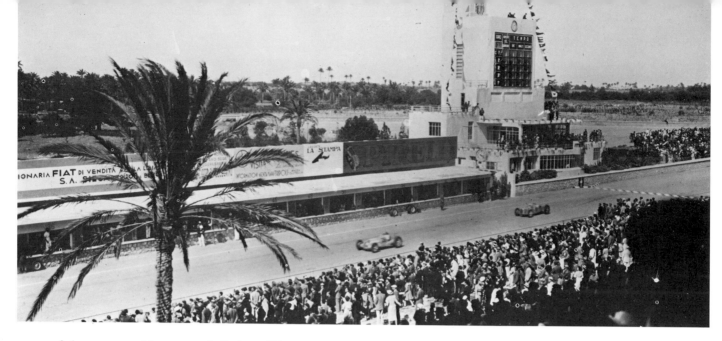

some of the most exciting cars of all time. They were so light and powerful that only a handful of the most skilled racing drivers could safely unleash them and Hitler (contrary to expectations) had to invite foreigners to drive for him. Englishman Dick Seaman and the top driver of them all, Italy's Tazio Nuvolari were thus signed onto the driving strength.

By now, independent suspension was better understood and softer springing mediums, permitting greater road-wheel movement, were possible, which enabled these great cars to hold the road rather better than the older, harshly sprung, racing cars had done. Even so, the sight and the sound of these new 750 kg-Formula cars were astounding, as were the smell and the eye-watering-propensities of Mercedes-Benz methanol fuel! The cars, especially the rear-engined Auto Unions, tended to oversteer. It took a driver with very quick reactions to cope with this by adding opposite steering-lock and using just the right amount of throttle for the conditions, which varied with every type of corner, road surface, car weight and weather condition. It was truly the Age of Giants – of both men and machines.

In the end, as another war loomed large, the Germans dominated motor

Left : one of the most picturesque circuits ever
to be used for Grand Prix racing was at Tripoli,
set amidst palm trees and sand dunes. Hermann
Lang's Mercedes is seen leading the 1937 event
past the impressive pits and control tower

Below right : 'B' Bira in his 3-litre Maserati at the
1939 JCC International Trophy at Brooklands

Below : by 1937 German domination of motor
sport was bringing magnificent machinery such
as this W125 to the circuits. The 5.66-litre
supercharged eight-cylinder engine gave a
massive 646 bhp at 5800 rpm, making it the most
powerful Grand Prix car of all time

racing. Mercedes-Benz topped everyone else. However, in spite of the enormous amount of finance available and the great armies of mechanics, spares and racing cars that the two Hitler-inspired teams brought to every race, these revolutionary new designs took time to perfect. For a short time, Mercedes-Benz were in trouble technically and Auto Union had the edge over them. The rest – Maserati, Alfa Romeo and Bugatti – did what they could, by opening-out obsolete engines, toying with independent front suspension (except for Bugatti, who was never to adopt it for racing, apart from a slight permitted movement in the centre of the tubular front axle of his last GP cars) and by taking, while they could, the top racing drivers. In the end, Germany gained complete ascendancy, up to the outbreak of war.

Mercedes-Benz quickly developed their W125 until, by 1937, it was the ultimate in the brute force field of thinking, as well as a perfect piece of road-racing machinery. It had, in this form, a Roots-blown, twin-cam engine of 94×102 mm for its eight, in-line cylinders, giving the power unit a swept volume of 5.66 litres. It developed no less than 646 bhp at 5800 rpm, and at only 2000 rpm gave as much power as most of the earlier 1930s racing engines had available at peak revs! Prior to this, Mercedes had raced the W25 cars, which had gained performance by continual increases in engine size. With the know-how they had attained from these, they applied not an independent system but a De Dion rear axle to their W125 chassis. They had already learned how to defeat wheel-spin out of corners by placing the final-drive and differential unit on the chassis frame, thus obviating the lifting of one wheel under torque, as suffered by a beam back axle. Now, they were able to combine this desirable characteristic with driving wheels which remained vertical as they rose and fell over road undulations. This gave them a much better driving force and killed the inherent oversteer of the swing-axle rear independent suspension systems. A skilled driver could now spin the car's wheels to promote oversteer when required, in a car that was otherwise neutral or deliberately set up to understeer. A very rigid chassis of oval tubes was used, in accord with these suspension arrangements, the front wheels being given coil spring and wishbone ifs, while the De Dion back-end used torsion bars. With a sleek aluminium shell of a single-seater body, these W125 Mercedes-Benz were classic cars, able to reach a top speed of some 195 mph, depending on the gearing in use.

Deciding that God is on the side of the Big Battalions, and that a maximum weight limit had entirely failed to hold racing-car speeds down, the authorities brought in a 3-litre maximum engine capacity ruling for 1938. This gave some consolation to the other European racing teams who had almost wilted away under the German onslaught. Even Ettore Bugatti's very handsome 3.3-litre GP car with its piano-wire-spoked wheels, the Type 59, had achieved little, even when given a 3.8-litre engine; Bugatti's last fling before the war centred around a 4.7-litre single-seater, again to no avail. Maserati tried to hold the German supremacy under the new Formula with their 3-litre cars, again without much success, and Alfa Romeo fared little better, although they experimented with three engines of this size: a straight-eight, a V12 and a V16. The last-named gave about 350 bhp, which was no match for the 3-litre Mercedes-Benz cars' 420 bhp. Mercedes achieved this by designing a new 67×70 mm, V12 engine of 2.96 litres, that gave the aforesaid power at 7800 rpm. It followed the general specification of the engine used in the W125 Mercedes-Benz, with twin overhead camshafts actuating four valves per cylinder, roller-bearings, Roots supercharging, fixed cylinder heads, and welded steel water-jacketting. An important advance was the employment on the 1939 version of the W154 of two blowers in series, driven from the nose of the crankshaft, to provide two-stage supercharging. One blower fed the other and remarkably high boosts were obtained satisfactorily, to an ultimate 34 psi. The mixture was sucked from the Mercedes-designed carburettor, a system to which they had changed their W125 engines in 1937. The 3-litre W154 in its final form gave 485 bhp at 7000 rpm.

Mercedes-Benz proved themselves masters of racing-car design and construction at this period, just as they had in the past and were to do again. Apart from their significant successes in the Grand Prix field, when the 1939 Tripoli GP was deliberately limited to 1½-litre cars to encourage the Italians (who were on top in *voiturette* racing at the time). Mercedes-Benz very quickly built two cars of this capacity using V8 engines, and won again. The car was designated the Type W165. Its ninety degree vee engine had dimensions of 64×58 mm and, from these 1.49 litres, the excellent power output of 260 bhp at 8500 rpm was realised. The twin superchargers, five-speed gearbox and De Dion rear suspension were like those of the full-scale Mercedes-Benz GP cars and, eventually, two-stage supercharging was adopted, when 278 bhp at 8250 rpm was spoken of for this 1½-litre engine.

Going back to the commencement of the 750 kg Formula, Auto Union, who were to oppose the Mercedes-Benz entries throughout the 3-litre Formula up to the outbreak of war, used a completely different approach. Dr Ferdinand Porsche had been encouraged by Hitler to design world-beating racing and record cars and, as he was engaged in giving Hitler his 'Peoples' Car' in the guise of the rear-engined Volkswagen, he put the engine of the Auto Union at the back. It was a very different proposition from that in a VW, however, being at first a V16, supercharged, 6006 cc power-pack developing a rumoured 600 bhp, and driving through a five-speed gearbox. This was enough to cower the opposition from the start, as stories of the fabulous performance of these secretly constructed P-wagons on early tests, in March 1934, filtered to the rest of Europe and to Britain. Dr Porsche had provided all-round independent suspension for his new racer, using trailing arms and torsion bars at the front (with which every VW Beetle owner will be familiar) and swing axles and torsion bars at the back. The chassis was made up of tubular members, the main tubes of which conveyed the cooling water from the nose radiator to the engine (and which tended to leak), and the engine had a central camshaft and push-rods to operate the inclined overhead valves. These A-type Auto Unions – the name was based on the Audi, Wanderer, Horch and DKW amalgamation – were difficult cars to drive. Their swing axles led to oversteer which was aggravated by the big 6-litre engine in the tail. However, while Mercedes-Benz sorted out their new straight-eight, 32-valve racers, Auto Union got their cars home first in a number of races.

For the 3-litre Formula, Auto Union put in De Dion rear suspension and

Top: the Bugatti type 59 first appeared in 1933 with a 2.8-litre engine, subsequently enlarged to 3.3 and 4.7-litres. This was the last Bugatti racing car produced in any quantity, and despite wins at Spa and Algiers the works cars were sold to private owners at the end of 1934

Above: the supercharged V12 Mercedes W154 developed 420 bhp and won five Grands Prix in 1938. Auto Union, the chief rival, scored two

Above right: the original 4.4 litre V16 Auto Union A type Grand Prix car of 1934, the development of which was fostered by the German Government

used a 65 × 75 mm, V12 engine, with two-stage Roots supercharging and inclined overhead valves, worked from triple overhead camshafts. The engine was still mounted behind the driver, but in this model the wheelbase was two inches shorter than in the C-type cars, at 9 ft 4 in, and the cockpit was further aft. Even so, it took Nuvolari, soon to be *the* crack Auto Union pilot, some time to get used to the handling characteristics of this 3-litre, 185 mph car which gave him 400 bhp at 7000 rpm to control, which was not surprising since the daring driver could provoke wheel-spin at 150 mph on a dry road.

Before we leave these outstanding contributions to motor-racing history, let us note down the principal engineers responsible for each car. They were as follows.

Mercedes-Benz: W25, Nibel and Wagner;
W125, Max Seiler, Wagner, Hess and Uhlenhaut;
W163, Wagner and Hess, under Dr Seiler;
Auto Union: A-type, Dr Ferdinand Porsche and Adolf Rosenberger;
B-type, Dr Ferdinand Porsche;
C-type, Dr Ferdinand Porsche;
D-type, Dr Werner, Dr Feuereisen and Professor Eberan von Eberhorst.

While all this intense top-formula work was going on, with the most exciting cars and racing of all time, the *voiturette* class had not been neglected. Raymond Mays had been instrumental in creating the ERA – its initials stood for English Racing Automobile – by using a supercharged, six-cylinder, short-push rod engine, based on that of the Riley Six, and a high 'cart-sprung' chassis, designed by the land-speed-record engineer, Reid Railton, to take a single-seater body. In 1½-litre form, these ERAs, which were sold to private owners, were decently successful. However, Dick Seaman had a 1927 straight-eight Delage, developed to give a reliable 195 bhp which, by virtue of needing fewer stops for refuelling, could beat the works ERAs. The Continental opposition came from 1½-litre Maserati and Alfa Romeo cars, but these were to have a greater importance after the war. Had hostilities not intervened, some very interesting 1½-litre racing must have resulted, because Auto Union were known to be working on a car to compete against the W165 Mercedes-Benz. It was thought to be capable of giving 327 bhp at a rousing 9000 rpm from a V12 of 53 × 56 mm bore and stroke, using a higher compression ratio, in conjunction with supercharging, than Mercedes-Benz had yet dared try.

THE RACES: 1914-39

Although World War I stopped European and British motor racing, it did see some of the valuable lessons of competition converted into effective aeroplane engines, at first by Mercédès and then later by Rolls-Royce and others. Until America became involved in the hostilities, it was able to continue an indulgence for the world's fastest sport. There was, however, still a strong European flavour, even across the Atlantic, because many successful pre-war Grand Prix cars were shipped there to continue their track careers. The Peugeot and Sunbeam 1914 Grand Prix cars appeared in the USA, and Ralph de Palma, the great American driver, secured one of the 1914 French GP-winning 4½-litre Mercédès racers. With the Peugeot, Dario Resta won many titles in 1915 and 1916, but de Palma took the important 500-mile race on the oval Indianapolis track (a race which started in 1911) in 1915 at an average of 89.8 mph; he also set the fastest lap at 98.6 mph.

Four 1914 GP Delages arrived for the 1916 Indy 500, but this was won, in the absence of the Mercédès, by Resta's Peugeot which averaged 83.26 mph for 300 miles, at which point rain stopped play. The Mercédès/Peugeot but de Palma also changed to the Mercédès, to win at Omaha.
rivalry, originating at Lyons in the eve-of-war Grand Prix, was continued at the Chicago board-track for the 300 Mile Chicago Derby which ended in a victory for Resta's Peugeot at 98.6 mph when, right at the end, after four hours of intense battling, a plug cut out on the Mercédès and the car was forced into the pits. Incidentally, the Peugeot proved able to lap at 109 mph.

These Henry-designed cars won many other American war-time triumphs, but de Palma also changed to the Mercédès, to win at Omaha, averaging

Howdy Wilcox won the Indy in 1919 with a 1914 4½-litre Peugeot, now privately entered, at 87.95 mph. One of M. Ballot's new, Henry-designed, straight-eight cars, built in remarkably quick time, was taken to Indy by René Thomas where he set fastest lap at a record 104 mph.

A varied assortment of pre-war, Henry-engineered Peugeots turned up when the Targa Florio was run over Sicilian mountain roads late in November 1919, with the 2½-litre car of André Boillot leading the team. The Targa was a punishing race over atrocious road surfaces, but André triumphed, although he crossed the finish line backwards because spectators had run onto the course and caused him to spin under braking. It was M. Ballot, however, who advised him to drive back down the course, turn around and finish with his car facing the proper way in case of disqualification. After this, it is said, Boillot collapsed over the steering wheel and cried '*C'est pour la France*'. His car had been off the road six times but he had averaged 34.19 mph for the 268 eventful miles.

With racing on the Continent moribund through 1920, it was at Indianapolis where the action returned. The Americans had now imposed a 3-litre engine capacity limit, so new straight-eight, twin-cam Ballots had been built, ready

Far left: the engine of the C type Auto Union, a 6.1-litre, 520 bhp, supercharged V16 which produced enormous low-speed torque. It was said that wheelspin could be provoked at 150 mph on a dry road

Left: with the change of formula for 1938, Auto Union produced a supercharged 3-litre V12 engine for the new D type chassis

Above: the ERA B type, number R10 of 1935. This car belongs to Jack Williamson who raced the car in its early days; his son Jonty campaigns the car in vintage events today

Below: André Boillot, younger brother of Georges, in a 2.5-litre Peugeot of 1914 at the start of the 1919 Indianapolis 500 Miles race. Tyre trouble precluded success

for the resumption of Grand Prix road racing; at Indy, they met the straight-eight Duesenbergs. The Ballots were fast, with de Palma's car dominating practice. However, in the race, his car caught fire and then ran out of petrol. The race was, however, won by another 'Henry crib', in the form of a Monroe, the engine of which was outwardly the same as a 1913, 3-litre Peugeot. The Monroe was driven by Gaston Chevrolet and averaged 88½ mph for the 500 miles; de Palma and the Ballot had to be content with fastest lap, at 99.15 mph. Thus, for the time being, a four-cylinder engine had triumphed over the new, small multi-cylindered units.

Racing resumed its former significance in 1921, with the return of the French Grand Prix, run to the same 3-litre formula as Indianapolis. Firstly, however, the Americans had their traditional Indy 500 again and this time the straight-eight motor car was in the ascendant. However, Tommy Milton's Frontenac, yet another crib of a four-cylinder Henry-type engine, won, at 88.16 mph, from half-a-dozen eights, three Ballots and three Duesenbergs. After this, it was to the Grand Prix, run at Le Mans over a course that was soon a sea of jagged stones, that attention was directed. Inspired by what it had done during the war, America decided to go for the road-racing 'blue riband', and sent over their left-hand-drive, three-speed, straight-eight Duesenberg cars, with hydraulic four-wheel brakes.

The state of the course, which used part of the pre-war circuit, was most unfortunate, as much work had been done to prevent dust, and to bind the surface. However, puncture-promoting flying stones did not stop Jimmy Murphy from beating the European runners, his Duesenberg finishing the 322 miles with its driver bruised and dirty and the car's straight-eight engine ready to seize after a piece of rock had holed the radiator. Nevertheless, Murphy was comfortably ahead of the Ballots of de Palma and Jules Goux. It was a convincing victory, in a race mostly of trouble for the Ballot and STD cars. The winner had averaged 78.10 mph and achieved fastest lap at 84 mph. Of the rest of this first post-war GP field, Guyot, Dubonnet and Joe Boyer made up the four-car Duesenberg team; Mathis drove a tiny Mathis more to demonstrate than race it; Guinness, René Thomas, Segrave and André Boillot drove the Anglo-French STD (or Talbot-Darracq) straight-eights and Chassagne and Wagner had the remaining Ballots. Boyer retired with a seized big-end bearing, because, like Murphy, he had had a stone puncture the car's radiator which let out all the cooling water; Chassagne went out when the bolster fuel tank of his hastily prepared TD came loose; Guyot had a slipping clutch and a difficult-to-restart engine; and the STD entries were continually changing wheels due to defective tyres. Incidentally, Murphy had had the rigours of his great ride made more severe because he was driving with broken ribs.

This was an interesting commencement of post-war road racing, even if a devastating one for the European entrants. Fiat had entered but had non-started in this Grand Prix, and any hope of the Duesenbergs being matched against the new Italian cars at Brescia was dispersed by the news that they were returning to America. In this 3-litre contest, the Ballots at last came into their own for, although the Fiats were quicker and Bordino's made fastest lap, it was now the Fiat's turn to be delayed by tyre troubles. So, Goux's Ballot won, at 89.9 mph, from Chassagne's similar car, which was one mile per hour slower; Wagner's Fiat was a poor third.

For 1922, the governing body of the sport brought in a 2-litre engine-capacity limit, which meant that all the carefully conceived designs had to be scrapped and new ones worked out. The French Grand Prix was taken to a fast circuit at Strasbourg in 1922, where the local authorities were so keen to host the race that they contributed Fr350,000 towards the organisational expenses. The new ruling evolved the slowest and dullest racing cars for some time, with only Bugatti and Rolland-Pilain staying with straight-eight units. Sunbeam had the celebrated Ernest Henry design new four-cylinder, sixteen-valve, power units for them, but it was Fiat, with their sixes, who were the successful entrants. The wealthy Count Louis Zborowski was anxious to get into real motor racing and was sponsoring Aston Martins with twin-cam

Henry-pattern engines (it would be fair to say that Henry dominated racing-engine design during this period) but they were 1½-litre cars, and hence out-classed. Zborowski, however, had realised his ambition, but was to die for it two years later after having survived the Chitty-Chitty-Bang-Bang escapades at Brooklands without injury.

The Grand Prix, over a triangular course, started at 8.15 am, spectators being keen enough to rise early for their sport in those far-away days; they were to see both triumph and tragedy. Triumph, when the veteran driver Felice Nazzaro brought his Fiat home the winner, at 79.2 mph for the 500 miles, after he had been driving for 6 hrs 17 mins 17 secs, and tragedy because these Fiats had weak back-axle shafts. When one broke and let a wheel detach itself on Felice's nephew's car, the young Biaggio Nazzaro was killed. The third Fiat also suffered this alarming malady but Bordino, who had driven very fast in the opening stages of the race, survived. Thus, what would have been a Fiat 1-2-3 walkover was a lone and hollow victory for 'old-man' Nazzaro. Behind him, a long way back, two of the Bugattis, driven by de Viscaya and Marco, unexpectedly found themselves in second and third places. Another Bugatti, handled by Maury, finished outside the time limit; every other starter retired, the Sunbeams dropping out with valve-stem faults. So ended a dull Grand Prix that Bordino was apparently intended to win, and which his team-mate Nazzaro had walked away with (at mostly 4100 rpm and never exceeding 4500 rpm).

The rapidly built Monza Autodrome was used in 1922 for the 2-litre European Grand Prix and supporting 1½-litre Italian GP. Because the organisers were able to charge all spectators admission-fees, and 150,000 of them are said to have attended, it was possible to award prize money amounting to the equivalent of some £6000. A dismally dull race was run off in a drizzle of rain, with the Fiats dominating a miserable field of eight: everyone else was entirely outclassed. Bordino won from Nazzaro, averaging 86.9 mph, with the only other car still motoring at the end being de Viscaya's Bugatti which was flagged off. It is, however, interesting that Maserati had started in a Diatto, which he had driven so fiercely that he crashed and wrote it off.

Mercédès returned to racing in the 1922 Targa Florio. Moreover, their cars were supercharged. Ironically, it was Masetti who was the victor, driving a much revamped 1914 GP Mercédès, of the kind that had proved invincible at Lyons on the eve of war. Behind him, Jules Goux drove a great race to take second place in a 2-litre, twin-cam, four-cylinder Ballot, more a sports car than a racer. The Frenchman had had victory snatched from him because loss of brakes had caused him to crash and he had to complete that last, long Sicilian lap with a bent chassis and very bald tyres. He finished only 1 min 47 secs behind the Italian in his German 'veteran' Mercédès, however.

Above: the start of the 1919 Indianapolis 500 Miles race. The leading cars here are Packard, Peugeot and Ballot, and the race was won by American Howdy Wilcox in one of the 1914 model Peugeots at 88.05 mph

Below: Jules Goux pictured in 1926, the year he won the French and Spanish Grands Prix for Bugatti. He began racing for Lion-Peugeot in 1907, and won the Indianapolis classic in 1913 in a Grand Prix Peugeot. Goux was regarded as a good long-distance driver, and he excelled in events like the Targa Florio. He joined Bugatti in 1925, and continued to work for that company until 1955

Left: Le Mans in 1921. André Boillet's eight-cylinder Talbot Darracq at White House on its way to fifth place in the French Grand Prix

Right: in the 1922 French Grand Prix at Strasbourg Giulio Foresti's Ballot is chased through Duttlenheim corner by the two-litre, eight-cylinder Bugatti of Pierre de Viscaya, which ultimately finished second

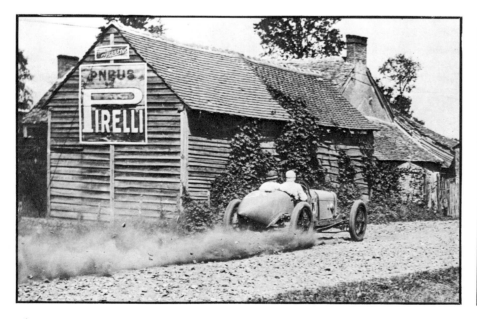

The year 1923 was to see the ACI continue the 2-litre engine-capacity limit, in spite of the retrograde happenings of the previous season. However, things improved and the French Grand Prix, held at Tours, was notable for its big and varied entry. Coatalen, of Sunbeam, as was his wont, had secured the services of the Fiat engineers, and his cars resembled nothing so much as the previous year's highly successful Fiats, but painted British racing green instead of Italian red! They had the same unblown, six-cylinder, twin-cam layout that had recently carried Bordino and Nazzaro to such great success. Henry Segrave had, by now, become an accepted driver in the STD racing team and it might be thought that he would have easily won the GP at Tours. It was not quite so easy as that but, when the faster supercharged straight-eight Fiats had trouble with stones and dust, making short work of their new-fangled blowers, Segrave did in fact manage to win. He was helped by a clutch that had slipped in the early stages of the race, leaving his engine unstressed, as he could not use maximum revs. The other Sunbeams were having a great deal of trouble: Guinness with his clutch and Divo with a jammed fuel filler-cap that delayed him as he could only continue by putting petrol into a small reserve tank every lap. The Fiat drivers had a bad time, Salamano thinking, from the behaviour of his engine, that he was out of fuel, whereas the blower had quit. His riding mechanic was dispatched for more fuel, but was told he had to run and not borrow a bicycle as he had done. In the midst of all this drama, Segrave realised he had taken the lead. He went on, with his mechanic Dutoit by his side, to win the first Grand Prix to fall to a British-built car although, as has been said, its design was really Italian. Segrave had averaged 75.31 mph, his race-time being 6 hrs 35 mins 19.6 secs. The luckless Divo, French driver of the other green Sunbeam, did not cross the finishing line until 19 mins 6.2 secs later! Following came Friedrich's Bugatti, with its odd tank-like body, and the Guinness Sunbeam, a sick car that lost a further two minutes on the final lap after its engine had stalled. The only other finisher in this 1923 Grand Prix, a race that had opened with such promise, was Lefèbvre, in one of the odd, ultra-streamlined, sleeve-valve Voisins.

In the wake of the open and technically advanced 1923 French Grand Prix was the Italian Grand Prix at Monza. Alfa Romeo had a new P1 model, but it was unfortunately withdrawn after one of the drivers, Sivocci, had been killed in practice – the car was never seen again. Germany had been refused an entry for the French race but produced a revolutionary rear-engined tear-drop-shape Benz for the Italian event. America, in the absence of the

Below: Henry Segrave, 1896–1930, was one of Britain's best drivers of the 1920s. He joined the Sunbeam-Talbot-Darracq works team in 1921 and drove brilliantly in virtually every race he entered. In 1927 he shattered the World Land Speed Record in a 1000 hp, 44.8-litre, aero-engined Sunbeam, travelling at 203.79 mph. Vying with Malcolm Campbell, Segrave raised the record in 1929 to 231.44 mph with his Napier-engined Golden Arrow, for which achievement he received a knighthood. Sir Henry had latterly become interested in speedboats, and died on Lake Windermere when his boat struck a log during record attempts

Bottom: Segrave's victory in the 1923 French Grand Prix was aided by Kenelm Lee Guinness, who drove his Sunbeam flat-out to break the opposition and, when Guinness fell back, Segrave went on to win

Right: the Benz of 1923 anticipated modern Grand Prix design by 35 years, being mid-engined. Here, Minoia's fourth-placed car visits the pits during the Italian Grand Prix; the streamlined body, fitted with side doors, was seen only at this particular race meeting

Below: Veteran Fiat driver Felice Nazzaro, who won three classic races in 1907, took first place in the 1922 French Grand Prix at Strasbourg driving a 2-litre six-cylinder Fiat

Bottom: the supercharged, 2-litre, straight-eight Fiat which Carlo Salamano, wearing the linen helmet, drove to victory at Monza in 1923. Nazzaro was second in a similar car

victorious Duesenbergs, was represented by Indy-type Millers, but they presented little menace to the European cars, which had better gearboxes and brakes more suited to a road circuit. Fiat had at last got their superchargers functioning properly and fielded a team of three effective cars, to be handled by Bordino, Salamano and the ageing Felice Nazzaro. Bordino broke his arm in a practice crash but insisted on competing, with his riding mechanic doing the gear-changing for him. The Fiats were the vastly superior cars on the course but, in the race, Bordino had to confess that he could not continue, due to fatigue. Salamano and Nazzaro finished in the first and second positions, the former having averaged over 91 mph and set a new Monza lap-record of 99.8 mph. Third place went to America, with Jimmy Murphy's Miller; he was followed in by two of the unconventional streamlined Benz projectiles.

In *voiturette* racing, the revised supercharged Darracqs (or Talbot-Darracqs)

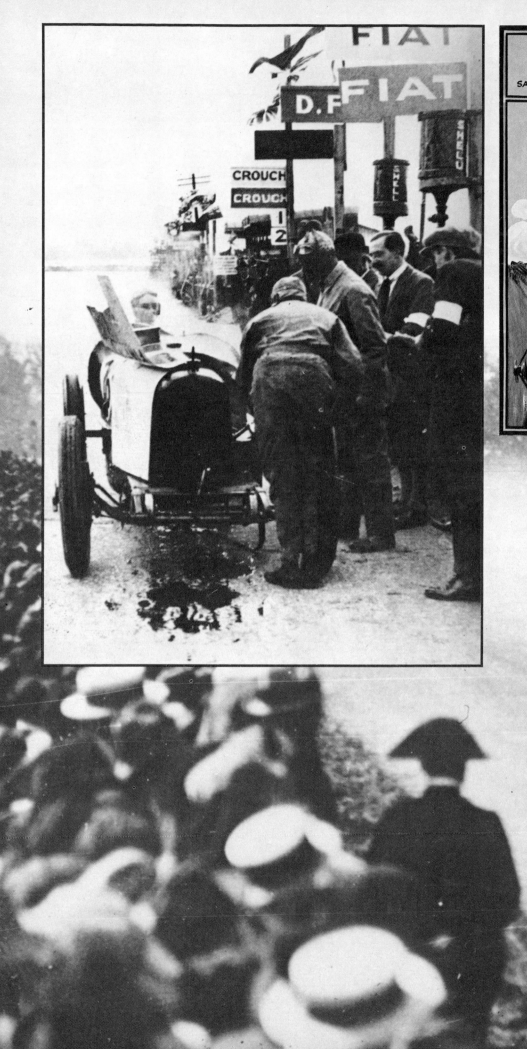

PROGRAMME

SAT. SEPT. 20TH   PRICE ONE SHILLING

200 MILES RACE

FOR LIGHT CARS UNDER 1500 c.c. AT BROOKLANDS.

ORGANISED BY THE JUNIOR CAR CLUB

maintained their 'invincible' reputation but so feared the new blown 1½-litre Fiats that they abstained from running in the Junior Car Club's 200 Mile Race at Brooklands in October 1923. The irony of this was that soon after both Fiats retired with dramatic mechanical failures. Salamano and Malcolm Campbell had not expected this, and a track-racing 12/50 Alvis, based on the well liked Alvis sports chassis, won instead. This shows how supercharging was now dominating both classes of motor-racing, for the 1923 Italian Grand Prix had been the first International race to be won by a supercharged car.

The racing season of 1924 opened with the Targa Florio and was won by a 2-litre 1923-pattern Mercédès improved in detail by Dr Porsche. Alfa Romeo had their effective new P2 racers ready for the Cremona event and their obvious superiority in this race, which Ascari won at a speed of over 98 mph, being timed at 123 mph for ten kilometres, must have made the Milan concern feel very confident about the forthcoming French Grand Prix at Lyons. Once they arrived there, however, they discovered that the 1923-type Sunbeams, which now had supercharged engines, were the faster cars. Rumour has it that this was so obvious that the Alfa Romeo personnel offered to let

Sunbeam win, without harassing the new cars from Wolverhampton, if they would, in turn, allow Alfas to come home in second and third places. Whether or not this was true, it seems that Louis Coatalen would have refused and that the great French race was as much an open battle as ever. In fact, Sunbeam chose to change to new German magnetos on the eve of the contest and, as a result, suffered from chronic misfiring. Thus, the newly evolving great P2 straight-eight supercharged Alfa Romeo had the considerable distinction of winning the most important motor race of the year on its first appearance there. The driver to pull this off was the portly opera singer Campari, at an average speed of 71 mph. The V12 Delage cars of Albert Divo and Robert Benoist followed the winning Italian home. Segrave in one of the stuttering Sunbeams had to make do with fastest lap, at 76.7 mph; the Bugatti drivers had lost out with continual tyre trouble and the Fiat pilots with braking maladies.

The circus – although it was not called this in 1924 – then moved to Monza for the Italian Grand Prix, which Alfa Romeo absolutely dominated while, in San Sebastian, Sunbeam had, to some extent, atoned for their French Grand Prix disappointment by Segrave's success there. However, while Henry Segrave had had a tough time winning in Spain, Zborowski had been killed driving one of the unpredictable straight-eight 2-litre Mercédès cars at Monza, leaving Clive Gallop to bring the Count's body back to England and disband the great stable of racing cars at Higham, much to the detriment of racing at Brooklands.

Everywhere, the increasing cost of racing was causing manufacturers to wonder if they could afford to continue to participate and drivers to question whether the low prize money made it worth their while continuing this risky profession. One solution seemed to be to concentrate on racing at specialised circuits, where maximum admission money could be extracted from the spectators, which it was not always possible to do at a closed-public-road course where the spectators were scattered about. Thus, the 1925 French Grand Prix was run over the combined track and road circuit at Montlhéry, where high attendance figures were expected.

It was not a particularly impressive affair, however. It began as an Alfa Romeo/Delage procession, with Antonio Ascari ahead of his team-mate Campari but, after setting up the best lap speed of 80 mph, the experienced Alfa Romeo driver who was in the lead, somehow misjudged a long fast bend and his car tangled with the wood-paling fencing and overturned in the ditch. When the news reached the circuit that Ascari had died in the ambulance, the other Alfa Romeo cars were withdrawn, as a mark of respect, and Delage, next in the lead with Benoist and Divo, gained a rather hollow victory, at 69.7 mph, with a Sunbeam in third place, followed by a host of Bugattis. Prior to this, Bugatti, with an unsupercharged engine, had won the Targa Florio and the European Grand Prix had been run off at the Spa road course in

Top: the Robert Benoist/Albert Divo 2-litre V12 Delage pursues a Bugatti, passing close to the edge on its way to victory at Montlhéry, Paris, in 1925 Grand Prix. In this race Antonio Ascari caught his Alfa Romeo's hubcap on the chestnut fencing and was killed when the car overturned into the ditch

Above: Giuseppe Campari, who gave Alfa Romeo their first racing victory in 1920 at Mugello. He owned one of the P2 Alfas which he raced independently, winning the European Grand Prix of 1924. Campari also drove works sports cars, winning the 1928 mille Miglia; he was killed in an Alfa P3 at Monza in 1933

Right: the Le Mans 24-hour race, 1924. This was the first time the classic was won by British drivers; here the John Duff/Frank Clement 3-litre Bentley races an Alfa Romeo at Mulsanne

Belgium, resulting in another 1–2 Alfa Romeo P2 success, Ascari winning at 74.56 mph, after the Delage entry had retired.

By now the greatest credit was due to Alfa Romeo, for their success with their beautiful P2 racers, but this made racing rather monotonous. For example, they had very little difficulty in winning the Italian GP at Monza, the No 1 driver in the team on this occasion being Count Brilli-Peri but at the end of this 1925 season, Delage won at San Sebastian only because the P2 Alfa Romeos were absent.

In 1926, however, the new 1½-litre Formula appeared. This marked the beginning of a Delage domination as great of that of Alfa Romeo's in the preceeding season – but not at first, however. Bugatti was by now reaping the benefit of outstanding roadholding and reliability and this enabled Jules Goux to win the French Grand Prix at the dull Marimas oval but, as the only runners were all in Bugattis, this race came to be known as the most ineffectual French Grand Prix of all time. Indeed, this impossibly dull race which was 500 kilometres in length, had only Goux as a finisher, the other two Bugattis having retired. He averaged a mere 68 mph, driving alone for the final fifty miles. The Talbots were unprepared for the European Grand Prix at San Sebastian, and, as the new straight-eight Delage cars were still addicted to roasting their drivers, it was Goux and the Bugatti that won again. The Delage cars had been stationary for something like an hour during this race but eventually the Bourlier/Sénéchal car was able to make up for lost ground and finish second, with Costantini, whose Bugatti developed last-minute trouble, in third place. This strongly reflected on the wide spacing of GP cars of that time and on the patience of the 1926 spectators. Racing was enlivened, nevertheless, by a 'free-for-all' ruling that prevailed for the Spanish Grand Prix, which enabled Segrave to run with a 4-litre V12 Land Speed Record-type Sunbeam and for 2.3-litre Bugattis to mingle with the 1½-litre and 2-litre cars. However, Segrave's front axle caved-in and the Delage entries also struck trouble so a Bugatti won again, with Costantini finishing ahead of Goux, at a speed of 76.8 mph for the 374½ miles.

The 1927 season was again for 1½-litre cars in the nature of a triangular battle between Delage, Talbot and Bugatti, with the emphasis on the superb little straight-eight Delages. Indeed, the experienced Robert Benoist, who lost his life in World War II working for the French resistance movement, won four of the 1927 *grandes epreuves*. He was first to receive the finishing flag in the French GP at Montlhéry, in the Spanish GP run at San Sebastian, and in the European GP at Monza, while he led the British Grand Prix, which was run at Brooklands Track over a course made into a parody of a road circuit by the use of a few sand-bank chicanes. Delage had managed to win this race the previous year in spite of their cockpit overheating, but it had required two drivers with Sénéchal helping out Wagner on that occasion, and, whereas the average speed had been 71.61 mph, Benoist averaged 85.59 mph for the 1927

race. Bugatti decided not to compete in either the French or Italian (European)
Grands Prix, and it is typical of Delage superiority that only one of these
cars was run in the latter race, with which Benoist made the fastest lap at
94.31 mph, winning easily at just over 90 mph for 50 laps of a wet course. Fiat
managed to win just one race, the Milan GP run at Monza, on an identical
circuit to the European GP, with their odd twelve-cylinder twin-crankshaft
concoction, which was entrusted to Bordino.

Racing after 1927 became more complicated. Many new events were
instituted and this, together with the free-engine-size formula resulted in a
situation whereby sports cars mingling with pure racing machines competed
for different honours. Picking out some of the more significant events, there
was that notorious occasion in the 1928 Targa Florio when Mme. Junek was
ahead of all the male drivers for a time, until her Bugatti finally dropped back,
leaving Albert Divo's 2.3-litre Bugatti in the lead.

1928 also saw the emergence of Tazio Nuvolari, who is regarded by many
authorities as the greatest and most versatile racing driver of all time. That
year his Bugatti took first place at Alessandria in a race called the Bordino

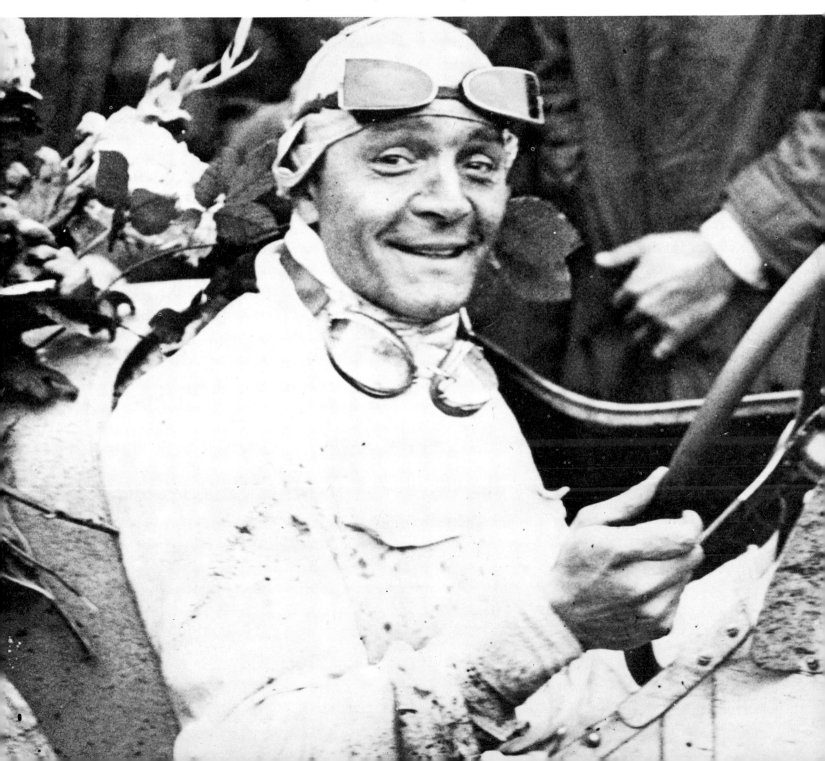

Prize, after Pietro Bordino. Louis Chiron, the volatile French ace, won the 1928 Rome, Marne and San Sebastian Grands Prix for Bugatti and clinched a fine successful racing season by taking first place in the European Grand Prix at Monza, at a speed of just under 100 mph. Arcangelli, who competed in a revised edition of the 1927 Talbot, was a fast challenger, and he won the Circuit of Cremona race at the high speed of 101.31 mph. He also set fastest lap, at 103.2 mph, at Monza while a Talbot driven by Materassi won at Montenero. The German Grand Prix, held at the Nürburgring, was nominally a sports-car contest. However, this arduous race was won by Rudi Caracciola in a 7-litre Mercedes-Benz at a speed of 64.6 mph, with two similar cars following him home, having vanquished the road-equipped Type 35 Bugattis, which would normally have been expected to out-handle the big and heavy Mercedes cars on this mountainous circuit. Count Brilli-Peri was now Bugatti-mounted, but could only average a speed of 62.2 mph. Altogether, 1928 was very much a Bugatti year, with drivers of the calibre of Chiron, Nuvolari and Caracciola much in evidence.

The trend continued in 1929. The International season commenced with

Left: car No 15 is a 1½-litre, twelve-cylinder Fiat Tipo 806, the last of the racing Fiats, with which Pietro Bordino won the 1927 Milan Grand Prix at Monza. Talking to Bordino is Felice Nazzaro

Right: from the cockpit of a Bugatti, following a Delage and a Sunbeam

Top: William Grover-Williams, who raced as Williams and was domiciled in France. He owned and raced Bugattis, and won the first Monaco Grand Prix in 1929. Williams joined the SAS during world War II, but was shot by the Gestapo in 1943

Above: the great Achille Varzi, who grew up with Nuvolari on racing motor cycles. The pair began racing Bugattis, but Varzi, feeling outshone, bought an Alfa Romeo P2 and enjoyed a great run of successes, culminating in the 1930 Targo Florio. From 1931–1934 Varzi returned to Bugatti, beating Nuvolari's Alfa P3, winning seven races, and the Mille Miglia. In 1935 he went to Auto Union and won his first race at Tripoli. After World War II he rejoined the Alfa Romeo team but at Berne in 1948, he was killed when his Tipo 158 overturned

a new, but now very respected street circuit race, at Monaco. It was won by the French-domiciled Englishman, W. Grover-Williams, in a Bugatti, at 50.23 mph, giving the well established professionals a nasty shock, as he made the fastest lap of this winding circuit, where drivers wore their hands to blisters continually changing gear, at 52.7 mph. The pending Alfa Romeo/Bugatti duelling was forecast when Achille Varzi, a dour driver who was to become an arch-rival of Nuvolari's, took the Bordino Prize at Alessandria at 68.24 mph, lapping a little faster than his average speed for the race. Divo again won the Targa Florio, over the Little Madonie circuit; his Bugatti averaged 46.21 mph

for his trip over the Sicilian mountains; driving adjacent to ravines, over stones and around hairpin bends. His car caught fire, until his mechanic used a cushion to quell the flames but he still managed to exceed his earlier speed of 45.65 mph. Minoia in another Bugatti could not get above 47.3 mph when establishing a new lap-record for this unique course. The Rome Grand Prix fell to Varzi's Alfa Romeo but Williams retaliated for Bugatti by winning the French Grand Prix at 82.66 mph. The fast Cremona Prize contest went to Brilli-Peri and Alfa Romeo. The pace rose to 114.41 mph, with Maserati in a car of his own manufacture making best lap (a record) at 124.4 mph. Held at Reims in the Champagne country, Phi-Phi Etancelin won the Marne GP for Bugatti at 85½ mph and the great Chiron, waving to the crowd, even managed a Bugatti victory at the German Grand Prix, around the Nürburgring, averaging

Below: Achille Varzi's privately owned Alfa Romeo P2 was updated by the works, and is seen here en route to victory in the 1930 Targa Florio. His faithful mechanic was Amedeo Bignami.

66.79 mph, or 2.19 mph faster than Caracciola's big Mercedes had managed to do in 1928. Louis also set the lap-record for the Nürburgring by a rousing 69.97 mph. The bitter duels between Chiron and Varzi were seen at the 1929 Coppa Ciano race at Montenero in July, when Varzi's Alfa Romeo, this being one of the old 1924 P2 cars, won at 54.17 mph leaving the lap-record to Nuvolari's Bugatti, at 55.3 mph; the low averages pointed to the difficulties the drivers had to contend with. Finally, for 1929, the now-important Monza Grand Prix was won by Varzi at a speed of 116.83 mph in a race of three engine-capacity heats and a final. Varzi drove one of the aged P2 straight-eight cars and Materassi, in a fearsome 16-cylinder 4-litre Maserati, set a lap-record for the 2.8-mile circuit of 124.2 mph. Nuvolari, in a rather dubious 1927-type Talbot, managed second spot, and a big privately sponsored sports Mercedes-Benz finished third. Incidentally, according to one English authority, one of these ancient Alfa Romeos was said to have reached 138.77 mph, in Count Brilli-Peri's hands, over ten kilometres of the Cremona circuit.

By 1930 the new Maserati cars were in the ascendant. Alfa Romeo's only important wins were at Alessandria, where Varzi dominated the field, winning the Bordino Prize race at 67.7 mph after he had lapped at the record speed of 70.7 mph and in the Targa Florio, which he won at 48.48 mph, again making a record lap speed of 49.1 mph. Once more, this was a staggering demonstration of the endurance of the old P2 Alfa Romeo, even though they had been modified for 1930 conditions and challenges. The Type 35 2.3-litre Bugattis were in the next two places. A private owner, René Dreyfus, had scored in the 1930 Monaco Grand Prix in his Bugatti, a Type 35C, at 64.63 mph, which was a very fine speed for this winding course. The new straight-eight 2½-litre Maserati had quickly come into its own, taking Arcangeli to victory at Rome, when Chiron's Bugatti failed right at the end, and Maserati cars gave wins to Fagioli in the Coppa Ciano and to Varzi at San Sebastian. Not only that; at Monza, Varzi drove a magnificent race to win the Monza GP in a 2½-litre car of this new make, having passed both Arcangeli, who was leading in a Maserati of the same type, and Maserati's own V16-engined model. Etancelin took the French GP for Bugatti, at Pau, with Birkin behind him in a stripped blower 4½ Bentley sports-car. Clearly, Alfa Romeo needed the new Monza and monoposto cars, for the aged P2 chassis could no longer stand up to the tuned engines

which were used in them. With the advent of Maserati, a new star had arisen, for the drivers to steer towards.

All thoughts of a Formula to control design had gone overboard by 1931, but it was stipulated that Grand Prix races should last for ten hours. This meant that two drivers would usually be nominated for each car and gave rise not only to an increased necessity for pit-work but to a new headache for team managers in deciding whether or not to take a top-ranking driver out of a disabled car and allow him to take the place, in one of their fitter vehicles, of a slower driver. It was an interesting though not enthralling period of racing; one of the highlights was the intensifying of the Bugatti–Alfa Romeo duel.

The 1931 season opened with the Targa Florio race, over a new and longer circuit adopted because a land slide had obliterated much of the former course. Chiron had already won the Monaco Grand Prix for Bugatti, who now had his new twin-cam, 160 bhp engine in the excellent and beautiful Type 35 cars. This updated version was designated the Type 51. Alfa Romeo replied with the Monza model and in the Targa Florio, over the Long Madonie course, Nuvolari, driving one of these new cars from Milan, gradually wore down the

Above: the 1931 Italian Grand Prix, at Monza, was won by Nuvolari and Campari in the new 2.3-litre 'Monza' Alfa Romeo, No. 26

Above left: Philippe 'Phi Phi' Etancelin began his racing career in French hill-climbs in 1926 with a Bugatti. His first win was at Reims in 1927, and he went on to achieve very many successes with Alfa Romeo, Maserati, including Le mans. Enthusiast Etancelin drove a Talbot-Lago in post-war Grands Prix with some high placings, retiring in 1952. He was always distinguishable at the wheel by his reversed cloth cap

Left: the Bugatti of Count Czaykowski is about to be passed by Sir Henry 'Tim' Birkin's stripped-down 4½-litre blower Bentley in the 1930 French Grand Prix

lead established by Varzi's faster Bugatti, to win at 40.3 mph. The low average speed was indicative of the road and weather conditions. Front mudguards were used on Nuvolari's Monza to keep streams of rain water out of the cockpit. Varzi had some consolation in setting fastest lap at a mere 43.8 mph.

The first really big race of the season was the Italian Grand Prix at Monza where strong works teams from Alfa Romeo and Bugatti clashed in full force. Apart from the Monzas, Alfa Romeo had a remarkable new twin-six-cylinder *monoposto*, of 3½-litres, and developing some 200 bhp. This was entrusted to Tazio Nuvolari. It was not as successful as had been hoped; Nuvolari only managed to reach third position, after three out of the ten hours' racing. He then retired but in the later stages of the race he aided the veteran Campari in bringing his Monza home first, at 96.17 mph. Varzi's Type 51 Bugatti had dropped out earlier, while leading, with back axle failure, only four hours into the race. Alfa Romeo also set a new lap record at 105 mph, although this was actually only a very small improvement over the old, 1924, record for the full Monza Autodrome course. A sports Mercedes-Benz was able to take victory at Nürburgring, with Rudolf Caracciola winning at 67.67 mph and then the French Grand Prix, held at the Montlhéry road circuit, saw a resumption of the French/Italian inter-marque rivalry. This time, Bugatti were the victors, Chiron and Varzi, usually great rivals, united for once and won, at an average speed of 78.21 mph.

It had been a good race for the newcomers, Maserati & Luigi Fagioli, driving one of the 2½-litre straight-eight racers that had shown up well in 1930, established the fastest lap, at 85.6 mph, which was a record for this much-used circuit. Indeed, Fagioli had been well placed for four of the ten hours over which this historic title was defended, but he then dropped back with brake maladies. Despite the Maserati's promise, the battle in this race was still very much between the Alfa Romeo and Bugatti cars and a Monza Alfa driven by Campari and Borzacchini finished in second place. Their Monza ran 27 fewer miles in the ten hours of the race than did the winning Bugatti, but then the victorious French car had lost only 10½ minutes at its depot, during just five stops, while the Alfa Romeo spent 24 minutes refuelling and being generally resuscitated.

After this, Bugatti more or less dominated the 1931 season, with victories at Reims, Spa and in Czechoslovakia, the winning drivers being, respectively, Lehoux, Williams, with Count Conelli, and Chiron. At the Nürburgring for the German Grand Prix of 1931, Caracciola in a big, even when stripped, 7-litre Mercedes-Benz sports-car triumphed over all the smaller racing cars, averaging 67.4 mph. Campari's Alfa Romeo won the Coppa Acerbo at 81.68 mph, the lap-record going to Nuvolari, also driving for Alfa Romeo, at 83.4 mph.

The heavy metal got going with a vengeance at Monza for the non-Formula Italian Grand Prix. Run over an abbreviated, 4.3-mile, course, the 14-lap event was a walk-over for the Maseratis which had been enlarged to 3.8-litres for the occasion and finished with Fagioli first and Dreyfus second. The unlimited-capacity contest saw such great cars as the twin-eight, sixteen-cylinder Maserati and the 4.9-litre Type 54 Bugatti locked in combat. The big, 152 mph, Maserati was totally unsuitable for this kind of race and it was Varzi who won bravely with a 4.9-litre Bugatti, at 98.5 mph. Nuvolari set a short-course lap-record of 101¼ mph in a twelve-cylinder Alfa Romeo. From within a field of some of these road-racing giants, the final showed up the superiority of the smaller 2.8-litre Maserati and Fagioli took the honours with victory at 96.6 mph, including the time for a pit-stop to change tyres. Borzacchini was second in a Monza Alfa Romeo, while Nuvolari had to be content with third place in the twelve-cylinder Alfa Romeo. Achille Varzi gave of his best in the dangerous, Type 54 Bugatti but was hampered by bursting tyres.

Whether ten hour Grand Prix races were enjoyable to drivers and spectators is best left to the imagination; one can only wonder for example how Robert Sénéchal felt after bringing one of the old, 1½-litre, eight-cylinder Delage cars home fifth in the French Grand Prix, for he drove the entire ten hour duration himself. He is remembered as the enthusiast who, when the Delage team was in dire trouble with roasted drivers in 1926, leapt onto the track to take over, clad in a gent's natty suit and presumably with no experience of this particular hot-seat.

Fortunes changed in 1932 and Bugatti was out of the running, except for the Czechoslovakian GP which Chiron won at 67.67 mph. Otherwise, it was the season of the P3 *monoposto* Alfa Romeo ably supported by the older model. Honours were divided between Nuvolari and Caracciola, a new addition to the Alfa ranks. Nuvolari won at Monaco at 55.81 mph in the Targa Florio at 49.27 mph, at Monza (for the Italian GP) at 104.13 mph and in the French GP at Reims at 92.26 mph. He also won the Coppa Ciano and Coppa Acerbo races. Caracciola soon settled down in the team and the German driver scored at the Eifel races at Nürburgring, at 70.2 mph, in the German GP over the same demanding circuit at 74.13 mph, and again in the Monza Grand Prix, averaging 110.8 mph. Nuvolari set fastest lap in the latter race at 113.7 mph, which was another record for the Monza course.

The following year, 1933, was one of economic recession, with the German Grand Prix cancelled as a result and Maserati and Bugatti once again racing their Type 51 and 2.9-litre cars, respectively. Moreover, Alfa Romeo retired from racing and their former successes were only slowly retrieved by the Scuderia Ferrari, which, at first, entered modified Monza cars. The race distance demanded by the regulations was reduced to 500 kilometres and the major races of 1933 were the Monaco, French, Belgium, Italian, and the revived Spanish Grands Prix.

Monaco displayed the full drama of the times, with the antagonists, Nuvolari and Varzi engaging in a ferocious battle round and round the town, until Nuvolari's Monza broke a vital oil-pipe and caught fire on the final rush down to the finish. Nuvolari jumped out of the cockpit and sought to push his flaming car over the line but it was Varzi's Type 51 Bugatti that received the victor's laurels, his winning speed being 57.04 mph. Umberto Borzacchini brought a Monza Alfa into second place. It is interesting that, at the insistance of Charles Faroux, the great French motoring journalist, the start at Monaco had been based on a grid assembled on practice times, predating the modern system by many years. It was felt that on this narrow and tortuous circuit it would be unfair to draw the positions out of a hat, as was the usual method. The system made Varzi's victory entirely convincing, but did not come into general use in Europe until 1935.

Bugatti did not manage a win in the French Grand Prix, because his new 3.8-litre racers were not ready. Instead, a host of privately-entered cars of this famous make ran, but they were no match for Campari's 2.9-litre Maserati, which commanded the race and won at 81.52 mph and also set a new lap record for the Montlhéry road-cum-track circuit of 86.6 mph. Out of a dozen Monza Alfa Romeos that started, those of Philippe Etancelin and George Eyston took second and third places, while Nuvolari was so upset over the preparation of his Ferrari-sponsored car that he afterwards changed his alligiance to Maserati. This paid off for the little maestro, because he won the Belgian Grand Prix at the fine Spa road circuit, at 89.23 mph, after breaking the lap record, at 92.33 mph. Varzi was some three minutes behind Nuvolari, in a Bugatti, a close finish for those days, with another Bugatti, handled by Dreyfus third. So the bitter battle between Nuvolari and Varzi continued unabated.

Alfa Romeo managed to win the Targa Florio (Brivio, at 47.56 mph), but at the Coppa Ciano race Maserati was again in the ascendant over the aged Monzas. The same thing might well have happened in the Coppa Acerbo race had not the Scuderia Ferrari been permitted by the Alfa Romeo company to have the use of the new P3 single-seaters. Even so, Nvuolari proved able to out-race them in the Maserati, but he was obliged to come into the pits. Then Campari's P3 Alfa, which had been tailing Nuvolari, retired, so that by virtue of a non-stop run, Fagioli, in his Alfa, was the first past the finish, at an average speed of 88.03 mph, although Nuvolari had broken the old lap record, at 90.4 mph.

This was all a good augury for the remaining important Grand Prix contests. At the Italian event, run over a full fifty laps of the complete Monza Park

Above: Bugatti and Alfa Romeo maintained a fierce duel from 1931 to 1933, and here one of the greatest battles is shown, between Achille Varzi in his type 51 Bugatti (No 10) and Tazio Nuvolari in his Alfa Romeo Monza. This is the start of the 1933 Monaco Grand Prix, in which the tussle continued until Nuvolari's car caught fire just before the finish; he made an attempt to push the Alfa across the line before Varzi caught him, but did not succeed

Right: Tazio Nuvolari, after giving the Alfa Romeo type B 2.6-litre car its first win in the 1932 Italian Grand Prix

circuit, Nuvolari's 2.9-litre Maserati met formidable foes, in Louis Chiron and the wily Luigi Fagioli, both driving P3 Alfas. Nuvolari put up his expected terrific performance, but a burst tyre slowed him down and allowed Fagioli to win, at 108.58 mph. Towards the end, Fagioli lapped at the record pace of 115.82 mph, but Nuvolari the master still finished second, only 0.63 mph slower.

In the afternoon of the same day, the Monza Grand Prix was run, using the short Monza circuit. It was a tragic race, in which oil on a corner cost the lives of Count Czaykowski (Type 54 Bugatti), Guiseppe Campari (Alfa Romeo P3) and Umberto Borzacchini (Maserati 8C). The winner proved to be Lehoux's Bugatti, at 108.99 mph, with a posthumous lap-record, to the credit of the Count at no less than 116.81 mph.

Still to come in 1933 was the Spanish Grand Prix and in this race Ettore Bugatti campaigned his new 2.8-litre cars. The design for these cars led directly to that for the next season's fine 3.3-litre models, but on this initial occasion there was no way that they could equal the performance of the P3 Alfa Romeos, one of which, Chiron's, won at 83.32 mph. However this victory was possible only after Nuvolari, comfortably in the lead for Maserati, had gone off the road into a tree.

During the last two seasons, it had become evident that political factors were creeping into motor racing, which initially had been a contest between nations (the Gordon Bennett races) and later, with quite lucrative money to be earned by the top drivers, had become a means of gaining publicity and improving design for the automobile manufacturers (the French Grands Prix etc). Mussolini was apt to send the Alfa Romeo drivers—and those of other Italian-made motor cars—telegrams before a race, saying in effect, 'Win for Italy'. He had also been known to try to smooth out the rough passage between Nuvolari and Varzi, in the hope of securing further Italian-based successes. Now, with Herr Hitler planning to annex the non-German constituents of Europe, racing took an even more obviously political turn: henceforth Mercedes-Benz and Auto Union were expected to dominate all the major motor races for the prestige of the Nazi régime and Hitler somehow saw to it that enough finance was made available to each of these racing teams for them to conquer all before them (or, more correctly, alongside them).

This they eventually did, with fabulous cars, the like of which, in speed, sight, sound and smell, no-one outside German had previously seen, as they stormed the bastions of European motor-racing circles.

It took time, of course. The first of the new 3.3-litre, independently sprung Mercedes-Benz racing cars and the highly unconventional Auto Union rear-engined projectiles arrived on the scene in 1934, but for the 1934 Monaco race they were not ready. It was pipe-smoking Count Trossi who lapped at record speed for Alfa Romeo, at 59.7 mph, and Guy Moll who won for the same Italian racing stable, in the P3, now of 2.9-litres capacity, averaging 55.86 mph.

278

Below: Rudi Caracciola, arguably the greatest pre-war racing driver of all, screams past the Montlhéry stand in Mercedes-Benz's first offering for the 750 kg formula in 1934. The Nazi-sponsored W25, with its swing axles and unlimited budget, did not shine in France, however, as the Scuderia Ferrari Alfas stormed to a 1–2–3 victory

The much-feared German onslaught commenced with the Avus race on that fast course near Berlin in May 1934, but after lapping in training at 143 mph Mercedes-Benz decided that their cars were unready and required more work to be done on them. The Auto Unions remained to fight and although two of them retired, leaving Moll to win for Alfa Romeo in a special Scuderia Ferrari car, with faired body and 3.2-litre engine, at an average of 127.56 mph, the inexperienced Momberger came in third for Germany, behind Varzi's Alfa Romeo. Auto Union had lapped fastest, at 140.33 mph.

At the Nürburgring, the writing on the wall received its signature, for in the Eifel races Manfred von Brauchitsch, in one of the new Mercedes-Benz cars, led throughout, followed by the Italian Fagioli in another of the German cars. Fagioli had the edge on Brauchitsch and wanted to lead but he was signalled to let the German driver stay in front. Not liking Nazi orders he stopped, got out of the Mercedes-Benz, and walked away. This let the Auto Union of Hans Stuck, the hill-climb ace, into second place, and the best Chiron could manage for Alfa Romeo was third place, even though the two German cars had needed to stop for fuel and the Alfa Romeos had run non-stop.

Following a walkover for Alfa Romeo in the Penya Rhin GP, the German cars returned to challenge them at Montlhéry for the French Grand Prix in July. However, both Mercedes-Benz and Auto Union ran into countless troubles and left the race to the Italian cars, Chiron, Varzi and Moll carrying out a 1-2-3 drubbing with their Alfas and the new 3.3 Bugattis being completely out-classed. Louis Chiron was the hero of France, having trounced the terrible German opposition, winning at 85.5 mph.

Alfa Romeo then pulled off the Marne GP at Reims at 90.71 mph, Chiron winning and Varzi setting best lap, at 97.65 mph. The great run of success for the P3 Alfa Romeo drivers was on the wane, however. From now on, apart from isolated Bugatti joy at Spa, where Dreyfus won at nearly 87 mph and Brivio, likewise Bugatti-mounted, put the circuit lap record to 96.38 mph, it was German domination all the way. The Bugatti victory was carried out without opposition from either of the German teams after Chrion had overturned his Alfa Romeo and Varzi had broken a piston trying to prove that not only Nuvolari could take lap records. After that, there were only the Bugattis left in the hunt.

Below left : a grid-full of Alfa Romeos, Bugattis, Maseratis *et al* line up for a pre-war French road race, the Grand Prix de la Marne at Reims. In the right foreground, by Alfa No. 14, is Tazio Nuvolari who won the 1932 Grand Prix de l'ACF at this circuit – also in an Alfa. It is interesting to note the proximity of the crowd to the track, typical of the period

Below right : Achille Varzi's Alfa Romeo seen at the 1934 German GP at the Nürburgring. In Nuvolari's short absence from the team, he won seven races with this car

Apart from this, the rest of the season made dull reading for any but the German Nazi Party, with Hans Stuck taking the Auto Union first past the flag at the Nürburgring to win the German Grand Prix at 75.14 mph. He set the best lap at a record 79.29 mph in the process. Fagioli made up for his show of nationalistic temperament at Spa, by winning for Mercedes-Benz at Pescara (80.26 mph average) after Moll's Alfa Romeo had increased the lap record to 90.5 mph and then crashed with fatal results. In this race Nuvolari was second in a Maserati and Brivio's Bugatti managed to finish third. Stuck won the Swiss Grand Prix at 87.21 mph for Auto Union, Momberger also showing form by putting the lap record for the course up to 94.42 mph, Brivio's Bugatti was again well up until it needed water. The Italian Grand Prix over the short Monza course was a victory for the Mercédès-Benz of Caracciola and Fagioli at 65.37 mph, with Stuck, troubled by brake weakness, second and an Alfa Romeo third. The German domination was not yet complete, however, for in the Spanish Grand Prix it was Mercedes-Benz drivers Fagioli and Caracciola first and second, but Nuvolari was third for Ettore Bugatti. In the Czech Grand Prix, the final race of this astonishing 1934 season, while Stuck's Auto Union

trounced Fagioli's Mercedes-Benz, the resolute Tazio Nuvolari, now driving a Maserati, again came home in third position. The winning averages for these two races were 97.13 and 79.21 mph, respectively. Clearly, motor racing was becoming faster and far more exacting and although Germany intended to win, how wise was Hitler to ensure that she had two rival teams in the field!

The remainder of the 1934–36 period is quickly told, for German domination had now been achieved. In 1936 Auto Union played while Mercedes-Benz mainly fiddled with mechanical troubles, but 1935 had been a Mercedes-Benz year. For example, they won at Monaco (Fagioli), the Eifel (Caracciola), Penya Rhin (Fagioli), Montlhéry for the French GP (Caracciola), at Spa (Caracciola), at Berne for the Swiss GP (Caracciola), and at San Sebastian for the Spanish GP (Caracciola), leaving only the Tunis GP (Varzi), the Coppa Acerbo (Varzi), the Italian GP at Monza (Stuck) and the Czech GP at Brno (Rosemeyer) to Auto Union. Yet in the German Grand Prix, played on their home ground at the Nürburgring, it was the talented Nuvolari who vanquished the entire might of Germany, before all those German spectators, driving an aged P3 Alfa Romeo. He achieved this great victory after an infuriating fuel stop when the refuelling pump broke down and cans has to be substituted, so that the P3 was stationary for over 2 minutes, compared to the Germans' pit-stop of well under one minute!

Nuvolari was also the winner in the Coppa Ciano for Alfa Romeo, and he made fastest lap in the Italian GP in one of these cars. Otherwise, apart from a win for Dreyfus' Alfa Romeo at the Marne GP, it was Germany all the way.

As has been said, Auto Union were in the ascendant in 1936. With the formerly important Belgian, Marne and French Grands Prix relegated to sports car status and the Czech and Spanish Grands Prix abandoned, it was victory after victory for the odd rear-engined cars. Mercedes-Benz pulled off a solitary win at the Tunis GP at Carthage (Caracciola), and at Monaco (Caracciola) and there

Left: like some of the Italians, Bugatti were not too happy with being GP 'also rans' so the French introduced a sports-car formula. Here, Jean-Pierre Winmille in his 3.3-litre Bugatti wins the 1936 French GP at Montlhéry

Left: Bernd Rosemeyer, the only man successfully to get to grips with the odd-handling Auto Unions (mainly because they were the first cars he drove and he did not know any different!) came to grief at the Tunis GP at Carthage in 1936. Here, is the wreck of his C-Type after it caught fire. However, 1936 was a brilliant year for the German who escaped this particular incident

was lingering Alfa Romeo success when Nuvolari took the Penya Rhin, Hungarian, Milan and Coppa Ciano races for Italy. Otherwise 1936 was Auto Union's year, with victories over Mercedes at Tripoli with Varzi first and Stuck second, the Eifelrennen (Rosemeyer), in the German GP (Rosemeyer first, Stuck second), the Coppa Acerbo (in the order of Rosemeyer, von Delius, Varzi), in the Swiss GP (Rosemeyer beating Varzi and Stuck), and in the Italian GP, which Rosemeyer won from Nuvolari's Alfa Romeo with von Delius third. Auto Union were very fortunate to have secured the services of the young Bernd Rosemeyer, a former motor cycle racer, and it was an enormous loss to them when he was later killed attempting to break high-speed records for them when a savage cross wind upset his car. In the Eifel Grand Prix of 1936 he had to drive in heavy rain which turned to mist, but he won all the same, at an average speed of 72.71 mph as well as lapping faster than the old-timers of greater experience, at a speed of 74.46 mph. It is noticeable that although Germany would have preferred to have used entirely German drivers for their two winning teams, so fast and difficult to handle were these cars, particularly the over-steering Auto Unions, that French and Italian drivers had to be called in, and Nuvolari, and Dick Seaman from Britain were to follow.

Under political influence, racing had become more exciting in respect of speed and spectacle, and more intense as the well organised and capably engineered German teams came to show the rest of the world their superiority. In 1937, the FIA in Paris had intended to curb speeds by introducing a maximum weight limit of 750 kg, but the advances in metallurgy, readily available to the government-financed Mercedes-Benz and Auto Union teams, opened the door to enormous power from ultra-lightweight motor-cars. But the new use of softer and increased-travel suspension systems was not yet fully understood, so that the high speed and very quick acceleration of the new racing cars put a great strain on their drivers as well as making Grand Prix contests a fine sport to watch. The Titans were in action!

Right: always a hazard in motor racing is oil dropped by an ailing car. The Monaco GP is thrown into confusion after Tadini's Alfa Romeo has dropped its engine lubricant at the chicane

The 1937 season opened in Rio de Janeiro, for Grand Prix racing was increasing in popularity and new countries sought Grand Prix status. Here the winding course allowed Carlo Pintacuda to bring the 400 bhp, all-independently-sprung, 4-litre, V12 Alfa Romeo in first, at 51.5 mph, ahead of Stuck's Auto Union, four seconds in arrears. Also, in the Milan Grand Prix Nuvolari got his Alfa Romeo in front of Hasse's Auto Union, winning at 64.4 mph and setting the lap record to 67.8 mph. But Formula racing as such did not start until the Eifel races in June and now superior German speed and preparation prevailed, Rosemeyer winning for Auto Union at 82.56 mph from the Mercedes-Benz of Caracciola and von Brauchitsch, these latter cars having been troubled by fuel-

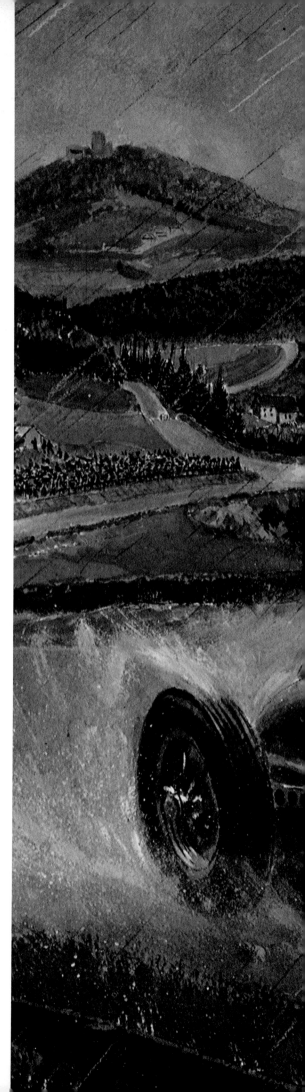

Right: hard at work earning his nickname, 'the Ringmaster' Caracciola in his 3-litre Mercedes in Germany in 1938

Inset: things did not always go so smoothly for the crack German Mercedes team. Manfred von Brauchitsch, the *Pechvögel* (unlucky bird), has some bad luck here in 1938 in Germany. While leading, he came in to the pits for a routine refuelling stop, only to have the car catch fire. Neubauer, team manager, rushes to the car, here. In an attempt to get back into the hunt after the flames were extinguished, von Brauchitsch's car ran off the road. However, Dick Seaman played a good number two and won for Mercedes instead

feed problems. Nuvolari could only manage fifth. Playing far away from home, the German and Italian teams then went to the Roosevelt Speedway in New York State for the Vanderbilt Trophy and found rather unexpected conditions. Even so the American cars could do no better than seventh, although Rex Mays, driving a 3.8-litre Alfa Romeo with a centrifugal blower, was a threat to the German cars. As it was, Rosemeyer sailed away into an easy lead to win for Auto Union at 82.95 mph, with Seaman second in a Mercedes-Benz.

Back in 1937 it was not possible to get the teams back over the Atlantic soon enough to compete in the Belgian Grand Prix at Spa, but Mercedes-Benz and Auto Union had cars and drivers in reserve. Their might was evident when Lang's Mercedes was timed over the flying-kilometre at 193 mph and the old lap record was pulverised again and again. But in the race these very quick Mercedes cars ran into various troubles, leaving Hasse's Auto Union to win at the very high pace of 104.87 mph, after Caracciola had left the Spa lap record at 108.8 mph. From then on it was Mercedes dominance all the way, with victories at Nürburgring in the German Grand Prix (Carracciola, 82.77 mph), at Monaco (von Brauchitsch, 63.25 mph) in the Swiss Grand Prix at Berne (Caracciola, 97.42 mph), in the Italian Grand Prix at Leghorn (Caracciola, 81.59 mph), and at Brno (Caracciola, 85.97 mph), with many new lap records *en route*. Behind these statistics lies some of the most exciting and worthy motor racing of all time. The brilliant Rosemeyer brought Auto Union some consolation with wins at the Coppa Acerbo at 87.61 mph and a new lap record of 92 mph, and in the Donington Grand Prix, at 82.86 mph, where he shared the lap record with Caracciola's Mercedes at an impressive 85.62 mph.

By 1938 the 3-litre Grand Prix cars were the vogue, with highly-supercharged, short-stroke engines, not much slower than the bigger cars that had preceded them, but not quite so dangerous to handle, for the new-style springing was now beginning to be understood by racing-car engineers. Alfa Romeo came up with their new Tipo 308 but were entirely outclassed, and Auto Union, who lost Bernd Rosemeyer at the beginning of the 1938 season, had hardly better luck, although Nuvolari managed to give them a win in the Donington Grand Prix. In this event many of the other ace-drivers had been eliminated because of oil dropped on the course. The crowds were again of immense proportions for a race meeting in Great Britain and the roads leading to the Leicestershire circuit were jammed with traffic. With good reason, too, for the German teams with their supporting fleets of vehicles and armies of mechanics plus the legendary Herr Neubauer controlling the Mercedes-Benz racing, were worth going far to see. The occasion was all the more dramatic because of the threat of imminent war and Nuvolari won at 80.49 mph and made a fastest lap of 83.71 mph. During the year, Auto Union netted only one more win, at Monza, and all the other races were Mercedes-Benz victories. At Pau, however, René Dreyfus took first place for Delahaye, by a whole lap, as Mercedes grappled with heavy fuel consumption, calling for pit stops in under ninety miles, and

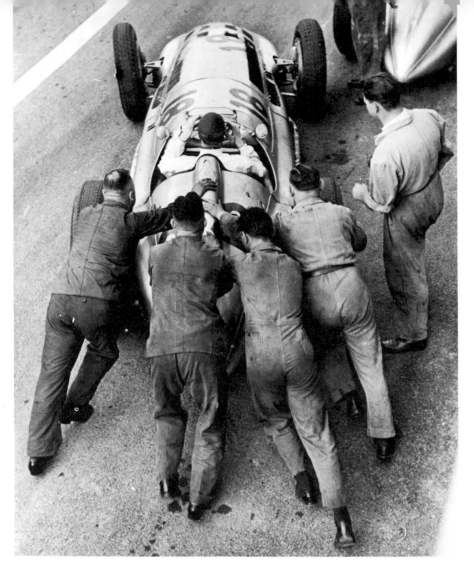

gear-shift troubles. Nuvolari did not start, having suffered burns when his Alfa Romeo caught fire in practice. The remaining Auto Union victory at Monza was less spectacular because the race organisers had toned down the great pace of the 1938 racers by building chicanes on the course. Tazio Nuvolari drove the winning car at 96.7mph but Lang had set fastest lap in his Mercedes-Benz at a record 101.38mph.

Otherwise, 1938 and the shortened 1939 3-litre seasons were full of Mercedes successes. In 1938 Caracciola took the honours at the Coppa Acerbo at an average speed of 83.69mph but, surprisingly, Villoresi's Maserati did fastest lap, at 87.79mph. He also won the Swiss Grand Prix at 89.44mph, while Manfred von Brauchitsch scored at the French Grand Prix at Reims averaging 101.3mph. Britain's hero, Richard Seaman, won a memorable German Grand Prix at the Nürburgring at 80.75mph, also setting fastest lap at 83.76mph (and being noticeably shy on the victor's rostrum of returning a full Nazi salute). Very soon after, he was tragically killed at Spa, skidding into a tree in the wet and being dragged from his blazing Mercedes-Benz to die in hospital. Lang, a former racing mechanic, won the Coppa Ciano at 85.94mph, sharing the record lap of 89.17mph with his team-mate von Brauchitsch, and it was Lang who showed us a lap of 101.38mph at England's first Grand Prix road racing circuit, Donington Park.

With the outbreak of war in September 1939, that season came to a premature close, but not before several races had been contested. Mercedes-Benz took all but the French Grand Prix and the Yugoslav Grand Prix; the latter event was actually held after war had broken out and marked an even greater spread of political international motor-racing. This, the last European race for many years, was won by Nuvolari's Auto Union at 81.21mph, after he and von Brauchitsch (who was a nephew of the German Field Marshal), had roused Belgrade with a joint lap record of 83.9mph. Otherwise, the season was dominated by the cars from Stuttgart. Caracciola was victorious in the German

Left : proving that it was an awful lot of car to move, four mechanics struggle to push start the 1939 W163 Mercedes-Benz of von Brauchitsch at the French GP at Reims

Below : still on the British club circuits, Raymond Mays takes the chequered flag at London's Crystal Palace in 1939 . . . again with his famous ERA fitted with twin rear wheels

Grand Prix at the Nürburgring. The classic circuit was built with previously unemployed labourers after World War I. Caracciola averaged 75.12 mph, and lapped at 81.66 mph in the last pre-war race. Lang took the Swiss Grand Prix at Berne at 96.02 mph but team-leader Rudi Caracciola set a very fast new lap record, at 104.32 mph. The last pre-war French Grand Prix at Reims had been even quicker, and Lang lapped at a record 114.87 mph. Even so, Muller's Auto Union won at 105.25 mph, after a smoking Mercedes announced that Lang was in dire mechanical trouble. Lang was certainly in the ascendancy however, having won at Pau and in the Eifel races.

Thus the 1939 season ended with German cars supreme, in the world's most exacting sport, if 'sport' it still was. Motor racing had come a long way since that first proper motor race over French roads from Paris to Bordeaux 44 years earlier.

Naturally, the war put paid to international motor racing, although the Tripoli Grand Prix was held in 1940, and won by Farina's Alfa Romeo at 128.22 mph from the Alfas of Biondetti and the veteran Count Trossi. It was to be some years before racing found its feet again, however.

Chapter 5

Weathering the Utility Years

ON THE ROAD: 1945-60

Victory in Europe didn't bring the expected millennium for the British motorist, for motoring was very low on the list of priorities of the post-war Socialist government – although restricting and taxing the car owner seemed to be higher up the list. New cars *were* available in 1945, but you needed a Ministry of War Transport Licence to order one, and then had to wait an indeterminate period before it was delivered (unless you had the money and the contacts to buy on the Black Market).

Purchase tax, introduced during the war to discourage the market in so-called luxury goods, remained on cars, although it was removed from household appliances, such as electric fires and refrigerators. Said the Chancellor of the Exchequer, Hugh Dalton: 'There is too much congestion on the roads at home . . . the industry should concentrate on exports . . . I have been asked to take the purchase tax off cars sold in this country, but regret that I cannot do this now. I have been told that the trade want a definite statement, and I shall give it. I cannot hold out any hope of removing the tax for some time to come . . . The motor industry and would-be purchasers of private cars in this country should, therefore, proceed on the assumption that the purchase tax is here to stay.

'I hope that the motor industry is going to export a lot more than it sells at home. There is a great block on the roads at home and great opportunities for trade abroad. There is today a sellers' market for cars, as for other British exports, in many different parts of the world, and I hope that the motor industry will fully exploit it. This is a time for exporters not only to renew contacts with old markets but to find their way into new ones – and there is, of course, no purchase tax on cars which manufacturers export. To this extent, therefore, the export trade is stimulated, as it should be'.

This was pure doctrinaire claptrap, and only Dalton's parliamentary colleagues applauded it: the unfortunate manufacturers, beset by material shortages of all kinds, coped magnificently with the order to export half their production, despite the fact that most of their products were only pre-war models with minimal updating, and had originally been designed for the peculiar requirements of the British market with no view to sales overseas. Both Government and industry were unrealistic in their view of the situation, for the manufacturers had forecast a production of 600,000 cars in the year 1947, but only managed to build 147,767: the Government set an export target of 100,000 cars for 1946, which turned out to be 80 per cent of total output for that year!

The motor industry had one particular bugbear among the ranks of the Government, and his name has become part of the mythology of austerity: ask anyone to recall the evocative images of the late 1940s, and it's inevitable that among a list that's bound to include things like snoek, whalemeat, Civic Restaurants, ration books, Dick Barton and the Berlin Airlift will be Sir Stafford Cripps.

Right: the American motor industry was considerably straitened after the conclusion of World War II, with a paucity of raw materials and a rigorous control on prices and production volumes. Ironically, in defeated Germany the motor industry was rapidly gaining momentum with the realisation of 'the people's car' – the Volkswagen. In 1948, Henry Ford II, who had taken over the family empire from his ageing grandfather, visited Cologne to test an early 'Beetle'

Below: a 1938 Hillman Minx. It was with the Minx that Hillman moved into the mass market in 1932, when the 1185cc, side-valve-engined car sold for £159. The car was improved by the addition of a four-speed gearbox before the outbreak of war and when hostilities ended it again found an enthusiastic market

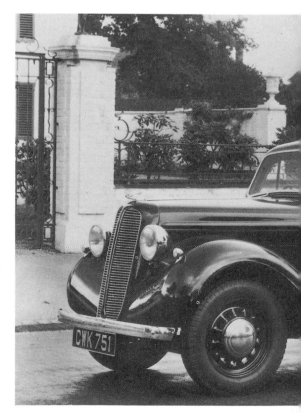

Cripps, whose thin, bespectacled, ascetic face seemed to personify austerity, was president of the Board of Trade and later became Chancellor of the Exchequer; although he made many statements which were received with scorn by those to whom they were addressed, few of his remarks attracted more attention than his speech to the Society of Motor Manufacturers and Traders in November 1945 in which he attempted to dictate the future marketing policy of the car industry.

'We must provide a cheap, tough, good-looking car of decent size,' said Cripps, 'not the sort of car we have hitherto produced for the smooth roads and short journeys of this country. And we must produce them in sufficient quantities to get the benefits of mass-production. That was what we had to do with aircraft engines, and so we concentrated on two or three types only and mass-produced them – not a dozen different ones in penny numbers. My own belief is that we cannot succeed in getting the volume of export we must have if we disperse our efforts over numberless types and makes'.

Commented a Manchester motor trader: 'Sir Stafford Cripps has told the motor industry how to build cars; no doubt another wise guy in the Government will now show us how to sell them . . . The retention of the purchase tax will reduce the sale of new cars in Britain to negligible proportions. That means relatively few cars will have to bear the overheads of selling and distributing costs, and prices must therefore be high'.

Certainly there was no comparison with pre-war prices: the cheapest car on the British market in November 1945 was the 8 hp Ford Anglia, at a basic price of £229, boosted by purchase tax to £293 7s 3d, against its 1940 price of £140. Some post-war prices were totally unrealistic: while a Hillman Minx

Below: Armstrong-Siddeley was the first
British company on the market with an
all-new postwar design exemplified by this
1947 Hurricane drophead coupé. The marque's
reputation was for solidly built, comfortable
touring cars, although in reality many had a
certain sporting flavour. This model used a
2-litre, 16 hp, overhead-valve, six-cylinder
engine which had originated before the war.
Several Armstrong-Siddeley models –
Hurricane, Typhoon, Whitley and Lancaster –
were named after illustrious fighting aircraft of
the parent company, Hawker-Siddeley

cost £396 17s 3d (inc PT), a Sunbeam-Talbot Ten, which was virtually identical apart from a better-finished body, was priced at a total of £620 9s 6d, which fact attracted some irony from enthusiasts.

With tyres almost unavailable and 'Pool' petrol rationed to enough for around 270 miles a month, motoring was a fairly gloomy business, and those who can remember the empty streets may well wonder where Hugh Dalton got his vision of unacceptable congestion, for car ownership was far from universal. At the end of the war there were only just over a million private cars on the road; the author can recall only two motor owners in his own fairly long street at that period, a builder who ran a three-wheeled James Handyvan and a family with an aged Morris Minor saloon which spent more time, it seemed, being pushed than running under its own power. Some mornings the only traffic was the leisurely milk cart, although he discovered the relentless onward march of progress when the milkman's horse was supplanted by an electric milk float (which broke down more frequently than the horse, and didn't know the round so well . . .).

Fortunately, one threat of State intervention in motoring proved empty – although it was a forecast of things to come . . . Late in 1945 *The Star* carried a disturbing feature: 'A people's car? State may enter motor industry. The Government contemplates entering into the motor trade in competition with the manufacturers'.

Although Americans had torn up their petrol coupons on VJ-Day, they too had discovered that the State was not finished with its interference, although in this case it was the manufacturers who were to be incommoded. Once the war in Europe was over, the American industry was granted permission to build 200,000 cars during the remainder of 1945, provided it could obtain enough of the necessary materials to do so. But raw materials were rare, and a series of wildcat strikes made them even rarer – and far more expensive. Into this situation was flung one Chester Bowles, the Price Administrator, who blandly announced that maximum prices for new American cars should be 2 per cent less than 1942 prices in the case of General Motors models (Chevrolet, Oldsmobile, DeSoto, Cadillac) while Ford, Chrysler and Studebaker were restricted to increases of 1 to 9 per cent. This meant, for instance, that a 30 hp Ford now cost the equivalent of £210, while a Studebaker was less than £225.

Complained Henry Ford II, who had taken over the running of the Ford Motor Company from his octogenarian grandfather: 'It costs us $1041 to make a car . . . but we are restricted to selling it at a maximum of $780'.

Retorted the altruistic Mr Bowles: 'Mr Ford is selfishly conspiring to undermine the American people's bulwark against economic disaster', (but weren't the motor manufacturers American people, too?).

As in Britain, restrictions of this kind served mainly to bolster the sales of aged derelicts, pre-war cars often changing hands at well over their price new . . . often over the post-war price for the same model. American buyers did have the advantage that their war had started in 1942, and that therefore pre-war models were that much newer, but it was a mixed blessing, for the exaggerated styling of the early 1940s had not been to everyone's taste. A survey of American motorists in 1945 showed that most of them wanted four-door saloons, painted black, light grey or dark blue, with ample headroom, larger windscreens and side windows and – the view of 75 per cent – cars with a plain exterior finish rather than chromium-plated ornamentation on grilles, louvres and wings. Needless to say, the stylists ignored this latter remark, for this was the era of the full-width 'dollar grin' radiator grille.

One New York motoring correspondent was in no doubt about his feelings on seeing the new 1946 Oldsmobile: 'The grille has been further widened and lessened in height. The bumper is more massive and wraps further round the front wheels. Alas, the effect is more and more like some nightmare creature coming up for air from a thousand fathoms!'.

However, the fickle public bought the cars anyway . . . they liked the novelty of their cars to be restricted to mere external show, and there was no future for the unconventional, like Powel Crosley's sub-compact Hotshot, Preston Tucker's rear-engined Torpedo or a bold design proposed in 1945 by the

Alsatian motor manufacturer, E. E. C. Mathis, who had destroyed his factory in Strasbourg and escaped to New York when the Germans overran France. Mathis and Ford had had an uneasy alliance in the 1930s to produce the Matford car, but now the Frenchman had no intention of competing on the mass-production market. Instead he planned to make an 'ultra-light car, utilising plastics and weighing less than its five passengers'. He had, in fact, built some prototypes in France before the war, and such a venture would probably have succeeded in his homeland, but there was no future for it in America.

Americans didn't even trust new marques of car, for when Henry J. Kaiser, who had a formidable reputation as a wartime producer of military material, attempted to break into the monopoly of the Big Three – Ford, Chrysler, General Motors – he couldn't build up a sufficiently strong marketing network for his Kaiser-Frazer and Henry J lines, took only five per cent of the market in 1948 and faded away completely thereafter.

Although the world was car-hungry, it could still be quite finicky about its motoring diet . . .

Above: the Kaiser-Frazer Corporation set up shop in 1946 and soon bought Henry Ford's wartime Willow Run plant, from where they proceeded to display advanced and imaginative prototypes, with unit construction, front-wheel drive and torsion bar suspension. Alas, when the Kaiser reached the market, economics and engineering limitations had dictated conventional springing and a simple box-section frame. Nevertheless, the Kaiser is remembered as a car that was too innovative to survive in the conservative American market. This six-cylinder Manhattan, built in 1953, virtually marked the end of the line for the company

This was odd, because the public was clamouring for new cars: in fact, if you believed a somewhat equivocal comment by *The Times*, they would buy anything on wheels that was offered to them.

'In most countries today,' reported the paper, 'the shortage of motorcars is so acute that motorists exercise very little discrimination in buying a car. They consider themselves fortunate if they can acquire any new car, of any make, nationality and engine power. This partly accounts for the present demand for British small cars in the United States, where motorists normally prefer cars of high power and large body size'.

In fact, it didn't account for it at all, for the 'small British cars' which were making such an impact on the American market were cars which didn't compete with existing US models at all, and attracted an entirely different kind of customer. One British model which particularly enshrined itself in American automotive mythology was the MG TC Midget, a sports car of pre-war character which offered lively handling and quick acceleration, and could consequently run away from any large American gin-palace on a twisting road, although the larger car was very likely faster in a straight line.

Austin exported many small cars styled on transatlantic lines, although again it was almost certainly their 'nippiness' which sold them rather than Americans buying in desperation: the Austin A90 Atlantic even set up a number of American speed records, and so the old bomber factory which housed Austin's export division was kept fully occupied.

There were some curious features about the British export drive, but none more odd than the case of the Citroën factory at Slough, where components were shipped in from France, assembled into complete cars for the British market – and fifty per cent of them were then solemnly exported overseas again!

By 1950, British factories were exporting some 350,000 cars out of a total output of 522,515, although the impetus of the export drive was now beginning to fall away, partly because the countries to which Britain was exporting were now building cars to meet their own requirements, partly because the British products were said to lack reliability and to deteriorate at an unacceptable rate.

Fortunately, the old taxation system based on cylinder bore had vanished in 1947, replaced for a year by a tax of £1 for every 100cc of engine capacity, thereafter by a flat-rate tax of £10; this did at least give British designers the

Below right: Sir Alec Issigonis's first design for the Nuffield Organisation was the Morris Minor of 1948. It had a unitary-construction body and torsion-bar front suspension (National Motor Museum, England)

Below: American influence on English styling is seen in the Austin A90 Atlantic of 1950, a design strangely out of character with the Austin tradition

opportunity to design cars for world markets, although not all availed themselves of the chance.

Austerity and shortages, indeed, meant that some new designs had to remain on paper: Morris designer Alex Issigonis designed a bulbously streamlined light car with torsion-bar independent front suspension, front-wheel drive and a flat-four engine. It emerged in production form with the chassis and styling intact, but with the side-valve Series E engine of pre-war vintage driving the rear wheels through a conventional transmission. It didn't matter, however: the Morris Minor would prove to be a car with inbuilt longevity, and even after production had ended some two decades later, Morris Minors of all ages would still be a common sight on British roads.

Oddly enough, the Morris Minor had rather similar styling to the German Volkswagen, which had been put into limited production in 1945 in a factory gutted by Allied bombing, after British experts and Henry Ford II had rejected the design as having no commercial future. Commented the British: 'This car does not fulfil the technical requirements which must be expected from a motor car. Its performance and qualities have no attraction to the average

buyer. It is too ugly and too noisy. Such a type of car can, if at all, only be popular for two to three years at the most'.

This was the car that would become the most popular model of all time, with sales considerably exceeding the all-time record of fifteen million plus set up in 1927 by the immortal Model T Ford (although it must be admitted that the Model T achieved its record in far less time and in a much smaller overall market).

The end of the war had left the German motor industry in poor shape. Most of the production was concentrated in the 'Bizone' (the area occupied by British and American forces) and in 1946 only managed to turn out 9900 cars and 11,200 trucks. The Russians had dismantled most of the car companies in their zone, leaving only the old BMW works, at Eisenach, in operation, while in the French Zone, only the Daimler-Benz factory at Gaggenau was working.

In 1947, production in the Bizone was again between 21,000 and 22,000 but the following year over 57,000 vehicles were built; this was, however, little more than a quarter of the annual output from the same area in the immediate pre-war period. Most of those 1948 vehicles were needed to meet demand within Germany and the total value of exports from the Bizone amounted to only £1.4 million.

Even so, that was enough for British manufacturers to complain of the potential threat from German cars in export markets, for German cars were already making inroads in Holland, Switzerland and Belgium, where the VW was exhibited at the Brussels Motor Show in January and February 1949.

Despite steel shortages, the potential of the German industry seemed good, especially until the summer of 1948, for up to that time an exchange rate of 24 Reichsmarks:£1 was in operation for export contracts for the Volkswagen and this gave an ex-works price equivalent to £200, and a retail price on Continental markets of under £350. Contracts made on this basis were still being honoured in the early part of 1949.

In mid-1948, however, the German currency had been revalued, and the new Deutschmark was being used for contracts signed after that time, at a rate of only 11.75 DM:£1. This revaluation raised the price of the VW to around £700, and took the edge off its competitiveness, making it – for the time being – less of a competitor for British small cars.

France's concept of the utility car was the 2 cv Citroën – 'four wheels under an umbrella' – with an 8 bhp, 375 cc, flat-twin engine driving the front wheels, a project developed in secret during the German occupation, as indeed had Renault's postwar offering, the 4 cv, which had its four-cylinder engine at the rear. This was the first model to be produced by Renault after its nationalisation in 1944 – the company's founder, Louis Renault, had been accused of collaboration with the Germans and died in prison – and was nicknamed 'Cockchafer' or 'Little pat of butter' because it was painted with yellow ochre confiscated from the Afrika Korps. This was to become the first French car whose sales exceeded a million, and it was to be built for fifteen years, up to July 1961.

Overall, however, the French motor industry was ill-equipped to meet demand. Partly this was as a result of wartime bombing – the Renault works, for instance, had been badly damaged – and partly because the Germans had dismantled plants and taken the machine tools and equipment back to Germany. Even without these problems, the French industry was a sick one and had been in decline since the late 1920s, mainly due to heavy taxation on petrol and a low national average income.

Recovery after the Liberation was slow – in 1946 car production was less than one-sixth the 1938 level – and the situation was not helped by a shortage of sheet steel and tyres. There were grandiose Government plans for the industry; under this 'Monnet Plan', 1947 production was to be 396,000 vehicles. In fact, the total output was 133,100 cars and trucks. A total of 460,000 cars and 75,000 trucks was anticipated for 1951. 'It seems most unlikely that so large an increase in car production will be realised' said a 1949 industry review, and the actual results (319,881 cars and 125,774 commercials) proved that the private vehicle market was taking longer to recover than had been anticipated, despite optimistic comments like those of *L'Action Automobile* in its review of the 1949 Paris Salon, the first French show since the lifting of post-war restrictions. 'Production brilliant in conception', eulogised the magazine. 'Our cars are ahead of all others. Lightness, roadholding, suspension, fuel economy, harmony of line, aerodynamic qualities . . . these are the areas in which our superiority is most marked . . .'

A British commentator showed the view of the customers outside France: 'A noticeable drawback of French cars compared with the British is the poor quality of the finish . . . it may be doubted whether the industry is equipped, technically and financially, to withstand price competition, particularly in the smaller cars'.

In any case, technical expertise was not always a guarantee of success. The situation of Ford-France during this post-war period was a striking instance.

Above: France's estimable interpretation of the car for the people theme was the Citroën 2CV, 'four wheels under an umbrella'. It was introduced in 1948 with an 8 hp, 375 cc, flat-twin engine and, in true Citroën style, front-wheel drive. Although the 2CV grew up over the years, it never lost its essential character and even in the 1980s retained something of a cult status, especially in the 'special edition' Charleston version. The 2CV is currently produced in the world's oldest car factory still in use, built in 1902 at Levallois, Paris, by Adolphe Clément

Right: the French equivalent of the Morris Minor was the 4CV Renault saloon. Cheap and easy to produce, it was, along with the 2CV Citroën, the 'motoring for everyone' car in France

Its factory at Poissy, just outside Paris, had been completed just before the war and largely rebuilt since, to repair considerable wartime damage. It was now Europe's most modern car factory – 'a witness to the renaissance of French industry'.

The only snag was that Poissy was producing the wrong car. The American-styled Vedette had the 2158cc Ford V8 engine, with a taxable rating of 12CV, nearly double that of any other popular mass-produced French car. Daily production in 1949 was fifty Vedettes. By comparison, the contemporary Peugeot 203, rated at 7CV, was being built at a rate of almost two hundred daily. Without a complete about-turn in policy, and the development of a totally new model more suited to the post-war French market, there was no way of saving the Poissy operation. Ford weren't prepared to make that kind of investment, and in 1954 sold Poissy to Simca, who had made their debut in 1934, building small Fiats under licence.

Simca – the name stood for '*Société Industrielle de Mécanique et Carrosserie Automobile*' – had begun operations in the old Donnet-Zedel factory at Nanterre and within less than two years were among the five biggest French constructors. Their post-war offerings included the Simca-8 (available with either 6CV or 7CV four-cylinder power units), the Simca-6 and the Simca-8 Sport, an elegant open two-seater whose price (880,000 francs) was twice that of the basic Simca-8, but still attractive for such a limited-production vehicle.

It was proof, too, that the day of the specialist producers of '*voitures hors série*' was drawing to a close, for out of all those companies – Delahaye, Delage, Hotchkiss, Salmson and Talbot – only Hotchkiss, justifying its slogan, '*le juste milieu*' and Salmson could come anywhere near the price of the Simca-8 Sport, and that with rather dull-looking saloons.

Talbot, whose competition-developed Lago-Record and Lago-Grand-Sport were the most expensive models on the market, attempted to move into a more 'popular' price bracket with the 15CV Lago-Baby, fitted with a 2.7-litre four-cylinder engine instead of the 4.5-litre six used in the big Talbots. As the Lago-Baby cost a hefty 1,198,000 francs, its appearance could only delay the inevitable demise of the Talbot company.

Nevertheless, there was still a limited market for very costly special-bodied cars and there were no fewer than thirteen *carrossiers* exhibiting at the 1949 Salon, among them such great names as Antem, Chapron, Figoni et Falaschi,

Below: last fling of the flamboyant *carrossier*; this Cadillac, bodied by Saoutchik features the brightwork accents typical of this designer

Franay, Letourneur et Marchand, Pourtout and Saoutchik. Their elegant vehicles, however, were no more typical of the future of the French industry than was the curious little voiturette built at St-Denis by De Rovin. This was, if anything, even more utilitarian than the 2CV Citroën, with an open, two-seater body, like that of a dodgem car, and a 425cc flat-twin engine. With an output of only five to six cars a day, the Rovin was scarcely competitive . . .

Italy's biggest manufacturer, Fiat, was concentrating on economy, too, with the post-war version of their 500cc Topolino ('Mickey Mouse') and its larger 1100cc and 1500cc sisters.

The Italians had great hopes for their car industry. 'Since the end of hostilities', wrote *l'Action Automobile*, 'the Italians have had the wish to give their car industry once again the maximum of gloss, for they will largely rely on it to give, at one and the same time, prestige in foreign markets and an economic renaissance for their country'.

The quickest way to gain prestige was of course, in competition, and many of the post-war Italian cars had been developed in sporting events. Alfa Romeo, Maserati, Cisitalia and Ferrari had all won international events in the late 1940s, successes reflected in models like the Ferrari 166 Mille Miglia or the supercharged 2.5-litre Alfa Romeo Super Sport. Even so, these prestigious marques took only a tiny percentage of a market dominated by Fiat. Experimental models like the front-wheel-drive Caproni and the rear-engined V8 Isotta-Fraschini Monterosa stood no chance at all.

Other countries seemed to play little part in the picture of world car production in the late 1940s. 'The use of motor vehicles in Japan has never been extensive', noted a 1949 report. 'The mountainous character of the country and its poor roads have made it dependent chiefly on shipping and railway facilities for long-distance traffic. There were only 140,000 civilian motor vehicles in 1941, of which 64,000 were trucks'.

The Japanese motor industry did not become significant until the mid-1930s, when production rose almost five-fold in three years, thanks to the Motor Car Manufacturing Enterprise Act of 1936, which cut taxes on motor manufacturers and set up protective tariffs. Three companies – Nissan, Toyota and Datsun – dominated the industry and employed some 21,000 people between them.

They came through the war without direct bomb damage and by 1946 were producing over 14,800 vehicles annually, almost all of which were commercials. By 1947, production had risen to almost 19,500, of which only 1700 were cars:

Below: Sydney Allard created magnificent cars described as 'motor cycles on four wheels'. This is a 1950 J2, which is powered by an Ardun-Mercury V8 engine of 3917cc (National Motor Museum, England)

Japan, it seemed, would never become a force to be reckoned with . . .

Czechoslovakia, now behind the Iron Curtain, was nevertheless still exporting to the West, mainly to Belgium and Holland and, following a 1949 trade agreement, to Argentina. The country's four export offerings were two Tatra models, the big V8 and the four-cylinder Tatraplan, both of course air-cooled; the Skoda 1100, with its backbone chassis; and the little, two-cylinder, 615cc Aerominor, which achieved success in its class in the 1949 Le Mans 24-hour race.

Sweden, after a flurry of activity during the war years, had dropped to an annual output of 6500 vehicles – less than the 1938 total. Most of those 6500 were built by Volvo and only 2300 of them were cars. The Philipsen company, which had assembled American and German cars before the war, introduced small cars to replace the German models in the late 1940s. The country's 1948 exports were of little significance on the international scene, totalling only 650 cars and 2000 commercials.

So the 1940s came to an end, with Europe concentrating on economy and America exuberantly extravagant. Automotive engineering was certainly moving forward: unfortunately good taste was heading in the opposite direction and, whatever else the fifties might be remembered for in the automobile industry, restraint was not on the menu.

Above: despite styling similar to that of many pre-war American motor cars, the Jowett Javelin was rather different underneath, with its flat-four engine; unfortunately, the car-buying public thought it was too radical, so it was not a great success; nevertheless, 30,000 examples were manufactured (National Motor Museum, England)

Above left: one of the more significant postwar British cars was the Ford Consul launched in 1950, the first overhead-valve, unit construction British Ford – and the first car with MacPherson strut front suspension; this is a 1955 drophead coupé version converted for Ford by Carbodies of Coventry (National Motor Museum, England)

Top: by 1954, the American industry was well on its way to the styling excesses of later in the decade, but, one year short of the memorable record sales year of 1955, cars like this Mercury Monterey could still boast quality engineering under the lurid skin

Left: three famous works MGs. They are Y-type 1½-litre saloons of 1953, seen here at Carlisle during the Daily Express Rally

Right at the start of the 1950s, the British motor industry was staggered by a merger which was more of a shotgun wedding than a marriage of convenience, bringing two great rivals together. William Morris had become Lord Nuffield, but had now lost interest in the empire he had created, and was finding increasing solace in his prolonged cruises to Australia; his former lieutenant, Sir Leonard Lord, now headed Austin and had once sworn that the only reason he would return to Morris would be to take it apart 'brick by bloody brick'. But Austin and the Nuffield Group did merge to form the British Motor Corporation, although there was little rationalisation of model ranges, and the old Austin-Morris rivalries seemed to persist. The group's share of the market, originally about fifty per cent, began to slip steadily downward.

Of course, this may have been due as much to the fact that the rest of the British motor industry was catching up technically as to any residual bitterness between Nuffield and Lord: Ford introduced its first truly modern range in 1950 with the Consul, with an ohv four-cylinder engine, hydraulic brakes, independent front suspension and integral body/chassis unit, and followed this soon after with the similar, six-cylindered Zephyr.

'Judged both on performance and on value for money, the Zephyr is a very satisfactory car,' commented *The Autocar*. 'It is quiet yet lively, roomy without being cumbersome, and it had a quiet modern line without the vulgarity often produced by the addition of excess ornamentation.' The test concluded with a masterly piece of ambiguity: 'It goes and stops and handles well'.

Soon after this, Ford announced a unit-constructed small car, the 100E Anglia, whose 1935-designed power unit was also used in a remarkable survival from the Mesolithic age of motoring, the Ford Popular, the cheapest real car on the British market, whose styling dated back to 1937. It was produced in the old Briggs Motor Bodies factory at Doncaster, which meant that manufacture of bodywork for the unorthodox Jowett Javelin had to stop: and Jowett ceased car production. Remarkably, the crude little Ford Popular remained in production until 1959.

Unfortunately the new-look Fords seemed to attract the attentions of the gadget-lover, for above all the early 1950s were the era of the bolt-on gimmick: amber plastic bug-deflectors in the shape of birds decorated the bonnet top, chromed masks sat like eyelids above the headlamps, windscreens were given overhanging peaks like the eyeshade of a Hollywood newspaper editor, 'portholes' lined the bonnet. Bad taste was rampant.

It was, it seems, the efforts of the motor industry to come to terms with the new technology that resulted in many of the styling gaffes of the early 1950s; that, plus the determination of the mass producers that their products should not look *too* different from their competitors. Describing the 1954 Earl's Court Motor Show, *Autocourse* commented: 'The post-war tendency to add more and more chromium plate to a previous year's model and then to present it as new and original was continued, and it would seem that for the "middle line" of transport, at least, fashion has settled down to a common shape . . . the discerning eye will not find this shape offensive, nor for that matter will it greatly please . . . many manufacturers have simply scaled down their more commodious brainchildren into, for example, the Austin A30, the Fords Anglia and Prefect, the Fiat 1100 and the Standard 8. This shameless copying is hardly stimulating . . .'.

There were still, however, nationalistic tendencies; some of the 'upper crust' British manufacturers were still using the razor-edge line in their bodywork, though this rather ugly design feature had a *passé*, 1930s, air to it. Italy, noted a contemporary journalist, 'enjoyed the charmingly elegant fantasies which made a nonsense of any close collaboration between pure engineering and design'; France 'concentrated on voluptuous curves'.

However hard the manufacturers tried, the praise always seemed to be qualified: 'The Frazer Nash hard-top also has a plainly defined radiator intake, though the effect is partially offset by the quasi juke-box adornment on the carburettor intake' . . . 'on the Lancia Gran Turismo the glass is recessed, giving a somewhat clumsy effect', and so on.

Below: the styling of the 1953 Ford Popular, in essence, dated back to 1937, but this was cheerfully overlooked by the buying public on the grounds that the 'Pop' was the cheapest real car then available on the British market. Remarkably, it survived with few changes until 1959

Above: by American standards of the early 1950s, when bad taste was rampant in the automobile industry, the design of the 1956 Ford Fairlane might even be considered conservative

Perhaps, too, the spirit of the age was shown in the adoption of brighter paint and trim schemes. After the war, most car interiors were trimmed in a dull brown; by the early 1950s, more colourful seats and fascias were in demand and bright synthetic plastics gave the opportunity to provide interior design colour-keyed to the overall paint scheme of the car. Not that this was always in very good taste . . . two-tone finishes became popular on many saloon cars, and metallic colours were increasingly used, including some particularly nasty shades of green. One 1955 Rolls-Royce appeared in two-tone orange and cream, while the 1954 London Show saw a flamingo-pink Triumph!

Nowhere was bad taste more evident during this period than in the United States. American cars smirked their way into the 1950s behind chromium-plated radiator grilles of surpassing vulgarity: they ended the decade with front-end styling reminiscent of the head of some deep-sea fish and tailfins like rocket-powered guppy. Nor is the piscine analogy far-fetched, for a promotional film made by Ford of America around 1956 showing a car stylist at work, bathed in a dim, religious light, emphasised that he took inspiration from natural forms – like a tank-full of tropical fish. Then the film showed this Renaissance

man take up his pencil, as though he were a medieval monk about to illuminate a psalter – and design a futuristic car that was as impracticable as it was repellent. Fortunately this was a flight of fancy that was not about to be launched on an unsuspecting public.

'Cars of the future' were very much in the corporate minds of the American motor moguls in this period, although quite why is something of a mystery, save that their appearance at motor shows did go some way to accustoming the public to the shape of cars to come – a sort of cushioning against bodyshell-shock.

Cadillac started the tailfin vogue in 1950, the modest kick-ups at the tips of the rear wings acting as something of a relieving touch to the ponderous styling of the new models, which were the first Caddys to sell over 100,000 in a year; the fin vogue reached its peak on cars like the 1959 Buick LeSabre, on which these lethal-looking appendages were half-a-car long.

For America, the 1950s began badly, with the outbreak of the Korean War; yet this major international disturbance had little effect on the sale of motor vehicles, which that same year exceeded 8,000,000 for the first time ever (6,665,863 of these were cars).

Despite their excesses of styling, American cars were all pretty much alike

Left : the famous Mercedes-Benz 300SL
'gullwing' of 1957; this car had what was
probably the nearest thing, in a production
model, to a true space-frame chassis, made
possible by the high sills and the lift-up doors

Below : seen at the 1952 London Motor Show,
this Bentley R-type had bodywork by
Freestone & Webb

underneath: most had V8 engines of around 100 hp, with six-cylinder power units reserved for the lower price ranges; suspension was generally by independent coils at the front and leaf springs at the back; sealed-beam headlights, radio and heater were regarded as virtually indispensable. On models with manual gearboxes, a steering-column gearchange made room for three on a bench front seat, but removed all precision from the operation of changing speed. The provision of a column change, with all its complex linkage, must have been extremely costly compared with the simplicity of the 'stick shift', especially to an industry reputed to count the cost of every washer.

There was an alternative, however, and motorists were prepared to pay extra for it. Automatic transmission, which had made its first tentative appearances in the 1930s, was now reliable enough to be put into mass-production. The fact that many of the early automatic boxes only possessed two forward speeds was immaterial, for those big V8s made up in torque what they lacked in economy.

One of the first manufacturers to go automatic was Buick, who in 1950 became the fourth manufacturer to achieve sales of over half-a-million cars in a year – and nearly 430,000 of these were fitted with the new Buick Dynaflow

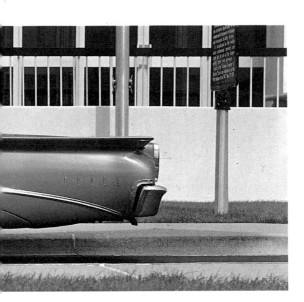

Above: perhaps the most famous of all motoring flops was the Edsel, a car which showed just how fickle public opinion could be. The market which millions of dollars worth of planning had foreseen for the new car flatly rejected it and in two years only 35,000 cars were sold. This is a 1960 Edsel Ranger, from the cheaper end of the range and the marque's final model year

Left: the AC Greyhound used a 2.2-litre Bristol engine, front disc brakes and coil-spring/wishbone suspension. It was similar in basic outline to the Ace and Aceca models, but had a larger, four-seater coupé body on a slightly longer wheelbase

Below: Citroën's DS19 caused a sensation when it was announced in 1955, setting standards of aerodynamic efficiency by which others were to be judged even into the late 1970s. The car used hydraulic power for brakes, steering, clutch, gear engagement and suspension trimming, but thanks to its outstanding efficiency a 1.9-litre, four-cylinder engine was quite enough to endow sparkling performance

torque-convertor transmission. Madison Avenue outdid itself in coining names redolent of speed and power for these early automatic transmission: 'Tip-Toe Hydraulic Shift with Gyrol Fluid Drive', 'Hydra-Matic', 'Powerglide', 'Ultra-Matic', 'PowerFlite'.

It was definitely marketing, not engineering, which sold cars in the America of the 1950s: in fact, these Rockets and Firedomes and Silver Streaks were only in their element on the dead-straight turnpike highways, and under more demanding conditions their road-holding deficiencies were emphasised to the full. However, the great marketing dream turned to a nightmare in 1959 when Ford introduced the Edsel, designed after thorough market research, and discovered that public taste could be expensively fickle. The motorists for whom the Edsel had been designed failed to buy it, and production was curtailed inside two years, with only 35,000 cars sold. The marketing men had failed to anticipate a move away from large cars, an error of judgment that cost Ford an estimated $250,000,000.

By the end of the decade, America was definitely warming to the compact, partly to combat the success of imported European cars, which were introducing American drivers to new standards of economy and roadholding (and if you can remember just how vague the steering was on some European small cars of the late 1950s, you'll get some measure of the directional imprecision that the average American monster of the epoch must have possessed).

Mind you, America's idea of 'compact' was a long way from Europe's concept of small cars. Oldsmobile and Buick entered the field late, in 1960, with a 3.5-litre V8 power unit which was to be adapted for the British Rover later in the decade. Oldsmobile's F85 compact was 15 ft 8 in long, two or three feet longer than the average medium-sized European car.

Europe, though, didn't have the advantages of wide-open spaces and cheap petrol which had encouraged Americans to think big (though growing urban congestion was showing the US industry the disadvantages of this policy); imported petrol and, on the Continent, taxation systems which penalised large engines, had conditioned Europeans to regard the optimum size for a power unit as being below 2 litres. Citroën's advanced and sharklike DS19, introduced in 1955, for instance, was a big car in everything but engine size. Despite having hydraulic power for steering, brakes, clutch operation, gear engagement and suspension trimming, the 22 cwt DS had a four-cylinder power unit of only 1.9 litres, relying on its slippery shape for efficient speed.

If the DS represented a practical production version of the 'car of tomorrow', across the Channel Rover were developing a futuristic vehicle which stood little chance of seeing any sort of production; unlike the American 'dream cars', however, this car was *avant-garde* in its engineering rather than simply in its styling. Its secret was its power unit – a gas turbine. Rover had pioneered this method of propulsion as far back as 1946, when they began work on the world's first gas-turbine car, 'JET 1'. A second prototype was built in 1955 and this had a rear-mounted gas turbine in a normal saloon body.

Towards the end of 1956 Rover unveiled the 'T3', using a compact gas turbine developed from Rover's IS/60 industrial power unit, half the size of JET 1's engine. A heat exchanger helped to keep fuel consumption within reasonable limits – in a track test, the T3 returned 13.8 mpg at a steady 40 mph, and 12.8 mpg at 80 mph.

While the T3 was the first practicable Rover gas turbine car, the company warned: 'This model is in no way a final design, representing only another stage in Rover gas turbine development. There are still several problems to be solved, both in respect of body style and engine arrangement, before a truly operational car can be produced'.

The main advantages of the gas turbine engine were its excellent power-to-weight ratio, and the absence of radiator, clutch and gearbox. In the T3 the engine was mounted at the rear of a two-seater saloon body made from glass fibre, with wrap around windscreen and large rear window; because of the engine's high torque to weight ratio, the specification included four-wheel drive, with a De Dion axle at the rear. Rover were to persist with their gas-turbine development programme for some time but the power unit never found

Left: a toothy grin from a 1950 Buick perhaps sums up what the car designers in America were doing at that time

Right : one of the most popular British sports saloons of the 1950s was the Sunbeam-Talbot; this is a 1954 example (Coventry Motor Museum, England)

Below : Jaguar's XK 140 was not only a magnificent sports car in terms of engine and chassis, it was also well styled; the XK series has become one of the most revered sporting lines ever built

its way into a production vehicle. The only practical benefits to the Rover customer lay in refinement of engineering specification on piston-engined cars and a subsequent styling study on a jet chassis that formed the basis of the 2000 saloon of the 1960s.

In the year of the introduction of the T3, Europe had been given a salutary reminder of the finite nature of petroleum resources in the wake of the Suez War when the fuel supply routes were closed and fuel rationing had to be imposed. There followed a brief period of happy hitch-hiking for the majority of the British public, those without transport being given lifts by those who could get petrol. By careful choice of which vehicles you waved your thumb at, it was possible to extend your motoring experience in the most intriguing way. On one day during this adventurous period, the author rode in (or on) vehicles as diverse as a mid 1920s Sunbeam tourer and a window cleaner's ex-WD BSA motor bike!

Even when the rationing was over, there was always the thought that it could happen again, and manufacturers and the motoring public suddenly began to take seriously a new breed of cyclecar which had, indeed, begun to appear before Suez, but was then regarded as something of a joke. One of the first such cars was the Isetta, a strange device like an Easter egg mounted on a roller skate, powered, if that is the appropriate word, by a rear-mounted 245cc engine with only one cylinder.

It was followed by the Heinkel, a similar vehicle (similar enough for the two makers to go to law about design resemblances) with a 198cc engine capable of returning 86mpg and propelling the vehicle at over 50mph on the level.

Their shape naturally earned these little creatures the nickname 'bubble cars', although their makers liked to think of them as 'cabin cruisers'. One of the strangest was the little Messerschmitt Kabinenroller, built by the erstwhile German aircraft manufacturer; this had tandem seating for two moderate-sized adults and a child under a plastic cockpit cover. It had handlebar steering and a 191cc Sachs two-stroke engine which had to have its direction of rotation reversed to achieve a 'reverse gear'. There was also a supersports version of this car, the KR500 Tiger, which had a 500cc engine and four wheels instead of three, as obstructions like manhole covers were liable to upset the roadholding of the original model.

The bubble-car vogue was a short-lived one, for these little cars were noisy, cramped and not over-reliable, although at one stage in 1960 the British-built Scootacar was, at £275, the cheapest enclosed car on the market (it looked rather like a perambulating phone box and was built by the Hunslet Engine

Below: JET 1, seen here preparing for a demonstration run at Silverstone, was the world's first gas-turbine-engined car; it was built by the Rover company in 1946, but although Rover continued to produce gas turbine prototypes, and racing cars, culminating in the T3 of 1956 they never satisfactorily solved all the problems which prevented the gas turbine being put into volume production

Above: the mid 1950s had their own share of economy models. This is an Isetta Moto Coupé, commonly referred to as a 'bubble car'; access was via the opening front of the vehicle, the steering column hinging with the door

Right: this is the 'supersports' KR500, four-wheeled version of Messerschmitt's strange Kabinenroller, the Tiger. Inside and out, the cockpit bore more than a passing resemblance to that of one of the company's more familiar aircraft
(National Motor Museum, England)

Company, who in 1903 had produced a car with the ominous name of Attila).

The car which was to prove the downfall of the bubbles arrived in the autumn of 1959, and stemmed directly from the swing to small cars caused by Suez. This was no cramped two-and-a-bit seater with a minuscule scooter engine, however, but a proper four-seater, four-cylinder car in which maximum use had been made of a minimum of space by clever design ideas like a transverse engine, with the gearbox in the sump, driving the front wheels and variable-rate rubber suspension. It was called the Morris Mini-Minor, and its designer was Alec Issigonis, who had previously been responsible for the Morris Minor. There was an attempt to market an Austin version of this car under the annoying title 'Austin Se7en', but it was the 'Mini' title which stuck (and coincidentally gave a new word to the English language). The Mini proved to have outstanding handling, and was soon being used for racing and rallying; its major fault was one which was not apparent to the public, but to the manufacturer, for this advanced design was expensive to produce in relation to the price which could be asked for the finished product. Ford engineers took one of the early examples apart for analysis, concluded that on the sort of production volumes then being achieved it would be hopelessly uneconomical for them to try and build a similar car, and instead designed the thoroughly conventional,

Left: Alec Issigonis's front-wheel drive idea finally achieved fruition with the Mini, introduced in 1959. The Mini came with incredible roadholding as standard equipment. This 1976 1000 model shows just how little the car changed over the years

Above right: a 1962 Daimler SP250 Dart. The glassfibre-bodied sports car used an all-aluminium, 2½-litre, V8 engine, which gave 120 mph performance for just £1395

Right: when the Mini appeared it became an instant success in the world of racing and rallying and the addition of the name of Cooper, then on top of the world as a racing car manufacturer, to special versions of the Mini was a brilliant sales exercise. Ford countered with the Cortina powered by Lotus, not only a masterful way of capitalising on the Lotus reputation, but also a splendid car. The Ford-based 1558 cc, twin-cam engine produced 105 bhp and gave the Lotus-Cortina, introduced in 1963, 100 mph performance

Below right: a 1959 Aston Martin DB4, which used the straight-six, twin-cam engine. Producing 240 bhp, the engine gave the car great performance

Below: at the sporting end of the British post-war market was the Healey, the first British car to be developed in a wind tunnel; the prototype had 'pop-up' headlights. This is a 2.4-litre model designed by Donald Healey and A. C. Sampietro, which was the fastest series-production saloon of its day; this actual car was raced into thirteenth place in the 1948 Mille Miglia by Count Lurani (National Motor Museum, England)

313

roomier Cortina, which appeared in 1962 after the space in the Ford range between the Anglia and the Consul had temporarily been plugged by two short-run 'stop-gap' designs, the Classic and the Capri, and which, selling in similar price ranges to the little car, proved its most serious competitor.

'You've never had it so good' was the political slogan which ruled the Mini's natal year, and indeed 1959 had seen an unparalleled crop of new designs; apart from the Issigonis baby, there had been the Triumph Herald, designed by Harry Webster, the Aston Martin DB4GT, 6¼-litre V8 light-alloy engines for Rolls-Royce and Bentley, the Ford 105E Anglia, the Daimler SP250 (a rather ugly glassfibre-bodied sports model), the MGA 1600, the Sunbeam Alpine, Hillman Minx with Easidrive automatic and new models from AC and Armstrong-Siddeley.

There was another slogan which was soon to affect motoring in America, however. Chevrolet had broken away from tradition to produce the Corvair compact, which had a flat-six air-cooled engine mounted at the rear and swing-axle independent rear suspension. Its unfamiliar handling characteristics led to a crop of accidents and a book written by a crusading lawyer, Ralph Nader. The book's title? *Unsafe at Any Speed . . .*

Right: a 1963 two-door Chevrolet Corvair Monza convertible. The Corvair was a brave effort to break with American tradition, using a rear-mounted, air-cooled, flat-six engine and independent rear suspension by swing axles. Any hope that might have been had of changing the style of the American automobile was comprehensively destroyed by Ralph Nader's safety-crusading book, *Unsafe at Any Speed* – a damaging indictment of the Corvair's design

Left: Ford's answer to the Mini was the mechanically conventional, if visually imaginative, new Anglia, introduced in 1959 and available with 997 and, later, 1200cc engines. The Anglia's most striking feature was the backward raked rear window, designed to resist rain and road grime and increase boot capacity

Right: a 1956 Armstrong-Siddeley Sapphire is typical of the British luxury motor car of the 1950s, with very conservative styling

Below: this 1952 Lea-Francis London Motor Show car is a 2½-litre sports model, which used a 2496cc, four-cylinder engine. It could reach a top speed of 102 mph, by courtesy of its 125 bhp power unit
(Stratford Motor Museum, England)

Chapter 6

The Racer Comes of Age

THE CARS: 1939-60

Below and right: the French Talbot concern had to resort to adapting its big sports cars for use in the Grands Prix of the immediate post-war years; they were very heavy, but this disadvantage was offset to a certain extent by the cars' ability to carry more fuel and therefore pit fewer times then their purpose-built rivals. The car shown here was built in 1950, with a 4½-litre Talbot-Lago engine, and was one of three used by the works team at Le Mans, before being driven by Froilan Gonzales in the French Grand Prix (Totnes Motor Museum, England)

Wars may disrupt and eventually quell motor racing but they have never spelt the end of its continuity. So it was in 1914–18 and again in 1939–45. World War II may have changed the whole way of European life as had the conflict of a quarter of a century earlier and it certainly left Europe in a shattered condition: her motor car manufacturing plants were either destroyed or converted for the production of aircraft and munitions. All through the dark years of this tremendous struggle for power, with bombs raining down on towns and factories, the enthusiasm for motor competitions never wained.

Racing was revived by the French in the Bois de Boulogne in September 1945, and international Grand Prix racing was resumed in 1947. The Germans, who had carried all before them before the outbreak of war with their phenomenal Mercedes-Benz and Auto Union racing teams, were not exactly popular at this time. British and American bombers had dealt with their production facilities, and they were in no way able, or allowed, immediately to resume the conflict even with racing cars over the great road circuits.

If Germany was still *hors de combat* in 1947, France was eager to resume motor racing and Italy was well prepared for it. What kind of cars these nations used would depend on the rules and regulations announced in Paris by the governing body of the sport, which was soon revived and operational again. The new Grand Prix Formula was announced as early as February 1946 and it had been carefully planned to provide for the prevailing post-war situation.

Before the war, the Grand Prix racing car had reached a high degree of efficiency, both in the power developed from its small supercharged engines and in its road-holding qualities, which had been enhanced by soft non-leaf-spring suspension systems of an all-independent action, or by the employment of De Dion rear suspension. Such racing cars were so very fast and accelerative that they called for highly skilled drivers to conduct them and they were a very exciting sort of vehicle to watch when on 'full-song' and engaged in a tense battle with others of the same ilk. However, they had been possible in their final costly pre-war form only because first Mussolini and then Hitler had seen a valuable means of fostering national prestige by racing cars of Italian and German manufacture (but not always driven by nationals) in world-wide international contests. This had made available to Alfa Romeo and Ferrari and, especially, to Mercedes-Benz and Auto Union, the enormous sums of money needed to research, build, develop and operate such fabulous racing cars.

By 1947, the picture was very different. Europe was impoverished and the motor industry, in war-damaged factories big and small, was attempting to salvage something from the aftermath and to get ordinary motor cars back into production. Those who sought to go racing, whether because they thought it good publicity for their customer products, an important laboratory for automotive research, or just because they enjoyed it, had to tread warily. This was if they were to afford the luxury of participation by convincing their mostly impoverished shareholders that it was worthwhile, or even profitable.

With these inescapable factors in mind, the new controlling body, known as the FIA, sensibly came up with a Grand Prix Formula which provided for two very different types of racing car to compete together. It was for cars of not more than $1\frac{1}{2}$ litres engine capacity supercharged, and of not over $4\frac{1}{2}$ litres capacity without a compressor or supercharger. As a matter of fact, this Formula was the one which the former AIACR had been intending to introduce in 1940, had the war not intervened. However, it was a Grand Prix stipulation well suited to post-war conditions. It meant that the expensive, small, high revving superchaged engine (two or multi-stage supercharged if the designer so wished) would be pitted against the more easy to render reliable, lazy-revving and big-capacity power unit, providing the latter used normal carburettors. It was a Formula that was of immediate interest to Great Britain, France and Italy. Britain had been concentrating on *voiturette* racing from 1934 onwards, with its top capacity figure of $1\frac{1}{2}$ litres, and Raymond Mays' green supercharged ERAs (English Racing Automobiles) had done very well in this field. France was more inclined, in the terrible plight in which the

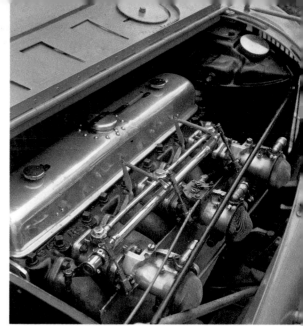

nation found itself after the end of the war, to hope that big, reliable and
enduring sports cars, stripped of their road-going wear, such as windscreens
mudguards, hoods, starter motors, lighting equipment, would serve as Grand
Prix cars; the non-supercharged 4½-litre engine-capacity limit looked after
them very nicely. The Italians were in the strongest position in 1947 however,
because Alfa Romeo raced the very beautiful and effective little 'blown'
1½-litre Tipo 158 cars, the Alfettas, before the war and Maserati, a small
company devoting themselves to racing-car production, brought out the 6C
and then the 4C sixteen-valve, twin-overhead-camshaft, four-cylinder *voiturette*
racing models before hostilities broke out. They were ideally suited to the
conditions and rules of the day.

That was the state of technical play as the post-war teams lined up on the
grids of circuits that had been abandoned, but certainly not forgotten, during
the past eight or nine years, to try their prowess at the resuscitated game of
international Grand Prix motor racing.

Apart from her economic and productive 'non condition', Germany would
not have been allowed by the FIA to return to international motor racing in
1947. Italy was, as has been said, in a fortunate position to resume, but even
she had to be content to develop pre-war designs. Profiting, perhaps, from pre-
war German technology, the Alfa Romeo engineers put two-stage supercharging on the Tipo 158 engine, which raised its power output to 265bhp
at 7500rpm, the blowers being paired in line along one side of the beautifully
constructed, straight-eight 1½-litre engine. This was compared to the 254bhp
at the same crankshaft speed which these engines had been producing back in
1939. Maserati, too, began to experiment with two-stage supercharging and
also designed a new chassis, using tubular construction. ERA had brought out
the very handsome E-type car of advanced conception, but it was never a
success, in spite of having a highly developed version of the well known ERA
six-cylinder engine that had itself been developed from the hemispherical head,
dual-high-set-camshaft Riley Six engine, as raced by Raymond Mays. The
idea of feeding this 63mm × 80mm power unit from a vast Zoller vane-type
compressor, and using Porsche trailing-arm front suspension and a De Dion
tube at the back, should have paid high dividends but led instead to frustration.

France had but her big sports cars to adapt to post-war Grand Prix racing,
in the guise of the heavy Talbots and Delahayes, which did not look very
promising, but which might not need to pause at the pits quite as frequently
as the highly boosted fuel-consuming 1½-litre racers. In addition, the French
Government, belatedly striving to gain prestige from motor racing, got
the Centre d'Etudes Technique de l'Automobile et du Cycle to prepare a
world-beating proper 1½-litre Grand Prix car. This showed enormous promise
(on paper) as had its talented designer, M. Lory, who created the great 2-litre
V12 and 1½-litre straight-eight Delage Grand Prix cars of 1924–27. Called the
CTA-Arsenal, as it was to be built at the Government Munitions Factory, the
car was a 90 degree V8, 60mm × 65.6mm, with a conventional, two-valves and
two-plugs-per-cylinder-head layout, the valves being prodded by two overhead camshafts. However it had all the trimmings including two-stage blowing,
of up to 30lb per sq in, from twin Roots instruments driven from the front of
the engine. The aim was to achieve 300bhp from this engine which, on the
test-bench, did show around 270 at 8000rpm. A chassis with all-round independent suspension was prepared for the CTA-Arsenal but, alas for French
hopes, nothing more was heard of it.

It was the Tipo 158 Alfa Romeo that was the truly significant Grand Prix
car of the period 1947 to 1950. By adopting the sensible attitude of continued
advancement of their existing design, instead of messing around with ingenious but untried new cars, Alfa Romeo of Milan managed to outpace
(on paper, at least) the impressive Type W165 Mercedes-Benz V8 of 1939.
Their now very highly supercharged straight-eight engine produced 310bhp.
Its chassis, too, underwent very little modification, although naturally the
braking system had to be adapted to the increased performance by fitting
stiffer brake drums and getting more heat away from them, thus cutting down
the considerable brake fade.

Apart from the big Talbots and Delahayes and the wonderful contribution of Alfa Romeo, there were numerous offshoots of lesser designs during this period of motor-racing revival, such as the Maserati-based OSCA, the Veritas and Meteor, which were really sports cars using pre-war Type 328 BMW six-cylinder engines. There was also the 2-litre V12 Ferrari sports car that competed in stripped form as a racing car. The Maserati now appeared under Omar Orsi's direction as the two-stage-blown, tubular-chassis 4CLT model thus reinforcing their chances of success in motor racing.

In Britain, Alta were busy with a new Grand Prix car. The pre-war four-cylinder twin-cam engine now had the cylinder dimensions of 78 mm × 78 mm, and was thus of truly 'square' conception, and still with roller-chain-drive to its overhead camshaft. It was used in a brand-new frame with tubular side members and an ingenious method of suspension was by double wishbones. This gave all-independent action when used with rubber blocks as the damping medium, pressed on by bell cranks formed at the lower wishbones. Unfortunately, for the hopes of Geoffrey Taylor and his little factory at Tolworth, off the Kingston by-pass, near London, this Grand Prix Alta was not a

wildly successful racing car and the marque gradually faded away.

After two years or so of the new régime, Ferrari came up with his Colombo-designed 2-litre racer, which owed much to his satisfactory sports car of that engine capacity. The new GP Ferrari was something of a sensation, because of its very compact size and therefore light weight, into which chassis Ferrari had put a supercharged V12 power pack producing 230bhp. This engine was of 55mm × 52.5mm bore and stroke, so now there was an 'over-square' engine, the first since that of Mercedes-Benz which had trampled on the Italians at Tripoli in 1939. Like its Alfa Romeo rival, this Ferrari ran at 7500rpm but was content with one Roots supercharger, and a single overhead camshaft operating valves inclined at 60 degrees. It was fitted with a five-speed gearbox, but the handling was not particularly good, the swing-axle rear suspension no doubt responsible for the high degree of oversteer produced on corners. Double wishbones were used at the front, and transverse leaf-springs were employed both front and rear. This, the first of the post-war Ferraris, fell between the winning form of the Tipo 158 Alfa Romeo and the lesser capabilities of the 4CLT/48 Maseratis.

Below: the 1948 Maserati 4CLT/48 was the ultimate development of the 4C, introduced in 1938 as a supercharged Voiturette racer. Following a debut win in the hands of Ascari and Villoresi, at San Remo, the model was immortalised as the 'San Remo' Maserati. It enjoyed a position of near-dominance between 1948 and 1950, with Ascari, Bira, Fangio and Parnell among an illustrious list of drivers, before a rapid decline of fortunes brought its famous career to a sad close. The car shown is the ex-Parnell example
(Donington Collection, England)

Below and inset: the straight-six Lago-Talbot of 1950 had a capacity of 4482 cc and produced 240–260 bhp. The advantage of using an unsupercharged engine against a forced-induction unit was in the fuel consumption. This car could return a respectable 9–10 mpg, which stood it in good stead against the thirsty Italian opposition

At quite the opposite extreme were the big Lago-Talbots, which Anthony Lago of Paris hoped might have their racing chance when the very highly boosted $1\frac{1}{2}$-litre cars had to go into their pits to refuel. Lago had built a single-seater version of what were otherwise purely sports cars in 1939, and he now introduced what seemed a rather unconvincing answer to the fast and furious small supercharged machines. It had a long-stroke engine, with six cylinders measuring 93×110 mm bore and stroke, respectively, so the capacity was actually 4.48 litres. The valve gear consisted of inclined valves in the cylinder heads, opened and closed by means of short, light, pushrods moved by a couple of camshafts located high up in the crankcase as on a Riley engine. A sort of 'refined lorry engine', some said. The drive went through a Wilson pre-selector gearbox, which had been used from 1934 to 1939 by ERA, and which enabled the driver to pre-select the required gear before a corner, and then to make a lightning change by merely pressing a pedal. This arrangement had the disadvantages of being very weighty and also of having fairly wide gear ratios. The $4\frac{1}{2}$-litre Lago-Talbot did have an off-set prop-shaft which enabled the driver to sit low in the car, and to some degree overcome the drag of such a

Left: by 1947, the Alfa Romeo was well on its way to being one of the most successful post-war racing cars. This car, which was first seen briefly before the war, was two-stage supercharged and produced 265 bhp from its 1479 cc, eight-cylinder engine. Fuel consumption was a great handicap, the car returning fewer than two miles per gallon

Below left and right: a post-war 'Auto Union'. This is the Porsche-designed Cisitalia 1½-litre GP car, first seen in 1950. It was hoped that its flat-twelve engine would produce 550 bhp, but 385 bhp was all that was seen, albeit briefly. An interesting feature of this car was that it was able to enter corners in two-wheel drive, but exit (at the driver's will) using all four wheels for propulsion, giving extra traction

large and heavy motor car. The rigid back axle was again a retrograde feature, judged by the number of independent suspension systems in use at the time, and it was suspended on half-elliptic leaf springs. Front suspension was independent, by a simple system of a transverse leaf spring and lower wishbones. The power output of 250bhp, and the car's weight, were not a happy combination, but these rather appealing 'heavy-metal' Lago-Talbots scored in those races where the lighter and far more powerful cars either ran into mechanical troubles or forfeited their superior speed in stops to take on more fuel or change their tyres. The interest in atmospheric-induction 4½-litre Grand Prix cars was very limited however.

As the scene moved closer to the pre-Hitler concept of road racing, the cost of participating began to move upwards again and the game became mainly one between wealthy manufacturers. To encourage participation at a lesser level, the FIA contrived Formula Two, for supercharged cars of up to 500cc, and non-supercharged cars of up to 2-litres. No-one seemed able to cope with a blown half-litre beast, so this racing was at first a 2-litre Ferrari benefit.

The 1949 season was disappointing if you were an Alfa enthusiast, because the great Milanese firm decided to drop out of racing while the Tipo 158 cars were at the top of their exceptional form. True, they had ready a remarkable 52 × 52 mm flat-twelve-cylinder racer dating back to 1940, but this was never raced. Nor was the very sensational Dr Ferry Porsche-designed, space-frame, flat-twelve-cylinder Cisitalia, which was intended to run at 10,000 to 12,000 rpm, anticipating a power output of 500bhp. This car had two superchargers, a five-speed gearbox, cylinder dimensions of 56 × 51 mm and, most notably, a centrally mounted engine driving all four wheels. A clutch enabled the driver to disconnect the drive to the front wheels at his discretion. Built at the Cisitalia works in Turin, the car was tested in South America and, although Nuvolari expressed interest in driving it, its sponsors went bankrupt and the project folded up.

The British BRM (British Racing Motor) was another dubious racing car of intended Grand Prix calibre, which made its debut during 1949. It was inspired by racing driver Raymond Mays, of ERA fame, and he persuaded the British motor and accessory companies to contribute in cash and in kind to the building of this highly advanced V16-cylinder 1½-litre, supercharged, all-British racing car, to the design of his friend Peter Berthon. It was, unfortunately, a disaster from the word go, except in lesser races, and then only after an enormous amount of mostly fruitless development.

The BRM design sought to use the 1½-litre supercharged part of the prevailing Formula to the fullest advantage. The engine had sixteen cylinders, in blocks of four, in a 135° Vee. Between each pair of blocks rose the drive for the twin overhead camshafts, which operated two valves per cylinder. The camshaft drive was by means of a gear train, from which the final drive was taken, and then via a short shaft to the clutch. The dimensions of this

ambitious V16 racing power unit were microscopic, being 49.53 × 48.26mm,
a swept-volume of 1.48-litres. Such small pistons and light moving parts were
intended to enable a maximum crankshaft speed as high as 10,000 to 12,000
rpm to be reached, and a power output in the region of 400bhp was visualised.
Very lofty supercharge pressures, of up to 70lb/sq in were obtained by twin
centrifugal blowers mounted on the front of the engine, drawing from two
horizontal carburettors. To save weight, ignition was of the coil-and-distributor
type. This BRM was a very courageous attempt to put paid to Alfa Romeo
and any other opposition on the circuits to British prestige, but it was to prove
far too complex and the unusual system of centrifugal supercharging meant
that the immense power came in over a very limited rev-band. This made the
car extremely difficult for even top Grand Prix drivers to control or use to its
full effect.

The V16 BRM had a chassis that had borrowed a great deal from the pre-
war Mercedes and Auto Unions, and the front trailing-arm independent suspension was very like that of the 1937 C-type and 1939 E-type ERAs. The
difference here was that the torsion bars had been deleted, in favour of Lockheed oleo-pneumatic struts, which relied on air under compression for suspension and oil for damping, operated from an extension of the upper suspension arm. More complication! At the rear of the BRM there was de Dion
semi-independent suspension, with the same kind of Lockheed suspension
struts as at the front. The transmission incorporated a five-speed gearbox and
the open propeller shaft ran at an angle, so that the driver's seat could be
positioned low down beside it. This was mostly a crib from the pre-war 1½-
litre, and 3-litre Mercedes racers. The chassis frame consisted of two side
members, united by tubular cross members, and the special fuel was carried
in a saddle tank over the luckless driver's legs, with an additional fuel tank
in the tail. This unfortunate BRM was announced with much aplomb, but
apart from missing the 1949 racing season, it was uncompetitive for the reasons given, and initially suffered from embarrassing starting-line breakdowns.

Ferrari must take the credit for a more sensible approach to racing in those
days. By increasing the length of his 1½-litre chassis and adopting twin
overhead camshafts and two-stage supercharging for the V12 engine, Ferrari
ensured a decent increase in performance and obtained better roadholding by
altering the rear suspension. This car was still the work of engineer Colombo,
but at the end of 1949 Enzo Ferrari decided on a complete change of policy.
Employing Aurelio Lampredi as the development engineer and designer,
Ferrari switched from the blown 1½-litre to the opposite non-supercharged
4½-litre format. His reasons were two-fold: in the first place he wished to
avoid the very high cost of maintaining between races his delicate supercharged engines, and in the second place Ferrari had much experience of
normally aspirated power units from his successful 2-litre V12 sports-cars
and he now realised that a bigger version could almost equal the power outputs

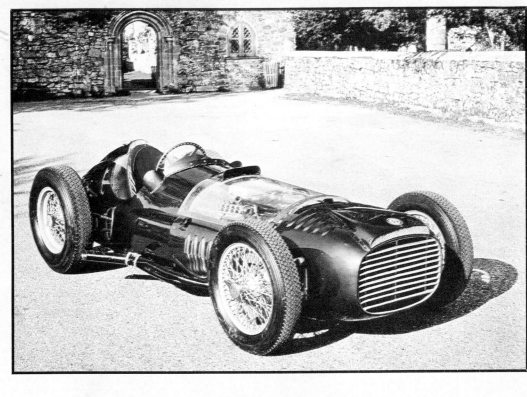

Left: proving that the war did not slow down their progress at all, Mercedes-Benz produced the W196; this is the streamlined version

Below and below right: the Alfettas, although thirsty, were remarkable racing cars. Their final race, the 1951 Spanish GP at Barcelona, gave them a win: a fitting time for the company to withdraw from the sport

which were being squeezed from little high-revving blown motors, and more reliably too. He may also have preferred a closer link with the sort of cars he was selling to his customers.

However, the Grand Prix scene was immediately rendered more interesting when Alfa Romeo announced that they intended to stage a come-back in 1950. Now would be witnessed a battle-royal between the two great Italian makes of Ferrari and Alfa Romeo, using diametrically opposite kinds of racing car: the former large and heavy, but reliable and fuel-thrifty, the latter small, compact and beautiful. Would these little racers last the distances, or have sufficient performance over the Ferraris to balance-out the time that they would presumably lose during refuelling pit-stops? One of the most interesting periods of Grand Prix racing was about to begin, and the race-by-race aspect will be looked at in the next chapter.

From the foregoing it will be realised that what Alfa Romeo of Milan intended to do was to return with their already very convincing little Alfettas, developed into what were to become known as the Tipo 159 cars. They were compact, with a wheelbase of 8 ft 2 in, and capable of 180 mph.

The revived 1951 Alfettas were at first credited with having increased their maximum revs from 7500 to 8500 rpm, enabling the power output to reach 350 bhp. It was also said that these effective straight-eight engines, at the end of their useful run, had shown a little over 400 bhp at 9000 rpm on the test rig. It seems more likely that, as raced during the 1951 season, they were delivering some 385 bhp at the former top limit of 7500 rpm. To achieve such outputs it was essential to use fuel of the alcohol 'dope' variety that would go far towards cooling the tortured engine internals, and it is certain that as a consequence of this, the Tipo 159s had the very heavy fuel consumption of only $1\frac{1}{2}$ miles per gallon. To carry as much fuel in the tail tanks of the cars as possible, without affecting the roadholding characteristics was a problem; it will be appreciated that as the fuel level drops in the course of a race, a car's weight distribution is altered, often very drastically. The Alfa Romeo engineers used de Dion instead of swing-axle rear suspension for the 159s, but they retained the transverse leaf springs of the 158 design. The axle was located by means of radius arms and an ingenious A-bracket. Wider brake drums were fitted to the Tipo 159 cars and to try to reduce the refuelling problem, a tankage of 65 gallons was contrived about the cockpit. In the engine department the original bore and stroke dimensions were retained, *ie* 58 × 70 mm, and the increase in power was obtained from subtle improvements to supercharger boost, valve timing, exhaust system and porting.

The $4\frac{1}{2}$-litre Ferrari which was soon to fight it out against these much smaller Alfa Romeos had a very similar chassis to the previous cars, except that Lampredi preferred a de Dion rear end. It was used in Formula Two as well as in Formula One races with the old 2-litre unsupercharged engine until the bigger F1 power unit was ready for it. Weight was saved in the de Dion assembly by having side radius arms to locate it, thus eliminating the need for a rotating joint. Strength for the chassis frame was gained from a spaceframe structure that at first merely formed the scuttle of the body. The big engine had a single overhead camshaft, driven by chain, over each cylinder bank of the 60 degree vee engine with 24 inclined valves. The engine started life as a 72 mm × 68 mm, 3.3-litre unit, but was soon expanded to 4.1 litres by opening out the cylinder bore to 80 mm and then, finally, to 4490 cc, by keeping the bigger bore in conjunction with an increase in piston stroke to 74.5 mm. It is significant, especially as most modern Grand Prix engines are non supercharged, that this $4\frac{1}{2}$-litre Ferrari engine was producing a claimed 380 bhp at 7500 rpm by the end of the 1950 season, which made the car only slightly slower than the Tipo 159 Alfa Romeos on the straights, a deficit which could often be wiped out by the Ferrari's fewer pit stops for petrol. For 1951, the $4\frac{1}{2}$-litre Ferrari was further improved by altering the combustion-chamber shape and using two spark plugs per cylinder. This pushed the horsepower to rather more than the previous 380 and that this engine had plenty of development left in it is shown by a special which produced no less than 430 bhp.

Right: the racing cars of the 50s demanded not only courage and skill of their drivers, but also great physical strength. Froilan Gonzalez, 'The Pampas Bull', is seen here at the wheel of a 1951 Ferrari 375. The car was powered by a $4\frac{1}{2}$-litre V12 engine, notable for its remarkably large piston area; at 93.6 square inches, it was larger than all but the C-type Auto Union and some ancient behemoths

Below: surely the most magnificent failure in motor racing: the V16 BRM had tiny cylinders and a Rolls-Royce-designed supercharger running at an astonishing 39,000 rpm. Although the engine never reached its projected 600 bhp output, 525 bhp was seen in the workshop. The engine was unfortunately better known for its exquisite sound than for its longevity

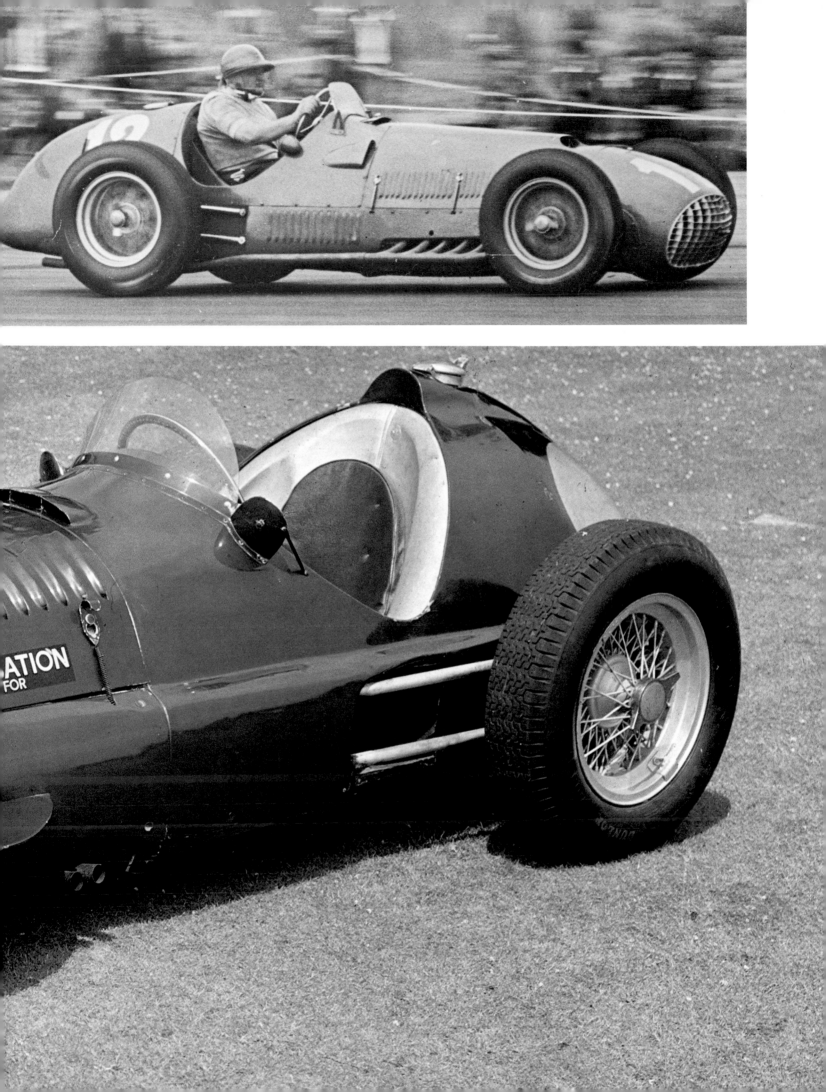

Left: the Ferrari 500 with which Alberto Ascari won two consecutive World Championships in 1952 and 1953. The original engine was a 1980cc, twin-overhead-camshaft, four-cylinder unit of Formula Two derivation. It developed 170bhp at 7000rpm. The engine shown here is a 3-litre unit, also with four cylinders, installed many years ago by a former owner for the 1954 Tasman racing series in Australia and New Zealand. This chassis is possibly the most successful in Grand Prix history
(Donington Collection, England)

The BRM was proving an embarrassment to poor Raymond Mays and the 'big but unblown' theme of Ferrari, Talbot and Delahaye was followed by OSCA, who brought out a V12-cylinder engine of 78mm × 78mm, 4.47 litres, to be accommodated in a 4CLT Maserati chassis. This is how racing recovered from the war years and proved so very interesting. However, when it was announced that the $1\frac{1}{2}$ litres blown/$4\frac{1}{2}$ litres unblown Formula was to hold good until a new Formula was announced from Paris to take effect in 1954, Alfa Romeo again withdrew from the scene, not wishing to build the necessary new cars for only two more seasons of the then current Formula. Mercedes-Benz had hinted excitingly that they intended to return to motor racing, but not until the new Formula came into use. So, F1 tended to take on a subdued aspect, in 1952, with only Ferrari ready to race his $4\frac{1}{2}$-litre cars. For this reason, many organisers took a look at the situation, with the V16 BRM still giving much trouble, and then decided to hold only Formula Two races, which attracted big and varied fields. Lampredi had brought out one new F1 car for Ferrari, as he found that the big $4\frac{1}{2}$-litre model lacked the torque desirable for certain kinds of race circuits. This was a four-cylinder unit of 90mm × 78mm, 1.98 litres, which was installed in the Formula Two frame, with de Dion rear suspension. Using twin spark plugs per cylinder and a dual-choke Weber carburettor for each pair of cylinders, it was an effective tool. The attention bestowed on ordinary, as opposed to supercharged, power units in the 1950–54 period was responsible for the introduction of ram pipes for the carburettor air intakes, tuned in conjunction with the valve timing and the exhaust system of an engine to give a mild boost without resorting to mechanical complications. It is thought, however, that J. G. Parry Thomas had played with the idea of ramming a little extra air into the engine of his racing Leyland-Thomas at Brooklands back in 1925.

Before we leave the declining Formula One years leading up to 1953, it must be mentioned that in Britain the courageous performances of the ERA *voiturettes* were followed by an attempt on the part of HWM to break into full-time racing. Their car was an Alta-engined single seater, using a wishbone and coil-spring front suspension system and a de Dion rear-end, in which quarter-elliptic springs both located and sprung the de Dion tube. The 1952 season may have been less than stimulating in respect of new cars, but it did witness more different makes of cars competing in important races than ever; Colombo left Ferrari to collaborate with Bellantani and Massimino in creating a new Formula Two Maserati with a tubular chassis, a twin-cam six-cylinder engine, two exhaust pipes, and the now-fashionable carburettor ram-pipes; Gordini evolved his successful racing version of the French Simca into a difficult-to-drive, 75 × 75mm bore and stroke, six-cylinder car, employing the former $1\frac{1}{2}$-litre-type chassis, and HWM went over to the use of torsion bars for their de Dion axle and adopted inboard brakes at the rear.

Two very significant developments took place at that time. The first was

Below: leading up to their own Vanwall Grand Prix racing car, Vandervells experimented with a modified Ferrari, the *Thinwall Special*. The name came from the thin-walled bearings used in the engine

the installation of a 2-litre Bristol engine into the sort of chassis that Cooper of Surbiton had evolved for their 500 cc, rear-engined, Formula Three racers, and in which Stirling Moss had his racing baptism. The larger car had its six-cylinder, triple-carburettor, BMW valve-geared engine mounted at the front, under a conventional bonnet. The second development was a very strong bid for British motor racing victories by Rodney Clark and Mike Oliver with the Connaught, a car financed by McAlpine and built in Surrey. The power unit of the latter was at first a modified Lea-Francis engine. It must also be mentioned that this period of racing-car development saw British engineers refining the disc brake, which BRM now fitted, as did Vandervell, who were using a 4½-litre Formula One Ferrari the *Thin Wall Special* for their early experiments. These experiments were to lead to Mr Tony Vandervell realising his life's ambition, which was to win Grand Prix races with a British car – his 2½-litre Vanwall. At this time his team's successes were still some way in the future.

In what remained of F1 racing under the existing regulations, Ferrari was persuading 400 bhp from the unblown 4½-litre motor and was seeking better

Below and below left: the Maserati 250F epitomised the racing car of the 1950s, with the tyres now looking fatter, the body smoother and finer contoured and the engine ever more efficient. The overhead camshaft 2460 cc engine of this car, which was driven by Perdisa, Mieres and Collins, produced about 250 hp in 1955 when it was built. Of course, it was with one of these cars that Fangio continued to create his own niche in motor-racing legend (Donington Collection, England)

cooling and greater rigidity from the drum brakes. Meanwhile, both Ferrari and Gordini had been trying out 2½-litre versions of their 2-litre, Formula Two power units, so as to be fully prepared for the coming new Grand Prix Formula.

So to 1954 and the new 2½-litre Formula. It had been introduced not to kill the speed of current Grand Prix cars, as had once been the aim behind restrictive rulings, but to encourage research into non-supercharged engines, which were rightly thought of as being of more value to production-car engineers than the highly supercharged power units which the preceding Formula had encouraged. This was sensible thinking, because in a road-going auto the expense, noise, and fuel-thirst of supercharged engines was unpalatable and in any case the normally aspirated type was now known to give 100 bhp per litre in Formula Two racing cars. All the Grand Prix contenders went for these 2½-litre, carburetted, motors. There was a general move towards chassis frames constructed of small-gauge tubes, de Dion rear suspension, and a concentration of weight in the centre of the car to make it controllable on corners, where a dumb-bell effect of weight at each end was detrimental.

Ferrari came up with an engine of 94 mm × 90 mm bore and stroke, the Type 625, for installation in the Type 500 car, and then produced the 2.49-litre, 100 × 79.5 mm, engine with big valve areas and two sparking plugs in each cylinder. This was used in the bulbous 'Squalo' model, with fuel carried in side tanks, as a sop to the aforesaid low polar moment of inertia or dumb-bell effect. Maserati raced a six-cylinder car, developed from their old Formula Two machine, which incorporated a compact gearbox on the back end of the car, turned 90 degrees from normal, spur gears taking the drive to the differential, from which jointed-shafts took the drive out to the wheels. This was the Maserati that was to become justly famous – the great 250F, which is still raced in suitable historic car races to this day. In 1954 guise

it had the 84 × 75 mm six-cylinder engine using twin overhead camshafts, triple, double-choke, Weber carburettors, and an exhaust system of three pairs of outlet pipes; ignition was by magneto to twelve sparking plugs. Connaught were trying hard, on a slender budget, with the $93\frac{1}{2}$ × 90 mm, four-cylinder Alta engine, on which they used fuel injection into the inlet ports. The gearbox used in these British-green racers was an Armstrong Siddeley-type pre-selector and the company even made a fully streamlined Connaught for the faster circuits. It all paid off, when one of these cars won a Grand Prix for Britain for the first time since Sunbeam had done so in 1924.

It was now that Vandervell set out on what was to be an even more successful effort for Britain. The Vanwall used a $2\frac{1}{2}$-litre, four-cylinder engine with a cylinder-head design based on that of the single-cylinder Norton motor-cycle engine, the engine of the bike on which millionaire Tony Vandervell had started his racing career. Hairpin valve springs were fitted to the twin-overhead-camshaft, four-cylinder engine. There was much trouble with throttle connections at first. Vanwall had previously bought one of the big, $4\frac{1}{2}$-litre Ferrari cars and from this many valuable lessons had been gleaned.

The 2½-litre Vanwall used a similar kind of four-speed gearbox, incorporated in its back axle, and the Goodyear disc brakes they had fitted to this bigger Ferrari were adopted for the exciting new car. BRM had fortunately been persuaded away from contesting the 1954–57 Formula with a blown 750 cc engine and were about to embark on restoring their very tarnished reputation, with a new 2½-litre, four-cylinder car.

Most exciting news of all was that Mercedes-Benz were returning to Grand Prix participation. The great German company, which had heard it all before, had done most of it, and knew, from painstakingly documented experience and experimentation, how to wring the best from any Formula, saw the new challenge as best met with 76×68.8 mm straight-eight-cylinder engines. This new W196 design used twin overhead camshafts, driven from a train of gears rising from the centre of the crankshaft in the middle of the paired cylinder blocks. The combustion chambers were conventionally hemispherical and the gear-drive to the overhead camshafts was as on the BRM and pre-war Alfa Romeos, but the inlet ports were arranged to run vertically into the cylinders, as on pre-war 328 BMW sports-car engines. Where this new Grand Prix

Below: the magnificent W196 Mercedes-Benz was brilliantly engineered in every detail. The chassis was a true spaceframe and the engine was a delightful straight-eight unit with overhead camshafts and desmodromic valve gear. With these cars, Fangio and Moss were seldom beaten

Mercedes-Benz was so very advanced was in the use of desmodromic, or positive, valve opening and closing and the employment of fuel injection directly into the cylinders. Cams closed and opened the overhead valves without the aid of springs. Moreover, this advanced engine had the full roller-bearing treatment, for big-end and main bearings, with a built-up crankshaft and one-piece connecting rods, and the traditional Mercedes-Benz method of welding steel water jackets round the cylinders was again made use of. This fine power producer was planned in unison with the entire W196 car, so that it was tilted over in the space frame to reduce height and therefore wind drag. The chassis was a stressed tubular affair of one-inch diameter tubing, with double wishbone and torsion-bar front springing, and a return at the rear of the chassis to swing-axle suspension, but on a new low-pivot system, in conjunction with torsion-bars. The drive was taken from the centre of the engine's crankshaft, passing through a five-speed gearbox, mounted at the back, behind the differential assembly. All the wheels were retarded by means of inboard drum brakes of enormous size, cooled by turbine-type finning, and thus having no effect on unsprung weight. These

great Grand Prix cars were the work of Rudolf Uhlenhaut and Dr Nallinger. They were at first given all-enveloping streamlined bodywork, enclosing the road wheels. This proved to be a mistake on normal road and semi-road circuits, even the great Fangio hitting the markers at Silverstone as vision was badly impaired. Ordinary bodies were soon substituted.

It is significant that, at this period of racing, these non-supercharged engines were able to develop at least 100 bhp per litre, and soon 300 bhp was to be released, while the power was transmitted to the road through tyres of rival makes, Mercedes-Benz using those made by Continental, other racing-car constructors relying on the products of Dunlop, Pirelli and Englebert. The day of the wet/dry tyre compound, which has been such a vital aspect of modern motor racing, was still far distant. Weights were down to around $13\frac{1}{2}$ cwt, Mercedes-Benz, for example, using bodywork made of Electron sheeting only 0.028 inches thick. Speeds varied from about 165 to 170 mph with the Vanwalls nudging 180 mph. In 1954 Lancia joined in, with their new D50 cars. Here was seen yet another step forward, as the Lancia's ninety-degree V8 engine was used to stiffen the chassis frame and the front suspension was attached to it, as is done with the rear suspension of today's lightweight Grand Prix cars. Lancia used the popular multi-tubular frame, composed of small-diameter tubing, and the also popular transaxle at the back for the de Dion suspension and they also located the clutch at the end of this transmission line, operating it hydraulically. The engine was of conventional twin-cam formation, breathing through Solex instead of the customary Weber carburettors, and was said to produce 260 bhp. Pannier fuel tanks on the Lancia D50 were a distinguishing feature, the idea being to gain some reduction in air turbulence between the road wheels, as on some of the pre-war Land Speed Record cars. This also kept the weight of the fuel within the compact wheelbase, so that the emptying of the tanks would not adversely affect cornering powers and road-clinging, as would have been the case with a tank in the car's tail.

The other rather stubby car was the Ferrari Squalo, or Type 555, which emerged for the 1955 season with several improvements to the unchanged basic design. The former multi-tube frame was abandoned for one with longitudinal tubes of large size and the fuel load was now accommodated in the centre of the car, thus giving the fattened appearance that caused this Ferrari to become known as the 'Supersqualo'. Ferrari also persevered with the older Type 625 cars, and for 1955 gave them coil-spring front suspension and a five-speed gearbox. Maserati went on racing the effective Type 250F cars but had evolved a revised cylinder head for them, with enlarged valves, and triple Weber 45DCO carburettors, flexibly mounted to keep a stable fuel-level in the float chambers. Fuel injection had been tried on the Maserati which Stirling Moss was driving but a reversion was made to Weber carburettors; disc brakes too were useful to Moss in enabling him to brake later than his rivals into corners.

Top and above: the Jano-designed Lancia D50 brought only the second completely new design to the grids of 1954. The very stiff 90° V8 engine was utilised as an integral part of the chassis and incorporated the mounting points for the front suspension. The clutch, gearbox and final drive were all mounted at the tail of the car. The distinctive pannier fuel tanks not only stabilised the centre of gravity within the wheelbase but also contributed to reducing aerodynamic turbulence between the wheels (Lancia collection, Italy)

Above: BRM's P25, 2½-litre car made its debut in August 1955 and continued to be raced, albeit in modified form, during 1956, 1957, 1958 and 1959. The four-cylinder engine was very much oversquare and produced 272 bhp on an AvGas. This particular car was built up from the remains of car number 2510, which was crashed in spectacular fashion at Avus in 1959, when Hans Herrmann suffered brake failure on Berlin's highspeed banked track
(Donington Collection, England)

From this it will be appreciated that chassis design was beginning to have as important an effect on the speed of a racing car round a circuit as engine power. In these exciting mid-nineteen-fifties years of Fangio/Moss domination, the modern art of 'setting-up' a racing car, and tuning its suspension characteristics to suit a given circuit, had not emerged. The reliability of the racing engine was much improved and it is a startling thought, or was to all those who had been in charge of the temperamental racing power units of the pre-war decades, that although sparking plugs could still oil-up, or cut-out from other causes, in the W196 Mercedes-Benz, with its deeply canted-over engine, it was necessary to remove one of the front wheels before a plug could be changed on the eight-cylinder unit. The aforesaid effect of chassis design and layout on lap speeds was portrayed when Mercedes-Benz, whose substantial financial resources enabled them to field a large number of variants of the W196, found that appreciable advantage was derived from having three different lengths of wheelbase; although these differed by only 2½ inches in the case of the short and medium-length chassis, the lap speeds set by Moss and Fangio at the Nürburgring improved by 5½ seconds when they drove the 7 ft 1 in wheelbase Mercedes. However, there was a difficulty! The short-wheelbase car was so difficult to drive that it was the medium-length Mercedes that was used for road racing – which is a nice illustration of the sophisticated state of the game at that period.

It was not entirely to the big battalions that racing successes were going. At Syracuse the Connaught of Tony Brooks won, from the Maserati of Musso, a car that the Connaught was capable of out-accelerating, although possibly not of out-braking, even with disc brakes. The Alta engine had had the fuel-injection system by SU removed from it and it was now getting its fuel via two twin-choke Webers. The Connaught may not have been delivering more than a mediocre 240 bhp but it had been deliberately planned to give power over a wide range of engine speed and good torque from low speeds, achieved by the timing of its valves and the shape of its inlet and exhaust piping. It would run to 7000 rpm but was not usually extended beyond 6500 rpm, whereas both of the current Ferrari racing engines would peak at 7500 rpm.

As 1956 dawned, the 2½-litre BRM was seen to continue its conservative design, which conformed to the prevailing formulae, except for the fact that oil-damped Lockheed suspension struts were fitted, borrowed, as it were, from the disastrous V16, 1½-litre, BRM. The Vanwall had been suspect in handling and during the winter Colin Chapman, later of Lotus fame, had been engaged as a technical consultant. This one-time civil engineer had designed for the wealthy Mr Vandervell a very impressive, scientifically stressed, full spaceframe chassis. Nor was this all. The Vanwall now appeared with sleek aerodynamic coachwork, devised by Frank Costin, Chapman's aircraft-expert friend, and the 2½-litre, four-cylinder engine with its Norton-type cylinder heads, hairpin valve springs on exposed valve stems, and its high-pressure

Bosch fuel injection was continually being developed. There were inboard rear brakes, air-cooled, of Goodyear make.

Maserati went on with the Type 250F cars, both in five-speed and four-speed forms, and with some experimentation with a fuel injection system of their own devising. Gordini were still in the hunt, with their ladder-frame, eight-cylinder, petrol-burning cars, the engine being based on that of their Le Mans sports-car, and the chassis having all-round independent suspension.

Historians would never forgive us if we omitted to refer to the return of the Bugatti Company to Grand Prix racing. This was done with the Type 251; of highly original design, its straight-eight twin-cam engine was placed transversely behind the cockpit, which was itself in the centre of the box-section, spaceframe, chassis. To the latter was attached a de Dion rear system of springing, employing an ingenious crank-and-rod connection to coil springs. From the centre of the transverse crankshaft came the spur-gear drive, to a five-speed gearbox of the Porsche synchromesh kind and at the front of the car, Bugatti tradition had been firmly upheld by the fitting of a beam axle! Although everyone, the writer included, wished the new Bugatti well – two

had been built – the Type 251 appeared only in the French Grand Prix at Reims and was hardly a success. However, for the record, let us mention that it was of 75 × 68.8 mm bore and stroke and ran up to 9000 rpm. Moreover, as one writer of note has pointed out, its telescopic shock absorbers were a glimpse into the future and this Bugatti's engine and gearbox arrangements gave a foretaste of the Lamborghini Miura, a roadgoing sports car of over a decade later. The 250F Masers had reverted to the well known twin exhaust tail pipes and Vanwall was, in employing a body in which the driver was enclosed up to his shoulders, very gently leading us towards the present-day conception of a Grand Prix car which is seen, but in which the driver is all but out of sight.

The next important GP racing car was a V12 Maserati with twin overhead camshafts to each bank of cylinders, 24 coils to attend to the firing of its two sparking plugs in each cylinder, and six Weber 35IDM downdraught carburettors. It was, however, not raced. 1957 saw the significant introduction by Ferrari of a V6-cylinder, 1½-litre, Formula Two car, rumoured to develop no less than 190 bhp, on petrol, at 9200 rpm. It was a pointer to future Ferrari F1 plans.

Then there came the most radical departure of all, the move to put the engine behind the driver, as is so in all modern GP cars. This happened when Rob Walker entered Jack Brabham in a Cooper, with the sting in its tail represented by a Coventry Climax engine enlarged from its customary Formula Two size. This far-reaching trend was continued first when the Cooper Car Company itself installed a 1.9-litre Coventry Climax power pack into the back of such a car, with disc brakes, and subsequently when Bob Gerard contrived a six-port, 69 × 100 mm, Bristol engine of 2250 cc for the back end of his Cooper chassis.

The 1954–57 Formula went out on some technically interesting and important notes. Ferrari had introduced the famous Dino Ferrari, its type name being that of Enzo Ferrari's son; the car's Formula Two V6-cylinder power unit was gradually enlarged, the first stage taking it to 1860 cc, with megaphone exhausts. Maserati had more power than anyone else in the field, their 2½-litre, 68½ × 66 mm, engine giving over 4½ bhp for every square inch of its piston-area, which measured an aggregate of 67 square inches, while the gallant Vanwalls were now giving 310 bhp and were safe up to a top crankshaft speed of 10,000 rpm. In due course the Dino Ferrari unit was opened out to the full 2½ litres, or more precisely, two versions were run in 1957, one having a capacity of 2417 cc and the other being of 2200 cc.

Although the Formula governing GP racing was much the same to the end of 1960 as it had been for the preceeding four years, the FIA now stipulated that the racing engines must function on petrol, at once dispensing with the artificial cooling effect of alcohol fuels. The mixtures used had provided engine reliability for those who were prepared to put large quantities of fuel of this 'forgiving' nature in the tanks of their cars before the start of a race and at the refuelling stops. Ferrari had the happy advantage of their Formula Two engines already being petrol burners, and now enlarged them into proper Grand Prix Formula cars. Maserati, however, withdrew from racing as a consequence of the changed ruling, even though the definition of petrol was stretched to mean 'AvGas' aviation spirit, of 130 octane rating. Vanwall and BRM were also very hard hit by the change. The Vanwall had relied on extreme nitromethane mixtures to produce its claimed 290 bhp, as installed in the car, and this engine would lose nearly 30 bhp if run on petrol; their fuel-injection system had to be drastically retuned for straight petrol fuels to release even that much horsepower. The four-cylinder BRM engine, with its stroke/bore ratio of 0.73:1, while giving an effective piston-area figure and very high rates of rotation, was very dependent on cooling from alcohol for its internals. Particularly prone to overheating were its valves, of which the inlet valves were much larger than normal and the exhaust valves were of more usual size.

The Ferrari, now called the Type Dino 246, its 65-degree, V6-cylinder, engine being of 85 × 71 mm (2417 cc), was good for 9400 rpm according to some authorities and probably gave 280 bhp in its 1958 guise.

Lotus now came onto the scene, with Formula Two-type cars, powered by the 'stretched' Coventry Climax engine. At first of only 2-litre and 2.2-litre capacity, these new Lotus cars were not only extremely light but they had suspension refinements that were the first of the great Colin Chapman innovations that have become the hallmark of the Lotus stable down the years. The BRMs were heavier but had been developed into effective racing cars with good torque characteristics, liked by most drivers. The rear-engined Coopers were on the way to absolute success and by 1959 had double wishbone independent suspension at the back, still in conjunction with a transverse leaf spring. Although tyre sizes were generally increasing, BRM changed from 16 in to 15 in diameter covers. Dunlop were rapidly ousting all opposition as leaders on racing-tyre techniques, with the new R5 racing tyre, which was finding favour with several teams.

Aston Martin entered F1 racing with the too heavy DBR4/250, developed from the better known Type DBR/300 sports-car, but of old-fashioned chassis conception, for all its close resemblance to a Maserati 250F. Maserati, in fact, had been in the ascendant up to their retirement from racing, having carried Fangio to his fourth successive World Championship. This was a triumph, really, for the conventional, well constructed, sensibly developed product of a factory well versed in racing, and employing the top drivers. Although there was far more to winning a 1959 motor race than absolute power, it must be remembered that whereas the Dino V6 Ferrari was pushing out a useful 290 bhp at this time, the Coventry Climax, although its fire-pump power unit background had been transcended, was only good for about 240 bhp, at the most. Yet by the close of the 1959 racing season the rear-engined genre had made it, very definitely, over the front-engined cars, whose now superseded layout had dated back to the Panhard-Levassor conception of 1895.

All manner of things had emerged during this 1958–1960 Formula. Vanwall had gone back to normal racing bodywork, but Connaught had come up with their semi-faired-in creation, nicknamed the 'toothpaste tube', and Porsche had brought out a single-seater RSK. To their credit, BRM had an early attempt at building a rear-engined car, although at the beginning of the 1960 season their old front-engined models were the ones which they raced. Lotus had been defeated in 1959 by poor roadholding qualities, so Colin Chapman started again, with a clean sheet of drawing paper. The result was the Lotus 18, which had the notably light weight of 980 lb (empty) and also boasted an impressively low frontal area. Behind the driver, in an almost genuine space-frame of multi-tubular type, there lived the Coventry Climax FPF engine, while fuel, oil and water were accommodated in the nose of the Lotus, which was of a mere 9 square feet frontal area. Low roll centre rear springing was a very deliberate aspect of the new car, but Chapman retained the magnesium-alloy disc wheels, of the shape that had distinguished his Type 16 Lotus from other contemporary racing cars.

Left: the first GP contender from Lotus was the 1958 Lotus 16, with lines reminiscent of the Vanwall; both cars' bodywork was designed by Frank Costin. The design was aimed at reducing frontal area and had the engine both inclined and angled to the car's axis to run the drive line alongside the low-seated driver. The Chapman-strut rear suspension was so efficient that the car was plagued with persistent understeer and it was never very successful

Right: the six-cylinder, 2493 cc engine of the 1959 Aston Martin DBR4/250 produced 280 bhp at 8250 rpm

Below: the DBR4/250 had de Dion rear suspension and disc brakes, but by the time it was introduced the writing was on the wall for front-engined cars

The lesson was that by putting the engine behind the driver it was possible, in a short, compact car, to save weight and reduce frontal area, and therefore wind drag. Chapman had only 240 bhp to play with, but from an engine weighing but 290 lb, which can be compared to the 450 lb of earlier GP engines. In this context, the rear-engined BRM was 100 lb below the avoirdupois of its earlier front-engined ancestors and also had nearly two square feet less body-work area exposed to frontal drag. So Cooper with the benefit of experience were on a very good wicket, especially after they had introduced coil-spring rear suspension and gone over to five-speed gearboxes. Ferrari had also turned to the use of a Dino 246 motor, behind the driver, in his factory cars. It was the Scarab, sponsored by the American Lance Reventlow, which was now looking old-fashioned, although just introduced to the European Grand Prix scene; the car had a front-located engine, a Chevrolet gearbox, and was of heavy conception, with a very upright driving position. Its saving grace was that it made up in beautiful finish what it lacked technically.

So the 2½-litre years ran out, characterised by the emergence of the new theory that the engine should be placed behind the driver to gain a compact body form. The BRMs of this kind were steadily improving, and the day of the Lotus was obviously soon to dawn, being held back for the moment by obscure carburation maladies that for some peculiar reason did not trouble the Coopers. Both the latter makes, Lotus and Cooper, if one can use 'make' in this context, were of less weight and could therefore out-strip the BRM on acceleration. This led to a new version of BRM with some 60 lb in weight lopped off it and with double-wishbone rear springing, which Vanwall had also adopted. Although the so-called European Grand Prix of 1960, run at Monza, was won by a front-engined Ferrari, the day of the conventional racing car in this sphere was over.

Thus came the beginnings of the change that was to render a road-racing motor car, the highest form the racing automobile could take, something quite different from the cars used for business and pleasure by the ordinary citizen. As the years advanced, the gulf widened. There was also the fact that much importance was being placed on the new Drivers' World Championship, which drew public interest more to the drivers than to the technical quality and performance of the racing cars. This was the commencement of the 'circus' aspect which has engulfed modern Grand Prix motor racing.

By 1960, the Driver's World Championship had run for a decade. It had seen Farina, Fangio (five times), Ascari (twice), Hawthorn and Jack Brabham (twice) in the seat of honour, these aces relying on Alfa Romeo (twice), Ferrari (three times), Mercedes and Maserati, Mercedes alone, Maserati alone, Lancia-Ferrari and Cooper (twice). It is significant that it was Brabham who took the crown in the last two years of the 2½-litre Formula, with Cooper cars, and that it was he who had pioneered the rear-engined conception of Grand Prix racing car, which was soon to dominate the sport.

Top and above: Cooper were the progenitors of the modern rear-engined layout for GP cars, although several manufacturers had used the configuration earlier. Before they went into the F1 arena, Cooper were already well known for their 500 cc F3 cars and machines such as this 1957 F2 car. This model is powered by a 1½-litre Coventry Climax four cylinder engine, producing 106 bhp. After a successful career in F2 it was campaigned by Patsy Burt in hill-climbs, gaining over 160 awards
(National Motor Museum, England)

Above: the first post-war motor race meeting was held in the Bois de Boulogne, Paris on 9 September 1945. This is the start of the Coupe Robert Benoist for 1500cc cars, which was won by Henri Louveau, seen on the right of the first three cars. Left is Deho (Maserati) and in the centre is Bonnard's unusual special single seater, composed of an MG R-type chassis and an eight-cylinder supercharged engine

THE RACES: 1939-60

Racing was somewhat slow to resume after the war had ended, although the delay was not the result of any lack of enthusiasm; all through the dark years of the fighting, bombing, and food and petrol rationing, plenty of enthusiasts made it clear that they wanted to witness racing cars in action just as soon as possible after the foes had been defeated. When hostilities ceased, it was lack of resources which proved the major stumbling block to an immediate resumption of full-scale motor racing. There was also the inescapable fact that the 1936–39 era of racing would be a difficult one for the post-war sport to live up to.

When racing began again it did so on a modest scale. The scene was Nice, where they contrived to hold a Grand Prix race in 1946; the race was won by the greying Luigi Villoresi – he has been called the man who *was* motor-racing – at the wheel of a 1½-litre Maserati. Only three weeks later a similar joyous occasion unfolded at Marseille, with something of the pre-war sounds, sights and scents to thrill the onlookers. It was Raymond Sommer who won this time, also in a 1½-litre Maserati; Tazio Nuvolari, a wiry little man, and ailing now, but perhaps still the very greatest of them all, set fastest lap speed and then went on to win at Albi. Nuvolari accomplished this with a Maserati, being followed home by Louveau and Raph in the same make of car. In spite of Maserati's early success, the sport had to wait only as long as the return of the Alfa Romeo 'Alfettas' to see a walk-over for the Milanese manufacturer.

Below: the Isle of Man circuit could have been Britain's Nürburgring; here are the Maseratis of Bob Ansell and Reg Parnell in the 1948 Empire Trophy

Ten years after making their racing debut, the splendid Tipo 158s ran away with the 1946 Grand Prix des Nations, which was staged, ambitiously, at Geneva. The winner was Dr Farina, and he was followed home by Count Trossi and Jean-Pierre Wimille, pre-war aces again in action; Wimille made fastest lap at 68.76 mph and the race average, set by Farina, was 64.1 mph. Two more races of this calibre were staged during 1946. There was the Circuit of Turin, longest of the revived races, at 174 miles, which saw Achille Varzi, another pre-war *pilote*, take the honours from Wimille, at 64.62 mph, both in the victorious Alfa Romeos, with third place filled by Sommer's Maserati. Once again fastest lap went to Wimille, at 73.58 mph – things were warming up. The year 1946 concluded with the shortest of these resuscitated Grands Prix, the Circuit of Milan, over 52 miles; the race was dominated by the Alfa Romeo team, with Trossi winning, from Varzi and works test driver Sanesi, the winning average being 55.59 mph. The Alfa driven by Varzi, but taken over by Farina, set fastest lap, at 56.7 mph.

Motor racing had well and truly started again and all looked forward to 1947, especially those who had watched Varzi beat Wimille by a mere half-second in that race at Turin. Five races to the prevailing Grand Prix status

Right: Raymond Sommer

Below: Alfa Romeo 158s in full cry at the 1946 GP des Nations, at Geneva

were organised. There were about twenty lesser events in which the independents, including a number of British drivers, like Reg Parnell and bespectacled Bob Gerard, had a chance of success, but it was the professionals who claimed the limelight. In the Swiss and Belgium Grands Prix the Alfa Romeos continued to make the pace, the order in both races being Wimille, Varzi, Trossi; the average speed of the former race, over 137 miles, was 95.42 mph, and at Spa, where the distance was 310 miles, the average was 95.28 mph. In the first of these 1947 contests Maserati had the honour, such as it was, of making fastest lap, when Sommer motored round at 97.03 mph, but at Spa the best time was done by the winning Wimille, at a speed of 101.94 mph.

Varzi and Sanesi, in that order, held off the Maserati of Grieco at Bari, the winning Alfa averaging 65.15 mph for the 165½-mile race, and at the Italian Grand Prix, back to almost former glory, the expected Alfa Romeo grand-slam was seen once again, with Trossi, Varzi and Sanesi in the order of finishing, and the winning speed was 70.29 mph. The terrors of Milan were absent from the 314 mile French Grand Prix, giving the unsupercharged cars their chance; popular (and pre-war) veteran Louis Chiron pulled off victory in a Talbot, at 78.09 mph, from the Maserati of Louveau.

Left: the cars line up for the eighteenth Italian GP, at Monza in 1947, with the grid dominated by works Alfa Romeos and Maseratis. Trossi, Varzi and Sanesi led an Alfa grand slam

Right: the start of the 1946 Turin GP, again with Alfa Romeo and Maserati to the fore. The race, which was won by Varzi's Alfa, decided the result of a 20 million lire national lottery

Below: the Alfetta of Dr Giuseppe Farina at the shortest of the 1946 Grands Prix, the Circuit of Milan. Alfa Romeo again scored a 1-2-3 victory in the event, with Trossi winning

Below: Jean Pierre Wimille in 1948. The action picture shows Wimille on his way to victory in the 1948 French GP, at Reims, with an Alfa Romeo 158. Had there been a World Championship in that year, Wimille would have won it, but he was killed in Argentina the following year before the championship was instituted

Right: the only real opposition to Alfa in 1948 came from Maserati. This is Louis Chiron racing in Jersey

It wasn't GP racing, but in the great Mille Miglia sports-car contest Nuvolari made a memorable swan-song; although he was by now a very ill person, he defied adversity and heavy rain, to bring a 1100cc Cisitalia home in second place, only a quarter of an hour behind the winning 3-litre Alfa-Romeo, driven by Biondetti.

The new Formula began to take hold for the 1948 racing season. In the European GP, held at Berne, Switzerland, it was the compact, highly-supercharged, Alfa Romeos that dominated, driven into first and second places by the experienced, pipe-smoking Trossi, and Wimille, the former averaging 90.81 mph from start to finishing-flag, and the latter setting up the fastest lap of the Swiss circuit, at 95.05 mph. Third place was secured by Villoresi in a Maserati. These Alfa Romeos continued to be the racing sensation of the age, for in training for the French Grand Prix of 1948 at Reims, Wimille lapped at 112.2 mph and although in the event he was not able to do better than 108.14 mph, this gave him victory, at 102.1 mph; Wimille's team-mate Sanesi was second and the rising star, Alberto Ascari (son of the Antonio Ascari

Left : Luigi Villoresi in a 4CLT/48 Maserati won the 1948 British GP at Silverstone, from Alberto Ascari in a similar car. The race was a revival of an event last held at Brooklands in 1927

Right : Achille Varzi, a few months before his death at Berne in 1948

Below : Raymond Sommer having a hard time in the wet with his Ferrari 125 at the Italian GP in Turin. Villoresi, seen here following in his Maserati 4CLT, beat Sommer for second place, behind Wimille's victorious Alfa Romeo

who had been killed at Lyon in this very race, before the war) third, also in an Alfa Romeo. In the Italian GP Wimille won again, after the other Alfas had met with trouble, from Villoresi's 4CLT Maserati and Sommer's Ferrari, at 70.38 mph. The *marque* from Milan had been placed 1-2-3 in the Monza GP, in the sequence Wimille, Trossi, Sanesi. The race-average was a remarkable 109.98 mph and Sanesi lapped at 116.95 mph, with one of these 1500 cc cars. Achille Varzi had been killed while practising at Berne, when his Alfa Romeo overturned, Wimille was the victim of a fatal accident in South America, at the wheel of a Simca *voiturette*, and during 1948 Trossi died from cancer.

At the difficult round-the-houses Monaco Grand Prix Maserati returned to the forefront, when Farina won at 59.61 mph from Chiron's Talbot, with de Graffenreid, the keen Swiss driver, third in another Maserati. The winner lapped the Monaco course at 62.32 mph. The British Grand Prix was run over the new aerodrome circuit at Silverstone and was a victory for Villoresi, who averaged 72.28 mph and also set fastest lap, at 76.82 mph. His new Maserati team mate, Ascari, backed him up with second place, and third place went to Bob Gerard's ERA.

Perhaps it was the loss of some of their best drivers that persuaded Alfa Romeo to drop out of racing in 1949. The Tipo 159 racers, which were then scattered unceremoniously about the factory, or tucked into odd corners gathering dust, had started in 19 races since 1938, of which they had won 16, finishing 1, 2, 3 on no fewer than ten occasions. They suffered defeat only at the hands of Maserati (twice) and the W165 Mercedes-Benz of Hermann Lang. It was an impressive record.

With Alfa Romeo out of contention, and the strong, level-headed, enormously talented Juan Manuel Fangio now occupying the driving seat of a Maserati, this Italian make dominated the 1949 races: Fangio won at San Remo (62.78 mph for 178 miles) and at Pau (52.7 mph for 87 miles), being followed in by the Maseratis of B. Bira and Baron de Graffenreid in the former race, and by Gerard's ERA and Rosier's big Talbot in the latter. Bira, the diminutive Siamese Royal driver who had been sponsored and managed by his cousin Prince Chula before the war, was still on form, for he made fastest lap at San Remo, at 64.66 mph, and repeated his show of speed at Silverstone in the British Grand Prix. This race was a victory for E. de Graffenreid in a Maserati, with the irrepressible ERA second, and Louis Rosier's Talbot placed third, an interesting mixed outcome, the winner averaging 77.31 mph. In the Belgian Grand Prix Rosier came into his own, winning with a Talbot at 96.95 mph, outclassing both Villoresi and Ascari in their Maseratis. Dr Farina also in a Maserati, since Alfa Romeo's withdrawal from racing, made fastest lap at over 101 mph.

The scene then shifted to the Swiss GP and here Alberto Ascari was in the ascendant, coming first past the finish; Farina's Maserati averaged a fraction more than 95 mph to establish the fastest lap speed, and the winner himself averaged 90.76 mph for this 181-mile contest. This year the Italian GP at Monza took on the mantle of the European GP and it was another victory for the chubby, Roman-nosed Ascari. He was now in a Ferrari, and averaged over 105 mph, though in practice he had lapped even faster, at 112.72 mph. Phi-Phi Etancelin was second in a Talbot and Prince Bira third in his Maserati. The GP de France had previously been won by Chiron's Talbot from Bira's Maserati, and Britain's Peter Whitehead had taken third place in a Ferrari. Whitehead was later to go on to victory in that years Czechoslovak Grand Prix at Brno. At the converted Silverstone airfield circuit, the newly formed British Automobile Racing Club had revived, under its new colours, the pre-war Junior Car Club's International Trophy Race, this being won in 1949 by Ascari, at 89.58 mph, after he had lapped triumphantly at 93.35 mph – Silverstone was already a fast course. Ascari was followed home by his teammate, Villoresi, but only in third place, for Farina had forced his Maserati between the two Ferraris.

So it was that motor racing started up again in the post-war years. It was well established by the time the 1950 season opened.

Far left: French Champion from 1949 to 1952, Louis Rosier raced Lago-Talbots to victory in the Belgian, Dutch and Albi Grands Prix. The Clermont-Ferrand garage proprietor won Le Mans with his son in 1950, and raced his own Ferraris and Maseratis in Formulae 1 and 2 and sports car events. Rosier, normally a safe driver, was killed at Montlhéry in 1956 aged 51. Jean Behra, *centre left*, instantly recognisable in his chequered helmet, was France's greatest driver of the 1950s

Left: the Maserati 4CLT/48 of Swiss Baron Emanuel de Graffenried, on his way to victory in the 1949 British Grand Prix at Silverstone

Below: the 1949 French Grand Prix was a sports car event, but Louis Chiron won the country's premier Formula 1 event at Reims in the ageing unsupercharged 4½-litre Talbot

357

The remarkable aspect of the 1950 season was the return of Alfa Romeo to the fray, with the revised Tipo 159 cars, which, once again, swept all before them. Indeed, they won all ten races in which they started, in spite of some notable setbacks. It is not always a good thing when one make of car dominates racing, except for the manufacturer and the drivers of that make, of course, but no-one could challenge Alfa's superiority. After Farina had been involved in an accident, Alfa Romeo used the services of the great Fangio at San Remo and the lone Alfa won, in wet weather, from Villoresi's two stage supercharged Ferrari, while Ascari spun and crashed his Ferrari. Next, it was to England, where for once the sun shone, and the Royal Family, led by HM King George VI, were present at Silverstone to watch the racing. This event, which was the British Grand Prix with the added status of the title of the European Grand Prix, was another entirely convincing triumph for the 'Alfettas', which would have arrived at the end of the race in 1-2-3-4, order, Briton Reg Parnell having been invited to drive one of them, had not Fangio's car developed valve trouble eight laps from the finish. So the result was first Farina, second Fagioli and third a very happy Parnell.

Below: the handsome Italian Doctor of Political Science, Giuseppe Farina racing at a very wet Silverstone in 1950. He took his Alfa Romeo 158 to victory twice at Silverstone that year, winning the British Grand Prix, the very first World Championship event, and the rain-soaked *Daily Express* International Trophy race

Above: the first lap fracas at Monaco during the 1950 Grand Prix, caused when race-leader Farina spun at the Tabac corner, wet with sea-water. Several other cars were involved, but Fangio managed to squeeze his Alfa Romeo through the gap and motor on to victory. In the photograph a Talbot and a Maserati thread their way through the carnage; this kind of accident is always a possibility at Monaco, where there are no run-off areas and few legitimate passing places

At the Monaco Grand Prix, with Prince Rainier in attendance, there was a historic pile-up on the very first lap, when the usually wily Farina skidded on the harbour front and half the entry was, so early, unfortunately eliminated. Fangio proved his skill in getting through the *melée* and, although both the other Alfa Romeos were out of the hunt, Fangio just motored on, to win with no-one challenging him. It is worth comparing his times with those of the mighty pre-war Mercedes-Benz, over this round-the-town course. Fangio had lapped at 64.56 mph. In the race he managed 64.09 mph and his winning average speed was 61.33 mph. Caracciola's fastest lap in the last pre-war running of the event had been 66.79 mph, a record which was to stand for eighteen years. Behind the Master came Ascari and Chiron. At Berne the race was rather dull after the Ferrari challenge to the 'Alfettas' had ended with both retiring early. The stage was then all set for another Fangio walk-over, but his car dropped a valve nine laps from the finish and it was Farina who took first place, his fellow Alfa Romeo *pilote* Fagioli being but 0.4 of a second behind him and Rosier coming in next, in one of the big Talbots. Sommer was the hero of Spa in 1950, in a Talbot, but even his inspired driving and the pit-stops for fuel necessary to the Alfa Romeos could not stop Fangio, who won from Fagioli. Sommer's early pace probably resulted in the loss of oil pressure which sidelined Farina before Sommer himself dropped out of the race with engine failure after 20 of the 35 laps; Rosier was third.

The French Grand Prix had returned to its full glory by 1950 and it remained to be seen whether the flying Fangio could equal the sort of performance put in at the fast Reims circuit by the pre-war monsters. He was timed over a lap at 116.2 mph in practice, against the actual pre-war lap record of 117.5 mph. In the race he went round the course that winds through the fields of the champagne country at 112.35 mph and won at 104.83 mph. Fagioli was second but Farina had been delayed by fuel feed problems after nine laps. These Alfa Romeos victories were becoming monotonous! Suffice to say that Farina and Fangio contested Bari, and Fangio and Fagioli Pescara, with Fangio the victor in both races, although Fagioli suffered a broken road spring on the last lap of what was intended to be his race at Pescara. Rosier had been actually pressing Fangio and the latter was obliged to rush over the line to prevent a disaster, instead of allowing Fagioli to limp to victory.

There was a confrontation between the big, unblown Ferraris and the super-charged Alfa Romeos at Geneva and the challenge was strongly apparent, in spite of Ascari, driving for Ferrari, retiring six laps from the end with water pouring out of his car's exhaust system, allowing the race to go to Fangio, with his new team-mates, de Graffenreid and Taruffi, second and third. Villoresi had also been pressing the smaller cars but crashed, taking Farina with him. The challenge of the big Ferraris came to a head in the Italian Grand Prix, when five Alfas met two Ferraris, Serafini replacing the injured Villoresi. The smaller cars would stop twice for fuel, the non-blown Ferraris only once.

Alfa Romeo, on the day, did some intelligent swopping about of their drivers and Farina won, from Ascari and Fagioli. Fangio had two cars blow up on him, but lapped at 117.445 mph, which was a race lap record. The forthcoming Barcelona race promised to be a most exciting return round, but Alfa Romeo stood down, leaving the interesting sight of two V16 BRMs running in a continental race for the first time, with Walker and Parnell nominated to drive them. That debut evaporated when Parnell's car succumbed to a sheared drive to the notorious centrifugal blower and Walker retired with a lack of power, a grave disappointment for the English onlookers, after Parnell's car had been timed to do 186 mph over a kilometre in practise. The result was a Ferrari 1-2-3, in the order Ascari, Serafini and Taruffi, the last named having lost a couple of laps after spinning off.

This Alfa/Ferrari battle continued into the 1951 season. Villoresi won at Syracuse and at Pau, while Ascari took the honours at San Remo in a full 4½-litre Ferrari. At Silverstone the rain was so heavy that the *Daily Express* International Trophy Race had to be stopped after a mere six laps. It was a race run in heats, however, so some racing was seen beforehand. In the Final

Right: a freak storm brought chaos to Silverstone's 1951 International Trophy meeting, with hailstones and nine inches of rain falling in half an hour. Here, Baron de Graffenried's Maserati struggles blindly through the impossible conditions, which caused the race to be stopped after six laps. Reg Parnell's Thinwall Special was leading at the time, and was awarded the Trophy

Below: Juan Manuel Fangio in an Alfa Romeo 159 at the European Grand Prix of 1951. This turned out to be a race-long duel between Fangio and Ascari, enacted at the ultra-fast Reims circuit. Such was the pace that both drivers used up their own cars and had to borrow from their slower team-mates, the Fangio/Fagioli Alfa beating the Ascari/Gonzales Ferrari by one minute

three English drivers held off the ace Italians during the thunderstorm, and Parnell's Thinwall Ferrari, forerunner of the latterly invincible Vanwalls, was actually placed first, Duncan Hamilton's big Talbot second, and Fangio third, after Fangio had taken one heat and Farina the other, for Alfa Romeo, both at over 90 mph. At Berne the Ferraris were in trouble and it was Fangio who gave a masterly performance in very wet conditions. He led all the way, except when in the pits for fuel. After Ascari had developed trouble and Villoresi had hit the markers, it was Sanesi who harried the Alfas, actually coming in second, between Fangio and Farina. Spa provided excitement of a different sort, apart from the sheer speed. Fangio lapped at over 120.5 mph and while in the lead, on the 15th lap, he stopped to refuel and for a change of wheels. A wheel jammed on its spline and lost the swarthy Argentinian all chance of World Championship points – yet he remained ice-calm throughout. The race was won by Farina, followed by Ascari and Villoresi, the Alfa Romeo the victor by a narrow margin, at 114.32 mph. Alfa Romeo won again at Reims in the French/European GP, with a car shared by Fangio and Fagioli, and at last, in practice, Fangio bettered Lang's 1939 Mercedes-Benz lap record with

a speed of 119.99 mph (against 117.5 mph). There could now be no looking back. Moreover, Neubauer and Lang were among the spectators! In the race Ascari's car threw a rod but, after the Alfa Romeo had won at 110.97 mph, the Ferrari, jointly handled by Gonzales – the 'Pampas Bull' – and Ascari, was second and Villoresi's Ferrari third, a nice balance of technical perfection against the might of 4½ litres.

In the British GP it finally happened: Ferrari defeated Alfa Romeo. It was a terrific battle between Gonzales, in his furious style of sliding his corners and Fangio holding a classic line through them in his Alfa Romeo. Fangio went ahead, but to yells from the crowd, the podgy 'Pampas Bull' took the lead again on lap 39, after being in arrears to his Argentinian friend by as much as six seconds. From that moment on, it was Gonzalez' race. He even refuelled without losing the lead. He won at 96.11 mph, from Fangio, with Villoresi's Ferrari third. Farina, after lapping within an ace of 100 mph, retired while in 3rd place, with his engine on fire, and Ascari had gearbox trouble.

The BRM position was only slightly improved in this 1951 British Grand Prix for, although both cars finished the course in fifth and seventh places,

drivers Reg Parnell and Peter Walker suffered great physical exhaustion, due to the heat and fumes, and the effort of keeping the ill-handling cars in the right gear. The limelight of the Grand Prix circus had now settled on Fangio and Gonzalez, both of whom showed their great prowess by quickly mastering the difficult Nürburgring circuit in readiness for the 1951 German Grand Prix. Another pre-war German driver was now to be found racing again, for Alfa Romeo had contracted Paul Pietsch for the occasion. It was the Alfa/Ferrari battle all over again, except that this time the Alfettas ran into a series of troubles. Farina went out with over-heating and no oil-pressure, Bonetto had supercharger failure, and Pietsch damaged the car after charging over a bank. This time it was Ascari who brought his unblown Ferrari home first, and, even with an unexpected stop for fresh rear tyres, he finished half-a-minute ahead of Fangio's Alfa and Gonzalez in another big Ferrari. At Pescara the Alfa challenge was absent, but Gonzalez' Ferrari was the only one to shine. He finished first some 7½-minutes ahead of the nearest Talbot, Rosier's 4½-litre car with Etancelin's Talbot third. At Bari Fangio had a fine victory, finishing over a minute ahead of the redoubtable Gonzalez, who had driven well after a poor start. Much mechanical trouble befell the others – Ascari's engine caught fire, Farina's Alfa suffered a burnt-out piston, and a shunt caused Villoresi's Ferrari to lose its oil-pressure. Meanwhile, Taruffi brought a 2-litre Ferrari home third. So it can be seen that the blown/unblown conflict was still wide open. In the Italian Grand Prix four Alfas with de Dion suspension and new air-intakes were to meet four big Ferraris, which had bigger fuel tanks and other minor improvements. Both BRMs were withdrawn before the start due to gearbox lubrication problems. After a race of much fluctuating fortune, the reliability of Ascari's Ferrari won the day at a speed of 115.45 mph, from Gonzalez' Ferrari and Farina who had lapped at a rousing 120.97 mph but had been delayed by slow Alfa pit-work and a leaking fuel tank. Next came the Ferraris of Villoresi and Taruffi.

In Italy, Fangio had retired with a blown-up engine, nevertheless he led the World Championship by two points from Ascari, a very satisfactory outcome of the Alfa/Ferrari duel. So it was in far away Barcelona that the 1951 World Championship would be settled. Tyre troubles marred the Ferrari attack and Fangio finished at a canter, his Alfa Romeo averaging 98.76 mph. Gonzalez was second for Ferrari, Farina third for Alfa, and Ascari fourth. Fangio, when in a hurry, had lapped at over 105 mph. Before we leave this interesting 1951 season it is worth mentioning that Dr Giuseppe Farina came to Dunrod with the Alfa Romeo for the Ulster Trophy Race, and to Goodwood. He beat Reg Parnell in the Vandervell-Thinwall-Ferrari on both occasions and left the Goodwood lap record at a stirring 97.36 mph. It is also of interest that Mercedes-Benz carefully unwrapped their 1939 3-litre Grand Prix cars and took them to two formula libre races at Buenos Aires. On both occasions they experienced a similar problem to that which beset them before the war, poor carburation, and both times a 2-litre two-stage supercharged Ferrari sufficed to vanquish them, but its driver was the great Froilan Gonzalez.

The 1952 season was not a particularly notable one for Alfa Romeo had again dropped out of racing and the Grand Prix organisers chose to run the races for Formula Two cars. Therefore neither the BRM nor the out-dated Talbots were eligible, and opposition to the Formula 2 Ferraris came from Gordini, Cooper-Bristol, Maserati and Connaught. Ascari won all seven World Championship qualifying rounds, and he was well on his way to a good season when he won the first three races of the year, at Syracuse, Pau, and Marseilles. His chief rival, Fangio, was out of racing for most of the year following a crash at Monza. The works Ferraris were not at Silverstone for the *Daily Express* Meeting. After Hawthorn in a Cooper Bristol and Manzon in a Gordini had won the heats, Lance Macklin and Tony Rolt went on to finish first and second for HWM. Ferrari was back in the Swiss Grand Prix with three 'works' cars for Farina, Taruffi, and Simon, the former Alfa-Romeo drivers having found new employment, and it was Taruffi the perfectionist who won.

At Spa-Francorchamps it was Ascari and Farina from Manzon's Gordini and Hawthorne's Cooper-Bristol. Much the same picture emerged at the three-hour race against the clock at Rouen-les-Essarts, but the new names of Maurice Trintignant on Gordini and Peter Collins on HWM figured on the results sheet in fifth and sixth. From the British point of view the results looked better at Silverstone, with Hawthorn's Cooper-Bristol third and the Connaughts of Dennis Poore (later to mastermind the Norton-Villiers motor cycle concern) and Thompson fourth and fifth, albeit three laps in arrears.

The great Jean Behra placed his Gordini fifth at the Nürburgring, breaking the monotony of a run of Ferraris. Ascari's tutor, Luigi Villoresi, finished third in his Ferrari at Zandvoort and at the final race at Monza, whilst Gonzalez placed his Maserati second at the latter. Gonzalez had more success in non-championship events in 1952, winning the Easter Goodwood meeting with the Thinwall Special and also leading the BRM 1-2-3 in an end-of-season meeting there.

It is interesting to note that points scored in the Indianapolis 500 could also be counted towards the World Championship, a provision only abolished in 1960. Ascari won from Villoresi, with Gonzalez third and Hawthorn fourth. The Dutch Grand Prix was to much the same pattern, with Ascari winning,

Right: Alberto Ascari won sixteen Grands Prix in 1952 and 1953 and, not surprisingly took the world championship title in both years. In 1955, while recovering from an accident in Monaco, Ascari crashed fatally testing a Ferrari sports car at Monza

Far right: the Villoresi brothers, Emilio and Luigi, were quite successful in motor racing, although Luigi lived long enough completely to overshadow his brothers achievements before the war in an Alfetta; 'Gigi' is seen here winning the 1951 Marseilles Grand Prix in a Ferrari 166

Below: in 1952, Frenchman Jean Behra was just beginning to show signs that he was soon to become a force to be reckoned with on the circuits. Here at that years Pau GP, however, he finds things difficult with his Gordini after spinning on oil dropped by Villoresi's car

and Farina's Ferrari, finishing second. Gonzalez climbed into Bonetto's Maserati after the final drive had gone on his own ASS6G, and brought the car in third, ahead of Hawthorn's Ferrari. It was all drama at Spa during the 1953 Belgian Grand Prix. Gonzalez opened with his customary fire, building up a useful lead over Fangio and Ascari, until his accelerator-pedal snapped right off! That gave Fangio the lead for three laps. Then his Maserati engine

Far left and left: Mike Hawthorn and Juan Manuel Fangio who are seen again *below* dicing for the lead on the last straight, at the 1953 French Grand Prix, held on the fast Reims circuit. The race-long duel came out in the favour of the Englishman from Farnham, Surrey. He was a mere one second ahead of the Argentinian at the finish line, after averaging 113.65 mph.

Right: Italian *marques* in battle on their home ground in 1953, Monza. Here, the Ferraris of Farina and Ascari head the Maseratis of Fangio and Marimon. On the last lap, Ascari spun when passing a slower car and took with him Farina and Marimon. Fangio, however, scraped by to win

blew up, so the *maestro* leapt into Johnny Claes' Maserati, got back up to third place, then slid on some oil and crashed. So it was his young team-mate Marimon who took third spot, behind the Ferraris of Ascari and Villoresi. The French Grand Prix, held in the sweltering heat of the Reims countryside, was a sensation. Hawthorn in the Ferrari and Fangio in the Maserati ran side by side along the final straight, after a race-long battle. Hawthorn thought that Fangio had lost bottom gear and staked all on a last-second spurt out of Thillois hairpin to win by one second. Mike then collapsed with emotion and exhaustion, his name made from that day on. Gonzalez, never to be entirely outdone, had closed to within a tenth of a second of Fangio, so the finish of this race had all the appearances of a sprint event. Ascari finished fourth.

In the British Grand Prix at Silverstone, Ascari returned to his unbeatable form, and nothing Fangio could do would stop him from winning, while Farina was third and Gonzalez was fourth, turning a convenient blind-eye to the

black flag held out for him, as his car was thought to be dropping oil. At the Nürburgring there was drama again, as Ascari lost a wheel when leading. Unhurt, he jumped into Villoresi's car to pursue Farina, but the Ferrari's engine blew up. Clearly here was a man keen to collect World Championship points. So it was Farina, Fangio and Hawthorn. Stirling Moss, new to Grand Prix racing, was sixth in a Cooper-Alta. Monza, the final Championship round, was almost unbearable – an all-time classic! Four cars of Ascari, Farina, Fangio and Marimon raced within a second of one another, with continual passing and repassing. Even a long pit-pause did not stop the last-named from rejoining this fierce battle. Then Ascari spun round and round as he overtook a slower Connaught, and he was hit by Marimon. Fangio found a gap and won for Maserati. Farina came second, Villoresi third and Hawthorn fourth.

The World Championship returned for Formula One cars in 1954, and marked the revival of Mercedes-Benz in Grand Prix racing. BRM were saved from oblivion when Alfred Owen stepped in to re-finance the British team and build new cars. Lancia took on Vittorio Jano's new ideas and had Ascari and Villoresi to drive their D50s. Millionaire Tony Vandervell was developing his Vanwalls, and the season looked decidedly promising! At the Argentine Grand Prix the new Mercedes were absent. Fangio scored the first victory for the 250F Maserati although the Ferraris were superior in the dry. When rain came Fangio stopped to change to ribbed tyres, an early example of rain-tyre, and continued, catching all the others to win. This was Fangio at his best. Ugolini had thought that more than the regulation number of mechanics had officiated at the Fangio tyre-change, so had signalled Farina to slow. His protest was not upheld, however.

Spa Francorchamps also went to Fangio and the Maserati, with Farina, injured in a sports-car race, driving pluckily in a Squalo Ferrari. The Mercedes-Benz debut came at Reims, for the French Grand Prix. With Fangio transferring to them, and backed up by Hans Hermann and Karl Kling, it was as if the pre-war story had come to life. Ascari's Maserati lasted but a lap and with others falling by the wayside it was a Mercedes benefit, the streamliners of Fangio and Kling finishing one-fifth of a second apart, and Hans Hermann set fastest lap at 117 mph before his machinery exploded. Twenty-one cars started, and only six survived. Mercedes were outclassed in the British Grand Prix because their all-enveloping bodies were ruinous to vision from the cockpits. So Gonzalez won for Ferrari, with Hawthorn's Ferrari second and Marimon's Maserati third. At the German Grand Prix Mercedes had the orthodox bodywork, and Fangio's W196 took the honours. But Hermann over-revved his engine and blew up, and Hermann Lang spun and could not restart his engine. Kling actually got past Fangio but his rear suspension broke. Hawthorn's Ferrari was second, Trintignant's Ferrari third, and Kling's Mercedes-Benz fourth. Sadly, Marimon was killed when his Maserati crashed in practice. It was not all Mercedes' year, however. Fangio led all the way at Berne, in the rain, Gonzalez being second and Hermann third. At Monza Fangio just won, with a sick car, although Moss was the moral victor, his Maserati 250F having retired with a split oil tank. The Ferraris of Hawthorn and Gonzalez were second and third. At Barcelona Hawthorn won from Luigi Musso's Maserati, with Fangio third in a Mercedes with an air-intake choked with dead leaves.

Fangio netted his third World Championship in 1955, a year dominated by Mercedes-Benz. In the second round of the Championship at Monaco, Ascari's Lancia dived over the harbour wall into the sea. Ascari swam to shore none the worse for wear, but he was killed a week later in an inexplicable crash at Monza while driving a sports Ferrari. Mercedes had the British Grand Prix at Aintree buttoned-up, Moss being permitted to lead Fangio home. Mercedes withdrew from racing in 1956 after the Le Mans tragedy of 1955 when Levegh's car disintegrated in a grandstand killing over 80 spectators. Fangio was driving for Ferrari, who had taken over the V8 Lancias, and he was again World Champion. At Monaco, Moss in a Maserati beat Fangio, with no holds barred, Fangio battering his Ferrari about to such an extent that he stopped, and resumed in Peter Collins' car. Collins won at Spa, with Paul Frère, the journalist second in another Ferrari. Stirling Moss was third, after losing a wheel, in Pedisa's Maserati. Fangio won the British and German Grands Prix and Moss just took the Italian, in spite of a worn rear tyre, from Fangio, who had taken over Luigi Musso's Ferrari.

The year 1957 was a jubilant one for Britain, because all Tony Vandervell's hard work and investment paid off. Vanwalls won three Grands Prix, although Fangio, back in a Maserati, took his fifth World Championship. At Monaco there was an enormous crash which eliminated Moss, Collins and Hawthorn. Fangio had held back and he went on to win, from Tony Brooks' Vanwall. Then, at Aintree, Moss won a memorable victory for Vanwall and the same

Below left: the two great Argentinian racing drivers of the 1950s, Froilan Gonzales and Fangio. They are standing on the rostrum after finishing first and second in the 1954 Swiss GP at Berne, with Fangio leading his compatriot home

Right and below: the Lancia-based Ferrari in action, piloted by two of the most successful British drivers of the 1950s, Peter Collins and Mike Hawthorn. Aintree is the setting in 1955, *right,* while Collins is seen at Reims busy winning the 1956 French Grand Prix

combination had a very convincing victory at Pescara. Yet before this Fangio had driven the race of his life in the German Grand Prix to catch the Ferraris of Hawthorn and Collins, after his Maserati had refuelled. He set a new lap record of 91.52 mph for the Nüburgring, smashing his own lap-time ten laps running. At Monza three green Vanwalls occupied the front row of the grid, a sight to gladden the Englishman's heart, and Moss won from Fangio's Maserati and von Trips' Ferrari, after Brooks had set fastest-lap for Vanwall, at 124.04 mph. The following year saw the Vanwalls really 'on song', so that Hawthorn was lucky to win the World Championship, driving a Ferrari, by a single point from Moss's Vanwall, but at Reims, Musso was killed and at the German Grand Prix Peter Collins lost his life, robbing Hawthorn of two close friends. Brooks won the Italian Grand Prix for Vanwall and when his car blew-up at the Moroccan event, Hawthorn was able to finish second to Moss. After Vanwall had retired from racing, the rear-engined cars came into their own, the lightweight Coopers being a match for the Ferrari and the 1959 World

Championship being won by the steady Australian, Jack Brabham. Thus did this new era of racing establish itself, with the rear-engined Cooper-Climax cars winning five Grands Prix in a row during the 1960 season, and bringing 'Black' Jack Brabham his second World title. The BRMs were now doing better, with Graham Hill and the American driver Dan Gurney in their cockpits, and the Lotus team was out in force, with Jim Clark, Alan Stacey, John Surtees and Innes Ireland in the team. Outside sponsorship had arrived, too, the Yeoman Credit Team, for instance, having Tony Brooks, young Bristow and Henry Taylor, together with Oliver Gendebien, as its drivers. Enthusiast Rob Walker had a rear-engined Lotus for Moss to drive, as an independent, and

Inset far left: a smiling Tony Brooks is seen before the start of the 1958 Italian GP at Monza; he had a lot to smile about for he and his Vanwall won the race, as seen *inset above*

Right: Hawthorn and Collins snatch the lead at the start of the 1957 German GP at the Nürburgring. Fangio, on the far left, made an unscheduled pit stop, but still went on to win. In doing so he broke the lap record ten times and clinched his fifth World Championship

Inset right: leader of the rear-engined revolution, three times World Champion Jack Brabham

Inset far right: Phil Hill's Ferrari Dino 246 at Reims during the 1960 French Grand Prix. The car's transmission broke just after half-distance

Moss used this to very good effect at Monaco, driving a memorable race in the rain. But mostly it was Brabham's year, and he even held off the Ferraris of Phil Hill and 'Taffy' von Trips in the French Grand Prix at Reims. It was a measure of the effectiveness of the new type of rear-engined racing car that Brabham there averaged 131.8 mph, this speed beating the previous lap record, which Jack lifted to a sensational 135.05 mph. In the British Grand Prix Graham Hill, after a bad start in his BRM, stormed through to catch Brabham, but with victory in sight Hill spun, stalled again, and so it was Brabham's race, in the Cooper. Moss had an appalling accident at Spa, when his Lotus shed a wheel, but he was back before the year was out.

Chapter 7

Styling Brings Sales

ON THE ROAD: 1960-83

It was clever packaging rather than engineering which sold cars in the early 1960s: two-tone paint jobs and vestigial fins were common on middle-range British cars, although interior appointments were distinctly spartan. Dashboard design was generally of a low standard, with much pressed metal in evidence, and instruments of poor design, although models as diverse as the De Luxe Mini and the MkII Jaguar range featured 'instrument-shaped instruments' of admirable clarity. The Jaguar, indeed, also offered a high standard of interior luxury – leather seating and polished wood – at reasonable prices. On the whole, however, the average car of the first part of the decade was a pretty dismal prospect, although it obviously pleased the customers, for sales continued to rise until 1964, when they dropped back slightly. Annual sales had first passed the million mark in Britain in 1958: in 1964 they were up to a record 1,867,640 of which some 600,000 went for export.

All, however, was not well with the industry: Standard-Triumph, having just announced the new Herald model, found themselves unable to finance the necessary expansion, so combined in 1960 with the Leyland Group, hitherto more closely connected with commercial vehicles. Not long after the merger the Standard marque was allowed to celebrate sixty years of production and then quietly phased out, as it was felt that the word 'standard' had become so debased since the make's debut in 1903 that it was no longer relevant. Once it had signified a criterion; now it just meant 'basic'.

The Standard story was just one example of the way in which the British motor industry was ignoring trends, resolutely refusing to recognise which way the tide was running.

'Few non-British cars offer . . . the leather-upholstered comfort of an armchair in quiet club surroundings . . . to a wide public,' commented *The Motor* in 1960. Nor, indeed, was there any good reason why they should. The concept of pointing a club armchair at the horizon was becoming increasingly irrelevant. Indeed, in the same issue of *The Motor*, the (literally) hidebound traditionalism of a large section of the British motor industry was lampooned: 'No doubt visiting American journalists (to the London Motor Show) will be having a hearty laugh at the traditional British polished walnut . . . "Just like a pre-war radio set", as someone remarked of a famous instrument panel'.

In fact, the early 1960s marked a watershed in the history of motoring; it was, perhaps, the last golden age of the car, before bureaucracy began to erode precious freedoms and the albatross of petty restrictions and regulations began to weigh down motorists and manufacturers alike. Fuel was still cheap – in Britain you could buy five gallons of petrol for a pound and get a few pence back in change – parking was easy and the roads uncrowded. It was still possible to drive for hours without meeting another car.

Motoring, in short, was still *fun*; the choice of cars was wide, and classic pre-war vehicles were available, if not exactly for a song, at a great deal less than the grand opera that is their present-day asking price . . . One dealer in rural Kent,

Right: the 1960 Jaguar Mark II carried on the company's tradition of luxury motoring and high-performance, with remarkable value for money. The Mark II range was powered by variants of the ubiquitous twin-overhead-camshaft engine which had first appeared in 1948 in the now-legendary XK120 sports car. Versions of the engine powered five Le Mans-winning Jaguars. Initially, the Mark II, introduced in 1959, used the 2.4-litre and 3.4-litre sixes, but in 1960 the 220bhp, 3.8-litre unit was added to the options. Disc brakes all round, good roadholding and a liberal helping of leather and walnut inside made the Jaguar an outstanding car in an era of general mediocrity

Right: the Jaguar Mark X was the Mark II's big brother, powered itself by the famous twin-cam six and introducing independent rear suspension to Jaguar's range for the first time. This system has been fitted, in the same basic form, to all Jaguar's subsequent models and features twin coil springs with unequal-length wishbones, the upper one being the drive shaft

who the author used to visit regularly, offered a choice of vintage Bugattis at under £200 each, a Siddeley Special tourer for £90, a Fiat 501 two-seater with a dickey full of spares at £60, and so on.

Breaker's yards were still places of romance, not the dreary eyesores full of spavined, rusting, totally useless monocoque bodyshells that assault the eye nowadays. Brooks of Edenbridge, Goodey of Twyford – these were names to be conjured with in the early 1960s, though they were already a vanishing breed. Their mounds of obsolete spares played a considerable part in the motoring economy of those days, helping to keep the many orphan vehicles still in use – Beans, Swifts, Crossleys, Trojans and a host of other quadragenarians – in running order.

Even the mass-producers expected *some* skill of their customers, for the large majority of popular cars had no syncromesh on bottom gear; although the gearchange may have been rubbery and vague, it still helped to know how to double-declutch . . .

There were many reasons why the car changed from being a glamour symbol to what it had been in America for many years – a necessity of life. True, the Americans tricked out their cars with styling gimmicks, but that was to induce the motorist to change his car for a later model on grounds of fashion, even though its utility was unimpaired.

One reason why Britons, especially in rural areas, began to place more emphasis on car ownership, was almost certainly Doctor Beeching's celebrated 'Axe', which closed down uneconomic railway branch lines all over the country. Bereft of reliable public transport, country dwellers were forced to become motorists if they wanted to travel. The growing network of motorways helped, too, enabling journeys to be made at speeds rivalling those of the fastest express trains, in greater comfort and convenience and from door to door as well.

There were great changes in design: the early 1960s saw the last of the mass-production side-valve models, although only a few years earlier this configuration had dominated the popular car field. The last of the side-valves were both – originally – Ford designs, although only the 100E Popular retained its parentage, and used a power unit whose basic design dated back to the early 1930s. Of equally venerable origin was the V8 engine of the Simca Vedette, basically the 22hp 'Alsace' power unit designed for Ford-France in 1935, and taken over with that company's Poissy factory when Ford stopped building cars in France in 1954. Those had been among the first power units designed for international, rather than narrow national, markets. Now there was great cross-fertilisation of ideas and components between the car-producing nations.

Surveying the decade's first Earls Court Show, in 1960, the motoring press noted that the exhibits included 'British Vauxhalls with an American automatic gearbox, a Swedish Volvo which is shortly to be built in Birmingham, and has a Scottish-made body of Italian styling, German Borgwards with Hobbs

Above: the AC Cobra was the last 'hairy chested' sports car built in England. This car, a seven-litre Shelby Cobra, was constructed in America. Boasting a genuine 550 bhp +, this actual car could reach 60 mph from rest in a shade under four seconds. A British constructor would revise the Cobra in the 1980s and produce a 'Mark IV' version on the original jigs and framing bucks used by AC in the 1960s

automatic gearboxes from Britain, French Facel Vegas with American V8 engines, Italian Ferraris, Lancias and Maseratis with British disc brakes . . .'.

As yet, however, there was little sign that the big multi-national corporations like Ford and General Motors would use their international expertise to produce a range of vehicles of common design, with parts interchangeable across Europe. The concept of personal mobility hadn't advanced that far. A Vauxhall was still a Vauxhall, with very little in common with its German sibling, the Opel; and the same went for British Fords and German Fords, where even the basic technology differed, with the British favouring rear-wheel drive, the Germans front-wheel drive. It was a very wasteful way of utilising a European organisation, with two lots of research and engineering being used to produce dichotomous model ranges aimed, ultimately, at similar market sectors.

Yet it had not always been so. In the early 1930s, Fords had followed the same design across Europe, with the little Ford 8hp Model Y being built in Britain, France, Germany and Spain. That pioneering venture had been immured behind the protectionist tariff barriers erected by the nations of Europe during the depressed years of the 1930s, and the model strains had been developing in

Below: a classic sports car, the Pininfarina-designed Ferrari Dino 246GT. The Dino, named for Enzo Ferrari's son, was introduced as the Dino 206 in 1965, going on general sale in 1967. The engine capacity was increased from 2 litres to 2.4 litres in 1969 – bringing the designation 246GT. 195 bhp from the mid-mounted V6 give the car a top speed of 148 mph and acceleration from rest to 60 mph in around 7 seconds. Exceptional roadholding, handling and braking made the Dino a truly outstanding driver's car

isolation for three decades, their national differences accentuated by the war.

Then Ford of America made a massive cash bid, which brought Ford of Britain entirely under their control. However, fuelled by successful models like the Anglia and the Cortina, Ford was in expansive mood, marked by the construction of a modern headquarters building costing several million pounds at Warley in Essex in 1963, and the opening of a new factory at Halewood on Merseyside the same year. Halewood, representing an investment of some £70 million, was a major step in a policy of decentralisation which created, in effect, production lines several hundred miles long, engines from Dagenham being shipped to Halewood and the truck factories at Langley and Southampton by special trains, and gearboxes from Halewood and back axles from Swansea being moved cross-country by the same method. This was theoretically the best interpretation of Henry Ford I's dictum that a factory must have the best possible transportation links. Stoppages at one factory can disrupt national production however.

There were complaints from some political quarters that, with Vauxhall owned by General Motors, the new set-up at Ford brought half the British

Left : Chrysler's small car for the 1960s was the Hillman Imp, a diminutive, rear-engined saloon distinguished by its splendid, if fragile, all-alloy, four-cylinder, 875cc engine. The Imp first appeared in 1963 and was followed by the Super Imp, as shown here, and Singer and Sunbeam variants

Left : for many people the Ford Capri, which the company introduced in 1969, was the answer to a prayer. Its '2 plus 2 coupé' styling made it a sports car for the man whose family had outgrown the sports car, but whose wallet could not support a grand tourer. Once again Ford had filled a glaring gap in the market. The Capri could be had with engines ranging from the four-cylinder 1300 to the 136 bhp, 3-litre V6, later replaced by a fuel injected 2.8-litre six, and with a wide variety of trim packages

376

Above: in 1964, Volkswagen obtained control of the Auto Union group from Mercedes-Benz and a year later the disused Audi name was revived. The 1½-litre Audi 60, shown here, joined the 80, 90 and 100 ranges in 1968, to give the company a stylish and technically impressive spread of models

Above right: a 1964 Alfa Romeo Giulia Berlina saloon. In common with many other manufacturers, Alfa Romeo were no strangers to the art of clothing the same mechanical basics in differing styles of bodyshell to produce ostensibly different cars. The Giulia succeeded the 1300cc, twin-cam Giulietta in 1962 and was offered with 1570cc engine, disc brakes and a five-speed gearbox

industry under direct American rule; there was little justification for such anxieties, however, for, quite apart from the fact that both Ford and Vauxhall were left to operate as virtually autonomous units, producing cars specifically designed for their own markets, the massive cash resources of their respective parent companies were used to finance the building of new factories, and thus the creation of many new jobs. It was during the early 1960s that Vauxhall built a new factory at Ellesmere Port, also in the Merseyside development area, to produce a new version of its 1-litre Viva model.

It was American cash which was to prove the salvation of the Rootes Group which, having just opened a Scottish factory to build its new rear-engined Imp light car, found itself in financial trouble, and needed bailing out. With Government approval, the Chrysler corporation took a £27 million stake in the company in 1964, and three years later put in another £20 million; the final takeover came in 1973.

As for the other two big companies in the British market, these began the Sixties as rivals and ended the decade as a unity. For seventy years, the groups which were now known as the Leyland Motor Corporation and the British Motor Corporation had been rolling along like corporate snowballs, gathering company after company, although by the mid 60s both seemed to have run out of inertia. The last act of rivalry was the acquisition of Jaguar in 1966 by the BMC, which gave the corporation an entrée into the prestige-car market; shortly afterwards, Leyland bought Rover to prevent BMC from having it. Even during the 1950s, the economic signs pointed towards a merger between the motoring giants, and a succession of Managing Directors, including Leonard Lord, Joe Edwards, Sir William Black, Sir George Harriman and Lord Stokes, had paved the way for the eventuality. In association with the Labour Government's Industrial Reorganisation Corporation, Leyland and BMC considered a rescue operation for the ailing Rootes Group. This was not a commercially sound proposition and Rootes was acquired by Chrysler. The Government-supported concept of a British corporation large enough to compete with the increasingly sophisticated continental manufacturers was sufficient to create the basis for the merger, which took place, not without considerable difficulty and bitterness, in the February of 1967. The company is still evolving through rationalisation of model ranges and streamlining of internal administration procedures, and is now the second largest automotive company in Europe.

Against the understandable complexity of the BLMC range, the other big European companies relied on simple model ranges of perhaps three or four distinct types: small, medium and large. Sporty cars gained sufficient variety to appeal to the mass of car-buyers by offering a wide range of trim and equipment, so that two identical bodyshells could leave the factory, one as a basic spartan model designed for fleet use, the other as a comfortable limousine with, for instance, wooden door-cappings and a high level of interior appointment.

From such companies it is therefore possible for a customer to choose, within the options offered, the size of car, performance, degree of sophistication and accessories to suit his own requirements.

The only real exception to the rule that a big company should keep its range simple seemed to be Fiat, which in the mid 1960s had a basic lineup of eleven different models, but as the company had a virtual monopoly of the Italian market, with something like 75 per cent of total sales, perhaps they could afford to be a little profligate in their marketing.

On the other hand, Volkswagen, who during the decade joined the Mercedes-Auto-Union group, found that stark simplicity had its drawbacks, too. At the start of the 1960s, the old VW Beetle was still selling strongly, backed up by enthusiastic press reports of its durability, but technical progress during the decade began to leave the Beetle behind – it was, after all, a child of the '30s – and Volkswagen began tentatively to diversify, offering models with the same basic layout but modern styling, although with hindsight these 'modernised' VWs seem to have dated far more quickly than the Beetle.

The unfortunate Beetle was one of the victims of Ralph Nader's *Unsafe at any Speed* campaign, although it seems that the crusading American lawyer was over-emphasising his arguments to gain the maximum of publicity. Especially in America, the motor industry and the legislature over-reacted, and the environmentalist lobby, boldened by the success of its onslaught, moved in for the kill. Figures were issued claiming – although exactly how such things could be measured was unclear – that, annually, motor cars emitted 60 million tons of carbon monoxide, 12 million tons of hydrocarbons, 6 million tons of nitrous oxide, a million tons of sulphur oxide . . . and a million tons of 'smoke'.

These arguments were given some credence by the freak atmospheric conditions prevailing around Los Angeles, where atmospheric pollution can form a dense smog layer over the city, although the inhabitants' predilection for using a car to go even the shortest distances, and to regard anyone actually seen

Right: after some three decades of building the 'Beetle', Volkswagen's association with Auto Union, perhaps helped a little by the power of Nader's *Unsafe at any Speed*, prompted the company to diversify its designs. The first 'conventional' Volkswagen saloon, the K70, appeared in 1970, inherited from NSU. It was a front-wheel-drive saloon with a water-cooled engine in 75 or 90 bhp options and was, in essence, a more universally acceptable version of the NSU Ro80

walking as some kind of freak, did not aid the situation.

Politically, there were easy pickings to be made out of the situation, and Senator Ed Muskie put a bill before Congress proposing that exhaust emissions from a motor vehicle should be 95 per cent clean before they were released to the atmosphere. This virtually meant that the exhaust gas had to be purer than the air sucked into the carburettor, but it sounded impressive, and soon manufacturers were attempting to meet this impossible standard by fitting all kinds of 'de-toxing' devices to ensure that engines ingested all their own harmful waste-products. Needless to say, power units did not benefit from their coprophagous diet, and performance and efficiency deteriorated. So much underbonnet equipment was needed to meet these requirements that Ford's engineering laboratories jokingly announced that the standard test to see whether a European Capri converted to meet California emission laws had all the appropriate plumbing was to empty a bucket of water over the engine. If any ran out underneath, there was sure to be something missing.

Having now forced the makers of all cars sold in America to conform to a standard intended to beat freak weather conditions, the environmentalists launched a campaign aimed at the additives included in fuel to promote more efficient combustion. Tetra-ethyl-lead, which had permitted increased engine

Above: NSU was another element in the Volkswagen Audi conglomerate of the early sixties and its chief claim to fame during the period was through its licensing of and experimentation with the Wankel rotary engine. The Wankel Spyder, an open version of the Sports Prinz, powered by a single-rotor, 60 bhp engine, became the world's first rotary-engined car – introduced in 1963 and going into production in 1964. The fuel crisis of the early 1970s sounded the death-knell for NSU's Wankel project, whose forte had never been good fuel consumption

Above: the Mercedes-Benz 600 was presented as the world's most automated production car. It was introduced in 1964 and used a 6.3-litre, fuel-injected, V8 engine, self-adjusting pneumatic suspension, with dampers which were adjustable while in motion, automatic transmission, power steering and electric window lifts. It also offered powered central door locking, a power sunroof, power-assisted boot and bonnet lifts, and a powered passenger compartment division. The whole was clothed in a huge, long-wheelbase limousine body

compression – and hence efficiency – when it was first put on the market at the end of the 1920s and regarded as a miracle additive and personified by a Betty Boop-like character called Miss Ethyl, was now reviled as a causer of brain damage, and plans made to phase it out.

Engines thus became less competent at burning their fuel, petrol consumption went up and in a world increasingly aware of the finite nature of its oil reserves, could one argue that the environmentalists were proposing the right solutions?

Many of these environmental lobbyists seemed to be non-motorists, misunderstanding completely the role of the car in society, and instead of encouraging manufacturers to produce cars with impeccable steering, braking, roadholding and acceleration – cars which were safe to *drive*, a criterion which the majority of manufacturers were already aiming at – they forced through legislation to ensure that a car was safe to *crash*!

In order to be able to sell in many markets, therefore, manufacturers now-adays have to spend vast sums of money in deliberately writing-off brand-new cars in carefully controlled crashes to prove the integrity of the passenger compartment. One particularly regrettable aspect of the situation was that the environmentalists succeeded in killing off the mass-produced convertible

Left: the 1971 Plymouth Hemi-Cuda development of the Barracuda was the epitome of the American 'muscle car', with staggering straight-line performance imparted by an elephantine, 7-litre, V8 engine and scant regard for fuel consumption. Such cars were the final extravagant fling before the industry, and the market, became conservation conscious

Right: safety was a major preoccupation of the 1970s. This is the 1973 Volvo Experimental Safety Car, a rolling laboratory for safety ideas. Many of the systems tested on this car found homes on subsequent production models, the nose and front light layout, for instance, being adopted on the 240 series. Some experimental features like the air bag have still to gain acceptance

in America at the beginning of the 1970s, as open tops were dangerous in the unlikely situation of a car being inverted. It apparently did not occur to these people to insist on the standardisation of roll bars.

One expensive blind alley followed by manufacturers in response to such hostile lobbying was the 'Safety Car', various concepts of which were built in America and Europe in the early 1970s, and most of which succeeded in looking like high speed bulldozers. Heavy, clumsy and inelegant, it seemed that the only thing that they could do successfully was to run into solid obstacles!

Mark you, some of the manufacturers seemed to have brought trouble on their own heads: the early part of the decade had seen American car makers, who had earlier mutually abandoned the 'horsepower race', suddenly burst forth once again with advertising extolling the power and speed of their products. Sherwood Egbert, President of Studebaker (which was fast approaching the end of its long life of vehicle manufacture), announced his company's 1963 models with the fatuous boast: 'If the customer wishes to buy more horsepower than he can use, he will be able to buy it from Studebaker'.

However, the new emphasis on performance did have some worthwhile results: of the new generation of American cars, some were destined to become classics, like the Ford Mustang, which set new records for first-year sales, and the Anglo-American Ford GT40 sports-racer, which won Le Mans four times in a row. Pontiac pioneered the use of a cogged-belt-driven overhead camshaft among American mass-producers on their 1966 Tempest range. Hitherto, this means of driving an overhead cam had only been used by the small, German, Glas company.

Right: for off-road motoring with style, Leyland's Range Rover was an absolute must before 'look-alikes' proliferated. The Range Rover was launched in July 1970 as a luxurious alternative to the Land-Rover. The all-alloy, 3½-litre Rover V8 engine gives the Range Rover a top speed of around 98 mph and 0–50 mph acceleration in 10½ seconds.

Another unusual model introduced for the 1966 season was the Oldsmobile Toronado, with front-wheel drive; the Toronado's running gear was used, a year later, on the Cadillac Eldorado, an 18ft 5in long 'personal car' which re-introduced, in vestigial form, the famous (or infamous) Cadillac fins, although these were now evident at front *and* back . . .

General Motors made quite a notable contribution to the British motor industry in 1965, when they agreed to let Rover take over the discontinued Buick-Oldsmobile-Pontiac, 3.5-litre, V8 alloy engine, which gave an extra boost to Rover's car range, going into production in 1966.

It was not, however, a happy year to introduce a high-powered new model to the British market, for the Government had decided to hit the motor industry hard. Purchase tax was increased by ten per cent, road tax went up by sixteen per cent, hire purchase conditions were stiffened; yet the British road user was already contributing over £1000 million in taxes to the Government – eleven per cent of the total national revenue. The effect on the motor industry was 'chaotic', and the result was a crisis which saw redundancy, short-time working and a drop in sales.

Commented Sir Patrick Hennessy, Chairman of the Society of Motor Manufacturers and Traders: 'It is hard to reconcile the situation with the

Right: in the quest for fuel efficiency, with performance and controlled exhaust emissions, the turbocharger has much to recommend it. One of the first serious attempts at producing a turbocharged road car was the 1974 BMW 2002 Turbo, which would accelerate from zero to sixty miles per hour in just 6.6 seconds

Government's avowed intention of helping industries of high productivity and export performance. Last year (1965) the British motor industry's exports reached £785 million and represented sixteen per cent of our total visible trade. Yet this industry, whose success overseas is so dependent on volume in the home market, is – once again – being forced to bear the brunt of Government economic policy.

'Government researchers have estimated that the country loses hundreds of millions of pounds every year because of the sheer inefficiency of road congestion – but the Government says we cannot afford to save that money. Is this the new way ahead? Every industry has to move every day materials, parts and supplies, using expensive sluggish transportation and meeting inevitably with congestion and inefficiency on arrival at the docks. So here again we are not competitive – particularly on the Continent.

'Instead of export exhortation, suppose we built some roads from the industrial areas to the docks: what a practical contribution that would be! But we are told we cannot help exports in that way unless we sacrifice hospitals and schools. A red herring – and an unpalatable one at that. Sooner or later, we in

Left: the Hillman Imp was the basis for this small sports car built first in Essex and then in Lincolnshire. It is the Ginetta G15

382

industry have to tackle this road problem. It isn't only a motor industry problem child. All the nation's industries know that roads are a continuation of their manufacturing processes and supply costs, and it is now evident that until they join together in a national effort, we shall have no effect on Government'.

Although many major road-building programmes were instituted during the 1960s, the constraints on the use of cars were multiplying with equal rapidity. For instance, in 1965, Britain's new non-motoring lady Minister of Transport announced that as a temporary experiment, a nationwide maximum speed limit of 70 mph would be instituted. It gives some idea of the credence that can be given to a politician's concept of 'temporary' when one considers that fourteen years later, that 70 mph maximum was still in force in spite of almost constant lobbying for its reappraisal.

Since then, the cancer of overall speed limitation has spread to most countries, either as a result of fuel economy measures or because of the attitude of the safety lobbyists. The facile argument that 'speed kills' is not really defensible, because the majority of drivers keep to self-imposed limits, and the faster driver is normally more aware of what is going on. It's the slow, half-asleep

Below: a 1965 Saab 96; unveiled in February 1960, the 96 featured a redesigned rear end grafted onto what was otherwise virtually the same shell as the 95. The 96 also used the same 841 cc, 38 bhp two-stroke engine as the 95 but had more luggage capacity, more passenger room, a new instrument layout, new ventilation system and a larger fuel tank. It was an immediate success and, even with the opening of Saab's new factory at Trollhättan, the company could sell all the cars it could build. Eventually, the two-stroke engine was ousted by a 'cleaner' four-stroke V4

Left: a Rolls-Royce Silver Shadow, photographed in August 1965, just prior to the model's public announcement. The styling found favour with the company's discerning clientele and the new Shadow was a resounding success. The 6750 cc, V8 engine, as is traditional in a Rolls-Royce, had 'adequate' power and gave the car a top speed of almost 120 mph

motorist who often causes accidents by his total oblivion of what other road users are doing. But of course when an image of 'responsibility' for such exponents of creeping paralysis has been created for political ends, one can hardly accuse those slow drivers of being a menace to the more rapid drivers on the road!

Faced with such unreasonable legislation, and fearing that the situation could only deteriorate in the future, the keener motorists began to seek solace in the ownership of cars built in happier days, whose driving required some little skill and which, in short, made driving within the limits still bearable. During the 1960s, therefore, demand for veteran and vintage cars grew apace, and prices began to rise. Unfortunately, the increase in value of such vehicles also attracted the 'investor', who just saw an interesting car in terms of its potential increase in capital value, and was prepared to salt it away and rarely, if ever, use it. The activities of such gentlemen priced many of the true enthusiasts out of the market, and forced them to look to more recent cars of interest for their recreation.

In that context, when one looked back on the 1960s, one realised how very few truly classic designs had appeared in that decade. Maybe the future held something better?

Left: the Jaguar E-type caused a sensation when it first appeared, in 1961. It offered 150 mph performance at a modest price and in a sleek and elegantly styled package, which looked fast even at a standstill! The car was launched with the 3.8-litre, six-cylinder unit, but this was finally superseded by the magnificent 5.3-litre, V12 engine in 1971, the year in which this Series III roadster was built

Above: the Vauxhall Viva was the Luton company's staple production car through the 1960s and early '70s; this is a Deluxe four-door HC from 1975. After struggling through the '70s, Vauxhall forged new links with Opel to regain their former strength

With the decade almost over, the 1970s were revealed as one of the most dramatic episodes in the history of motoring, with the motor industry lurching between optimism and despondency as the victim of international politics which at one stage seemed to threaten its entire future.

The 70s opened well enough for the British industry, although Ford, Vauxhall and Chrysler all had their share of industrial unrest. By 1973, optimism was the keynote.

Reported *The Times*: 'The fruits of a bumper 1972 are already being reflected in plans for 1973. The Society of Motor Manufacturers and Traders says that the British industry is geared to produce 2,500,000 cars and car sets (for assembly overseas) this year. This compares with 1,900,000 last year. Mr Gilbert Hunt, the society's president and also chief executive of Chrysler UK, talks of a four to five per cent rise in home demand and a twenty per cent rise in exports . . . Much is at stake for the country's biggest earner of foreign currency this year'.

Mr Hunt's optimism was, however, misplaced; at the end of 1973 the Arab–Israeli War erupted, bringing the Arab oil embargo in its wake. For maybe half a century, there had been forecasts that one day there would be problems in obtaining Middle East oil: faced with the reality, European governments instituted all kinds of restrictions, from limits on the amount of petrol that could be bought at one time to car-less Sundays. Most of these measures were mere windowdressing, introduced to bring home the seriousness of the crisis to the general public, for cars used only a tiny proportion of oil imports, the bulk being used by industry and public services.

Far from rising, British sales fell by almost 200,000. Soaring raw materials prices and wages caused new car prices to rise at an alarming rate – nearly 40 per cent in a year in some cases – and savage taxes were placed on petrol to curb demand.

The worst of the oil crisis was soon over, but it left a vastly changed motor industry in its wake. The salvation of British Leyland, faced as it was with massive losses, lay in the hands of the government, and the company was 'taken into public ownership'. Whilst it is arguable that such a drastic step might not necessarily be certain to increase the company's commercial efficiency, there is little doubt that without Government intervention at the time, Leyland would look quite different today. Chrysler, too, was in trouble, although as it was an American-owned company, the British Government could hardly take it over as it had British Leyland: but again millions of pounds were handed over to keep Chrysler in Britain.

To an outside observer, it might have seemed like unfair preference; after all, the other British motor companies were trading in the same market. But both Ford and Vauxhall, using shrewd marketing and attractive model ranges, actually increased their share of overall sales, Ford, indeed, nudging the British Leyland makes (lumped together for statistical purposes, although still market-

Top: the body style which carried Aston Martin through the 1970s and into the 1980s

Above: the Fiat 126 replaced the ageing but still much loved 500 in 1973. With the adoption of a slightly larger, 594cc, engine (albeit still with only two cylinders) and a completely revised bodyshell, the 500 continued in spirit if not in substance. With 23bhp on tap, the 126 would reach 65mph and would travel close to sixty miles on a gallon of petrol. Even at this end of the motoring spectrum, there is a call for a touch of creature comfort and Fiat catered for it with this version of the basic 126, the Personal

Left: Ford were late into the proliferating market for the small hatchback car, but when their contender, the Fiesta, finally arrived in July 1976, it soon found acceptance in the very discerning market place. The Fiesta was launched with a choice of 957cc or 1117cc engines, later supplemented by a 1300 option, and it followed many competitors in using front-wheel drive

ed under their old marque names) out of first place during the early part of 1976, although Leyland made efforts to retaliate.

There were, indeed, doubts about the government's understanding of business management: the civil servants didn't always seem to be pulling in the same direction as the Leyland management. As witness the announcement by Whitehall in September 1976 that British Leyland was planning to invest some £100 million on the development of a successor to the Mini. As this car wasn't due to be put on the market for another three to four years, the announcement was premature to say the least, and broke all the industry's normal rules of confidentiality over forthcoming models. The press reported that the Leyland directors were 'furious', and that the leak had caused a drop in the sales of the current Mini. There were also doubts about the economic viability of such a model, as all the leading European companies were already active in this area of the market, known to the manufacturers as the 'B' car class.

The main problem with building small cars – and the fuel crisis had really only advanced a swing to such economical vehicles – is that a great deal of them needed to be built before they become financially attractive. After all, the plant and labour costs are virtually those of a larger car, the only saving being on metal and other raw materials.

Ford solved the problem neatly by building their Fiesta in three strategically-placed factories; at Dagenham, at Saarlouis in Germany and in a new, purpose-built plant at Almusafes, near Valencia in Spain, where Fiestas would be built not only for the booming Spanish market but also for other southern European countries. The necessary raw materials could therefore be bought in quantities sufficient to keep these three factories supplied, the 'economies of scale' meaning that components could be purchased or produced at the minimum unit cost. Typical of the new generation of small cars, the Fiesta was a two-door model with hatchback tailgate, and offered a wide range of options and trim – even a luxury Ghia model. Small no longer meant 'austere'.

The launching of the Fiesta in 1976 also proved a new truism: in order to think small, a company had to be very big. And, in general, the climate of the 1970s was inimical to the limited-production, specialised manufacturer. Aston Martin almost vanished and Jensen *did* vanish; only those specialists like Rolls-Royce or Morgan who catered for a readily identifiable minority of well heeled motorists could face the future with some assurance.

In fact, the period was marked by huge groupings, both national and international, either as straight commercial mergers, or as looser comings-together where companies retained their independence but pooled resources for the development of some technical resource, such as a new design of power unit. Typical of the latter type of arrangement was the Comotor company, formed jointly by Citroën (who were owned by Pardevi, a Swiss company owned 51 per cent by Michelin, 49 per cent by Fiat) and by Audi-NSU (who were a subsidiary of Volkswagen); Comotor, whose factory was in the Saarland, produced Wankel Rotary engines, a type of power unit which seemed to hold out possibilities of being more easily adapted to meet American exhaust pollution levels. Just to complicate the merger picture still further, by 1976

Citroën had come under the control of the privately-owned Peugeot company (which for a decade had been operating a joint research, development and investment programme with the state-owned Renault company!). First fruit of the Peugeot-Citroën alliance was the Citroën LN minicar, referred to in the French press as 'a little lion with Javel sauce', which used a two-door Peugeot 104 bodyshell and a 602cc, flat-twin, air-cooled power unit and transmission from the 3cv Citroën.

Above: the NSU Ro80 was the second car to feature Felix Wankel's rotary-engine design, the first being the rare NSU Spider. The front-wheel-drive Ro80 also featured a three-speed manual gearbox, with a torque converter and a clutch operated by a touch-sensitive switch in the gear lever knob

Left: in spite of being subject to one of the longest waiting lists for delivery anywhere in the motor industry, the Morgan Plus 8 still maintains the Morgan tradition of open-air motoring with few compromises. The Plus 8's 3½-litre Rover engine endows the car with anything but vintage performance, 0–60mph being possible in 6.7 seconds

Right: the Jaguar XJS, seen in automatic form, used the 5.3-litre V12 two-cam engine first seen in the last E-types. Not only did the XJS have magnificent acceleration and top speed (155mph), but it was one of the quietest tourers ever available. The XJS, despite its conservative instead of *avant guarde* styling, represented luxury motoring in the 1970s: sophisticated, silent, quick and expensive

Above : Rolls-Royce turned to Pininfarina of Turin to design the coachwork of their top of the range car, the Camargue, which was introduced in 1975. The resulting shape was not to everyone's taste, many people thinking the car less elegant than the Fiat 130 Coupé to which it obviously owed its basic line. Mechanically, the Camargue relied on the 6750 cc, all-alloy, V8 engine

Above right: in the 1970s, Citroën produced the CX series which was as futuristic as its predecessor, the DS. Here is a CX2200 Pallas

So the new generation of cars for the late 1970s were really quite conventional restatements of established themes. Comfort, of course, was greatly improved on the majority of them, and features like heated rear windows, servo-assisted disc brakes became common standard fitments; but most of the refinements were relatively minor ones. Faced with the reality that motorists were changing their cars less frequently, manufacturers began using phrases like 'the long-lasting car', and Porsche came up with a car that would 'last for twenty years' (although as there were still fifty-year-old cars in daily use, one felt that they could have been a little more ambitious). Such trends caused the prophets of the automotive future to trade in their crystal balls for utility models.

In 1966 the *Wall Street Journal* looked ahead to transportation in the year 2000, and forecast a 'dazzling, Buck Rogers-like world of plush, electronically controlled ground vehicles and 6000-mile-an-hour airliners'.

Ten years later, their view of the future was more cautious: 'Today's airline passenger or motorist should be able to step into a vehicle of the early 21st century and feel right at home'.

Coupled with this attitude was that of the protagonists of public transport, who wanted to drive people away from the privately-owned motor car and force them to use what Americans called 'mass-transit vehicles' – buses and trains. But these were no longer economically viable alternatives to the car: however expensive owning a motor vehicle had become, public transport had become more expensive still, and with services pared to a minimum, especially in rural areas, the use of public transport became only a desperation measure for many people.

Politically-biased 'consultation groups' talked grandly in their big brotherly way about increasing the cost of petrol still further so that the motorist would be frightened out of his car and on to the public transport by the 'perceived cost

Above: the 1978 Citroën LN, a Peugeot 104 by any other name, was an example of badge engineering, European-style, brought about by the polarising of the industry during the 1970s

Left: a 1973, 8.3-litre Cadillac Eldorado, which had everything either automatic or power operated. This front-wheel-drive car even had lights that came on automatically when the daylight faded

Right: the 1977 Porsche Turbo, with turbocharged, 3-litre, flat-six engine, clearly demonstrates its lineage from the company's 911 series, which was launched in 1964 and gradually treated to more and more power and the essential aerodynamic and chassis changes to cope with it. The 3-litre Turbo had truly spectacular performance, with sixty miles per hour attainable from rest in just 5.2 seconds

of his journey'; but what they seemed unable to comprehend was that for the family motorist the car would always win. On a train and bus four travelled at four times the cost of one, but in a car, four travelled at a quarter the cost of one. Nevertheless, the pressure groups continued to press for cars to be abolished, despite opposition from many people.

When, in 1975, Henry Ford II was called to testify before the US Joint Economic Committee, he was questioned persistently about his attitude towards Federal aid to the car industry to enable it to make the 'inevitable' (or supposedly inevitable) conversion from building motor cars to building mass-transit vehicles.

Commented Mr Ford: 'That's one problem we at Ford are not worried about. The real mass-transit system in the United States is the Highway system and the automobile, which are responsible for more than 80 per cent of all trips to work and all trips between cities, and for more than 90 per cent of all trips within cities. The automobile business is now about 75 years old. Most of the United States has been built within that period, and the building pattern has been made possible by the unprecedented convenience, flexibility, comfort and low cost of motor vehicle transportation.

'Even if it were possible, the United States has better things to do with its resources than build a 19th century transportation system – and then build a 19th century country so that we can somehow make do with primitive transportation.

'There is room and need for better public transportation in many places. But better public transportation will take few people out of cars and probably will not even halt the long, steady decline in public transportation usage. The few new rapid transit systems built in recent years all have drawn their riders from buses, not cars. They can be built only with enormous outlays of public funds,

and generally can be operated only with additional large subsidies to cover the growing gap between revenues and operating costs'.

What, however, of the car's alleged over-use of non-replaceable fuel and raw materials? The latest statistics available in 1976 showed that the known recoverable reserves of petroleum totalled 660,000,000,000 barrels, enough for some 34 years. And much of the world's surface remained undrilled – ninety per cent of all the oil and gas wells ever drilled in the world had been drilled in the United States. Other potential fuel sources included oil shale, tar sands, coal and organic waste matter: it seemed as though the internal combustion engine would be around for a long time yet. And 80 per cent of the materials used to build a car could be recycled to build new cars.

Meanwhile, governments were understandably taking a parsimonious look at their oil imports. In America, Congress decreed late in 1975 that the average fuel economy of all cars produced in a year by each manufacturer should rise in stages to 27·5 miles per (US) gallon by the 1985 model year, representing a 100 per cent improvement over the fuel consumption of 1974 models.

'To achieve so big a change in so huge an industry in so short a period,'

claimed Henry Ford II, 'we must start right now and we have little time to hesitate or change direction along the way'.

The motor industry world-wide, it seemed, was entering a period of unusual uncertainty, although there was evidence that the public was becoming tired of excessive government interference in their freedom to buy and use motor vehicles. Henry Ford II summed up the problems ahead in a speech to the Automotive World Congress at Dearborn, Michigan, in July 1976: 'Outside the United States, will the trend towards government control and ownership of auto companies continue, and how far will the march towards social democracy go? How will world trade in motor vehicles be affected if manufacturing and marketing are increasingly aimed at protecting jobs and generating export income rather than profits? Can private, profit-orientated enterprise survive in anything like its present form in the face of growing support for such measures as worker participation in management, compulsory profit sharing and compulsory distribution of stock to workers and unions?'

That feeling of uncertainty was certainly present when America's biggest manufacturer, GM, unveiled its 1977 models; one got the feeling that the General's product planners were waiting eyes shut, fingers crossed and holding their breath awaiting the reaction of the public and press. For they had, in one season, reversed the trend of the previous half-century; their big-car ranges, instead of getting bigger and more powerful, had become smaller. Engine lineups were trimmed; the biggest gas-guzzling engines, V8s of 7438 cc, 7454 cc and 8192 cc, were summarily dropped from the range and Chevrolets and Pontiacs, after a four-year gap, once again offered six-cylinder engines. The Chevy line now consisted of three power units only in the marque's big cars – a six of 4096 cc and V8s of 4997 cc and 5734 cc, with the previous 6554 cc and 7438 cc V8s axed.

Similar changes were wrought at Buick, Oldsmobile, Pontiac and, most significantly, at Cadillac, where the US industry's biggest production engine, the massive 8192 cc V8, no longer had a place in the range. Now the Caddy owner had to settle for a modest little 6963 cc engine; this philosophy ran completely counter to GM's previously stated dictum that coupled 'bigness' with prestige.

Now the engineers and salesmen were insisting that the smaller engines actually represented increased performance, because the new 'downsized' big cars were smaller and lighter than their predecessors, and also returned a better fuel consumption. GM claimed that, far from being an economy measure dictated by the energy crisis, the decision to downsize had been taken a year before the crisis struck. The smaller cars were on average nearly 11 inches shorter than comparable 1976 models at 211.9 in long, as well as 4.1 inches narrower and with 5.5 inches off the wheelbase. The ratio between length and wheelbase was already greater than on European cars, which were based on the ethos that the nearer the wheels were to the corners the better; shorter wheelbases made the big American cars look as though their bodies were squatting on a skateboard, and didn't do much for their handling, either. But since Americans were also to end the 1970s with a nationwide speed limit of 55 mph – a political decision of even greater irrelevance than the European limits – maybe the incentive to provide European-style handling characteristics just wasn't there. In any case, the engineering costs of meeting the government's Corporate Average Fuel Economy (CAFE) standards were, literally, astronomical: by the end of 1978 it was reckoned that the cost to American manufacturers of meeting the CAFE standards already equalled the cost of putting the US astronauts on the Moon, and that by 1985 the industry would have spent around $80 billion more – three times the $26 billion budget for the Apollo lunar landings!

In the face of all this concentration on economy, the American big-car market seemed amazingly resilient; in mid-1977 it was reporting that sales were at peak levels while registrations of small cars were flagging. In contrast to the situation of three years earlier, the plant shutdowns were taking place at small-car factories, and extra overtime was being worked on large-car assembly lines.

Right: the 1975 American Motors Pacer had a futuristic body housing the traditional American package of V8 engine, three-speed transmission and independent front/non-independent rear suspension. Drum brakes were considered adequate to restrain a 4228 cc top-of-the-range engine

Far right: the Citroën GS continued admirably the Citroën tradition of superior front-wheel-drive engineering and outstanding aerodynamic efficiency. Flat-four engines of a mere 1015 cc or 1222 cc, gave maximum speeds of up to 94 mph with remarkable fuel economy, in the region of 40 mpg

Below: the only American sports car in production in the 1970s was the Chevrolet Corvette Stingray, this being a 1973 7.5-litre automatic

By the beginning of 1978, the future for the motor industry seemed a good deal brighter than it had done in the period immediately following the oil crisis. Car sales in Western Europe, which had overtaken America as the biggest producer of motor vehicles at the end of the 1960s, looked set to exceed ten million for the first time. However, overall production was not quite back to 1973 levels, and it was unlikely that that year's record of 11,250,000 cars would be equalled for some time.

A main cause of this was the tremendous inroads made by the Japanese into the markets traditionally served by European manufacturers. In the late 1960s, the European industry regarded Japanese cars as a source of humour, and certainly as no sort of threat to their livelihood. Although Japanese cars *had* been technically retrograde and stylistically dreadful, things were changing.

From 1966, Japanese manufacturers invested heavily in development of new designs, even to the extent of buying styling packages from the Italians.

By 1970, the annual Tokyo Motor Show had gained a reputation similar to that of the Turin Salon as a showcase for concept cars and advanced prototypes alongside the normal production cars, and the Japanese industry, which had doubled its output every two years since 1961, had soared into second place among the world's motor manufacturing countries. Eager to gain a piece of the Oriental action, the American motor industry was seeking inroads into this glittering automotive shogunate.

Already, Chrysler had entered into an agreement with Japan's Mitsubishi company, an offshoot of a vast engineering empire that had built its first cars as early as 1917 (but concentrated on trucks and military vehicles between 1921 and 1959, when the 500 minicar made its appearance). Under this agreement, Chrysler held 35 per cent of the stock, Mitsubishi 65 per cent; the newly introduced Colt Galant 1.5-litre model was to be sold in the United States as the Dodge Colt through Dodge dealers. Meanwhile, Ford was talking to Toyo Kogyo, makers of the Mazda, in a series of discussions that would eventually lead to Ford's taking a 25 per cent interest in Toyo Kogyo, and GM was seeking a similar accord with Isuzu.

Mazda was certainly a company with a keen interest in advanced technology; among the prototypes they showed at Tokyo in 1970 were the RX500, which had a mid-mounted twin-rotor Wankel engine, and the EX-5 runabout with electric motors in the wheel hubs fed from a generator driven by a constant-speed Wankel engine.

But, more significantly from the point of view of the Western car industry, the Japanese were already beginning to transform their products from small utility models to a wider range of vehicles, even challenging the European sports car manufacturers. The philosophy was the same as that which had given Japan its dominant position in the fields of cameras, motorcycles and

Above left: the 1970s saw the beginnings of links between the world's largest manufacturing nations, Japan and America. American cars remained fairly thin on the ground in Japan, but America, bowing to the in any case inevitable Japanese influx and pursuing its own continuing trend to smaller cars, adopted several Japanese designs under domestic brand names. This is the 1982 model of the long-running Dodge Colt, the Americanised 1.5-litre Colt Galant which featured an innovative 'twin-stick' transmission with dual range final drive as well as the usual gearbox

Above: Mazda were only a matter of weeks behind NSU with their introduction of a rotary-engined car, the RX3 model being revealed in 1973. The engine was equivalent to a reciprocating engine of 1964cc and produced a useful 110bhp. While NSU struggled with their Wankel development programme, Mazda's version went from strength to strength and appeared to overcome many of the problems

electronic goods; to establish a firm base line and then build outwards from this solid foundation, with the aim of eventual market domination. So the 1970s opened with the Japanese offering such export-orientated sports models as the Datsun 240Z, which could actually challenge Western marques in rallying. Like Japan's large-capacity motorcycles, the 240Z, with its 2.4-litre engine, was solely intended for overseas markets; for the domestic market, only a 2.0-litre version was available. With its all-independent suspension and ohc six-cylinder power unit, the 240Z was very far from being a tin box from Tokyo. Advanced technique, too, was evident in Mazda's range of three rotary-engined cars, this manufacturer having far more success than NSU in commercialising Dr Wankel's trochoidal motor.

Mazda's rotary-engined R100, Cosmo 110S and R130 were all being produced in significant numbers; and to hedge their bets, the Hiroshima-based company, which had begun its corporate life as a manufacturer of cork products, offered the piston-engined 'Capella' version of the R100 coupe. They claimed an output of 120 bhp and a top speed of 120 mph from this 1175 cc model, though the power outputs emanating from Japanese press handouts at that period all seem to have been more than a little exaggerated. The 58 bhp advertised for the new Datsun Cherry, with its transverse 1000 cc engine driving the front wheels was, for instance, almost equal to the output claimed for the equally new 1200 cc Vauxhall Viva from Britain. Nevertheless, it was the level of specifications offered at prices that seemed more than competitive with the home-grown products that made motorists in those markets on which the Japanese had already begun their onslaught look with interest at the Oriental models.

Already Japanese imports had made a considerable impression on the West Coast of America, but Europe felt itself safe from invasion. Japanese cars represented only a tiny fraction of total sales and as late as 1970 an eminent British motoring journalist could write: 'By the time import duty has been added to the enormous cost of transportation halfway around the world it is quite obvious that no model designed to be competitive on, say, the West Coast of America can possibly hold its own on the home ground of one of the manufacturers it is thrashing into the ground out there in the export territories'.

Japan's marketing philosophy, however, was vastly different from that of the European companies. Typically, the Toyo Kogo company, makers of Mazda cars, operated their own shipping line of some sixty ships to deliver cars to

Right: Japanese companies such as Datsun made huge inroads into European markets with cars such as this 1977 120Y Sunny saloon through offering exceptional value for money, albeit usually coupled with mechanical mediocrity. Japanese companies may occasionally have overstated the power outputs and handling of their products but there was no need to overstate the customer-attracting levels of equipment. What European manufacturers still regarded as 'extras', the Japanese invariably included as standard

export markets, and operated on the basis that when there was a slump in home market sales, exports were to be doubled, so that overall sales volume should remain constant.

It was tactics like this which put Japan into the big league. In 1977, Japanese manufacturers were selling a million cars a year in the United States, and had six per cent of all new car sales in Europe, including over ten per cent of the British market.

Indeed, the British industry had requested Japanese manufacturers to restrict imports and claimed, in 1977, that the Japanese had agreed to keep their share of the British market down to the 1976 level of 9.4 per cent. The 1977 Japanese penetration of 10.6 per cent came as something of a shock, therefore, reinforced by the news that at the beginning of 1978 their share had risen to 13 per cent, and the Japanese industry association told the British Society of Motor Manufacturers and Traders that it would no longer give any undertaking – official or unofficial – that it would restrict UK sales during 1978.

Perhaps the Japanese industry had become too export-based for its own good. European manufacturers had attempted to move into many overseas markets by setting up local plants, thereby creating local employment; press reports accused the Japanese of exporting unemployment along with their cars. With Japan now selling almost a quarter of the world's cars, it seemed that they had reached a level of tolerance beyond which stringent curbs would be enforced.

European experts claimed that the Japanese had made a major tactical error by choosing to supply major overseas markets solely by export, rather than utilising local manufacture, and that, especially in the Third World, nationalistic demands for local assembly plants would increasingly threaten those exports.

The doors seemed to have been closed against the Japanese buying into an existing European company. They had made advances when Citroën was in trouble, before that company merged with Peugeot, but the French Government had prevented any takeover from occurring. Any chance of Chrysler releasing idle production capacity to Mitsubishi (in which it held a fifteen per cent share) seemed likely to meet with a similar fate.

Faced with a dramatic fall in the car exports essential to its economic success – twenty per cent of Japan's industry manufacturing activity was centred on the car industry – the Japanese industry was seen to be planning for the change. Forecasts indicated that Japanese companies would shift an increasing

Above: having taken the two-wheeled world by storm in the early 1960s, Honda turned their attentions to the manufacture of cars and, after a hesitant start with several motor cars in miniature, they gained acceptance with cars such as the Civic and this 1977 Accord

Above: once Volkswagen had broken away from the constraints of a 'Beetles only' policy, they began to produce a splendid series of cars, including the Scirocco, the Golf and the Polo. The front-wheel-drive Polo was available with 895cc and 1092cc engines. This is a 1976 example

Below: another challenger from Japan to the medium sized car market sector was the 1970 Toyota Crown De Luxe sedan. Like all Japanese cars the Toyota offered a comprehensive list of standard equipment within the basic price

percentage of their resources into truck manufacture and could be competing strongly on a global scale in the commercial vehicle market by the 1980s.

Another factor which was seen likely to slow down the Japanese growth was the rising value of the Japanese currency, which added to the cost of their cars.

Some indication of future trends was given by Honda's decision to open a motor cycle factory in the United States in 1979, with plans to follow this by a car factory which would be in production by 1981.

It was a policy already followed by Volkswagen, who began building cars in the United States in the spring of 1978, with plans to open another factory at a later date. Currency fluctuations played a major part in the VW decision: any manufacturer setting up operations in widely scattered countries seeks immunity from the fluctuations of the currency market. Moreover, it is possible to even out labour costs, so that the expense of building cars in a high-wage country, which can represent a considerable hindrance to an export-seeking manufacturer, could be countered by further production in low-wage countries.

The 1970s saw several of the larger manufacturers moving eagerly into the less developed countries. Fiat was one of the more interesting examples. Aware of the problems which could arise from its dependence on the relatively small Italian market, in which it held a dominant share of new car sales. Fiat diversified within Italy, so that less than half its industrial energies were concentrated on car production. The company moved into new fields, like tourism and hotels, and expanded existing technologies such as aircraft production.

Outside Italy, Fiat held thirty per cent of Seat, the Spanish car manufacturer, in partnership with the Madrid government, and sold production know-how to Poland and the USSR, who set up huge car plants to produce cars based on obsolescent – in Western terms – Fiat designs. The size of these ventures can be gauged from the fact that in 1976, Lada, the Russian end of the deal, turned out 740,000 cars, virtually equal to Leyland's 1978 output.

In April 1978, Fiat and Seat joined forces in a venture to establish an Egyptian motor factory in conjunction with Egyptian financial and motor engineering interests, although at the same time it was reported that Seat was developing its own design of sports car for the Spanish market, so as to reduce the amount of royalty payments due to Fiat.

Another North African country which went out of its way to attract European motor manufacturers was Morocco, which by 1978 could count several vehicle plants in the Casablanca area, most recent of which was a Renault component factory which – with the agreement of the French trades unions – supplied items such as mirrors and seat belt anchorages to Renault-France factories.

Further afield, Third World countries were eager for the benefits that the motor industry could bring: Korea had its own car producing plant, Vietnam was courting European car companies with attractive financial concessions, Volkswagen was still producing the old Beetle in Brazil, after production of this best-selling car of all time had stopped in Europe, in volumes which made it Brazil's biggest car manufacturer.

Within a very few years the emphasis of car production had changed radically, and the chances were that it would undergo still more dramatic changes in the years ahead. Volume production, distribution networks, service and model rationalisation would be the keys to survival for hard-pressed manufacturers. It would be essential that parts for a car produced, say in Australia, should be interchangeable with those of an identical model produced half a world away.

Just how small the automotive world was becoming was proved one day in 1978 when Bernard Vernier-Palliez, the President of Renault, boarded Concorde in Paris, flashed across the Atlantic at twice the speed of sound, signed an agreement with American Motors Corporation to sell the Renault R5 (ungrammatically known as 'Le Car') through AMC's 2300 dealers in the US and Canada, got back onto Concorde and was once again at work in his Paris office that same evening. A neat and deservedly popular little car, the R5 was now available with an 'in-house' electronically-controlled automatic transmission, while there was also a 'hot-shoe' Alpine variant on offer, developing 93 bhp from 1.4 litres, against the 36 bhp and 845 cc of the basic R5. Hardly surprisingly, it also cost nearly twice as much.

There were some interesting developments announced by the French industry as the 1970s drew to an end. For instance, the new Peugeot-Citroën-Talbot grouping came out with an all-new variation on the eternal 2cv theme, the Visa, intended to replace the ugly-duckling Ami with a model of wider appeal. Very recognisably a Citroën, in its basic form the Visa employed a flat-twin air-cooled engine redolent of its 2cv ancestry, while the more powerful variant played on family ties to borrow the transverse watercooled four of the Peugeot 104, thus neatly reversing the trend of the LN. Fitted with typically idiosyncratic controls, the little Visa broke new ground for what was ostensibly an economy model by specifying electronic ignition on the 602 cc flat-twin.

Electronic wizardry also featured on the Visa's new cousin by marriage, the

Below: the Renault R5 was introduced in 1972 with a 782 cc engine and quite ordinary lines for a French car. Later versions included this 1978 1.3-litre TS, the 93 bhp, 1.4-litre Alpine, the turbocharged Gordini and even a staggeringly quick mid-engined, turbocharged 'silhouette' variant, specifically aimed at racing and rallying. While other American car makers formed links with Japanese manufacturers, the beleagured American Motors Corporation turned to Renault for the all-important broadening of horizons and had great success with various Renault cars, including the R5 sold as 'Le Car'

Chrysler-Simca (shortly to become Talbot) Horizon. In a relationship worthy of the Byzantine complexity of the old Sunbeam-Talbot-Darracq empire whose distant descendant it was, the Horizon was built in Coventry as a Sunbeam by the UK end of the operation; its SX version carried a mini-computer which gave details of fuel consumption, journey time and average speed among its functions and heralded a growing trend among the better-specified small cars. Moreover, the Chrysler Sunbeam emerged in a neat Lotus-engineered version with a 16-valve head and striking black-and-silver decor.

At the distant end of the Peugeot-Citroën-Talbot line-up, Peugeot brought out a turbo charged version of their 2.3-litre diesel engine in the 604; but it is only in markets where sufficient price differential exists between petrol and diesel fuel that the turbo diesel engine becomes a worthwhile proposition.

Advanced technology of a different kind was apparent in Italy where Fiat launched the little Ritmo, whose production was robotised to an extent new in Europe; 'handmade by robots' was the way its makers advertised it, capturing this cybernetic legerdemain in a highly-praised television commercial orchestrated to Mozart opera.

For the Italian luxury car makers, there was, conversely, nothing to sing about. Since 1969 Ferrari had been sustained by Fiat cash, so they at least were cushioned, but Lamborghini was in crisis. A potentially lucrative arrangement with BMW to build the latter's mid-engined M1 coupé collapsed on the eve of production, with the tooling complete and several prototypes in the metal, because of Lambo's economic problems which led to a re-organisation under French ownership in the autumn of 1980.

Even state-owned Alfa Romeo, despite its production of the excellent Alfasud, was haemhoraging cash at an alarming rate; in 1979 it was revealed that the group had lost some £400 million in six years; nevertheless, development of a new, big, 2.5-litre six proceeded, with this model appearing in 1979, the excellent GTV6 following a year later.

For another state-owned firm, British Leyland – or 'BL' as it now preferred to be known – the end of the decade showed continuing strengths in luxury lines which were not echoed by the volume models' slipping share of the home market. Like Gaul, the car side of BL was now divided into three parts: Austin Morris, building Austin, Mini, Morris, MG and Princess; Jaguar Rover Triumph, which also manufactured Daimler, Land Rover and Vanden Plas; and BL Components, the profitable parts division. The old '2000' Rover shape, revolutionary in the 1960s but now dated, had been replaced by the slippery SD bodyshell, initially with the Buick-based 3500 alloy V8, then with

Above: the Fiat Ritmo (known as the Strada in Britain, where this 1981 Super 85 version was sold) was a fairly conventional car built by 'unconventional' machines which soon became the industry norm

Below: serious financial problems did not stop Lamborghini building cars such as the stunning mid-engined Countach

the smaller Rover in-line sixes; with its overtones of Ferrari styling, the SD was initially criticised by Rover's more hidebound clientele as being too *avante garde*, though it was obvious that the aerodynamic hatchback route followed by the SD was the right approach to the 1980s and that the days of wall-to-wall walnut veneer were numbered.

Jaguar, too, were improved by design, though here it was in the standardisation of petrol injection on the 4.2-litre six, bringing this classic engine back to the performance standards that had made it legendary before emissions legislation had garotted its induction.

Triumph introduced a drophead version of their TR7 sports car; this was to have a short, unhappy life, with Leyland's Merseyside factory at Speke closed down under it, followed by a brief continuation in the Midlands. A V8 derivative proved a production rarity, though it was claimed that the bigger engine removed some of the shortcomings that made the TR7 a less appealing car than its MG cousin (though as the poor old Pavlova Works at Abingdon-on-Thames that had been cradle to the MG for half-a-century were summarily shut down as they celebrated their jubilee, one might think that BL loved the Triumph more, despite its unhappy styling, which seemed to marry the front and back of entirely different cars . . .).

Indeed, the closure of Abingdon and the (temporary) extinction of the MG name seemed symptomatic of the deep-rooted ills of BL which, throughout its corporate existence, had sought to homogenise its image by burying well-loved marques alive: Riley and Wolseley had gone, to be followed into limbo by MG; Standard had been choked off in 1963 because its 60-year-old name had lost its value and now there were rumours that BL's new chairman, Michael Edwardes, was about to sign a deal whereby a Honda design would be assembled in Britain under the Triumph banner.

So far, the 1980s have proved a decade of surprising contrasts: dominating the industry have been the new generation 'world cars', a concept far removed from old Henry Ford's Model T 'universal car', built the world over in exactly the same style, specification and colour – black – for the larger part of its 19-year production life. Such cars, typified by the General Motors 'J-cars' and the Ford Escort, have a common basic design, but the finished vehicle is very much a native of the continent in which it is built, with American versions very different in appearance and equipment from their European counterparts. Alongside these models have mushroomed a new breed of 'muscle cars' with the buzzword being 'Turbo'. And, as a curious substratum, came a not entirely healthy preoccupation with nostalgia that resulted in a curious race of cars that aped the styling features of the 1930s, with an alarming lack of taste a recurrent failing (though there were also some praiseworthy, but expensive 're-creations' of classic sports cars).

Above: Alfa Romeo, usually regarded, in spite of its previous sporting saloons as a sports car builder, entered the desperately competitive small hatchback market in 1971 with the excellent Alfasud. The 1186 cc, overhead cam, flat-four, front-wheel-drive car made the mass-market breakthrough and gave rise to this more angular, 1977, fastback Alfasud Sprint, but it could not keep Alfa from near fatal financial problems in the early 1980s

Below: the energy crisis did not stifle the desire for performance but it did prompt turbocharging as an acceptable form of boosting performance through efficiency. Otherwise wasted exhaust gases are used to drive a supercharger, giving considerable power gains with no mechanical loss. The Saab 99 Turbo was one of the first and one of the best

Above: the styling of Leyland's Triumph TR7 did not prove universally popular, but the car itself was a solidly built, ultra-conventional medium priced sports car, with outstanding roadholding and handling and a reasonable turn of speed. The TR7 was powered by a 2-litre, four-cylinder engine derived from the Dolomite saloon. Successes in rallying were gained in 1978 by TR7s fitted with the $3\frac{1}{2}$-litre Rover V8 engine

First of the 'world cars' to make its appearance was the Ford Escort – one of the first mass-production cars to be designed from the ground up since the oil crisis. Right on the heels of the traumatic increase in oil prices in the early 1970s, Ford engineers in Detroit had begun work on a new small power unit intended to take the company into the uncertain days of the 1980s. As the development cycle of an engine is around seven years, against four for a car, the decision to go ahead with the considerable investment for the proposed engine programme – which included the construction of a totally new engine plant in Europe and the rebuilding of the Michigan engine plant to give a combined capacity of a million engines a year – required considerable faith in the future of the motor industry.

Three different engine configurations were tested, and eventually the choice fell on a competition-inspired layout with hemispherical combustion chambers and an overhead camshaft operating inclined valves through hydraulic tappets. Because Ford's European operations had great experience with the design and development of competition engines, the project was handed over to them, though they maintained the closest possible links with the US design centres, not least through the medium of Ford's transatlantic computer linkup which, thanks to the time difference between Europe and Michigan, permits Ford engineers in the British and German engineering centres to use the vast computer facilities in Dearborn while America sleeps.

Equally, development of the car, which began in mid-1977, was a joint project, with the bulk of the development work carried out in Europe, where experience of small front-wheel-drive cars was greatest. Particular attention was paid to good aerodynamics allied to efficient utilisation of fuel and low maintenance costs, these being the criteria expected by the public of the 1980s, to whom economical operating expenses have become of paramount importance. But while in the past economy has only been associated with utilitarian creepabouts, today's motorist expected a reasonable road performance in keeping with the motorway age.

Representing a considerable advance over the model it replaced, the Escort also marked a new direction for Ford which was moving away from its old image as a maker of sound, unadventurous, moderately-priced vehicles – this unadventurous end of the market was being energetically usurped by the Japanese, whose radically-different society underwrote far lower manufacturing costs – and becoming a technologically-advanced maker of exciting, efficient vehicles which offered, as the then Chairman of Ford of Europe, Bob Lutz, commented, 'an equally compelling sort of value', the value of superior engineering, design and dynamics.

For General Motors, the creation of the J-Car line, which made its début

shortly after the Escort, the aim was more simple – to meet the imported cars that were making such inroads in the US market head-on. It also helped with the fusion of image of their European subsidiaries, Opel of Germany and Vauxhall of Britain, giving Vauxhall a much-needed image boost. In the US, the J-Car range was initially launched as the Chevrolet Cavalier, Pontiac J2000 and Cadillac Cimarron at a time when GM's corporate ego badly needed boosting, for in 1980 the world's biggest carmaker had reported its first loss-making year since 1921, despite a record 62.6 per cent share of the US market. Though 1981 saw a return to (modest) profit, that market share was slipping, and in the first six months of 1982, GM recorded 61 per cent of registrations of US-built cars. That apparently modest 1.6 per cent drop actually represented something in the order of $560 million in lost sales. The reason, said critics, was that the traditional differences between GM's five car lines – Chevrolet, Pontiac, Oldsmobile, Buick and Cadillac – had been eroded by the introduction of new models like the 1979 X-Car and the 1981 J-Car which were common, save for trim and minor sheet metal changes, to several GM divisions. How, for instance, could GM explain why the outwardly similar Chevrolet Cavalier and Cadillac Cimarron had a difference of some $6000 in basic price?

The easy solution, it seemed, would be merely to do away with one or more of the GM divisions – but that ran counter to GM philosophy that was virtually as old as the corporation itself, which relied on what a leading market consultant called 'aspiration order' in GM's product line, the belief that once a customer had started at the foot of the car-buying ladder with the low-priced Chevrolet he could proceed upward through the other GM lines as his circumstances improved until he reached Nirvana in a Cadillac. Less divisions, less sales, claimed the GM gurus and the corporation agreed with them, though to an outsider it did seem as though the General was seeking to launch more lifeboats than the sea would hold. For instance, *Business Week* magazine reported in the autumn of 1982 that GM was selling two midsized car bodies through four divisions under 12 different nameplates, as well as offering new car lines alongside the old models they were intended to replace. To regain the old frontiers, GM divisions began lobbying for 'exclusive deals' on forthcoming model lines, led by Pontiac, which had developed a two-seat sports 'P-Car' for launch in 1983 'to stimulate a youthful, exciting image'.

Then, said the Motown rumour mongers, things would get really convoluted: Cadillac wanted to keep its big deVille into 1985, though the Buick and Olds divisions would be replacing their equivalent models by a new, front-wheel-drive 'C-Car' in 1984, since petrol prices had stabilised and the demand for large cars had therefore revived. For the same reason, Chevrolet wanted to keep its Impala/Caprice lines in production for a year of two after smaller 'B-Cars' had been introduced in the equivalent slots in the Buick and Olds ranges. And Chevrolet was demanding a one-year 'exclusive' for the all-new 1985 'N-Car', the front-wheel-driven replacement for the GM personal coupé line (Chevy Monte Carlo, Pontiac Grand Prix, Olds Cutlass, Buick Regal), so that the other divisions would have to wait until 1986 for *their* N-Cars.

Then GM had contracted with its Japanese associate Isuzu for 300,000 minicars to supplement the US-built subcompact offerings in 1984–85, followed by 'well under 100,000' 800 cc three-cylinder Suzuki 'micro-minis' from 1985 on. Then, in October 1982 GM announced tentative agreement with Toyota to use the GM plant in Fremont, California, for the first phase of a joint car production, probably a front-wheel-drive subcompact to replace the ageing Chevy Chevette subcompact.

The preponderance of front-wheel drive in the GM plans underlined America's almost obsessive preoccupation with *traction avant* in the 1980s. Quite forgetting the way pioneers of front-wheel-drive like Christie and Cord had been regarded as eccentric in their day, and apparently oblivious of the fact that fwd and rwd had been happily co-existing in Europe for over half a century, the US industry and public embraced front-wheel-drive with born-again fervour, regarding any car driven by the rear wheels as 'old-fashioned', despite the proven dynamic advantages of rear drive on medium and large cars. By opting exclusively for fwd, manufacturers make a rod for their own backs, since the range of engine and transmission options is necessarily reduced.

The vast cost of the changeover to meet not only popular demand for different technologies but also not always realistic Government demands represented a crippling burden on the American manufacturers. GM, as we have seen, was involved in a vast programme of retooling and redesign that was budgeted at $40 million, and all the 'Big Four' were spending record sums on new model development against an economic backdrop that was solidly gloomy.

The speed with which the American industry had descended into the abyss was nothing short of cataclysmic. From 1978, with its record sales of 15.4 million vehicles and record Big Four profits of $4.9 billion, the industry bellyflopped to sales of 11.5 million vehicles and a combined loss of $4.2 billion in 1980. Chrysler nearly went bankrupt and had to be rescued by the US Government. A year later, sales were down further, to 10.8 million vehicles, but the industry had taken dire measures to plug the financial haemhoraging – plants were shut down and over 200,000 workers laid off indefinitely – and losses were down to $1.8 billion. The 1981 car output was just 6.3 million, letting Japan into the lead as the world's biggest car-producing country, with

Right: undeterred by slow-to-fade sales resistance to subcompacts, General Motors laid plans for the import of a limited number of Suzuki 'micro-minis' beginning in 1985 and probably similar in size to the three-cylinder Alto sold in Europe from 1982

an output of 6.9 million (though Europe as a whole had been ahead of America in terms of car output for many years).

And for 1982 the signs were that car sales could fall as low as 5.8 – even 5.5 – million, the worst results since 1959.

And, in spite of all the staff reductions and economies, the three biggest companies – GM, Ford, Chrysler – still had to sell 9.1 million vehicles to break even, against 12.1 million in 1980. With a projected market of 8 million in 1982, clearly there was still a gap to bridge. And the more optimistic Detroit watchers were forecasting that 1983 could be the year of the upturn, with the Big Three all in the black.

The US scene remains unpredictable; Volkswagen, who had established a factory in the US to build the Rabbit (a federalised Golf) and planned a second plant, had to shelve their expansion plans when 1982 saw a plunge of over 40 per cent in their sales. And Japanese manufacturers, who had planned to ship minicar models to the States as part of their import quota, quietly shelved these plans in the autumn of 1982. Said Nissan vice-president Masataka Okuma: 'The trend of larger cars has increased recently and the demand for minicars, thanks to stable oil prices, is levelling off and is rather weak . . . if we were to put a minicar into the US market under the current export restrictions, it would take away from the sales of our larger cars'. But he felt that there still might be a future for minicars in the US commuter market. Summed up another Japanese executive: 'The minicar bound for the US isn't dead – it's just waiting for the American market to become more attractive'.

But with America showing growing signs of protectionism – it would be a brave man who drove a Japanese-built car through recession-hit downtown Detroit – maybe the US market would be a long time regaining its appeal to importers . . .

To overcome the rising tide of protectionist action, often irrational, Japan's Nissan set out to conquer from within by establishing manufacturing footholds in prime export markets. Within one year – 1980 – Nissan bought into Spain's biggest truck maker, Motor Iberica (which had its origins in the old Spanish Ford company, closed after the Civil War), set up a US light truck company with a proposed factory site in Tennessee, concluded a deal whereby Nissan and Alfa Romeo would jointly operate a factory in southern Italy and announced that in the early 1980s his company would start building VWs in Japan for that market and South East Asia.

Other Japanese companies were also finding strange bedfellows: the BL/Honda deal bore its fruit in the Triumph Acclaim, a thinly-disguised Honda Ballade, with a second 'joint model', code-named 'XX' and executive model shrouded in mystery, due in 1985. And in 1983, a joint Toyota/Lotus was due to make its bow delayed by Lotus's precarious financial position. Recognising that their domestic styling talent was somewhat deficient in originality, Japan's manufacturers began to turn to Europe for advanced design; one of the first and neatest Euro-designs for a Japanese manufacturer was Guigaro's Isuzu Piazza. So far, Japanese manufacturers have, for the most part, despite their lead in production automation, remained some years behind Europe in design and engineering; the indications are that they may be about to close the distance . . .

There's no doubt that, at present, most of the bright ideas are coming out of Europe and that America is, at last, beginning to learn from the experience of the Old World. And for Europe, the 1980s have so far been particularly exciting. For beleaguered BL, the decade had opened with some pretty crucial decisions. Having cancelled the ADO 1 replacement for the Mini, they decided to go ahead with a 'supermini'; a poll among their workforce chose the name Metro for the new car and the model was duly launched in 1980. Its début was clouded by an advertising campaign that claimed fuel consumption figures attainable only under the most ideal of conditions; its inability to reach the claimed 83 miles per gallon in the hands of the average customer detracted from fuel economy figures that were competitive enough without needing such padding.

Right: two very different cars each played a major part in the recovery of British Leyland, the Metro (left), launched in 1980 as BL's 'supermini' and the long running Rover SD1. Although both cars included small engined versions among the options, they also offered high performance variants, the top of the ranges in 1983 being the MG Turbo Metro and the Rover Vitesse. Both were reflections of BL's growing commitment to racing as a way to sales, the Metros having their own 'one-make' MG series as well as dominating the small class of the British Saloon Car Championship in which the Rovers had taken over from the Ford Capri as the outright winners

404

To some, the decision to launch Metro at that time in that market segment seemed an odd one, for it was in the medium car sector that BL really needed a new model. But the explanation was simple; engineering for the Metro was further advanced than for BL's LM 10 medium car project, and so it was the smaller car that was pressed ahead to the delaying of its big sister. BL, it seems, were in such dire straits that they just had to have a new car in 1980 to revitalise their image and claw back some of their vanishing market share. Their problem was a fairly crucial one; the volume car divisions weren't really big enough, and the company's perceived strengths lay in its prestige models like the Jaguar and Range Rover. When Sir Michael Edwardes stepped down as Chairman in 1982, handing over power to a triumvirate of executives, the company's losses had certainly diminished; BL was only losing £750,000 a day in the first half of 1982 against nearly £1.24 million a day for the same period of 1981. Sir Michael's farewell prediction was: 'We aim to approach break-even at the trading level (before interest and tax) in 1983'. Such qualified optimism relied on the LC 10 achieving its objectives; as it would be appearing well after more modern designs like the Vauxhall Cavalier (the British J-car) and the Ford Sierra, the LC 10 was going to have to meet some pretty exacting targets.

Indeed, the fate of BL as a whole seemed to be in the balance; Britain's conservative government, with its commitment to 'rolling back the state' seemed anxious to hive off the more desirable offshoots of BL to the private sector. If these went – and it seemed as though Honda, for one, would be willing to buy – what would happen to the volume car division? Had BL the chance of surviving as an independent company or had the root-and-branch pruning carried out by Sir Michael cut back production capacity to such an extent that BL would need to merge with another company to stay alive, for its volumes weren't enough to cover the costs of adding new models to the line-up. Indeed, BL's curious attitude to the volume market seemed underlined by an announcement that the Morris marque-name was doomed to extinction, 'because market research had shown that it was regarded as being linked to commercial vehicles . . .'

'The problem with DeLorean was that he was planning to sell 20,000 cars a year in a 5000-car market', a specialist car manufacturer told the author on the day that John DeLorean's dream collapsed in ruins; 24 hours later

Above left: if there was one concept that divided the 1980s from the 1970s, that concept was aerodynamics. In an age of motorway travelling, the savings in fuel consumption that can be achieved by clean aerodynamic design are remarkable and when Ford conceived the shapely Sierra as a 1980s replacement for the staggeringly successful Cortina it at least looked strikingly different. In time honoured fashion, public reaction to the Sierra shape had been judged through Ford show cars such as the Probe series but, although Sierra was a best seller, Ford had to work very hard to overcome early market resistance

Left: John Zachary DeLorean, having failed to persuade investors in the United States, South America, mainland Europe and the Republic of Ireland to back his ambitious plans to produce his gull-wing sports car, found substantial finance from the British government to build in Northern Ireland. In February 1982 receivers were called in to the troubled Belfast company and shortly after DeLorean himself was arrested in America on

charges of smuggling cocaine – allegedly to raise finance to alleviate his company's debts

Above: many cars have acquired the tag of 'supercar', mostly quite erroneously but in a very few cases with total justification. Very near the top of *any* list of true supercars must come the superb Aston Martin Vantage, of which this is a 1978 example. The Vantage is based on the Aston Martin V8 but has an uprated version of the hand-built all alloy 5.4-litre V8 engine, uprated suspension and subtly revised bodywork for improved high speed stability. With 0–60 mph acceleration in the 5 second bracket and a top speed of over 170 mph all in the utmost luxury, the Vantage is probably the most outstanding remaining example of a Grand Touring car

DeLorean himself was arrested in Los Angeles on drug-smuggling charges, apparently desperately trying to raise the capital to buy time for the doomed company (which had, anyway, started life as a cynical gamble by a minority socialist government anxious to buy Northern Irish MP's support for its survival by creating jobs, even though the Irish Republic, Puerto Rico and the US had all rejected the project as too risky. 'Put your money into wine, women and song,' advised a Wall Street business analyst. 'You'll get the same return but you'll have much better fun!')

The demise of DeLorean emphasised the problems of the specialist car manufacturers in the face of a recession that had added to their many other problems, such as the disproportionately large costs of meeting the increasing tide of safety and emission legislation, much of which represented the whims of national governments rather than genuine progress. But, mostly run by genuine enthusiasts with an unshakeable faith in their products, the specialists seemed remarkably resilient in an increasingly hostile environment, buoyed up by the benevolent interest of the mass manufacturers on whom many of the specialists depended for their power units and transmissions.

One of the most interesting cases is that of Aston Martin, which in its sixty-odd years of existence has built less cars than the US motor industry can make in twenty minutes and changed ownership nine times. Its present owner, Victor Gauntlett, is the head of a petrol company as well as a vintage Bentley enthusiast, who has returned the company to profit by completely altering the company's marketing strategy for its 5.3-litre V8 'musclecars', switching sales into export markets where there has been a resurgence of interest in quality British sports cars. Over half the 1983 output of Aston Martin's 'high-tech' Lagonda luxury car was earmarked for America, where there was felt to be a rich clientele willing to pay around $150,000 for such a sophisticated four-door saloon.

But alongside their high-priced models – total production around 200 cars a year – Aston Martin moved into a totally-different bracket for 1983 with a £14,000 development of the 2.8-litre Ford Capri with a coachbuilt interior allied to aerodynamically-restyled bodywork and a turbocharger installation that boosted the already good performance of the fuel-injected Capri to give a maximum speed 'in excess of' 140 mph.

The engineering of the conversion – carried out by Aston Martin's Tickford division – was aimed at overcoming one of the major disadvantages associated with turbocharging, the fact that on many installations the engine has to be turning fast before the turbo boost comes in. In theory, turbocharging is a 'something-for-nothing' means of increasing the volumetric efficiency of an engine, using the flow of exhaust gases to spin a turbine wheel to force more fuel/air mixture into the cylinder; but as experience teaches us, there is

Left: initially, Audi produced the turbocharged, four-wheel-drive Quattro as a car suitable for its competition programme, specifically for rallying where the combination of high power outputs (near 400 bhp in the most extreme rally guise) and exceptional traction to make that horsepower usable were unbeatable. The Quattro, however, turned into a remarkable success story, for not only did it scare the pants from the rally fraternity but it also transcended the traditional, spartan image of 'homologation special' to become a highly desirable, superbly equipped and *very* quick road car. In 1983 Audi introduced a four-wheel-drive version of the smaller Audi 80, known as the 80 Quattro and announced that four-wheel-drive options would eventually be available throughout the company's range

no way of increasing engine power that has no consequent penalties. So it is with turbocharging: the loads on the mechanical components are increased and greater heat is developed – in some installations, oil jets are directed against the underside of the piston crown to cool it – and, since the exhaust-driven impeller of the turbocharger is 'downstream' of the engine, there has to be an inertial lag in response to the throttle. Equally, because the boost supplied by a centrifugal blower is not directly proportional to its speed of rotation, but increases as the square of that speed (double the revs gives four times the boost), 'wastegates' have to be fitted to dump the excess boost pressure once it exceeds a preset level.

With many turbo installations, nothing much seems to happen below 3000 rpm, when the boost suddenly comes in with a rush, which can make such 'hotshoe' models seem nervous and jerky to drive; in the better installations like the Tickford Capri, particular attention has been paid to low-speed performance so that as low as 2000 rpm, torque is doubled.

One advantage claimed for turbos is that they enhance fuel economy; but, if the performance of the turbo model is used to full advantage, this gain is purely theoretical – because supercharging an engine increases its power output by around 1.5 times, an engine of 2.2 litres with turbocharging would have the power output of a normally aspirated engine of 3.3 litres BUT would use less fuel than the larger engine, even though its consumption was up against a normally aspirated (and therefore less powerful) 2.2-litre . . .

In countries where diesel fuel enjoys a price advantage against petrol, there may be some argument for turbocharged diesel cars, for the turbo puts back some of the 'lost' performance that comes from fitting a diesel engine; but in countries like Great Britain, where taxation makes diesel fuel almost as expensive as petrol, the added cost and complication of the turbo diesel are not justified.

Stripped of the 'economy' arguments, and regarded as a contribution to hedonistic motoring (not yet legislated out of existence, thank goodness), the petrol turbo can offer much to the enthusiastic driver. Some interesting turbo installations appeared in the early 1980s, not the least of them the ingenious Audi Quattro, launched at the 1980 Geneva Show, which, created largely from existing VW/Audi production parts, is a remarkable 200 bhp turbocharged

four-wheel-drive car with outstanding road performance. Far more than a 'homologation special' to qualify its rally derivative for international competition, the Quattro soon attained a production rhythm of ten cars a day.

Another technically-competent turbo installation was that of Saab of Sweden, whose 1982 Automatic Performance Control Turbo incorporated three sensor units to monitor heat, humidity and fuel quality, this information being fed to an electronic 'brain' which analysed it and adjusted the boost level accordingly so that the turbo always operated at maximum efficiency, even on low-grade fuel or in extremely hot or dry conditions.

As for Maserati of Italy, which after various vicissitudes had come under the control of Allessandro de Tomaso, the end of 1982 saw a move towards a more popular slice of the market with the launch of the V6 Biturbo 2-litre, a very different concept from the 4.9-litre Quattroporte which Maserati's Modena factory was turning out at the rate of just two a day. The Biturbo, as its name suggested, had twin turbochargers running at 150,000 rpm to raise the power output of the engine to 180 bhp (against around 103 hp for a normally-aspirated version), yet having low inertia to give good low-speed response with virtually no throttle lag. A technical novelty of the Biturbo engine was the use of two inlet valves of unequal size in each cylinder, the small one for economical cruising and the larger one to admit extra fuel/air mixture through an auxiliary port at wide throttle openings.

That a market existed for such specialised sporting vehicles in the early 1980s must have surprised the professional doomsayers, who had forecast the imminent death of the automobile during the energy crisis of the seventies; they must have been even more surprised by the interest taken by the mass-producers in cars that were fun to drive. This interest ranged from Ford of America's reintroduction of a convertible Mustang in 1982 to the disinterment by BL of the MG name that same year for a sporting derivative of the Metro (inevitably available with a turbocharger).

But perhaps this urge to put some excitement back into motoring was inevitable, given the fierce competition for a share of a market that had just undergone a traumatic recession and was not recovering as quickly as expected, a competition that had evidenced itself in fierce discounting by all major manufacturers in order to move the metal off the dealership forecourts. The creation of exciting variants of those popular models could have a two-fold effect; firstly, it would give the company a distinctive image in the eyes of the buying public and secondly it would widen the available choice of models within the manufacturers' range, so that the customer, once having bought a car of that make would be less inclined to move outside it for his next car purchase.

Whatever the reasons behind the revival of exciting motoring in the eighties in the face of all the odds, it did underline one sure fact; that anyone who confidently predicts the future course of the car industry must be prepared to have his predictions completely confounded by the future turn of events.

Of course modern technology is going to shape the cars of tomorrow; in 1982 the author rode in a prototype whose five-speed gearbox was controlled by an onboard computer which took its instructions from the throttle pedal and the load on the road wheels and selected the appropriate gear and throttle opening for the best economy and road performance, while cars whose ignition advance is gauged by a 'computer map' of optimum ignition points under all road and load conditions are already in the showrooms. So tomorrow's car will incorporate more electronics, and will almost certainly be aerodynamically styled; so much is obvious from the latest cars to have appeared at the time of writing.

Now that manufacturers have learned to cope with the energy crisis, the prospects look remarkably bright. Aided by the most modern technology and spurred by competition, the mass-producers are vying to make their products more desirable. Having been privileged to see some of the proposed designs for the late 1980s and beyond, I can say, with a certain degree of anticipation: 'I have seen the future – and it works!'

Above: after years of absence initially brought on by federal legislation, the soft top returned to American motoring in 1981 with the Dodge 400 convertible, soon to be joined by several others. The automobile had survived the energy crisis and the messages of doom of the legislators and now it was bringing back the message of driving for fun

Left: the car is adopting the technology of the computer age apace. Silicon chip electronics have made possible voice synthesis and electronic instrumentation, both of which appear on the top of the range 'Electronique' TSE models of Renault's excellent 11, the dashboard of which is shown here. The electronic voice conveys warning messages and the digital and graphic displays offer a vast choice of information at the touch of a button. It is as far removed from the mechanical instruments of today as those instruments are from the capillary tubes and glass thermometers of the Edwardians. This *is* the future – and it works!

Chapter 8

The Age of Reason

THE CARS: 1960-83

The decade and a half from 1960 to the mid 1970s saw drastic changes in many aspects of motor racing; the new wave of thinking that began to emerge at the end of the 1950s gathered impetus as the commercial rewards for motor racing snowballed. The old order was rapidly changing: from being a sport, with a playboy image, motor racing was growing into a brash, commercialised and utterly professional business. For all the purists' scorn of the path of modern racing huge financial rewards have bred more intense competition than ever before, spawned innumerable racing car manufacturers and technologists, pushed the state of the art to new frontiers and brought the sport a bigger following than at any time in its history. The revolution can be traced through the cars.

1961 saw the birth of a new formula for Grand Prix cars of a mere 1½ litres, with a ban on supercharging, a minimum dry weight of 450 kg and with commercially available petrol as the obligatory fuel.

The remarkable success of the rear-engined Coopers towards the close of the 2½-litre formula had made a profound impression on the sport, and to even the most conservative observer it was apparent that the days of the front-engined racing car were at an end. The adoption of the 1½-litre formula, and the attendant advantages inherent in its compact mechanical elements, hammered the final nail into the coffin. Already the move to the 'kit-car' had begun, when a competitive engine, in the guise of the Coventry Climax FPF, became freely available. No longer did the building of a Grand Prix car have to begin with the enormous technical and financial resources necessary to

Below: the Lotus 18 was designed as a multi-formula car and was raced in events as diverse as the one-litre Formula Junior and the Grands Prix of the 2.5-litre formula. It had a spaceframe chassis and was clad in aluminium and glassfibre panels. Front suspension was independent by wishbones and coil-spring damper units, and the rear suspension was also independent, by coil springs, transverse links and radius arms. The car illustrated is Rob Walker's Grand Prix 18 which Stirling Moss drove to victory in the 1961 Monaco Grand Prix

Above: Jack Brabham gives the first F1 car to bear his name its debut at the Nürburgring in 1962. The BT3 is seen at the famous little Karussell bend

design and build engine and transmission. The way was open for more constructors to emerge and for chassis development to benefit from the attention that had so long been absorbed in the search for power.

The successes of Vanwall and Cooper had lifted British motor racing from the doldrums in which it had so long languished. Cooper were joined in the revolution by BRM, Lola and Lotus and British Racing Green became a colour to be feared rather than ridiculed. Simplification came to be the path to pursue and the work of designers like Colin Chapman of Lotus brought a new elegance to racing engineering. Although Cooper were the progenitors of the modern rear-engined layout, it was Chapman who realised its greater implications and began the gradual refinement which still continues.

The Lotus 18 made its first appearances in $2\frac{1}{2}$-litre form, under the previous formula, and when the formula changed in 1961 the car was given a $1\frac{1}{2}$-litre, four-cylinder Coventry Climax engine and thrown back into the fray by Rob Walker's private team. It was typical of the position in which the British teams found themselves. When the $1\frac{1}{2}$-litre formula was announced, the British constructors dug in their heels and clung steadfastly to the notion that, by boycotting the new formula, the days of the $2\frac{1}{2}$-litre cars could be extended. The FIA dug in with even more verve and, although they conceded a reduction in the weight limit, from the originally agreed 500 kg to 450 kg, the $1\frac{1}{2}$-litre limit stood. While Lotus, BRM Cooper and, particularly, Coventry Climax procrastinated, Ferrari had forged quietly ahead under the guidance of designer Chiti. Their new Formula One car was built around a massive tubular chassis, like that of the Cooper, with the sting in the tail coming from a 65 degree V6 engine, the Dino 156. In its earliest form this engine gave almost 180 bhp at 9000 rpm, an advantage of some 30 bhp over the ageing Climax four. At Monaco, the wire-wheeled, shark-nostrilled Ferraris appeared with a 120 degree V6, giving another 5 bhp, and only an inspired performance by Moss in a Lotus 18 robbed the new car of victory. While the 18 was showing that it could, in the right hands, still perform miracles, Chapman, with his works cars, was pursuing his quest for lightness, compactness and simplicity. His offering for 1961 was the Lotus 21, which aroused great interest at its debut in Monaco, in the hands of Jim Clark.

In his attempts at further reducing the frontal area – equatable with increasing usable power – Chapman had laid his drivers even lower in the multi-tubular chassis, inclined the engine 18 degrees and moved the front springing inboard of the bodywork, where it was operated by a cantilevered upper wishbone of streamlined section. The rear suspension featured transverse links to relieve the drive shafts of suspension duties and enable rubber doughnut couplings to be utilised at their inboard ends.

413

While the aerodynamic advantages were of little consequence at Monaco, the car soon proved its worth on the faster circuits, scoring Lotus's first ever Grand Prix victory at Watkins Glen. It was clear that when Coventry Climax's new V8 engine appeared, the Lotus would be a force to be reckoned with. The V8 did appear briefly in 1961, being used by both Moss and Brabham, but it was plagued by overheating problems.

Like the FPF it had a stroke to bore ratio of 0.95 with twin, chain-driven, overhead camshafts on each bank. The 90 degree engine had a two-plane crankshaft, which necessitated the use of a crossover exhaust system; this was the only system which could fully utilise the pressure pulses associated with such an engine. Its accommodation was to give chassis designers some severe headaches.

The new BRM V8 unit was also revealed that year, at Monza. For once BRM seemed to be on the right track. This engine was a 90 degree V8, with gear drive to the twin overhead camshafts. A stroke to bore ratio of 0.74 and consequently large piston area promised adequate rewards. The engine had Lucas fuel injection, transistorised ignition and, in spite of its two-plane crank, separate exhaust banks.

For the time being, the challengers to Maranello's superiority had to plod gamely along with outdated designs and the only serious competition came from Moss in the Lotus 18 – more a reflection of his talent than of the car's prowess. Ferrari, of course, won the Championship by a handsome margin.

The second season of the new formula dawned with more promise: Ferrari were now faced with real opposition. Coventry Climax had supplied their new engine to Cooper, the new Brabham team, Lotus, Bowmaker-Lola and Rob Walker. Porsche too had developed an eight-cylinder engine, of flat, air-cooled

Below: Porsche's contribution to the 1½-litre formula was the 804. It featured an air-cooled flat-eight engine of 1498 cc which produced 185 bhp at 9200 rpm. Even though the car won several Grands Prix, its driver likened its performance and handling to that of a roadgoing Volkswagen Beetle

configuration, and BRM had the V8 that was to win them the Championship, in a cliff-hanging finale.

Ferrari themselves had changed the 156 but little, perhaps a sign that the lack of competition had inspired too much confidence. Significantly, the poor showing of the experimental, front-engined, four-wheel-drive Ferguson car in 1961 had not encouraged others to pursue that course. The major bombshell came again from Chapman's fertile brain, in the form of the sensational Lotus 25. This car, which made its debut at Zandvoort, was a milestone; gone was the multi-tubular chassis and in its stead was a tremendously light and rigid aluminium 'monocoque' or, more accurately, stressed-skin chassis with transverse bulkheads. Its success was to sound the death knell of the traditional tubular designs and, if any one car can be so described, the 25 was surely the father of all subsequent Grand Prix cars.

With the exceptional improvement in torsional stiffness that this chassis, with its rigidly mounted engine, offered, Chapman was able to treat the suspension in isolation from the vagaries of the rest of the car. Although little more than half its weight, the 'monocoque' was three times stiffer than the 21's 'spaceframe'. With the driver even more reclined and inboard suspension at the front, the frontal area was down to eight square feet. The rear suspension was by wishbones, radius arms, transverse links and coil spring/damper units.

After a season-long battle with Hill's BRM, Clark needed to take the final race, in South Africa, to win the title. He was beaten by an engine oil leak and BRM were at last on top of the world. Their Championship winner was, in comparison, very conventional. It had a light, compact, multi-tubular chassis with outboard wishbone suspension. Its only distinctive feature was the use of eight individual, upswept exhaust pipes, which earned this P56 the nickname

of the 'Stack-pipe BRM'. By Spa even these individual pipes, which had a tendency to fall off, had been replaced by an integrated system.

Cooper's T60 was memorable more for its looks than its performance and, although McLaren scored a victory for the team at Monaco, their days in the vanguard were over. Porsche too were among the winners in 1962, Gurney won at Rouen and Solitude with the torsion-bar suspended, flat-eight car.

A famous name appeared in the constructors' ranks that year when Jack Brabham introduced the Ron Tauranac designed Brabham BT3 at the Nürburgring. The car was 'British Standard F1', a tubular chassis pushed along by a Climax V8. The only other significant car of the season was Eric Broadley's first F1 Lola, built for Reg Parnell's Bowmaker Finance team. With John Surtees at the wheel it scored two seconds and several lesser placings, but it was to be the last F1 Lola until 1974.

1963 was the year of Jim Clark and the Lotus 25, the much modified car helping Clark to seven victories from ten Grands Prix. It was Lotus's first constructor's title and Clark's first Drivers' Championship. No one had expected that things could have been different. The Coventry Climax engine had been redesigned with a single-plane crankshaft, allowing the use of a much simpler exhaust system, and a stroke to bore ratio of 0.76 – improvements which netted 195 bhp at 9500 rpm. Its only opposition came from Hill's BRM P56, which won in Monaco and the USA, and from the latest Ferrari. The 156B still had a tubular frame, but with a new body, suspension and – at last – alloy wheels. The 120 degree V6 boasted Bosch fuel injection and four valves per cylinder. Surtees rewarded Ferrari with victory at the Nürburgring. The company also revealed a new car with a monocoque chassis and V8 engine. This was the car in which Surtees was to capture the 1964 World Championship. Although Ferrari were to rely on the V8 for the following year, too, 1964 also saw them reveal the flat-twelve-engined type 512. The engine in this latter car used the engine as an integral part of the chassis, a practice which was later to become universal.

The Coventry Climax was now producing marginally over 200 bhp with a further reduction of stroke to bore ratio to 0.63; the addition of four-valve cylinder heads took the output to 210 bhp for 1965. Either Lotus or BRM could have taken the 1964 championship in the final round, Lotus with the latest version of the 33 or BRM with their monocoque type 261. The 61 had been introduced in 1963 and was notable for its use of a full monocoque, which extended over the drivers legs and behind his shoulders, in contrast to most other manufacturers' linked-pontoon types. For 1964, the 261 monocoque extended right back around the engine, but on some four-valve cars this had to be cut away to accommodate the exhaust system! Also in 1964 a young BRM engineer, Mike Pilbeam, had experimented with a four-wheel-drive car, based on a P56 chassis and designated P67, but four-wheel drive was again rejected as a failure.

Above: the engine of the 1961 World Championship winning Ferrari was designed for the new 1½-litre formula by Carlo Chiti. The cars started the season with a 65 degree V6 unit, the Dino 156, running on carburettors and producing 180 bhp at 9000 rpm. This was soon replaced by a 120 degree V6, a fuel injected version of which is shown here. It is also interesting to note the massive tubular chassis and Ferrari's continued use of wire wheels.

1965, the final year of the 1½-litre formula, saw Lotus dominant again, with the latest 33 winning six races for Clark. BRM relied once again on updated P261s, which often proved to be the fastest cars of all. With the induction tracts between the camshafts, the V8 was now able to better 210 bhp.

The swansong of the formula was to have been a flat-16 engine from Coventry Climax, for Lotus, Brabham and Cooper only. This FWMW had a crankshaft compounded of two separate single-plane units, phased at 90 degrees to each other and joined by a central, spur gear, driving the eight cams and all ancillaries. This effectively divided the engine into four banks and demanded four separate cylinder heads. Although the engine showed 220 bhp at 12,000 rpm on test, it never raced, as the company withdrew from the sport, for financial reasons.

While Climax tested the FWMW, the final race was being won by possibly the most powerful and imaginative car of the formula, the Honda V12. The Japanese motor cycle company had revealed their car at the Nürburgring in 1964. Extensive use of needle roller bearings, common to motor cycle practice, allowed up to 13,000 rpm, and large piston area and four valves per cylinder

Top: BRM's 1.5-litre V8 on the testbed. This was the company's final shot at the one-and-a-half litre formula which ended in 1965. The engine used fuel injection and produced 200 bhp at over 11,000 rpm

Above: everything finally clicked for BRM in 1962 when Graham Hill captured the World Championship in this Type 56. Powered by a 1498 cc V8 engine, this car marked the beginning of a four-year run of success for the marque

coaxed from it a reputed 230 bhp, on Keihin carburettors and coil ignition. This engine and a six-speed gearbox were mounted transversely in the monocoque chassis, which featured inboard front suspension. The beautifully prepared car's undoubted speed silenced most sceptics.

Far from being dull and underpowered, the cars of the 1½-litre formula had provided fast, close and technically fascinating racing. In five brief years, Grand Prix design particularly of chassis, tyres and suspension, had made huge strides. No less than 22 ostensibly separate makes had attempted to qualify for World Championship races in the period, and a handful of them will long be remembered.

It remains a matter for conjecture what stirring contests might have ensued between the V12 Honda, flat-12 Ferraris and the Climax flat-16 Lotuses *et al* had the formula not changed again for 1966.

The new rules were heralded as 'The return of power'. Engine capacity had

been doubled, to a maximum of 3 litres, while a category for supercharged engines (of $1\frac{1}{2}$-litres) made a return. The minimum weight limit was raised by only 50 kg – to the 500 kg limit which was originally envisaged for the $1\frac{1}{2}$-litre formula – and the requirements for use of pump petrol and open wheels remained. One might have been forgiven for thinking that after the fiasco of the start of the previous regulations perhaps this occasion would have found the teams in a better state of readiness. It was not so. Although the new formula had been announced in 1963, the withdrawal of Coventry Climax had left most of the 'kit car' teams in a sorry predicament, and once again they were faced with a situation of compromise. Ferrari, of course, were more ready than most. Their new car was based on a scaled up $1\frac{1}{2}$-litre-type chassis, carrying a V12 of a full 3 litres. The engine used two valves per cylinder and fuel injection in the centre of the Vee. The chassis was a semi-monocoque, with stressed panelling on a tubular structure. The 312 initially looked as though it might follow the path of the 156 of five years earlier, but reliability proved not to be its strong suit.

Full 3-litre cars were few and far between in the first season but the ones that were around were technically interesting. Following in the path of fellow Antipodean Brabham as a constructor, Bruce McLaren entered the arena with a very interesting machine. The chassis of the first McLaren was usual in that it was of monocoque configuration, but rather than the traditional riveted and bonded aluminium panelling, this car employed an aviation-type material called Mallite. This consisted of two much thinner aluminium skins sandwiching a core of balsa wood, with the grains running from face to face, the whole being bonded together into an enormously light and stiff sheet. The very advanced chassis which was thus built up was unfortunately let down by the lack of power from the de-stroked Indianapolis Ford engine which propelled it. While losing 1.2 litres from its original 4.2, the engine unfortunately lost much of its specific output and very little of its excess weight.

The season was to belong to the man in whose footsteps McLaren was following, Black Jack Brabham himself. In slightly opportunist vein, Brabham and Tauranac penned the BT20, a simple spaceframe chassis with even simpler outboard springing all round and of the smallest dimensions possible. Into this they fitted their master stroke, a cheap, light and unusually simple V8 engine built by the Australian Repco organisation around the bones of a mass-production Oldsmobile V8. The engine had all the right basic ingredients, with a very short stroke and single-plane crankshaft; the addition of single-overhead-camshaft cylinder heads, with two valves per cylinder, netted an initial 285 bhp at 8000 rpm. That in itself was far from spectacular, but in such a mild state of tune the engine had a wide spread of usable power, lots of torque and a miserly thirst for fuel. Capitalising on this simplicity the two Australians made the car by far the lightest on the grids and one of the most reliable. The car took the Championship with consummate ease.

Left : the 36-valve V12 engined Ferraris of Ludovico Scarfiotti and Mike Parkes at Monza before their first and second place triumph in the 1966 Italian Grand Prix. Scarfiotti was the first Italian to win his home Grand Prix since Ascari in 1952

Below : the screaming 3-litre Honda RA273 made its debut at the 1966 Italian Grand Prix. Its engine was a large, 60° V12 four-cam unit with four valves per cylinder. Drive was taken from the centre of the crankshaft to negate whip, and this heavy engine produced 430 bhp at 11,000 rpm. Richie Ginther was lucky to escape unhurt when the car crashed at high speed during the race. Its best showing was at Mexico City when Ginther finished fourth and set fastest lap.

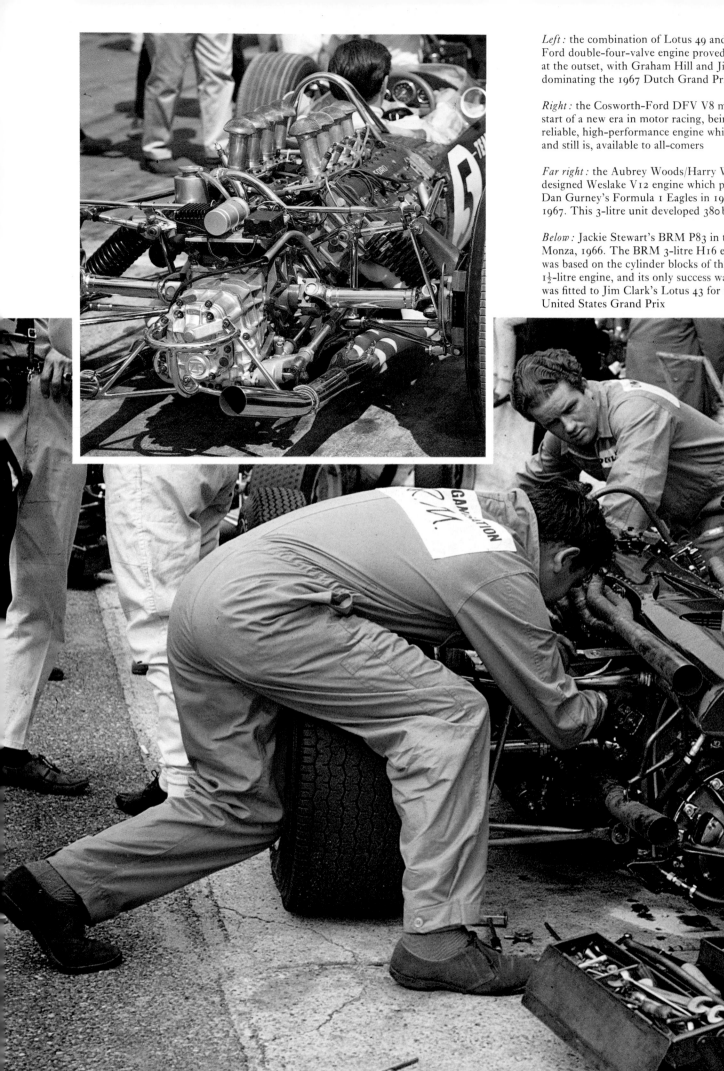

Left : the combination of Lotus 49 and Cosworth-Ford double-four-valve engine proved unbeatable at the outset, with Graham Hill and Jim Clark dominating the 1967 Dutch Grand Prix

Right : the Cosworth-Ford DFV V8 marked the start of a new era in motor racing, being a reliable, high-performance engine which was, and still is, available to all-comers

Far right : the Aubrey Woods/Harry Weslake designed Weslake V12 engine which powered Dan Gurney's Formula 1 Eagles in 1966 and 1967. This 3-litre unit developed 380 bhp.

Below : Jackie Stewart's BRM P83 in the pits at Monza, 1966. The BRM 3-litre H16 engine was based on the cylinder blocks of the old $1\frac{1}{2}$-litre engine, and its only success was when it was fitted to Jim Clark's Lotus 43 for the 1966 United States Grand Prix

Of the others, Lotus initially relied on yet another development of the 33, whose superior handling could not compensate for the paucity of power of its 2-litre Climax or BRM engines. BRM themselves started the season with 2.1-litre versions of the P261, using a 2070cc, 270 bhp engine, developed for the Tasman series. It was enough to give Stewart victory in the opening race but thereafter every race was won by a 3-litre car. BRM's own 3-litre was another 16-cylinder concoction, with a reputation akin to that of their first example. Aero-engine thinking had been cribbed to make a 16-cylinder unit short enough for rear mounting; two flat-eight units were mounted one atop the other, with their two crankshafts coupled to a common output. Use of major components from the successful V8 should have ensured both power and reliability but, owing to severe vibrational problems, neither was forthcoming. The most power ever seen from the unit was 420 bhp – far short of target – and its most memorable characteristic was sudden and violent self destruction. BRM used the engine as a stressed, suspension-carrying unit in the monocoque P83 car but the H16's only success came in a Lotus 43 chassis, at Watkins Glen, with Clark driving.

Three other full 3-litre cars appeared in 1966. Having started the season with a Coventry Climax 2.7-litre four, Dan Gurney's All American Racers' Eagle appeared at Monza with an all new V12 engine, designed by Harry Weslake and Aubrey Woods. Both car and 380 bhp engine were beautifully made and very purposeful.

Cooper began the season with 3-litre engines in their T81s, by courtesy of Maserati. Unfortunately, the sports-car-derived V12s were massive and thirsty and gave only 320 bhp to propel the equally bulky 'bathtub' monocoque chassis. The car was developed to some extent during the season and won the final race in Mexico. The Cooper may have been heavy but the latest Honda was even more so. To compensate, their V12 engine was again the most powerful of all. It was of 90 degree, four-camshaft configuration, with induction between the cams and a tangle of exhaust pipes emerging from between the cylinder heads. Honda claimed 420 bhp and, again, none argued, but the power was wasted on the grossly overweight chassis.

Some of the cars of 1966 were effective but there was little sophistication; the real technical advances came from the tyre industry. After several years of near monopoly, with their R5, 6 and 7 designs, Dunlop suddenly had competition, from the radical ideas of American manufacturers Firestone and Goodyear. The wide, concave-moulded, low-profile tyres which then emerged were the forerunners of the huge slicks of the mid seventies.

1967 was the most significant year in recent racing history: it marked the genesis of the Ford-financed Cosworth DFV V8 engine which filled the void left by Climax's departure. The engine was to dominate F1 racing for many seasons to come.

Again it fell to Chapman to set the trend: for 1967, the DFV was available exclusively to Lotus. The Lotus-Ford 49 made its bow in Holland, and a spectacular bow it was. The car itself was a logical development of previous

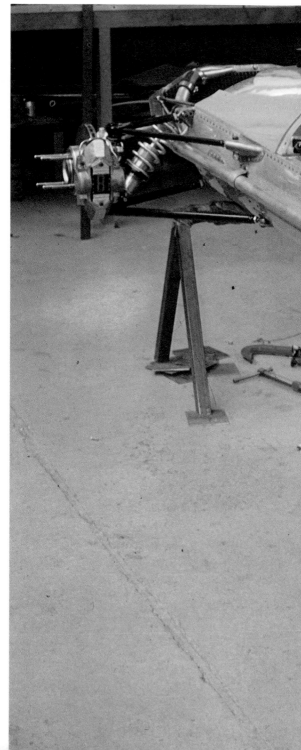

Left: the complexity of the 1968 Matra MS11's V12 engine made it a difficult car to develop. With the original six-pipe exhaust system the V12 was a good match for early DFVs in terms of power but not tractability: with this later, four-pipe, system flexibility improved but maximum power suffered as a consequence

Below: McLaren were among the first to join the Ford–Cosworth DFV users after the engine became generally available in 1968. This M7A, taking shape at the McLaren works, shows the use of the DFV as a stressed unit on the monocoque

Lotuses, with refinements aimed at better handling and brake cooling; the engine, which was suspension bearing and fully stressed, bolted directly onto the vertical back of the abbreviated monocoque. It was straightforward and beautifully conceived; individually, car and engine were interesting, together they were sensational. At Zandvoort Hill took pole position and Clark won the race. The writing was on the wall.

Although the 49 was dominant throughout 1967, reliability cost it the results that it promised, and it was the Repco Brabham that emerged again as champion. The Eagle won in Belgium and the Honda, now with a Lola-inspired chassis and Surtees driving, won in Italy. Everthing else was shared between Lotus and Brabham.

For 1968, the DFV was available to all-comers and, at last, the constructors had access to an engine which was a match for any other. Examples were quickly snapped up by McLaren for their M7A, and by Matra, to be used pending completion of their own V12. The only intruder into a Ford grand slam was Jacky Ickx, with the latest Ferrari 312, with a four-valve V12. This car won at Rouen, where the Honda was second. Honda also produced an air-

cooled, V8-engined car at that race but Jo Schlesser crashed it, with fatal results, after the engine cut out on the fast downhill sweeps. No further cars were built.

BRM abandoned the H16 in favour of the ubiquitous V12, which also found its way into the Cooper T86B. That car and the Alfa Romeo-engined T86C were the last of the Coopers. Honda's ambitions in F1 seemed to die with Schlesser and the Eagles returned to their USAC eyrie in 1968. After Clark's tragic death at Hockenheim, Hill's capture of the world title was a much needed morale booster for Lotus. The 1968 car was the 49B, a long wheelbase development of the 49.

Technically, 1968 was most significant for the proliferation of fins, spoilers and, ultimately, huge, moveable, suspension-mounted aerofoils, on both ends of many cars. Several near tragedies, directly attributable to these devices, led to their size and location being strictly limited by new regulations. While rules on wings had been tightened up, limits on advertising on cars were relaxed and racing took on a colourful new face.

1969 saw a clean sweep by Ford-powered cars, the DFV being used by everyone except BRM, Ferrari and the Matra prototype. Stewart took the Championship for the Ken Tyrrell run Matra-Ford team. Lotus, Brabham (with the BT26A) and McLaren (with the M7A) all won rounds; in spite of the new wing and safety regulations – which demanded fire extinguisher systems and leak proof fuel tanks, and increased the minimum weight limit to allow for them – lap speeds were generally quicker.

Interesting from a technical standpoint was the appearance of four-wheel-drive cars from Matra, McLaren, Lotus and Cosworth. Again, the system was not the sought for panacea. The McLaren M9 made only one race appearance and the Matra MS84 was overshadowed by the conventional car. The Robin Herd designed Cosworth was a strange looking device which never reached fruition. The possible advantages of four-wheel drive could now be reproduced by much simpler, and cheaper, aerodynamic means – without the penalties of extra weight, power losses and unpredictable handling. Even Chapman's four-wheel-drive venture was short lived. The Lotus 63 owed much of its design to the 1968, turbine-powered, Indianapolis car and was a stop gap, pending the introduction of a similarly powered Grand Prix car. The Matra MS84 and the Brabham BT26 were the last tubular-framed cars to appear in Grand Prix racing.

Having taken a back seat in 1969, Chapman yet again rocked the establishment in 1970 with his type 72. By relocating the radiators at the sides of the cockpit, Chapman was able to give the car a distinctive wedge shaped profile, with low polar moment of inertia and tremendous aerodynamic efficiency. The rest of the car was equally novel; suspension and brakes were both inboard and the suspension medium was torsion bars. Few people could have foreseen the extraordinarily long competitive life that lay ahead of the 72.

Left: the Tyrrell 001 as it appeared at its auspicious debut in 1970 when Jackie Stewart set fastest lap in the non-championship Oulton Park Gold Cup, before retiring. In 1971, Stewart won six Grands Prix in this car and took the World Championship. The hammerhead shaped nose-cone, which still housed the radiator, was intended to reduce the drag imposed by the ever-widening front tyres and produce down thrust

Below: the trend-setting Maurice Phillipe/Colin Chapman designed Lotus 72 as it first appeared in 1970, at the start of its five-year racing career. Featuring such attributes as a smooth ride, excellent traction through torsion bar suspension, good aerodynamics with its wedge-shaped body, and inboard mounted disc brakes, the car was driven to victory in four Grands Prix in 1970, enough to give Jochen Rindt the World Championship. Sadly, Rindt was killed at Monza whilst trying for a greater maximum speed by running the car without aerofoils

The first four races of the season went to four different marques, including Lotus, but the sequence of successes in mid season by Rindt and the 72 were enough to secure the title, even though Rindt was killed in Italy with three rounds remaining. After Rindt's death, the flat-12-engined Ferrari 312B became the car to beat. Only Fittipaldi with the Lotus 72 succeeded.

Three new marques appeared in 1970. Amid a blaze of publicity, March entered the arena with both works and privately entered cars. Most significant was Ken Tyrrell's example for World Champion Stewart. Other than its use of aerofoil section side fuel tanks, the March 701 was quite conventional. Tyrrell himself was already at work on one of the best kept secrets in racing; at the Canadian Grand Prix Tyrrell 001 started from pole position. It was an auspicious debut. Slightly less successful was the Surtees TS7, another offering from a driver turned constructor.

For 1971, designer Derek Gardner refined 001 and produced 002 and 003. The car's bulbous aluminium monocoque was designed to keep the fuel load central and the cars were distinguished by wide, shovel noses, designed to give maximum downthrust. The final form of the nose also improved top

Right: the March 711 chassis was designed by Robin Herd, with bodywork influenced by Frank Costin. The car handled well but the engine cooling was not particularly efficient and the car was usually raced in 1971 without the engine cover and radiator ducting

Below: the Ralph Bellamy designed McLaren M19B with its rising-rate front suspension took first place in the 1972 South African Grand Prix, giving Denny Hulme and the McLaren team their first Grand Prix win since 1969

speed and stability. Others were quick to copy but the originators reaped the rewards, with Stewart taking his second championship. One of the tweaks tried on the cars during the season was an ingenious double-disc-brake system, with floating calipers, but its advantages were dubious.

March's 711 caused quite a stir, with its aerodynamic, Frank Costin-designed, body. Although the design was very effective in wind tunnel testing, it suffered badly in the turbulent company of other cars.

1971 saw a revival for BRM, with two mid-season victories for their P160, V12-engined cars. The only other winner was the Ferrari 312B2, whose ever improving flat-12 engine was now giving around 460 bhp. The car briefly featured troublesome inboard rear suspension. The Matra MS120B was very quick on occasion but driver Amon's luck was as bad as ever. Brabham's 'lobster claw' BT34, with split front radiators introduced an interesting new shape but had little success.

Probably the most interesting car which will be seen under the 3-litre formula was the Lotus 56B of 1971. This, the world's first gas-turbine-powered Grand Prix car, was a direct descendant of the Type 56 Indianapolis car, which came within an ace of winning the 500 in 1968. The 56B used a Pratt and Whitney STN6/76 turbine to a 3-litre equivalency, determined principally on intake area. Power was transmitted to the four-wheel-drive system through a 2-inch wide Morse chain and two pedal control was all that was required. The chassis was a complex monocoque wedge with brakes and suspension inboard all round. The car's main drawback was one of controllability, or lack of it. The 450 bhp turbine suffered a lag in throttle response, committing the driver to making all his judgements in advance. More important, it offered no engine braking, putting the onus on the car's massive ventilated disc brakes. With the Lotus 72 far from outclassed, the 56B was quietly shelved.

1972 was a hard fought season from which Chapman emerged with his bi-annual championship, the 72D taking five victories to Tyrrell's four. The interlopers in the Lotus/Tyrrell show were Ferrari, McLaren – with the M19A, featuring rising rate suspension – and BRM. BRM's victory was more a result of Beltoise's brilliance in the wet at Monaco than of the car's competitiveness.

March had an innovative but dismally unsuccessful season. Their search for a low polar moment of inertia car led to the 721X, on which Herd mounted the gearbox between the engine and the final drive. Enforced use of Alfa Romeo mechanicals prevented a direct comparison with its competitors. This 721X was superseded by the 721G, based on the firm's successful F2 design. Also on the scene in 1972 with varying levels of success were the Matra MS120C, with a very wide and flat chassis and a magnificent engine note, but no luck, and the Tecno, whose flat-12 engine drew obvious comparisons with its Italian compatriot.

Stewart and Tyrrell were back in the ascendancy in 1973; Gardner's 006

Left: the office from where Jackie Stewart worked to get the 1973 World Championship, his Tyrrell 006. Unlike the days of yesteryear when drivers sat on top of their machines, the modern Grand Prix driver is strapped very securely into his car: with cornering forces of over 2g, the driver would collapse with fatigue and exhaustion if he had to physically sit upright in the car without being held. In fact, all movements by the pilot in a car like this have to be kept to a minimum and here it is almost possible to change gear without letting go of the steering wheel. Also to make things easier, the gauges are set in such a way that all the needles are vertical when things are going right. That way, the driver will subconsciously notice that something is wrong whereas the instruments will be 'ignored' if everything is in order. However, the basic driving technique has not changed much from the very earliest days and, when it comes down to basics, the driver has to get the car as fast as possible through corners, using honed reactions, skill and no small amount of guts. That applies to both the flat-capped and goggled pioneers of the last century and the flame-proof cocooned motor racing executives of the present day

design took five victories, in a season dominated by three Ford-powered makes – Tyrrell, Lotus and McLaren. 006 was a typical Tyrrell, with a wedge-shaped monocoque, side radiators and the highest of high airboxes – designed to collect cool undisturbed air from above the body-induced turbulence. It was a year of elation and tragedy for Tyrrell, the championship success being tempered by Stewart's retirement and Cevert's death in America. The remarkable Lotus 72D again provided most of the opposition but McLaren's new M23 proved to be very quick. The Gordon Coppuck designed car was very much a second generation Lotus 72, embodying the side radiator, wedge layout of that car. The latest regulations demanded wider deformable structures on the flanks of the cars and the M23 used these to good effect to achieve excellent aerodynamic penetration. The M23 was to share another feature with the Lotus 72, its long competitive life.

Involvement from America returned with the appearance of the UOP Shadow DN1, designed by former Eagle and BRM man Tony Southgate. The young Englishman Lord Alexander Hesketh entered James Hunt in a March 731, looked over by the former March designer Dr Harvey Postlethwaite; the car proved consistently faster than several works entered cars.

At the end of 1973, Hesketh announced that the team would build their own car and V12 engine for the following season. Although the engine never materialised, the Postlethwaite designed Hesketh 308, bearing a fair resemblance to the March, did.

Much driver shuffling in the closed season saw Emerson Fittipaldi in the latest McLaren M23. In a season where McLaren tried numerous variations of track, wheelbase and aerodynamics, Fittipaldi emerged as 1974 champion. It was one of the most competitive seasons ever: McLarens took only four of the season's fifteen races, the rest being shared between Brabham, Ferrari, Lotus and Tyrrell. Brabham's winner was one of the most attractive cars of the whole formula, the BT44 designed by Gordon Murray. In this car, Murray had used a monocoque with sloping sides whose angle matched that of the cam covers of the DFV engine, resulting in a beautifully neat and compact car. The Ferrari team was at last emerging from the doldrums and the performances of the 312B3s were more impressive than their results record. The car had been constantly developed around the very powerful flat-12 engine, until it had superb traction and handling to match its near 500 bhp. Lotus's wins came once again from the 72, now in 72E guise, the team having quietly abandoned the revolutionary Lotus 76. That car was introduced with an automatic clutch and split, two-footed brake pedal. These features and a two-tier wing which was on the original car were soon dropped and the team reverted to the ever faithful 72. Tyrrell's fortunes seemed to take a turn for the better with the introduction of 007, which was again a development rather than a revolution. 1974 was a year which saw many other new cars, none with much distinction and all built to virtually the same formula of simple monocoque chassis and Cosworth engine, the major differences being in the aerodynamics of the cars. One that did stand out a little way from the crowd was the BRM P201, another slope-sided monocoque, this time using a V12 engine, and flattering in its early performances only to deceive. Attempts at breaking into Grand Prix racing at the bottom end of the financial scale, by teams such as Token and the disastrous Japanese Maki, foundered rapidly. Even the reasonably wealthy, Frank Williams run, Iso team found it very hard to break into the big league. The emergence of two new American teams, Parnelli and Penske came too near to the end of the season to show much other than that the cars were totally conventional and superbly presented.

All Ferrari's earlier promise finally netted the results in 1975 and Niki Lauda took the world championship away from the Ford-powered cars for the first time since 1968, once more fuelling the longstanding pronostications that the DFV's reign was over. The introduction of the Ferrari 312T marked the beginning of a long run of successes for the Maranello *marque*. The outstanding feature of the 312T was its use of a transversely mounted gearbox, yet another variation on the low polar moment theme, but this time one that worked. One other car that looked as though it was on the road to success was the latest Shadow, the DN5; a sterling performance in Argentina, in practice, and another in the Brazilian race were highspots in an otherwise frustrating season. New cars appeared from Lola, Ensign, Frank Williams and the Brazilian Copersucar team, formed by Wilson Fittipaldi. The return of Lola to F1 was not a successful one and before the end of the season the Hill team, which was running their cars, had built their own contender. Alas the potential of the team was never fully realised as the key personnel, including Hill and the designer Andy Smallman, were killed in a flying accident in November 1975.

The Hesketh team's swansong was the 308C which made its debut in Italy. The car featured an extremely shallow monocoque tub with the fuel load carried centrally, and low line air intakes which anticipated the 1976 rules, which banned high air boxes. Alas, the Hesketh team were to be disbanded at the end of 1975 and the car was never developed to the extent it deserved.

Before the end of the 1975 season, Tyrrell dropped a bombshell when he revealed his new car – known then as Project 34 – to a disbelieving world; Project 34 had six wheels. Far from being the publicity grabber that many dubbed it, P34 was developed over the closed season and the early part of 1976 to be among the top three competitors. Gardner's thinking in providing the car with four mini-sized front wheels was to maintain – or even improve – the tyre contact area and consequently braking and steering power, with a reduction in frontal area to give a higher top speed. When early brake-cooling and setting-up problems had been overcome the car showed that its major advantage was that the narrow front track allowed the drivers to go much deeper into the corners before turning in, allowing them to brake a little later and harder. Perspex windows in the cockpit sides, to allow the drivers to see the tiny wheels, also let spectators in on the fact that the six-wheeler was something of a handful to drive. Whether P34 would have been quicker than a newly developed conventional Tyrrell is a matter for conjecture but several other teams were rumoured to be thinking along similar lines. The other departure from the wheel on each corner theme came from March whose 1977 car featured four small rear wheels, all driven. The advantage was again supposed to be aerodynamic, aimed at producing a smooth airflow underneath the rear wing, as well as above.

Even without the six-wheelers, 1976 was a year with plenty of interest on the machinery front. Ferrari brought a de Dion suspension system back into racing for the first time since the mid fifties, on the rear of their 312T cars. A de Dion front end was tried, too, but not raced. Colin Chapman's interest had turned towards building a fully adjustable car that could be changed quite dramatically in track and wheelbase to suit various circuits. The car originally had a complex front suspension system with the brake calipers in the air stream between the wheels and the body and acting as an intermediate suspension upright. During the season the car was gradually simplified and became

Right: Lord Hesketh, James Hunt and the 1975 Hesketh 308C; the car was very low, apart from the turret-like cockpit, and featured rubber springing. After the demise of the racing team from Easton Neston, the Frank Williams equipe took over the project

Below right: Vittorio Brambilla's March 751 of 1975. While other manufacturers were striving to build more advanced cars, March made their car as simple as possible. When it held together, it was faster than most in a straight line

Below: March in 1977 surprised many by deciding to take the six-wheel route, although they differed in having four of theirs driven. It was quickly adaptable to the more normal four-wheeled configuration, they hastened to add

competitive, winning the final race of the season to restore some faith in Lotus's flagging fortunes.

Two 'new' engines made their bow with Brabham introducing the BT45, designed around the Alfa Romeo flat-12 unit, and the Ligier team making an impressive debut with their Matra engined car. The Ligier-Matra JS5 was originally dubbed the 'Flying Teapot' because of its enormously high airbox but that soon disappeared in deference to the new regulations and the car proved extremely quick. The Alfa-engined Brabham was less successful, occasional bursts of speed being wasted by a notorious lack of reliability.

New cars abounded during the season but all the others were very ordinary offerings which were rewarded with varying degrees of success. The four-wheeled Marches were very quick and very unreliable; the new Copersucar did not reward Emerson's faith with any speed; and the new Surtees TS19 was disappointing after an extremely promising early showing. One high spot was Mo Nunn's showing with his shoestring-budgeted Ensign team who ran a very economical and simple chassis with results that often embarrassed the bigger teams. A sign of things to come may also have been seen at the final round of the championship at Mount Fuji where James Hunt clinched the title with his McLaren M23, leaving the M26 to make its real debut in 1977: among the quicker cars at Fuji were local entries – promising to be back.

Formula One now has such a crowded calendar that making real changes to the cars in mid season is a thing of the past, steady development is all that can now be undertaken. In spite of regular rumours, the day of the big manufacturer is over and the face of motor racing is very different from the earliest days.

Above: McLaren's successor to their twice world championship winning M23 was the M26, introduced in July 1976. The M26 owed much to designer Gordon Coppuck's aircraft design experience. Like the first Grand Prix McLaren, the monocoque tub of this car utilised composite materials in its construction. Unlike the Mallite, aluminium/balsa sandwich, used on the M3, the material used on the M26 was an all aluminium sheet and honeycomb sandwich. The driver protection structures used Nomex honeycomb material. The major suspension features of the M23 were retained but the new car had less frontal area and weight plus considerably more rigidity

Below: putting six wheels on the Tyrrell P34 was a brave departure from the norm, which met with mixed fortune over two seasons of racing. In the 1976 Swedish Grand Prix the cars romped home first and second, but in 1977 they simply couldn't make the best of the latest Goodyear rubber

Bottom: the Wolf WR1 came from the pen of former March and Hesketh designer Dr Harvey Postlethwaite and was a straightforward offering with an aerodynamically efficient shape, outboard suspension, and side radiators. In deference to saving weight, the bodywork was made in Kevlar and carbon fibre – claimed to save 20lbs in comparison with the more commonly used glassfibre

In spite of its early introduction, protracted testing and use of aircraft inspired honeycomb chassis materials, the M26 was a late developer. Hunt put the M23 (latterly fitted with driver adjustable rear anti-roll bars) on pole three times before the M26 made its race debut in Spain. The car's main problem was in the steering, which was heavy and inclined to severe understeer. By mid-season, suspension changes and a switch to front radiators made the M26 a formidable weapon in Hunt's hands.

1977, however, was not to be dominated by any one car—at least not in terms of results—and it was the newest team of all which opened the scoring. The Wolf WR1 was designed by ex-March and Hesketh man Harvey Postlethwaite and was a thoroughly conventional Ford kit car, blessed with excellent traction and the ministrations of a dedicated team. Its debut win in Argentina probably owed more to Scheckter's fitness than to the car's outright speed, but it is significant that – aside from engine breakages – the team did not suffer a single mechanical failure all season.

After two doubles – for the Ferrari 312T-2 in Brazil and South Africa and for the remarkable Lotus 78 in Long Beach and Spain – Scheckter took the original WR1 chassis to a memorable win at Monte Carlo, marking an unsurpassed century of victories for the splendid Cosworth DFV.

In its ten year history, the DFV had powered eight World Champions and taken seven constructors' titles. It had scored more points and more fastest laps than any other engine in the history of the Championship. From around 408 bhp in 1967, its output had risen to a touch over 480 bhp a decade later. Most important of all, it had undoubtedly kept Grand Prix racing within financial reach of more than a privileged few, had shaped the whole character of the sport throughout the 'seventies and, it might be argued, saved a branch of racing otherwise doomed by spiralling costs.

Cosworth, however, were not without their problems, and their fortunes played an important role in a highly competitive season. In the face of increasing opposition from the Ferrari, Alfa and Matra twelves, Cosworth made available to Lotus, Tyrrell and McLaren a total of nine 'development' engines. These had various features, including magnesium heads and cam

Left and below: the start of the revolution. The Lotus 78 used a very narrow monocoque chassis, housing most of the fuel between the driver and the engine and flanked by the aerofoil section side structures revealed here by the removal of the side plates. The radiators were mounted in the leading edges of the 'wings' and air flow was kept under the car by flexible skirts which bridged the gap between the side plates and the ground. Chapman's 'wing car' not surprisingly soon brought a host of imitators, but by the time they had arrived on the scene Lotus had taken the idea another step forward . . .

carriers on some engines, giving a two per cent power increase and, more important, a nineteen pound weight saving. Alas, longevity was not the engines' forte and on too many occasions they cost their users valuable points as they failed.

One of the development engine users was unquestionably the car of the year. It was the Lotus 78, and, as so often before, with it Colin Chapman introduced a new concept, brilliant in its simplicity and devastating in its efficacy. The 78 brought a new term to the Grand Prix glossary: wing car. By building the chassis as narrow as possible and locating all the fuel in the centre of the car, behind the driver, Chapman was able to use the whole of the car's side pod area to good aerodynamic effect. In essence the side structures were large inverted aerofoils, carrying the cooling systems and supplemented by flexible skirts to keep the airflow over the lower, working, surface. The 78 incorporated lessons of weight distribution learned from the later developments of the 77, moving more weight (including the oil radiator) to the front to help in generating efficient front tyre temperatures. It also featured such niceties as an oil tank incorporated within the engine bellhousing, which also held an annular clutch slave cylinder, and a Salisbury-type differential which, on occasion, could be run virtually as a locked unit. Lotus's own gearbox proved troublesome however and the car relied mostly on the trusty Hewland FG400. Just as the 25 and 72 before it, the 78 was destined to spawn a host of imitators.

Also among the winners, of course, were the 312T-2 Ferraris and it was with this car that Niki Lauda was to take his second World Championship. He was also to notch up the season's second winning century, this time for Goodyear tyres who had opened their account through Ritchie Ginther way back in the 1965 Mexican Grand Prix. It was in a way ironic that a Ferrari should score Goodyear's hundredth win, for relations between the two companies were becoming very strained. Ferrari owed their success much more to the strength of the flat-twelve engine than to the cars' handling, which for most of 1977 was dreadful. Characteristically, and in this case perhaps with some justification, the Maranello company could not shoulder the blame for such inadequacies and pointed the finger at Goodyear. The root of the problem was that Lotus now dictated tyre parameters and the smooth way in which the 78 got on with the job allowed it to use a much softer – hence grippier – compound than the rest. Ferrari made no secret of his pique and was soon to be seen talking to other possible tyre suppliers – backed no doubt by the size of the potential Fiat market.

For their part, Goodyear had played a role as important in its way as that of Cosworth, creating general availability and being fundamental in most development work. The company's test and development programme was a major part of the sport by the mid 'seventies. The Vehicle Dynamics Programme, instituted in 1975, set out to lend testing more of a scientific basis.

Above: the 1977 World Champion, Niki Lauda, in the Ferrari 312 T-2. The lusty and reliable flat-twelve engine, transverse gearbox, and wide monocoque gave the car a very square configuration in plan

With the aid of applied mathematician and polymer scientist Karl Kempf, a means of interpreting and recording the cars' dynamic behaviour through on-board instrumentation was evolved.

Goodyear's development programme and their advice to circuit owners on eliminating some of the causes of punctures led to much closer racing with less of an element of chance about it. Their testing sessions and their own test facility in Luxembourg speeded chassis development for many a team.

To Goodyear's credit, the company did not abuse the monopolistic situation, but in a highly competitive sport there was a natural frustration in having no-one else to beat. Japanese Dunlop and Bridgestone tyres had made a brief incursion into the Goodyear monopoly at Fuji in 1976 but a more formidable rival arrived on the scene in 1977 when Michelin radial tyres appeared on the Renault RS01.

Aside from its tyres, the Renault was one of the most significant cars to appear for many years; it marked the return of *direct* participation by a major manufacturer (coincidentally, the one which had won the very first Grand Prix in 1906) and it marked the first time since 1954 that anyone had pursued the supercharging option. At the British Grand Prix, encouraged by the success of their Formula Two and sports car engine programmes, Renault wheeled out their turbocharged $1\frac{1}{2}$-litre challenger.

The turbocharging option was an attractive one to Renault for several reasons: first of all, the Gordini-developed engine could be used in this

Left: the Renault RS01 of 1977 was the first car in 23 years to make use of a supercharged engine, the last being the Italian Giaur which was raced in the 1954 Rome Grand Prix. The Renault's 1492 cc turbocharged engine did not lack power but its appetite for valve springs and its tendency to blow up hindered performances

Below: after several years of using the ubiquitous Cosworth engine, Brabham changed to Alfa-Romeo power for their BT45, seen here in B form with John Watson at the wheel. Small problems with fuel injection couldn't disguise the car's ample power and speed, even though it was some way over the minimum weight limit

Bottom: David Purley's 'Cosworth kit car' Lec proved reliable if unspectacular in 1977

Formula One guise, turbocharged 2.1-litre form for sports car racing (it was to win at Le Mans in 1978) and as a normally aspirated 2-litre unit for Formula Two: furthermore, it bore more relation to the way Renault foresaw the passenger car engine developing than did a highly stressed, larger capacity motor. Turbocharging in itself is an attractive way of achieving good thermodynamic efficiency and hence providing ample power without incurring the penalty of an increased fuel load. The turbocharger is essentially a centrifugal supercharger (which works most efficiently at very high rotational speeds) driven by a small turbine powered by otherwise waste exhaust gases. The considerable dynamic and heat energies of the fast moving exhaust gases are therefore channeled back into the engine instead of simply being thrown away. As an engine works better on cooler, hence denser, fuel charges, the pressurised air from the Renault's turbocharger is piped forward to an intercooler placed between the driver and the engine and is then fed back to the inlet ports via short pipes each equipped with Kügelfischer fuel injection nozzles. A waste gate controls the upper limit of boost and also allows some control over the slight lag caused by the fact that the turbine must be spinning very quickly before the engine produces sufficient power. This, however, remains one of the turbocharged engine's major drawbacks.

The Renault engine itself was a relatively simple V6, with exaggeratedly oversquare bore and stroke dimensions of 86 × 42.8 mm and a nominal compression ratio of just 7:1. The large bore allowed plenty of valve area, the two inlets and two exhausts being set in a very flat pent-roof arrangement, and it also gave lots of piston area to aid internal cooling. With four belt-driven overhead camshafts, a cast iron block and Marelli electronic ignition the engine was immediately good for around 510 bhp at 11,000 rpm, with an impressive spread of power. Unfortunately, in spite of not being *per se* a highly stressed unit, the engine did lack reliability. Early turbocharger problems prompted inlet and exhaust manifolding changes and a change to the turbine but then gave way to valve and piston problems. However, imitation is the sincerest form of flattery and Ferrari and Alfa were far from reticent about the fact that they already had their own turbo motors under development.

For the most part the rest of the year's offerings were mundane in comparison, but at least their numbers reflected the healthy state of the sport during the late 'seventies. The other race winners were the Shadow DN8 (helped along by an inspired Alan Jones in appalling conditions in Austria) and the Matra V12-powered Ligier JS7. Both teams had long been bridesmaids and both had come very close to winning in the past, so their victories were popular ones. With a claimed 520 bhp delivered at 12,300 rpm, the screaming Matra MS76 engine was probably the most potent and high revving engine of the current crop. It had been a long road to victory since

438

the first Matra V12 appeared in 1968 but it was the sweeter for the waiting . . .

The car which at last looked most likely to succeed, but in the event never quite made the winner's circle, was another 'twelve'. The Alfa-powered Brabham BT45B was often capable of running near the front but all too often it was not around when the flag dropped. It too was laying claim to 520 bhp, at 12,000 rpm, and its performance gave no reason to doubt the figure. On the debit side, the engine was notably thirsty and demanded a big chassis to accommodate it, its 615 kg being surpassed only by the Tyrrell P34 at a hefty 630 kg.

In spite of the ministrations of Karl Kempf's computer analysed on-board monitoring systems, P34 had a dreadful year. Its main problem was incompatibility with the latest Goodyear compounds; during a troubled season it gained some ten inches in the front track, reverted to its old style bodywork and put on a good deal of weight, but to no avail.

The Penske PC4s became known as ATS but continued to perform like Penskes. The new Fittipaldi F5, designed by ex-Lotus and Ensign man Dave Baldwin, showed occasional pace as did the very similar Ensign N177 itself. None of the numerous March offerings or the Surtees TS19 had much success and of the remaining runners the most interesting was perhaps Dave Purley's Lec CRP1, designed by Mike Pilbeam. Alas the Lec's promising career was cut short by Purley's dreadful accident in practice for the British Grand Prix. His survival spoke volumes for the strength of the car's chassis. Of Pilbeam's earlier employer's offering, the overweight, overheating, underpowered BRM P207, the less said the better. . . .

'1978' cars began to appear before the wheels had stopped turning in '77 and there was plenty of technical interest on one of the first, Gordon Murray's elegant Brabham BT46. Retaining the ever improving Alfa engine, Murray evolved a compact triangular monocoque chassis with integral surface coolers, obviating the need for separate radiators. In theory the surface coolers would save a lot of weight and eliminate a significant amount of cooling drag. The outer skin of the chassis was formed of a double-skinned element of high strength aluminium, ribbed on its exposed surface, through which flowed the oil and coolant. Murray's innovative approach did not stop with the cooling system; digital instrumentation with information modes selected by the driver was backed by a pit-triggered lap time display, all the information appearing on a panel on the steering wheel. Borrowing from longstanding USAC practice the BT46 was also fitted with on-board pneumatic jacks with a quick action connector for a pit air bottle. Murray also gave some thought for the driver, with a built in cooling panel and immensely strong protection areas. The braking system used steel discs with a carbon fibre skin as the friction surface, and the pads were also carbon fibre based – the system owed much to Dunlop's work on Concorde.

Sadly, Murray's radical new approach met with problems from the start and, although the oil cooling systems worked, the water cooling effect was seriously inadequate and the car reverted to conventional radiators (in the front nose wings) even before the season started. The BT46 did manage to win two races during 1978, but both were in controversial circumstances. At Anderstorp, Sweden, the team arrived with a BT46 equipped (à la Chaparral) with an engine driven fan, mounted, vertically, at the rear – which turned out to be the only view most people saw. The fan sucked air from under a completely sealed engine cover which was also sealed to the ground by a perimeter of sliding skirts. Brabham pointed out that it was for cooling purposes but those who saw it disappear into the distance thought otherwise and the protests came thick and fast. It was considered to infringe the rules regarding moveable aerodynamic devices; it was feared that it might pick up track debris and hurl it at its pursuers; it was thought to corner just too fast for safety – with probably dire consequences if something caused the suction to fail in mid-corner; and it was argued that to compete with 'the fan car' everyone else would have to take the same, expensive, route. The Swedish win was allowed to stand, but the car was declared illegal and reverted to its more conventional guise. In this form it 'won' at Monza, but only after two

cars which led it over the line had been penalised for jumped starts.

The car which won on the road at Monza was Chapman's own version of the 'ground effect' theme but, with another touch of genius, Chapman managed to achieve much the same ends without resorting to an extractor fan. In the Lotus 79, the flow of air over the car did the job itself, exhausting air from below the bodywork and sucking the car on to the road. The 79 was a development of the 78, true, but it took the state of the art a step further. The 78's major shortcoming had been a lack of straightline speed. With the 79, Chapman retained the narrow monocoque but tidied up the elements intruding into side airflow, tucking front and rear suspension well inboard and adopting an up and over exhaust system. The crucial part of the design, however, was the adoption of very efficient sliding skirts around the lower edge of the monocoque which effectively sealed the car to the ground; air was now exhausted from above the car and not allowed back in underneath, sucking the car down on to the road and giving the tyres all the down force they needed. The only part of the 79 which did not work was the troublesome Lotus gearbox around which the car had been designed. Had it worked it

Top: Carlos Reutemann in action in the flat-twelve Ferrari 312T-3 of 1978. The engine was reputed to develop about 510 bhp and the T-3 gave Michelin their first Grand Prix win

Above: Clay Regazzoni in the Shadow DN9 at Long Beach in 1978. The DN9, powered by the ubiquitous Cosworth DFV engine, came out on top of a High Court action with the Arrows team

Left: designer Gordon Murray's imaginative Brabham-Alfa BT46 of 1978, as originally introduced, with surface cooler radiators

Far right top: the car of 1978: this is the 'ground effect' Lotus 79 which took Mario Andretti to his world championship title

Bottom right: designed by Patrick Head, the Saudia-backed, Williams-Ford FW06 was driven to good effect by Alan Jones during 1978

would have allowed clutchless gearchanges and two pedal control – shades of the Lotus 76. Instead the team was forced to revert to the heavier Hewland box once again. In this form the 79 won six Grands Prix (seven disregarding the penalty at Monza) and with the 78 having won two more, Lotus took the Drivers' and Constructors' Championships once again.

Naturally there were many imitators of the 78 now in circulation but they were already a step behind. The next 'wing car' to appear was the Arrows FA1, designed by Tony Southgate and Dave Wass and the product of an outfit born over the winter out of the Shadow team. The next wing car was the Shadow DN9, also designed by Southgate and Wass before their departure to Arrows. The remarkable similarity of the cars led to cries of plagiarism which landed Arrows in the High Court where it was deemed that FA1 owed more to DN9 than just its parentage and FA1 was promptly banned. It was quickly followed by the new Arrows A1 which never quited lived up to the promise of the earlier car; nor, strangely, did the near identical Shadow. . . .

The only car which presented a real threat to Lotus dominance was the Ferrari 312T-3, which appeared right from the beginning of the season shod

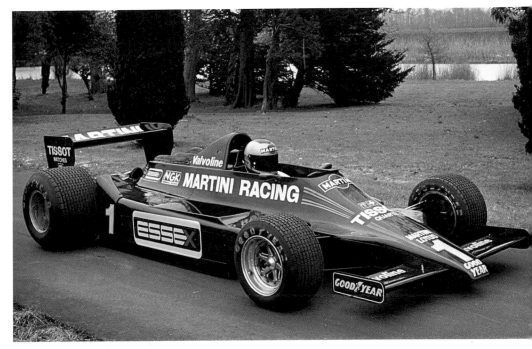

with Michelin radials. The T-3's record was rather chequered and the Michelins ranged from faultless to fragile with no apparent reason. Michelin did have the whip hand over Goodyear in that supplying only two teams they were able to try many more compounds on each without having to carry vast stocks of covers. Goodyear for their part limited their supply of special qualifying tyres to selected teams and those who showed most potential in practice. They usually included the latest Ligier – the JS9 – and the beautifully simple and compact Williams FW06, designed by Patrick Head for Frank Williams' Saudi Arabian sponsored team. The Williams showed that it was still possible to be a front runner with a simple, well engineered lightweight car and a determined driver.

With the departure of Derek Gardner back to the motor industry, the design onus at Tyrrell passed to Maurice Phillippe who rapidly shunned what was proving to be an expensive blind alley with the six-wheeler and penned a very straightforward successor, Tyrrell 008, distinguished mostly by its very low, flat monocoque and the fact that it won at Monaco.

Wolf brought a new shape to the circuits with WR5, a 'wing car' with the radiator sitting on the front of the cockpit over the driver's legs. After such a good start in 1977 the Wolf team sadly lost much of its impetus and although Scheckter put in some stirring drives, notably in Monaco, he was obviously losing heart and looking forward to a new challenge at Ferrari.

There was little else of much import in a year in which Lotus superiority seemingly demoralised more than one team. There were new names on the grids in the form of Martini (the French Formula Two championship winners soon finding Formula One to be a much tougher proposition and quietly fading away), the Theodore TR1 from Ron Tauranac and the crude, March-based Merzario A1 for Arturo himself. ATS moved on from re-dubbing Marches and Penskes to building their own cars – the D1 – which showed occasional turns of speed. The latest incarnation of the Hesketh team persevered with the 308E; Surtees traded in the TS19 for the equally mediocre TS20; Emerson struggled on with Fittipaldi F5A and Ensign did likewise with the N177, which probably suffered more from a lack of finance than from a lack of technical promise; at McLaren, the M26 had an absolutely dismal season and the feelings of relief at Colnbrook when the season came to a close were doubtless mirrored in many other camps.

All thoughts of the invincibility of the Lotus 79 went out of the window as the 1979 season opened in South America; confirming its testing performances, the Ligier JS11 – now Cosworth powered, allowing it to make the

most of a beautifully engineered ground effect chassis – simply pulverised the opposition. It was a spectacular demonstration of the importance of tyre compatibility for, it seemed, the latest, slightly taller, Goodyears suited the Ligier to perfection but left the Lotus struggling for rear end grip.

For once there was much of technical interest to be seen on the grids. A completely new engine is a rare happening and so there was much interest in the new V12 Alfa Romeo unit, around which Gordon Murray had designed the spectacular Brabham BT48, taking advantage of the narrowness of the new unit to allow a proper ground effect chassis.

The new engine was a sixty degree V12, retaining the heads and some of the internals of the boxer engine. It was used, of course, as a stressed unit, and had an up and over exhaust system in deference to ground effect requirements.

Predictably, 1979 started with a good sprinkling of Lotus 79 look alikes on the grids, the most blatant of which were without doubt the Tyrrell 009, McLaren M28 and the Wolf WR7. It did not take a very gifted seer to predict the arrival of many more variations as the season progressed.

Above left: after a fairy tale season in 1977 with the WR1, great things were expected of the Harvey Postlethwaite designed Wolf WR5 in 1978. Handling problems plagued the car and driver Scheckter wanted better so left the team at the end of the year

Left: Maurice Phillippe's first car for Tyrrell was the 008 with shallow monocoque, forward pointing canard wings and Karl Kempf's on-board computer. Depailler won at Monaco through determination, but thereafter the car's weight was too much of a handicap

Above: the Ligier team honed to perfection the Lotus ground-effect principle with their JS11, and the car was by far the quickest in the early part of 1979 with drivers Laffite and Depailler

Right: with ground effect cars becoming necessity rather than luxury, Alfa forsook the centre of gravity advantage they had with their flat-twelve for the necessary lateral compactness of a V12 seen here in the 1979 Brabham BT48

There was some original thinking to be seen however. The new Fittipaldi F6, designed by Ralph Bellamy, appeared with very abbreviated side pods (through which passed the exhaust system) flanking the slimmest of monocoques, devoid (initially at least) of wings. From Mo Nunn came a new Ensign, the N179, which carried its water and oil radiators immediately ahead of the driver and over his legs. By cleaning up the side pod area the Ensign proved exceptionally quick in a straight line but its development was delayed by overheating problems, in an attempt to cure which the radiators were quickly moved back into the side pods!

Best of all was the new Ferrari, the 312T-4, disproving the widely held belief that the flat-twelve precluded the use of a ground effect chassis. The T-4 moved all its fuel into a single central tank behind the driver and swept the exhausts up through the rear of the side pods. The very slim front end was supplanted by a curiously shaped but apparently effective aerofoil section upper deck and the whole lot was wheeled out on its Michelin radials to take a convincing one-two on its maiden outing in South Africa, followed by the same result with apparently equal ease for Villeneuve and Scheckter at Long Beach....

Once again, however, Colin Chapman was aiming one step ahead; on a snowy March day at Brands Hatch he unveiled the Lotus 80, with not a wing in sight. In fact there were two wings, one was a venturi section – sealed by skirts – under the elongated nose, the other was the rest of the car. Now only the front suspension intruded into the side airflow, even the drive shafts being taken through the side pods which filled all the space between the rear wheels. When the 80 began testing it soon became apparent that all was far from well, with the detail design if not with the concept. The sliding skirt system, on which the ground effect relied, proved troublesome and was redesigned, but sceptics could not entirely suppress an 'I told you so' attitude as the car donned wings during further trials. Such problems, however, are the stuff on which the Colin Chapmans of this world thrive and the Lotus, once again, was but the vanguard of a new philosophy.

The prime technology of Formula One had now moved firmly from chassis and suspension design to aerodynamics. While Chapman struggled for once, and McLaren learned that having a larger car was a poor way to generate more downforce, a new leader was emerging in the unlikely personna of the long-time underdog, Williams. At Long Beach, Williams showed off the elegantly simple FW07, designed by Patrick Head and being no more than a beautiful interpretation of current convention. Air was channeled through a venturi created by the road and a carefully shaped underbody profile. The

Above: with the 312T-4, Ferrari dispelled, by a convincing one-two victory on their maiden outing, any notion that using a flat-twelve engine precluded building an efficient ground effect chassis. By locating all the fuel load in a central tank behind the driver, adopting a very narrow centre section and taking the exhausts well upwards at the rear, the sides of the car were left relatively clear for aerodynamic appendages, supplemented by the strange 'foredeck'.

Above: after years of shoestring struggling, made possible only by exceptional dedication and sacrifice, Frank Williams, helped by Saudi finance and the design expertise of Patrick Head (*background*) finally made it to the top in 1980

Right: the combination which took Williams to the Constructor's Championship in 1980, Alan Jones, who won the Drivers' Championship and the elegantly simple FW07, seen here in the 1979 Dutch Grand Prix, which Jones won

air was kept in laminar flow along the length of the car by sliding skirts, sprung to stay in constant contact with the road throughout all suspension movement and tipped with ceramic rubbing strips to minimise wear. This controlled air flow, escaping only at the rear, effectively sucked the car onto the ground without recourse to fans or motors. Cornering speeds took another leap and as 1980 dawned, Williams, not Lotus, was the team to be copied.

It was no more than just reward for Williams that he maintained the momentum of 1979 and scored a memorable Drivers and Constructors World Championship double, with Alan Jones leading the team. They won against ever more effective opposition. Towards the end of 1979, Brabham had reverted from Alfa Romeo to Cosworth power in the BT49 and this provided the most effective opposition to the Williams, in the hands of Nelson Piquet. The emphasis placed on clean underbody airflow may be judged by the fact that Brabham experimented with specially made taller and narrower Weisman gearbox casings simply to clean up further the air exit area. Ultimately, Williams won six races (plus the unsanctioned Spanish Grand Prix) and Brabham won three. The other winners were Renault and Ligier, with three and two wins, respectively. The latest Renault, the RE20-25 series was a development of the previous car, the engine now with twin turbochargers, better intercooling and 520 bhp at 11,000 rpm, compared to the 470 plus of a good Cosworth. Sadly, although the Renault was potent it still lacked reliability, being particularly prone to valve spring failures. Cosworth engines on the other hand won no less than eleven races (plus Spain) to bring their total to 136.

Undeterred by Renault's problems and probably spurred by uncharacteristically dubious reliability with their own normally aspirated flat-12, Ferrari joined the ranks of the turbocharged engine builders after Monza. Like the Renault EF1, the Ferrari engine, designated 126C, was a V6, a configuration well suited to the narrow chassis dictates of a true ground effect car but inevitably nullified to some degree by the need to locate complex exhaust plumbing, the turbocharger itself and the vital intercooling within the airstream. The Ferrari engine was less oversquare than the Renault at 81 × 48.4 mm but it was also lighter and more powerful. With a compression ratio between 6.5 and 7.5:1 the 126C claimed 540 bhp at 12,000 rpm. The turbos suffered a further disadvantage in their compatibility with ground effects in that their more pronounced thirst (typically 15 to 20 per cent more than a Cosworth) demanded a bulkier and heavier fuel load.

Little else was new in 1980, virtually all the remaining cars being developments of previous chassis with largely speculative aerodynamic revisions.

Left: although Gilles Villeneuve looks pleased during early tests of the early 126CK turbo-engined Ferrari, the car never really fulfilled its potential. The KKK turbocharged engine was powerful but reliable only to a point and the power was wasted on a chassis which was years behind the despised 'kit-car' front runners in terms of modern thinking and materials

Below: another team which introduced turbo power in 1981 was former European Formula Two Champions Toleman whose 1494 cc four-cylinder unit, developed by Brian Hart again squandered its obvious power on a chassis possibly even worse than that of the Ferrari

Lotus derived the 79X from a mixture of 79 and 80 ideas but neither that nor the subsequent 81 produced any results. Ensign, Shadow and Arrows produced new designs, the N180, DN11 and A3 respectively and although all three showed promise on odd occasions they were never more than 'best of the rest'. The increasingly frustrated Fittipaldi team took over the assets of the disbanded Walter Wolf Racing and produced some very conventional and mediocre hybrids dubbed F7 and the one newcomer to the F1 ranks, Osella's FA1 was disastrously overweight and served principally to underline how far Formula One technology had recently progressed.

The turbo revolution continued to gain momentum in 1981, with the eventual appearance of Ferrari, BMW and Hart engines, the last two for Brabham and the new Toleman team respectively, and both in-line fours as opposed to the usual V6. Nevertheless, as Brabham developed the BMW engine for full time use in 1982, the team scored yet another Cosworth powered World Championship in 1981, with Piquet reversing the Williams-Brabham stranglehold. The Williams drivers, Reutemann and Jones, in that order won four Grands Prix (two each) while Piquet won three, FW07s to B and C specification and similar BT49s being simple developments of the previous cars.

Ferrari used two forced induction systems on their 126 cars in 1981, the Comprex pressure wave supercharger and the exhaust-driven KKK turbocharger, the 126CX Comprex engine soon being dropped, however, in favour

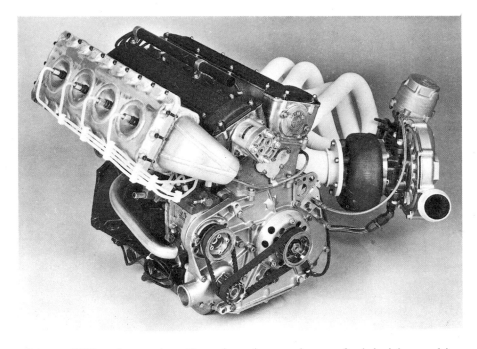

of the 126CK turbo version. Ferrari used a novel way of minimising turbine inertia induced throttle lag, allowing a rich overrun mixture to burn within the turbine housing, the combustion driving the compressor much like a gas turbine, quite independent of exhaust pressure. The turbine was therefore kept spinning even on closed or small throttle running and lag was minimised. The price was unreliability due to overheating of the turbine and its bearings and they eventually reverted to a more normal boost transfer system. The 126C won two races but that was largely due to Gilles Villeneuve as the turbo's 560 bhp was wasted on a very agricultural chassis.

Even from the beginning of testing, the BMW M12/13 turbos were at least in a decent chassis, Gordon Murray doing a characteristically neat adaption of the BT49 into the BMW powered BT50. The four-cylinder KKK turbocharged BMW engine had bore and stroke of 89.2 × 60 mm, or 1499 cc, and four relatively large valves per cylinder. Compared to most it was quite low revving, claiming (with typical German precision) 557 bhp at only 9500 rpm. Its one public outing, in practice for the British Grand Prix, suggested that it did indeed have a great deal of power.

The other four-cylinder turbo, Toleman's Hart 145T, was 1494 cc, 88 × 61.5 mm, used a Garrett AiResearch turbocharger instead of the otherwise universal KKK and offered 540 bhp (minimum) at 10,500 rpm. Again, its power was not in doubt but like Ferrari's it was rather wasted on the bulky and difficult TG181 chassis (designed by Rory Byrne and John Gentry). The car was variously nicknamed the Flying Pig, in deference to its handling, or the General Belgrano, a comparison with the unfortunate Argentine battleship . . .

Alfa Romeo had a V8 turbo engine on the drawing board, but they continued to rely on their 540 bhp, 1260 series V12, being joined in the V12 ranks by the latest Matra MS81 engine making another return with Ligier – successfully too, with two wins during the year and threatening several more. Its advertised 510 bhp may even have been somewhat conservative, for the beautifully engineered Talbot-Ligier JS17 was certainly no lightweight and the V12 was fairly thirsty.

1981 was also a busy year on the chassis engineering front, with new regulations dictating 6 cm ground clearance and an end to sliding skirts. Without the channelling effect of skirts, ground effect is largely lost, so a new approach was necessary. The ever innovative Gordon Murray found one answer – albeit exploiting a loophole and eventually spawning a breed of imitators which the drivers universally abhorred. In that the 6 cm clearance could only be measured at rest, Murray contrived a soft, pneumatic suspension system on the Brabham which aerodynamic downforce at speed pushed into

a fully down position, at which time solid, vestigial 'skirts' ran close enough to the ground to approach the efficiency of the sliding skirt systems. The penalty was that once into the down position, suspension movement had to be minimised to maintain constant, minimum clearance and so the car ran astronomical spring rates – or, put another way, virtually solid suspension – subjecting drivers to a terrible pounding and making the cars *extremely* nervous on anything less than a perfect surface.

As FISA made little protest at the blatant rule bending, every team was soon obliged to imitate the Brabham system and before long cars even had driver controlled ride height systems and flexible (yet still fixed and therefore within the letter of the law) skirts with rubbing strips. A limit was eventually put on the dimensions, rigidity and fixing of the skirts but it really only served to make the cars even more rock hard.

There was one other attempt to achieve the same end but retain a degree of concern for the driver and that was Colin Chapman's 'twin-chassis' Lotus 88; the 'primary chassis' comprised the bodywork, sidepods, aerofoils and radiators, suspended on coil spring damper units at each wheel and intended to absorb aerodynamic loads while being unaffected by braking, cornering or acceleration loads. Those loads were fed to the 'secondary chassis' which comprised a monocoque, fuel tank, engine and gearbox and suspension, thereby isolating the driver from the need for constant aerodynamic trim and allowing him a degree of suspension movement. While accepting single chassis cars which blatantly ran in contact with the ground, FISA, after numerous and acrimonious protests, counter protests and technical tribunals, banned the 88 before it had a chance to prove its worth or otherwise.

The only other real technical innovation on the chassis front was John Barnard's beautifully neat McLaren MP4 whose monocoque was not rivetted or bonded from sheet metal but moulded in the extraordinarily light and strong carbon fibre. The car won at Silverstone and proved its strength in several very severe accidents.

With the return of Goodyear and the arrival of Pirelli (with Toleman),

Top: the rules banning skirts but allowing the loophole of hydropneumatic suspension systems led to the ludicrous spectacle of cars like Carlos Reutemann's Williams running with enormous ground clearances such as here at low speeds but then hugging the ground at racing speeds

Above, left to right and top right: while FISA tacitly accepted the patently illegal hydropneumatic suspension cars, they banned Colin Chapman's innovative, double chassis Lotus 88 virtually before it ran

competition returned to the tyre scene after Goodyear's early season withdrawal but Michelin generally looked the better bet and Pirelli's steel belted radials suffered not so much from compounding problems as from being simply too heavy to allow competitively hard spring rates.

After 1981, 1982 was relatively calm once the early season controversy about disposable ballast had been resolved. Unable to beat or even approach the turbo runners in terms of power, the Cosworth users could only pursue their weight advantage over the thirstier and bulkier turbos. Through the hideously expensive use of exotic materials such as titanium and carbon fibre and the equally exotic manufacturing methods which they imposed, the best of the Cosworth teams, with the help of designs of exceptional engineering quality, could now build cars substantially below the minimum weight limit, but how to use that advantage without breaking the rules? Well, the rules would bend before they would break and suddenly teams were exploiting the interpretation of the rule which allowed cars to be topped up with essential coolants after the race and before the weight check. The lighter cars now developed a need for water cooled brakes and as a rule of thumb the water in the cooling system generally weighed about as much as the car was shy of the weight limit. With the water quickly jettisoned in the approximate direction of the brakes, these cars could race underweight, giving a performance edge and easing the suspension problems. For once, FISA, protecting the interests of its closely

Above: from the middle of the 1982 season (starting at the British Grand Prix and seen here practising at the Italian Grand Prix) the Brabham team used (or when engines expired early prepared to use) tactical pit-stops. Faced with the dilemma of marginal fuel capacity for their thirsty BMW turbos, the team started the cars on half full tanks and soft tyres, theoretically allowing the drivers to build a big lead before pitting at roughly half distance for fuel and fresh rubber, preheated in an oven but still cool enough by racing standards to be a problem for a couple of laps. Given a chance the system showed some promise and by the beginning of 1983 many teams were copying it – even the Cosworth powered Williams. The more teams used the idea the less relevant it obviously became, FISA became increasingly concerned with the safety aspects and pit stops for fuel were due to be phased out by 1984

Left: the beautifully constructed Marlboro MP4 introduced carbon fibre monocoques, soon to be copied by virtually every team

aligned turbo and V12 teams, was quick to react and by mid–April the cheat was specifically banned.

With the arrival of Harvey Postlethwaite, Ferrari developed a 'modern', carbon fibre composite chassis to match the prodigious power of their latest turbo engine, with water injection and a relatively reliable 580 bhp (or probably more than 600 in short bursts during qualifying). Alas, Ferrari's dreadful misfortune made real assessment of the new car rather academic. The BMW turbo now began to race and showed terrific power coupled with appalling reliability, largely with the fuel system which often resulted in the BMW Brabhams making a spectacularly pyrotechnic departure. During the year

Right: with improving reliability from the Ferrari turbo engine, the carbon fibre and aluminium composite chassis of the 1982 Ferrari was seen by most as a potential champion in the hands of the brilliant Villeneuve but the car's worth was totally overshadowed by the team's dreadful run of luck. Ferrari did however win the Constructors' title

Brabham also introduced a tactical ploy which showed promise on the rare occasions when the cars lasted long enough to employ it. Starting on soft tyres and light fuel load, the Brabhams would endeavour to build a commanding lead before stopping for more fuel and fresh, soft tyres, preheated in an oven to speed their subsequent warmup. The cars were adapted with fast fuel fillers and the pit crews were impeccably rehearsed and equipped but the benefits were at best moot.

'Pull-rod' suspension, which operated in tension rather than compression and allowed for lighter and slimmer suspension arms without allowing unwanted bending spring effects (a Gordon Murray original idea) proliferated, as did the use of carbon fibre for anything from aerodynamic appendages to complete monocoques. Once early problems with pad compatibility and nearby component cooling had been overcome, carbon fibre brake discs, again pioneered by Brabham and offering a tremendous weight saving came to be seen more and more.

Yet in the end of course, the Championship went to a driver in a now 'conventional' car and with a Cosworth engine, although Ferrari, to their utmost credit, slavaged a worthy Constructor's Championship from this dreadful season. Rosberg and the Williams FWO8 just might have represented the pinnacle of Cosworth achievement. For 1983, sweeping changes in the regulations, inspired by an urgent need to slow the cars through corners for safety's sake, banned skirts completely and introduced 'flat bottoms' to limit ground effect. At first it seemed that this new breed could be a great leveller, putting renewed emphasis on driver skill and engine response, giving the latest, short stroke, lightweight Cosworth, the DFY, a control advantage if not a power advantage, but it soon became apparent that power is still the name of the game and turbos will eventually rule the roost, perhaps ultimately coupled to a fuel consumption formula.

After years of sprouting wings and squandering fuel, there is still a glimmer of hope that this most specialised of vehicles might yet have a few lessons to be applied to cars on the world's highways; which, after all, was how it all began . . .

Below: in spite of the proliferation of the turbos, the Drivers' Championship went once again to a Cosworth-powered team and the Williams FWo8, a simple design refined to the absolute state of the art

THE RACES: 1960-83

Below: by the 1962 season, British manufacturers had wiped out Ferrari's early lead in the 1½-litre formula, and Graham Hill was able to score his own and BRM's first championships. He is seen here in the championship-winning V8's four-cylinder predecessor during the 1961 Dutch Grand Prix, at Zandvoort

The change of formula in 1961 brought more than a change in the cars; it heralded a new hierarchy of drivers. The names which permeated the history of motor racing in the 1950s were gone and a new generation was born. The image of motor racing was changing and the sport's afficionados were finding a different breed of hero.

The first season of the new formula saw the first American World Champion, 34-year-old Phil Hill from Santa Monica. Hill, a member of the powerful Ferrari team, took the title when his German team mate, Wolfgang von Trips, was killed at Monza. Hill won the Monza race, and also won at Spa – at 128.151 mph; von Trips had won at Zandvoort and at Aintree and Ferrari's 'rookie' driver, Giancarlo Baghetti, scooped a sensational debut win at Reims. the only break in Ferrari's monopoly came from the Lotuses of Moss – with Rob Walker's 18 – and Innes Ireland in the works 21. Moss scored spectacular victories, against the odds, in Monaco and Germany, through sheer driving skill; Ireland's first, and only, championship race win came at Watkins Glen, in the absence of the Ferraris. In the Principality, Moss led from lap fourteen onwards and had to use every ounce of his skill to fend off the works Ferraris of Hill and Ginther. He won by 3.6 secs, at an average speed of 70.70 mph, and shared fastest lap with second man Ginther, at 73.13 mph. In Germany, Moss gave everything to win by 21.8 secs from von Trips, at 92.34 mph.

The season was marred by the death of von Trips and fourteen spectators at Monza when, on the second lap, his and Jim Clark's cars touched at Vedano and the talented German's Ferrari was launched into the crowd. A happier statistic came from the Dutch Grand Prix, the first ever world championship race at which every starter finished without incident.

It had been a good start to the new formula for the Maranello cars but by 1962 the British teams had caught up some of their lost impetus and the season saw a sterling battle between Clark's Lotus and Graham Hill's BRM. The championship was eventually resolved at the very last round, in favour of Hill – who had taken four superb victories during the season in Holland, Germany, Italy and that final race in South Africa. Clark scored in Belgium, England and the United States and was within a few laps of winning his first world title when his engine failed.

The season started in Holland where Hill scored his own first Grand Prix win and BRM's second – at the same circuit where they opened their tally in 1959. Hill won at 95.44 mph from Lotus's new driver Trevor Taylor, who surprised many by his performance. John Surtees, making the switch from two to four wheels, in a Lola, had a lucky escape when a wishbone on the car broke at high speed.

One driver who was not so lucky in 1962 was Stirling Moss who crashed heavily and inexplicably during a non-championship race at Goodwood on Easter Monday. 32-year-old Moss was released, bleeding and partially paralysed, from his wrecked Lotus and, although he recovered to what would be regarded as full fitness by any other person, his racing career was over: the fine edge had gone forever from his judgement and reactions. Moss never did gain the world title he so thoroughly deserved, a mixture of national pride, when he drove sub-standard machinery simply because it was British, and wretched luck keeping that honour from him. He had risen from his first appearance at Prescott hill-climb, in a 500 cc Cooper on 9 May 1948, through almost every kind of racing, to be a works Formula One driver for Mercedes, Maserati, Vanwall and Connaught. He also drove BRMs, Lotuses, Coopers and many more. He was second in the World Championship for Drivers four times but he never won. The end of Moss's career severed a link with an earlier generation of drivers and left a space at the pinnacle of racing for someone else to fill.

The man who was to fill it was the young Scot who finished second in the 1962 championship, Jim Clark. Clark was born on 4 March 1936 and began his motoring career in the early 1950s, first in local rallies and then in circuit races. Early support from the Scottish Border Reivers team led Clark through saloon, Formula Junior, sports car and Formula Two racing, to a contract for Formula One with Lotus. In all his career, Clark never lost faith with Lotus and never drove for another Grand Prix team. Clark and Lotus were a combination whose story is woven into the web of racing for many years; he was a worthy successor to fill the void left by Moss.

Clark collected his first Grand Prix win at Spa in 1962, beating Graham Hill and Phil Hill into second and third places and averaging 131.89 mph in the process, with a fastest lap at 133.98 mph. The season saw the first championship victory for both Porsche and their lanky Californian driver, Dan Gurney, who inherited victory at Rouen when race leader Graham Hill's engine went off song twelve laps from home.

Top: before his death in a Formula Two race at Hockenheim in 1968, Jim Clark had dominated motor racing for several glorious years. His two World Championships, in 1963 and 1965, were gained with seemingly consummate ease and only mechanical misfortunes prevented him from claiming the title in other years. It became rare for Clark to be beaten in a straight confrontation in Grand Prix racing, mechanical failure notwithstanding; he was regarded as almost invincible

Above: Californian Dan Gurney was the mainstay of Porsche's first venture into Grand Prix racing; he gave the German team their first Grand Prix win at Rouen in 1962

Right: the master of Monaco at work – Graham Hill powers his BRM P56 through Casino Square on his way to victory and setting fastest lap during the 1963 Grand Prix. In the picture, he is pursued by John Surtees' Ferrari, a chase which lasted until the latter's goggles became covered with oil. By the end of his career, Hill had won the Monaco event five times

Below: Jim Clark led the 1963 Dutch Grand Prix from start to finish, lapping the whole field and setting the first 100 mph lap record at the Zandvoort circuit. Clark's Lotus-Climax 25 was fitted with an air-deflector screen for the first time

The only other winner in 1962 was Bruce McLaren, who won the Monaco Grand Prix at an average speed of 70.46 mph, after leader Graham Hill retired with no oil pressure. Phil Hill was just 1.3 seconds behind for Ferrari after making a tremendous effort to catch McLaren. 1963 was the year of 'the Flying Scot', Jim Clark. On his way to his first World Championship, Clark scored seven victories from the season's ten Grands Prix, with one second place, one third and a single retirement, in Monaco, to wrest the title from Graham Hill and BRM. Hill and his BRM team-mate Ritchie Ginther shared second place in the championship, albeit 25 points in arrears of Clark's perfect score of 54, from his best six results. The season began without Porsche, who had retired at the end of 1962. Their top driver, Gurney, joined the newly formed Brabham team, while the withdrawal of Lola from the scene sent John Surtees to Ferrari, alongside Willy Mairesse of Belgium. The Lolas did in fact appear again in 1963 in the colours of the Reg Parnell team and driven by Chris Amon, newly launched on a career to become notorious for its ill fortune.

With Clark retiring from a strong lead, when the gearbox of his Lotus broke on the 78th lap, Graham Hill scored the first of his famous series of Monaco victories in the opening round. At Spa, Clark scored the first of four consecutive 1963 victories at 114.1 mph and by almost five minutes from Bruce McLaren's Cooper. The race was held in appalling conditions with thunderstorms sweeping the daunting Belgian circuit and it was sheer good fortune that none of many incidents had serious outcomes. After Spa, Clark simply ran away and hid from the opposition at the Dutch Grand Prix, lapping the entire field. Dan Gurney improved Brabham's standing by taking second place –

Left: after early leaders Brabham, Gurney, McLaren and Hill had dropped out, Jim Clark comfortably led the British Grand Prix of 1963, winning by a large margin from Surtees' Ferrari

Right: John Surtees looks pensive after his victory in the 1963 German Grand Prix. This was his first Grand Prix win, and he repeated the success in 1964, his World Championship year

Below: Richie Ginther's works BRM leads Jo Bonnier's Rob Walker-entered Cooper-Climax, Dan Gurney's Brabham and the debutant Chris Amon in Reg Parnell's Lola through the Zandvoort sand dunes in 1963. Ginther eventually finished fifth and Gurney second

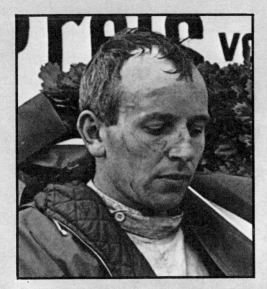

having scored an encouraging third in Belgium. Surtees raised Ferrari's spirits with a fighting third place, ahead of Innes Ireland's BRP BRM. Young Italian Ludovico Scarfiotti collected his first championship point for sixth place in this his first Grand Prix. Despite a continual misfire, Clark won at Reims, averaging 125.31mph and collecting fastest lap at 131.14mph in the process. Second place, a minute and five seconds behind, went to South African Tony Maggs in a Cooper and third went to Graham Hill – even counting a one minute penalty for a push start.

Clark's fourth successive victory was gained with consummate ease at Silverstone, followed home by a stirring battle for second place between Hill and Surtees, resolved on the last lap when Hill ran out of fuel to coast home third. Mike Hailwood followed in Surtees' footsteps, turning from two wheels to four for the first time at this race; he finished eighth.

It was Surtees who finally broke Clark's winning streak with a hard-won victory at the Nürburgring, with Clark bringing his ailing Lotus home second. Surtees' average speed was 95.83mph and he set fastest lap at 96.8mph. Clark was back to form in Italy and won from Ginther and McLaren after early leader

Surtees and his strongest challengers, Hill and Gurney, all retired. Clark drove a masterly race to finish third behind the BRMs of Hill and Ginther at Watkins Glen, having been left at the line with a flat battery. Clark's fastest lap of 111.14 mph was not enough to catch Hill who won at 109.91 mph. Clark rounded off a magnificent season with wins in the first ever Mexican Grand Prix and in South Africa. Brabhams wcrc second in both races, Jack himself scoring in Mexico and Gurney in South Africa, a promising season for the team.

Clark's luck was not at its best in the 1964 season, which was one of the closest ever raced, being decided in favour of John Surtees at the final round in Mexico after a three-cornered fight with Hill and Clark. Surtees amply justified Ferrari's faith on his way to becoming the first ever man to win championships on both two and four wheels.

Hill and Ginther opened the season with another one-two finish at Monaco. Clark's Monaco gremlins struck again and he finished fourth behind his team-mate, Peter Arundell. Hailwood scored a championship point with sixth place in a BRM-powered Lotus. Clark scored his traditional easy victory at Zandvoort while Surtees showed his ever growing talent with a good second place.

Below: Dan Gurney's Brabham at the Nouveau Monde hairpin at Rouen, during the 1964 French Grand Prix. Gurney, who started from the middle of the front row of the grid, went on to score Brabham's first Grand Prix victory after Jim Clark retired from the lead of this race

Right: Jim Clark's Lotus-Climax 25 has just gone through the Monaco chicane, while Graham Hill's BRM P56 follows Bob Anderson's Brabham-Climax into the same bend. On the first lap, Clark had hit the straw bales on the exit from the chicane, breaking the anti-roll bar. His engine expired on lap 93, and Hill dominated this, the 1964 race. Ginther was second and Clark was classified fourth behind team-mate Arundell

Chris Amon finished fifth to score his first championship points, as did former motor cyclist Bob Anderson in sixth place. The Belgian race was again packed with drama and saw Clark take another victory at the one circuit which he openly hated. The victory was one of the luckiest of Clark's career; the Scot was lying fourth behind Gurney, Hill and McLaren with two laps to go when Gurney ran out of fuel and had none available in the Brabham pit. Hill took the lead only to go out with fuel pump trouble on the last lap and McLaren also ran out of fuel within sight of the finish, handing victory to a disbelieving Clark.

After so much promise, Gurney finally gave the Brabham team their first victory at Rouen, winning at 108.77 mph from Hill and Brabham himself who took fastest lap at 111.37 mph. At this stage in the season Surtees was way behind in the championship race with only a third of Clark's points total, but the German Grand Prix marked a turning point for the Italian team. Surtees scored another great Nürburgring victory from Hill, and Bandini's Ferrari. Surtees averaged 96.57 mph and set fastest lap at 98.3 mph. The meeting was marred by the death in practice of the Dutchman Count Carel Godin de Beaufort, a popular and dedicated privateer.

Austria's first championship Grand Prix was run at Zeltweg and won at 99.20 mph by Ferrari's Lorenzo Bandini, from Ginther and an inspired Bob Anderson in a private Brabham. Making his debut was a young Austrian who was to become the sport's first posthumous champion, Jochen Rindt. With most of the favourites, Rindt was on the list of retirements. Surtees won again at Monza in a thrilling slipstreaming battle at an average speed of 127.78 mph, with McLaren giving Cooper a rare high spot with second place. Graham Hill had gone no further than the start line in Italy due to clutch failure, but he kept his hopes of a second championship alive by winning at Watkins Glen from Surtees and Jo Siffert, who had a splendid outing with his Brabham.

All this left the championship open into the final round, with Surtees, Hill and Clark all in a position to win the title. Hill led with 39 points to Surtees' 34 and Clark's 30. With 9, 6, 4, 3, 2 and 1 point at stake for the first six places Clark had to win the race to take his second title. With Hill out of the race fairly early, Clark looked all set to take his second championship but, as in the South African race two seasons earlier, Clark was robbed almost within sight of the flag by engine trouble. In a classic example of team work, Bandini moved politely over to let Surtees through to second place, enough points to scoop the championship and a place in motor sport's history books.

The following year, 1965, was the final year of the very successful $1\frac{1}{2}$-litre formula and it was dominated again by the man who had always been the one to beat, Jim Clark. Clark scored six more victories to add to his growing tally, at a time when the competition was stronger than ever. Clark won in South Africa, Belgium, France, Britain, Holland and Germany; Hill scored his Monaco hat trick and won at Watkins Glen and his young Scottish team-mate at BRM, Jackie Stewart marked himself as the greatest find for some years with several good performances culminating in victory in Italy. The final race of the formula saw a new make of car on the list of winners when Ritchie Ginther gave Honda a popular win in Mexico.

Hill's Monaco victory was a classic, achieved through pure skill and determination, after he had to go down the escape road at the chicane after 24 laps, to avoid Bob Anderson's Brabham. Hill gradually caught and passed the field to win a memorable race by just over a minute from Bandini's Ferrari and his own team-mate, Stewart, at an average speed of 74.30 mph. Hill's fastest lap was 76.72 mph. Clark and Gurney had both been missing from Monaco, driving for Team Lotus in the Indianapolis 500. Clark won. During the Monaco race, Paul Hawkins had a lucky escape when he crashed his Lotus 33 into the harbour, without injury!

Clark returned from America to score his fourth successive victory at Spa, again in atrocious conditions which kept visibility and lap speeds down. Clark's winning average was 117.16 mph and his fastest lap was 124.72 mph. The other 'Flying Scot', Stewart, was second, from McLaren, while Ginther gave Honda their first championship point with sixth place. The circus then moved on to a

Far left: Jim Clark, who won the Belgian Grand Prix four years running, is pictured here in June 1963. In the foul weather conditions which can so unexpectedly occur at Spa, Clark's Lotus Climax 25 leads Count Carel Godin de Beaufort's private four-cylinder Porsche, which eventually finished sixth. Team managers Rudd of BRM and Chapman of Lotus asked, in vain, for the race to be stopped. Only six cars finished

Left: Just before winning his sixth Grand Prix of the 1965 season, Jim Clark appears quietly confident. His Lotus 33 led the German Grand Prix from start to finish and thus clinched the Championship by half-season

Below: Yet another rain-soaked Spa-Franchorchamps, this time 1965, and Jackie Stewart drove an excellent race in his BRM P56 to finish second, 45 seconds behind Clark

new venue for the French Grand Prix, Clermont-Ferrand, a very difficult addition to the championship stage. Again it was Clark and Stewart who led the field, followed home by burly New Zealander Denny Hulme in a Brabham. They were Hulme's first points in the championship.

The British Grand Prix was at Silverstone and, in spite of a sick engine, Clark made no mistakes about winning, leading arch-rival Hill home by just 3.2 seconds. Clark used the four-valve engine at Silverstone and Surtees was at last given a flat-12 Ferrari to replace the V8 he had used until then. Clark scored another victory in Holland, after being pressed hard by Stewart, who finished only 8 seconds behind the maestro. Gurney was third, a further 5 seconds adrift with the Brabham. The Honda actually led for a few laps and Ginther eventually brought it into sixth place. Clark at last broke his Nürburgring duck with a splendid win in the German race from Hill and Gurney, while Jochen Rindt scored a good fourth place in his Cooper. Clark's winning average was 99.796 mph and his fastest lap 101.226 mph. His win clinched his second championship.

Stewart's championship winning days may have been a few years into the future, but he did not show it at Monza where he scored his first Grand Prix win from Hill in the other BRM. Even at this late stage in the 1½-litre formula there were plenty of revised cars to be seen, notably from Honda and Ferrari. Clark set fastest lap at 133.43 mph, before retiring on lap 63 with fuel pump problems; Stewart's winning average was 130.31 mph.

The final two races of the season, in the United States and Mexico, were without John Surtees, who had had a huge accident in a Can-Am race and was still seriously ill. The Ferraris were entrusted to Bandini, Rodriguez and local

Above: Jim Clark made a typical start at the 1965 United States GP at Watkins Glen where he is seen leading the pack from Hill, Ginther and Spence. Clark's hastily rebuilt engine broke a piston on lap 11 and the race was won by Hill's BRM with the Brabhams of Gurney and Jack Brabham second and third

Above right: Spa in 1966 saw the kind of race that every driver dreads. Fifteen cars started the first lap and only seven completed it; of the others seven were victims of the appalling conditions and Jim Clark's Lotus suffered an engine failure. The race was kept alive by this stirring battle between Surtees' Ferrari and Rindt's Cooper which was resolved in Surtees' favour, with the pair a whole lap ahead of Bandini in third place

star Bob Bondurant for the American race, but none of them could catch Graham Hill, who drove to his Watkins Glen hat trick at 107.98 mph, setting fastest lap at 115.16 mph on the way. Ginther wound up the 1½-litre years by giving the Honda team a well deserved win in Mexico by leading from flag to flag at 94.26 mph. Gurney set fastest lap with his Brabham, at 96.59 mph.

While the Japanese team celebrated their victory, everyone began to look ahead to the new 3-litre formula whose start was only months away.

The advent of the 3-litre formula was heralded as the 'Return of Power' and many foretold that it would bring forward a different type of driver to control the powerful new cars. These seers were only partly right, for although the drivers did change it was not their talent or determination that changed but rather their whole attitude to motor sport, which finally became a totally professional occupation with no place for the enthusiastic amateur of years gone by.

1966, the first years of the new rules, again caught the manufacturers in their natural state of unreadiness and it was Jackie Stewart who opened the scoring at Monaco with a 2.1-litre BRM. The race was one of attrition, with only four classified finishers from sixteen starters. Bandini was second and triple Monaco winner Hill was third, after racing with a slipping clutch. A fine day for BRM was completed by Bob Bondurant who brought his privately entered car home fourth. It was a rare highlight in a not very good year for BRM.

After Monaco all the other races went to full 3-litre cars, the next round, at Spa, being taken by Surtees in the V12 Ferrari from Rindt's Cooper-Maserati and Bandini in the second Ferrari. Surtees' winning average was 113.395 mph and he also set fastest lap at 121.91 mph, in a race again marred by the weather conditions and numerous accidents; no less than eight of the fifteen starters were eliminated on the first lap. Into fourth place came Jack Brabham in the new 3-litre Brabham-Repco, with which he was to win his third world title.

'Black Jack' opened his account with victory in the next round, at Reims, beating Mike Parkes' Ferrari by 9.5 seconds. Denny Hulme made it a convincing showing for the new Brabhams by bringing the other car home in third place, and Dan Gurney gave encouragement to the Eagle team with a fine fifth place. Brabham's winning average of 136.9 mph made this the fastest race ever run in France. Brabham continued his winning streak at Brands Hatch, leading Hulme to the flag by 9.6 seconds. Hill and Clark took the next two spots, albeit a long way in arrears with their smaller engined cars. The Ferraris missed the race through industrial problems. Jack collected his third win in a row in Holland with a hard fought victory, at 100.10 mph, over Hill and Clark – who led for much of the race before falling back with overheating. Brabham's fourth consecutive win, at the Nürburgring, virtually clinched the championship with three races remaining. He was pressed all the way in Germany by John Surtees, now driving for Cooper-Maserati and displaying all his old mastery of the Ring. Rindt, in another Cooper, was third and Surtees' fastest lap was 96.44 mph, compared with Brabham's winning average of 86.75 mph.

Ferrari fans had something to cheer in Italy when Ludovico Scarfiotti led team-mate Mike Parkes to a one-two triumph at Monza, following the demise of most of the regular front runners, including Ginther who was lucky to escape from a huge accident caused when his Honda threw a tyre tread at around 150 mph. While Brabham was confirmed as the new champion after Monza, despite his not finishing, Jim Clark brought a ray of light into an unhappy season by taking his BRM H16-engined Lotus to victory at Watkins Glen, scoring the engine's only Grand Prix win. The season finished in Mexico where John Surtees gave the Cooper-Maserati a well deserved win at the end of a season in which they had tried desperately hard with a basically poor car. Brabham and Hulme filled the next two places, ahead of Ginther's Honda and Gurney's Eagle. Already the new formula was bringing a host of new names to the winner's circle.

1967 started with another victory for Cooper and ended with another championship for the Brabham team, this time with Denny Hulme taking the title to New Zealand. It was a year of great strides in car design, and tragedy with Bandini's death in a terrible fiery accident at Monaco.

Pedro Rodriguez scored his first championship win with the Cooper-Maserati in South Africa after a sensational race, which looked as though it was going to be won by local hero John Love in an ancient Cooper-Climax before he ran short of fuel. Love was second and John Surtees, now driving for Honda, was a good third. Denny Hulme scored his first win in the tragic Monaco Grand Prix, from Graham Hill, who was making his debut alongside his old rival Clark in the Lotus camp. Chris Amon's magnificent third place on his first appearance with Ferrari was completely overshadowed by Bandini's accident on the 82nd lap. The talented Italian died a few days later from his terrible burns.

At Zandvoort, Lotus introduced the new 49, powered by the new Cosworth DFV engine. Hill claimed pole position but he retired from the race, leaving Clark to win in fine style at 104.49 mph, setting fastest lap on the way at 106.49 mph. It was a real *tour de force* for the team. Brabham and Hulme showed that they were not going to relinquish the championship without a fight, taking second and third places ahead of Amon's Ferrari. Dan Gurney put the Eagle on to the list of winners with a magnificent performance in Belgium where he averaged a sensational 145.74 mph to beat Stewart's H16 BRM by over a minute. Amon again came home third and the pace of the event can be judged by Gurney's fastest lap of 148.85 mph. Ferrari were lucky not to lose another driver when Parkes survived a huge first lap accident with no more than a broken arm and leg.

Brabham himself was back on top in France where the Grand Prix was held on the Bugatti circuit at Le Mans. Hulme finished second and both Lotuses retired, showing the gap in reliability between the two teams which would net Brabham's second championship, despite the Lotuses' undoubted speed.

Above left: the Dutch Grand Prix of 1968 was run in extremely wet conditions, and many drivers were caught out. One such was Jean-Pierre Beltoise, who spun his V12 Matra MS11 when lying second. After calling at the pits to have sand removed from the throttle slides, he rejoined the race, and re-took second place after a superb drive up from seventh place

Top: Jackie Stewart began racing in 1961 using a variety of borrowed sports cars, and in 1964 he drove Formula 3 Coopers for Ken Tyrrell, winning eleven of the thirteen races he entered. A full Formula One season with BRM in 1965 gave him third place in the Championship, but a bad accident at Spa in 1966 caused him to campaign vigorously for greater safety precautions. His long-standing rapport with Tyrrell paid off in 1969 when he took the Championship in Ken's Matra-Ford. Champion again in 1971 and 1973 driving Tyrrell-Fords, Jackie won an unsurpassed 27 Grands Prix He is now a businessman, but he and his wife Helen are still to be seen at the Grands Prix as Stewart is much in demand as a commentator

Top: Jackie Stewart at Kyalami during the 1969 South African Grand Prix, a race he won easily in the Ford-powered Matra. Soon after this the excessively high-mounted aerofoils were banned

Above left: Jacky Ickx's career began on motor cycles and he was Belgian Trials champion three years running. He was Belgian saloon car champion in 1965, and spotted by Ken Tyrrell, he won the European F2 Championship in 1967. Ickx drove for Ferrari in 1968, Brabham in 1969, and back with Ferrari was runner-up to Rindt in 1970. After a disjointed season in 1973, Jacky joined Lotus for two seasons. A man of very many interests outside the sport, he appears happiest at the wheel of sports cars, having won Le Mans six times

Above: Mike Spence was a works Lotus driver from 1963 to 1966, then he drove for the Parnell team until 1968 when he joined BRM. In 1967 he and Phil Hill won the BOAC 500 miles at Brands Hatch in the Chaparral. He was killed at Indianapolis in 1968 in the Lotus 56 turbine car

Clark's Lotus did not let him down at Silverstone however and he scored his fifth British Grand Prix win in six attempts, 3.8 seconds ahead of Hulme and 14 seconds ahead of Amon. The gremlins hit Lotus again in Germany and Hulme and Brabham were again ready to pounce for the first two places. Hulme's winning average was 101.47 mph. The Formula One establishment was almost dealt a severe shock by young Belgian Jacky Ickx, who held fourth place in his Formula Two Matra before retiring.

Canada hosted her first Grand Prix in August and saw yet another one-two for Brabham and Hulme, from Gurney's Eagle.

The Monza race was sensational. After early problems, Clark drove the race of his life to retake the lead, only to lose it again on the last lap when he ran short of fuel. Surtees and Brabham swapped places all the way round that final tour until Surtees took the flag by just 0.2 seconds at an average of 140.5 mph. In making up a deficit of a whole lap Clark left the lap record at a staggering 145.3 mph. It was Lotus's turn to score first and second in the USA with Hill winning from Clark, whose suspension was rapidly falling apart! Hulme kept his sights on the title with third place, and finally resolved the battle by finishing in the same position in Mexico, behind Clark and Brabham. Clark's victory brought his total tally to 24, the same as that of Juan Manuel Fangio. Alas there was to be only one more.

The 1968 season lost all meaning to many people on 8 April when Jim Clark was killed in an inexplicable accident in a minor Formula Two race at Hockenheim in Germany. With Clark, motor racing lost one of its greatest-ever exponents and a true hero to hundreds of thousands of people. Once again there was a void to be filled at the top.

Clark's team-mate and greatest rival eased the burden, if only by the smallest amount, for Team Lotus, by taking the 49B to the title. On his way to his second championship, Hill won in Spain, Monaco and Mexico. Clark had given Lotus another victory in the opening race of the season in South Africa taking his number of wins to the quarter century – one more than Fangio. Lotus were given another memorable victory when Jo Siffert won the British Grand Prix at an average speed of 104.83 mph in a Lotus 49B entered privately by Rob Walker. The other winners of the season were Bruce McLaren, scoring his first victory in his own car at Spa (at a remarkable 147.14 mph), Jackie Stewart with the Ford-engined Matra in Holland, Germany and the USA, Denny Hulme – now McLaren mounted – in Italy and Canada, and Jacky Ickx at Rouen. Rouen was marred by the death of Jo Schlesser, giving the air-cooled V8 Honda its debut. Mike Spence and Ludovico Scarfiotti were also victims of their cruel sport, the former dying at Indianapolis and the latter in practice for a hill-climb. What did emerge from 1968 was that if any driver might be a future heir to Clark's crown it was his countryman, Stewart, who shone out of a galaxy of new talent which was taking over from the old brigade.

After finishing second to Hill in 1968, Stewart took his first title in the

Right: Lorenzo Bandini made his competition debut in 1957 and became a works Ferrari driver in 1963. A promising career, which included wins at Le Mans in 1963 and in the Austrian Grand Prix in 1964, was tragically cut short in 1967: while chasing Denny Hulme at Monaco, he crashed at the chicane on the 82nd lap and was trapped in his blazing car. He was released and flown to hospital, but died three days later

Far right: Hulme drove brilliantly at Monaco in 1967 to win by a whole lap from Graham Hill. He is seen here leading Bruce McLaren, who took his McLaren-BRM to a creditable fourth place after a pit stop to change the battery

Below: on his way to his third World Championship, in 1966, Jack Brabham won at the Nürburgring after a monumental battle with John Surtees and Jochen Rindt – both in Cooper-Maseratis

following year with a series of magnificent performances with the Ken Tyrrell entered Matra-Ford. With Cooper, Eagle and Honda all withdrawing from the fray, and Brabham building Ford-powered cars for the first time, the championship became virtually a straight fight between Ford and Ferrari, BRM's fortunes being at a fairly low ebb and Matra's own V12 project still being in need of much development. Driver changes too were a new element in the struggle, with new found advertising revenue tempting several stars to new seats. Rindt left Brabham to join Hill at Lotus and was replaced by Ickx, while Surtees made a brief flirtation with the troubled BRM team.

Stewart started the season in style at Kyalami for the South African Grand Prix. He led from start to finish to beat his former team-mate, and reigning champion, Hill, into second place. The Brabham team suffered problems at Kyalami with their large, high-mounted aerofoils and in the next race, at Barcelona's Montjuich Park, the problem came to an ugly head when Hill and Rindt were lucky to survive major accidents directly attributable to the devices. The newly installed Armco barriers – for whose use Jackie Stewart had become a vociferous and much criticised campaigner – earned their keep on that day by keeping the errant Lotuses out of the packed crowds. Stewart himself took a lucky win in the race after early leader Amon again fell victim to his appalling fortune, his Ferrari engine digesting its bearings after 34 laps.

The new, wingless, look was enforced by new regulations coming into force – during practice – at Monaco but it didn't stop Graham Hill from taking his fifth victory at the demanding circuit. Piers Courage enhanced his reputation with a stirring second place in Frank Williams' privately entered Brabham and Siffert brought the Walker Lotus home third. Hill's winning average was 80.18 mph and Stewart confirmed that his sights were on the title by taking fastest lap at 82.67 mph before retiring.

The next three races, in Holland, France – at Clermont Ferrand – and Great Britain, saw three clear cut victories for Stewart. After Rindt dropped out, Stewart beat Siffert to the flag in Holland; he led his team-mate Beltoise home to a classic one-two victory in France, averaging 97.71 mph and at Silverstone he drove Beltoise's car, after wrecking his own in a practice accident. It did not deter him from a running battle with Rindt which was resolved when the new low-mounted wing on Rindt's Lotus came adrift, vindicating the new rules by the absence of spectacular consequences. Rindt eventually finished fourth behind Ickx and McLaren. Four-wheel-drive cars from Lotus and McLaren had very disappointing outings.

Ickx scored a classic win for Brabham at the Nürburgring after hounding Stewart for many laps. His fastest lap on the road to a 108.43 mph victory was 110.13 mph. American ace Mario Andretti drove one of the works Lotuses, but lasted only as long as the first lap. Stewart clinched the title in an epic slipstreaming battle at Monza in which 0.2 seconds covered the first four finishers. The order was Stewart, Rindt, Beltoise and McLaren. Stewart averaged

Above: Jochen Rindt's Lotus 49B on its way to victory in the 1969 United States Grand Prix and the 200,000 dollars prize fund.

Left: Winner Rindt and his close friend Piers Courage share the spoils of victory after the US Grand Prix. Courage came second in Frank William's Brabham BT26A

Above right: Bruce McLaren won New Zealand's 'Driver to Europe' award in 1958, and at age 22 had won the 1959 US Grand Prix. He was a pioneer of the Can-Am sports car championship as well as Le Mans winner in 1966. His cars virtually monopolised Can-Am until 1971, and Bruce won the 1968 Belgian GP in his own car. Sadly, McLaren was killed in 1970 while testing his latest Can-Am car, but his name lives on in Fittipaldi's and Hunt's World Championship-winning cars

146.96 mph and Beltoise put the lap record over 150 mph, to 150.96 mph. Ickx won again in Canada, after a coming together with Stewart in the early stages had eliminated the Scot. Black Jack backed up his young team-mate with a popular second place ahead of Rindt.

In the USA, Rindt showed that Stewart may not have been the only heir to Clark's crown by scoring the victory that he had threatened for so long. He finished 46.99 seconds ahead of Piers Courage followed two laps later by Surtees, giving the BRM its best result of the season. Graham Hill had a terrible accident in the closing stages of the race, breaking both legs when he was flung from his cartwheeling Lotus. It was only sheer determination that brought Hill back to the grids for the opening round of 1970. The one race that he missed, Mexico 1969, was a triumph for Hulme over Ickx's Brabham, but the championship was already Stewart's by a clear 26 points from Ickx.

1970 was a black year for the sport with the championship being awarded posthumously for the first time. The champion who did not live to receive his acclaim was Jochen Rindt. As well as the death of Rindt the sport was rocked by the loss of Bruce McLaren, killed at Goodwood while testing a Can-Am sports car, and Piers Courage, who perished in his burning de Tomaso after crashing heavily at Zandvoort.

Ickx returned to Ferrari, and the World Champion found himself equipped with one of the new March cars to start the season, while Matra now had their own cars for Beltoise and Henry Pescarolo.

Brabham won the season opener in South Africa, with Hill earning the hardest point of his career for sixth place, in his comeback with the Rob Walker team. Stewart gave heart to newcomers, March, with a flag-to-flag win in Spain, at Jarama. McLaren was second, a lap down, and Andretti completed a great day for March with third place; Hill was fourth. Ickx's Ferrari and Oliver's BRM were totally destroyed in a fiery accident from which they were lucky to escape intact.

Monaco will be remembered as a race where Jack Brabham made one of his rare mistakes to let Rindt, who was hounding him all the way, slip through on the last corner. Pescarolo drove well to bring the new Matra home in third place. Rodriguez brought a smile back to the glum faces from Bourne by giving BRM a rare win at Spa, by just over a second from Amon's March. Beltoise rewarded Matra with another third place at the ultra-fast Belgian circuit, which Amon had lapped at 152.07 mph in his chase of Rodriguez, who averaged 149.94 mph for the race.

Zandvoort saw the debut of a new Lotus, the 72, and like Clark with the 49 Rindt made no mistake at all in winning the race. It brought him little joy though, his great friend Courage was no longer alive to share it. Stewart gave March another second place from the Ferraris of Ickx and Regazzoni, making a promising debut. Rindt's sequence of mid-season triumphs, at Clermont Ferrand, Brands Hatch and Hockenheim, gave him an unassailable lead in the

title race. The British race saw a near replay of the Monaco finish, with Brabham this time running out of fuel almost within sight of the line to let Rindt through. Post race protests over the height of the Lotus's wing were eventually rejected and Jochen celebrated his third successive win. A new face joined the Lotus team that day, a young Brazilian by the name of Emerson Fittipaldi whose steady drive to eighth place gave little clue to the future that lay ahead of him. Hockenheim saw Rindt's last Grand Prix win, by 0.7 seconds from Ickx's Ferrari after a race long duel. Rindt averaged 123.90 mph and Ickx's consolation was fastest lap at 126.02 mph. Fittipaldi was fourth and a promising French newcomer, François Cevert, was seventh in a March.

Ickx and Regazzoni gave notice of a Ferrari revival by taking the first two places in Austria, where Rindt lost the chance to win in front of his home crowd due to engine failure.

After Rindt's death at Monza during practice, the race was of academic interest. All the other Lotus entries, works and private, were withdrawn – both out of respect for Rindt and respect for the possibility that a mechanical failure had caused the accident. It was a pity that a fine victory, in his first season, by Regazzoni should have been so overshadowed. The lap speed at Monza was again over 150 mph, Regazzoni turning in one lap at 150.96 mph and the whole distance at 147.07 mph. The authorities began to look seriously at the circuit's future. Victories by Ickx in Canada and Mexico, and by Fittipaldi in America were not enough to wrest the title from Jochen and no one begrudged him his posthumous triumph.

The March drivers had not been without their successes in 1970, with Stewart scoring one win, and at least one of the cars being well placed in most

Top: Niki Lauda's first Grand Prix was in his native Austria in 1971 with a March 711. He retired after only 20 laps with handling problems and did not race in Grands Prix again until 1972. In 1975 at the age of 26 he won the World Championship for Ferrari, taking the title from Ford-powered cars for the first time since 1967

Above: 1971 saw François Cevert, with the guidance of team-mate Jackie Stewart and manager Ken Tyrrell, mature into a fast and consistent competitor. He is seen here in the French Grand Prix, at Paul Ricard, where he finished second to Stewart to complete a great day for the French-financed Tyrrell team. Parisian born Cevert was killed at Watkins Glen in practice for the final race of the 1973 championship. He was then 29

Top: motor racing can be a cruel sport and one of its cruellest blows was the death of Jochen Rindt in practice for the Italian Grand Prix at Monza in 1970: his death left the sport with its first posthumous World Champion. The 28-year-old Austrian was widely regarded as one of the all time great drivers and his loss was a great tragedy

Above: with the possible exception of the drivers, the most important part of a motor racing team is the team manager; perhaps the most respected manager in the business is Ken Tyrrell. Tyrrell is a former driver himself and his business as a timber merchant earned him the nickname 'Chopper'. It was Tyrrell who 'discovered' the young Jackie Stewart and developed his talents to world championship class. When the March 701 which he was running for Stewart in 1970 left doubts over its potential Tyrrell entered the ranks of the car constructors. His cars were immediately front runners and have stayed that way ever since

races, but Ken Tyrrell had long wanted more control of his own team and, early in 1970, he had introduced Tyrrell 001. With the latest Tyrrells, Stewart and his new team-mate, Cevert, were to have a remarkable season in 1971.

The year got off to a bad start even before the season started, when Ferrari's Italian rising star, Ignazio Giunti, was killed in a sports car race in Argentina. Jean-Pierre Beltoise was rather hastily held by the organisers to be culpable, and lost his licence for much of the year. Ferrari started the season proper on a happier note when their American ex-patriot-Italian, Mario Andretti, scored a sensational first Grand Prix win, by 20.9 seconds from Stewart. Regazzoni with the other Ferrari was third, ahead of Reine Wisell's Lotus.

Stewart opened his 1971 account – and Tyrrell's Grand Prix score – in Spain, where he beat Ickx's Ferrari by just 3.4 seconds after a race-long struggle. His 97.19 mph win was his third Spanish victory in a row. He followed it up with a start to finish win in Monaco, but that day it was second man Peterson who caused the sensation by driving a brilliant race in the works March 711 to beat Ickx and Siffert – the latter now in a BRM. Graham Hill had joined the Brabham team with Jack's retirement at the end of 1970, but he was out of luck at his beloved Monaco, writing off his BT34 on only the second lap. Stewart was off form at a very wet Zandvoort, but Ickx and Rodriguez put on a great display of their wet weather skills to finish first and second, in that order, Rodriguez giving the BRM team a needed lift. Regazzoni was third and Peterson fourth. Emerson Fittipaldi was out of commission following a road accident and Dave Walker, deputising, crashed both a 72 in practice and the debutante turbine Lotus in the race.

The French Grand Prix had yet another new home, at the Circuit Paul Ricard near Marseilles, a new purpose built circuit which met with mixed feelings from the purists. Stewart obviously liked the place though, disappearing into the distance with Cevert in pursuit to give the French-financed team a great day, in front of a partisan crowd. Emerson showed that his brief absence had taken away none of his fire, with a brilliant drive to third place less than six seconds behind Cevert. Ferrari and the works March team could not boast a finisher between them.

Stewart did not take long to overhaul the leading pair of Ferraris at Silverstone to score another comfortable victory, with Peterson recording another fine second place; Fittipaldi was third and again no Ferraris finished. From England, the circus moved to Germany, where the Tyrrell twins were first and second again, Stewart leading Cevert home by 30.1 seconds at 114.46 mph, although Cevert took fastest lap at 116.07 mph. Regazzoni and Andretti in Ferrari 312 B2s filled the next two places and Peterson was fifth. When Stewart ignominiously crashed out of the Austrian Grand Prix he was consoled by the fact that Ickx's failure to score in the race had handed him his second championship on a plate. The race was won in style by Jo Siffert, for BRM, who needed a morale booster after the death of Rodriguez in a minor sports car race a week before the British race. The rising stars had a good day with Fittipaldi second, Tim Schenken – in a Brabham – third, and Reine Wisell fourth. Not-so-new boy Graham Hill had a better day than of late with the 'lobster claw' Brabham, to finish fifth. A young Austrian in a rented March retired with handling trouble, his name was Niki Lauda and it was his first Grand Prix. The Ferraris both retired again and for once so did the Tyrrells.

The traditional Monza slipstreamer was won after a momentous struggle by BRM's new signing, Peter Gethin. Gethin, Peterson, Cevert, Hailwood (in a Surtees TS9) and Howden Ganley (in a BRM) finished in that order and with just 0.61 seconds covering all five. Chris Amon was sixth and had looked like winning until his cruel luck struck again and he lost his visor a few laps from home. The winning average was 150.76 mph and Pescarolo's fastest lap, for March, was 153.49 mph. The Canadian race ran only 64 of its scheduled 80 laps, due to bad weather conditions, and when the flag was hung out Stewart was first beneath it for the sixth time of the season, with Peterson again following him home and Mark Donohue in a privately entered McLaren M19A taking a popular third place. Cevert completed a happy season for Tyrrell by scoring his first win in the final round at Watkins Glen, the richest race on the

calendar. Siffert was second and Peterson was third, to claim the runner-up spot in the championship. This was Siffert's last Grand Prix, the season ending as it had begun, with tragedy in a minor race, when 'Seppi' was killed at Brands Hatch in a race to celebrate Stewart's victory.

After two seasons of tragedy, 1972 was free of incident and Lotus came out of the shadows to score another world title, through Emerson Fittipaldi, who, at 25, was the sport's youngest ever champion. The Brazilian took the championship in style with wins at Jarama, Nivelles (in Belgium), Brands Hatch, the Österreichring and Monza. He was second at Kyalami and Clermont Ferrand and third in Monaco, to win by a handsome margin. Emerson's nearest rival was Stewart, who won the opening round as the championship returned to the Argentine for the first time in twelve years, plus the French, Canadian and American races. Denny Hulme won in South Africa, Jacky Ickx won at the Nürburgring and Jean-Pierre Beltoise scored a memorable triumph for BRM at an extremely wet Monaco. Stewart, in taking second place in the championship, revealed some of the pressure of modern racing when he had to miss the Belgian Grand Prix through stomach ulcer problems. Chris Amon looked all set for his first ever win at Clermont Ferrand before a puncture stole his glory. Carlos Reutemann was a new name on the grids and impressed many people with very fast performances in his Brabham, scoring pole position at his first ever Grand Prix, appropriately in his native Argentina. With a new World Champion and a promising new star, the South Americans again had something to shout about in motor racing.

1973 was a year symptomatic of the modern trend of racing, with as much competition off the tracks – mostly concerning money – as on. Fortunately the quality of the racing diverted the public eye from the more unseemly side of things and it was another vintage championship year, though one again tainted by tragedy.

The first race, in Argentina, saw Ronnie Peterson alongside Fittipaldi in the black and gold Lotus 72Ds and the reigning champion won the race after Regazzoni, Cevert and Stewart had problems ahead of him. Regazzoni was newly ensconced at BRM and was sensational in practice, giving the team their first pole position since 1971. He led for 29 laps before overheating tyres forced him out. Fittipaldi won again in his native Brazil, at 114.88 mph and the stage looked set for him to retain his title. Stewart thought otherwise and followed up second place in Brazil and third in the Argentine (behind Cevert) with his first win of the season in South Africa. It was a meeting of high drama; Stewart had crashed in practice, local man Jody Scheckter shared the front row with McLaren team-mate Hulme (who used the new M23 to give him his first ever pole position) and Mike Hailwood earned himself a George Medal during the race for a heroic rescue of Regazzoni from his blazing BRM. George Follmer also survived all the dramas to give the new Shadow team their first point.

The Spanish Grand Prix was back to the round the houses circuit at Mont-

Above: keeping it in the family at the French Grand Prix, at Paul Ricard, in 1973 are the Fittipaldi brothers, with Emerson's Lotus 72 ahead of Wilson's Brabham

Above left: while Denny Hulme, with the new McLaren M23, claimed his first ever pole position at the 1973 South African Grand Prix, local hero Jody Scheckter put his older McLaren M19 onto the front row too. Scheckter led the race for several laps, with his McLaren team-mate Peter Revson on his tail as seen here, but his race ended with a blown engine. An inspired Jackie Stewart took the lead on the seventh lap and beat Revson into second place. The race was marred by an accident in the opening stages in which Clay Regazzoni was trapped in his blazing car. The Swiss was rescued by Mike Hailwood, whose Surtees had also been involved in the accident, and Hailwood was later awarded a George Medal for his bravery

Left: Jo Siffert will be remembered as a driver who always gave his utmost. He started racing on motor cycles in his native Switzerland and graduated to cars in 1960. In 1968 he scored a memorable Grand Prix victory at Brands Hatch with Rob Walker's privately entered Lotus 49B. He only won one other Grand Prix, in Austria in 1971, but his reputation as a driver of the enormously powerful Porsche 917 sports cars made him a man to respect. At the end of the 1971 season a race was organised at Brands Hatch to celebrate Jackie Stewart's World Championship. During the race Siffert's BRM crashed heavily and burst into flames. Inadequately equipped marshals were unable to release Siffert and he perished in the blazing car

juich and the drivers must have been glad of the new deformable structures on the cars, which became mandatory at this race. Peterson was again on pole, but the race went to Fittipaldi after Peterson, Hulme, Cevert and Stewart were all sidelined. Emerson's 97.86 mph win gave Lotus their 50th Grand Prix victory. Emerson's win was a close thing as he had a tyre deflating over the closing laps, and Cevert, recovering after a puncture of his own, drove as hard as he knew how in his efforts to take the lead. Follmer brought his Shadow home in third place.

Politics reared their head at the Belgian Grand Prix, which was transferred from Nivelles to Zolder. The newly resurfaced track began to break up during practice and for a while it looked as though the race might be cancelled. An idea of the conditions can be gained from the fact that Peterson, having gained pole position, crashed twice during the race-day warm up and again in the race. He was not alone: as car after car left the circuit, Stewart and Cevert pounded through to a one-two, from Fittipaldi. There were plenty of statistics to note at Monaco: Graham Hill was making his 150th Grand Prix appearance and Stewart was aiming for the 25th win of his meteoric career. He collected it, too, beating Fittipaldi by 1.3 seconds at an average of 80.96 mph. Making his debut in the race at the wheel of the flamboyant Hesketh team's March 731 was James Hunt. His engine blew up five laps from home, while he was lying sixth and silencing many critics.

Sweden was a new country to be added to the championship trail and all eyes at Anderstorp were naturally on Peterson. From pole position he led until less than two laps from home, when a deflating tyre forced him to give way to Denny Hulme who had stormed through the field in his McLaren M23 after early problems. McLaren's new boy, Jody Scheckter, sprung some surprises in France, leading from the flag and disputing the lead until he collided with Fittipaldi, eliminating them both. On his 40th attempt, Peterson won his first Grand Prix, by 40.92 seconds from Cevert; Hunt scored his first point at his second attempt with sixth place.

The British Grand Prix, at Silverstone, saw one of the biggest accidents of all time when, at the end of the first lap, Scheckter – lying fourth – lost control coming onto the start-finish straight from the very fast right hander, Woodcote. He bounced off the pit wall and into the pack, which was soon reduced to so much wreckage. The only injuries amidst the mechanical carnage were to Scheckter's ego and Andrea de Adamich's ankle. The race was restarted after a long delay and was no less of a sensation with Peter Revson winning from Peterson, Hulme and Hunt. 3.4 seconds covered the four of them and Revson's average speed was 131.75 mph. Hunt pleased his local crowd with fastest lap, at 134.06 mph.

The sense of security lent by the efficiency of the new deformable structures in the Silverstone melée was shattered at Zandvoort. Roger Williamson, in only his second Grand Prix with Tom Wheatcroft's March, crashed heavily on lap eight and the car burst into flames. Although David Purley tried heroically to rescue Williamson – virtually unaided by the marshals – the promising young Englishman perished. Stewart went on to win his 26th Grand Prix, from Cevert, but there were no celebrations, only bitterness.

Stewart and Cevert pulverised the opposition at the Nürburgring, finishing 1.6 seconds apart and a long way ahead of third man Ickx, who was making a 'guest' appearance with McLarens. The winning average was 116.82 mph and fastest lap went to an inspired Carlos Pace at 118.43 mph. Peterson won in Austria, from Stewart, after Fittipaldi had retired only five laps from victory. Ronnie won again at Monza, with Emerson second, but Stewart, who drove a magnificent race to finish fourth after a puncture, clinched his third championship. The Canadian race was won by Peter Revson in total confusion after rain forced pit stops for tyre changes and an accident brought the newly introduced pace car out to slow the action. Unfortunately, it came out in front of the wrong car and the race degenerated into a shambles.

What should have been the crowning of a magnificent career for Stewart with his 100th and last Grand Prix at Watkins Glen was completely over-shadowed by the death of Cevert in practice. The Tyrrell team withdrew,

Stewart announced his retirement a week later as Champion, and Peterson won the race from a hard charging and very impressive Hunt.

Stewart's retirement again left a throne to be filled and the sport was now so competitive that no single driver could fill it. 1974 began with doubts over the very future of the sport, brought on by the energy crisis of the winter months. Out of the gloom came one of the most exciting championships ever. With Stewart gone, drivers began a major reshuffle of their services. Fittipaldi went to McLaren, Ickx to Lotus, Lauda to Ferrari and Regazzoni *back* to Ferrari; Revson joined Shadow and Ken Tyrrell set out to rebuild his team with Jody Scheckter and Frenchman Patrick Depailler.

At last, the domination of the Cosworth DFV was being challenged by Ferrari's flat-12. Reutemann, leading his home Grand Prix in Argentina had his own fuel crisis one and a half laps from home and handed victory to Denny Hulme, followed by the Ferraris of Lauda and Regazzoni. Fittipaldi scored his first win for his new team in front of his home crowd in Brazil after a duel with Peterson. The race was shortened to forty laps after a sudden cloudburst. Regazzoni's second place for Ferrari put them on top of the title table.

Below: Ronnie Peterson's John Player Special-Lotus 72 leads team-mate Emerson Fittipaldi and Jacky Ickx's Ferrari past the Monza pits during the 1973 Italian Grand Prix. Peterson was out to win, and did not repeat his gesture of the preceding Austrian Grand Prix of waving Fittipaldi past for maximum points in order to retain the Championship. Meanwhile, Stewart, who could not know what the Lotus tactics would be, was having the drive of his life, storming from twentieth to fourth place after a puncture. This was enough to guarantee him the Championship, so Peterson's race victory was vindicated

Below: Carlos Reutemann's Brabham sandwiched between the Ferraris of Regazzoni and Lauda at the start of the 1974 South African Grand Prix, and *inset*, a delighted Lole after his victory. It had been four years since Jack Brabham had won the same race in a Brabham, and Carlos was the first Argentinian to win a Grand Prix since Fangio in 1957

The South African Grand Prix was put back into the calendar at the end of March, having been cancelled during the winter. It seemed that there was something to be happy about after all, but it was all forgotten when Peter Revson's Shadow crashed head on into the barriers during practice, killing the very popular American instantly. The race saw the introduction of the new John Player Specials, or Lotuses by any other name, but it was an inauspicious debut, with the type 76s eliminating each other on the first lap. Lauda started the race from pole but the glory went to Reutemann who gained his first win and the first for Brabham for four years. Into a sensational second came Beltoise with the new BRM P201.

Ferrari finally came in from the cold with a magnificent one-two finish at Jarama after a race turned topsy turvy by rain. Ronnie Peterson had a more encouraging outing with the Lotus 76, now running with a conventional clutch. He started from the front row and roared away in the lead with Ickx backing him up in third place but when the rains came the Lotus pit work was shambolic while Ferrari's was exemplary; Lauda won his first Grand Prix at an average speed of 88.48 mph. Fittipaldi took victory at Nivelles by the narrowest of margins (0.35 seconds) from Lauda, after driving the race of his life. It put him into the lead of the championship by one point.

In Monaco, Lotus reverted to using the 72Es and Peterson showed that there was life in the old cars yet by claiming victory in a race which saw almost everyone, including Ronnie, fall off at some stage. His average speed was 80.74mph and he took fastest lap at 83.42mph. With this win in the bag, Lotus went to Sweden full of confidence but the establishment was stood on its ear by the new Tyrrell twins who filled the front row of the grid and finished first and second in the race, with Scheckter beating Depailler by 0.38 seconds. James Hunt was now equipped with Hesketh's own car and gave it its first points with a fine third place, while Graham Hill with a Lola was sixth; Scheckter's win made him the sixth different winner from the first seven rounds! Ferrari steamrollered all the Ford opposition at Zandvoort with Lauda winning his second race of the season from Regazzoni, while Fittipaldi and Hailwood in McLarens headed the vain chase by the 'Formula Ford' cars.

Notions that the reign of the DFV was over were firmly quashed when Peterson led home Lauda and Regazzoni at Dijon, the fifteenth new home of

Below left : Niki Lauda was desperately unlucky in the 1974 British Grand Prix at Brands Hatch when his Ferrari suffered a deflating rear tyre only six laps from the finish. Lauda, who had been leading, rushed into the pits for a new tyre, but he was prevented from rejoining the race by a course car and the many officials, mechanics and personnel who had gathered at the end of the pit road to watch the finish. Lauda was classified ninth, and his protest that he could have taken fifth place was rejected, although the FIA later awarded him two championship points

Right : Jody Scheckter took the lead of the 1974 British Grand Prix after Lauda's puncture and went on to win. Scheckter is pictured with the John Player girls about to be taken on his lap of honour. He left Tyrrell at the close of the 1976 season and he gave the Wolf Team an auspicious debut by winning the 1977 Argentine Grand Prix

the French Grand Prix. Lauda thus went to Brands Hatch with a four point lead in the championship. After leading all the way from Scheckter's Tyrrell 007, the flying Ferrari became one of many to fall victim of a puncture. Lauda struggled on, falling to third place by the closing stages. With only two laps to go, the tyre had disintegrated completely and Lauda was forced into the pits. By the time the new wheel was on, Scheckter was well on his way to the flag and the pit exit road was so crowded that Lauda was unable to rejoin the race. It was not until two months later that a tribunal awarded him fifth place. Ferrari honour was restored at the Nürburgring where Regazzoni was uncatchable. Lauda was eliminated in the season's sixth first-lap accident – a sure sign of the extraordinary intensity of the competition. Scheckter set fastest lap at 118.49 mph on his way to second place and Reutemann was third. Mike Hailwood's career came to a sad and premature end at Pflanzgarten when he landed all awry and smashed into the barriers, severely damaging his legs. Reutemann won his second race of the season in Austria, heading Hulme and Hunt by a healthy margin.

Regazzoni's fifth place sent him to Italy with a five point lead over Scheckter in the championship and the kind of support that comes only to Ferrari at Monza. Alas, both Maranello cars were sidelined by engine failures and Peterson went on to win from Fittipaldi – by 0.8 seconds. Fittipaldi won in Canada with Regazzoni finishing second which resulted in the amazing situation of those two drivers going to the last round at Watkins Glen with 52 points each. Scheckter, with 45 points, also had a mathematical chance of winning. It turned into something of an anticlimax. Reutemann disappeared into the distance while Regazzoni fought unpredictable handling back in ninth place and Scheckter dropped out when a fuel pipe broke. Fittipaldi's fifth place was unspectacular but enough to earn him his second championship in one of the most closely fought series ever. Once again, the end of the series was overshadowed by tragedy. Helmuth Koinigg was killed when his Surtees ploughed under a guard rail on lap nine.

The DFV engine's incredible run of success was finally halted in 1975 when Ferrari put everything right at the same time to take the championship away from the Ford-powered cars for the first time since 1967. Niki Lauda applied all his single minded determination to winning the title and win it he did. Ferrari started the season with the latest 312B3 cars but they were soundly beaten in the opening round in Argentina by Fittipaldi and by Hunt – with the Hesketh 308; Regazzoni was third and Lauda sixth. Jarier had been sensationally quick in practice to put the new Shadow DN5 on pole but the car broke on the warm up lap and did not start. Carlos Pace was the second Brazilian race winner in two events when he delighted everyone by storming home first in Brazil. His Brabham BT44B led home compatriot Fittipaldi's McLaren M23 by 5.79 seconds; Jarier had led with ease before the Shadow again failed.

Right: the Armco barriers were in such a poor state of neglect at Barcelona's Montjuich Park circuit prior to the 1975 Grand Prix that the team mechanics were forced to do what they could to rebuild them. Even Ken Tyrrell lent a hand, but it was not enough to prevent a tragedy when Rolf Stommelen's Hill-Lola crashed, fatally injuring three officials and a spectator

Below left: Emerson Fittipaldi's McLaren M23 won the Argentine Grand Prix of 1975 after Reutemann and Hunt had dropped back

Below right: Jean-Pierre Jarier astonished everyone by setting pole position time for the Argentinian and Brazilian Grands Prix in 1975. Such promise was unfulfilled, however, for the Shadow broke a crown-wheel before the Buenos Aires race, and a metering unit failed when Jarier was in the lead at Interlagos

South Africa saw the debut of the Ferrari 312T, with transverse gearbox, which was to end Ford's domination. It was not to happen in this race, however, for Scheckter became the second 'home' winner of the season by beating Reutemann into second place.

The Spanish race started with arguments and ended with tragedy. On arriving at Barcelona's Montjuich Park, the teams took one look at the shoddily erected safety barriers and said 'no way!'. After much wrangling and work by the teams themselves, the race was grudgingly staged – albeit without Fittipaldi, whose principles were more important to him than his contract and who withdrew. Tragically, the Embassy-Hill-Lola of Rolf Stommelen, which had inherited the lead as others fell by the wayside, crashed heavily on the 25th lap, seriously injuring the driver and hurling debris over the barriers which killed three officials and a photographer. The race was stopped four laps later and Jochen Mass was declared the winner for McLaren and awarded half points. Lella Lombardi of Italy came home in sixth place with her March 751 to give a rare break in the total male domination of Grand Prix racing and collected half a point. It was not, however, a weekend for celebration.

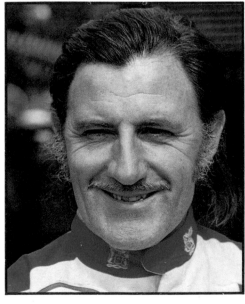

Above: Graham Hill retired from race-driving in 1975, but his team was on the threshold of success when Hill and his young protégé, Tony Brise, were killed in a senseless air crash at the end of the year. Four team members died with them and the team was disbanded

Below: Tony Brise drove a fine race at Sweden's Anderstorp circuit to take sixth place. He might have finished higher had his Embassy Hill GH1 not been jammed in fourth gear

Left: Emerson Fittipaldi at the Rascasse hairpin during the 1975 Monaco Grand Prix. The Brazilian, seen leading Mark Donohue's Penske PC1, finished second after a race interrupted by tyre changes when the wet track dried out

Monaco, with some similarity to Montjuich as a true road circuit, was obviously in the public eye and happily it was a classic race with no squabbles or major incidents. The organisers made great efforts to make the race safe by limiting the grid to 18 cars, but this prevented Graham Hill from qualifying on the circuit of his greatest triumphs. Lauda gave the new Ferrari its first win at 75.55 mph after a race dominated by the weather and pit stops. Fittipaldi was second, 2.78 seconds adrift. The race was shortened by three laps as the rain came down again and whether Emerson might have caught Lauda's ailing Ferrari remained a matter for conjecture. It did not seem to trouble Lauda unduly as he reeled off the laps to win in Belgium and again in Sweden after a rousing battle with Reutemann who came home second. One of the most impressive performances in Sweden came from young Tony Brise in the new Hill GH 1: he finished sixth. His promise was lost to the world when he was killed with Hill himself and other team members in a plane crash in November 1975 at Hendon.

The Dutch Grand Prix was again influenced by tyre changes: James Hunt judged the time for a change to slicks to perfection on a rapidly drying track

Far right : this is how the 1975 John Player British Grand Prix ended, when twelve cars, including most of the leaders were eliminated on the 56th lap. The race had been dogged by foul weather, necessitating as many as four tyre-changes, act conditions became so bad at Club corner that most of the drivers crashed into the catch fencing. The race was abandoned after Emerson Fittipaldi had completed the 56th lap, but it took three days for the official finishing order to be established

Centre : it was a sad day for motor racing when Mark Donohue died. One of the nicest people in his profession, he was fatally injured in a crash while practising for the 1975 Austrian Grand Prix. An experienced development engineer, Donohue had been Trans-Am Champion in 1968, 1969 and 1970 in Roger Penske's Camaro, Can-Am Champion in a Porsche 917 in 1973 and Indianapolis winner in 1972 and he was hoping for Grand Prix success

Below : World Champion in 1972 with Lotus and in 1974 with McLaren, Emerson Fittipaldi finished the 1975 season second in the points standings. He did not enjoy the same success in 1976, driving for his brother's Copersucar-backed team

and his pit crew were ultra quick. James went back out and built up a commanding lead before the others read the signs and then fought a magnificent running battle for many laps as Lauda reeled in his advantage. He beat the Ferrari by 1.06 seconds to give the Hesketh team a well deserved win. The French Grand Prix at Paul Ricard saw the status quo restored, with Lauda turning the tables to beat Hunt by 1.59 seconds at 116.60 mph. Mario Andretti brought the Parnelli VPJ-4 into fifth place. The British Grand Prix was at Silverstone and again the weather decided the outcome. A deluge of rain on the 56th lap sent car after car crashing into the barriers, leaving Emerson Fittipaldi – who had called at the pits while everyone else was slithering off – as the winner.

Reutemann showed his skill at the Nürburgring to win at 117.73 mph from a very surprising Jacques Laffite in Frank Williams' Williams FW04. A host of punctures and mechanical failures decimated the field. The Austrian Grand Prix was wet. Race day was marred by an accident in unofficial practice which was to cost the life of Mark Donohue, driver of the Penske PC1. The race itself was shortened by rain once again and the winner was surprised and delighted.

Vittorio Brambilla had driven magnificently to give March their first ever works win. In his enthusiasm he spun and knocked the nose off the car only yards past the flag.

Lauda's third place behind Regazzoni and Fittipaldi at Monza was enough to wrest the title for Ferrari and give the Italian crowd their greatest day in many years. James Hunt debuted the Hesketh 308C and finished fifth. With chicanes now slowing down the cars and breaking up the slipstreaming bunches, the race average was 135.48 mph and Regazzoni's fastest lap 138.87 mph. Lauda celebrated his championship in the United States with his fifth win of the season. The race had a sour note when Regazzoni held up Fittipaldi's challenge to Lauda by putting his Ferrari between them. Regazzoni was eventually black flagged and fists flew in the pits between the Ferrari team and the organisers. It was not a very decorous end to a season of fine achievement.

1976 was the season to end all seasons in terms of political wranglings, with the results being decided as much by the rule books as on the circuits. Fortunately, it was also a season with plenty of close racing and several new cars to enliven the scene. The main feature of the year, on the circuits, was the terrific struggle between Hunt and Lauda. Hunt actually took the chequered flag first at seven races, in Spain, France, Great Britain, Germany, Holland, Canada and at the US Grand Prix East at Watkins Glen. Lauda scored four first places, in Brazil, South Africa, Belgium and Monaco but the second half of his season was badly affected by his accident in Germany which almost cost him his life. Five other drivers put themselves onto the list of winners in 1976, Regazzoni at the US Grand Prix West, Scheckter in Sweden, John Watson in Austria, Peterson in Italy and Mario Andretti at Mount Fuji in Japan where Hunt finally clinched his title.

The season opened with three victories in succession for Ferrari; Lauda beat Depailler in Brazil and Hunt, by a mere 1.3 seconds, in South Africa; then Regazzoni made amends for his display in the last American race by winning the first US Grand Prix West at the newly laid out 'round the houses' circuit in Long Beach, California. Lauda was second there and Hunt was pushed out of the race by Patrick Depailler, driving the Tyrrell 007 while the six wheeler was being developed. The protests started to flow after Hunt won the Spanish Grand Prix at Jarama by 20.97 seconds from Lauda. Hunt's McLaren M23 was found after the race to be marginally over the maximum allowable width and, although the team protested that the discrepancy was due to manufacturing tolerances in the rear tyres, Hunt was excluded from the results. Laffite's Ligier-Matra JS5 was also excluded from twelfth place for an alleged wing infringement; both teams appealed.

Lauda went on to score two successive victories at Zolder and Monaco; at Zolder, he was followed home by Regazzoni and Laffite, and in Monaco by Scheckter.

The Swedish race was a historic one. After Mario Andretti, with the new Lotus 77, had started from the front row and led for the first 45 laps, unaware of a one minute penalty for a jumped start, his engine blew up allowing Scheckter and Depailler to coast home to an easy one-two finish with the two six-wheeled Tyrrell P34s; Lauda was third and Hunt was fifth. James Hunt 'won' two races within 24 hours at Paul Ricard in France. As well as beating Patrick Depailler on the road, he learned that his appeal over the Spanish result had been upheld and that he was reinstated as winner. To add to James's joy, Lauda failed to score in France, retiring with a broken engine.

His satisfaction was to be short lived, however, and the British Grand Prix, at Brands Hatch, was to result in more wrangles. After a first corner shunt caused by Regazzoni's over enthusiasm, the race was re-started, but it was contended that Hunt, among others, had not completed the first lap under his own power and should be excluded. He was allowed to restart and went on to win by almost a minute from Lauda's ailing Ferrari and Sheckter. The race was later taken away from Hunt after a series of appeals by Ferrari and the points awarded to Lauda which made Hunt's championship position look bleak both mathematically and psychologically.

Although Hunt had troubles they were nothing compared to what awaited

Top: determination has certainly paid off for 30-year-old Niki Lauda, who began his Grand Prix career driving for March. He was a member of the five-car BRM team in 1973, and for 1974 joined Ferrari with Regazzoni. By mid season in 1975, the Ferraris displayed a significant torque advantage over Cosworth-powered rivals and Niki won the Championship. The 1976 season developed into a needle match between Lauda and James Hunt. His super-human recovery from his crash at the Nürburgring did not prevent Hunt from taking the title

Above: Clay Regazzoni was one of the stalwarts of Formula One. Although the popular Swiss was never World Champion he achieved many good results with Ferrari, the last of which was at Long Beach in 1976. His Grand Prix career took him from Ferrari in 1970, to BRM in 1973, back to Ferrari in 1974, to Ensign in 1977 and in 1979 to Frank Williams' Saudia team whose first win he scored. His career was ended by an accident at Long Beach in 1980

Left: In 1976 Ken Tyrrell introduced his Derek Gardner designed six-wheeler Formula 1 cars. Jody Scheckter and Patrick Depailler won the Swedish Grand Prix. It was Scheckter's (inset) fourth Grand Prix Win

Below left: John Watson from Belfast scored his first well deserved Grand Prix win at the Österreichring in the Penske, but despite this, the American team withdrew at the end of 1976

Far left top: rated by many as the fastest Grand Prix driver of the 1970s, Ronnie Peterson spent three years with March before driving for John Player Team Lotus from 1973 to early 1976. His eighth Grand Prix victory came at Monza in 1976 at the wheel of a March 762. He rejoined Lotus in 1978 enjoying great success until his tragic fatal accident at Monza

Below: the race at the rain-soaked Mount Fuji circuit put Mario Andretti and Lotus back in the winner's circle. Andretti had rejoined Lotus in 1976 after a spell with the Parnelli team and became World Champion in 1978

Lauda at the Nürburgring. The race was stopped after rain had swept the circuit to allow the drivers to change tyres if they wished. After the restart, Lauda was quite far down the field and trying hard to catch the leaders. His Ferrari crashed in flames and he was fortunate that several following drivers stopped or were involved in the accident and were able to pull him from the blazing wreckage, which was some way from the nearest marshals. Even so, his life hung in the balance for a considerable time and his future looked bleak. With Lauda in hospital, no Ferraris were sent to Austria and John Watson won his first Grand Prix, after years of promise, with the Penske PC4.

When it seemed that Lauda might make a miraculous comeback before the end of the season, Ferrari relented and sent Regazzoni to Holland where he finished under a second behind a very 'on form' Hunt; it was just one year since Hunt's first Grand Prix win at the same circuit with the Hesketh.

Italy saw Lauda make a miraculous return and, although Hunt was openly pleased that Niki was back to fight the title, he was barracked by the crowd and sent to the back of the grid, with Watson and Mass, for allegedly using fuel of more than the permitted octane ratings. It was a decision made on very

dubious evidence and effectively robbed Hunt of all chance of a good result. In his efforts to come to terms with the leaders, he crashed, without personal harm, on lap 12. The race was won by Ronnie Peterson who gave both himself and the March team a much needed morale booster.

The circus now moved on to Canada and the United States, East – or Watkins Glen where Hunt knew he had to win to pull back some of the lead which Lauda still clung to. In both races, he did everything that was necessary to score two superb victories and go to the final round, in Japan, with a reasonable chance of winning the title. Lauda had scored a courageous fourth place in his comeback at Monza and, despite obvious problems, he was a magnificent third at the Glen. It seemed that he was not going to give up the championship without a fight.

As things turned out, that assumption was wrong and, as the rain swept Mount Fuji circuit where Japan was hosting her first Grand Prix and getting a thrilling finale for her money, Lauda made one of the most courageous decisions of his life in deciding not to race. After a few brief moments of exploring the circuit, Niki came to the conclusion that the conditions were simply not fit for him to race under, troubled as he was by problems with his eyelids, burned at Nürburgring. As he climbed from his car, the race went on in truly appalling conditions which were tailor made for a huge accident. The accident did not come, though, and the circuit even began to dry a little. Hunt, who had charged away into a commanding lead – intent on winning the title in style – tried desperately to preserve his wet-weather tyres but with only five laps to go and having lost the lead to Mario Andretti his left front tyre deflated. He rushed into the pits where the McLaren mechanics changed all four wheels with amazing rapidity and stormed out again knowing only that he had to make up several places. Those last few laps saw Hunt give the performance of his life to pull back to third place behind Andretti and Depailler and to take the title by a single point from Lauda. It was quite some time before James could be convinced that he was really World Champion.

It was a remarkable ending to a season which would have been dismissed as incredible had it been written as a film script but then motor racing sometimes can be much larger than life.

Below: it took James Hunt only three seasons to become World Champion – from a flamboyant beginning with Lord Hesketh's March in 1973 and with the same team's Harvey Postlethwaite designed cars until he took over Fittipaldi's seat at McLaren for 1976. An excellent third place at Mount Fuji clinched the title for Hunt after a very hard-fought season

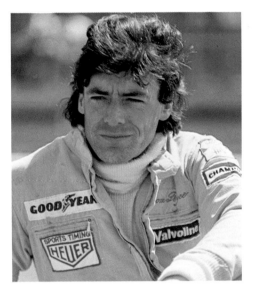

Top: Jody Scheckter enjoyed a fairy-tale start with the brand new Wolf WR1 at the Argentine GP in 1977. The debutant Wolf demonstrated the reliability that distinguished it throughout the season, even at the hands of a hard driver like Jody

Above: Welsh driver Tom Pryce in pensive mood. His death at Kyalami in 1977 was one of those particularly unfortunate and needless accidents that periodically mar the sport.

Above right: Pryce's Shadow DN8 in action at Buenos Aires during the very hot Argentine Grand Prix. Unlike many cars, the Shadow did not succumb to the heat, although it ran a rather undistinguished race, finishing out of the points

While 1977 never repeated the high drama of the previous year, it was nonetheless a see-saw season which saw eight Grand Prix winners and a very open run for the title. It was much less tainted by political in-fighting but there were inevitable rumblings about the scoring system when it was realised that the champion had won fewer races than the man who was placed third.

After Japan, Niki Lauda might well have been written off as a championship challenger but in the end it seemed almost inevitable when he regained his coveted title. He won in South Africa, Germany and Holland, but his championship was earned more through dogged insistence on finishing in the points than on a need to win at all costs; to Lauda the championship was all important, the races relatively incidental. Mario Andretti seemed intent on winning races at whatever cost and the occasional impetuous moment helped snatch the championship from his grasp. In spite of this and a spate of Cosworth 'development' engine failures, Andretti won at Long Beach and in Spain, France and Italy, yet he did not even take the runner-up spot to Lauda; that went to Scheckter, who had left the struggling Tyrrell team and put his faith in Walter Wolf Racing – as their sole driver.

Scheckter opened the season in fairy-tale style, taking the debutant Wolf WR1 to victory in Argentina. His was not the fastest car in Buenos Aires but as the intense heat took its toll of cars and drivers he outlasted the opposition. A strong military presence and volatile political situation added tension to the stifling heat and when the fire extinguisher bottle on Andretti's Lotus exploded during practice (at very high speed, in front of the pits) there were mutterings of terrorist bombs. Hunt, on pole position with the latest M23, was one of four leaders, the others being the winner and the much improved

Brabham-Alfas of John Watson and Carlos Pace. Hunt and Watson fell foul of suspension failures while Pace succumbed to the heat, surrendering the lead to Scheckter just six laps from home.

Speculation about rivalry between Lauda and his new team-mate, Carlos Reutemann, was fuelled when the latter scored a convincing first win for the team in Brazil. Hunt was on pole again but, after a storming start, local hero Pace led for six laps before being caught out by the crumbling track – forfeiting his nose cone to the pursuing McLaren. As the track surface began to break up in the heat, eight cars came to grief on one corner alone. From thirteenth on the grid Lauda avoided the mayhem to snatch third place, behind Hunt and ahead of a delighted Emerson Fittipaldi who at last seemed to be making progress with the home grown FD04.

Lauda retorted by winning at Kyalami, but his win was not to be fêted as the race was marred by the death of Welshman Tom Pryce and a young South African marshal. Ironically, an incident involving Pryce's new Shadow team-mate precipitated the disaster. On lap twenty, Renzo Zorzi pulled off the pits straight with a dead engine. As he walked away, leaking fuel flared up briefly, sending Zorzi back to activate the car's extinguisher. As the flames fizzled out two marshals, one carrying a heavy extinguisher, ran across the track to the Shadow. The unencumbered one made it but the other was hit head on by Pryce who was probably killed instantly. The car continued out of control along the straight until it clipped the Armco, collected Laffite's Ligier and crashed headlong into the barriers. It was a needless end to a career which had the utmost promise. Pryce started racing with a Formula Ford car, won in a newspaper competition. He progressed to Formula Three and trounced the opposition in the prestigious Monaco race in 1974, earning himself a Formula One contract with Shadow. He won only one Formula One race, the Race of Champions, at Brands Hatch, in 1975. That his unbounded enthusiasm and abundant talent should never be rewarded was a sad blow.

Two weeks later Carlos Pace died in a flying accident in his native Brazil. He had never lost faith in the difficult Brabham-Alfa and his death was a major setback to the team just as it seemed he had transformed the car into a winner.

As always, the circus recovered from its too oft felt sense of loss and returned to the fray with a stirring, three-cornered, flag-to-flag battle at Long Beach. Having avoided a first corner barging match involving Hunt, Reutemann, Watson and Brambilla, Jody Scheckter demonstrated the Wolf's worth. For 75 of the eighty laps he held off determined challenges from Andretti (the Lotus 78 now sufficiently reliable to show its pace) and Lauda,

Below: Niki Lauda on his way to victory in the Ferrari 312 T-2 in the 1977 South African GP

Below left: Lauda's team-mate Carlos Reutemann in the incongruous setting of California's Long Beach circuit during the 1977 US Grand Prix West. His interest in the race ended on lap five when he collided with Brett Lunger's McLaren

Below right: another street scene, this time from Monaco in 1977 where Jody Scheckter in the Wolf WR1 won his second Grand Prix of the season, ahead of Niki Lauda, bringing up the Cosworth engine's 'century'

but now he was fighting the effects of a slowly deflating right front tyre. On lap 76 he could hold off his pursuers no longer and both Andretti and Lauda slipped past. At the end less than five seconds covered the three and Lauda had left the lap record for the increasingly well respected waterfront circuit at 87.87 mph.

Andretti made it two in a row with a demoralising walkover in Spain, where he sat on pole by the margin of .72 seconds. A very on-form Carlos Reutemann was sixteen seconds adrift at the end. The only remote threat to the Lotus came from Jacques Laffite who had the Ligier JS7-Matra flying to be second on the grid and set fastest lap, at a record 94.24 mph. Laffite lost over a lap early in the race but fought back from nineteenth place to seventh – just outside the points. Third place for Scheckter put him into an outright lead in the championship as Lauda missed the race, having cracked a rib (without apparent reason) during practice.

Andretti's hat trick was scotched in Monaco by an absolutely stunning performance from Scheckter which, coincidentally, brought up the hundredth win for the ubiquitous Cosworth engine. Lauda missed his Monaco hat-trick by less than a second in beating Reutemann into third place. A race long battle between Andretti and Jochen Mass finally went to the McLaren driver and the final point went to new Shadow team leader Alan Jones.

Belgium showed again the superiority of the Lotus 78. Andretti was on pole by a demoralising 1.54 seconds from Monaco pole man John Watson but in dismal conditions the two collided in the chicane on the first lap and went no further. As the weather went from wet to dry to wet six drivers led: Scheckter, Watson, Mass, Brambilla, Lauda and Gunnar Nilsson. Having outbraked Lauda on lap fifty, it was Nilsson who led them home. Lauda was second and Ronnie Peterson gave Tyrrell a rare moment for celebration by wrestling the six-wheeler into third place.

Sadly, Zolder was to be Nilsson's only Grand Prix win. He began experiencing health problems and early in 1978 it was learned that he was suffering from cancer. He never drove for the Arrows team for which he had signed for 1978. In October the 28-year-old Swede died in a London hospital. He had taken Formula Three and Formula Atlantic by storm but instead of the world title which many predicted, his monument became the Gunnar Nilsson Cancer Treatment Campaign.

Andretti was one of the few who did not rejoice in Jacques Laffite's all-French win in Sweden; Andretti led for all but the last two laps when a fuel metering fault finally resulted in the inevitable fuel shortage.

The tables were turned two weeks later at Dijon where Andretti was

forced to settle for second place to John Watson's Brabham until almost within sight of the flag when it was Watson's turn to run out of fuel!

By this time in the season there were so many entries for most races that organisers were making life very hard for privateers who, on occasion, had to resort to legal action even to gain the right to practice. For the British Grand Prix, at Silverstone, the organisers set aside a separate 'pre-qualifying' session to determine which of the many second string entries would go forward to qualifying proper. During this session David Purley survived what was later billed as racing's most severe non-fatal accident, when his Lec went straight on at Becketts, hitting the barriers at about 110 mph. Sticking throttles were to blame. It was a happier weekend for James Hunt who (having put the M26 on the front row and led briefly at Dijon) at last scored his first win of the season. Watson again led much of the race before succumbing to fuel feed problems and Lauda cruised home second, to extend his lead in the championship.

He extended it still further with a sweet victory, just one year after his accident, in the German Grand Prix – now transferred from Nürburgring to Hockenheim.

In Austria Alan Jones drove the Shadow magnificently in poor conditions to haul himself to second place behind James Hunt and was delighted to inherit a well deserved first Grand Prix win when Hunt's engine expired eleven laps from home. Yet again Niki Lauda stayed clear of everyone else's problems to take home six points from second place, stretching his lead to sixteen points....

At Zandvoort he virtually sewed up his second title by overhauling and just staying ahead of Laffite's very quick Ligier. Andretti threw away all hopes of challenging Lauda in an early incident with Hunt when both laid claim to the same piece of road.

With his sixth second place of the season, this time behind an uncatchable Mario Andretti, Lauda put the championship beyond all doubt at Monza and finished his season with a cool drive to fourth place in the wet US Grand Prix behind Hunt, Andretti and Scheckter. Thereafter he earned few friends by

Right: Alan Jones enjoying practice for the 1977 Austrian Grand Prix, a race he went on to win

Below right: Jacques Laffite only managed to give the beautifully built Ligier JS7, with its distinctive sounding V12 engine, one victory, here at Anderstorp in the 1977 Swedish GP

Below: the immensely likeable Gunnar Nilsson's promising career was cut short by cancer. The action shot of Nilsson's Lotus 78 is from the 1977 Belgian Grand Prix. Although this was to be Gunnar's only Grand Prix victory it was a particularly impressive one earned through great skill in poor conditions.

taking no further part in the championship after Ferrari had co-opted young Gilles Villeneuve into the team for the Canadian and Japanese races. Lauda expressed his feelings by heading for Brabham with his faithful mechanic, Ermanno Cuoghi, in tow. . . .

Scheckter scored his third win in Walter Wolf's adopted country, Canada, and no doubt reflected on what could so easily have been a first time championship but for a disastrous loss of form in mid-season. James Hunt too, no doubt, thought back to the previous season as he won the Japanese Grand Prix at Fuji. Hunt's results for the season did not do true justice to his title defence for he led many races and was inevitably competitive but dogged by cruel luck. The Fuji race was marred by a dreadful accident involving Gilles Villeneuve's Ferrari which cartwheeled off the end of the straight after hitting Peterson's Tyrrell and killed two onlookers standing in a prohibited area. Villeneuve was unhurt and as third place man Patrick Depailler climbed alone onto the victory rostrum the circus tramped wearily home for a short rest after a long and not always happy season.

Anyone who thought Andretti the moral victor in 1977 needed no recourse to semantics at the end of 1978, for Mario won the title in convincing fashion. He won six Grands Prix – Argentina, Belgium, Spain, France, Germany and Holland – and crossed the line first in one more – Italy. Such was the superiority of the Lotuses that his only serious challenger was his team mate. Ronnie Peterson was employed by Lotus as number two driver and although he won in South Africa and Austria (with Andretti out of contention) he dutifully maintained that role, finishing second to Andretti on four occasions.

Come Monza, only Ronnie had a mathematical chance of challenging Andretti, but by the next morning Peterson was dead, the victim of a fiery accident as the cars funnelled into the first chicane.

Reutemann, now Ferrari's number one, took obvious pleasure in beating Niki Lauda into fourth spot in the championship. He won in Brazil, Long Beach, Great Britain and at Watkins Glen, while Lauda's wins in Sweden and Italy were both tinged by controversy. First-time winners picked up the re-

maining crumbs; Patrick Depailler's Monaco victory ended years of near misses, but when Gilles Villeneuve won in Canada he had not had to wait quite so long. . . .

Andretti, with the Lotus 78, won as he pleased from pole position in Argentina, with Lauda a distant and calmly calculating second for Brabham. Depailler rewarded Tyrrell with an encouraging third place in the new 008, while at the other end of the scale Hesketh's lady, Divina Galica, and Theodore's talented youngster, Eddie Cheever, failed to qualify.

Only half the 22 starters survived the heat in Rio and none looked remotely close to catching Reutemann's Michelin-shod Ferrari. 'Lole's' third Brazilian win looked very easy as Andretti dropped back with gearbox problems and a delighted Emerson Fittipaldi came home second ahead of Lauda.

Michelin's jubilation was short-lived, for in South Africa they were simply not competitive. In a sensational race, early leaders Andretti and Scheckter dropped back with tyre troubles, leaving a hard charging Riccardo Patrese in a commanding lead with the new Arrows FA1. There he stayed until the engine inexplicably exploded after 63 of the 78 laps. A surprised Patrick Depailler

Above: the crowded start of the 1978 South African Grand Prix. Star of the race was, without a shadow of a doubt, Riccardo Patrese in the Arrows FA1 – shown here to the left of the picture behind Jabouille's troublesome turbocharged Renault RS01. Ronnie Peterson was the eventual winner after Patrese's engine expired on lap 63

took the lead but in the last five laps Ronnie Peterson (having *carte blanche* as Andretti had fallen back with fuel starvation) remorselessly hauled him in. The two completed most of the last lap side by side, touching wheels occasionally but giving nothing away. At the Esses it was all over; Ronnie was through and Patrick was second yet again.

The undoubted star of the show at Long Beach was Alan Jones in the neat Williams FW06, latest and much the best in Frank Williams' long line of enthusiastically fielded contenders. In the end, however, Reutemann scored again as the Australian dropped from second to seventh place with fuel problems and a deranged front wing. His consolation was a new lap record at 88.41 mph. Reutemann's 26-year-old French Canadian team-mate, Gilles Villeneuve, veteran of snowmobile racing and 'round the houses' Formula Atlantic racing, Canadian-style, showed why so many people predicted a bright future for him by leading comfortably for many laps. He eventually crashed when attempting an impossible overtaking manoeuvre on former Long Beach winner Clay Regazzoni – now driving for Shadow – leaving tyre marks all over Regga's helmet!

From street racing American-style the circus moved to Monaco, for street racing European-style, and in spite of his third places in Argentina and Long Beach and second in South Africa few would have predicted that Patrick Depailler would at last put himself on the winner's rostrum here. This was a classic motor race; pole man Reutemann threw it all away at the start, getting away slowly and puncturing a tyre through hitting Lauda's Brabham. John Watson in the other Brabham stormed away into the lead but under intense pressure from Depailler he overcooked the brakes and finally made an un-

Left: Brazilian Emerson Fittipaldi, very much at home in the Copersucar Fittipaldi F5A during the Brazilian Grand Prix in 1978 where he took the F5A to a well earned second place behind Carlos Reutemann: its highest ever position. It was a just, if rare, reward for the former World Champion's perseverance with his Anglo-Brazilian project

Right: at long, long last . . . Patrick Depailler's first Grand Prix win. The scene is Monaco, the year 1978 and the car the Tyrrell 008. Depailler drove faultlessly to finish ahead of a spectacularly charging Niki Lauda to give the somewhat frail 008 its one and only GP win

dignified exit down the chicane escape road. Lauda, second for a while, dropped to sixth in having a rear tyre replaced and in a truly memorable drive he fought back to second place ahead of Scheckter, Watson, Pironi and the impressive Patrese. Lauda left the lap record at a remarkable 83.57 mph, but Depailler now moved into the lead in the championship.

In Belgium, Andretti gave the Lotus 79 the best possible debut with pole position and a flag to flag win – followed by Peterson, who also took the lap record at 114.68 mph. Three former world champions – Hunt, Lauda and Fittipaldi – were eliminated in a multiple accident on the grid, precipitated by some rather over exuberant starts and Reutemann missing a gear.

Andretti and Peterson repeated their performance in Spain, both now in 79s. James Hunt, so far well out of contention, led initially and Jacques Laffite underlined his current form with a dogged third place. Carlos Reutemann was lucky to escape unscathed from a spectacular accident which left his Ferrari perched between the Armco and the paddock.

Controversy reared its head at the Swedish Grand Prix which followed. The Brabham team, struggling to make the BT46 a front runner arrived with the

car equipped with an engine-driven fan which sucked air from under the car. Lauda soon disposed of Andretti and simply drove away into the distance. Patrese took the equally controversial Arrows into second, a whisker ahead of Peterson who had recovered from seventeenth place after a puncture. Not surprisingly the protests about the Brabham flew thick and fast but although the FIA subsequently declared it illegal, the Swedish result stood.

Andretti and Peterson were now first and second in the points table and they reflected this with another dominant one-two in the French Grand Prix at Paul Ricard but then in the British Grand Prix, at Brands Hatch, both the black and gold cars were out within 28 laps. Peterson went out first, after six laps, and Andretti conceded the lead to Scheckter when his engine let go. Scheckter in turn succumbed to gearbox failure, leaving Niki Lauda to be hauled in by a hard charging Reutemann. By lap sixty they were running together when, at Clearways, they came up to lap Bruno Giacomelli in the third McLaren. Giacomelli waved Lauda through and then inadvertently moved across on him. In an instant Lauda had half spun and Reutemann had ducked through on the inside to take the lead. Although Niki set a new lap record, at 119.71 mph, he was 1.23 seconds adrift when the flag came out.

In stifling heat, Andretti won the German Grand Prix at the soulless Hockenheimring, from Jody Scheckter who drove a magnificent race after making a mess of his start. It was Andretti himself who did it all wrong in the opening moments of the Austrian Grand Prix, colliding with Reutemann's Ferrari. The race was stopped after seven laps as the rain came down and from the restart Peterson was uncatchable. Although, nominally at least, the Drivers' Championship remained open, this result clinched the Constructors' Championship for Lotus yet again.

Didier Pironi and Riccardo Patrese put the cat among the pigeons shortly after the start of the Dutch Grand Prix by having a monumental (yet, miraculously, non-injurious) accident near the front of the pack. When the dust died down and the track was cleared, Andretti stayed out of trouble to score his sixth win of the year – followed again by Peterson.

Above: Brabham designer Gordon Murray's use of the rear mounted fan to glue the Brabham BT46 to the road was only allowed to have one moment of glory, here at the 1978 Swedish Grand Prix. Lauda easily showed the way home to second place man Patrese, and could probably have gone considerably quicker if need be. Although the win at Sweden stood, the BT46 'fan car' never turned a wheel again in anger

Tragically, Zandvoort was to be Peterson's last race. When the teams arrived at Monza, Andretti had amassed 63 points and only Ronnie, with 51, could possibly take his title away – but he was adamant that he would abide by his 'number two' status. It was immaterial; the two Lotuses started from the front row (with Andretti on pole) and as the field – many of whom had taken a rolling start as the lights flashed green – crowded into the first chicane, disaster struck. As the whole grid bunched up into the corner, cars began to touch and run out of control. James Hunt's McLaren was pushed into Peterson's Lotus which ran across the track to the right, head on into the barriers at enormous speed and bounced back, the front totally demolished, in a horrifying ball of flame. For once, the marshals were magnificent and, aided by Hunt, they quickly had the fire out and the critically injured Peterson out of the car. After what seemed an age he was taken by helicopter to hospital with shattered legs and minor burns and eventually news filtered back that he was critically injured but would survive. Vittorio Brambilla was also seriously injured when a flying wheel struck him on the head.

After a further delay to replace a barrier which Scheckter flattened in the second warm up, the remaining cars restarted. Again the start was chaos and after a race long battle between Andretti and Villeneuve had gone to the new champion elect, both were penalised for jumped starts and relegated to sixth and seventh places. Niki Lauda thus took his second controversial win of the season, followed home by John Watson, and Mario Andretti's championship was confirmed. There were no celebrations, for Monza had been a disaster. All interest in the championship was lost the next morning when Peterson died after emergency surgery on his shattered legs. He was 34 and unquestionably the fastest driver of his era. His loss was deeply felt.

The final two races of the season were sombre formalities. As Carlos Reutemann crossed the line to win the US Grand Prix, from Alan Jones in the Williams, he gave a derisory salute to the Ferrari pit which left them in no

Below: Ronnie Peterson showing his absolute mastery in the rain during the 1978 Austrian Grand Prix at the Österreichring. Andretti's over exuberance on the first lap put him out of the race and gave Ronnie *carte blanche* to win, rather than simply trail round behind his team leader. Sadly this was Peterson's last victory before the Monza tragedy

doubt as to his feelings about his imminent departure to Lotus.

Ferrari, however, were perhaps not too concerned, for their continued faith in Gilles Villeneuve was amply rewarded when he took his very first Grand Prix win at the closing race of the season. Fittingly, it was on home ground as the Canadian Grand Prix was fought out on a new circuit on the Ile Notre-Dame, in Montreal. Only cruel luck kept temporary Lotus recruit Jean-Pierre Jarier from winning as a brake pipe fractured on his 49th lap.

Villeneuve's home win brought some joy to a sad end of season as everyone went home to think of some way of challenging the flying Lotuses. . . .

During winter testing it became apparent that the Ligier team, with a switch to Cosworth engines and a 'ground effect' chassis, had found the answer. In the opening South American races, Jacques Laffite and his new team mate, Patrick Depailler, were simply untouchable. They started side by side from the front row in both Argentina and Brazil. Laffite won both races without challenge and, but for handling and fuel vaporisation problems which dropped him to third place in Argentina, Depailler would have been second again.

At Kyalami, for the 1979 South African Grand Prix, the tables were turned again with the arrival of the Ferrari 312 T-4s, which gave Gilles Villeneuve and Jody Scheckter a splendid one-two win in dismal weather conditions.

The start of the 1979 season simply confirmed what motor racing has shown throughout its history – even when you are winning, someone will always find a better idea. . . .

Top left: Gilles Villeneuve, not exactly on rails as the sign behind him might suggest, but nevertheless travelling quickly during the 1978 Canadian Grand Prix at the futuristic Ile Notre-Dame circuit in Montreal, which replaced Mosport as the venue for the Grand Prix

Above left: a variation on 1978's theme of Lotus 1-2 was seen in the opening races of the 1979 season. Here in Argentina, Jacques Laffite's Ligier leads the similar car of Patrick Depailler. Laffite went on to win easily although Depailler went astray with handling and fuel vaporisation problems. That situation was corrected in Brazil when the Ligiers did finish 1-2. The new 'ground effect' Ligier JS11, now with the Cosworth V8, Engins Matra having withdrawn from the fray, proved shatteringly quick from the word go

Above: the 'brilliant young French Canadian' Gilles Villeneuve

498

Right: at Long Beach, Ferrari scored their second 1–2 of the season, Villeneuve and Scheckter leading Depailler, Andretti, Hunt and the rest away from the start and staying there to the end, with Villeneuve leading them home. Jones and Regazzoni raced the FW06 Williams here but the ultimately dominant FW07 made its bow in the pit lane

Below: once Williams began to race the FW07, there was little doubt that it was only a matter of time before it became a regular winner. In Monaco, Regazzoni gave an inspired performance to chase Scheckter home in second place and it was Regga who went on to score Williams' first ever Grand Prix win, with the FW07 at Silverstone in July

So far, Lotus, so dominant in 1978 had been somewhat overshadowed by Ligier and now it seemed that Ferrari was also back in the hunt, a suspicion confirmed next time out with another one-two at Long Beach. Villeneuve again led Scheckter and set an 89.56 mph lap record in the process. Depailler's Ligier and Jarier's impressive yet still unsponsored Tyrrell split the Ferraris until Depailler ran out of brakes and gears and Jarier succumbed to serious tyre vibrations. Into third place came the ever improving Alan Jones, having his last outing in Williams FW06 as the elegant, ground affects FW07 waited in the wings. Williams was suddenly anything but the poor also-ran.

In Spain it was the Ligiers again, this time with Depailler taking his first win for the team in a convincing demonstration which might have netted a one-two had Laffite not missed a gear and blown his engine in the early stages. This time, Lotus, thanks to a determined Reutemann and Andretti's efforts with the new 80, beat the Ferraris into submission and both Tyrrells, of Jarier and Pironi, finished in the points.

At this stage Villeneuve was leading the Championship from the two Ligier drivers and Reutemann, but now his team mate Scheckter scored an unexpected win in Belgium. Again the Ligiers were running away with the race but Depailler crashed and Laffite's tyres wilted. Either way, Alan Jones had convincingly shown that the FW07 was already a potential winner by building an increasing lead before electrical problems intervened. Villeneuve drove an absolutely remarkable race to pull back from last place to third after a pit stop, only to run out of fuel a lap from home. There was still the nagging doubt that he sometimes tried *too* hard but there was no denying his masterful car control and sheer speed.

With Scheckter and Laffite tied on points, the Championship moved to Monaco where Jody led from pole to chequered flag in a race far more interesting than that bald statement suggests. He was shadowed first by Villeneuve, running second to team orders, then pressed remorselessly by Jones. Finally, after Villeneuve retired and Jones deranged his front suspension by untidily clipping a barrier, Scheckter was hounded all the way to the flag by Jones's Williams team mate, Clay Regazzoni. Regga carved the gap down to less than half a second at the finish after an inspired performance. Only five cars were actually running at the end of this memorable race – Scheckter, Regga, Reutemann, an exhausted John Watson and Jochen Mass, taking sixth place after a splendid drive in his ultimately brakeless Arrows. Depailler was classified fifth in spite of stopping two laps from home with a blown engine; it was to be the end of his season as he broke his legs, very badly, in a hang gliding accident shortly afterwards. There were plenty who questioned his wisdom at pursuing such a 'dangerous' hobby when he at last had a realistic chance of winning the world championship.

The Monaco race also marked the end of James Hunt's career; the former

World Champion retired his uncompetitive Wolf on the first lap and promptly announced that he was retiring from the sport too, frustrated by the changing emphasis from driver skill to machinery and unwilling to continue the risks for so little return.

As the season moved into its second half with the French Grand Prix, Renault at last fulfilled all their promise and rewarded the staggering investment of the last two years. Frenchman Jean-Pierre Jabouille won the French Grand Prix in a French car and even on French Michelins – and he won fair and square. It was just reward for his unwavering dedication to the project. Having forced his way past Villeneuve just after half distance, Jabouille was untouchable, while Gilles and Arnoux, in the other Renault, put on a display of *racing* on the final lap which should be remembered forever. All out, side by side, passing and re-passing, even touching occasionally; neither driver gave or asked any quarter and they loved it. In the end, the Ferrari took the flag by inches and the two saluted each other and a tremendous fight.

France was for the French but Britain saluted another great patriot as Frank Williams, so long the frustrated underdog, finally fielded a Grand Prix winner. Had Alan Jones won, the result would have been popular and predictable, but Jones, starting from pole after some astonishingly quick practice laps, went out with a water pump leak at around half distance. He had already lapped all but six cars, with almost contemptuous ease. As it was, Clay Regazzoni picked up the reins to win by over 24 seconds from Arnoux – the only unlapped runner. The crowd's reaction to Regga's first victory since 1976 and Frank Williams' first ever was tremendously emotional.

Jones had only to wait for the next race for his own first Williams win. In Germany he was absolutely untouchable, in spite of a slowly deflating and rapidly chunking rear tyre, and Regazzoni followed up to complete Williams' first one-two. By finishing a distant if hardworking fourth, Scheckter retained his championship lead, but Laffite's third place brought him a little closer.

Whatever the situation in the championship, Williams was indisputably the team of the moment and in the next two races, Austria and Holland, Jones completed his own hat trick and made it four wins in a row for the FW07. Actually the situation in the championship was rather sad, because

Above: Jean-Pierre Jabouille kept faith with the often frustrating Renault turbo development programme for two long years before he scored his own and the revolutionary car's first Grand Prix win. Sadly, Jabouille's career as a driver was effectively ended by an accident in the 1980 Canadian Grand Prix which badly broke his legs

even had Jones won all the remaining races he still could not win the title. Having scored very little in the first half of the season he was allowed by the absurd scoring system to count only four results in the second half, from eight races.

As things turned out, Jones won only one of the three remaining Grands Prix, in Canada, but by then the championship was already decided, Scheckter clinching it on Ferrari home ground at Monza where he led an emotional one-two for the team. Fast as he was, consistency had been Scheckter's long suit; on top of his third win he had been second in South Africa, Long Beach and Holland, fourth in Spain, Germany, Austria and (later) Canada, fifth in Britain and sixth in Brazil. He spread his scoring performances (twelve out of fifteen races) handily across both halves of the season and emerged at the end with 51 points (from 60 scored) to Villeneuve's 47 (from 53) and Jones's 40 (from 43). In spite of three consecutive third places for Laffite, in Germany, Austria and Holland, and fifth for Depailler's replacement, Jacky Ickx, in Holland, it all went rather downhill for Ligier in the second half of the season and Laffite finished only fourth. Whichever way you looked at it, Scheckter was a worthy Champion and the rapidly changing fortunes of the sport were highlighted by Mario Andretti's lowly tenth equal, with just fourteen points for a season's dogged effort.

One driver who ultimately thought the effort was just no longer worth it was another former Champion, Niki Lauda. Lauda practiced the new and very promising Brabham-Cosworth in Canada and having done so announced that he was retiring from the sport forthwith, leaving the circuit without even taking his helmet or overalls and with never a look back. He left to develop his airline business with the classic observation that he was no longer interested in driving around in circles. The sport had undoubtedly lost a great champion but the manner of Alan Jones's hard won victory over Gilles Villeneuve in Canada and Villeneuve's own third win of the year in the American finale suggested that there would still be some quality at the top. And then there was Lauda's promising replacement at Brabham, one Nelson Piquet.

1980 was the years of skirts, turbos, arguments about who should control the sport, and of the fastest Grand Prix cars yet seen. In the very nature of the sport, the new order will always challenge the old and 1980 saw several young chargers score their first Grand Prix wins. In the end the title went to a driver who had been chasing it in hope and frustration for years and to a constructor who had been trying for even longer: Alan Jones and Frank Williams.

Right from the start of the season it was apparent that Williams' designer, Patrick Head, had developed the sliding skirt ground effect concept of the FW07 into an equation to keep the lead which he had taken so convincingly at the end of the previous season. On his way to the championship, Jones would score six Grand Prix wins (although only five would be rewarded with points) to add to his four of the previous year.

His first came in the blisteringly hot Argentine race in January, where he started from pole position. it was a dramatic race; Jones was forced into the pits by an overheating engine after he had spun off the crumbling track surface and picked up a plastic bag in his Williams' air intakes. He fought back, challenged by Villeneuve's Ferrari until the hard charging Canadian crashed when his car's suspension failed. Jones won in spite of two more trips onto the grass as the track deteriorated even further and second place went to the man who would dispute Jones's title throughout the year, the young Brazilian Nelson Piquet. There was more joy for the South American fans as Keke Rosberg brought Emerson Fittipaldi's latest offering, the F7, into third place ahead of Derek Daly's Tyrrell.

When the drivers eventually agreed to race in Brazil, having first argued that the spectacularly fast Interlagos circuit was just too dangerous for the new breed of car, the turbocharged Renault of René Arnoux – probably the most powerful of all the cars – took the honours, but only after Renault team leader Jabouille had retired from the lead with engine failure. The Renaults continued to be fast but they were all too often embarrassingly fragile.

Below: with Jabouille having broken the Renault duck in 1979, 1980 was widely predicted as being the turbo's year and when Arnoux won on successive outings in Brazil and South Africa, the French team looked set for championship success, but they could not match their performance with reliability

Brazil was Arnoux's first Grand Prix win, but he quickly made it two in a row at the South African Grand Prix where the thin air of Kyalami's high altitude favours the turbo engines. Jabouille led again until he retired, this time with a puncture, and the Ligier due, Laffite and his new team mate Didier Pironi, were second and third. Piquet, who had crashed out of his home Grand Prix in Brazil, took a valuable fourth place but it was a bad weekend for McLaren's promising new recruit, Alain Prost (a scorer in both previous rounds) and for ATS driver marc Surer; Prost broke his wrist and Surer broke his ankle, both in practice accidents.

Arnoux now led the championship but when the circus moved to Long Beach for the US Grand Prix West Piquet added his name to the list of Grand Prix winners for the first time. Sadly, Long Beach marked the end of Clay Regazzoni's career. The popular Swiss survived a terrible accident when the brake pedal of his Ensign broke as he approached the hairpin from the fastest part of the circuit. His injuries left him with paralysed legs and he would never race again. Less serious accidents at the demanding street circuit took away much of Piquet's potential opposition, including Jones and his new team mate, Reutemann, but Piquet was on devastating form. Patrese's Arrows finished second, a delighted Emerson Fittipaldi was third, Watson took fourth for McLaren, reigning champion Scheckter scored Ferrari's first points of the season in fifth and Pironi was sixth for Ligier – six makes of car in the first six places!

With newcomers Arnoux and Piquet sharing the lead of the championship, the first European round, Belgium, saw yet another first time Grand Prix winner as Pironi led from start to finish at Zolder with Jones his only challenger.

The banning of qualifying tyres had brought a few changes, especially in practice, but the Michelin-shod Ferraris continued to be totally uncompetitive and only heroic efforts from the never-say-die Villeneuve earned a point for sixth place. This time, five makes in the top six said just how competitive in depth Grand Prix racing had become.

There were just four points covering the top four in the championship, Arnoux, Jones, Piquet and Pironi, before the glamorous setting of Monte Carlo. In untypically awful weather, for the first time since the world championship began there would not be a British driver on the grid, John Watson having

Anyone who thought that modern Grand Prix cars cornered on rails should have been watching Alan Jones with the Williams at Long Beach (*above*) or Jean-Pierre Jarier with the Candy Tyrell in the wet at Zolder (*above right*)

Right: even before the dramas of later in the season, there was little love lost between Alan Jones and Jean-Marie Balestre as Pironi took the laurels in Belgium

Above: considering the dreadful handling and seemingly inevitable tyre problems with the Ferrari 312T4s, it was just as well that Gilles Villeneuve simply did not know how to give up. Here at Monaco he salvaged fifth place while his team mate Scheckter threw in the towel, so bad was the car

narrowly failed to qualify. The race was seen on television in no less than 26 countries and millions of viewers were treated to the sight of another spectacular first corner accident. Derek Daly braked too late, rode over the back of Alain Prost and cartwheeled over several other cars to land on top of his own team mate, Jean-Pierre Jarier, eliminating both Tyrrells, among others, on the spot. Pironi meanwhile pulled out a convincing lead before crashing on lap 55 when his car jumped out of gear. The race was won, as rain began to fall, by Carlos Reutemann, his first win for Williams. Villeneuve wrestled his Ferrari to fifth in spite of dreadful handling and a stop for tyres, while his more circumspect team mate, Scheckter, eventually gave up in frustration after two stops for tyres had failed to make his car much more than undrivable. Third place moved Piquet to the lead of the championship, by a single point.

As the teams moved to Jarama on the outskirts of Madrid for the Spanish Grand Prix, the political arguments began. Several drivers had been fined by FISA for failing to attend the briefings before the Belgian and Monaco races and as most had not paid, Jean-Marie Balestre, autocratic President of FISA, first attempted to stop the Spanish Grand Prix from happening at all and having failed to do that declared the race outlawed and any results void. The constructors and drivers ignored the edict (except for Ferrari, Renault and Alfa Romeo who played safe and complied) and the race went ahead, making history of a sort as the first race where the entire field was powered by a single type of engine, the Cosworth DFV. It was won by Alan Jones after early leaders Reutemann and Laffite had tripped over each other while passing Spanish driver Emilio de Villota. Piquet's gearbox failed and Pironi lost a wheel – also while leading.

The argument between FISA, the constructors and the drivers really went much deeper than the issue of the fines and it would drag on for most of the season and beyond, almost resulting in a split into rival championships for the following year.

Nevertheless, the show went on and the French Grand Prix saw a full grid once again. Jones was the delighted winner, beating strong French opposition on home ground to make a heartfelt gesture to the predominantly French rule makers, including Balestre who diplomatically stayed away as Jones mounted the rostrum. Locals, Laffite and Pironi could only manage second and third, while Piquet's fourth place now left him three points adrift of Jones – or a little more if, like Jones, you counted the results from Spain. In finishing fifth, Arnoux worked so hard with the struggling Renault that he chewed right through his bottom lip . . .

Jones completed his hat trick of wins at Brands Hatch, although Ligier again dominated with Pironi leading from pole until a puncture sent him to the pits, from where he stormed back through the field until another puncture stopped him for good. Tyre trouble also caused Laffite to crash heavily out of the lead, handing victory to Jones with Piquet second. Scheckter continued to struggle with the hopelessly uncompetitive Ferrari, but now he announced that he would retire at the end of the year. Unlike some, who had walked out of the sport which had made them rich and famous, on the spot, Scheckter tried his very hardest right to the end and then retired with dignity.

The German Grand Prix, at the unloved Hockenheim, was run under the appalling shadow of Patrick Depailler's death in a testing accident. The Frenchman died from multiple injuries when his Alfa Romeo crashed, inexplicably, into unprotected barriers at the end of the very fast straight. The race saw a change of fortune for Ligier; for once, Laffite not only led convincingly but he survived to win, albeit with a little luck. Both Renaults suffered valve breakages while running away from the field and Alan Jones lost the lead with a puncture, with just five laps to go. He did storm back to fastest lap after changing the offending wheel and held off Nelson Piquet by less than a second for a very important third place. Bruno Giacomelli salvaged fifth place for Alfa Romeo, after a very fine drive, but it was little compensation for the loss of their popular and talented team leader.

Renault made the most of the fast sweeps and high altitude of the Österreich-ring, victory in the Austrian Grand Prix going to the 'old man' of the team, Jean-Pierre Jabouille, chased all the way to the flag by Alan Jones. Derek Daly was lucky to keep his head when he spun so far across the grass that he almost went under a farmer's barbed wire fence!

It seemed that Jones was racing away to the championship he so much wanted, seven points clear of Piquet with the rest beginning to trail, but in Holland Jones made a terribly uncharacteristic mistake in the most exciting Grand Prix of the year. On only his second lap, but already in a comfortable lead, the Williams driver bounced over a kerb at the hairpin, breaking one all-important skirt and losing all chance of a good result. Piquet made the most of the mistake, going on to win in style from Arnoux's Renault which snatched second place at the very last moment from a temporarily unwary Jacques Laffite. Jacques had been forced to fight most of the way by an on-form Giacomelli, until the Alfa driver crashed. With the pressure apparently off, Laffite relaxed just a little too much! Derek Daly was lucky to escape from yet another huge accident, caused this time when his Tyrrell's brakes failed at the end of the straight. When the Goodyear technicians took the tyres off his wrecked car they found one of the left front brake calipers *inside* the wheel. Once again there were six makes of car in the first six places and this time there were nine makes in the first ten.

Now the gap between Jones and Piquet was only two points and there were three races to run. The last of the European races, the Italian Grand Prix, this year at Imola, saw the debut in practice of the turbocharged Ferrari 126C and almost saw the end of Jody Scheckter who walked away from the biggest accident of his career just weeks before he was due to retire. To complete Ferrari's weekend, Villeneuve too had a simply enormous accident in the race following a puncture at some 180 mph. The rear of the car finally came to rest a long way down the road from the front, in which Villeneuve was still sitting. Away from all this drama, Piquet got on with the job of winning by almost half a minute from Jones to take a one point lead in the championship, Williams having already won the constructors' title, to Frank's unbridled joy.

So, the World Championship would be decided in North America; first stop Montreal and the Canadian Grand Prix. As things turned out, Jones

Above: throughout the season, Nelson Piquet, pitched in at the deep end at Brabham following Lauda's unceremonious departure, was Alan Jones's closest challenger. When Jones made an unforced error at Zandvoort, Piquet was ready to score a faultless win

Below: the sensation of Long Beach was the oft-maligned Ricardo Patrese who took pole position and was showing Carlos Reutemann's Williams the way home until succumbing to fuel feed problems

would win the title at this race. Piquet was fastest in practice by almost a second from his arch-rival, but as the two charged into the first corner Jones edged into a half length lead; Piquet, of course, was not about to let him go and the two touched wheels, spinning wildly across the track and unleashing chaos in the pursuing pack. In the inevitable accident, seven other cars were damaged, three written off. One of those eliminated (giving up his car to his team leader) was Mike Thackwell, who at 19 had, for a few hundred yards, been the youngest driver ever to compete in a Grand Prix. The race was stopped immediately, to be restarted over an hour later, with Piquet, among others, in a spare car. At the second start, Jones forged ahead while Pironi beat Piquet for second place only to be penalised a minute for jumping the gun. It did not take Piquet long to force his way to the front and proceed to pull away to what it seemed would be an effortless win, but on lap 23 Piquet was out when his reserve Brabham's engine suddenly exploded. Pironi actually took the chequered flag at the head of the field but his jump-start penalty dropped him to third place and the laurels went to Jones, for the fifth time of the season. Jones's nine points meant that Piquet (who was only eight points behind but would have to drop at least two points under the still controversial scoring system) could no longer take the title; Alan Jones was World Champion.

Any thoughts that with the championship won the Australian would relax at the final round were soon forgotten at Watkins Glen for the US Grand Prix East. Jones celebrated by driving a truly brilliant race to win for the sixth time of the year, having briefly been down to twelfth place after taking to the grass on the first corner. He had driven his race of the year just for the love of it, to pull back to second place behind Giacomelli's flying Alfa Romeo before the unlucky Italian was brought to a halt by electrical failure.

Piquet ended his season with a spin, Jody Scheckter ended his career with a hardworking drive to eleventh place and a champagne celebration, and Alan Jones simply looked forward to doing it all over again in 1981; but it was not to be.

The FISA–FOCA war dragged into 1981 with FISA unwilling to backtrack on its revised regulations and FOCA refusing to concede an ounce of commercial muscle. The so-called 'grandee' teams, principally the technically autonomous Ferrari, Renault and Alfa Romeo organisations (as opposed to the 'kit-car' Cosworth teams) aligned with FISA, partly because the revised regulations would favour turbos and V12s and partly for political expediency. In February, with the threat of a split remaining, FISA declared the approaching South African Grand Prix illegal. Ferrari, Renault, Alfa Romeo, Ligier and Osella diplomatically stayed away and once again we had a 'Formula Ford' Grand Prix, the cars running the supposedly outlawed sliding skirts as before. Having dominated practice, Piquet led the wet race comfortably on wet tyres until a drying track allowed Reutemann, gambling on slicks, into a lead which he held to the end. Alan Jones retired, ironically, with a damaged skirt, but in the end it was immaterial because for the first time since 1966 the South African Grand Prix did not carry championship points.

Somewhat surprisingly, the next round, Long Beach, saw a full turn out and apparent peace; the oil of threatened commercial interests had smoothed the troubled waters and paved the way for the fancifully named 'Concorde' agreement between FISA and FOCA in March.

At Long Beach the cars complied with the letter of the regulations, without skirts and with a nominal 6 cm ground clearance – at rest at least. The 'grandee' teams had the advantage of considerable testing in this configuration and as Goodyear, disillusioned by the all too public bickering, pulled out, most teams were left to rely on Michelin rubber, further favouring regular Michelin runners Ferrari and Renault.

Alan Jones rose above such factors. Not since Jack Brabham scored in 1959 and 1960 for John Cooper has a World Champion retained his crown, but although Jones was not to emulate Brabham's successive titles it would not be for want of trying. He opened his defence as he had clinched his championship, with a near faultless win – although not without an unexpected challenge. Riccardo Patrese took a surprise pole for Arrows and was going away until he succumbed to fuel feed problems. Thereafter, Reutemann led until he made a rare mistake which let Jones through with the Argentine signalled to hold station in second place. Piquet stole home third to signal Brabham's continued threat to the Williams pair, Brabham having tried the ingenious hydro-pneumatic suspension system on the BT49C for the first time. While the Brabham was deemed legal, Colin Chapman's equally innovative, double chassis Lotus 88 was outlawed after protests from other teams, sparking yet another long-running row.

Ultimately, Piquet, much matured, enviably consistent yet rarely obvious, would snatch the championship and that was all he really wanted. As with his Brabham predecessor, Niki Lauda, to Piquet the championship was the ultimate goal, Grand Prix wins a mere, if desirable, incidental. On his way to the title he would win three races, more than any other driver, but perhaps the ultimate factor was the rivalry within the Williams team between the two outstanding drivers of the year.

After Long Beach, Frank Williams reiterated that Reutemann *was* number two and would be expected to move over for Jones if the need arose. Williams thought the situation unlikely, but as the rain-soaked Brazilian Grand Prix edged to a premature conclusion under the two-hour 'guillotine', Reutemann led Jones. The Williams put hung out the signal JONES-REUT, but to no avail. The board went out again and again but Reutemann stayed put and won as the flag came out a lap early.

Neither Jones nor Frank Williams was very impressed that the two drivers now shared the championship lead and Jones now had an almost frightening singleness of purpose. Where other reigning champions had slipped into complacency, Jones breathed fire. Still, his opening round win would be his last until his spectacularly barbed parting gesture in Las Vegas. In between, in spite of several performances of pure brilliance, his best efforts were frustrated.

Piquet's pole position with the hydro-pneumatic Brabham in Brazil had been one thing, but in Argentina, as Piquet waltzed into the distance his oft maligned Mexican team mate Hector Rebaque sailed past Reutemann into third place, heading for second; and that, said everyone sagely, simply *had* to be unfair car advantage. Rebaque saved face by retiring as Piquet cruised to victory over Reutemann, but the protests over the Brabham flew — only to be rejected. Soon, everyone would be obliged to run a version of the Brabham system and the unpopular, rock hard suspension which it dictated. A hard fought sixth place for Elio de Angelis in the old Lotus 81 did little to calm Colin Chapman who left the circuit in high dudgeon having seen the 88 rejected at scrutineering. Jones, having wound up the army of Reutemann supporters in fine style endured the ignominy of a sick engine and fourth place.

The first San Marino Grand Prix, held at Imola in Italy, saw Piquet close the championship gap on third placed Reutemann with another win, in spite of a compromise car to satisfy the diligent scrutineers. Among the surprises at Imola were a fine second place for Patrese's Arrows, a staggering pole position for Villeneuve in the powerful but unwieldy Ferrari turbo, the debut of the Toleman team, and the complete absence of Lotus, withdrawn in disgust as Chapman smarted over a fine imposed by FISA in the wake of his comments in Argentina. Villeneuve and Pironi both led for Ferrari and in spite of falling back to seventh and fifth both finished, Villeneuve with fastest lap.

That was the best news for Ferrari for an uncomfortably long time, but there was more to come. In Belgium, Villeneuve kept going for fourth place as rain brought a mercifully premature end to a thoroughly miserable weekend. In practice an Osella mechanic fell between the wheels of Reutemann's moving car in the overcrowded pit-lane, dying a couple of days later. Then there was confusion and acrimony at the start following a drivers' protest; an Arrows mechanic, on the grid as the flag fell was badly injured, tragically by the team's own driver, Siegfried Stohr. With the mechanic being tended on the track the race, incredibly, was allowed to continue until Pironi took the

Above: John Watson with the impressive Marlboro McLaren MP4 at Monaco. Since his first Grand Prix win in Austria in 1976, Watson had had none of the supposed luck of the Irish and had been written off on more than one occasion as a no hoper. An emotional win at the British Grand Prix at Silverstone in 1981 was just a foretaste of some truly stunning 1982 performances which re-established Watson as a real front runner

initiative and forced a halt. From the restart, Reutemann won as Jones spun out of the lead, Piquet having already retired after an inelegant barging match with the reigning champion which marked the beginning of open hostility between the pair. Reutemann for the moment could derive little satisfaction from his growing championship lead.

In Monaco, Villeneuve won when Jones began to slow with a mysterious misfire. Jones had driven a great race, including pressuring pole winner Piquet into a rather ignominious exit while lapping Tambay's Theodore. Piquet had earlier made some somewhat ill-advised suggestions that he was out to get the Williams driver and Jones had not been terribly impressed . . .

Notwithstanding Jones's problems, Villeneuve drove superbly to give the V6 turbo Ferrari its first win and he raised eyebrows even further in Spain by winning a thrilling Grand Prix in scorching heat. Alan Jones having lost a runaway lead by a rare driving error, Villeneuve was left to hang on grimly with the evil-handling 126CK at the head of a line of five cars covered by less than two seconds at the flag. Second place for the impressive Jacques Laffite and his Ligier kept him in the championship chase, although Reutemann was now thirteen points clear at the top and looking very secure.

Until now the vaunted Renaults had been disappointing, frequently fast but with only a third for Prost and fifth for Arnoux in Argentina to show. On home ground though, the French team made the most of a split race to give Alain Prost his first Grand Prix win. Renault were on form all weekend, with Arnoux taking pole by some margin, but Piquet (back on Goodyears as the American company returned) led from a confused start as the lights faltered, to an equally confused finish as the heavens opened. The first 'heat' ended one lap short of three-quarter distance, meaning the remaining laps would be run. From the restart, Prost, who had been running second with no fourth gear, made the most of a repaired gearbox and soft Michelins to overhaul Piquet. John Watson scored a tremendous second place after leading briefly, while a disconsolate Piquet in third could only take solace from the fact that Reutemann was out of the points.

If the last couple of races had seen a revival for John Watson, then Silverstone was a fairytale, the Ulsterman winning for the first time since Austria 1976 and, amazingly, for only the second time in 116 attempts. He was helped by a spinning Villeneuve taking out Jones, by Piquet crashing heavily after a tyre failed and by both the leading Renaults going out with engine failure, but he had fought hard for the most popular win of the year.

With Reutemann and Laffite second and third at Silverstone, the title still looked to be going Carlos's way and Williams was positively romping away with the Constructors' Cup. Alan Jones must have been wondering what he was doing wrong. In Germany he was in a class of his own, even overhauling Prost's Renault to lead until the mysterious Monaco misfire returned and handed victory to Piquet.

With Reutemann retiring from fourth place, third in Germany was bringing Jacques Laffite into distant contention with five races to run. By winning, brilliantly, in Austria as the pace setting Renault and Ferrari turbos again faltered, he closed the gap to eleven points, with Piquet still in between. Then came high drama in Holland as Reutemann and Laffite, fighting for fourth place eliminated each other when Reutemann made a rather optimistic dive for a non-existent gap. A remarkable drive from Jones could not prevent the power of the Renault from giving Prost a well-earned win. The Australian, his tyres shot by his efforts to beat Prost, was also finally overhauled by Piquet who now led the championship with the dejected Reutemann.

Prost gave a convincing repeat performance at Monza, again pursued relentlessly by Jones, who had a broken finger, apparently caused by someone's jaw during a discussion following a minor road accident. Piquet had the agony of a blown engine on the last lap, dropping him from third place (eagerly snapped up by Reutemann) to sixth. John Watson's fortunes had been all downhill since Silverstone but luck was with him as he survived a violent accident which left his McLaren scattered all over the track.

Five drivers, Reutemann, Piquet, Jones, Prost and Laffite now had a mathematical chance of taking the title and there were two races to run. In

Canada, Laffite put himself firmly into contention with another fine win. To say the race was wet would be an understatement; the conditions were the worst that many could remember. Nevertheless, Jones stormed away from the start, sights undoubtedly on the championship, but tried a bit *too* hard for once and spun off. Piquet finished fifth, Villeneuve took the impossible Ferrari by the scruff of the neck and positively shook it into third place and Reutemann simply gave up. With the championship his for the taking he still could not rise above his moods; with a perfect car he was invariably magnificent, with anything less he was abject.

In the bizarre setting of a new circuit laid out in the car park of Caesars Palace Hotel, Las Vegas, Reutemann – leading Piquet by one point and Laffite by six – played for the championship. In practice Reutemann was simply devastating and the outcome looked settled. In the race, having talked himself into feeling first handling and then gearbox problems, Carlos just wasn't going anywhere – certainly not to the World Championship. Once again, with the championship all but in the bag, he gave up; he didn't even fight as Piquet cruised past into sixth place and the vital points. Laffite, with everything to gain, was going even better, up into second place before tyre problems sent him scurrying into the pits and out of the reckoning. In the end Jacques finished sixth and Piquet, utterly exhausted and hanging on from sheer will was fifth. He was incapable of driving another mile at the end and one more lap would undoubtedly have seen Laffite past and handing the title to a little deserving Reutemann. As it was, Reutemann was a forgotten and desolate eighth and Piquet was World Champion by a single point.

Meanwhile, Alan Jones put the whole sad affair into perspective, destroying the opposition with a pointed victory of the utmost quality before retiring to his farm in Australia. Motor racing had found a champion, and a worthy one, but it had lost a hero – for the moment at least.

Jones may have been thankful to miss 1982, another year of controversy over rule bending, of all but undrivable cars and of tragedy contributed to by ineffectual government. During practice for the Belgian Grand Prix in May, the championship lost much of its meaning. Gilles Villeneuve, going all out for pole position in the final minutes, rode over the back of Jochen Mass's slow moving March and cartwheeled to destruction. Villeneuve was thrown from the disintegrating car and died from his injuries during the evening. Two weeks earlier at Imola, Pironi had beaten Villeneuve, against team orders, and the two had not spoken to each other since. In the closing minutes at Zolder, Pironi was fractionally quicker than Gilles. Ludicrously, the rules allowed each driver just two sets of super sticky qualifying tyres, good for only two or three quick laps each. On his last lap on his last set, Villeneuve, as so often before, had faced the choice of slowing for another car, thereby sacrificing his last banzai lap for pole, or taking a, literally, life or death chance. Characteristically, he took the chance, and he lost. Mass, blamelessly, moved the wrong way and the sport lost a driver widely ranked with the greatest ever. He was 30 years old and had won six Grands Prix in his tragically short career. Like most drivers, he had openly deplored the qualifying tyre situation which forced him into exactly the situation which claimed his life, but the rule had remained.

Villeneuve's death was only one of the tragedies of 1982. Riccardo Paletti died in a start line accident in Canada and Pironi was critically injured at Hockenheim. It might have been so different; following the arrival of Briton Harvey Postlethwaite, Ferrari at last had a chassis more equal to the prodigious power of the V6 turbo and either of the Ferrari drivers might have emerged as champion. In the end, Pironi, in spite of missing five races, missed the title by only five points as Keke Rosberg clinched another championship for Williams. The resurgent John Watson ran Rosberg even closer, missing the championship by one point after a disastrous run of mid season problems. Watson summed 1982 up nicely when he remarked that it was a championship just crying out to be won by somebody . . .

Somehow, it was appropriate that, given the tragedies, it was Rosberg who came through. Ultimately, his was the outstanding style and the fighting spirit and ultimately his were the rewards. Following Jones's retirement, Williams started the season with Rosberg and a seemingly revivified Reutemann. The Finn was highly rated for ability but had so far struggled, successively, with Theodore, Wolf and Fittipaldi. Although he failed to score a single point in 1981, Williams saw him as an obvious successor to Jones.

Yet again, the season got off to a shaky start as the South African Grand Prix endured a drivers' strike. Niki Lauda, returning to Grand Prix racing with McLaren, drew other drivers' attention to clauses in the Super Licence form which restricted their transfer between teams and generally required them to toe the FISA line. On the first day of practice the drivers refused to drive, melodramatically barricading themselves into a nearby hotel to promote solidarity. Having slept overnight on matresses on the ballroom floor, the drivers negotiated a settlement of sorts and went to work. There was little enthusiasm for the new cars either; although hydro-pneumatic suspensions had gone, the cars were allowed solid skirts – and that in effect dictated solid suspensions. The cars were physically punishing and potentially even more dangerous than their sliding skirt predecessors, but they were forced by the regulations and the desire to win at whatever cost.

The race itself was a Renault *tour de force*, if not to quite the extent that the team believed. Prost won after an outstanding recovery from a pit stop and Arnoux, the only other race leader, *thought* that he was second, but in fact he was third. Five laps from home and misinformed by his pit, he let Reutemann through, apparently only to unlap himself; he was in fact letting the surprised Williams driver into second place. The turbo domination of practice, with six of the seven turbo entries heading the grid, was expected in the rarefied Kyalami air, but the Cosworth teams took solace from the turbos' continuing fragility. Only the Renaults broke the Cosworth hold on the top six, the remarkable Lauda, Keke Rosberg and Watson filling the places. No sooner had the race ended than the trouble returned, the drivers being suspended and heavily fined.

Right: all for nothing: Nelson Piquet and Keke Rosberg fought a stirring battle to finish first and second in the blistering heat of the Brazilian Grand Prix only for both to be disqualified for running underweight cars with supposed brake cooling systems

After the Argentine Grand Prix had been cancelled and the fines and suspensions either reduced or quashed by an FIA court of appeal, there was an uneasy truce in Brazil, but, of course, it was too good to last. With the FISA aligned turbo teams and the FOCA Cosworth constructors, hamstrung for power, were desperately seeking, within the rules, to lose weight. In Brazil, the first and second placed cars – among others – only made the weight limit by using putative water cooled brake systems. The loosely worded regulations allowed replenishment of coolants before post race weighing. With the supposed brake coolant the cars were above the limit, in the race they undoubtedly were not. In a superb race in blistering heat, Villeneuve *just* held off Piquet, Rosberg and, initially, Arnoux until the Brazilian pressured him into a spin and retirement. Piquet then held onto win as Rosberg's tyres gave up, but the strain of driving these latest generation cars with virtually no suspension movement showed as Piquet collapsed, exhausted, on the rostrum, and what was more it was all for nothing – a month later both Piquet and Rosberg were disqualified as an appeal court reversed the immediate decision on a protest by Ferrari and Renault, the latter benefitting most as Prost was thereby declared winner – remaining so in spite of protracted subsequent counter appeals.

Long Beach was full of surprises. For a start it was surprising, given the current backbiting, that it happened at all, then none other than Alfa Romeo's Andrea de Cesaris snatched pole with a single remarkable practice lap. To cap it all, the Rat was back, Niki Lauda winning, ahead of schedule, in the third race of his second coming. De Cesaris spun away the lead on a crumbling track and ultimately only Rosberg, his hard charging in telling counter-point to Lauda's unruffled precision, offered a challenge. This time Ferrari were the butt of the protests, with Villeneuve disqualified from a well-won third place for running a double rear wing arrangement which most saw as a rather tongue in cheek gesture to the rulemakers and their glaring loopholes.

There was no joy for Villeneuve at Imola either for the so-called San Marino Grand Prix. As the majority of FOCA teams stayed away in protest at the

Brazilian disqualifications, Pironi, against team orders, led a furious Villeneuve to a Ferrari 2–1.

With Villeneuve still not speaking to Pironi, the scene moved to Zolder and the terrible accident which took the young French Canadian's life. Rather academically, Watson won the race, quite brilliantly, robbing long time leader Rosberg two laps from home as the Williams again destroyed its tyres. Cheever inherited third for Ligier as Lauda was excluded for being underweight and the desperately sad weekend dragged to a merciful end.

If Zolder was tragedy, Monaco was farce. With rain falling steadily and three laps to run, Prost, leading comfortably, crashed heavily just past the chicane. Riccardo Patrese inherited the lead and promptly threw it away on his penultimate lap with a gentle gyration at the Station hairpin. Now Pironi, frantically signalling that the race should be stopped, led for just as long as it took to suffer electrical failure in the tunnel. De Cesaris might have been leading next but for the fact that he too had just run out of fuel and Derek Daly, in his second race at Williams replacing the finally retired Reutemann, *could* have won but for losing his gearbox oil having swiped the rear wing and gearbox tail off on the barriers at Tabac. Suddenly a Lotus one-two, for Nigel Mansell and Elio de Angelis was a real possibility but no, Patrese was running again to take the chequered flag and what he only later realised was his first Grand Prix win . . .

From one street circuit the circus moved to another, less steeped in tradition but typical of Grand Prix racing's present: Detroit. Yes, Motor City turned its streets into a circuit and ran a Grand Prix – just. With the best will in the world, the organisers struggled to make the grade, struggling even to complete the circuit, plagued by appalling weather in the much curtailed practices, rather hasty to stop the race after a relatively minor shunt on lap seven and saved from total ignominy by an absolutely glorious display of *racing* by John Watson. In thirty laps, Watson carved his way through from thirteenth to first and that was where he stayed, the opposition destroyed to an extent rarely seen. it moved Watson into a well-deserved six-point championship lead, ahead of Pironi, Prost, Rosberg and the rest.

Nelson Piquet had failed to qualify the new turbocharged Brabham BT50 in Detroit, but in a remarkable turnaround he won the Canadian Grand Prix in Montreal a week later, with Patrese second in the Cosworth powered BT49D. Watson was third and the only unlapped runner in Canada, but it was another sad weekend with the death of Riccardo Paletti whose Osella crashed headlong into Pironi's stalled Ferrari at the start.

Zandvoort, back in the calendar at the last minute for the sake of the all-important TV commitments, was free of tragedy and largely free of controversy, ending in a morale boosting win for Pironi and Ferrari and an encouraging eighth place for new Ferrari recruit Patrick Tambay.

At Brands Hatch, Rosberg took his first pole position purely on the strength of his fantastic driving – the first non-turbo pole of the year – but then he was forced to start from the back of the grid after his Williams proved reluctant to start. The other front-row qualifier, Patrese's Brabham, stalled on the line and was promptly wiped out as the flag fell, by Arnoux's Renault. Piquet fairly flew into the lead, his Brabham running a light fuel load and soft tyres in the first attempt at Brabham's planned pit-stop ploy, but before he could make the elaborately rehearsed stop he was out, handing the lead – and ultimate victory – to Niki Lauda. For John Watson the run of bad luck that would cost him the championship was beginning as he was sidelined by someone else's accident and a fine second place now edged Pironi into the championship lead after briefly being frightened by the pace of Derek Warwick's Toleman before it broke a driveshaft.

As René Arnoux and Alain Prost cruised to a comfortable Renault one-two at Paul Ricard, ahead of the two Ferrari turbos, the Grand Prix world pondered the horror of what might have been as Jochen Mass's March touched Baldi's Arrows on the approach to the dauntingly fast Signes corner and tore through catch fences, over the barrier and through a debris fence before coming to rest upside down, briefly on fire and comprehensively wrecked.

Above: Derek Warwick couldn't have chosen a better place to give the struggling Toleman team its moment of glory than in front of the huge and fervently patriotic crowd at Brands Hatch

Miraculously, Mass was unhurt and although there were some minor spectator injuries there was no mistaking the enormity of what might have been. During testing earlier in the year, Pironi had had a similarly massive accident at the same spot, again ending his flight in what would have been a spectator area. Even Ricard, a 'new' circuit previously vaunted as safe, could no longer contain ground effect induced cornering speeds. Things had to change.

For the championship, things did change, tragically, at Hockenheim where Pironi crashed heavily during wet practice when he ran, unsighted, into the back of Prost's slow moving Renault. Faultless circuit rescue and brilliant surgery saved Pironi's shattered legs, but his championship hopes were gone. For Ferrari, scant consolation came with cautiously optimistic news of their stricken driver and a poignant first Grand Prix win by Tambay, from Arnoux, Rosberg and Tyrrell's Michele Alboreto who was steadily proving himself to be the find of the season.

With Pironi hospitalised, the championship fight devolved to Rosberg, Watson, Prost and Lauda. As Watson's bad luck continued with retirement from third place in Germany, retirement in Austria and a struggling twelfth place at Dijon, Rosberg was beginning his run to the title. In Austria, with

Above: for the first time since Mike Hawthorn won the World Championship in 1958, the Champion won only one Grand Prix. That was more a reflection of the competitiveness of Grand Prix racing in the 1980s than a comment on the ability of 1982 champion Keke Rosberg, seen after his win in the 'Swiss' Grand Prix at Dijon. Above all, Rosberg proved that, whatever the regulations governing the cars and whatever apparent advantages others might hold, there will always be room for pure natural ability

a carefully planned tyre advantage in the closing stages he failed by just five hundredths of a second to stop Elio de Angelis from scoring his first Grand Prix win, Lotus's first win for what seemed eternity and an almost unbelievable 150th for the magnificent Cosworth DFV. The Cosworth won because it was around at the finish when the turbos were not. Piquet led, Patrese led, Prost led but de Angelis survived. The Brabham pit-stop finally happened, superbly, for Patrese at least. But three laps later and still leading he was pitched into the scenery as his BMW engine siezed.

It was only one more race for Rosberg to wait for his first ever Grand Prix victory, as with the front running Renaults breaking yet again, the Finn scored his long expected and very popular first win in the 'Swiss' Grand Prix, at Dijon. It was a near thing though; with two laps left to run and a fast ailing Prost clinging onto a tenuous lead a patriotically inclined official was ready to show Prost the chequered flag until the error of his ways was pointed out by the Williams team! He then let the race run for one lap too many, but Rosberg was not denied his victory. With Patrick Tambay withdrawing because of a pinched nerve aggravated by the pounding of rock hard suspension there was no Ferrari on the grid and although the Brabhams'

BMW engines for once ran faultlessly, the blue and white cars were off the pace for the race. With John Watson failing to score again after another gritty but unlucky drive, Rosberg now had a three point lead over Pironi.

From no cars in Dijon, Ferrari were back to full strength at Monza with Tambay being joined by former World Champion and firm Monza favourite, Mario Andretti. What's more, Andretti guaranteed a full house on race day by taking a spectacular pole position. In the race however Andretti was plagued by a sticking throttle and had to be content with third place behind Arnoux's untouchable Renault and a very on-form Tambay. The Italian crowd more or less forgave Arnoux his Francophile victory as he had earlier signed to drive for Ferrari in 1983. Rosberg would have clinched the title with a single point here but while running sixth he had a rare mechanical failure as the rear wing parted company with his Williams, leaving John Watson in a superb fourth place here, with an outside chance of taking the championship in the final round.

That finale was in the unlikely setting of the car park of the Caesars Palace Hotel in Las Vegas on a circuit as artificial as the city's tinselly glamour. With an appeal still pending over his Belgian disqualification, Niki Lauda still had hopes too of another World title, but really this race was between Rosberg and Watson and, whatever else, Watson had to win. In the event he finished only second after yet another drive of the utmost quality to recover from a lowly twelfth place. Watson was beaten fair and square in the end by the young Italian who had been so impressive all year, Michele Alboreto. His win was the first for a Tyrrell since Monaco in 1978 and it probably surprised only the local bookmakers who never having *heard* of this new superstar had been offering a generous 20–1!

Of course, Alboreto's win was only part of the Las Vegas celebration; by finishing a careful and calculated fifth, Keke Rosberg clinched his first World Championship to bring a little cheer to the end of a dreadful season. Already, the rules for 1983 were in the melting pot, heralding the arrival of a new breed of skirtless, flat-bottomed cars which many thought would return more of an emphasis to driver skill and bring back to racing more of the spectacle to old. To most people neither the skill nor the spectacle had ever been gone.

Above: at the beginning of the year in Long Beach, Michele Alboreto was little more than Tyrrell's new boy going into his first full season of Grand Prix racing. At the end of the season, having put together several excellent performances in between, Alboreto won in Las Vegas to underline his reputation as one of the sport's many rising stars

INDEX

518